A Tangled Web

A TANGLED WEB

The Making of Foreign Policy

in the Nixon Presidency

WILLIAM BUNDY

HILL AND WANG

A division of Farrar, Straus and Giroux

New York

Hill and Wang
A division of Farrar, Straus and Giroux
19 Union Square West, New York 10003

Copyright © 1998 by William Bundy
Distributed in Canada by Douglas & McIntyre Ltd.
Printed in the United States of America
Designed by Debbie Glasserman
First edition, 1998

Library of Congress Cataloging-in-Publication Data
Bundy, William P., 1917–
    Tangled web : the making of foreign policy in the Nixon Presidency
/ William P. Bundy. — 1st ed.
        p.   cm.
    Includes bibliographical references and index.
    ISBN 0-8090-9151-8 (cloth : alk. paper)
    1. United States—Foreign relations—1969–1974.   2. Nixon, Richard
M. (Richard Milhous), 1913–   .   3. Kissinger, Henry, 1923–   .
I. Title.
E855.B85   1998
327.73—DC21   97-35585

For Mary

Contents

Illustrations

16: Gerald and Betty Ford say goodbye to the Nixon
        family, 1974

Maps

Preface

Winston Churchill is said to have rejected a fancy dessert with the blunt comment "This pudding has no theme." A reader confronting a largish book on the Nixon era has every right to ask what distinguishes it from the shelves of books that have already been written by and about President Richard Nixon and his National Security Advisor and later Secretary of State, Henry Kissinger.

First, this book focuses almost entirely on foreign policy. I discuss the personalities of both men, which have fascinated many writers, only as they bear on their conduct of foreign policy. Domestic policy has little place, except where it involved foreign policy (as with oil supplies and exchange rates). On the other hand, political strategy and struggles at home (not always on partisan lines) often affected foreign policy moves and must be considered with care. It is hardly news that Nixon was a "political animal," often first and almost always.

Second, I examine the views and actions of both Nixon and Kissinger, usually together. It would be simpler to focus on one of the two, and many books have done so. But these inevitably leave gaps, and may even blur the focus. For most of the time the two were close collaborators, whose inter-relationship and relative input in particular cases must be understood for a rounded picture. Other senior officials must also be taken into account, as well as professional military men and civilians, who for the most part get short shrift in the memoirs of the two chief actors.

Third, I discuss foreign policy issues as they arose, not in sometimes misleading separate packages. Nixon and Kissinger were almost always active on several fronts at once. These must be kept straight, but also considered together where they affected each other. In one particular period of multiple crises, April and May 1972 — the breakpoint of the first Nixon term — Nixon had to use U.S. sea- and air-power in beating back a climactic North Vietnamese offensive, but sought at the same time to preserve a critical first summit meeting with the Soviet Union. How and why it was possible for him to do this is a fascinating story, in which I offer an interpretation very different from those of Nixon and Kissinger themselves.

Fourth, I emphasize what was actually done, why, and with what result. Effective presentation has an important place in any foreign policy, and the principles and grand strategies propounded by the two leading figures have bemused many writers, especially in the academic community. It is important to sort out their true meaning and effect on the actions that comprised the core of their foreign policy.

Next, I devote a lot of attention to the foreign policies of other nations. The Nixon era was a time of striking changes only marginally related to American policy. The emergence of outright hostility between China and the Soviet Union in 1968–69 opened the way for new American moves. Less noted (and scanted by Nixon and Kissinger themselves) was the effect of the new "Eastern Policy" (*Ostpolitik*) initiated by West Germany's Willy Brandt in 1969 — a pioneering move with major future implications, by an individual member of the Western Alliance. Nixon's opening to China, justly praised, was not the only change in international geometry during his presidency.

Moreover, the Nixon era was a time of colorful and important figures in many countries. Golda Meir and Willy Brandt were Prime Ministers for periods almost parallel with Nixon's presidency, Anwar el-Sadat came to power in Egypt in October 1970, and Leonid Brezhnev in the Soviet Union and Zhou Enlai in China rose to new levels of power and influence in 1970–71, giving coherence to their countries' foreign policies to a remarkable degree.

Finally, I confront squarely the most crucial historical issue about foreign policy in the Nixon era. In his first four years Nixon scored great successes: a Paris Agreement that ended American participation in the Vietnam War and appeared to give the South Vietnamese regime a chance of surviving; the opening to China; and important agreements with the Soviet Union. In the next 28 months, however, South Vietnam collapsed, détente with the Soviet Union became shaky, and the relationship with China inactive: only in the Middle East, during and after the October 1973 War, was American policy a success story. Was this confounding of high hopes largely due, as Kissinger in particular has argued, to the impact of the greatest scandal in modern American political history, known as Watergate, which broke open in March 1973 and for the next seventeen months riveted the attention of the American public, eroded Nixon's power, and finally forced his resignation? Was the Democratic-controlled Congress substantially to blame? Or did the principal reasons lie deeper? Had the new "structure of peace" been oversold, timed and framed too much for domestic political effect? Had serious errors of judgment and execution entered in? Was that structure flawed and almost bound to weaken and become "tangled"?

These questions are a main focus of this book, and one reason for its title. The other is its literal origin, as many may recognize, in the well-known lines of Sir Walter Scott:

> Oh, what a tangled web we weave,
> When first we practice to deceive!

Deception, including frequent concealment and resort to covert operations, as well as misleading the public in larger ways, was a hallmark of Nixon's handling of foreign policy throughout his presidency. It must occupy a big place in any serious study of that policy and how the American people and their Congress responded to it.

So much for the scope of the book. For its sources I have relied mainly on contemporary reporting and comment, and on the host of memoirs and studies published since the early 1970s. Nixon and Kissinger themselves have published thousands of pages, perhaps the most determined effort ever to fix the image of their period. In recent years the diaries of H. R. Haldeman and the memoir of the Soviet Ambassador, Anatoly Dobrynin, have been especially illuminating. Now the flow of memoirs has probably peaked, as participants pass from the scene. It may therefore be a good time to take stock. Release of the massive official U.S. records, including more of the famous tapes, is probably many years away, at least in usable transcribed form. So too the release of the papers assembled by Henry Kissinger, almost all recorded on government time by government personnel, which he has been able to classify as "personal" and to deposit in the Library of Congress to be opened only five years after his death. Any historian must feel the lack of such materials. On the other hand, I suspect that they will in due course tell us more about personalities and political factors than about the substance of policy. I doubt they will change the important judgments already made possible by available sources.

A word about my personal perspective. I was a Washington lawyer when Richard Nixon was in Congress. I then joined the CIA and from 1953 to 1956, when he was Vice President, served as CIA staff assistant with the National Security Council's Planning Board, which under President Eisenhower prepared and coordinated policy papers for NSC meetings. In that period the Planning Board received fairly full oral accounts of NSC meetings, in which the interventions of the Vice President showed a serious and professional approach to foreign policy problems. It was a symptom of those times, when bipartisan consensus on foreign policy was greater than before or since, that a Democrat like myself could participate in this way in a Republican administration, and that all of us who did were trusted to refrain from keeping systematic records and to restrict what we heard to a very few superiors and colleagues, telling them only what they had a "need to know." For me, it was a special exposure to the thinking that formed a large part of Richard Nixon's makeup.

Overall, my government service was wide-ranging. From mid-1951 to January 1960, my CIA job (including my NSC duties) concerned what were called "national intelligence estimates," seeking to judge situations and the policies of nations all over the world, on an all-source basis. During 1960 I took leave to be staff director of a Commission on National Goals, set up at President Eisenhower's request but carried out by the American Assembly, independent of government. From January 1961 to March 1964, I served in the Defense Department's Office of International Security Affairs (ISA), again with a worldwide scope, then for five-plus years in the State Department, devoted to policy in East Asia. These positions gave me an extensive firsthand familiarity with the making and carrying out of foreign policy, amplified by frequent trips abroad; I also came to know well a great many civilian and military officials who went on to play significant parts during the Nixon presidency. In writing this book, I have had advice and information from many of these (listed in the acknowledgments), as well as from the wide range of people with whom I worked as editor of *Foreign Affairs* from 1972 to 1984. Such personal sources are not just a supplement or check on documentary sources. On many matters they provide a more reliable basis for interpretation and understanding, especially of a highly secretive presidency.

The Vietnam War (more properly the Second Indochina War) occupies a quarter of the book, probably less than its share of Nixon's and Kissinger's attention. The next-to-last chapter contains my reflections on Nixon's Indochina policies and on the whole American involvement there, in which I was marginally engaged from 1951 to 1960, then closely from 1961 to 1969, as published records have shown. The choices successive Presidents faced, including Nixon, were always difficult. I approach the subject with humility, in the hope that what I have written may help in some small degree to further national understanding of that tragic and still-searing experience.

In my government service, I dealt extensively with members of Congress, individually and in committee settings. These contacts left me with great respect for the basic honesty, compassion, and competence abundantly present in the Congress of those years. Most of those whom I knew were still on Capitol Hill during the Nixon period; some wrote or became constant points of reference for *Foreign Affairs*. Though my government experience was in the executive branch, I think of U.S foreign policy as in every respect a shared enterprise, with Congress and with the American people. In my policy-connected years, I spoke to gatherings of all sorts and appeared on television as often as time permitted, and have continued to make myself available to scholars and students since leaving government. This attempt to write history is in the same spirit; every American has a "need to know." It is aimed in part at those who remember the Nixon era, but in larger part at those who were not then alive or old enough to follow foreign policy. For these last in particular, I have tried to explain background events and describe key personalities so that the whole may be not only an interpretation but a living human picture of an important presidency.

Princeton, N.J.
July 1997

Acknowledgments

A writer of history, especially one inexperienced at book length and working without full-time assistance, accumulates numerous debts to individuals. Without their help and advice, I could never have accomplished the necessary research or completed the writing and revision.

My first debt is to Dr. David Hamburg for a generous start-up grant from the Carnegie Corporation — simply to write — when I retired from *Foreign Affairs* in 1984. After an interval in which, among other things, I taught part-time at Princeton, Arthur Rosenthal signed up the book with Hill and Wang on the basis of a limited draft and outline.

For the past four years of more intensive work, my mainstay, publisher, and editor has been Elisabeth Sifton, who patiently accepted a major enlargement of the original outline, made excellent basic suggestions, and worked incredibly hard for months to improve my prose and guide me to rethinking as well as rewriting the text. Lauren Osborne has joined in the editing and kept the manuscript, the endnotes, and all the auxiliaries straight with great care and skill, along with her assistant, Susan DeCarava. It has been a pleasant as well as constructive relationship, for which I am indirectly indebted also to Roger Straus, the legendary head of the parent firm of Farrar, Straus and Giroux.

I have had priceless help from a series of research assistants, mostly graduate students at Princeton University. Over more than five years, Jennifer Delton in particular not only did useful research and typed voluminous notes but handled the bibliography throughout and was in the last phase a superb decipherer of text changes, editor, and critic. Kara Stibora Fulcher did research and typing with great ability for more than two years, and Karen Vasudeva came to my rescue on several occasions, notably in handling text changes in the last phase. Before them, Sheila McNeill Riggs was the pioneer, and Mark Easton, Mark Sandy, and Patricia Labaw all helped at the early stages.

Many friends have read and criticized draft sections of the manuscript. Gail Ullman, John Zentay, Robert Bowie, and my onetime colleagues Blanche Moore and Daniel Davidson did so for the whole draft text, supplying a host of valuable comments. William Roth, Harry McPherson, and my brother McGeorge read chapters and gave me solid advice at an intermediate stage, and my colleague at the State Department and lifelong friend, Marshall Green, not only read and criticized large parts of the manuscript but contributed important recollections of his own association with President Nixon. Others who read and commented usefully on individual sections were Alfred Atherton, Nayan Chanda, Cyrus Ghani, G. McMurtrie Godley, John Holdridge, Paul Kreisberg, Winston Lord, Douglas Pike, Robert Pursley, John Rhinelander, Harold Saunders, Robert Scalapino, and Emory Swank. Needless to say, the responsibility for content remains wholly mine.

I have profited from wide-ranging interviews with William Hyland, Charles S. Levy, Jonathan Moore, Elliot Richardson, and Ted Van Dyk. On individual points, I have turned, usually by telephone, to a number of former colleagues and senior figures in the Nixon period, as well as to authors or sources from my time at *Foreign Affairs*. These have included James Akins, George W. Ball, Lucius D. Battle, Joseph Califano, Jeffrey Clarke, Kenneth Dam, Nathaniel Davis, Jonathan Dean, Raymond Garthoff, Robert Goheen, Philip Habib, Norman Hannah, Richard Helms, Seymour Hersh, Arthur Hummel, John Irwin, U. Alexis Johnson, Max Kampelman, Nicholas Katzenbach, A. James McAdams, Charles Meyer, Thomas Moorer, Russell Mott, Paul H. Nitze, Don Oberdorfer, Rutherford Poats, Stanley Resor, Walt Rostow, Kenneth Rush, John Sawhill, Paul Sigmund, Monteagle Stearns, William H. Sullivan, Cyrus Vance, and Christopher Van Hollen.

For written materials, the staff of the Princeton University Library has been uniformly helpful. For certain CIA materials (in the public domain) I have been greatly helped by my old colleague Harold Ford, and on one key matter by Ben Fischer of the Agency's Center for the Study of Intelligence, to whom I was guided by Diane Snyder. Jane Smith of the recently established Center for Diplomatic Studies and Training in Arlington, Virginia, introduced me to their rapidly expanding collection of oral histories by diplomats. Likewise Alfred Goldberg, Historian at the Office of the Secretary of Defense in the Pentagon, showed me useful oral histories and a massive file of daily media summaries that only distance kept me from using properly.

To thank all these people is to realize again how far my researches have fallen short of the standards of my mentor in diplomatic history, William L. Langer. This is not a fully scholarly account of its subject—but then I doubt that, with the explosion in information technology, there will ever be even the semblance of one for the Nixon period, or perhaps for any other in recent American history.

I owe special thanks to Dr. Andrew Costin, whose resourceful care restored my health and energy after a lull two years ago.

Finally, our children, Michael, Carol, and Chris, have been wonderfully understanding of my distracted state for now many years. My wife, Mary, has encouraged and supported me at every stage, criticizing intermediate drafts trenchantly and, in the crunch of the past year, reading and annotating the complete text three times with great care and insight, as well as bearing the whole household load. Her taste, her eye for precision and clarity, and her ear for tone have made incalculable improvements, and her humor and patience have lifted us over many shoals. The dedication of the book to her is the merest token of my gratitude and love.

A Tangled Web

Chapter One

AN HOUR AND A MAN

The election year of 1968 was as eventful and tumultuous as any in American history—a war in Vietnam that had turned sour yet offered no easy exit; an antiwar movement at home, chiefly among a generation born during or after World War II to great expectations and ideals, with many both resenting and profiting from a conscription system loaded in favor of the educated and well-to-do; new movements such as feminism just starting to take hold; and above all a deep-seated racial division between African-American and white citizens, as old as the nation itself but attacked more forthrightly by President Lyndon Johnson than by any predecessor, with the result, common in history, that as the possibility of improvement showed itself, bitterness and frustration became all the greater.

There had been election years of equally deep domestic discontent and convulsion—in 1932, at the depth of the Great Depression, bonus marchers and breadlines in the cities conveyed a whiff of revolution. In other intense election years the nation faced and debated issues of peace and war—1860, 1864, 1916, 1940. But never before had the two elements come together powerfully in the same election year. That they did in 1968 is basic to understanding the Nixon presidency. This was an hour of testing, and the experienced Republican candidate in that year was, in the eyes of a plurality of the American voting public, ready for the test.

For twenty-plus years, Richard Nixon had cut a wide swath in American public life and made a deep impression on two fronts. One was political campaigning. He had raised to a high level the art of imputing subversive tendencies to liberal opponents, acquiring early the nickname "Tricky Dick." Almost every campaign he fought was etched in the memory of his contemporaries for some extraordinary event: 1952 for a "Checkers speech" in brilliant defense of his own honor; 1960 for woebegone handling of a TV debate with John F. Kennedy; 1962 for a bitter farewell press conference in California before the despised media. This Nixon was emotional, capable of igniting deep chords of feeling for and against his personality and positions, and at the same time of masterly expository speeches. He was a superb practitioner of politics, occasionally with the raw side showing.

The other feature that stood out in Richard Nixon's record was his extensive foreign policy experience. As a member of Congress, Vice President in the collegial Eisenhower structure, and then as a much-traveled private citizen, his exposure to the world and to foreign leaders stood near the top among the political figures of his time and among twentieth-century candidates for the presidency. He had been particularly involved in and articulate over policy toward East Asia, stressing the threat from China after the Communists won power there in 1949, and had made dramatic impressions of competence and coolness on two occasions — under the physical threat of a crowd in Caracas, Venezuela, in 1958, and in a dramatic kitchen debate in the Soviet Union in 1959 with the redoubtable Nikita Khrushchev. On the other hand, both in public and in government councils, Nixon demonstrated on many occasions a strong inclination to deal with problems by decisive action, violent and military if necessary, and not to be constrained by potential opposition at home or by the attitudes of allied countries. Both in domestic politics and in his foreign policy views, he had the temperament of a "true believer," fervent, intolerant, sure of his own positions.*

An hour and a man had come together. The story of Nixon's pre-presidential career, his years of preparation, is not only an account of the personal development of an extremely energetic and intelligent American of his generation, but a study of what the American nation itself went through, especially in East Asia, in the first twenty-five years of the Cold War.

1. The Making of a True Believer

Richard Nixon grew up next door to the Pacific Ocean. His wartime service was as a Navy officer in the South Pacific. Elected to Congress in 1946 over a popular liberal Democratic incumbent, in a campaign that he made markedly negative by the standards of the period, Nixon made a strong impres-

---

*In his 1951 book, The True Believer, which gave currency to the label, Eric Hoffer used the term in the sense of a fanatic prepared to lay down his life for a cause. In common usage, however, a less extreme meaning has generally dominated, and is the one used here.

sion at once as an articulate younger voice in a Republican Party that
retained many elements of its prewar isolationism.

When the Marshall Plan for Europe was announced in the spring of
1947, Christian Herter of Massachusetts picked Nixon as a junior member
of a special bipartisan House committee, which spent several weeks exam-
ining the European situation. The committee soon endorsed the Plan, and
Nixon went all out to turn around his skeptical California constituents. The
experience did much to establish him as a serious worker and thinker on
foreign policy.[1] In his own account of the trip, Nixon dwelt on what he
learned about Communists, whom he insisted on meeting face to face and
found to be men of great ability to be taken extremely seriously. He concluded that the only thing Communists would respect and deal with was
"power at least equal to theirs and backed up by willingness to use it" and
that a basic rule with Russians must be "never bluff unless you are prepared
to carry through, because they will test you every time." At the same time,
Nixon saw that it was essential to improve economic conditions in Europe,
the main object of the Marshall Plan. (The question of military measures
was not then to the fore.)[2]

At the opposite extreme from this high-toned committee was the House
Un-American Activities Committee, dominated by right-wingers from both
parties and often accused of irresponsibility in exposing supposed Communist activity. Doubtless on the strength of his election campaign, in
which he had so successfully attacked his Democratic opponent for leftist
leanings, Republican leaders put Nixon on HUAC, where he rapidly distinguished himself as an active participant and articulate questioner. By the
summer of 1948 he was the lead figure in the committee's investigation of
a just-retired State Department official, Alger Hiss, on charges of association
with Communists leveled by a confessed Communist informant, Whittaker
Chambers. A dramatic confrontation between the two was inconclusive, but
Nixon kept pressing Chambers, who finally came forward that fall with
microfilm of State Department cables, stored for years in a pumpkin on the
farm of a friend. These so-called Pumpkin Papers became the key evidence
leading to the conviction of Hiss, in early 1950, for perjury concerning his
relationship with Chambers.

Nixon was also in the lead in linking the celebrated Hiss case to alleged
Communist influence on American policy in China during and after
World War II. As the Chinese Civil War turned in favor of the Communist side in 1947–49, he consistently supported attempts to increase American military aid to the Chiang Kai-shek government, and when Mao
Zedong took over China in October 1949, became a strident proponent of
the charge that the "loss" of China had been the fault of President Harry
Truman and his Secretary of State, Dean Acheson. While Nixon steered
clear of some of the wilder attacks mounted by the mostly conservative and

Republican "China Lobby," he remained close to its members in and out of Congress.

When North Korea attacked South Korea in June 1950, Nixon fully supported Truman's decision to commit American forces to the defense of South Korea. Unlike many Republicans—Senator Robert Taft of Ohio, for example—he never challenged Truman's refusal to seek a declaration of war or any other congressional approval, apart from the voting of appropriations. Nixon consistently took an expansive view of presidential authority in matters of war and peace. On the other hand, he was also one of the first to charge that the Truman Administration had invited the North Korean attack, particularly by a speech Acheson had given in January 1950 that omitted Korea from a geographically defined American "defense perimeter" in East Asia. Whether the charge was valid or not, a great many Americans, then and later, found it persuasive; it was repeatedly invoked not merely for partisan purposes but to show that the United States ought to clarify its attitude toward military intervention in all regions. Ironically, Acheson had intended primarily to stir up latent conflicts between the Soviet Union and a now Communist-controlled China (which were to become central in Nixon's presidency). Only secondarily did he draw on the known views of the Joint Chiefs of Staff that, given the reduced postwar U.S. military forces, defense perimeters should be defined only for areas that could realistically be defended. Yet the episode came to be a main argument for drawing lines firmly and fixedly, first in Northeast Asia and in the mid-1950s in Southeast Asia as well.[3]

In the turbulent summer and fall of 1950, as forces under General Douglas MacArthur held on precariously in South Korea and then rebounded in the brilliant Inchon landing, Richard Nixon was winning an invective-laden Senate campaign against a Democratic incumbent, Helen Gahagan Douglas, whom he charged, often in nasty ways, with being "soft" on the threat of Communism. It was a campaign that, even more than the pursuit of Alger Hiss, made him anathema to a great many Democrats and not a few independent voters and observers.

That September, the Truman Administration enlarged its objective from simply restoring South Korea to unifying all of Korea by force. Authorized to go into North Korea with care and caution, MacArthur did so with maximum fanfare and aggressiveness. As his forces approached the Yalu River boundary with China, the Chinese intervened massively and to devastating effect.

Under the field command of General Matthew B. Ridgway, the war became a grinding struggle near the 38th parallel, with the Truman Administration effectively abandoning the objective of unifying Korea. The unchastened MacArthur, declaring that "war's very object is victory," urged stronger action against China. In March 1951, the charismatic general stated his views in a public letter to Congressman Joseph Martin, Republican Minority Leader. Truman, who had put up with earlier critical statements from MacArthur, finally relieved the general for insubordination and for publicly advocating a policy opposed to that of the government. It was an epic confrontation: legendary war hero versus upstart President. Many wondered whether the very principle of civilian control of the military could survive, or whether MacArthur's views might sweep the country and make Truman's position untenable.

On the day the firing was announced, April 11, 1951, Richard Nixon, in a role rare for a freshman senator, was picked to lead his party in a long and acrimonious debate on the Senate floor. He did not challenge the President's power to relieve a commander, but urged simply that General MacArthur be reinstated. Nixon also did not lend himself to attacks by other Republicans on Secretary of Defense George C. Marshall, who had joined in recommending the President's action. He went beyond familiar Republican attacks on past policy to urge all the immediate steps MacArthur had proposed. Seeing no hope that the war could be ended successfully "with concerted United Nations action," he argued that the United States unilaterally insist on strategic bombing of key targets within China and on allowing Chiang Kai-shek's Nationalist forces on Taiwan to threaten the mainland and thus divert some Chinese forces from Korea.[4]

As the historian Stephen Ambrose rightly sums up, the debate that spring was "between those who wanted to crush the Communists in Asia and those who wanted to contain them." The Truman Administration — through Acheson, Marshall, and General Omar Bradley — stressed the fundamental strategic importance of ground forces, of accepting geographical limits and taking account of the views of allies; the MacArthur side advocated drastic use of airpower, enlarging the war zone, and making political and alliance factors subordinate to military needs.[5] (This sharp division of opinion over American policy in East Asia continued for the next two decades.) In 1951, exhaustive joint congressional hearings, impressively chaired by Senator Richard Russell, convinced many Americans that Truman had been right both to fire MacArthur and to reject his advice. Nixon did not return to the fray during or immediately after those hearings, but he had clearly aligned himself with the MacArthur school, in favor of drastic military action with maximum objectives.[6]

At the same time, Nixon continued to distance himself from Taft Republicans by his strong support of the U.S. commitment of major forces to the North Atlantic Treaty Organization and of the designation of General Dwight D. Eisenhower as the Alliance's supreme commander in Europe. Nixon was an early supporter of Eisenhower as the Republican nominee in 1952, and his own selection as Vice President fell naturally into place, highlighting the issue of Communism and balancing the ticket geographically.

In the campaign, much of Nixon's oratory repeated his earlier litany of attacks over the "loss" of China and "softness" on Communism. Calling Acheson the dean of a "college of cowardly communist containment" was a sample of rhetoric that endeared him to the right, enraged liberals and many moderates, and left a deep mark.

Nixon was more involved in foreign policy than any previous Vice President. He formed close and friendly ties with both Secretary of State John Foster Dulles and CIA Director Allen Dulles. And whereas the custom in most administrations was for the Vice President to air his views only directly and personally to the President, Eisenhower allowed the Vice President to participate frequently and apparently frankly in meetings of the National Security Council. All in all, Nixon got a training in foreign policy that was comparable to the kind of apprenticeship that is usual in Cabinet-style governments but a rare exception in the American system.[7]

By 1953, with a stalemate in Korea, Eisenhower took the secret step of warning the Chinese, through an Indian intermediary, that if the war went on the United States might feel impelled to attack China; the clear implication was that it might use nuclear weapons. It was an action consistent with Eisenhower's New Look strategy of defending outlying areas by making a threat of "massive retaliation" at places and times chosen by the United States—a strategy Nixon accepted and was surely much influenced by.[8]

North Korea and China did accept an armistice in July 1953: whether the secret Eisenhower warning was decisive has been much debated among historians. But there can be little doubt that Eisenhower and Nixon (whenever he learned of it) believed that the warning had been a crucial and perhaps the single most decisive factor. Nixon repeatedly said so in later years, and must have marked down stern private messages and threats of all-out war as special and important tools of policy.

By the fall of 1953, the Eisenhower Administration had scored a noteworthy series of successes, including the armistice in Korea, the election of Ramon Magsaysay as President of the Philippines (with substantial American advice and a strong public campaign to make the election fair), and a CIA-assisted coup in Iran that restored the pro-American Mohammed Reza Shah Pahlevi to power.[9] NATO was firmly established, Latin America and the Middle East at peace. The greatest remaining worry was Indochina, where the French position was deteriorating rapidly, so that Eisenhower decided in September on a major increase in military aid.

At this apogee of American power and prestige, Nixon embarked on a seventy-day "goodwill" trip to nineteen different countries. This had no ceremonial purposes; rather, it was a down-to-earth survey with little formality and a great deal of direct talk with senior foreign officials and Americans in the countries visited. The format gave Nixon the chance to refine his already great capacity to digest written materials and to conduct searching conversations with foreign leaders, usually without tension. On the trip he also formed a number of strong impressions of individuals. Carrying with him the ideas that were soon to be embodied in treaty links with Pakistan, he was drawn to the bluff and downright Pakistani generals, but found Jawaharlal Nehru in India iniquitously neutral ("immoral" was John Foster Dulles's label); similarly, although Prince Norodom Sihanouk in Cambodia was a non-Communist leader with legitimacy and popular support almost unique in Southeast Asia, Nixon found him intelligent but "vain and flighty," above all naive about Communism.[10]

With American officials likewise, his assessment depended heavily on evidence of hard-line anti-Communist views. In Tokyo, Samuel Berger, a Foreign Service officer with a labor background, briefed Nixon on the important labor federation SOHYO. Under Nixon's stern cross-examination, Berger stuck to his judgment that SOHYO was not then Communist-dominated or likely to become so — a judgment confirmed by later events. The result, at Nixon's behest, was the early reassignment of Berger to a less important post.[11]

The overall situation in Southeast Asia made by far the greatest impression on Nixon. He came to believe that holding off the Communist threat in Vietnam, Laos, and Cambodia was essential to a stable East Asia and the top priority for American policy. He found the French too tarred with the colonialist brush to be effective; locally rooted regimes were essential, but so was outside support in some form, to deal principally with the threat of Communist China.

On his return, Nixon made a two-hour report to the National Security Council. He urged that the United States forge mutual-defense links from Turkey right around to a rearmed Japan — an Asia-wide security structure to deter and resist Communist expansion in any form, with the United States in the central role as it already was in Europe. He was thus an early advocate of the "pactomania" that characterized John Foster Dulles's foreign policy, with its great emphasis on formal defense commitments.

The situation in Indochina became critical even sooner than Nixon had feared. In April 1954, Vietminh forces besieged the remote fortress of Dien Bien Phu, and Eisenhower had to decide whether the United States should intervene directly. Intense discussions with the French produced a plan for strategic air attacks, in line with the Administration's New Look military strategy. But the French public was sick of the war, the British government was cool to taking military action, and Eisenhower's old colleague, General Ridgway, now Army Chief of Staff, argued strongly that a land war in Indochina would be costly, unpredictable, and unwise. In early April, a Gallup poll found 68 percent of the American public against armed intervention.[12]

Within the Administration, Nixon for a time joined with Admiral Arthur Radford, Chairman of the Joint Chiefs of Staff, in favoring the air attack plan. He also expressed his views in a dramatic public fashion. At the important annual meeting of newspaper publishers in Washington, he said in response to a question that if the situation required he would favor a decision to commit U.S. ground forces to help the French. Although the response was theoretically "off the record," it was far too explosive for him or anyone else to suppose it would remain private. Both comment and speaker were at once reported in the media, bringing the issue of American intervention to a head.

Eisenhower did not rebuke or repudiate Nixon — part of a cool and somewhat detached position in the crisis that continues to puzzle historians. When the President met with congressional leaders shortly afterward, he found them strongly opposed to military action and decided to pursue a more diplomatic policy of "united action," designed less to prevent a Communist takeover in North Vietnam than to forestall further Communist gains after that. As in the MacArthur crisis three years earlier, Nixon was for taking risks with strong action, especially air attacks. But when Eisenhower moved in a more moderate direction, Nixon supported his policy loyally.

The upshot was that France gave up the fight when Dien Bien Phu fell in early May. A July conference in Geneva set the 17th parallel as the demarcation line between the Communist-held territories in the North and the Western-supported non-Communists in the South, with an ambiguous provision for elections after two years to determine whether the country should remain divided. The United States accepted these 1954 Accords, but did not sign them or participate in the hasty final decisions that produced them.

That fall, "united action" took shape in the Southeast Asia Treaty Organization (SEATO) that John Foster Dulles designed and promoted. The signatories — the United States, Britain, France, Australia, New Zealand, the Philippines, Thailand, and Pakistan — pledged to come to each other's aid against armed aggression and to consult on common action against "indirect aggression." Laos, Cambodia, and South Vietnam (called the Republic of Vietnam) became "protocol states" under the treaty, entitled to call on the signers for help against direct or indirect aggression — a status that Sihanouk in Cambodia promptly rejected as part of a determined policy of neutrality.

That the Senate readily ratified the SEATO treaty reflected the Eisenhower Administration's prestige, relief that America had not become militarily involved in Southeast Asia, and belief in the "lesson of Korea," that drawing firm lines helped to deter Communist expansion and make war less likely. But it was a weak and unrealistic treaty: it offered no answer to subversion and guerrilla warfare, so everything depended on whether solid local regimes could emerge and win the support of their people.

The next few years saw remarkable apparent progress in South Vietnam. In July 1954, on the recommendation of Democratic senator Mike Mansfield (a long-standing expert on East Asia), Ngo Dinh Diem, a central Vietnam mandarin with a staunch nationalist record and some administrative experience, was plucked from a New Jersey retreat and persuaded to take office as Prime Minister of South Vietnam. The next spring, with strong support from some officials in a divided U.S. Embassy, Diem beat back threats from local sect forces and established himself in control. In the fall of 1955 his power was ratified by a formal, though hardly free, election as President.

Just what part Nixon played in these dramatic developments is not clear. His association with the activist Dulles brothers suggests that he may have been a significant force behind the scenes at critical points. Certainly he welcomed and publicly cheered for each successive move to strengthen South Vietnam and to enlarge American activities there. He was also one of the first U.S. officials to describe America's new relationship to South Vietnam as a "commitment."

July 1956 was the due date for the elections called for under the Geneva Accords, but by then a confident Diem had publicly refused to accept these, on the ground that South Vietnam had never signed the Accords and was not bound by them. A more persuasive argument, urged on Diem by Secretary Dulles and endorsed at the time by at least one senator, John F. Kennedy, was that any semblance of free choice was impossible in the territories controlled by the Communist regime in North Vietnam. Hanoi sharply attacked Diem's decision, but could do nothing.

Nixon came to Saigon again that July, to celebrate the second anniversary of Diem's taking charge. In the next four years, American aid to South Vietnam was massive and varied. Military equipment and training were provided to create a conventional defense force, organized in division units on the South Korean model, and designed to hold off a frontal attack from the North until help came. Large quantities of economic aid and training in public administration were also supplied. But the political situation was left almost entirely to Diem, who developed a system of personal rule, relying heavily on his brothers. It was apparent from an early stage that his regime was antagonizing Buddhists and other groups in Vietnam's varied society, and thus playing into the hands of the initially small Communist movement in the southern part of the country, but when a courageous American ambassador with experience in Communist situations, Elbridge Durbrow, tried to offer advice, Diem ignored him with impunity, believing rightly that the pliant American general in charge of military aid was the effective voice of Washington.[13] This passive and acquiescent American posture probably had an important influence on Diem's later behavior and on his refusal to take American advice seriously. Again, just what part Nixon played in this American posture has not been revealed.

Certainly the Eisenhower Administration saw its record in South Vietnam as a success story. When it invited Diem to Washington for a state visit in 1959, the exchange of statements was flowery—with the Vice President to the fore. In all, Nixon's record suggests that his sense of the need to support South Vietnam went beyond normal loyalty to Administration policy and took on a personal, almost evangelical character. Nixon had developed, as Stephen Ambrose concludes, "almost a lifelong commitment to saving the people of Indochina from Communism."[14]

In Laos, meanwhile, the Eisenhower Administration moved away from formal support of an unstable coalition regime, which had been prescribed in the 1954 Geneva Accords, and in 1960 gave its outright backing to a rightist general, Phoumi Nosavan. This set off a sharp conflict with "neutralist" forces, and by the end of the year small U.S. military detachments were in Laos supporting Phoumi's side. Wider hostilities seemed imminent.

In South Vietnam, 1960 saw widespread terrorist activity and increasing small-scale actions by local Vietcong (Vietnamese Communist) forces and a tremor of instability in the form of an abortive coup against Diem in November by Air Force officers. Much more important, but then unknown to the American government or public, was a North Vietnamese move in May 1959, which most historians regard as the start of the Second Indochina War. Hanoi decided to turn up the pressure by supporting and directing the already sizable Vietcong guerrilla forces it had helped to create in South Vietnam. Trained cadres flowed across the porous border and down the blossoming supply trail through eastern Laos (the Ho Chi Minh Trail). American intelligence soon detected a Hanoi-led radio command network, but American policymakers only dimly grasped the scale of the North's intervention. The Lao Dong (Communist) Party in the North wanted total control of Indochina—a goal that was encouraged, but never directed, by the Communist regime in China. Thus, what appeared to the American public—even, apparently, to the two presidential candidates in 1960—as a fairly stable Indochina situation was in fact drifting badly.

.   .   .

In all, Richard Nixon's performance as Vice President won high marks, especially among Republicans. When Ike had serious illnesses in 1955 and 1956, Nixon behaved with tact and restraint, and his personal performances in Caracas in 1958 and in the 1959 kitchen debate with Nikita Khrushchev added to his stature. By 1960, when he won the Republican nomination for the presidency after a brief contest with Governor Nelson Rockefeller of New York, he had established himself as a serious participant in and expert on foreign policy, holding the views then common among responsible conservatives. Bipartisan consensus was the order of the day, and differences between parties and between liberals and conservatives were less than at any other time in the postwar period. In fact, when Senator Kennedy went into action after winning the Democratic nomination, his campaign theme quickly became an attack on the Eisenhower Administration and Nixon, not for going too far but for being sluggish and unimaginative, both at home and in the conduct of the Cold War abroad.

In the 1960 campaign, U.S. support for South Vietnam was not an issue, nor was concern about China paramount: the Communist regime had first "let a hundred flowers bloom" in an apparently generous effort to encourage freer expression of opinion, then cut off the new freedom abruptly and embarked on "the Great Leap Forward," a draconian economic program that failed almost immediately. Even over the only foreign policy issue involving China—whether to help the Nationalists in Taiwan defend the islands of Quemoy and Matsu, lying between Taiwan and the mainland—the differences between the two candidates were "mainly rhetorical."[15] Throughout the campaign, neither candidate suggested any change in the nation's hard-line policy toward China, nor was the chain of alliances around the rim of East Asia questioned. Vietnam simply never came up.

The main foreign issue was Cuba. The Administration had begun, in the spring of 1960, with Nixon's knowledge and support, to create and arm a small force of Cuban exiles intended to overthrow Castro. Kennedy was not briefed before the election on this operation, but on his own suggested such a plan in one of the debates, to Nixon's intense annoyance.[16]

With the choice between Nixon and Kennedy turning finally less on substantive policy positions than on apparent fitness to lead, the election was extraordinarily close. Kennedy won by the smallest margin of both electoral and popular votes in the twentieth century, a result that seemed to many to turn on last-minute events: a sympathetic phone call from Kennedy to Mrs. Martin Luther King, Jr., when her husband, already famous, was briefly thrown into prison on an unconvincing charge; a late surge of Democratic votes from areas of southern Texas with dubious past reputations; and above all the "machine" vote in Cook County, Illinois, where irregularities were habitual. Since overturning the Illinois and Texas results would have reversed the whole election, Eisenhower and others urged Nixon to protest and force recounts, which would have consumed months. Although his defeat was a searing experience, Nixon declined to do so, in a decision widely regarded as wise and courageous. Undoubtedly, he came out of the election with more than a close loser's normal feeling that little things had tipped the scale; he was convinced that he had been done out of victory by shady Democratic practices.

2. The Years in the Wilderness

Nixon held his peace as President Kennedy moved to cope first with the mess in Laos and then with the decay in South Vietnam. We can only guess whether he would have made a stand in Laos with American forces, as Eisenhower appeared to urge when he had his only meeting with Kennedy just before the Inauguration.[17]

Kennedy chose to negotiate, and enlisted Soviet help in getting a new set of Geneva Accords for Laos in 1962, reaffirming its neutral status and barring the use of Laotian territory for military purposes. But the regime in Hanoi soon shook off any Soviet influence and cynically violated the Accords. Nixon in his memoirs called Kennedy's policy "an unqualified disaster," but he was silent at the time and, to judge from comments later in the 1960s, saw the point of having, as a goal of American policy, a formal neutral status for Laos, a theater always secondary to South Vietnam and dependent on the outcome there. He may or may not have noted how little leverage the United States had with the Soviet Union on issues related to Indochina, or paused to question the degree of Soviet influence over Hanoi.[18]

Would Nixon have gone further in South Vietnam in 1961 than the several thousand military advisors and massive military aid Kennedy sent late that year? Again, there is no public evidence. In 1961 and 1962, confrontation with Fidel Castro in Cuba and deadlock with the Soviet Union over Berlin were the centers of attention. Nixon concentrated on going after the governorship of California, where he unexpectedly lost out to the popular Pat Brown. In a notable farewell, he lashed out at the press—which he always saw as hostile to him and dominated by liberals—with the memorable quotation: "Now you won't have Richard Nixon to kick around anymore!" Humiliated, Nixon left the West Coast and came to New York to practice law and get back, quietly, into the national political arena. He attracted major clients, some with interests abroad, and was soon able to travel frequently and extend his contacts, and to renew his involvement in debate over foreign policy.

In the summer and fall of 1963, the Diem government in South Vietnam got into a political crisis brought on largely by Buddhist opposition. The worsening situation led the Kennedy Administration to draw back from the regime and set up covert links to dissident military groups. To Nixon, Diem remained "a foe of communism and a friend of the United States," and the repressive actions he took against demonstrators were no more than "embarrassing to us." Kennedy saw Diem as not only repressive but no longer effective, and in effect acquiesced in the coup that toppled Diem in early November, though he never intended, and tried to forestall, the ensuing assassination of Diem and his brother Ngo Dinh Nhu. Nixon, probably sincerely, remained deeply suspicious that there had in fact been American complicity in the killings.[19]

The clouded year of 1964 passed in the shadow of the assassination of President Kennedy in November 1963. In the spring, Nixon took a long trip to East Asia, stopping for two days in South Vietnam. Seeing that the situation was going downhill, and fortified by the expressed worries of mostly rightist Asian leaders at other stops, he began to speak guardedly of denying the enemy, through unspecified countermeasures, a "privileged sanctuary" in North Vietnam.[20] But as a long-shot potential presidential candidate that year, Nixon was cautious. American policy was still to support the regime in South Vietnam but not engage in military action against North Vietnam itself. Only in a *Reader's Digest* article in August, after Barry Goldwater had gotten the Republican nomination, did Nixon forthrightly urge attacks on the North–South supply routes. Even then he stressed that only South Vietnamese air forces should be used — a clear evasion to anyone who knew, as he must have, that their offensive capabilities were virtually nonexistent. Yet Nixon's inspirational appeals for the "will to win" and his totally dark picture of the consequences of defeat suggested that he was ready to go, in Ambrose's words, "all the way," and was "the most hawkish of all national politicians" during that eventful summer. In August, after an incident in the Tonkin Gulf, President Johnson got Congress to pass a resolution authorizing strong measures, including military force, to hold Southeast Asia, but in his campaign speeches he stressed that Americans should not do the job of Asians in this war. In November, with the Republicans badly divided, Johnson won a landslide victory.[21]

With Goldwater's defeat, Nixon quickly reemerged as a leading Republican spokesman. In late January 1965 he came out for U.S. naval and air bombardment of North Vietnam, while saying that ground forces would not be necessary and (as he had already argued in the 1964 campaign) that nuclear weapons should not be considered. When Johnson decided in February to bomb North Vietnam, Nixon applauded, and as North Vietnamese pressure increased and with it American involvement (culminating in the commitment of major U.S. ground combat forces in late July) Nixon was always ready to call for more. In September he visited South Vietnam again, predicting that the war might go on for two or three years; on his return he urged air attacks against military targets near Hanoi and a naval blockade of Haiphong, North Vietnam's main port of entry for equipment — part of a constant emphasis on airpower rather than getting "bogged down" in a ground war, as he saw Johnson doing. At the same time, in a widely noted TV appearance, he "strongly opposed" a suggestion by Congressman Gerald Ford that the United States declare war on North Vietnam, saying this might lead the North to seek the open intervention of the Soviet Union and China.[22]

At the same time, Nixon consistently opposed any negotiating concessions and insisted that the objective had to be "victory"—defined as an independent and secure South Vietnam. In December, when Johnson decided on a long pause in the bombing to see if North Vietnam showed any signs of compromise, Nixon commented that the United States "should negotiate only when our military superiority is so convincing that we can achieve our objective at the conference table."[23]

Throughout 1966, the drumfire of his criticism went on. Whereas he had spoken in late 1965 of a maximum of 200,000 American ground forces, in August 1966, after another visit to South Vietnam, he called for a rapid increase to 500,000. He did, however, criticize Johnson for going too far, on the basis of an inaccurate story that the President planned a force of 750,000, saying that the South Vietnamese must "carry the brunt of the responsibility."[24]

In October 1966, with dramatic Republican gains in the House and Senate races appearing likely, President Johnson decided not to campaign hard, but to dramatize the American role in East Asia by a tour of the countries directly supporting the war effort, culminating in a conference at Manila. Nixon at once saw the trip in domestic political terms. When Johnson announced at Manila that the United States was prepared to withdraw its forces from South Vietnam six months after the North Vietnamese had pulled out all of theirs, as part of a verifiable peace settlement, Nixon erupted in a sharp attack on the eve of election day. His argument was that in such a situation, even if North Vietnamese regular forces truly withdrew, the South Vietnamese armed forces could not be sure of being able to handle the indigenous Vietcong forces who would remain in place. Stung, Johnson responded angrily and in a personal vein, which only helped Nixon's standing.[25]

The Republicans did indeed score great gains in the 1966 congressional elections, and Nixon's important and highly visible participation in the campaign reestablished him solidly as a potential presidential candidate. It was an extraordinary comeback from the depths of late 1962. From then on, every move he made was calculated in terms of winning the nomination and then the election. He assumed that Johnson would run again and, if the Vietnam War was still inconclusive, would be increasingly vulnerable. For his part, Johnson considered Nixon the most dangerous Republican candidate and watched his every move and statement. Nixon may well have come to symbolize for Johnson a fear that he often expressed to his closest confidants: that the really sharp backlash over Vietnam policy might easily come—as earlier, over Korea—not from the vocal liberal left but from the hard-line right.

To refurbish his foreign policy credentials, Nixon made another series of trips abroad in 1967, again including a stop in Saigon. Here he made an upbeat public statement that Communist defeat was inevitable, although his private view, stated in his memoirs a decade later, was that the strategy of attrition was not working. By then, it must have been clear to him that the war was not likely to be under control by the 1968 campaign season, and he knew well (from Korea) how much Americans hated long, bloody, and inconclusive wars.

Nixon drew on his travels for a major article on U.S. policy in East Asia, which was published by *Foreign Affairs* in October. In later years there grew up a considerable mythology, furthered by Nixon supporters, that this article foreshadowed his later policy toward China. In fact, the tenor of the article was generally tough and uncompromising. He had found in Asia "an extraordinarily promising transformation," in which the "U.S. presence" had been "vital" to the 1965–66 turnaround in Indonesia and the emergence of an anti-Communist government in that key country, "by far the richest prize in the Southeast Asian area." It was "beyond question that without the American commitment in Viet Nam, Asia would be a far different place today."

As he saw it, most non-Communist leaders "recognize a common danger, and see its source as Peking." "Red China's threat is clear, present, and repeatedly and insistently expressed." What was being attempted in Vietnam was a Communist advance by proxy, and a similar threat of "externally supported guerrilla action . . . is even now being mounted in Thailand, and . . . could be launched in any one of a half-dozen spots in the Chinese shadow."[26] The major thrust of the article was to urge a regional military grouping, based on the core group of nations who had just set up an Asian and Pacific Council: South Korea, Japan, Taiwan, Thailand, Malaysia, South Vietnam, the Philippines, Australia, and New Zealand. Even India might be enlisted, he thought, since it had been a "target of overt Chinese aggression" in 1962.[27]

Interestingly, the four countries he saw as most important for the future of the area were the United States, Japan, China ("the world's most populous nation and Asia's most immediate threat"), and, again, India—leaving out the Soviet Union on the ground that "its principal focus is toward the west" and its Asian lands were essentially "an appendage of European Russia."[28] He looked especially to Japan to take more responsibility "both diplomatically and militarily," and (as he had done as far back as 1953) advocated lifting the restraints written into Article 9 of the Japanese Constitution, which forbade the creation of any Japanese military forces other than for self-defense narrowly defined.

Only at a late point in the article, after these major themes, did Nixon discuss future U.S. policy toward China. He urged the United States to [recognize] the present and potential danger from Communist China, and [take] measures designed to meet that danger. . . .

Taking the long view, we simply cannot afford to leave China forever outside the family of nations, there to nurture its fantasies, cherish its hates and threaten its neighbors. There is no place in this small planet for a billion of its potentially most able people to live in angry isolation. But we could go disastrously wrong if, in pursuing this long-range goal, we failed in the short run to read the lessons of history.[29]

Looking to the next decade, Nixon saw two prospects that, together, "could create a crisis of the first order":

(1) that the Soviets may reach nuclear parity with the United States; and (2) that China, within three to five years, will have a significant deliverable nuclear capability [and would be free to] scatter its weapons among "liberation" forces anywhere in the world.

In his view, this combination required

that we now assign to the strengthening of non-communist Asia a priority comparable to that which we gave to the strengthening of Western Europe after World War II. [This means] . . . a marshaling of Asian forces [so that non-communist nations] no longer furnish tempting targets for Chinese aggression [and] the leaders in Peking . . . turn their energies inward rather than outward. *And that will be the time when the dialogue with mainland China can begin.*[30]

It was a carefully crafted article, with eloquent generalizations to appeal to moderate and liberal sentiment, but specific proposals that were distinctly more cautious and appealing to conservatives. Most notably, it postponed even a "dialogue" with "mainland China" to the day when China turned inward—a vague condition that Nixon plainly did not think would be met for many years.

Any such major statement must be interpreted in context. In the spring and summer of 1967, Chinese policy was particularly hard to make out: the Cultural Revolution had been under way since late 1965, spread to massive repression by June 1966, and in the summer of 1967 included attacks on the British and other foreign embassies in Beijing. China seemed out of control, but it had taken no threatening external action. Nixon mentioned none of these uncertainties. He seems to have seen the Cultural Revolution, at that stage, as simply accenting the radical-threat component in Chinese policy, a view common among hard-line China watchers.

Moreover, it is striking that he did not mention the Soviet Union as a threat in East Asia, or North Vietnam and Ho Chi Minh as forces in their own right, or the ancient and deep-seated hostility between China and Vietnam. Rather, the several references to "aggression by proxy" suggest that he still saw China as the moving force and Ho as essentially a client or puppet—a view totally at variance with the long-standing judgment of the Johnson Administration and of the great majority of East Asian experts worldwide.[31]

In all, there was a great deal more revived and reframed 1950s thinking in the article than any foretaste of communication, let alone a real easing of relations, with China. Along the spectrum of serious American thinking about China by that time, Nixon's views were still on the hard-line side.[32]

. . .

In mid-October 1967, Nixon paid a visit to Eisenhower at his farm in Gettysburg. By Nixon's account, Ike was strongly opposed to stopping the bombing and criticized Johnson for restricting it; he also thought LBJ "had been a year and half late at every stage: in committing U.S. troops, in initiating the bombing, and in building up public support for the war." For his part, Nixon again put forward his idea that North Vietnam's harbors should be mined, but Eisenhower demurred on the ground that this would need a declaration of war—which apparently neither man favored.[33]

In late November, Eisenhower publicly urged that U.S. troops be allowed to cross the demilitarized zone at the 17th parallel (the DMZ, the border between North and South) and to pursue Communist forces into Cambodia and Laos. Campaigning in Oregon, Nixon responded to a request for comment by saying that Ike was "absolutely right" from a "military standpoint," but that such a move would be both diplomatically and politically unsound "at this time," for it might "run a substantial risk of widening the ground conflict in Vietnam."[34]

In sum, Nixon wanted to mine Haiphong but Eisenhower did not, while Eisenhower wanted to send U.S. forces into Cambodia and Laos, but Nixon demurred on political grounds. The two top Republicans thus tended to cancel each other out over expanding the war.

. . .

Such was the record Nixon made in his years out of office. He remained a "true believer" in the cause of resisting Communism in East Asia, in the crucial importance of supporting South Vietnam, and in the strong use of airpower. More than most, also, and certainly more than the Johnson Administration by this time, he saw China as the greatest threat and as the mainspring of Communist efforts. The Nixon of late 1967 remained a confirmed hawk, although more sophisticated and less reflexive than he had been in the 1950s.

3. *The 1968 Campaign: Through August*

When Nixon formally announced his candidacy on January 15, 1968, he was at once the clear favorite to win the Republican nomination. His anti-Communist record, his extraordinary familiarity with international affairs, and his hard-line positions on law and order issues made him almost invulnerable to any challenge from the Republican right. But he could also reach out to the party's moderate wing and to the important independent vote and concentrate, with increasing success, on his effort to shed the negative images of his past and present himself as a "new Nixon." The assessment of the veteran political writer and historian Theodore H. White was typical. In contrast to 1960, White now found a "total absence" of earlier bitterness and rancor, and was also impressed by how diligent and "driven to get to the bottom of things" Nixon was. White was still worried about "the ability of the man to stand up to the strain and heat of violent decision," and about the nature of his dreams. But all in all, "one must respect this man."[35]

Within a few weeks, the Tet offensive launched by Communist forces in Vietnam drastically changed the American people's view of the war and, thus, its place in the election campaign. Initial Communist successes, including a brief invasion of the U.S. Embassy compound in Saigon, attacks on many other cities and towns, and the occupation for several weeks of the key northern cities of Hue and Danang—all this was so different from the picture the Johnson Administration had been painting of slow but steady progress that public confidence was deeply shaken. Though the Vietcong suffered enormous casualties and were shortly driven out of the cities, the Communist side was winning on the American home front, where it most counted.

The Tet offensive was the decisive turning point in the war. For the first time, polls showed a majority of the public believing that it had been a mistake for the United States to get so deeply involved in Indochina. Opponents of the war renewed their efforts, while much moderate and even conservative opinion moved toward a conclusion that, valid as American objectives might still be, they could not be achieved in an acceptable time. In late March the majority of a group of bipartisan elder statesmen and retired military leaders who advised President Johnson in private—the so-called Wise Men—told him that the country would not accept further increases in the military effort and that the United States should start to reduce its effort and role. The Wise Men also urged entering into serious negotiation with North Vietnam if possible.[36]

As public opinion changed and Johnson tried to cope with the crisis, Nixon lay low. On March 5, campaigning in New Hampshire, he told an American Legion audience that "the war can be ended if we mobilize our economic and political leadership," and pledged "new leadership" to "end the war and win the peace in the Pacific." Pressed for details of what shortly became known as his "secret plan to end the war"—a media tag he himself neither used nor disclaimed—he refused on the ground that to do so would weaken his bargaining position if and when he became President.

He did say, at various campaign stops, that the objective should be an "honorable" peace that would not be regarded as a defeat—a considerable modification of earlier statements insisting that the United States must be in a commanding position to dictate terms. He also emphasized that the United States should engage the Soviet Union in efforts toward peace. Publicly he spoke only of doing this by unspecified political, economic, and diplomatic actions; in private he told Eisenhower he was thinking in terms of a combination of pressures (presumably having a military component) with a "carrot" of "economic détente" in Europe.[37]

By mid-March, the military situation in South Vietnam had stabilized. President Johnson and his advisors went through weeks of anxious deliberation over a February request from General William Westmoreland, the commander in Vietnam, for major reinforcements. Finally, President Johnson announced, in a nationwide TV speech on March 31, that he was providing only a modest force increase of 24,500 men, bringing the authorized U.S. force level to 549,500; that bombing of North Vietnam was being suspended except for the area near the demilitarized zone, and that it could stop entirely if this would lead to prompt peace negotiations and if Hanoi did not "take advantage" of the halt. Finally—to universal surprise—he announced that he was withdrawing as a candidate for reelection.

With the Democratic nomination now wide open, Vice President Hubert Humphrey quickly entered the fight against two antiwar senators, Robert Kennedy and Eugene McCarthy. When, on April 3, Hanoi declared its readiness to enter into talks about stopping the bombing completely, and implied that it was ready for serious substantive negotiations, the Vietnam War took on a totally different complexion as a political issue.

Nixon had a radio speech planned on the night Johnson withdrew, but naturally canceled the appearance. He was to have expanded on the Soviet Union as the possible key to peace, while reiterating sharp criticism of Johnson's policy of gradualism on the military front (without, however, advocating increased bombing) and urging that more of the war be turned over to the South Vietnamese. Thus, for practical purposes Nixon now abandoned his advocacy of tougher bombing, blockades, and (at intervals) higher force levels. Moreover, he never referred in the campaign to action in Laos or Cambodia.

Johnson named the veteran Ambassador Averell Harriman and the former Deputy Secretary of Defense (later Secretary of State) Cyrus Vance as U.S. negotiators, and the bilateral talks got under way in Paris in early May.

They focused only on the terms for stopping the U.S. bombing, not on peace terms.

Nixon made the obvious decision to refrain from comment lest this in any way affect the Paris talks. Through the horror months from April to July—months that saw the assassinations of Martin Luther King, Jr., and Robert Kennedy as well as a devastating racial riot in Washington itself—Nixon attended quietly to sewing up the Republican nomination and seeking particularly to limit the effect of the third-party candidacy of Governor George Wallace of Alabama by firming up his own support in the South. Challenges from the last-minute candidacies of Governor Ronald Reagan of California and Nelson Rockefeller were never serious, and served only to underscore Nixon's new "responsible" image. Wallace was a different story, with his often racist appeal to blue-collar voters North and South who in a straight two-party race would go mostly to Nixon. To head him off, Nixon made a private promise, through Senator Strom Thurmond of South Carolina, to help the textile industry, a political power and major source of political funds, by insisting that Japan, the leading textile exporter to America, accept firm quotas on its shipments.[38]

Meanwhile, as the Paris talks focused on the format and conditions for later peace talks, Hanoi's negotiators left no doubt of their ultimate terms, insisting over and over that the United States must withdraw all its forces from South Vietnam and dismantle the regime of Nguyen Van Thieu in favor of a coalition government formed with the National Liberation Front, or NLF—the Vietcong organizational title since 1961. In response, the initial American position rested on Johnson's March 31 speech: there could be a total bombing halt if Hanoi gave some assurance of reciprocal military restraint; the South Vietnamese government (the GVN) must participate in peace negotiations; and there must be agreement to move promptly to such negotiations. In the formal Paris sessions, as well as accompanying press interviews and releases, these three central points were repeated over and over, to no avail.

On the key issue of a cessation of bombing, Johnson all along shared the concern of his advisors, especially his military commanders, that any reduction in the bombing could increase the threat to American and other non-Communist forces. The format for peace negotiations was an equally difficult issue, not in U.S. eyes but for the Vietnamese on both sides. Thieu insisted, reasonably, on having a recognized position in substantive peace negotiations, in which the future of South Vietnam itself would be thrashed out. On the other hand, Hanoi predictably took the position that the only South Vietnamese representative must be the National Liberation Front and that the Saigon government was a puppet with no standing. Yet for the GVN to imply recognition of the NLF in any way would not only weaken its own legitimacy but seem to portend a future coalition government. The very word "coalition" evoked in Saigon the disastrous historical record of such coalitions in the years after World War II, when they had uniformly been manipulated to produce Communist governments. Thus, both the GVN and the NLF—indeed, all politically conscious Vietnamese of whatever stripe—saw any concession by either side about the legitimacy of the other as a matter of enormous importance.

To meet the problem, the South Vietnamese themselves came up with a formula. In April, Thieu and his Vice President (and perennial rival), Nguyen Cao Ky, suggested what came to be called the "your side–our side" formula: the South Vietnamese government would participate alongside the United States on a non-Communist "side," while Hanoi would be free to bring representatives of the NLF on its side.[39] Hanoi was bound to put forward the NLF as an ostensibly separate delegation, and neither the United States nor, ultimately, the GVN could resist or prevent this. But it was quickly agreed that the United States would continue to emphasize its categorical refusal to recognize that the NLF had any legitimacy. Each side devoted much attention and many press releases to justifying these opening positions and to expounding its view of the war. The two basic issues—military restraint and representation at the talks—were widely publicized and understood, certainly by a sophisticated observer such as Richard Nixon.

After hoping briefly that the failure of a follow-up Communist offensive in May, involving rocket attacks against several South Vietnamese cities, might produce a change, President Johnson in June and July accepted the advice of the Paris negotiators to initiate private and unannounced talks with the North Vietnamese at which the three central points of the basic American position were spelled out: Hanoi must accept the "your side–our side" formula; Communist forces (in practice, North Vietnamese) must refrain from significant violations of the demilitarized zone at the 17th parallel (the DMZ); and Communist forces of all types must refrain from indiscriminate or large-scale attacks on major cities in the South. At the same time, in a significant change of position, the U.S. negotiators did not demand that Hanoi commit itself expressly to the second and third points. Rather, they proposed informal "understandings," but Hanoi was left in no doubt that any significant breach of these would mean a resumption of the bombing. The use of such informal understandings had in fact been proposed publicly by Johnson in late September 1967, in a speech at San Antonio, so that the idea became known as "the San Antonio Formula."[40] As for the specific military restraints proposed, giving up attacks across the DMZ and on cities would amount to a major reduction in potential North Vietnamese and Vietcong operations.

In June and early July, Ambassador Ellsworth Bunker in Saigon at least twice went over the proposed position on military reciprocity with President

Thieu and got his assent, and Thieu repeatedly reaffirmed the "your side–our side" representation formula.[41] On July 15, Vance carefully spelled out the whole position in a private session with Ha Van Lau, his opposite number in the Hanoi delegation. Hanoi's negotiators obviously grasped all three key points, but remained totally unresponsive, thus reinforcing the public picture of stalemate and impasse.

. . .

In the last days of July, Johnson held unpublicized meetings to bring the main candidates fully into the picture. By then, Humphrey had a clear majority of the nomination votes lined up, mostly through state and local party leaders; a Gallup poll of professed Democrats also showed him ahead of Eugene McCarthy 53–39, though the same poll showed that a strong majority of Democrats in their twenties, and of those opposed to LBJ, were against Humphrey (34–58). Together with a great many older liberals, these groups passionately opposed the war and had come to focus, along with many moderates, on a demand for a total, immediate, and genuinely unconditional halt to all bombing of North Vietnam.

For some time Humphrey, even though he was Vice President, had not been brought into the government's discussions about negotiations. On July 25 he saw the President alone and asked his reaction to a draft statement that noted the recent drop in Communist operations and said that if this continued it might approximate the reciprocal action the Administration was seeking, in which case Humphrey would favor an immediate halt to the bombing. Tentative as this suggestion was, Johnson rejected it vehemently.[42]

On the next day, July 26, it was Nixon's turn to come to the White House for a briefing. Johnson related that a proposal had been made to the North Vietnamese, and to the Soviets, that called for a quid pro quo—that is, reciprocal military restraint on Hanoi's part—and that no bombing halt was planned "at that moment." In response, Nixon "pledged not to undercut our negotiating position just in case the Communists came around."[43]

This was the setting when Nixon, with the nomination as good as his, drafted a personal statement on Vietnam, which he presented to the Republican platform committee on August 1. "The war must be ended," he wrote. But until then "it must be waged more effectively. But rather than further escalation on the military front, what it requires now is a dramatic escalation of our efforts on the economic, political, diplomatic and psychological fronts." Nixon did not comment directly on the Paris talks or the terms for a bombing halt, but he did say that efforts toward peace should include "the most candid and searching conversations with the Soviet Union." His main theme was "a fuller enlistment of our South Vietnamese allies in their own defense." He also referred to his own past urging of stronger military measures: "The swift, overwhelming blow that would have been decisive two or three years ago is no longer possible today." Yet neither in 1965 nor in 1966 had Nixon offered any such drastic proposal, publicly or, as far as the evidence shows, privately.[44]

The Vietnam plank that the Republican Party adopted at its convention on August 6 was consistent with Nixon's ideas, which observers found "surprisingly dovish." The final version also reflected strenuous drafting sessions, in which Nixon's people joined forces with representatives of Nelson Rockefeller, notably Professor Henry Kissinger of Harvard, to fend off challenges from the more hawkish supporters of Governor Reagan.[45] It stressed the importance of "pacification" operations within South Vietnam and promised, "We will sincerely and vigorously pursue peace negotiations, as long as they offer any reasonable prospect for a just peace." By devoting itself mostly to sweeping criticisms of Johnson's handling of the war, the platform appealed to conservatives, while in its vague promises for the future it reached out to moderate and liberal opinion — "ambiguously peace-oriented" was *The New York Times* heading. A complete bombing halt was not mentioned, though the text appeared to assume that there would be early peace negotiations.[46]

Stripped of the hyperbole common to opposition party platforms, this one appeared to most observers to complete the process of removing from the campaign substantive differences between Democrats and Republicans over what to do in Vietnam. Reducing the U.S. role and stepping up that of the South Vietnamese had already been embraced by Johnson and Humphrey. The idea of new "economic, political and diplomatic" initiatives was vague, although in interviews at the convention Nixon spoke not only of bringing in the Russians but of negotiations "eventually" with the Chinese.[47] In effect, he was going along with the Paris talks, wishing them success (undefined), and holding the rest of his views to himself. Voters were asked to accept that he had been wise about Vietnam in the past, knew a great deal about it, probably had some kind of plan for moving toward peace and ending at least American involvement in the war, and was being a statesman in not commenting on issues that might be under discussion in Paris. It was a strong position, which he used to fend off all pressures to elaborate on his own proposals.[48]

Right after the Republican convention, on August 10, Nixon and the Republican nominee for Vice President, Governor Spiro Agnew of Maryland, were Johnson's guests for lunch at his Texas ranch, along with Secretary of State Rusk, CIA Director Richard Helms, and Cyrus Vance. The two hours of discussion and briefing included a presentation by Vance on the Paris talks and what the United States was "suggesting" there. The "your side–our side" formula was discussed as something already familiar and accepted by all present; and Vance almost certainly covered the San Antonio formula and the specific military restraints being insisted on.[49] After the meeting the press was told that Nixon had expressed support for Johnson's basic position that any total bombing halt should not be done unilaterally without Hanoi providing a meaningful quid pro quo—a public affirmation of what Nixon had said to Johnson privately on July 26.

Two days earlier, on August 8, Humphrey too had been received at the President's ranch, and this time Johnson filled him in much more fully on what was happening in Paris. He agreed to a public statement Humphrey could make that linked a bombing halt on the U.S. side to an "appropriate act of restraint and response" on the North Vietnamese one.[50] But this was not enough for the opposition within the Democratic Party. In addition to the pro-McCarthy delegates, a large number of younger liberals and antiwar protesters converged on Chicago, where the convention was shortly to begin, with "Stop the Bombing" as their principal cry. In the week before the convention, Johnson fed the antiwar fires when his speech to the Veterans of Foreign Wars on August 19 reiterated in strong terms his insistence on reciprocity. Speaking to the always hawkish VFW earlier the same day, Nixon also referred to the need for reciprocity.

Thus, when Dean Rusk started to testify before the Democratic platform committee on the evening of August 20, the stage was set for a bout of hostile questioning by dovish members of the committee and a widening of the split in the party. However, before the expected donnybrook could get under way, news came of a dramatic development abroad. Soviet tanks had rolled into Prague.

Earlier in the year a reform movement had taken power there, with a new Premier, Alexander Dubček, insisting on greater freedoms and more liberal internal practices. The reformers were all Communists, but they wanted "socialism with a human face" and hoped for democracy. The Dubček government during that "Prague spring" disavowed any intention to change Czechoslovakia's external policies or its adherence to the Warsaw Pact, but the Soviet leadership wavered on how to respond to what was obviously a challenge to Soviet dominance in Eastern Europe, and for months the situation hung in the balance. Many Sovietologists were inclined to think that Brezhnev and his colleagues might after all accept an unprecedented degree of internal change in Czechoslovakia, so the August 20 invasion came as a shock. Dubček and his colleagues were deposed and arrested, and a regime of hard-line Communists loyal to Moscow was installed. As in Budapest in 1956, Europe and the world saw a constant stream of pictures showing ruthless repression, with courageous civilians trying to defy tanks and dying in the process.

For a day or two, the events in Czechoslovakia took the limelight away from the Democrats' problems in Chicago. And, unknown to all but a very few senior officials in the Administration, they also forced Johnson to cancel plans for a dramatic move in U.S.-Soviet relations. Over the previous months, Soviet leaders had been slowly persuaded, largely by U.S. Ambassador Llewellyn (Tommy) Thompson in Moscow, to start serious talks on strategic arms limitation. Broad agreement to this effect had been mentioned publicly on June 30 when Johnson signed the multilateral Nuclear Nonproliferation Treaty, a worldwide undertaking on which the U.S.S.R. had almost for the first time collaborated with the United States, and on August 21 there was to have been a joint announcement that an opening meeting would take place between President Johnson and Soviet Premier Alexei Kosygin at the end of September, in Leningrad or Moscow.

LBJ's private discussions with Nixon in July and August had foreshadowed such a development and also put Nixon on notice that the President hoped to use these dealings with the Soviets to persuade them to exert effective influence on their North Vietnamese allies to move toward peace — precisely the policy Nixon was advocating on the stump. Certainly the announcement of a forthcoming "mini-summit" meeting with the Russians would have been considered a major move toward reducing tensions, and might have lessened the bitterness especially within the Democratic Party. But the Prague takeover dashed such hopes, and the fight over the Democratic platform quickly resumed. Johnson's friends submitted an "Administration" draft, which recommended a bombing halt only when there was clear evidence that it would not "endanger our troops in the field." The text also urged that negotiations seek "an immediate end or limitation of hostilities," the withdrawal of all foreign forces, and "a postwar government of South Vietnam . . . determined by fair and safeguarded elections, open to all political factions and parties prepared to accept peaceful political processes." Meanwhile, there should be accelerated efforts to train South Vietnamese forces, so as to permit "cutbacks in U.S. involvement."

Set alongside the Republican plank, the differences were slight. But the alternative Democratic plank offered by the antiwar forces of Senator McCarthy was very different: it favored stopping the bombing promptly and unconditionally, negotiating at once a complete withdrawal of American and North Vietnamese forces from South Vietnam, and "encouraging" the Saigon government to talk with all political elements, including the NLF, with a view to a new political regime in the South without the "prop" of American aid. The thrust was clear: peace soon, at whatever risk of a Communist-dominated South Vietnam.[51]

The resulting floor fight was long and disorderly, ending in the defeat of the alternative plank by a 1,567–1,041 vote. The bitterness that had marked the convention from the outset, accentuated by a feeling that it was dominated unduly by officeholders and professional politicians, broke open in physical battles within the hall and wild demonstrations outside it, which the Chicago police dealt with harshly. National television carried unforgettable scenes of policemen beating up helpless demonstrators, while old-line politicians, led by Mayor Richard Daley of Chicago, silenced respected liberals within the convention hall. By the end, on August 29, the Democratic nominees, Humphrey and Senator Edmund Muskie of Maine, stood at the head of a dispirited and sharply divided party, appealing to an electorate that had just seen another round of horror on its television screens. A few weeks before, after the Republican convention, Nixon had led Humphrey in the unofficial trial-heat polls by 45 to 29 (with 18 percent for Wallace), and ordinarily, the Democratic convention would have produced a substantial swing in the Democrats' favor. But after Chicago the polls still showed Nixon far ahead, 43–31–19.[52]

Given the condition of the Democratic Party at that point, pundits and public alike thought that Nixon was now virtually sure to win the election. So, too, must the leaders of the Soviet Union and North and South Vietnam.

4. Crescendo: The Last Weeks of the Campaign

As President Johnson turned back to the Paris talks after the convention period, it was clear that the domestic political implications of the negotiation had become greater. Neither he nor the two presidential candidates needed to be reminded of the potential importance of the "peace" theme, or that in 1968 it was even more powerful than usual. Yet at the same time, Johnson and Nixon were well aware that a peace move by Lyndon Johnson could produce disbelief or even a backlash, especially if it came close to the election. In the 1964 campaign he had twice burst out with statements that "Asians should fight Asians," appearing to say, even promise, that the government would not make a large-scale commitment of American forces in Vietnam. When such a commitment was made in 1965, the charge of deception and lack of candor contributed mightily to the "credibility gap" that dogged him thereafter.

Thus, Johnson knew well that his every move would be carefully scrutinized and suspiciously regarded, and that the initial reactions to any breakthrough were likely to be vehement and simplistic. Even the slightest movement toward peace might unite the Democratic Party and bring back those of its liberal wing who had opposed the Chicago platform and for critical weeks thereafter sat on their hands, often not expecting to vote at all. So it was natural for Nixon to feel that only a breakthrough in the Paris talks could wrest (in his eyes steal) the election from him at the last minute.[53]

In mid-August, the situation in Vietnam and in Paris suddenly changed. There was a surge in fighting between August 19 and September 3. The number of Americans killed in action rose to 308 and 408 in successive weeks, and attacks were made on several provincial capitals. Yet this was tame compared to Tet or even the May offensive. The steam seemed to have gone out of the Communist threat, and the performance of South Vietnamese forces had improved greatly.[54] As September went on with no renewal of enemy action, the overall situation seemed favorable for the government side, perhaps more so than at any previous time.

Yet for many Americans and certainly for most of the world, events in Eastern Europe held center stage, as the reversion to a harsh Soviet policy in Czechoslovakia was reinforced and extended to other Communist regimes. Unmistakably, by deed if not by any single statement, Moscow was asserting that it considered itself entitled to intervene wherever a Communist regime got out of line. This position, soon to be known as the Brezhnev Doctrine, also appeared to apply to China.[55]

The Soviet action in Prague was almost universally condemned. The European members of NATO were especially alarmed, and stayed on military alert even as the threat of wider action subsided. Although the reaction in the United States was also one of outrage, Lyndon Johnson did not want to give up the hope that he could end his term with U.S.–U.S.S.R. arms control negotiations under way. He also had in mind that warmer relations with Moscow might produce Soviet help toward peace in Vietnam. Official U.S. statements therefore used less harsh language about the Soviet action than those of many other governments, and the President continued to express hopes to the Soviet leaders for an exploratory summit. Using an indirect channel, he gave the Soviets an explicit picture of the U.S. three-point position on stopping the bombing in North Vietnam.[56] In response, Soviet Ambassador Valerian Zorin in Paris became much more accessible.

In mid-September the press stepped up its coverage of the Paris talks. When Harriman and Vance followed each other to Washington, the possibility of a U.S. initiative figured in several stories. (In fact the two visits produced no change in the U.S. position.) With the atmosphere expectant, Humphrey made a move. His campaign was still in great disarray, behind 28–43 to Nixon (and with Wallace still high at 21 percent). Finally, on September 30, responding at last to the urging of advisors led by former Under Secretary of State George Ball, he made a major speech in Salt Lake City saying that he would be prepared to risk a complete bombing halt, see what response might develop, and resume the bombing if there was no constructive response. This was a deliberately vague version of the San Antonio formula, not explicitly contrary to the Chicago platform but designed to shade it in a dovish direction—and above all to differ in tone from Johnson's public statements.[57] In domestic political terms, the speech was a resounding success, bringing back to the fold a great many idle Democrats and some independents and giving Humphrey a surge of personal confidence. It was a visible turning point in the campaign: thereafter Humphrey's stock rose steadily and an ultimate victory for him became conceivable. In Hanoi, the speech may have strengthened a preference for a Humphrey victory. In Saigon, more certainly, it added to distaste for Humphrey and fed the already evident desire to see Nixon win.

For whatever combination of reasons, on October 9 the North Vietnamese negotiators hinted at a major change in their position at the regular announced session in Paris, and confirmed the change in private on October 11. What would happen, they asked, if Hanoi agreed to accept official representatives of the Saigon government for a discussion of substantive terms? This implied offer to accept the Saigon government as a party to the peace negotiations was at once recognized as a simple but vital concession on a point where the U.S. negotiators had almost given up hope. The North Vietnamese again made clear that the NLF must also be there. In effect, they were no longer contesting the U.S. position that each side should have its South Vietnamese representative, with neither accepting the asserted status of the rival. The representation impasse had been resolved. The following day, October 12, the Soviet deputy in Paris visited Vance to deliver a message promising hopeful results if talks got under way, a message said to be on behalf of North Vietnam as well as the Soviet Union.[58]

Johnson at once cabled Ambassador Bunker and General Creighton Abrams, who had succeeded General Westmoreland, asking their comments on draft instructions for Harriman and Vance to go full speed ahead to get an agreement and to discuss convening the actual peace discussions immediately afterward. Bunker went over these instructions and the whole plan with President Thieu and cabled that "Thieu was for the plan without reservations."[59]

The next day, in Washington, Johnson met first with an inner circle of advisors and then with a larger group that included Senator Richard Russell as a special guest. The two meetings framed with remarkable clarity the advice the President got, and his own thinking. Bunker and Abrams cabled that they regarded Hanoi's move as a significant concession and its "shift to the conference table as a result of an unfavorable military situation. . . . 1968 has been a disaster for Hanoi." The Joint Chiefs agreed, with General Earle Wheeler, the chairman, going so far as to say, in substance: "The military war has been won." Secretary Clark Clifford was strongly in favor of going ahead, as was Secretary Dean Rusk, while noting that even if the proposal was accepted, "the negotiations will be long, difficult and troublesome."[60]

The most reserved participant was Senator Russell, who predicted that the proposal would be attacked as a "purely political trick," but thought most people would support it over such objections ("they want to get this infernal war over"). The President responded that the record since March "shows conclusively that no action has been taken for domestic political reasons," to which Russell replied that he did not need to be convinced of that, but that it would be difficult to persuade others, especially if the bombing was later resumed. In the ensuing discussion, according to one account, Nixon's possible reaction was mentioned. "[I]t was argued that Nixon had been honorable on the war issue and had said he wanted the peace talks moved along as far as possible by the incumbent President."[61]

In the end, Senator Russell agreed that the proposal was "worth a try," and the President made a moving statement:

> If this isn't the way to stop it, I don't have any way to end it. . . . [W]e couldn't survive if all of this became public and it became known that we had done nothing about it.[62]

The two crucial meetings ended with all present understanding that the President, well aware of the problems, had decided to go ahead. On October 16, Johnson instructed Harriman and Vance to press for agreement that peace discussions should get under way at once after a bombing halt, and that the announcement of the halt should specify the date at which delegations would meet in Paris for the new negotiations. Briefly, Johnson hoped to make a joint announcement that evening, but during the day both Hanoi and Saigon registered reservations about his plan. As predicted, Hanoi wanted a longer or indefinite interval; Thieu's plea was that he needed time to marshal and instruct a proper delegation.[63]

At this point, press speculation was feverish, and to keep it from making the final ironing out harder, Johnson put out word that there was "no change, no breakthrough."[64] He then made a conference telephone call to the three candidates, out on the campaign trail, still taking the "no breakthrough" line but indicating there had been "some movement." Nixon asked what assurances Johnson was seeking, and Johnson replied by listing the standard three points. Nixon later summarized his own reaction: "If these conditions were fulfilled, of course, I would support whatever arrangements Johnson could work out."[65]

Over the next ten days, Harriman and Vance met almost daily with their North Vietnamese counterparts in Paris. At Johnson's insistence, the Soviet Union was also brought more closely into the situation. Rusk and Harriman told Dobrynin and Zorin how serious it would be if Hanoi were to violate the understandings on military restraint, and by their replies the ambassadors in effect certified that Hanoi fully understood the American terms. In fact, Zorin came close to saying that the Soviet Union would make sure they were observed. This was the strongest Soviet diplomatic involvement in exchanges over Indochina in years, and seemed a useful and hopeful sign.

Notably, the North Vietnamese did not further debate the plans for participation in the peace talks. Everyone understood that Saigon would be at the table, and so would the NLF. But Thieu focused heavily on this issue. From May onward, the Americans had asked him to restrict the key exchanges to himself and his inner circle, which included Vice President Ky and his Foreign Minister. Only this inner circle, it appears, knew that Thieu had suggested the "your side–our side" formula, that he had accepted the American three-point position in July, and that he had concurred with the whole American plan, including the rapid convening of serious peace talks, on October 13.

By this time, a year after his election, Thieu had consolidated his personal power and was in control of the government, including the elected Assembly, on most matters. He had rallied his people after the Tet setbacks and put on a good performance in moving ahead with increases in the armed forces and somewhat greater military responsibility. But elements in both the Assembly and his National Security Council were hostile to him personally and especially to the idea of allowing the NLF at the peace talks, for fear that such a move would lead to a coalition government. The Johnson Administration (repeatedly) and both the Democratic and Republican Party platforms had expressly rejected the idea of a coalition in any form, but the bugaboo now reared its head again, and at the most difficult time.

As South Vietnamese politicians must have noted, moreover, the American presidential race was narrowing. In contrast to the mid-September Gallup reading of 43–28–21 for Nixon, Humphrey, and Wallace, respectively, the tally by the end of the third week of October was 44–36–15! Much of the labor vote was returning to its traditional Democratic home; the extreme nuclear bomb rattling of George Wallace's chosen running mate, retired Air Force general Curtis LeMay, weakened that third party's appeal; the Democrats were campaigning more effectively; and most presidential races tend to become closer as election day approaches. All the pundits were describing a Humphrey trend, with some suggesting parallels to Harry Truman's last-month overtaking of Thomas Dewey in 1948 and others recalling the close 1960 race Nixon had lost to Kennedy.[66]

Despite Thieu's earlier concurrences, he now made difficulties. Beginning on October 16, as the press reported, Bunker met with him no fewer than ten times, while Thieu in turn consulted with his National Security Council and a widening circle within South Vietnam's small political establishment. Most of these sessions were devoted to the question of NLF participation in peace talks. American officials knew that Thieu had a genuine political problem, but the "your side–our side" formula remained the only practical way to start talks. To walk back from the deal both Saigon and Hanoi had agreed to would have been difficult in any circumstances;

to do so on the basis that Saigon had to be accepted as the preeminent South Vietnamese representative would have been impossible to explain to the American people, let alone Hanoi.

On October 25, Nixon injected his voice, through a statement that he was hearing reports that Johnson was acting for political reasons, but did not believe these reports and assumed it was not so. As *The Washington Post* and many other papers noted, this was an old Nixon technique of maximum innuendo and pious dissociation. To the White House, it seemed an unpleasant political move but not more. The President still believed Nixon both knew and accepted Johnson's positions and knew that the timing had not been LBJ's to decide.

On Sunday, October 27, Harriman and Vance were at last able to report complete agreement with the North Vietnamese in Paris. In Saigon, however, Thieu had come up with a new list of demands, most notably that the United States must "guarantee" that Hanoi would talk directly and bilaterally with Saigon. This was just the kind of impossible demand the "your side–our side" formula was designed to avoid. To all the Americans involved, Thieu seemed to be backing off a clear commitment.

Facing this difficulty but also to be absolutely sure of his ground, Johnson that weekend brought in General Abrams from Saigon. Reporting immediately after his arrival, in the early morning of October 29, Abrams reiterated his judgment that a bombing halt on the proposed understandings was militarily tolerable and "the right thing to do." For Johnson, this was the clincher: he was now fully committed. That same evening, however, Bunker reported that in an extraordinary morning meeting on October 30, Thieu still refused to budge. All the following day, Johnson deliberated, and finally decided to announce on the evening of October 31 that the bombing would halt at once and peace negotiations would begin on November 6, with the South Vietnamese government "free to attend." His hope, encouraged by Bunker, was that the prospect of isolation would get Thieu to participate.

On the afternoon of October 31, Johnson made a second conference call to Nixon, Humphrey, and Wallace, to inform them that he was going ahead. He specifically stated that the Saigon government was not yet committed to attending the substantive negotiations — and his interlocutors did not seek to pursue the matter. That evening, on nationwide television, Johnson announced that the bombing in Vietnam would stop completely at eight o'clock the following morning, Washington time. The public response was enthusiastic and hopeful. Few doubted that difficult negotiations lay ahead, but the announced actions still seemed a big move toward peace.

On Saturday, November 2, however, Thieu made a dramatic speech to the National Assembly in Saigon, stating flatly that the South Vietnamese would not attend peace negotiations unless they were categorically accorded a superior position to that of the NLF. The result was a weekend of total confusion on the American political front, with the polls at first showing significant gains for Humphrey but then diverging. After Thieu's rejection was reported, Nixon made a short statement on Saturday, regretting that the prospects were not as bright as they had at first appeared. That evening he went further, by having his top assistant on the campaign plane, Robert Finch, tell reporters that Nixon had been surprised by the Thieu rejection, since Johnson had led him to believe that "all the diplomatic ducks were in a row." (This was untrue, as we have just noted.) Nixon's obvious purpose was to portray the President's action as sloppily prepared and politically motivated. The Finch story made banner headlines on Sunday, dominating Nixon's appearance that morning on the important national program *Meet the Press.* Asked about claims that the bombing halt was a political stunt, Nixon replied that Johnson had been "very candid with me throughout these discussions, and I do not make such a charge" — innuendo and dissociation once again. He went on in a statesmanlike tone to say that the South Vietnamese should attend the new peace talks and that he was willing to go to Paris or Saigon to help if that were deemed useful; he had assumed from the announcement that the South Vietnamese were "aboard," since their attendance was "the only quid pro quo we got from the bombing pause." (This was again untrue, in that it ignored the military restraint understandings.)

In further appearances on Sunday and Monday, Nixon again took the line that politics should not be a factor. He was sorry the "outlook was so bleak" and would do anything to get the early peace talks back on track, adding that he had conveyed this message to President Johnson, who had seemed grateful for it.

On Sunday evening, in Houston, Johnson finally pitched in and joined Humphrey in a dramatic rally, but by Monday the polls showed a swing back in favor of Nixon, giving him a hairline edge. Most people were persuaded that Nixon had handled Johnson's announcement in a correct and responsible fashion, while many believed that Johnson had been motivated in large part, if not entirely, by a desire to help Humphrey and the Democrats.

Finally, on Tuesday, November 5, the voters spoke, giving Richard Nixon a small margin in the overall vote (43–42), but a greater one in the decisive electoral college (302–191). It was a dramatic ending to a painful campaign. Humphrey conceded gallantly, and Nixon saw the outcome as the vindication of years of effort, a successful campaign, and (privately) his resourceful handling of the last days after Johnson's announcement.

To most Americans, it was a relief simply to have it over. In American elections, the dominant tradition has always been not to go back over the result unless the defeated candidate brings forward evidence of gross and exceptional misconduct. Close as the result had been, Nixon's election seemed confirmed and accepted. Only in later years, mostly after he had been forced from office, did the full story emerge of how he had personally organized in 1968 a covert operation to persuade Nguyen Van Thieu to defer joining in the peace talks—the very act that may have tipped the election result in Nixon's favor.

5. Behind the Scenes: The Chennault Affair

When President Johnson told the three candidates on October 31 of his forthcoming statement announcing the bombing halt, he added a thinly veiled warning aimed at Nixon. As recalled by members of his staff listening in, Johnson said there had been implications "by some of our folks, even including some of the old China lobbyists, that a better deal might be made with a different President."[67] The remark can hardly have been lost on Richard Nixon. He knew at once that the reference was to Anna Chennault, Republican activist and an official in his campaign, and at the core of what remained of the strongly pro-Nationalist-China groups loosely labeled the China Lobby.

Over the next four days, a rumor that Chennault had played some role spread to the press, which was already well aware that senior Republicans like Senator Everett Dirksen were fulminating that the bombing halt was an election stunt. Two normally shrewd election watchers, Theodore White and Tom Wicker, queried Nixon's campaign people. Both readily accepted that Chennault had done something, yet both knew her well enough to think it possible that she had acted on her own. In White's account:

> At the first report of Republican sabotage in Saigon, Nixon's headquarters had begun to investigate the story; had discovered Mrs. Chennault's activities; and was appalled. The fury and dismay at Nixon's headquarters when his aides discovered the report were so intense that they could not have been feigned simply for the benefit of this reporter. Their feeling on Monday morning before the election was, simply, that if they lost the election, Mrs. Chennault might have lost it for them. She had taken their name and authority in vain.[68]

Both reporters were convinced, and along with another reporter, Jules Witcover, who had also picked up the story, they decided not to pursue the matter.

Once the election was over, interest in what came to be called "the Chennault affair" ebbed rapidly. In January 1969 an article by Thomas Ottenad of the St. Louis Post-Dispatch spelling out what he had learned about her activities attracted only slight attention. Later in 1969, Theodore

White's third quadrennial campaign history, *The Making of the President 1968*, brought the episode to wider public attention but at the same time seemed to confirm that Chennault's actions had not involved Nixon himself. Witcover's book on the campaign left open whether Nixon had known of Chennault's activities, while painting a damning picture of the successive statements made by the Nixon camp in the final days. For a few years, the affair seemed to have been laid to rest.[69]

On Nixon's side, William Safire's 1973 memoir argued strenuously that Johnson's actions were politically motivated and Nixon's innocent, and went on to attack Johnson in harsh terms for the use of intelligence methods directed at Anna Chennault. That Johnson had information from official intelligence sources was part of the early rumors, and was confirmed in 1976 hearings on intelligence activities before the Church Committee of the Senate, with mention of wiretaps and other surveillance and intercepted diplomatic messages of the South Vietnamese Embassy. Working from these revelations and his own inquiries, Thomas Powers, in a book on the CIA published in 1979, spelled out that part of the story in some detail.[70]

Nixon's memoir, published in 1978, mentioned neither Chennault nor Johnson's several reports to him about the Paris talks. Instead, he went on at length about general warnings he received from Henry Kissinger and other sources alleging political motives among Johnson's advisors. This position — in effect avoiding direct comment on the charges while claiming this justification for whatever was done — was maintained thereafter by others close to Nixon. In 1980, the memoir of Anna Chennault herself appeared, though little noted; it went into great and revealing detail about her role in the campaign and her relationship with Nixon then and later. This was followed in 1986 by *The Palace File* by Nguyen Tien Hung and Jerrold Schecter, which tells this story and much else as seen by President Thieu, to whom Hung was a close advisor, and in 1987 by an equally revealing memoir of Bui Diem. On the Democratic side, Carl Solberg's 1984 biography of Hubert Humphrey contained an excellent account reflecting careful research. Most recently, the 1991 memoir of Clark Clifford dealt at length with the affair, using other materials by then available.

The sharp conflict among the various accounts must compel a historian to be especially clear in naming and evaluating sources. The chronological sequence of the published accounts is also relevant: each built on, or felt the need to rebut or modify, what others had said or published before.

. . .

On July 12, 1968, Nixon received three visitors in New York, either at his apartment or in a room at his campaign headquarters. The first was John Mitchell, his law partner and confidant, later to become his Attorney General. The second was Ambassador Bui Diem of South Vietnam. The third was Anna Chennault.[71]

Bui Diem had been shuttling back and forth to Paris since May, as South Vietnamese liaison officer to the talks there. As Assistant Secretary of State for East Asia, I was in regular contact with him whenever he was in Washington, and his memoir states that before going to see Nixon he asked me whether the Administration would have any problem with his doing so. I have no recollection of such a conversation, but would surely have told him that such a meeting (in itself) would not be objectionable or improper. In his inquiry, he did not mention who else might be there.

Chennault had proposed a meeting to Nixon in late June, but just how it was arranged is obscure. The evidence suggests that it was done clandestinely, circumventing everyone on Nixon's staff except Mitchell, and going to some lengths to keep even the fact of the meeting from becoming known to his staff or his Secret Service escort.[72] Nixon had known Anna Chennault for a long time; over the years the two came to regard each other as natural allies. By the 1960s Chennault was an established Washington character, moving in wide circles. Chinese-born and close to Nationalist Chinese leaders, she became in 1947 the young second wife of the legendary General Claire Chennault, who had left the U.S. air forces to organize and lead a group of American volunteers, the Flying Tigers, who operated in support of the Chinese against the Japanese before America came into the war. When the general died in 1958 she stayed on in Washington, working actively for various air transport organizations in Asia, some with CIA connections, as was widely known in Asia and generally surmised in Washington.[73]

Attractive, outgoing, always well informed and an excellent hostess, she was more and more active in Republican causes from the late 1950s on, close to many top senators such as Minority Leader Everett Dirksen of Illinois and John Tower of Texas. She also kept up her ties in Asia, not only in Taiwan but around Southeast Asia, with frequent visits to the area. Through a sister married to a Chinese (Nationalist) diplomat in Saigon, she was in constant touch with the situation there, and on her habitual visits, from the mid-1960s on, developed a friendship with Thieu through personal talks alone with him. In Taiwan her regular contacts included the South Vietnamese Ambassador, Nguyen Van Kieu, President Thieu's brother. Anna Chennault was totally dedicated to support for South Vietnam and had special feelings about any possibility of a coalition, from having lived through the 1946–47 phase of the Chinese Civil War, when the United States briefly promoted such a coalition between the Nationalists and the Communists. When this fell through and the Communists won, she, like most Nationalists, blamed the United States rather than the corruption and incompetence of the Chiang Kai-shek regime. In 1968, Chennault was undoubtedly sincere in opposing serious peace negotiations with Hanoi, fearing that, whatever their original intentions, the Americans would end up abandoning the Thieu regime, as she believed they had done shamefully in China.

In short, Anna Chennault was an ideal intermediary, bright, resourceful, acting from deepest conviction, with only the drawbacks of being a bit too conspicuous and not always discreet in speech and action. These same qualities made her memoir more revealing than she may have intended.

Bui Diem was a highly capable journalist turned diplomat, with a long record of anti-Communist activity in North Vietnam before he was forced to flee to the South. As editor of the leading English-language daily in Saigon, he was respected by Americans of all stripes, so that it seemed natural that when Thieu was elected President in October 1967, he sent Bui Diem to Washington. There he readily found his way around, keeping up with all shades of opinion, including vehement critics of the war, and in constant touch with leading Republicans, often through Anna Chennault's salon. As for John Mitchell, the best description of his position is that of Anna Chennault herself: "From the beginning it was clear that John Mitchell was commander-in-chief of the campaign. . . . [H]is presence was very much felt, his approval sought on all major decisions." By her own account, at the height of the campaign she was on the phone to Mitchell at least once a day![74]

The later accounts by Chennault and Bui Diem agree that the July 12 meeting went well beyond a courtesy call. The four talked together for a half hour, and Nixon, Mitchell, and Bui Diem then withdrew without her to another room and talked for another hour. The second session discussed the need for better weapons and training for the South Vietnamese troops, and Thieu's plans for a Honolulu meeting with Johnson the following week. The session that included Chennault centered on the election and the need for continuing close communication between Nixon and Thieu. According to both accounts, Richard Nixon used the meeting to confirm to the others that Anna Chennault was his channel to President Thieu. He told the ambassador that he should feel free to convey messages to her at any time, and that she in turn would relay thoughts from the Nixon camp, via Mitchell. He stressed that she "would be the sole representative between the Vietnamese government and the Nixon campaign headquarters," saying: "Anna is a very dear friend. . . . We count on her for information on Asia. She brings me up to date."[75] The relationship thus established was hardly a normal or customary one, and may have been unique. The opposition party's candidate for President was setting up a special two-way private channel to the head of state of a government with whom the incumbent President was conducting critically important and secret negotiations!

Soon thereafter, Anna Chennault attended the Miami Republican convention. She then made one or more trips to Asia, using one stop in Saigon to visit with President Thieu in what she described as "an informal presentation of credentials. I was delivering a message from Nixon requesting that I be recognized as the conduit for any information that might flow between the two." She also discussed the Paris talks, finding (and reporting to Nixon and Mitchell) that the South Vietnamese government "remained intransigent" in its "attitudes vis-à-vis the peace talks."[76]

In mid-September, with speculation growing that there might be progress in Paris, Henry Kissinger became a part of the story. As we have noted, Nixon knew his reputation and writing, and in August, Kissinger, acting for Nelson Rockefeller, had negotiated effectively on the contents of the Republican platform, showing himself receptive to Nixon's ideas, which were close to his own. After the conventions, Kissinger set out to prepare an article for *Foreign Affairs*, his habitual outlet for policy-related pieces, about the possible shape of substantive negotiations over Vietnam. He was completely familiar with the issues, and especially with the Administration's San Antonio formula on military restraint under a bombing halt, which had emerged from a secret 1967 negotiating effort in which he had been the principal American intermediary.[77]

With this interest and previous exposure, Kissinger planned a stopover in Paris in mid-September, on his way to a conference in England. Just before he left, John Mitchell, following up on an earlier suggestion from Nelson Rockefeller to Nixon, got in touch with him and on September 12 enlisted him to give judgment and advice to the Nixon campaign. The arrangement was apparently secret, or at least not to be publicized.[78] Kissinger was thus an undisclosed advisor to Nixon when he went to Paris and talked with several members of the U.S. delegation in September 18–22. On his return, about September 26, he reported to Mitchell that he felt, on the basis of his Paris trip, that "something big was afoot." According to Nixon's account, Kissinger was "completely circumspect" and did not reveal any details of negotiations, but simply warned against launching any new ideas or proposals that might be undercut by developments in Paris.[79]

But was this all? Did Kissinger learn something more concrete about the prospects and convey this to the Nixon people? In 1983 the investigative reporter Seymour Hersh made headlines by leading off his important book *The Price of Power*, which is sharply critical of Kissinger throughout, with the charge that Kissinger got inside information in Paris, conveyed it to the Nixon camp, and followed up repeatedly during October, ingratiating himself with Nixon to secure a high appointment. On a great many other points in his book, I have found Hersh reliable and often original, showing a solid grasp of problems and issues. But in this case, I believe his charge does not stand up under careful examination. There is of course nothing wrong in offering advice and judgment to a candidate in the hope of preferment. In any presidential campaign, many individuals do so. Such action is open to harsh criticism only if it involves the use of inside government information. Yet that is where the charge collapses.

As of September 18, and until at least the end of the month, not only was the American position unchanged on the terms for a bombing halt and start of negotiations (as it remained throughout), but there was no sign that the North Vietnamese were wavering in their rejection of that position. The most that Kissinger could have picked up was a sense of increased activity and possibly that an effort was being made to engage the Soviet Union. Even if one or more members of a disciplined delegation was ready to confide in a former colleague, there simply was no useful "inside information" at that point.[80]

Nixon's memoir goes on to say that in early October, Kissinger reiterated his warning of late September, suggesting that a bombing halt might be arranged for mid-October. About October 12, according to Nixon, a third Kissinger message suggested that this might happen about October 23. It is plausible that in the first three weeks of October, Kissinger did convey one or more warnings to Nixon, via Mitchell, that a break in the Paris talks might be imminent. His later rebuttal, however, saying that any such messages were based on his judgment alone—primarily his assessment that the North Vietnamese might see it to their advantage to move into peace talks while Johnson was President—is persuasive. Almost any experienced Hanoi watcher might have come to the same conclusion.[81]

On October 15, Bui Diem learned that a deal might be imminent—from Thieu himself and from Philip Habib, a member of the Harriman-Vance delegation who was back in Washington that day. Undoubtedly Bui Diem told Anna Chennault right away, and she passed the word on to Nixon, via Mitchell (as prescribed), making it plain that Johnson's "no breakthrough" line in his conference call to the candidates on October 16 was not to be taken literally. According to one source, Chennault wrote Nixon at once to protest the idea of a bombing halt; she also activated her lines to Saigon.[82] By her own account, her messages by whatever routing went direct to Thieu himself. As "the campaign neared its climax" and as Thieu came under "steady pressure . . . by the Democrats to attend the Paris Peace Talks," she was repeatedly in touch with Thieu through one or more channels.[83]

In these exchanges (again by her account) Thieu stated a consistent position: he opposed peace talks on the ground that no one was ready, and "would much prefer to have the peace talks after your election." Chennault would then ask if this was a message to "my party." Invariably, Thieu would respond that she should "convey this message to your candidate." Given her instructions, there is every reason to believe that she did so, via Mitchell or perhaps directly to Nixon himself.[84]

Important further exchanges occurred on the night of October 31, when

Chennault, at a private party, listened to Johnson's speech announcing the bombing halt. Mitchell telephoned her there immediately (showing how closely they were staying in touch), and when she went to a private place to return the call, he said at once: "Anna. I'm speaking on behalf of Mr. Nixon. It's very important that our Vietnamese friends understand our Republican position and I hope you have made that very clear to them."

According to her account, she was startled, believing that her instructions had been only "to keep Nixon informed of South Vietnamese intentions" and detecting in Mitchell's tone a request to go further. She responded, she says:

> Look, John, all I've done is to relay messages. If you're talking about direct influence, I have to tell you it isn't wise for us to try to influence the South Vietnamese. Their actions have to follow their own national interests, and I'm sure that is what will dictate Thieu's decisions.

Mitchell still "sounded nervous" and asked whether "they really have decided not to go to Paris." To which she replied: "I don't think they'll go. Thieu has told me over and over again that going to Paris would be walking into a smoke screen that has nothing to do with reality." At the end of the call Mitchell asked her to be sure to call him if she got any more news.[85]

In short, very soon after Johnson's speech, or earlier, Nixon knew that Thieu was adamant, unlikely to consent to an early bombing halt or to participate in any talks. Chennault's assertion to Mitchell, that she never tried to exert "direct influence" on Thieu, was at best a quibble: repeated inquiries, coming from an authorized Nixon agent like herself, surely conveyed Nixon's fervent desire that Thieu should not go along with the Johnson plan. She may have avoided direct appeals, but her message was hardly subtle or obscure.

The other principal in the story, Ambassador Bui Diem, has given an exceptionally precise account in his memoir. On October 23 (he wrote), he cabled Saigon: "Many Republican friends have contacted me and encouraged us to stand firm. They were alarmed by press reports to the effect that you had already softened your position." Then, on October 27, he reported that he was "regularly in touch with the Nixon entourage," by which he says he meant Chennault, Mitchell, and Tower; his memoir does not give further details of that cable.[86]

. . .

What did President Johnson learn and how did he and Hubert Humphrey react? Sometime on October 29, as President Johnson and his inner circle realized that Thieu was being more and more resistant and devious in his objections, they received a report that shook them. Almost certainly it was based on the deciphered and translated text of one or more intercepted cables from the South Vietnamese Embassy in Washington, most likely those of October 23 and 27, which were the basis of Bui Diem's later reconstruction of events.[87] One of those who saw the deciphered text of Bui Diem's personal cable to Thieu on October 27 kept notes of it, according to which Bui Diem reported that he had "explained discreetly to our partisan friends our firm attitude" and "plan to adhere to that position." He went on: "The longer the [impasse] situation continues, the more we are favored" and Johnson would "probably have difficulties in forcing our hand." The ambassador concluded that he had been told that if Nixon was elected he would first send an unofficial emissary to Thieu and would consider going to Saigon himself prior to his inauguration.[88] While there is no direct evidence that such a message came personally from Nixon, it is hardly the sort of semi-promise that would be made without his authority.

Aroused by this solid information, and by other evidence of Republican agitation, Johnson on October 30 ordered the FBI to conduct "physical and electronic surveillance" (a euphemism for phone tapping) of Anna Chennault. In so doing, he relied both on national security concerns and on possible violations of existing laws dealing with contacts between private citizens and foreign governments.[89] On November 2, the phone tap picked up a call from Chennault to Saigon (presumably Thieu or his office) specifically urging that Thieu stand firm and saying that they would get a better deal (unspecified) from Nixon. Asked if Nixon knew of her call, she responded that he did not but "our friend in New Mexico does." Spiro Agnew, as the candidate for Vice President, was campaigning in Albuquerque, New Mexico, on that day.[90]

As information about Chennault's activities flowed in to Johnson, he and his inner circle debated what to do. Clark Clifford strongly favored a confrontation with Nixon, or making the gist of the evidence public. Dean Rusk, on the other hand, thought that this would so blacken Thieu's standing with the American public as to make any further American support for South Vietnam difficult, if not impossible.[91] With conflicting advice, Johnson hesitated from Thursday till Sunday. He did, however, inform Humphrey about Chennault's activities on Friday, November 1. Returning to Washington, Humphrey went through agonizing hours on Sunday morning, trying to decide whether he himself should make an issue of this Republican intervention. He was urged to do so by his staff, and was told of the conflicting arguments being put to Johnson, along with a summary of the evidence. In the end he decided not to raise the issue, for two reasons: that the evidence did not on its face show that Nixon himself was involved and that "it would have been difficult to explain how we knew about what she had done."[92]

Theodore White later wrote that he "knew of no more essentially decent story in American politics than Humphrey's decision." Another acute observer, Jules Witcover, wrote: "The decision was either one of the noblest in American political history or one of the great tactical blunders. Possibly it was both."[93]

Johnson himself finally boiled over on Sunday afternoon, after listening to Nixon on television. Nixon said that his aide Robert Finch thought the Democrats must have plotted the bombing halt for election purposes, but piously added that he himself did not believe this. Since Johnson knew beyond doubt by this time about the Republican efforts to persuade Thieu to be obdurate, it must have been especially galling when Nixon volunteered to help straighten things out by going to Saigon himself! So Johnson telephoned Nixon, then in Los Angeles, to complain vigorously about what "Fink" had said and to ask point-blank whether Nixon was involved. Nixon responded with a categorical denial, saying flatly that whatever Chennault had done had been on her own, with no connection or knowledge on his part. This barefaced lie was his only tenable line of defense, and the word must have gone out to his top campaign people, accounting for the vehement denials Theodore White encountered at the Republican campaign offices on Monday.[94]

In the closing days of the campaign, therefore, Nixon artfully gave maximum play to the notion that Johnson was simply playing politics—while at the same time repeating that he himself made no such charge and that Johnson had been candid with him. In his 1978 memoir, however, Nixon shifted ground and adopted the position that Johnson's decision had been "sufficiently political to permit my taking at least some action."[95] For this view he claimed to have relied heavily on reports given him by Bryce Harlow (an old election hand and expert on defense matters who was working for the Nixon campaign) from "someone in Johnson's innermost circle," especially one on October 22 to the effect that Clark Clifford, Joseph Califano (of the White House staff), and Llewellyn Thompson (Ambassador to Moscow) were "the main participants" in "driving exceedingly hard for a deal," that George Ball (Humphrey's chief foreign policy advisor) was in on the effort, and that the wires were set up for Humphrey to take maximum advantage.

On its face, such a report should have sounded odd. An experienced White House hand like Harlow would surely have known that Califano was wholly concerned with domestic policy and that Thompson, in Moscow, was an apolitical diplomat who was hardly in a position to exert influence on Johnson. Neither was in fact involved in the policy discussions of those weeks, nor was Ball, who had left government many months earlier. The reports were indeed so implausible as to throw doubt that anyone at all near the actual center of decision was the source. They were the rawest sort of campaign rumor.

What did Nixon really believe, and why did he act as he did? He does not address or answer these questions frankly in his memoir, while other Nixon supporters who have written books, notably Safire, did not know what he was doing through Chennault.

In all, however, the weight of evidence should have left Nixon in no doubt that Johnson was hewing straight to the position with which he was familiar and that he had endorsed more than once, and most specifically on October 16. But the final days of campaigns are not notable for careful reflection, and the bedrock of his actions was surely that he simply could not accept having his candidacy founder over the timing of a peace move — even one that he formally supported. Still vivid were the memories of important last-minute developments in 1960 and 1962 that he believed had sent him down to defeat.

Yet this cannot excuse his lining up the Chennault–Bui Diem operation as far back as July, and his encouragement of Anna Chennault's contacts with Thieu through the summer, which must have made Johnson's task of persuasion much more difficult. Nor, in light of his sure knowledge, at least after October 31, that Thieu would not go along, is there any way to condone his public line on the final weekend. The pundits thought he was taking chances, but he was actually betting on a sure thing, and his Sunday offer to "go to Saigon" to bring Thieu around surely set some sort of record for hypocrisy, given what he had been doing via Chennault to cause Thieu to dig in!

A further word should be said about Nixon's technique. In selecting Anna Chennault as his emissary, he made it impossible to dissociate the Republican Party from the enterprise if it was detected. But by keeping himself at a distance, working only through the totally discreet John Mitchell, he could achieve what the covert-action trade always wants, "plausible deniability," that no action can be definitely linked to the key individual. Unless his other subordinates were guilty of mass lying—which I do not believe— he had them totally persuaded that he had not been involved. He was thus, of course, much better able to deny convincingly that it was anything but an unauthorized caper by a headstrong lady who happened to be also involved in his campaign organization.

In the 1950s Nixon had become fascinated with covert operations. His adoption of central principles of the trade in this case was wholly in character. It leaves a last question. By 1972, was his relationship with Mitchell so well established that when it came to getting whatever it was he wanted to get from Democratic headquarters in the Watergate complex that June, it was not necessary for him to express to Mitchell any more than the wish to learn, or nail down, something he deemed crucial to his reelection? Was the Chennault operation, in short, a preview of techniques used at Watergate—techniques designed to make it impossible to prove any direct Nixon connection to the burglary that set off that scandal?

As we have seen, no mention of Chennault appeared in the media until the following January. When the public voted, few were aware of the episode. By the time the election was over, however, the rumors were enough to make Anna Chennault radioactive. Nixon and Mitchell must have been very afraid that she would spill the beans at some point, and her memoir tells vividly how they treated her. In the ten days after the election, senior figures in Nixon's entourage repeatedly asked her to be the channel for further messages to Saigon (which she indignantly refused to do) and urged her in the strongest terms to protect "our friend," meaning Nixon. The final appeal came from Senator Dirksen, who told her he wanted "to make sure that I would not let my anger get the better of me by talking to the press."

Chennault got a showcase position on the Inaugural Committee and a visit from the man handling personnel in Nixon's transition, the veteran ambassador Robert Murphy. But she never got an offer of the kind of appointment, at least to some honorific commission, to which she would normally have been entitled on the basis of her overt campaign work and highly successful fund-raising alone, doubly so after she had run some risks. When, months later, she saw Nixon briefly at a large reception, he drew her aside to thank her for what she had done and especially for having been such a "good soldier" about it. Hurt and indignation shine through her account of these encounters, which surely reflected the bad conscience of Nixon and his people and at the same time their overwhelming desire to keep her out of sight, especially out of reach of any congressional committee considering a nomination of her for some post.[96]

In 1981, after the publication of her memoir, *The Washington Post* published a feature article on the career and personality of Anna Chennault. Her old friend Thomas Corcoran, asked about the 1968 events, replied: "People have used Anna scandalously, Nixon in particular. *I know exactly what Nixon said to her and then he repudiated her.* But Anna said nothing; she kept her mouth shut."[97] It was a fitting epitaph to an episode that from a personal standpoint alone was sordid.

· · ·

What was the effect of Thieu's decision on the election? How much was that decision influenced by Nixon's agents and by Republicans generally? Did the delay in getting into serious negotiations affect, even destroy, a real chance for peace?

The first question is easy. There can be little doubt that a joint October 31 announcement that included Thieu's participation would have had a powerful effect on the American voting public, which would have lasted through the election. The plan Thieu endorsed on October 13 called for this, and had Thieu done the things he promised, the effect would surely have been decisive in favor of Humphrey. Thieu's pulling back in those last days was crucial to Nixon's victory.

But did Thieu act as he did because of Nixon's urging (via Chennault and the various Republican senators talking to Bui Diem), or would he have taken the same course without that urging? On this key question, any judgment must be tentative. While those who have adopted the latter conclusion have not known how much Nixon actually did, their arguments are respectable. First, as we have noted, the mere idea of getting into negotiations was always suspect in Saigon, and the reality that the NLF would also be present at the table (a reality drummed in by their prompt appearance in Paris in the last week of October, with press conferences and maximum fanfare) raised fears of a coalition government emerging even though the United States disavowed this time and again.[98] Second, in South Vietnamese political circles the preference for Nixon over Humphrey was strong and deep-seated. Eleven members of the South Vietnamese Senate went so far on November 2 as to issue a statement endorsing Nixon.

Ambassador Bunker in Saigon, the American in the best position to appraise Thieu, gave this retrospective analysis in January 1969, after emotions had cooled:

> The idea of sitting down [in Paris] with the NLF in international negotiations has all along been very troublesome to Thieu and his colleagues. To their mind it gives a degree of recognition and respectability to a tool of Hanoi, and raises the specter of its inclusion in a future government. . . .
>
> Thieu's recoil from [including the NLF] at the moment of truth in October sprang from these basic factors: his inability adequately to prepare public opinion; his normal reluctance to bite the bullet; and his hope that with a new U.S. administration coming in he could postpone or perhaps evade entirely the bombing halt and the confrontation with the NLF it implied.

Bunker thought that American insistence on Thieu's keeping things to a very narrow group did not give him enough time to persuade important political figures in Saigon. Given the need on the American side to preserve security during the crucial mid-October period (to confirm the deal with Hanoi), "delay was inevitable" at the Saigon end.[99] This is an analysis with which I would have agreed at the time, before the evidence of the Chennault and Bui Diem memoirs showed how strongly the Nixon-established "Republican position" was pressed on Thieu and others. Bunker knew only generally of this pressure and thus, I believe, underestimated its importance.[100]

Moreover, there is good evidence that Thieu had a degree of personal animosity toward Humphrey, based apparently on a talk between the two at the end of Humphrey's visit to South Vietnam for Thieu's inauguration in October 1967. When Humphrey said that Thieu should start to think about a transition to self-reliance and a reduced American role, Thieu replied that U.S. forces would have to remain in South Vietnam indefinitely at their strength at that time, which was already over 500,000, whereupon Humphrey commented that retention of the full American military presence was "not in the cards." Thieu took this very badly.[101]

It is certainly plausible that when Thieu saw Humphrey's election suddenly as likely, this personal animosity and concern affected his actions. On the other hand, if he had not been told that he would have Nixon's support in holding back, he would surely have had to give greater weight to what refusing to go along could do to his chances of full support from any American President. He was, in effect, assured that the top Republicans would soften any immediate criticism of him, and would themselves hold him in greater favor for holding back.

In sum, a historical jury trying to decide whether Nixon's Chennault operation actually carried the day in Saigon and led Thieu to act as he did would, I believe, conclude that Nixon intended that result and did all he could to produce it. Yet there is no way to prove beyond doubt that the operation was decisive in Saigon.

Was a chance for peace lost? Here again one must be tentative. If North Vietnam was as hard pressed as Johnson's advisors believed and said at the decisive meeting of October 14, then immediate and serious peace negotiations might have produced useful concessions. Yet, as Dean Rusk then pointed out, complete negotiations would have taken months, and Hanoi might have reverted to a very hard line.

My conclusion is that probably no great chance was lost. Yet from a moral and political standpoint, Nixon's actions must be judged harshly. Certainly, if the full extent of those actions had become known then—or indeed at any point during his presidency—his moral authority would have been greatly damaged and the antiwar movement substantially strengthened.

At the practical level, Nixon (and, soon, Kissinger) must have learned from the experience that South Vietnam could not be made a full party to serious negotiations. Even formal concurrence by Thieu in a negotiating position did not prevent him from pulling back when he chose.

This leaves a final question—whether serious peace negotiations involving the United States are ever possible in the months just before a close election. If American forces are fighting and dying, and if the peace issues are debatable and in some respects painful, getting the concurrence of the opposition party may be as difficult as going ahead without it. Moreover, a serving President can easily be pressured—as Johnson was not—into unwise concessions. It is not hard to envisage situations in which the American national interest would suffer; it is one of the prices our country pays for holding elections in time of conflict.

What cannot be debated, however—and this may be the key point of the whole affair—is that Thieu emerged from it convinced that Nixon owed him a great political debt. On this the testimony of his closest advisor, Nguyen Tien Hung, was categorical: Thieu not only believed in 1968 that such a debt had been created, but attached great weight to it throughout his association with Nixon.[102] In most cultures, but perhaps especially in East Asia and in Vietnam, the sense of such a debt raises profound questions of loyalty and honor, even at the expense of other obligations. Over and over, throughout the war, orthodox American calculations about X or Y military or political figure turned out to be wrong because of some unknown favor (or slight) to the individual or, often, simply to a family member. The act might have taken place years ago, but its impact lingered.

American political figures can have a similar sense of debt, and help extended in the crucial phases of a presidential campaign has a special place. In this case, the help and the stakes were about as great as they could possibly have been, as Nixon knew well. Moreover, while it is possible that Thieu would have dug in for his own reasons, the fact that Nixon urged him to do so was bound to increase the debt.

The effect of such a debt on future dealings between the two men— which were at the core of American policy in South Vietnam—was in my judgment the most important legacy of the whole episode. As we have already seen and will have occasion to reiterate over and over, the greatest single problem for the United States in South Vietnam was how to bring effective influence to bear, so that the South Vietnamese government would improve its performance and take on more of the burden of assuring its own survival. That a new American President started with a heavy and recognized debt to the leader he had above all to influence was surely a great handicap, brought on by Nixon for domestic political reasons.

6. Aftermath and Transition

On the Saturday after the election, Ambassador Bui Diem was startled to receive an unannounced visit from Senator Everett Dirksen. The Republican Minority Leader came right to the point: he was conveying, in strong terms, a joint message from Richard Nixon and Lyndon Johnson that President Thieu should immediately announce that he was sending a full South Vietnamese delegation to Paris to participate in substantive negotiations.[103] Johnson had decided on this message on Thursday, November 7, and presumably it was he who chose Dirksen as his channel to Nixon.[104] There is no evidence whether Johnson referred in any way to the Anna Chennault affair, but he had already done so elliptically on October 31 and Nixon must have realized that, through the government's intelligence services, Johnson probably knew essentially what the Republicans had done.[105]

In the postelection week, Johnson also invited Nixon to the White House for a substantial briefing and discussion on all outstanding matters, with Vietnam at the forefront. The meeting came off on November 11, involving the principals (and their wives) and Johnson's assembled advisors. Dean Rusk and Walt Rostow (Johnson's National Security Advisor) reviewed the whole sequence of dealings with North Vietnam and the Soviet Union going back to June, which should have left little doubt that Johnson had acted all along for honest policy reasons. Nixon was totally supportive and cooperative, offering to do anything to help get substantive peace talks started and stressing that it was essential to have "a united front." He also asked whether it would help for him to "travel," but dropped the idea when Johnson reacted negatively.[106]

At the close of the meeting and lunch, Johnson assured Nixon that in line with Eisenhower's practice with him as ex-President, he would never criticize Nixon publicly. As Nixon saw it:

> [O]n that day our political and personal differences melted away. As we stood together in the Oval Office, he welcomed me into a club of very exclusive membership, and he made a promise to adhere to the cardinal rule of that membership: stand behind those who succeed you.

It was true that, in contrast to many past periods in American history, refraining from public criticism had become the common practice among postwar Presidents familiar with the crushing foreign policy burdens of the office and also well aware that they now lacked information they once had. In this case, the friendly atmosphere surely also reflected the compatible attitudes of the two men toward the Vietnam War and the considerable effort Nixon had made, for practical political reasons, not to seem critical of Johnson during the campaign. The objective of an early reconciliation had been achieved.[107]

As he left, Nixon said to the press that, on the matters on which he had been briefed, citing specifically Vietnam, the Middle East, and Soviet relations, "I gave assurance in each instance to the Secretary of State and, of course, to the President, that they could speak . . . for the nation, and that meant for the next administration as well."[108] Three days later, however, he backtracked, claiming a parallel understanding that there would be "prior consultation and prior agreement" before the incumbent took any major step. For this claim there was no basis according to Johnson, who responded with a crisp and constitutionally correct public statement that decisions up to January 20 would be taken by him and his Secretaries of State and Defense.

This confusing exchange surely weakened the message that Bui Diem carried to Saigon that week. Thieu had seen the first Nixon statement as pressure to act promptly. But then, in the words of one of his close advisors: "We saw Nixon as biding his time until he took office, letting Johnson do the dirty work."[109] Dirty work it was, with Johnson a lame duck. Clark Clifford vented his wrath at Thieu in public, in a series of statements saying that the Administration should consider going ahead without him, but this was a threat Johnson was unwilling to make. It would surely have confused the American public all the more.

The result was a further grinding series of talks between Thieu and Ambassador Bunker, in which Thieu was walking a narrow line. He did not wish substantive negotiations to start with the experienced Democratic negotiating team still in place; on the other hand, he knew that appearing to drag his feet could hurt his standing with the American public and Congress. Finally, on November 27, after the Johnson Administration had issued a formal statement that the United States had no intention of accepting a coalition government, Thieu agreed to send a delegation to Paris, and in early December, Vice President Nguyen Cao Ky duly arrived there. But six more weeks were then consumed fussing over the shape of the negotiating table — a ridiculous issue for American and other observers, but full of symbolic and psychological meaning for the Vietnamese.[110] Only in mid-January did Soviet diplomats mediate a compromise, in the form of a very oddly shaped table.[111]

Did the delay of two and a half months destroy what might otherwise have been realistic hopes of progress? Harriman and Vance thought so, basing their views in part on suggestions Le Duc Tho had made in mid-September that the Vietnamese were willing to discuss reciprocal troop withdrawals seriously.

Here it is useful to draw on a contemporary analysis of the situation by Henry Kissinger. In mid-December, *Foreign Affairs* published the article he had been working on during the fall; it had been essentially completed prior to the election, so that he wrote as a private citizen, not noting his negotiating activities the year before or his more recent tie to the Nixon campaign.[112] In the article, Kissinger approved and defended key features of Johnson's handling of the preliminary Paris talks, such as the insistence on prompt negotiations. Reliance on an understanding about military restraint should be a more certain protection against trickery than a formal commitment. . . . Hanoi can have little doubt that the bombing halt would not survive if it disregarded the points publicly stated by Secretary Rusk and President Johnson.

He also noted that in its main outlines the American position had "remained unchanged throughout the negotiations."[113]

In his last pages, Kissinger analyzed the issues he believed would arise in substantive negotiations. The United States should not withdraw unilaterally, he believed, and Hanoi would have to negotiate over what he saw as the two main objectives for U.S. negotiators:

(1) to bring about a staged withdrawal of external forces, North Vietnamese and American, (2) thereby to create a maximum incentive for the contending forces in South Viet Nam to work out a political agreement. . . . The primary responsibility for negotiating the internal structure of South Viet Nam should be left for direct negotiations among the South Vietnamese.

Perhaps not by coincidence, his proposals matched almost exactly what Johnson's negotiators would have suggested, and at the same time highlighted the difficulties Dean Rusk had foreseen. For North Vietnam to agree on reciprocal withdrawals would be to admit that its forces did not belong in the South, undercutting its claim that the conflict was a civil war in which only the United States was truly "foreign." Likewise, conceding that the South Vietnamese government had standing of any sort would go far toward surrendering the ambition that was central to its whole effort. Clearly, as Rusk had noted, an early agreement was not in the cards, even though Hanoi faced a difficult military situation. What might have been hoped for, however, was an early negotiation aimed initially at reducing the level of fighting, then the level of forces. This was how Harriman and Vance envisioned it, based on the September signals they had detected from Le Duc Tho. Equally important, if serious negotiations had got under way promptly, it would have been possible to observe and insist on North Vietnam's compliance with the understandings about military restraints. Kissinger's optimism that Hanoi could be held to these restraints was probably not misplaced during the fall. But by January, with Saigon dragging its feet, Hanoi could well argue that it had met the provision for prompt negotiations while the other side had not.

In November and December 1968, however, the public saw only the delay, found it hard to understand what the fuss was about or why South Vietnam was objecting, became more irritated with Saigon, but probably thought the problems reflected failures or errors on the part of President

Johnson and his advisors. The dominant reaction was simply vast relief that the hideous ten months since the Tet offensive had ended. On the whole, the country welcomed the advent of a new President who had managed to dissociate himself almost entirely from the turmoil of the year.

For his part, Lyndon Johnson was prepared to suppress doubts about Nixon's involvement in Anna Chennault's activities, and was ready to do all he could to make the handover of power smooth and effective. As columnist Kenneth Crawford wrote: "Never in living memory has national power passed from one party to the other as amicably and smoothly as it is passing this time from Democrats to Republicans."[114] On December 12, the Cabinet and White House staff of the outgoing Administration held separate receptions for the incoming team, and Johnson and Nixon had a second meeting. As many people noted, this was in striking contrast to the frigid Truman-Eisenhower transition and the skimpy and confused handover between Eisenhower and Kennedy.[115]

Nixon's key appointments were made rapidly and coherently. The first to be announced was that of Henry Kissinger as Special Assistant for National Security Affairs—"National Security Advisor," as it had come to be known. Although Nixon had only met Kissinger once before the election, he had read and studied his writings, and knew that Kissinger had handled easily, on behalf of Nelson Rockefeller, the final discussions on the Republican platform at the Miami convention. There is no evidence whether the information Kissinger conveyed to Mitchell during the campaign played any part in the appointment, although his capacity for secrecy must surely have appealed to Nixon. In addition, Kissinger's appointment would outwardly represent the Rockefeller wing of the Republican Party while justifying Nixon's making no move to enlist Rockefeller himself, whom he cordially disliked—just the kind of carom shot Nixon relished. Most of all, Kissinger fit well with Nixon's style of decision making. When the appointment was announced on December 2, Nixon piously rejected any intent to make the new man a "wall" between the White House and the Department of State, but this was in fact exactly what he had told Kissinger he wanted him to be—an example of the tendency in Nixonian discourse to disavow a true motive loudly and explicitly.

Kissinger quickly assembled a strong staff, mostly career people or civilian holdovers from the Johnson Administration. From previous work as a consultant, he had an excellent network of contacts. Nixon gave him his head, and even had Kissinger interview and give his judgment on William P. Rogers as a possible Secretary of State. It was a strange but appropriate beginning for a painful relationship, virtually prescribed by Nixon from the start. In the Eisenhower Administration, Rogers had been Deputy Attorney General and later Attorney General, and had worked closely with Vice President Nixon on many matters. A lawyer's lawyer, he had excellent practical judgment and sound political instincts but almost no experience of foreign policy. As Nixon judged him, he would be loyal and discreet, not likely to kick over the traces when differing on policy or even on being excluded from important matters that would historically have been the primary responsibility of the Secretary of State.

The other principal Cabinet appointment in the national security area, Secretary of Defense, was first offered to Senator Henry M. Jackson of Washington, a senior Democratic member of the Senate Armed Services Committee and a rising star on other matters. (Some other Nixon offers of positions to Democrats — such as Hubert Humphrey for Ambassador to the United Nations — were for show purposes and with little expectation they would be accepted.) Nixon well knew how seldom powerful senators, in the American system, have been lured into Cabinets even of their own party, but he needed, and felt a kinship with, a "strong defense" Democrat and wanted at least credit for making the offer. Jackson was briefly tempted but in the end refused, saying he could be more help where he was.[116] Nixon then turned to Melvin Laird, Republican congressman from Wisconsin and a longtime member of the Defense Subcommittee of the House Appropriations Committee, therefore thoroughly familiar with the budgets and problems of the Pentagon. Laird had a power base in Congress, through the respect he commanded on both sides of the House, as well as an independent mind and (as it turned out) considerable bureaucratic skills. He could not be easily circumvented, and was to become a more powerful Cabinet member than Nixon had bargained on.

For the Treasury, Nixon chose David Kennedy, a Chicago banker of no outstanding stature, and as Attorney General he installed John Mitchell, closest to him personally of all these men, though with a legal background that was very limited in terms of the range of Justice Department concerns. Kennedy's role in economic policy was to be secondary to that of Arthur Burns, a conservative veteran of the Eisenhower Administration, who was made a Cabinet-level Counselor in the White House.

With the rest of the new Cabinet, these appointments were announced with maximum fanfare on December 11. All were moderates, representing diverse geographical areas. Nixon privately thought that as a whole they were a little to the left of what he saw as his own "centrist" position. But even less than other late-twentieth-century Presidents did he intend to use the Cabinet as a serious forum for debate and advice, let alone decision.[117]

After some delay, Nixon decided to retain CIA Director Richard Helms, a career intelligence officer who had held the position since 1966. In contrast, Nixon instantly reaffirmed the status of J. Edgar Hoover, legendary head of the FBI since the early 1920s, with unctuous expressions of praise and confidence, despite his having passed the retirement age four years before. The members of the Joint Chiefs of Staff also remained in place, with Army general Earle Wheeler as Chairman (as he had been since 1964), William C. Westmoreland, former commander in Vietnam, as Army Chief of Staff, and Admiral Thomas Moorer as Chief of Naval Operations. To the surprise of some, Nixon also retained Ellsworth Bunker as Ambassador in South Vietnam, along with General Abrams as commander, Samuel Berger as Deputy Ambassador, and William Colby of the CIA in charge of pacification operations. It was, and was meant to be, a signal of continuity in the conduct of the war.

Elliot Richardson was chosen as deputy to Rogers. He was a veteran from the Eisenhower Administration, where he had served in the Department of Health, Education, and Welfare, and was well known to Nixon though never personally or professionally close. The rest of the new cast in State was drawn mostly from the career Foreign Service, led by the Under Secretary for Political Affairs, U. Alexis Johnson, most recently Ambassador to Japan and an old Asia hand who had held other senior positions in the Eisenhower years. One notable change was the retirement of the veteran Llewellyn Thompson as Ambassador to the Soviet Union; Thompson had served in Moscow twice, for a total of seven years, and between these tours had exerted considerable influence on President Johnson in favor of the "thaw" in Soviet-American relations initiated by President Kennedy in 1963 after the Cuban Missile Crisis.

Finally, for the apparently key post of Paris negotiator, Nixon picked Henry Cabot Lodge, his running mate in the 1960 presidential election and later twice Ambassador to South Vietnam, in 1963–64 and 1965–67. A distinguished moderate and internationalist Republican, symbolic of patriotism and of bipartisan support for a strong stand in Vietnam, Lodge appeared to be a highly qualified choice who would have Nixon's confidence. In fact, the two men were antithetic in personality and to a considerable extent in their underlying views.[118] As with some other Nixon choices, therefore, there was less to this than met the eye. From the beginning Nixon drew a sharp demarcation line between individuals genuinely in his confidence and those who, whatever their titles, were not.

Along with the necessary appointments, Nixon quickly initiated a major shift in the relative power of the institutions that make and carry out foreign policy. He had disliked the formal and collegial procedures of the Eisenhower Administration and been put off in lesser degree by the freewheeling way Kennedy and Johnson had operated on occasion; in all three Administrations, as he saw it, the State Department had had too much power. Under President Johnson, State had clearly become primary in formulating policy papers and options and in following up on presidential decisions, after 1967 through a Senior Interdepartmental Group (SIG) presided over by the Under Secretary of State.[119] (The two dominant policy problems, the Vietnam War and relations with the Soviet Union, however, were controlled closely and constantly by President Johnson himself.) This SIG system was Nixon's first target. To Kissinger, who already had a taste for power and scant regard for "bureaucrats," the assignment to prepare a memorandum defining the new system was right up his alley.[120] One reason for this important decision was undoubtedly Nixon's gut feeling about many of the Foreign Service personnel he had encountered over the years, especially during the out-of-office years in the 1960s. In Kissinger's words, "the Foreign Service had disdained him as Vice President and ignored him the moment he was out of office," while the CIA (meaning the analysis and estimating sections, not the covert operators) "was staffed by Ivy League liberals who behind the facade of analytical objectivity were usually pushing their own preferences."[121]

Yet the methods Nixon chose were not merely a matter of personal dislikes or even of a personal style that stressed solitude and working from papers. He sought White House control in part from a coherent view of what effective policy required in the situation he confronted in 1969. In this and in many other ways, it was significant that the contemporary statesman Nixon most admired was Charles de Gaulle of France. Secrecy, aloofness, an aura of mystery, limiting personal statements and achieving maximum surprise and effect with those he did make, frequent dissimulation of his true purposes in order to keep criticism at bay—all these were leaves from de Gaulle's book that Nixon was prepared by instinct and calculation to borrow. He must also have seen in his own foremost problem of disengaging from the Vietnam War a strong resemblance to de Gaulle's brilliant extrication of France from a fruitless war in Algeria.

In January, Nixon approved Kissinger's secretly produced blueprint for White House control of the foreign policy process, over the mild protests of a belatedly alerted William Rogers. Policy papers would now flow up through a structure of "panels" chaired by the National Security Advisor (Kissinger) and comprised of deputies from State and Defense and the heads of the CIA and the Joint Chiefs, with final decisions taken by the President sometimes in the National Security Council but often without any further meetings. The system permitted the President to intervene all along the way, through Kissinger, while making it difficult for the Secretaries of State and Defense to get hold of an issue until it had been virtually decided in one of the panels. It was a palace coup, entirely constitutional but at the same time revolutionary.

. . .

During the transition period, Nixon confronted one action decision, how to handle a Johnson project he definitely did not support. The Soviet takeover of Prague in August, as we have seen, aborted what was to have been an announcement of a summit meeting between Johnson and Soviet Premier Alexei Kosygin. The precise plans for a September meeting had never leaked, and after Prague most observers assumed the idea was dead. But Johnson had never given up on it, and in mid-September there was a further exchange on the subject, possibly linking it with the suggestion of an active Soviet role toward a bombing halt deal with Hanoi in Paris. When the Soviets duly played such a role, they may well have hoped that the summit too would come back on track and help them regain the respectability they had forfeited by the brutal Prague takeover.

On November 6, right after the American election, an article in a Soviet publication suggested that a top-level meeting could be useful, and on November 14, Soviet Ambassador Anatoly Dobrynin made the suggestion explicitly to Walt Rostow. While it had never been intended that the meeting would get beyond a general exchange on principles, with no precise agreement in view, any such meeting in the closing months of a lame-duck Administration presented problems. Nixon could hardly be asked to sign on to whatever positions Johnson might take, and would have been entirely right to consider himself not bound even by the tenor of the discussions. When Johnson consulted Nixon about the possibility of such a summit before the transfer of power, his reaction was noncommittal, but in early December the President-elect used two channels to dissuade the Soviets from going ahead. Kissinger, to the Soviet number two in Washington, and Robert Ellsworth, a prominent Nixon advisor during the campaign, to a Soviet official in New York, conveyed identical messages to the effect that any such meeting would not be taken seriously by the incoming Administration. The line went dead and the project was abandoned.[122]

In itself this was a simple decision for Nixon, wholly justified as a matter of realistic behavior during an interparty transition. But behind the decision lay a line of thinking stressed in the memoirs of both Nixon and Kissinger. The two men put great emphasis on what they called "linkage"—a constant weighing of all the points of contact with a given nation (above all the Soviet Union) so that these fitted with the intended overall line of policy. Moreover, they had in mind more explicit forms of linkage, such as telling the Soviet Union that certain actions were in effect preconditions to American actions thought to be desired by the Soviets. For such a policy to work, every strand of policy had to be inventoried and deployed in a concerted manner toward the desired end. Linkage was an important feature of Nixon's initial policies. Whether it could be used effectively remained to be seen.

In all, Nixon's handling of the transition period gave him a strong base and starting point. He had filled out his appointments to general approval, he had the policymaking process he wanted and the key man at its center, and he had conveyed a strong image of moderation and responsibility. From every standpoint it had been a good eleven weeks' work. He would land running.

Chapter Two

THE FIRST FIFTEEN MONTHS

1. *Dealing with the Vietnam War*

As he took office, Richard Nixon undoubtedly thought of Eisenhower, who achieved an armistice in the Korean War during his first months in office and was then able to turn to other problems. Nixon hardly thought the Vietnam War could be ended so rapidly, but it was his overriding initial priority. He began by allowing Henry Kissinger and his handpicked staff an increasing amount of authority while the State and Defense Departments were still finalizing their senior appointments. Kissinger set the agenda with directives for large study projects that kept the "bureaucracy" out of mischief and at the same time moved the key controls solidly into his own hands.

Washington observers caught on only gradually to the extent of the change to White House control, but the most important ambassadors, one in particular, soon learned of it. The Soviet Union's Anatoly Dobrynin had been accustomed to long private meetings with Secretary of State Dean Rusk and had always dealt primarily with the State Department. Now, after a short delay to show he would not be rushed, the President received Dobrynin on February 17 with only Kissinger in attendance. At the close he kept the ambassador alone to convey the message that he should henceforth deal directly with Kissinger on any matter of consequence. Thus was established what Kissinger called "the Channel," used over and over in the next four and a half years on every key problem in Soviet-American relations. The State Department was rarely informed even that a meeting had taken place, the meetings were almost always one-on-one, and the record of what was said, usually dictated by Kissinger, went only to the President and to selected members of Kissinger's NSC staff.[1]

Over time, the Channel was replicated with other ambassadors and visiting officials. With this practice went a far more extensive use than ever before of back-channel communication links to foreign countries and American officials abroad (using the facilities of the CIA or occasionally individual military services), circumventing the State and Defense Departments and almost always unknown to the Washington officials involved with the matters discussed. There were advantages in total White House control and coordination. But the main reason for the shift in control was the strong antipathy and distrust that both Nixon and Kissinger felt toward career officers in the State Department, in part for what they supposed were liberal tendencies verging on disloyalty and in part, somewhat paradoxically, for alleged stodginess and resistance to change. In addition, Nixon had an acute distaste for personal confrontations of even the mildest sort. He avoided giving oral orders in the presence of those affected, outside a handful of White House staff members, and shunned serious one-on-one talks with his Cabinet members or any kind of searching exchanges with members of Congress alone or in groups. It was not an unprecedented trait. Franklin Roosevelt, for example, rarely dealt frankly with difficult problems, especially personnel ones — but in Nixon the characteristic was unusually strong, remarkably so for the leader of a democratic nation.[2]

The primary beneficiary was Kissinger. To his uniquely extensive sources of government information and his assured position as chairman of any significant advisory group, he could add constant access to the President and Nixon's habit of thrashing out problems with a single staff person before making up his mind. An advisor with these advantages would have had to be stupid not to develop enormous power and influence and, if he were ambitious, to hoard and seek to increase that influence by all the techniques known to outstanding courtiers throughout history.

The primary victim was the State Department. Alexis Johnson, who had served in senior positions under Eisenhower, Kennedy, and Johnson, later gave a heartfelt summary of what it was like to work under Nixon. Responsibilities that once bulked large in State had become "hollow shells," as "Nixon and Kissinger systematically froze out the State Department from real influence on the subjects they considered most vital: ending the Vietnam War, détente, relations with Peking, SALT, and later the Middle East."[3] So the system had two tiers: except at rare moments of presidential decision, top priority problems were handled in the White House, the rest in the State and Defense Departments. Meetings with senior advisors, whether in the National Security Council or less formally, were frequently orchestrated and done for the record rather than being occasions where the President's mind was genuinely influenced by what was said.

While Nixon sought immediately to distinguish himself from his predecessors' style, at the same time he seemed to make policy changes only slowly and deliberately. Almost at once the change in style registered to his benefit: he was much less agitated than Johnson had habitually been, made fewer public statements and created initially a general impression of studying problems at length before deciding how he would deal with them. Nixon's first public action matched his intention both to establish a different tone and to reassure the European allies with a significant gesture. Johnson's trips abroad had been rare and usually Vietnam-related; Western European leaders in particular had a sense of having been neglected. Nixon decided to make a five-country visit to Europe beginning on February 23, earlier than any other President had traveled. He started at Brussels, home to NATO headquarters, and went on to London, Bonn, Berlin, Rome, and finally Paris. Everywhere he was warmly received, with no significant disturbances. Publicly, the trip usefully demonstrated continuing U.S. concern about Europe; privately, Nixon's experience and command of the issues left a strong impression among European leaders. The overall effect was reassuring and impressive.

For Nixon the key stop was Paris. He and Kissinger had separately dissented from the Johnson Administration's critical attitude toward de Gaulle, notably over his decision in the spring of 1966 to withdraw French forces from the NATO military command while maintaining France's membership in the Alliance itself. De Gaulle's emphasis on the nation-state and his low opinion of multilateral organizations were congenial to Nixon's (and Kissinger's) long-standing views; the President and his advisor also accepted France's go-it-alone policy on nuclear weapons. Sharing also the experiences of political exile and dramatic recovery, de Gaulle and Nixon had kept in contact during the 1960s, when Nixon had been received for long conversations and the French President had let it be known that he regarded him as a man of weight and wisdom. On this 1969 visit, de Gaulle showed his regard not only by having lengthy private meetings but by the almost unique gesture of coming to a dinner at the American Embassy after a gala at the Elysée Palace on Nixon's first night in Paris.

De Gaulle's advice was twofold: get out of Vietnam and cultivate China. Nixon listened politely to the first, avidly to the second. France at once became the bearer, through her ambassador in Beijing, of a general message to the Chinese leadership of Nixon's interest in changing the American relationship to China.

Having seen how foreign travel broadened not only the mind but his image at home, Nixon did a lot more of it in the next few months: in July and August he went right around the world, starting in Guam and with full-scale visits to the Philippines, Indonesia, Thailand, South Vietnam, India, Pakistan, Romania, and Britain. Again, the aim was partly to show that America under its new President stood tall, partly to cement ties to favorite countries and leaders, and in two cases, Pakistan and Romania, to open up possible channels to China. The visit to Romania, then hard-line Communist in its internal policies but occasionally deviant from Moscow's line in foreign policy, was intended also to suggest that Nixon did not regard Soviet control of Eastern Europe as immutable and that he would treat each nation there individually. Yet none of these formal visits revealed much about the substance of his policies or his priorities. These were as much changed from Johnson's as his policymaking process.

In the case of the Paris negotiations, Kissinger, at Nixon's direction, had made one move prior to the Inauguration. He had enlisted an old French Indochina hand, Jean Sainteny, whom he and Nixon had known separately over the years, to approach the North Vietnamese in Paris and inquire what their initial negotiating position was. Sainteny's inquiry was amateurish; he approached Mai Van Bo, an official junior even to the titular chief negotiator, Xuan Thuy, and far below the real power, Le Duc Tho, who by the end of the year was back in Hanoi. Between 1964 and 1967, before any kind of direct contact with North Vietnam existed, the Johnson Administration had occasionally used makeshift channels of this sort, but by 1968 these had been superseded by the formal Paris talks and by the private talks between Le Duc Tho and the team of Harriman and Vance. This time, Mai Van Bo gave what was surely a reflex response: U.S. forces must be withdrawn from Vietnam unilaterally and totally and the entire "Thieu regime" must be removed. Nixon and Kissinger took this answer at face value as the considered North Vietnamese position, immovable at least for the time being. This may indeed have been the case, but it was absurd to take the reply as the last word. One can only conclude that the contact had been effected to prove that Nixon and Kissinger had made a good-faith effort, and to offer them an excuse for sidetracking serious Paris negotiations, at least until they had given an approach to the Soviet Union their best try.

Formal meetings in Paris did start at weekly intervals in late January, with the same kind of fruitless press releases and background briefings as in 1968, but Cyrus Vance's offer to stay on for a while and lend his experience to the new team of Henry Cabot Lodge and Lawrence Walsh was not seriously taken up, and no effort was made to reopen private talks on central issues with Le Duc Tho and Xuan Thuy. Nixon did have a well-publicized meeting on March 1 with the new negotiating team. An apparent consensus was reached that the United States should negotiate privately with the North Vietnamese on a withdrawal agenda, while South Vietnam should be urged to relent and express willingness to talk to either Hanoi or the NLF. Thieu's announcement to that effect in late March was hailed as a big step forward, but on the American side no serious instructions were ever sent to Lodge. The private meetings, which started in March, never got beyond the old issue about the demilitarized zone.[4]

Back in Washington, in one of his now frequent talks with Ambassador Dobrynin, Kissinger asked that the Soviet Union give the North Vietnamese a message proposing totally secret talks between Le Duc Tho and a special U.S. negotiator. This message prepared the way for a secret July meeting in Paris between Kissinger and the North Vietnamese, but also had the effect of completely downgrading all the work being done in Paris, leaving an uninformed and uninstructed Lodge serving as a figurehead token of "serious" negotiations. Not surprisingly, Lodge resigned in November, and a succession of equally token senior negotiators succeeded him. The publicly known Paris talks were no longer a serious forum, as the press slowly came to realize.

Although negotiations were going nowhere, public statements did stake out modest changes in the American and South Vietnamese negotiating positions. On May 14, with Congress starting to stir, Nixon gave a major speech that highlighted a modest and obvious concession. In late 1966, when Johnson had first offered to withdraw all organized U.S. forces as part of a peace settlement, he had insisted that the withdrawal be completed only six months after all North Vietnamese forces had been pulled out. Now Nixon proposed that the two proceed in parallel and be completed at the same time, a sensible and realistic change. Moreover, in June, Thieu came around to saying publicly that the NLF could participate in an election in the South. Hanoi's scornful public rejection of this, and its renewed insistence that the whole "Thieu regime" be removed, at least showed that Nixon and Thieu had tried, and confirmed in Nixon's mind the conviction that negotiations were unlikely to produce an acceptable outcome until something more had been added.

Whereas Nixon could move at a slow pace on negotiations without serious criticism, early decisions about the conduct of the war were inescapable. As early as December 1968, Kissinger and his staff put together, in National Security Study Memorandum 1 (NSSM-1), a comprehensive set of questions about the state of the war and what might be done, which was sent to all the major agencies in January. The replies were in by March and confirmed a split that had emerged during 1968 between the military command in Vietnam (MACV) and the CIA. MACV continued to take a generally upbeat view of military events. By contrast, a long CIA study completed in December, which rested its conclusions both on observations from its large contingent in the field and on an analysis of reports in Washington, was much more pessimistic:

[It] focused on perennial South Vietnamese military problems . . . [and concluded that] given the current "social and psychological environment" in South Vietnam . . . little positive change could be expected and that Saigon would be unable to assume a greater share of combat operations.[5]

The State Department and civilians in the Pentagon generally shared this pessimistic CIA view, while the Joint Chiefs of Staff in Washington and Ambassador Bunker in Saigon agreed with General Abrams's more hopeful assessment that although "[poor] leadership, corruption, desertion, and political favoritism are problems endemic to South Vietnam," with MACV's efforts "progress is being made." As he summarized this view, however, Abrams had before him another prognosis, shared by each of his four corps area senior advisors, all of them general officers with substantial Vietnam experience. Answering the key question about the ability of South Vietnamese forces to handle various assumed levels of action against them, all four

were hopeful that the South Vietnamese could eventually deal with the insurgency [i.e., the Vietcong] by themselves, but none felt that they could ever handle a conventional North Vietnamese threat or a combined Vietcong–North Vietnamese Army opponent. In summary, the advisers doubted Saigon's ability to survive alone.[6]

Behind these conclusions lay fundamental characteristics of the war. Against the 130,000 to 140,000 North Vietnamese regulars in or near South Vietnam, and an estimated 150,000 Vietcong, battered and somewhat demoralized by their heavy losses at Tet, the South Vietnamese regular force (ARVN) had 800,000 men, with another 300,000 in the popular forces. If there had been an established front (as in Korea), these ratios would have ensured an adequate defense—but in an essentially guerrilla conflict, with the antigovernment forces able to move freely and to choose their points of attack—or to lie low—the defeat of a large and well-established threat had always required much higher ratios. Moreover, the mobility of the South Vietnamese forces was limited: for morale reasons, all but two elite divisions were kept essentially static, as near to their families as possible. Abrams and his predecessors never thought it possible to change this system and make the South Vietnamese Army truly all-purpose and all-area, which was in itself a measure of the only moderate unity, resolve, and will of the South Vietnamese nation as a whole, compared with the longer battle experience, cohesion, and ideological fervor of the North Vietnamese.

Abrams's formal response to NSSM-1 incorporated the judgments of his area commanders and advisors, though his own view remained guardedly hopeful. Perhaps he thought that Saigon would ultimately not be left on its own. For a time he certainly hoped that any U.S. withdrawal would leave a significant residual force behind, and he always assumed that negotiations would lead to at least a partial North Vietnamese withdrawal.

To Nixon and Kissinger the comprehensive review showed both important differences in judgment and a dearth of suggestions about new approaches or programs. The JCS urged that bombing of the North be resumed, which was clearly impossible (for domestic political reasons) in the absence of a strong provocation. There was also heightened concern for Cambodia. But for the most part the advice was to continue the old policy and execute it better.

As the NSSM-1 exercise was concluding, Defense Secretary Laird made a long visit to South Vietnam in early March for exhaustive discussions with Abrams. His long report noted the apparent progress in the percentage of South Vietnam's population under government control and the general effectiveness of the pacification program, then being specially accelerated. He urged an increase in supplies of key equipment for which the South Vietnamese Army (ARVN) relied almost wholly on the United States — fighter aircraft, helicopters, light tanks — plus a universal distribution to even local forces of the best rifles available, and greater emphasis on the training and advisory function of U.S. forces. But he did not recommend a further increase in the overall size of the South Vietnamese forces: at about 1.1 million men, these were all that could be adequately supported even with continued large-scale U.S. economic aid.

At a meeting on March 15, Nixon approved this program, which was now given a new and more emphatic name, "Vietnamization." Its intent and objectives were similar to what the Johnson Administration had called "de-Americanization" and pursued since 1967, vigorously in 1968. It quickly became a centerpiece of Nixon's policy.

Laird's thinking deserves a further word. On the one hand, he was perhaps the Administration official most sensitive to opinion in the Congress and among the public. A consistent supporter of the war effort all along, he had never been drawn to the more extreme proposals for military action, and in 1969 considered it impossible to imagine public support for them. Any form of "military victory" was now out of the question. In the words of one of his closest associates, Robert Pursley (in a 1994 interview), he had concluded that:

> one, the North Vietnamese had made it very clear that they could sustain losses that would be horrendous to anyone else and would be willing to do that. Or two, they had the capability of avoiding military contact so that they didn't have to sustain losses if they didn't want to, they could still stay in the game.

Laird firmly believed that South Vietnam would have true independence and self-determination only when it had pulled itself together socially and economically as well as militarily. This was bound to take time and to require patience on the part of the American Congress and public. Meanwhile "Vietnamization" had to go ahead, along with a measured program of troop withdrawals.

This was straightforward thinking. The test, as Laird well knew, was whether it could be consistently applied for the time it would take. He did not propose, or urge on Nixon, a fixed schedule for withdrawing U.S. forces, but he insisted that withdrawals must start soon and then continue whatever else happened; on the completion of one withdrawal, the Administration should be ready with an announcement of the amount and time frame of the next.

Vietnamization and withdrawals: almost certainly both would have been pursued by any American Administration in 1969, yet the Secretary of Defense was largely responsible for the broad strategic view and for how the program was transmitted and executed. Over time, as Henry Kissinger was grudgingly to note, the concepts became so ingrained in all planning and budgeting that the program became unchangeable, with just the kind of irreversible momentum that he (and probably Nixon) abhorred.

The announcement of the Vietnamization program helped ease domestic criticism for a short time, but the popular demand for large troop withdrawals remained strong, and in late May, Laird persuaded Nixon that a 25,000-man initial reduction could be completed during the summer. On short notice, Nixon invited Thieu to meet with him at Midway Island, where the South Vietnamese President, sensing what Nixon was about to tell him, presented the withdrawal proposal as his own, so that it was jointly announced then and there. According to Thieu's report of the meeting to his friend Chiang Kai-shek, Nixon promised continued U.S. military support during his first term and economic support in his second, and made one statement that appeared to be an assurance that North Vietnam too would withdraw its forces along with the complete American withdrawal—a remarkable set of promises and assurances if they were reported correctly by Thieu.[7]

Privately, Thieu pressed Nixon for more aircraft, artillery, and armor, but, on the advice of Abrams and Laird, the United States gave him little. Laird added a proviso that funding for the increase, and for a small increase in the force level, should come out of the already planned budgets of the American military services. For the Army in particular, funds for other forces, especially in Europe, had long been pinched by the Vietnam War, and the effect of the ruling was to inhibit Army officers or officials from pressing to spend more on helping the South Vietnamese forces. As Abrams kept insisting, the real limiting factor was that the South Vietnamese could not effectively handle an increase. The greatest problem was not inadequate equipment or even training, but rather South Vietnamese will and resolve, especially in senior military ranks, where there was always a high degree of favoritism and considerable corruption. General Abrams and his officers were doing all they thought they could, especially to get incompetent officers removed, but again and again Thieu did not adequately respond.

Yet neither at Midway nor in Saigon six weeks later does it appear that Nixon said anything on these crucial matters. Rather, he continued to reassure Thieu, avoiding both realistic discussion of withdrawal and the need for a drastic improvement in the South Vietnamese performance, especially in its military leadership. Perhaps the most trenchant report by an American official about Vietnam in 1969 was made by a member of Kissinger's staff, Sven Kraemer. After a lengthy visit in September, Kraemer (son of Kissinger's World War II mentor) concluded bluntly that American officials there had exhausted their credibility and that only "American *presidential* action, making improved leadership the condition of continued American support" could make possible the necessary improvement in South Vietnamese performance.[8]

Was Nixon ever tough with Thieu? The historical materials available contain no suggestion that he was, or indeed ever thought of being. Although he was never disposed to criticize leaders of allied or friendly nations, even in private, South Vietnam should have been different, since his Vietnam War policy depended enormously on getting the South Vietnamese to do better. This historian is bound to conclude that his kid-gloves treatment of Thieu was due in significant degree to the sense of personal debt he felt toward Thieu for his help in the 1968 election. Whatever the reasons, lack of a firm presidential policy on this key problem was a serious defect.

As the withdrawal policy evolved, there was confusion within the Nixon Administration about whether a small residual American force would remain in South Vietnam indefinitely, as American forces had done in Korea. Abrams initially assumed so—which may account in part for his upbeat judgments of South Vietnamese capacity—but by November a firm directive from Laird to the Joint Chiefs of Staff ordered that planning should assume that by July 1971 only a "support force" of 190,000 to 260,000 would be left, dwindling to a much smaller "advisory force" by July 1973.[9]

In public, though, Nixon shied away from defining such limits and target dates. In June, however, when former Defense Secretary Clark Clifford argued in an article that the war had become ever more pointless and that all U.S. combat forces should be out by the end of 1970, Nixon impetuously (and to Kissinger's dismay) told reporters that he fully expected to beat that target date! In any event, the withdrawal program rapidly and predictably developed its own momentum, along the very lines Laird had urged. Announcements of further cuts came successively—in September of 40,500 men, in December of another 50,000, and in April 1970 of 150,000 over the next twelve months.[10]

In public, General Abrams and the Joint Chiefs of Staff loyally supported these successive withdrawals, but in private many senior officers had grave reservations as it became clear that the timing and pace were being decided in Washington on the basis primarily of domestic opinion requirements. The program became a moral commitment to the American people that at least all American combat units would be out of Vietnam by the end of 1972. At the same time, as we have seen, senior military officers (and other informed observers) did not believe that this would leave the South Vietnamese—barring extraordinary reforms and much greater cohesion and will—in a position to deal with the North Vietnamese threat. To note this is not to suggest that the Vietnamization and withdrawal programs were faulty. Given the contradictory thrust of American congressional and public opinion—"get out but don't bug out"—the measured withdrawal program was simply inevitable. Laird and many others saw it in this light, and also, from an overall strategic standpoint, as the soundest way to deemphasize the Indochina War and concentrate on relations with the Soviet Union.

In that crucial March, the month of decision, President Nixon got similar advice from a special source, former Secretary of State Dean Acheson. The unpublicized reconciliation of these two once bitter adversaries was a remarkable event, engineered in part by Kissinger, who had long been in touch with Acheson on strategic and European problems and detected in him a willingness to give advice to a serving President despite past differences.

Called in by President Johnson a year earlier, Acheson had played a leading role in the judgment of Johnson's Wise Men that the war simply had to be wound down, but he was skeptical about the effectiveness of negotiations, in view of North Vietnamese implacability. Thus, in a long talk with Nixon on March 19, Acheson pressed for systematic withdrawal to start as soon as possible, without waiting for negotiations. Nixon apparently agreed. While Nixon may have agreed partly to establish a tie to a still respected Democrat, it is striking that they talked just as Nixon was adopting Laird's proposals and also as he was putting a damper on the talks in Paris.[11]

After a brief North Vietnamese offensive in February and March, sporadic Communist military activity avoided large-scale engagement, so that the pacification program was able to make some progress extending government control. Already in late 1968, Abrams had done away with the practical division of labor under which American forces undertook most major operations while the South Vietnamese engaged primarily in local security and pacification support. Moreover, in August 1969, Abrams initiated and Nixon approved an important change in Abrams's mission, replacing the earlier emphasis on offensive and attrition operations with a clear statement that henceforth the primary American mission would be improving the capabilities of the South Vietnamese forces and preparing them to take over, with even the protection of populated areas a lesser priority. To give it maximum effect, the change was announced in Saigon by Army Secretary Stanley Resor.[12] With this combination of factors, the level of U.S. casualties dropped sharply in the last half of the year.

. . .

Along with the troop withdrawals, and as another move to ease antiwar sentiment, the Nixon Administration also made basic changes in the draft, the keystone of the American military manpower system since 1941. All could see that the draft had become profoundly divisive and unequal in its effect. Better-off and more educated men could find ways out (through educational exemptions, for one). All the services, especially the Army, drew their manpower disproportionately from poorer, especially black, citizens. President Johnson had appointed a presidential commission to address this tragic failure of national policy, but its recommendations were rejected by key congressional leaders—a measure in its own way of the public's only moderate resolve and will to pursue the war.

Nixon appointed former Secretary of Defense Thomas Gates to chair a high-level commission to review all aspects of the manpower system. When the commission's interim report in late 1969 favored a volunteer army, President Nixon announced that the United States would move to an all-volunteer force by 1973. In the meantime, educational deferments were sharply reduced and an individual's exposure to the draft reduced to a single year. In November, Congress passed a bill to focus draft calls primarily on nineteen-year-olds and to base them on a lottery system using birth dates. This was more sensible than the previous system, and also helped to damp down protest in the colleges, which had been hotbeds of dissent. Nixon also replaced the legendary General Lewis B. Hershey, longtime head of the draft, who had come to symbolize the application of an unequal system.

. . .

Finally, the start of Nixon's round-the-world trip in July and August 1969 provided the occasion for announcing a basic change in U.S. national security policy worldwide. This had not been carefully prepared or discussed among his senior advisors, other than in general terms with Kissinger. A principal source was almost certainly the newly installed Assistant Secretary of State for East Asia, Marshall Green, whom Nixon had known in the Eisenhower days and from a long conversation in 1967 in Indonesia, where Green had handled with distinction a low-profile American policy during the transition from the Sukarno regime to that of General Suharto. (This was a major transformation in the Communist threat to Southeast Asia and, as we have noted, a part of Johnson's East Asia policy Nixon admired.) Green had consistently advocated lowering the American profile in East Asia and in the spring of 1969 gave Nixon a memo to this effect, the essence of which was in the State Department's proposed talking points for the President when he convened an informal press conference at his first stop, the Officers' Club on the island of Guam, on July 25.[13]

Speaking from notes, Nixon said that non-Communist East Asia had made such progress that nations there should now be able to ensure their own security with a less conspicuous American involvement. He defined future American policy under three headings: the United States would keep all its treaty commitments (but by implication be chary of new ones); it would "provide a shield" if a nuclear power threatened the freedom of an allied nation or of a nation whose survival was vital to American security or that of "the region as a whole"; and it would furnish military and economic assistance against aggression but would expect the nation directly threatened to assume the primary responsibility of providing the manpower for its own defense.[14]

When Americans applauded the announced policy, Nixon promptly named it the Nixon Doctrine. There were misgivings in East Asia, but these were eased as Nixon explained that his purpose was not to start an American disengagement from Asian security but rather to put continued U.S. involvement on a more solid basis. The Nixon Doctrine served Nixon's purposes admirably. It quickly became the fourth stated pillar of American policy in Indochina, alongside negotiations, Vietnamization, and troop withdrawals. Less visible, and never mentioned in public statements, was a fifth line of policy: stronger action in the countries bordering on Vietnam—Laos and Cambodia. And a sixth was perhaps in Nixon's mind the most important of all—namely, secret pressure on the Soviet Union to persuade or order North Vietnam to move toward peace.

2. *Laos and Cambodia*

From the beginning of the Second Indochina War, the North Vietnamese leadership and its Communist Party, the Lao Dong, had made clear that their objectives included the subjugation and communization of Laos and Cambodia. Both countries clung to their formal status of neutrality, pursuant to the 1954 Geneva Accords, which at least helped to keep the war from spreading wholesale to their territories. Yet the war kept creeping further into both countries.[15]

Concerning the ground war in Laos, Nixon decided to keep Johnson's policy while trying to make it more effective. This meant substantial aid to the Lao government of Prince Souvanna Phouma in the center of the coun-try and the Hmong (or Meo) forces to the north, along with tactical advice from the military attaché's office and the CIA—all this under the guidance of the American Ambassador in Vientiane, who for practical purposes had been virtually a military commander since 1964.

From early 1965 on, American forces regularly bombed the Ho Chi Minh Trail, part of which ran through eastern Laos. When the bombing of North Vietnam itself was halted in October 1968, that of Laos increased, and under Nixon it increased further. Whether in response to the stepped-up U.S. bombing or to extend its own territorial control, Hanoi conducted a more determined offensive in the north-central area of Laos in the summer of 1969 than it had for some years. The United States responded with a counteroffensive in the fall rainy season, retaking most of the lost ground and inflicting substantial losses on North Vietnamese forces and those of the Pathet Lao—the Laotian Communists completely under North Viet-namese control and direction.

American operations in Laos soon became the target of a politically in-spired investigation led by Senator Stuart Symington, Democrat from Mis-souri. In hearings devoted to many subjects related to the handling of the war, Symington pressed the charge that Nixon was enlarging what he and some in the media kept calling a "secret war" in Laos.

It was a phony label. As had been explained over and over to congres-sional committees, the Nixon and Johnson Administrations had refrained from public statements about operations in Laos, partly to keep alive Laos's facade of neutrality, which might be made real if all went well, but deci-sively because of the insistence of the sophisticated, admirably tough Prime Minister of Laos, Prince Souvanna Phouma, who was thoroughly informed of all that was happening in the north-central area as well as of the essentials of the Ho Chi Minh Trail bombing. Visiting senators and congressmen had been fully briefed for years in Bangkok or Vientiane, and many articles had appeared in newsmagazines and other media outlets. It was thus only in the most formal sense a "secret war"—any careful news reader or member of Congress knew basically what was going on.

Nonetheless, Symington got a lot of publicity for his hearings, which also emphasized the various arrangements the Johnson Administration had made with Asian countries sending troops to Vietnam. In the end, he focused on what he saw as a danger that American involvement in Laos would extend to sending organized military forces, or at any rate advisors on the model of South Vietnam in 1961–64, thus drawing the United States into direct participation in the ground fighting.

The result was an amendment to the basic military appropriation bill adopted in late 1969, which provided that no funds could be expended to support American military units or advisors in Laos. Since the Nixon Ad-

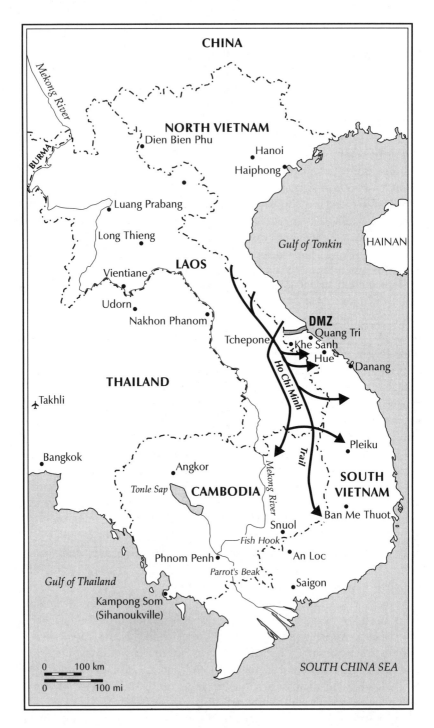

North Vietnam, Thailand, Cambodia, South Vietnam © 1997 *Chris Brest*

ministration had consistently disavowed any such intent, it accepted the amendment. Few noted that in the course of the Indochina wars this was the first time Congress had acted to control or limit military operations by explicit legislation. Its power of the purse, always present under the Constitution but rarely invoked, had now been used.[16]

Modern Cambodia—the remnant of the once far-flung and powerful Khmer Empire, broken up in the fifteenth century and memorialized unforgettably at Angkor—was like Laos in that it was targeted for conquest by Hanoi, had been a French colony, had a long border with South Vietnam, and was supposedly neutral under the Geneva Accords of 1954. In other respects it differed sharply: in geography, national feelings, and policies about the war in Vietnam.

Ever since 1954 the government of Prince Norodom Sihanouk had been genuinely neutral, refusing to accept the SEATO treaty's "protocol state" semi-protection. By 1964, Sihanouk decided that the Communist side was the likely victor in South Vietnam, and he broke off diplomatic relations with the United States and refused further aid. By late 1967, however, he had come to believe that the United States might after all prevail, and in January 1968 he received an American envoy, Chester Bowles, hoping to renew diplomatic relations and to limit occasional U.S. violations of his border. During the Bowles mission, Sihanouk suggested that he would not be disturbed by military operations in northeastern Cambodia, since the area was effectively under North Vietnamese control and few if any Cambodians remained there. But the Tet offensive in South Vietnam interrupted this diplomatic effort, and in the military campaigns of 1968 pressure from South Vietnamese and American forces increased the number of North Vietnamese forces taking refuge in the border areas of Cambodia; by early 1969 they were an estimated 40,000 men.[17] Sihanouk turned a blind eye to these border areas and to North Vietnamese activity generally; since 1966 he had permitted military supply ships to dock at the port of Sihanoukville, on the southwestern coast; almost all the supplies and equipment came from China and went to Vietcong forces in the Mekong Delta, but part of the shipments were retained for the ill-equipped Cambodian Army.

By early 1969, in addition to increased North Vietnamese forces in Cambodia, there were now many more supply bases in the border areas, including (or so American intelligence thought) the North Vietnamese headquarters, called COSVN, from which all operations in the south-central and southern parts of South Vietnam were directed. Nixon in early January noted to Kissinger that "a very definite change of policy toward Cambodia should be one of the first orders of business when we get in."[18] A Joint Chiefs proposal to renew the bombing against North Vietnam was thought by Laird to be politically insupportable, and the Chiefs proposed instead a series of air attacks on the base areas just across the Cambodian border.

This proposal lay on the table when President Nixon set off on his European trip on February 23. It then became entwined with the question of how to respond to a new and widespread series of attacks on U.S. units and installations, attacks that doubled the American casualty rate (to 336, 453, and 351 in successive weeks). Since the demilitarized zone was not substantially violated and action against cities was limited, the attacks were at most a marginal violation of the understandings accompanying the October 1968 bombing halt. Yet Nixon saw them as a test. In his quandary he turned naturally to the Abrams/JCS project for air attacks in Cambodia; on March 17 a large-scale B-52 attack was carried out against the "Fish Hook" area, about halfway up the border.

From the first, Nixon intended the Cambodian bombing to be totally secret. Even the Secretary and Chief of Staff of the Air Force were kept in ignorance. Nixon expressly rejected Melvin Laird's urging to inform selected members of Congress, and he had the military devise a system of double bookkeeping under which strikes on targets within Cambodia were reported as having taken place in South Vietnam.[19]

Clearly the decisive reason for the secrecy was domestic. Any disclosure of the bombing or supportive arguments for it would have aroused Congress and the public and contradicted the image of careful deliberation and gradual withdrawal.

On May 9, however, *The New York Times* carried a story by its Pentagon correspondent, William Beecher, that there had been B-52 raids on targets in Cambodia, that Sihanouk had said he would not object to them, and that the bombing was meant as a signal to Hanoi that Nixon was different and "tougher" than Johnson had been. To Nixon and Kissinger, this disclosure, which was of course accurate, seemed devastating. Within hours the FBI was ordered to use wiretaps to identify the supposed "leakers," and shortly installed taps on the phones of several members of the NSC and Pentagon staffs singled out by Kissinger or his deputy, Alexander Haig. Four years later, these wiretaps were disclosed and became part of the Watergate scandal.

Remarkably, however, neither the media nor anyone in Congress picked up Beecher's story. It simply died away. This was the more remarkable since the bombing had become by then a systematic program, in large part because of an incident over the Sea of Japan, off Korea. North Korean fighter planes shot down an unarmed U.S. EC-121 patrol aircraft, in daylight and with no possibility of mistaken identity, with the loss of the entire crew of 31 men. The American plane was on a routine reconnaissance mission of a kind that had been conducted for years without interference or protest, and was well outside any definition of North Korean territorial waters.[20]

Faced now with his own parallel crisis—and inclined as always to see it as a personal challenge—Nixon found his top Cabinet advisors, Rogers and Laird, opposed to a military response, while Ambassador William Porter in South Korea suggested that such a response might trigger further incidents (or more) on the main truce-line front in Korea. The President kept his own counsel, venting his rage and frustration only to Kissinger and Haig. In the end he limited the American response to providing fighter escorts for future reconnaissance operations.

Not to retaliate was for Nixon a painful choice, and one he claimed later to regret. Already he wanted to use the threat of drastic airpower as a clincher with the Soviet Union and North Vietnam; at the very least, he wished to depict himself as capable of such action, however irrational it might appear and however far from the norms of American behavior during even the gravest Cold War crises in 1948 and 1962. This was the "madman theory" he stated at intervals to his intimate associates. In the late summer of 1968 he spoke of it to his chief of staff, H. R. Haldeman, in a fashion that seemed genuine to a listener accustomed to his blowing off steam. Years later, Haldeman described the theory as "clearly one of the tools in his kit":

> He believed conceptually that it was important that the enemy and those counseling or controlling the enemy as then perceived in Vietnam, have, if not a conviction, at least a concern that he might be pushed to a point where he might do something totally irrational. That was a strategic concept, not a planned intent, and there was never any consideration given to doing anything to carry out the "madman" theory.

Asked whether the last part of this definition meant that it was in fact a bluff, Haldeman said that it was.[21] This much later interpretation is open to question. There were times, as other parts of this book suggest, when Nixon really meant to carry out the threats he made. But whether bluff or real intent, making such threats was a persistent element in Nixon's approach to his dealings with North Vietnam and the Soviet Union.

In April 1969, when he was persuaded to refrain from a drastic response to the EC-121 shootdown, Nixon cast around for a strong action that Moscow and its satellites would respect. The weapon to hand was the bombing of Cambodia—hurting the Communists there and also showing that the President was prepared to go to extremes even in minor situations.

Thus, what had initially been a one-shot policy now became systematic. It disregarded any uncertainty as to whether increased bombing in Cambodia would register forcibly on North Korea's President, Kim Il Sung, two thousand miles away, or on the Soviet leaders in Moscow. Nixon was simply acting from a reflexive desire to hit back at some Communist somewhere, a response rationalized only by his propensity to see all actions by Asian Communist countries as interlinked and perhaps coordinated. Since Kim Il Sung was a notorious rogue and maverick, few if any serious observers shared this way of thinking. It was the "true believer" at his truest.

When it became a regular program, the secret B-52 bombing of Cambodia acquired the unappealing name of Menu, with successive meal names assigned to individual groups of raids. Between May and August 1969 there were about ten more strikes on individual orders from Washington; after that, authority was given to Abrams and the regional air commanders to continue them as military needs and intelligence indicated. As this expansion got under way, a very few selected members of Congress were told about it, beginning with a "full briefing" (by Nixon and Kissinger personally) on June 11 of Senators Richard Russell and John Stennis. The two were chairmen, respectively, of the Senate Armed Services and Appropriations committees, the two congressional positions (usually the only two) that by long-standing tradition were informed by the CIA of covert operations. Later, according to Kissinger, a few other senators and selected congressmen were "briefed" as well.[22] But the briefings totally excluded the Democratic leadership and the Foreign Relations committees of both chambers, though the program was a major change in policy toward neutral Cambodia, not simply another military operation on a new scale, still less a covert CIA operation. In describing in his memoirs what was done, Kissinger was to write that he came to regret not having been "more frank" with the Congress, which suggests that even these disclosures to limited circles were less than all-embracing.

Even as the bombing went on, Nixon's State Department followed up belatedly on the Bowles visit by moving to reestablish diplomatic relations. In August a small mission was installed in Phnom Penh, headed not by an ambassador but by a medium-senior Foreign Service officer, Lloyd Rives, who had with him a skeleton staff that included no old Cambodia hands or intelligence experts on Communist movements in Indochina.

Thus, U.S. policy toward Cambodia was on two distinct tracks, one publicly restoring relations and reiterating total respect for the country's neutrality, and another secretly treating its eastern border areas as a war zone subject to massive air attack. Nixon and Kissinger later made much of the fact that Sihanouk never publicly referred to the bombing in any way, although the devastation of each raid can hardly have failed to come to his attention. No doubt he felt helpless; certainly no attempt was ever made to explain to him just what was going on. And almost certainly the secret bombing affected the situation within Cambodia. Its greater importance to Nixon, however, was as a possible warning to North Vietnam and above all as a demonstration to the Soviet Union that he was indeed capable of extreme and irrational response. In effect, the sixth element in Nixon's

Indochina policy—taking a leaf from Eisenhower's book—was to use the threat of drastic air action as an ultimate form of pressure on the Soviet Union to go all out to induce North Vietnam to move toward peace. Just such a threat was secretly conveyed to North Vietnam and the Soviet Union in what became the centerpiece of his Indochina War policy in 1969.

3. Rebuff and Recovery

Early in the 1968 campaign, Nixon had spoken of enlisting the Soviet Union to work for peace in Indochina by a combination of "political, economic, and diplomatic" pressures. But North Vietnam's relationships to China and Russia were complex and subject to conflicting and often directly opposed forces. On the one hand, Ho Chi Minh and the Lao Dong were fiercely independent; their ambition to control all of Indochina was totally their own. On the other, they had come to depend on moral and material support from the U.S.S.R. and China, first in their struggle to evict the French and then as they fought from 1959 onward. That Moscow and Beijing might put their own interests and concerns ahead of all-out support for North Vietnam had been amply demonstrated in 1954, when both — reluctant after the Korean War to have a new military confrontation—put great (and deeply resented) pressure on Hanoi to accept the division of Vietnam at the 17th parallel and neutrality for Laos and Cambodia.

To be sure, all three almost certainly believed that the partition of Vietnam would not last and that in a few years Hanoi would take over the South, by ballot or bullet, and go on to succeed France in controlling all of Indochina. But such a prospect was at best only tolerable to China, which had its own plans for increased influence in Southeast Asia as well as a long-standing hostility toward Vietnam.

To this complex brew was added the growing breach between China and the U.S.S.R. After the ouster of Khrushchev in October 1964, followed by Hanoi's decision to send regular conventional forces into South Vietnam and the start of U.S. bombing of the North, Soviet policy moved to take advantage of the opportunity to become North Vietnam's major supplier of sophisticated military equipment and thus to diminish Chinese influence.[23] Far from drawing China and the Soviet Union together, the serious fighting in Vietnam in 1965 led to friction over the passage of Soviet supplies through China, and then to a division of labor that beneath a veneer of cooperation was highly competitive. Hanoi remained able to play off one against the other, with the threat of moving closer to a generous donor at the expense of the less helpful one. When the chips were down and Hanoi really pressed hard, both came through handsomely, as in their support for the buildup before the Tet and later 1968 Communist offensives.

By early 1969, it was generally believed that Soviet influence in Hanoi was significantly greater than Chinese. On the other hand, to the extent that the Soviet Union got involved in any effort to bring peace in Vietnam, it would expose itself to a loss of influence in Hanoi and to the general charge, within the Communist camp, of letting down a fellow socialist state—violating "international solidarity." Most of all, it stood to lose ground in the continuing rivalry with China. These complexities almost certainly had little place in Richard Nixon's mind: to him the Soviet Union was potentially as decisive as it had been in getting the Korean armistice in 1953. The question was how best to put pressure on it.

In one of his early press conferences Nixon took the position that negotiations toward arms control should go alongside an easing of political problems in the Middle East and Southeast Asia. But even this modest form of "linkage" attracted critical comment, especially in the Eastern press. Kennedy and Johnson, like Eisenhower before them, had always accepted what might be called normal atmospheric links among Soviet-related matters— had seen that fruitful negotiations with the U.S.S.R. on any major subject were unlikely in periods of acute tension—but all three had believed that the main bilateral discussion track, especially on nuclear weapons, was and should be kept somewhat separate from ongoing rivalries in regional situations. Thus to link strategic arms talks to progress in a regional rivalry was in itself significant.

In fact, Nixon had much more in mind all along. In his first meeting with Johnson on July 26, 1968, discussing what then looked like a possible early meeting between Johnson and a top Soviet leader, Nixon interjected vigorously that the question must be: "Can we do anything until Vietnam is off the burner?"[24] For a time he meant exactly this. Over and over again, according to Kissinger, he told Dobrynin that there could be no meaningful progress or agreement *on any subject whatever*, no change in the atmosphere of the relationship, unless the Soviet Union really and usefully influenced North Vietnam toward peace. This secret policy went well beyond what he said in public. Given the apparent and latent importance of arms control and trade alone, it was the strongest kind of "political, economic and diplomatic" pressure possible to put on the Soviet Union—economic sanctions being in effect already in place under long-standing policies.

Basic to Nixon's approach was the judgment that if the Soviet Union truly chose to do so, it could exert decisive leverage on North Vietnam. From the first, Nixon and Kissinger considered that relationships within the Communist sphere were extremely hierarchical, with Communist movements controlled by nearby larger ones, and these in turn by either the Soviet Union or China, with the Soviet Union dominant where it chose to be. This view, evident again and again in their actions and decisions, stemmed in part from a general sense that internal or external power always flowed from the top. In larger part it reflected a predominantly ideological view of Communist nations and movements, downgrading and often totally discounting the influence of nationalist sentiment and national concerns. American Presidents before Nixon were often rightly criticized for inadequately recognizing these nationalist factors—such as the deep-seated historical hostility between China and Vietnam—but there had been important exceptions, for example the Truman Administration's recognition of Tito in Yugoslavia as more nationalist than Communist at least in his behavior toward Moscow. With Nixon and Kissinger, there were no exceptions: nowhere in the memoirs of either man does one find a remotely adequate recognition of nationalist factors in situations with Communist labels.

Always well aware that Moscow's military and economic material support of Hanoi was indispensable to North Vietnam's effort to take over the South, President Johnson and his advisors nonetheless treated Soviet relations as a top priority in their own right, seeking Soviet restraint and help for peace in Indochina but not making such action a prerequisite. At the height of American involvement in Vietnam there had been fairly close Soviet-American cooperation over the problem of nuclear nonproliferation, for example, as well as ready U.S. endorsement of NATO's 1967 Harmel Report, which made détente with the Soviet Union in Europe an accepted objective. Even in the Middle East, though the United States and the U.S.S.R. took opposite sides in the Arab-Israeli confrontation, Johnson did not make a big public issue of the Soviet Union's egging on Syria and Egypt before the 1967 War.

Essentially, both Nixon and Kissinger thought this position wrong and ineffective, "softheaded," as they said in private. They thought that serious talks about strategic weapons or concessions on trade and the conditions for private economic dealings were favors the United States could grant or withhold—and should now make conditional on specific Soviet help toward peace in Vietnam.

This was a major policy reversal, for which Nixon appears to have had extraordinarily high hopes. He, and on occasion Kissinger, repeatedly told their colleagues that they thought there would be crucial progress toward ending the Vietnam War within a year.

By July 1969, the stated negotiating positions of the United States and South Vietnam included several concessions: that eventual total withdrawals on both sides would be completed at the same time; that North Vietnam's withdrawal need only be carried out, not necessarily admitted; and that the NLF—just changing its name to Provisional Revolutionary Government (PRG), to give itself greater status—could participate in elections and even in a commission to lay down the rules for elections. These useful concessions underscored the two basic differences that remained: First, the United

States still proposed to leave Thieu's regime in control of the political process, a position totally at odds with Hanoi's continuing demands that it first
be removed, and that a coalition government be created with the PRG in
a strong position in it. Second, North Vietnam continued to refuse to discuss troop withdrawal on its part, a position obviously likely to become even
firmer as the United States went ahead with unilateral withdrawals. Why
give up something for what is coming your way in any case? These extreme
positions were plainly unacceptable, but it must also be noted that Nixon's
underlying readiness to accept an evenly balanced political process in South
Vietnam was always open to doubt, his firm objective all along being to
preserve Thieu's regime or its equivalent. On this point, his public statements throw little light. More revealing was his private briefing when he
stopped in Bangkok in the course of his world trip. He told a group of
American ambassadors in East Asia, as one present remembered it, that "any
satisfactory settlement must leave behind a government which would be
able to stand for at least five years." By this he plainly meant a non-
Communist government with no serious participation by the PRG or its
like.²⁵

In short, as everyone was becoming aware, no real progress had been
made at all. Nixon faced the prospect of a "massive new antiwar tide" of
demonstrations in the fall and winter, plus a possible renewed Communist
offensive in early 1970. By spring, with midterm congressional elections in
sight, this "would make congressional demands for more troop withdrawals
impossible to stop and difficult to ignore." At the same time, he noted an
apparent lull in the fighting in Vietnam, along with indications that some
North Vietnamese units were actually being returned to the North. Sometime in July he therefore decided to play what for him had always been the
key card:

> I decided to "go for broke" in the sense that I would attempt to end the
> war one way or the other—either by negotiated agreement or by an in-
> creased use of force. . . .
>
> After half a year of sending peaceful signals to the Communists, I was
> ready to use whatever military pressure was necessary to prevent them
> from taking over South Vietnam by force. During several long sessions,
> Kissinger and I developed an elaborate orchestration of diplomatic, mil-
> itary and publicity pressures we would bring to bear on Hanoi.
>
> I decided to set Nov. 1, 1969—the first anniversary of Johnson's bomb-
> ing halt—as the deadline for what would in effect be an ultimatum to
> North Vietnam.²⁶

One step in carrying out this plan was to give the Soviet Union a last
chance by offering it a mixture of "carrots," visions of rewards and gains,

with "sticks," hints that something more drastic might happen if it failed to seize the carrots. This task fell to Kissinger, using "the Channel" for an exceptionally long session with Ambassador Dobrynin on July 12. Dobrynin was about to leave for Moscow and perhaps the Crimea, where the top leaders usually vacationed; both trips were leading up to a possible serious high-level review of Soviet policies toward the United States and the Indochina War. In this rare instance, we have the *Soviet* record of what was said, rather than Kissinger's (or Nixon's) summary. Dobrynin's report to Moscow, which ran to nearly 4,000 words, showed Kissinger covering many subjects in a generally conciliatory tone—stating American acceptance of a divided Germany and especially of Soviet dominance in Eastern Europe, among other comments. After noting that China had shown no signs of readiness "to carry out a more peaceful policy towards the USA" but might be bidding for decisive influence in Hanoi, Kissinger came to the main point.[27] His appeal was twofold: On the one hand, he held out the prospect of many, perhaps annual, summit meetings for businesslike discussion of all current problems; this would be an elevation to continuing coequal superpower status, which he doubtless thought would have special appeal. On the other hand, he insisted not only that Soviet help over Vietnam was the prerequisite to "a really serious improvement in Soviet-American relations" but that "if Hanoi will endlessly 'obstruct' the negotiations, then it will be necessary for the [American] government to think about 'other alternatives in order to convince Hanoi.'" In his report to Moscow, Dobrynin added that this "sufficiently firm-sounding theme . . . cannot but be noted." He thought it suggested renewed bombing of North Vietnam or other military measures, and commented that it was not possible to "entirely exclude the possibility of such actions."[28]

Immediately after this, on July 15, Nixon sent a personal letter to Ho Chi Minh himself, secret at the time but meant to be made public at the right moment. This was conciliatory in tone, though it gave no new ground. Then, a few days later, Nixon was at pains to tell the heads of government in Romania and Pakistan that his patience was wearing thin and that November 1 was a deadline after which the United States might move to drastic action of some sort. Just what was never stated, but clearly his model was Eisenhower's equally vague threat directed at China in 1953. If, like Lincoln, this President had been a student of Shakespeare, the thought could have been summarized in the words of King Lear: "I shall do such things—what they are yet I know not, but they shall be the terror of the earth."

At the end of Nixon's trip, Kissinger stopped off in Europe, ostensibly to brief leaders there on the trip and the Nixon Doctrine, actually to have a first truly secret talk with the North Vietnamese Paris negotiator, Xuan Thuy. This took place on August 4 at the apartment of Jean Sainteny, and (by Kissinger's later account) consisted mostly of restatements of "established positions in a less contentious manner." Xuan Thuy indicated distaste for third-country intermediaries and they agreed that General Vernon Walters, U.S. military attaché in Paris, should be the channel to arrange future meetings.

What Xuan Thuy's report to Hanoi must have stressed most, however, was surely Kissinger's opening statement, a message from Nixon that concluded:

> In all solemnity . . . if by November 1 no major progress has been made toward a solution, we will be compelled—with great reluctance—to take measures of the greatest consequences.[29]

When the same message was conveyed to Dobrynin on Kissinger's return, the circuits were closed. Since February the Soviet Union had been on notice that everything in the relationship remained in abeyance until and unless it helped over Vietnam. Now Moscow was being threatened as well as Hanoi, with an ultimatum that in its directness, its explicit date, and its implied weight of threat, may have been as strong as any in the whole course of the Cold War.

At the end of August, Ho Chi Minh replied to Nixon's letter, in a stiff tone and with no give at all. He was in fact in very bad health, and died on September 3. Although people had occasionally speculated whether his death might in some way change North Vietnamese policy, it was at once clear that it did not.

By mid-September, then, as Nixon felt impelled to announce the second troop withdrawal, there was neither response nor action plan. At this point Haig and one or two other NSC staffers set to work with the Pentagon on various escalation measures. These plans, labeled Duck Hook, included intense renewed bombing of the North and mining of the port of Haiphong. Later in the month, Nixon met twice with Republican leaders and suggested the possibility of stronger military action. When this news predictably leaked out, it was the first Rogers and Laird knew of it; they urged against any such course.[30] With the antiwar movement set to conduct large "moratorium" demonstrations on October 15 and November 15, Kissinger and then Nixon were gradually persuaded (in part by courageous staff members) that any such escalation would trigger unbearable reactions in much of the Congress and public alike. Years later, Nixon said on television that abandoning Duck Hook was the worst decision of his presidency and that if carried through relentlessly it could have ended the war in 1969. This is typical of the bravado of his later years, expressed also in similar comments about the EC-121 incident. But it is unrealistic to suppose that, given the public mood at home—and in the face of likely Soviet reactions — drastic action could have been sustained for long enough to get Hanoi to back down.[31]

Nixon did make one further try at scaring the Soviet Union into action. When Kissinger and Dobrynin met in the usual way on September 27, Nixon by prearrangement called Kissinger and had him convey, as if impromptu, a message that "the train just left the station and is now headed down the track" — to which Kissinger added that it was up to Moscow to make a move.[32]

The Soviet leadership made no attempt to reply. Instead, on October 20, Dobrynin at his request saw Nixon to deliver the message that Moscow was now ready for the strategic arms talks formally proposed in June. Nixon took the occasion to speak very roughly about not being "diddled to death," and threatened to move ahead with China while piously disclaiming that this might be aimed at the U.S.S.R. He emphasized that

> the Soviet Union is going to be stuck with me for the next three years and three months, and during all that time I will keep in mind what is being done right now, today. If the Soviet Union will not help us get peace, then we will have to pursue our own methods for bringing the war to an end.

This was a less strong threat than the September one, and came with a carrot: if Moscow did help in Vietnam he might "do something dramatic to improve our relations, indeed, something more dramatic than could be imagined."[33]

As Nixon thus pulled back from what he himself described as "the ultimatum," his memoirs depict him as aware that without some "indisputably good reason" for not acting on it, "the Communists would become contemptuous and even more difficult to deal with." The indisputably good reason was, of course, the moratorium demonstrations, which had "undercut the credibility of the ultimatum."[34] This was a feeble excuse: Nixon himself had said publicly, three weeks before, that under no circumstances would he permit himself to be affected by public opposition to a resumption of bombing. One must conclude that his successive military threats were all along bluffs never intended to be carried out — of just the sort he himself had said should never occur in dealings with the Soviet Union.

From this low point — unknown to the public — Nixon made a remarkable recovery, as often in his career. On October 13 he announced he would make a major TV speech on November 3, for which he received advice from many quarters, of which two in particular registered in different ways. The Senate Majority Leader, Mike Mansfield, a consistent "dove" since at least 1963, urged that he announce a rapid and total U.S. withdrawal — a more extreme position than that of almost any of his Senate colleagues and a perfect target for Nixon to attack. In contrast, Dean Acheson urged that the speech soft-pedal the negotiating possibilities, avoid any firm timetable on withdrawal, continue to stress Vietnamization, and make a special plea to rally "emotionally around the flag," which he thought would drown out the demonstrators, "whom Acheson believed represented only a small fraction of the population."[35]

Probably Nixon was already thinking on similar lines. In his speech, conciliatory and reasonable in tone though sharply critical of Johnson's past policies, he argued that prompt withdrawal would be a catastrophe for America's standing worldwide and offered instead the twin recipe of negotiation and Vietnamization. Listing the several concessions in the formal U.S. negotiating position, he made special use of the exchange of letters with Ho and the two exchanges via Sainteny (without naming him) to show how far he had gone and what a rigid response he'd gotten, and also referred to efforts to enlist Soviet help. Not surprisingly, he made no mention of the clumsiness of his attempts, the failure to get into serious secret talks, or the threats he had made to the Soviet Union. He spoke proudly of the sharply reduced U.S. casualty rate under Abrams's newly defined mission (which the President had accepted only reluctantly), and offered a future program of withdrawals pegged to progress being made in the negotiations and above all to what he claimed was the increasing ability of the South Vietnamese to fend for themselves.

In short, he proclaimed a policy of controlled reduction in the U.S. involvement in Vietnam. He made no reference to the continued large-scale use of airpower in South Vietnam and gave no hint of the bombing of Cambodia. At the end, he appealed eloquently and explicitly to the patriotic instincts of a "silent majority" of the public, while linking his policy to the goal of "a just and lasting peace."

It was a superbly crafted speech, delivered at just the right emotional moment when the country was at a peak of anxiety over the antiwar demonstrations, undecided, and in need of a show of leadership. That it offered nothing that had not been spelled out over the past several months, that it contained nasty subliminal messages against the antiwar movement and all of Nixon's adversaries, were features scarcely noted by what probably was indeed a "silent majority" of the public. Beneath its appeal to unity, the speech was actually divisive and so intended, not least in setting up the media themselves as scapegoats for American distress about the war. But for most of Nixon's audience it was his presidential tone, clarity, and apparent candor that mattered most.

The response was highly favorable. The President's approval rating in the polls, which had been steadily in the 50–60 percent range, rose to 68 percent. As important, the House of Representatives shortly adopted, by an overwhelming vote, a resolution supporting the President's policy. In the

Senate, where it might have produced sharp dissent, a more general letter of support was finally signed by 58 senators. As Nixon claimed, the speech and its reception put him in a much stronger position to deal with Hanoi and other nations.

After that, a second moratorium demonstration on November 15 in Washington drew a tremendous (and orderly) attendance of an estimated 250,000. This was shortly followed by the revelation of a terrible massacre by U.S. troops in the village of My Lai in South Vietnam. The massacre had occurred in March 1968, before Nixon's time, and for some it simply added to a contrast between the war under his leadership and Johnson's. For others, it increased the feeling of disgust: public opinion polls by then showed a strong majority believing that sending large U.S. forces to Vietnam had been a mistake.[36]

On December 15, Nixon went on television again to announce a further withdrawal of 50,000 troops by April 1970. In his statement he made much of an upbeat assessment of the situation by Sir Robert Thompson, who had been a senior British official when a Communist insurgency had been defeated in Malaya in the 1950s and still had considerable prestige, especially with Nixon, as an expert on the Vietnam situation.[37]

In sum, Nixon did a remarkable job of staking out and getting public support for the policy toward the Indochina War represented by his public words and actions. What he had actually done and intended was in fact a very different policy, known only to a few White House officials. The outwardly confident Nixon must inwardly have been well aware of the discrepancy: he had, after all, planned it that way. He must also have known that his Communist adversaries in Hanoi and Moscow had in effect faced him down, showing up his threats as bluff. The memory of successive failures to act or to get a Soviet response must have rankled deeply and formed a big part of the mood in which he approached the new year.

4. Strategic Arms Control

Throughout Nixon's first year, as we have seen, there was constant reference to future negotiations aimed at a genuine agreement between the United States and the Soviet Union to control strategic nuclear weapons. Nixon encouraged this hope by an early statement that seemed to disavow the goal of maintaining U.S. nuclear superiority, and to adopt instead an objective of simple "sufficiency."

Strategic arms control, when first attempted under President Eisenhower in the 1950s, had focused on the testing of new nuclear weapons. Building on his efforts, in 1963 President Kennedy achieved a Limited Test Ban Treaty, putting an end to atmospheric testing and thus significantly restraining competition in nuclear technology. The focus then moved to means of delivery. Although Kennedy soon discovered that the Soviet Union did not, in fact, have more missiles than the United States, he pressed forward with programs begun by Eisenhower to produce more intercontinental ballistic missiles, or ICBMs, and more submarine-launched ballistic ones (SLBMs) on a new fleet of nuclear-powered submarines. The latter especially were produced at great speed. By the time of the Cuban Missile Crisis in the fall of 1962, the United States had a clear lead in numbers of strategic missiles, about five to one.

How much this superiority contributed to Nikita Khrushchev's backing down in the Missile Crisis has long been debated. The United States also had overwhelming conventional superiority in sea, air, and ground forces. It gradually became clear, however, that the Soviets themselves saw their failure largely in terms of the strategic nuclear balance. When the Soviet negotiator for the final evacuation of nuclear arms from Cuba told his American counterpart, "The Soviet Union is not going to find itself in a position like this ever again," he was referring to the nuclear balance and expressing a deep Kremlin reaction.

Soviet leaders then set in motion a crash program to catch up with the United States. The programs of the two superpowers, however, differed sharply. American policymakers, after flirting briefly with a primary objective of knocking out Soviet missile and aircraft bases ("counterforce" targeting), settled instead on a generalized capability to inflict "unacceptable" damage on Soviet society as a whole, even after a Soviet first strike. This was called "an assured second-strike capability," and meant emphasizing compact and accurate missiles of modest size, controllable and well protected, with a substantial portion at sea and thus invulnerable.[38]

Having reached a level that appeared to ensure such a capability, the U.S. program stopped and the production lines were closed down in 1966. At that point, the key elements in the U.S. arsenal were 1,054 land-based ICBMs and 656 sea-based SLBMs, supplemented in a so-called triad by about 400 long-range B-52 bombers dating from the 1950s. Seeking only an assured second-strike capability, American top officials hoped that the Soviet program would at least not be drastically incompatible. In a situation of "mutual assured destruction" the nuclear balance would not be insignificant in any confrontation, but the result would usually depend on other factors; in any case, the temptation for either side to launch an impulsive or preemptive nuclear attack would be sharply reduced.

The Soviet program took a different course. From the first it stressed bulky, land-based offensive missiles. Soviet submarine efforts lagged, and the program in general concentrated on the kind of "counterforce" policy the United States had moved away from. Moreover, the Soviets introduced as early as 1964 a missile defense system, Galosh, that was thought to reduce the damage from ballistic missile attacks on the Soviet capital.

On the U.S. side, two contrasting trends developed, affected as much by inventiveness among defense scientists as by doctrine or the perceived Soviet program. On the one hand, any serious defense against ballistic missiles seemed to present enormous technological difficulties; the idea had its fervent backers, but those closer to centers of decision believed that an effective and practicable antiballistic missile (ABM) system was unlikely. On the other hand, scientists working on offensive systems concluded as early as 1963 that it was possible to develop reliable multiple independently targeted reentry vehicles (MIRVs), several of which could be installed on a single carrying missile, each capable of being guided to hit its own separate target. At once, MIRV had great appeal, as an insurance against any swing of the numerical missile balance in the Soviets' favor, as a ready countermeasure that could saturate the Soviet defenses and negate Galosh, and, in the view of top people in the Air Force, as a highly effective weapon against Soviet land-based offensive missile sites. Even though "counterforce" was not the guiding doctrine for Johnson or Secretary of Defense Robert McNamara, the Air Force and many civilian experts continued to prefer it.

By 1966, MIRV development was going ahead secretly but at full speed, while ABM development lagged. At that point, congressional pressures multiplied for the United States somehow to match the Soviet Galosh program. Preoccupied with the Vietnam War, the Pentagon thrashed around and came up with a limited ABM program, about which McNamara himself remained skeptical. He urged that before embarking on it, a determined effort should be made to talk the Soviets out of their Galosh emphasis. This was the starting point for Strategic Arms Limitation Talks (SALT).

In June 1967, President Johnson met with Soviet Premier Alexei Kosygin for a short summit meeting in Glassboro, New Jersey. McNamara argued fervently that nominally defensive systems like Galosh actually affected the offensive balance seriously and should be abandoned by both sides. The argument made no impression on Kosygin, who replied that "giving up *defensive* systems was the most absurd proposition" he had ever heard.[39]

Curiously, nothing was said at Glassboro about *offensive* missiles, although by then the Soviet Union had 500–600 and was building and installing nearly 200 a year. Both the quantity and the technology lagged behind those of American missiles, and for a time the CIA expected that the Soviets would level off, as the United States had, at numerical levels consistent with parity.[40]

Disappointed at Glassboro, McNamara announced in September 1967 a hybrid ABM program called Sentinel, which emphasized the protection of key cities against attacks not just from the Soviet Union but also from a third country, with China most likely. This compromise program was modest, its justification uncertain, its technology unproven. Doubts quickly emerged in Congress, which stalled action on the program during the turbulent last eighteen months of the Johnson Administration.

On the other hand, the ongoing MIRV program was formally announced in December 1967. Feasibility tests in August 1968 were successful, and the program was slated to deploy its first MIRVed missiles by late 1970 or early 1971.

Concurrently, only days after the first American MIRV feasibility test, U.S. intelligence detected the first flight test of a much heavier Soviet ICBM than any previously observed. This new missile, labeled the SS-9, quickly became an object of special concern, since its additional carrying capacity—called "throw weight"—would enable it to deliver not only the heaviest single warheads then in existence but, conceivably, many of the still crude Soviet warheads at once. Did not the Soviets aim at a large MIRV capability as soon as they had mastered the technology? Many American defense scientists believed that Soviet scientists could achieve such mastery in roughly five years.

In the summer of 1968, Deputy Secretary of Defense Paul Nitze led an intense preparatory exercise for possible strategic arms control talks. The group drafted parts of an initial negotiating position. Its key features were: a freeze on offensive delivery systems, notably ICBMs but also SLBMs; an agreed limit on numbers of ABM installations; no numerical or research limitations on MIRVs, this at the insistence of the JCS; and verification by "national technical means"—that is, distant electronic detection, with no demand for on-site inspection.[41]

In short, Johnson's legacy to Nixon in this area consisted of a solid U.S. offensive missile posture, but with no production lines and no new delivery vehicles; a MIRV program of proven feasibility; a shaky ABM program; and a tentative negotiating position. Meanwhile, the SS-9 heavy missile threat briefly seemed compounded when analysis of an early SS-9 test showed that the missile had dropped three warheads in what appeared to be a systematic pattern.

Of course, U.S. policymakers faced enormous uncertainties in trying to make decisions on arms control. The tight secrecy of the Soviet system meant that one had to make crucial judgments by inference from limited data that often proved faulty. The Galosh system, for example, eventually proved to be technically backward and ineffective, and the SS-9 testing turned out to have involved only a triplet of warheads that were not independently targetable.

American decisions on strategic weapons, moreover, required congressional approval. In 1969, with the backlash against the Vietnam War strong, a near-majority of senators (though few members of the House) were critical of the general level of defense spending, and particularly of spending for strategic nuclear weapons systems (which comprised about 10 percent of the total defense budget).

Moreover, the Joint Chiefs of Staff had a special function concerning arms agreements. Traditionally loyal in supporting, to the Congress and public, budget and operating decisions reached by the Defense Secretary and the President, the Chiefs were expected to speak freely when an arms control agreement was presented for approval, giving their judgment as to whether it was acceptable from a military standpoint. No matter that the criteria for what was "acceptable" and what was truly "military" were bound to be vague: if the JCS testified against an agreement or expressed grave reservations, enough votes would almost surely be influenced to doom the deal. A prudent Administration had to take this into account at every turn. Nixon certainly did.

Finally, decisions on arms control engaged what could be described as an "arms control community," composed of citizens in and out of government—many of them scientists and with past government experience—who believed that control of the nuclear arms race should be a top priority of national and international security policy. Nixon had never paid much heed to the subject in his years in the Eisenhower Administration or those out of office. He approached strategic arms control skeptically, believing that the Soviet Union was sure to seek maximum advantage. He was also less persuaded than the arms control community that reducing, or at least capping, the nuclear arms race was a moral obligation.

Moreover, he was not by any means convinced, as Johnson had been, that controlling the spread of nuclear weapons to other nations (beyond the five countries then avowedly nuclear-capable: the United States, the Soviet Union, Britain, France, and, after 1964, China) was either feasible or highly important. He shared Kissinger's view that many countries, including France, Israel, and in due course Japan, were bound to have their own nuclear capabilities and it was constructive that they should. He also did not believe that efforts in this direction, given new impetus by the multilateral Nuclear Non-Proliferation Treaty (NPT) signed in 1968, would be weakened if the two superpowers failed to bring their own nuclear arsenals under control. Johnson had even considered a special session of Congress to get the NPT ratified at once, but Nixon from the first gave the treaty only formal support. In February 1969 he submitted it to the Senate, but with no fanfare or effort to move it rapidly; the Senate finally ratified it in March 1970, largely on its own initiative.

Whatever Nixon's underlying views, he and Kissinger rightly judged that Congress, especially the Senate, was not likely to support a defense budget at the levels he deemed necessary without a clear showing of effort to control nuclear arms. Moreover, he saw some agreement on this as an almost inescapable element in any changed relationship with the Soviet Union and, probably, the capstone of a summit meeting with the Soviet leaders toward the end of his first term, when it would have maximum domestic political effect. Such a summit stood, all along, as a major Nixon objective.

. . .

In early 1969, Nixon and Kissinger decided not to accept the initial negotiating position worked out under Johnson, but rather to put the interested agencies to work on a new detailed analysis. Careful work had already been done under Johnson, and a new directive on this scale would have been unnecessary in an Administration disposed to move. The directive was a device for delay.

The real action during Nixon's first seven months revolved around the U.S. ABM program. Johnson's Sentinel proposal had been widely questioned and Congress had never acted on it. On March 14 the President announced and submitted to Congress a new program called Safeguard, calling for a dozen ABM sites to defend not major cities but broad areas containing offensive missile bases. By this time many Americans, especially those living near cities, were alarmed that ABM installations in their neighborhoods would automatically make them targets of the first Soviet strikes in a hypothetical all-out war. A striking example was Senator Henry M. Jackson, a fervent advocate of ABM and of a strong nuclear posture, who at the same time rejected, early and vehemently, proposals to locate ABM installations in his home state of Washington![42]

The ABM discussion that spring and summer was exceptionally intense and bitter. Citizens' organizations, as well as respected scientists and engineers who seriously doubted that an ABM system would work well, fought against ABM. On the side of the Administration, a small committee of private citizens put together by Paul Nitze, with the strong support of Dean Acheson, produced trenchant papers that probably swayed several key votes.[43]

The legislation to authorize the Safeguard program cleared the House without difficulty but ran into heavy opposition in the Senate. For a time the opponents of any ABM system appeared to have the upper hand; in the end, the key August 6 vote on an amendment to deny funds for the program was a tie, 50–50, which would in any case have defeated the amendment. For good measure, Vice President Agnew added his ballot, as he was entitled to do.

In his memoirs Nixon called this "the biggest congressional battle of the first term." In his own mind, the decisive argument was that the United States could not go into a serious negotiation without a realistic ABM program under way. This "bargaining chip" rationale for a weapons program, much debated over the years, was at its strongest then; the record of the

Senate debate makes clear that it was fully understood and almost certainly decisive against strong arguments that the system could never do the full job or even work as projected.[44]

. . .

Most opponents of ABM had also urged at least a moratorium on testing MIRV, specifically a delay in the "on-board" tests scheduled for June 1969. But meanwhile the new hardware designed to carry MIRVed missiles—Minuteman III ICBMs and modified Polaris submarines—was already in production, creating Pentagon (and local) pressures to go ahead. MIRV was already a sure thing technologically. Its mission, to hit fixed targets at known locations, was vastly simpler than that of any antimissile defense, and it involved no new installations or fears of special local dangers. MIRVs would simply go into existing missiles.

Thus it was harder to make a practical case against MIRV. Its opponents relied instead on more general arguments, notably that such a large increase in offensive capabilities would greatly intensify the strategic arms competition, and that it would be an inherently destabilizing new factor, because of the unknowns and the problems of counting nuclear warheads once deployed. Another big reason for doubt and rejection was harshly realist and little noted in public comment, though it was clear to those who focused on defense matters. U.S. offensive missile types were compact and relatively small, whereas their Soviet ground-based counterparts were much bulkier, though less sophisticated or accurate. If the Soviets mastered the MIRV technology, the greater carrying capacity of their offensive missiles was bound to mean that their effective number of deliverable and targetable warheads would be multiplied much more than the equivalent U.S. capability. Moreover, if in time they also brought the accuracy of their missiles nearer to the U.S. level, the result would surely be greatly increased vulnerability of the land-based American strategic missile force. In short, an eventual "window of vulnerability" for at least the land-based component of U.S. strategic nuclear forces—which was to become a vivid alarmist vision by the late 1970s—was always foreseen. "MIRV will doom Minuteman" was the shorthand.

All these arguments were made in 1969 and early 1970, both within government and outside it. Yet, largely because it was abstract and long-range, the debate over the next MIRV tests never became so intense as that over ABM. It was a case of one issue at a time; some also reasoned that MIRV was bound to come up when arms control talks began and could be further addressed then.[45] Moreover, the Nixon Administration discouraged debate. For example, the bipartisan General Advisory Committee on Arms Control and Disarmament, chaired by John J. McCloy, which had been set up in 1961 by President Kennedy and was composed of prominent citizens, had carried weight in the Kennedy and Johnson Administrations. In 1969 its advice favoring a moratorium on MIRV testing was disregarded.

In June 1969, an effort to block MIRV appropriations was defeated in Senate committee. Yet forty or more senators favored a sense-of-the-Senate resolution (advisory, not binding) for a test moratorium, and Republican Senator Edward Brooke personally argued the case with Kissinger. But it was a scattershot opposition compared with the ABM fight, and in June, President Nixon announced that the "on-board" tests of MIRV would take place on schedule. It is probable that he never seriously considered postponement, although members of Kissinger's staff debated the question intensively.[46]

Going ahead with the tests made it progressively harder to stop the program. But just as the "bargaining chip" rationale for ABM envisaged a possible reduction or elimination of the program in negotiations, so going ahead with MIRV tests need not have ended the matter, and was not thought to do so. The next decisive question was whether, and how, MIRV might be dealt with when SALT I got under way.

Kissinger, at Nixon's direction, put his NSC staff at the center of the preparations for negotiations. This was natural, particularly because Kissinger was exceptionally well versed in the field.[47]

Nixon had appointed the veteran Gerard Smith to head the arms control agency (ACDA) and in August designated him also as the head of the negotiating delegation. The twin appointments were widely approved. Smith was a loyal but never partisan Republican who had served as a lawyer with the Atomic Energy Commission in the early 1950s, then as special assistant for atomic matters to Secretary of State John Foster Dulles, and from 1957 to 1960 as head of the Policy Planning Council in the State Department. He was strong both on technical matters and on broad policy. Nixon respected him for his dedication and integrity, although he remained suspicious of the ACDA staff generally. Another key player was Paul Nitze of the Defense Department, for whom Nixon had formed a special regard.[48] With Nitze, General Royal Allison of the Air Force, and an able, experienced staff, Smith quickly made the negotiating team an exceptionally collegial and disciplined group.[49]

As the framing of negotiating positions got seriously under way in early summer, the problem of verification at once loomed large. Civilian hardliners, led by the Pentagon's chief of research and development, John Foster, as well as the Joint Chiefs, were inclined to demand total precision in numbers and solid assurance against any undetected technological change. Most other civilian officials, though, notably those in the CIA and ACDA, argued that the test could be more pragmatic: it was necessary only to detect new developments in time to react effectively. Both groups agreed that the U.S. reconnaissance satellites by then available were sure to detect and count missile-launching sites and also submarines and their carrying capacity, as well as ABM or ABM-potential sites and numbers of deployed defensive missiles. MIRVs, however, being physically concealed within an offensive missile, presented major difficulties as to both numbers and characteristics.[50] So serious and persistent were arguments on this subject that by August the Administration's center for arms control policy had become the so-called Verification Panel, set up within the NSC structure and chaired by Kissinger. Nixon was supplied with the analytic papers and met frequently with the Verification Panel, but did not try to make decisions and usually confined himself to general reactions. The subject bored him.[51]

After Secretary Rogers's June 11 announcement of U.S. readiness to proceed, it was widely assumed that the Soviets would respond rapidly. That they did not was probably due in large part to the ABM debate in the Senate. A second reason, unknown to the public, may have been the secret Nixon ultimatum over Vietnam, leading the Soviets to hold back on all key matters. Still a third reason may have been the extremely tense state of Sino-Soviet relations right through the summer. Finally, on October 20, Dobrynin conveyed directly to Nixon the message that the Soviet side was prepared to start formal SALT negotiations on November 17. A joint formal announcement followed on October 25. By this time the churning machinery of planning under Kissinger had produced an array of options on the four main problems: numbers of offensive missiles, ABM, MIRV, and verification. Even if Nixon's mind had not been riveted on Vietnam, he might have had difficulty deciding what opening positions to choose. Instead he sent the delegation into the first round, in Helsinki, Finland, with only a general instruction to probe for Soviet thinking. (This was typical of Nixon's attitude toward negotiations. He hardly ever went in for hands-on supervision but instead would approve broad guidelines or initial positions, then stand aloof and inject himself only to insist on tough bargaining. Kissinger, on the other hand, loved both negotiation and one-on-one contact.[52])

The delegation was also firmly instructed not to bring up MIRV in any way. In a preliminary July instruction to Smith, Nixon had mentioned that he might consider raising MIRV, but now he expressly forbade it; he thought that raising MIRV first would indicate weakness. Most of those involved believed that other topics bearing on the overall balance were likely to lead the Soviet Union to bring up MIRV first.

Neither at this point nor thereafter did Nixon or Kissinger try to frame a coherent statement of what the U.S. objectives and strategy should be for the talks. Such a statement would have been difficult to draft in any case, yet surely discussion would have clarified the likely problems and trade-offs and identified the essential objectives. In the absence of such a statement, the preparations for negotiations ignored long-term goals in favor of details, with the result that Kissinger ended up with a remarkably free hand.

. . .

At the first round in Helsinki (November 17 to December 16), it quickly developed that the Soviets, too, were probing for general attitudes rather than concentrating on specific proposals. The Soviet negotiators surprised the U.S. side, however, by emphasizing that the balance of offensive weapons must take specific account of the so-called Forward-Based Systems (FBS)—American land-based and carrier-based strike aircraft with ranges that could reach Soviet territory. The American inventory then included about a thousand of each, capable of carrying nuclear warheads but deployed primarily for tactical and naval missions; the land-based aircraft were mostly based in allied territory and were part of joint defense planning with allies.[53]

No doubt these nuclear-capable aircraft did figure in some annex to American contingency plans, but in view of the vulnerability of land-based aircraft and the variable locations of the aircraft carriers, they can hardly have been significant. Moreover, it would have been damaging to allied relations for the United States to appear to bargain alone over assets committed to the Alliance. For these reasons the Americans argued consistently that the FBS should not be considered part of the strategic balance, while the Soviet side—always ready to try to divide NATO—never abandoned its demand that they be included. This disagreement was to haunt the negotiations for two years.

The major American discovery in this first round was that the Soviet Union—which in 1967 had wanted to talk primarily about limitations on offensive weapons—now had ABM limitation as its top priority. Congressional approval of the Safeguard program had triggered by December a series of important American tests, mostly successful, widely reported, and surely noted by Soviet intelligence. It was clearer and clearer that the United States had a wide lead over the primitive Soviet facilities in the technologies relevant to missile defense, including the vast and complex radar and reporting networks required. The revealed Soviet concern over ABMs both gave hope of an agreement sharply limiting ABMs on both sides and validated the "bargaining chip" approach.

A second discovery was the apparently relaxed Soviet attitude toward offensive weapons. The Soviets never once mentioned MIRV. Either they were worried but did not want to appear eager or they had their own plans and were resigned to MIRV development on both sides—knowing that the Americans might lead for a time, but that they could catch up in due course and even forge ahead, given the carrying capacity of their heavier missiles.

It quickly became clear that the Soviet military men knew many things the civilians, nominally their seniors, did not, and that scientific members of the delegation had special status. From the first, the delegations paired off with their opposites to talk outside the stereotyped formal meetings. One such pairing, between Paul Nitze and a top Soviet defense scientist, made a significant impression. Nitze had at one point been attracted to elements of a "counterforce" strategy, but had come in the mid-1960s to believe in assured second-strike capabilities on both sides. He now picked up the case McNamara had tried to make to Kosygin at Glassboro, with much more time to explore every facet of it. If the Soviets were to develop a serious missile defense system, he argued, the inevitable American response would be to build its own such system and go all out in offensive weapons that could overcome projected defenses. Moreover, if either side had even the theoretical possibility of knocking out the other's main offensive weapons while protecting its own, this was bound to create a hair-trigger atmosphere that might turn otherwise resolvable confrontations into catastrophic nuclear exchanges.

The response of Nitze's interlocutor to this line of thought, along with reactions from other Soviet negotiators, unfortunately left little doubt that the argument fell on deaf ears (if indeed it ever reached the top Soviet leadership). The inescapable conclusion was that the Soviet Union was not prepared to accept a common goal of assured second-strike capabilities on both sides; it continued to have in mind, though it did not necessarily have a firm resolve to achieve, "superiority" and the potential ability to destroy most of the American power in a first strike.[54] Back in May, as he settled into his job, Gerard Smith had written a memorandum to Secretary Rogers starkly concluding that "if either side is striving for or appears to be striving for an effective counterforce first strike capability, then there is no hope for strategic arms control." The Helsinki exchanges hardly proved that the Soviet leadership was dead set on achieving such a capability, only that it continued to see the future in terms of a sharp continuing struggle in which either side might gain such a position and profit greatly from it.

One can speculate how SALT I (and all later strategic arms negotiations) would have worked out if a bilateral consensus on an objective of strategic stability had been achieved—how differently, in fact, the whole nuclear rivalry would have unfolded over the next decades. The important fact for the historian is that Nitze made a serious attempt at Helsinki, and it was thrust aside. It does not appear that in the Kissinger-Dobrynin exchanges, which assumed central importance in 1970, Kissinger ever made a similar effort—though it would have stood much more chance of getting through to the Soviet leaders.

The general feeling within the delegation and in Washington was that Helsinki had usefully clarified attitudes and developed working relations. Meanwhile, the Soviet buildup of land-based strategic missiles continued: the total grew from 250 operational ICBMs in mid-1966 to 1,060 in September 1969 (just ahead of the United States' 1,054). Sea-based and bomber-carried weapons still gave the United States an overall numerical edge, but the trends pointed inescapably to a Soviet lead in weapons totals in another two years or so.[55]

As the U.S. side prepared for the second SALT round, to start in Vienna in April 1970, the Verification Panel developed several possible positions. From these Nixon picked two. One called for a ban on flight testing or deployment of MIRV, though permitting production of MIRV items already tested; the other for progressive reduction in numbers of offensive missiles, from initial agreed levels, while not restraining qualitative improvements such as MIRV. The decision to focus on these two options was shared with a representative congressional group from both chambers, which strongly approved the options as outlined. Senator Jackson was among those favorably impressed, but confirmed advocates of arms control were also pleased.

The members of Congress were not, however, told of — or at least did not come to grips with — a crucial modification in the first proposal on MIRV. The State Department and ACDA had recommended, via the Verification Panel, a MIRV ban on testing and deployment to be policed solely by national technical means, without physical inspection at the site, but the JCS and senior Pentagon civilians in the Defense Department insisted on on-site inspection. After a full airing of the subject at a climactic NSC meeting, President Nixon reached his decision in private, choosing, without explanation, the JCS view. As Smith's team and everyone who had read their reports knew well, any proposal for on-site inspection was almost bound to be summarily rejected. At Helsinki, the Soviet Union had made clear its expected aversion to having inspectors on its territory — and many American officials had similar reservations about Soviet inspectors in U.S. facilities. Nor was it at all clear that "on-site inspection" could effectively detect MIRV-related measures, given the small size of the components involved.[56]

By April, as deliberations within government continued, the idea of banning deployment of both MIRV and ABM, with equal priority, picked up public momentum. In March the Senate approved, by the overwhelming margin of 72–6, a nonbinding sense-of-the-Senate resolution urging that neither ABM nor MIRV be deployed by either side. John McCloy's General Advisory Committee took the same position and asked for backup documents. Although similar requests by that committee had been honored as a matter of course ever since 1961, this time the Administration refused to comply. McCloy and his colleagues were frozen out.

The conclusion is inescapable that Nixon, with Kissinger, thought that making a MIRV proposal in the SALT talks, but also linking it to on-site inspection, was a neat move that would duck the issue. Those who wanted a real negotiation about MIRV would be assured that it was indeed on the table, and the JCS and others opposed to any MIRV deal could readily deduce that it would never happen. It was the kind of plan that depended heavily on no official at any level airing to the press or Congress any suspicion or disappointment. Congress had in fact been misled and the press kept completely out of things—a pattern that recurred often.

In January 1970, Kissinger himself began to talk directly to Dobrynin about arms control, taking up the ambassador's suggestion that the Channel be extended to topics other than Vietnam. In conversations kept secret from the rest of the government, including Smith's negotiating team, Dobrynin probed to find out especially whether the United States visualized a "limited" or "comprehensive" agreement—"limited" meaning one confined to ABM, "comprehensive" meaning one covering both offensive and defensive weapons. In reply, Kissinger wound up making an extraordinary concession, that the United States had no strong preference! There is no record whether Nixon was consulted on this reply. Certainly neither the negotiators nor the Verification Panel were.

In his memoirs, Kissinger was to note that by then it was clear to him that the Soviet Union wanted a very low ceiling on the number of antiballistic missile complexes; at another point he acknowledged that this Soviet desire gave the American side major leverage toward an agreement on limiting offensive weapons to acceptable levels. Yet his reply to Dobrynin inexplicably failed to insist on connecting the two. The practical effect was that throughout 1970 the negotiations were much more serious on ABM than on offensive weapons and the two were never related. In effect, just when a realistic form of "linkage" was most needed and useful, one of its vocal adherents failed to invoke it![57]

A side effect, also, was to further downgrade the issue of MIRV. When Gerard Smith's opening presentation at the session in Vienna reached the subject of MIRVs, the Soviet note taker wrote feverishly, but when Smith went on to insist on on-site inspection, he simply stopped taking notes.[58]

Nor did the Soviets do what some Americans had thought they might: namely, counter by proposing a MIRV ban policed only by national technical means. Rather, whereas the U.S. proposal banned testing (which the United States had already done) but allowed deployment and production, the Soviet counterproposal turned this on its head, calling for no restraints on testing or deployment of MIRV but banning further production. Even this obviously one-sided proposal might have been matched by a U.S. offer to accept a ban on further production in return for a ban on flight testing and deployment—in effect a freeze leaving each side where it then was.[59] In May the Smith delegation in Vienna asked Washington if it could suggest such a proposal, but never got a reply. Thus it was clear that neither side was ready to bargain seriously about MIRV. The planned tests of MIRV aboard Minuteman missiles went forward in June, and similar tests on the newer Poseidon submarines were carried out later in the year. MIRV had been excluded tacitly from the SALT negotiations.[60]

To sum up, there were two major SALT decisions in early 1970. One, Kissinger's failure to insist on a comprehensive agreement linking ABM and offensive missiles, was a negotiating blunder that could be retrieved and in the end was, though at a heavy cost in delay and distraction. The second decision, however, not to put MIRV on the table in any serious way, was final. When actual U.S. deployment occurred, any effort to control MIRV became almost impossible even within the American government; deployment had to keep pace with that of the Soviets.[61] For all practical purposes, therefore, the decision to let MIRV run free was made, and the die cast, between mid-1968 and mid-1970. Not until 1974, when Nixon left office, did the two sides even find a way to count MIRVed missiles in the effort to reach some sort of numerical balance. Yet MIRV both enormously increased the destructive power of strategic nuclear arsenals and made them far harder to verify or even estimate. The absence of any limitation on MIRV weighed heavily on arms control negotiations for a very long time.

5. The MIRV Decision Examined

In December 1974, Henry Kissinger made a remarkable statement: "I would say in retrospect that I wish I had thought through the implications of a MIRVed world more thoughtfully in 1969 and 1970 than I did."[62] In 1980, Gerard Smith voiced a similar feeling, and pointed out that "[o]nly during the opening months was there a chance to stop MIRVs."[63] And William G. Hyland, Kissinger's close associate at the time, wrote in 1987: "Refusal to ban MIRVs was the key decision in the entire history of SALT. . . . It was a truly fateful decision that changed strategic relations, and changed them to the detriment of American security."[64]

These hindsight judgments, by men who had been deeply involved then and later, pose a difficult problem for the historian. Was there ever, in the critical 1968–70 period, a different possible approach that might have been more hopeful from the standpoint of both U.S. interests narrowly considered and the wider ongoing course of the Cold War?

To be fair, Nixon and his colleagues, and their Soviet counterparts, were feeling their way in an unknown area of policy and interaction, grappling with a new technology that drastically changed old assumptions and ways of thinking. Obviously, too, the two parties had a long history of rivalry, confrontation, and often justified suspicion. Both approached the MIRV problem from perspectives honed by years of Cold War. But let us try to be more specific. What were the obstacles and the factors behind what was done and not done?

Here the problem of *verification* has to come first. MIRV was perhaps the most difficult technological innovation of the Cold War to control. In importance, it deserved to be placed alongside the switch from the atomic bomb to the hydrogen bomb in the early 1950s, and the change from aircraft delivery to long-range missiles in the late 1950s and early 1960s. These two crucial changes were controlled only within wide limits, and MIRV was in many ways more difficult than either. It could be developed in the laboratory, and the key components were extremely small and did not involve any especially sensitive materials. A single MIRV warhead in a missile looked no different from a conventional warhead in a photograph.

In the 1968–70 discussions within the U.S. government, the strongest argument that verification was possible rested on a judgment that the Soviet Union would never deploy or rely on a weapon that had not been tested thoroughly under operational conditions—that is, through the actual test firing of MIRVed missiles carrying and aiming their several warheads at once. The United States could detect and identify such multiple firings and their targeting as MIRV tests, but those bent on deploying MIRV noted that once the technique was perfected, follow-on tests might not be necessary or revealing. In short, a convincing case simply could not be made that MIRV, once past the first testing phase, could be detected. This was an almost insuperable difficulty for those who urged a MIRV ban.[65]

Another major factor was delay and distraction, in large part related to the Vietnam War. Gerard Smith is right that the Johnson Administration

> perhaps missed a last clear chance to avoid MIRV missiles on both sides by not deferring or stretching out the developmental testing of MIRV systems until the degree of Soviet interest in banning them could be assessed.[66]

It is a fair comment, yet it is hard to see how that Administration could have acted differently. Only on July 1, 1968, was it agreed that there should be strategic arms control talks, and the initial operational test of MIRV was conducted in August. To have deferred the August test with no Soviet negotiation yet established would have required both great imagination and a willingness to ride out opposition not only from the Joint Chiefs but from many conservative and defense-minded members of Congress.

An alternative would have been to go ahead with the August test but to put the issue on the table at the summit meeting planned for September. Civilians in the Pentagon's Office of International Security Affairs (ISA), responsible for framing the initial negotiating position, considered such a course, but never seriously proposed it to President Johnson, and Congress was dispersed and not then involved.[67] If the Soviet action in Prague (in mid-August) had not intervened, it is conceivable that participation in a SALT-oriented summit would have at least started a serious discussion with Soviet leaders and thus perhaps produced a thought-through MIRV position on the U.S. side. The simple historical fact remains: the Johnson Administration did have the first and best theoretical chance to set about controlling MIRV, but did not pursue it.

When Nixon took over, the same possibility of deferring or stretching out MIRV tests had become more difficult to visualize, although outside members of the arms control community, as well as Gerard Smith, earnestly proposed it. Nixon's successive decisions to go ahead with the on-board tests, delay the opening of SALT I for many months, and then categorically forbid discussion of MIRV at the first session in Helsinki had the effect of losing a year. One senior Johnson Administration official, Walt Rostow, later called it "a terrible year to lose."[68] For these decisions, certainly, the onus must fall on Nixon's policy of focusing on putting pressure on the Soviet Union to help toward a Vietnam peace.

Inseparable from the consequent delay was the always present factor of inertia—the ongoing momentum of a project undertaken for what were thought to be sensible precautionary reasons. From the 1950s on, the arms control community argued that any new weapons system should be assessed as to whether it could be controlled if the other side caught up. That this was never really done was a human failure, perhaps characteristic of a twentieth-century society prone to consider all invention and innovation to be progress. Weapons competition was always encouraged by bureaucratic interests, by the argument that "if we don't do it, the other side will," and sometimes by scientific Micawberism, "some new and offsetting invention will turn up and prevent the bad consequences you claim." From the decision to manufacture the hydrogen bomb onward, all these arguments were heard, and mostly prevailed. It is hardly surprising that they weighed heavily in the case of MIRV.

Another key factor was misjudgment, as much outside the government as within it. Critics of weapons competition in 1969 concentrated on the Safeguard ABM project, erroneously rating ABM as at least as great a future threat as MIRV. They also failed to see the genuine Soviet interest in ABM limitation. In biblical terms, the critics and opponents strained at the "gnat" of ABM and ended by having to swallow the "camel" of MIRV.[69]

Let us turn finally to the decision-making process itself. Under Johnson, key civilians in the Defense Department favored a SALT negotiation and were open-minded about the positions to be taken; they were supported in State, the ACDA, and the White House staff. The JCS too were cooperative (except on the issue of deferring MIRV). But the balance shifted sharply when Nixon took office. In the Pentagon, Melvin Laird had a generally negative attitude toward arms control; he retained close ties with key leaders in the Congress, which added weight to his views. Under him the Office of International Security Affairs was virtually eclipsed by the scientist civilians, always strong backers and promoters of MIRV; John Foster was particularly influential. In effect, the Pentagon's voice now became "more royalist than the King"—that is, more skeptical and critical of arms control initiatives than the JCS.

Gerard Smith, as we have seen, urged both a freeze covering all aspects of MIRV (testing, production, and deployment) and a delay in on-board tests. He was supported by Secretary Rogers, whose inexpert opinion carried little weight with Nixon. As for Henry Kissinger, he appears never to have weighed in at all. There can be little doubt that he knew the issue thoroughly, in part through several discussions over the winter with old associates from Harvard and MIT. But his staff was divided and it seems likely that he had little appetite at this early stage to take a strong position against the visible inclinations of the President.

A President would in any event have to decide for himself. There were no group discussions whatever about the 1969 on-board tests of MIRV. Nixon made the crucial decision alone, and without showing his hand in the internal debate. Was there ever any doubt about his stance? Neither he nor any participant suggests that there was. On the contrary, the circumstantial evidence indicates that he brushed aside doubts and objections. One must conclude that he was at all times dead set to go ahead with MIRV.

Gerard Smith in 1980 stated his own view about the failure to control MIRV:

> In retrospect, the weak effort to ban MIRVs was a key aspect of SALT. . . . [But] it is far from sure that even if we had made a more reasonable offer on MIRVs the Soviets would have accepted it. It is doubtful that they would have locked themselves into a MIRV-less condition and it is most unlikely that the United States would, while stopping U.S. MIRV deployments, have permitted the Soviets to develop them through the testing stage. While there may have been an opportunity missed, it was not a clear one.[70]

My own conclusion is that a MIRV ban, whether by explicit negotiation or by parallel decisions not to deploy, was never conceivable under Nixon and extremely hard to visualize under any American President in 1969–72. There just was not enough trust or communication, and to have attempted it seriously would have set off a storm of controversy that would almost certainly have doomed the best-intended initiative. This said, was there anything else that might have eased the arms competition in the future, even if it failed to head off the emergence of MIRV? Was the choice solely between an agreed ban and letting MIRV run free? Only Gerard Smith has suggested such a middle course, and only in a single sentence of regret.

Let us at least look at the only possibility that seems even faintly realistic. This would have involved the United States making clear that it felt impelled to go ahead, but did not intend to achieve a strength that would genuinely threaten most of the Soviet land-based missiles (or bases for Soviet missile-carrying submarines). The Americans would have had to concede and accept that the Soviet Union too would go ahead and achieve a MIRV capability — and to argue that it, too, should be limited and made ascertainable in some fashion. The channel used for this discussion would of course have had to be totally private and secret, perhaps even after some sort of initial understanding had been reached: actions would speak for themselves, with the beneficial side effect that each would get credit for acting unilaterally and voluntarily.

The objective would have been to achieve by tacit parallel action a reduction in the major fear felt on both sides that the other side might be clearly superior and capable of a devastating first-strike attack. In practice, the effect might have been to level off the key category of land-based missiles at something like 3,000 deliverable warheads on each side, as opposed to the much higher levels both sides were to reach in the 1980s.

Farfetched? Dependent on a level of trust still well out of reach? Contrary to established custom, even law, in terms of the powers of a U.S. President to act alone? In any case, likely sooner or later to be surmised and become intensely controversial? All these objections, and others, can be made, but I believe it would have been worth serious consideration, even a trial run, considering how MIRV colored the strategic arms postures and overall behavior of the superpowers for the next two decades — and, as William Hyland wrote, not to U.S. advantage.

6. Signs of Change: China

There is a natural tendency among high-level writers of memoirs to emphasize a line of policy that turned out well and to ascribe to early efforts a prescient and systematic quality they did not in fact possess. This was emphatically true of the Nixon Administration's dealings with China, which were at first halting, uncertain, and indecisive. A new relationship with China was far from being a top priority from the start, as both Nixon and Kissinger later tried to suggest.

During the transition period after his election, Nixon took the modest step of concurring in President Johnson's reopening of the long-standing ambassadorial talks in Warsaw between American and Chinese representatives, a channel that for all its stilted formality had been at least a useful register of mood. Certainly by early 1968, when the talks were suspended in the chaotic atmosphere of the Tet offensive and its aftermath, it must have been clear to the Chinese that the Johnson Administration no longer held the deep fears of China that Americans had earlier. In refusing to depict the Indochina War primarily as a Chinese threat, the Nixon Administration was following the line taken by its predecessor for at least two years. It was a time of slack water, ready for the tide to turn.

At the outset, an unpredictable event entered in. With a late February date set for the resumption of the Warsaw talks, early that month a Chinese diplomat in the Netherlands defected and was given asylum in the American Embassy in The Hague. Although it had long been the practice not to accept Communist official defectors of this sort in any embassy, worldwide, the Hague Embassy was simply taken by surprise and reacted on a humane basis. Once it had done so, to return the individual to Chinese custody seemed both repugnant and likely to stir an outcry in many American quarters.

It was the kind of incident that might have caused only a ripple in other circumstances. But given the delicate state of feeling, the Chinese responded by canceling the Warsaw resumption. In early March, during Nixon's visit to Paris, President de Gaulle brought up the subject of China. Kissinger, who was present, later summarized the President's response thus:

> [I]n the short term there would be no change largely because of the unsettling impact of such a move on the rest of Asia; but over the long term — say ten years — we would have more communications with China, especially after it began to make progress in nuclear weapons.

Kissinger added his own commentary:

> This indirect reply by Nixon was a sure sign that he meant to keep his options open. It was as compatible with an intention to wait ten years as with the objective of moving at the first opportunity. At best it reflected the reality that the new Administration had no clear-cut plan.[71]

Then, on March 14, when announcing the Safeguard ABM program, Nixon gave the decision much the same twist President Johnson had, that it was in considerable part insurance against any rash act by China. Indeed, he suggested that the Soviet Union should approve of the program since it shared a common interest in containing China. Predictably, the official New China News Agency denounced this "collusion with the Soviet revisionists."[72]

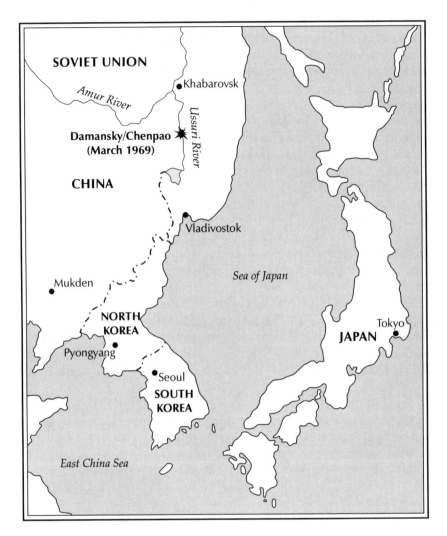

China, North Korea, South Korea, Sea of Japan, Japan © 1997 *Chris Brest*

In the meantime, however, a landmark event had taken place on a remote stretch of the Sino-Soviet border. This was a sharp armed clash, on
March 2, along the Ussuri River, at the extreme northeastern tip of Chinese
territory and between Vladivostok and Khabarovsk. While this particular
incident may have been triggered by the Chinese, as Nixon at first believed,
both sides had been sparring for some time and continued to do so after
March 2. Previous brushes had been hushed up, but this time the Soviets
let fly a torrent of verbal abuse, and the Chinese naturally replied in kind.

Already Soviet forces along the whole length of the border, which had been at roughly a seven-division level over the years, had been increased to twenty-four divisions (roughly 10,000 men each).

The Ussuri River incident marked a change to outright and total hostility between China and the Soviet Union. In the White House, however, its significance did not at once sink in. In his memoirs Kissinger later claimed that after this incident "ambiguity vanished, and we moved without further hesitation toward a momentous change in global diplomacy," but this over-states the speed with which he and Nixon grasped what had happened.[73]

Professors of Chinese studies at Harvard and MIT had sent a memoran-dum to Nixon during the transition period, advocating the widely held liberal view that the United States should relinquish its ties to the Nation-alist Republic of China, now based on Taiwan, and accept the People's Republic forthwith in the United Nations. At the opposite extreme was the "China Lobby" (of Anna Chennault fame) — conservative Americans, a few linked directly to Taiwan, who strongly opposed any change. Over the years this "China Lobby" had lost most of its influence and standing except in the right wing of the Republican Party, but it retained a considerable ca-pacity to kick up a fuss.

Between the two, and probably more widespread than either at least among the informed public, was a moderate position that considered a new relationship with Beijing inevitable and desirable, but also took account of the enormous progress the Nationalists had made, both economically and politically, on Taiwan, and the respect they enjoyed in much of East Asia. To this segment of opinion, the idea of "dumping Taiwan" seemed wrong and unappealing, to be avoided if possible. Yet few even in this moderate group had come to grips with the practical problems of disengaging the United States from Taiwan without leaving its 15 million people at the mercy of the regime on the mainland, and of persuading Beijing to accept what both Chinese regimes had always denounced, some sort of U.S. re-lationship with each, at least for a time.

In effect, Nixon had moved to this moderate viewpoint by the time he wrote his *Foreign Affairs* article in late 1967. But he was far from ready to say so out loud then, for fear of offending supporters like Anna Chennault. The Johnson Administration had meanwhile left two legacies: the renewal of the Warsaw talks and a number of possible measures that would ease the rigid trade and travel controls with China that had been in force since 1950. Each would signal to Beijing that a less tense relationship was possible. During the transition period, Johnson had told Nixon that he was prepared to go ahead with these measures on his own responsibility, but that if Nixon preferred, he would refrain from taking action and simply turn them over to the incoming administration to use as it saw fit. Nixon replied that he preferred the latter course.[74]

Both Secretary Rogers and the East Asian Bureau in the State Department were at least abreast of the White House and the NSC staff in grasping the new situation. Assistant Secretary Marshall Green had written a "toe in the water" speech suggesting change as far back as late 1963, and he and others had worked for years to craft the best actions to take when the right time came. The China hands in State saw clearly both the potentialities and the problems of changing U.S. policy toward China.

Initially slow to grasp the possibilities suggested by the Ussuri River clash, Nixon and Kissinger now saw that the Soviets' obsession with China meant that conciliatory American gestures toward China could be used to discomfit and worry the Soviets. Conflicting advice on this point came from two State Department sources. One was Green, to whom Nixon talked for a long time in June, on his return flight from conferring with President Thieu at Midway Island. In this talk Green commented that

> there was some merit in the Soviet Union being worried about our relations with China. Perhaps this would make the Soviet Union less prone to take us for granted and do things that might improve relations with the U.S. if only in order to prevent a U.S.-Peking drift.

His notes continue:

> The President agreed with my further comment that we should not do things designed to play on Sino-Soviet differences, but, if there were sound reasons for taking moves which have the incidental effect of exploiting Sino-Soviet differences, the advantage was double.[75]

Nixon got a different slant from two veteran and highly respected Foreign Service specialists on the Soviet Union, Ambassadors Charles Bohlen and Llewellyn Thompson. Concerned about rumors that the United States might make trade concessions to China, the two sought an appointment with Nixon, at which (according to Kissinger's possibly slanted account) they warned that any attempt to "use" China against the Soviet Union "could have nothing but dire consequences for U.S.-Soviet relations and for world peace." Nixon responded sympathetically, but then, when they left the room, mocked the "incorrigible softheadedness of the Foreign Service."[76]

This may have been an important breakpoint in Nixon's thinking. Faced with this long-standing difference between East Asian and Soviet experts, he apparently concluded that gestures toward China should be made not merely despite their effect on the Soviets but in fact because of it. He came to consider the easing of relations with China in large part as an anti-Soviet action. It was against this background that Nixon went ahead. In late June he approved the unilateral removal of several outdated restraints on trade and travel as an initial gesture to China.

The press conference in Guam announcing the Nixon Doctrine may itself have made a conciliatory impression in Beijing. At almost all his stops during his summer trip in Asia, Nixon expressed a clear view of U.S. policy toward the Brezhnev proposal for a wide anti-Chinese front, which had agitated the countries around the periphery of China far more than it attracted them. He put out the word that the United States was having no part of such anti-Chinese schemes; surely this reached the Chinese and usefully reassured them.

More pointedly, the President sought to create his own channels to China's top leaders through private talks with Yahya Khan in Pakistan and Nicolae Ceauşescu in Romania, with only Kissinger present and no others informed.[77] Each was receptive, especially Yahya Khan. At his order, a recent Pakistani visitor to China briefed Kissinger in a very upbeat way, saying that China's "domestic upheaval"—meaning the Cultural Revolution—was winding down and China would soon seek to end its self-imposed isolation. Contrary to widespread stereotypes of the Chinese leaders as fanatical ideologues, this visitor had found them "disciplined and pragmatic."[78]

From every standpoint, Pakistan was an ideal message bearer. One of Nixon's favorite countries since the early 1950s, it was under tight military leadership with strong security habits, and had outstanding ambassadors in Washington and Beijing. Moreover, the uniquely close ties between China and Pakistan, formed in the early 1960s and strengthened by China's support of Pakistan in the 1965 India-Pakistan war, had been unaffected by the Cultural Revolution. There was respect and trust on both sides. Yet Pakistan was not a disinterested party. In perennial fear of India next door—an obvious reason for cultivating ties with China—its leaders also welcomed having the weight of the United States on at least a corner of the scales. Pakistan could earn credit with both Beijing and Washington as a rigorously accurate intermediary, which might come in handy if things flared up again with India. Kissinger on his return confirmed the Pakistani connection with Ambassador Agha Hilaly.

Shortly after, Secretary Rogers, in a widely reported speech to the SEATO meeting in Canberra, referred to the "People's Republic of China" rather than to "Communist China," as had been standard in American statements for decades—another signal of slow change. A week later, in the first serious discussion of China at a meeting of the National Security Council, no decisions were reached. To Kissinger's surprise, however, the President did tell the group that he now regarded the Soviet Union as the more aggressive party and that it was against U.S. interests to let China be "smashed" in a Sino-Soviet war. It was a striking change from his long-standing emphasis on the threat from China.

At this point the most important fact was the high state of tension between the two great Communist powers. The Soviet military buildup along the long border with China continued: between March and August, estimated strength along this line went from twenty-four divisions to more than thirty. Even more important and ominous was a marked buildup in Soviet air strength within striking range of targets in China, notably the complex of nuclear facilities in western China, which were within easy range of Soviet bases. By early summer a CIA estimate concluded that the chances were significant (quoted as one in three) that the Soviets would launch air attacks on this complex. Confirming these fears, in mid-August a Soviet official in Washington asked a middle-level State Department officer what the U.S. reaction would be to just such an attack. It was a query almost invited by the emphasis Nixon had put on the Chinese "threat" in launching his ABM program in March.

Neither Nixon nor Kissinger has discussed in his writings how the response to this inquiry was decided upon, but it was considered and clear. Under Secretary of State Elliot Richardson told a New York audience on September 5 that "long-run improvements in our relations [with "Communist China"] were in our own national interest," but that

> we do not seek to exploit for our own advantage the hostility between the Soviet Union and the People's Republic. Ideological differences between the two Communist giants are not our affair. *We could not fail to be deeply concerned, however, with an escalation of this quarrel into a massive breach of international peace and security.*[79]

In other words, the United States would not take sides as the Soviets had hoped and the Chinese surely feared. This may have been the most important public signal on U.S. China policy in the whole year.

Concurrently, the funeral of Ho Chi Minh in Hanoi brought Soviet Premier Alexei Kosygin there, traveling via Beijing. He left before the Chinese did to go home, and indeed had left Beijing for Moscow when the Chinese suddenly asked him to return. Shortly, the talks there resulted in the resumption of discussions over the disputed border area. Tension remained high, but it now had a safety valve.

Kissinger and Richardson then worked out a plan to change the long-standing permanent patrol of U.S. destroyers in the Strait of Taiwan to frequent in-and-out visits by other warships. With Nixon's approval, this was conveyed via the Pakistanis as the first specific message to pass on. At the same time, Kissinger made a move presumably on orders from Nixon and apparently without informing the State Department: when the U.S. Ambassador to Warsaw, Walter Stoessel, paid a routine call to Nixon on September 9, Kissinger took him aside afterward and told him to seek out his

Chinese counterpart discreetly and say that the United States was now prepared for serious talks. The instruction was apparently not given urgently, and Stoessel found it hard to carry out in the intended informal fashion, given the long-standing habit of China's diplomats to avoid contact of any sort with an American. Only on December 3, and then by literally running after the Chinese No. 2 as he left a big reception, was Stoessel able to deliver the message.

China's response was immediate and positive: two informal meetings were held in the respective embassies in Warsaw on December 11 and January 8; the ambassadors' cars were fully visible to observers. January 20 was set for resumed talks in Warsaw.

In the drafting of the U.S. message for this first substantive exchange under Nixon, Kissinger has described himself as sharply at odds with the East Asian Bureau of the State Department. Assistant Secretary Green wanted to emphasize easing trade and travel and especially to propose that China make some gesture of good faith such as renouncing force as a means to solve the Taiwan problem. Only then, as State saw it, could high-level talks be undertaken with a clear promise of progress.

Moreover, State was sensitive all along, as Kissinger was not, to the effect of these talks with China on the morale and confidence in America of East Asian nations that had cast their lot with American policy over the years and were still fearful of China. As Green saw it, even changing the location of talks, which was likely to become known, might lead to confusion and wild speculation among America's allies; this would be hard to handle and damaging in itself to the strength of the U.S. position. He did not then see how this problem might be minimized and total secrecy achieved. In effect, State wanted to go slow and take careful account of East Asian reactions, not least in Japan.[80]

Kissinger on the other hand wanted to move fast, offer high-level talks right away, and tempt China less by making bilateral concessions on trade, travel, and the like than by promising a forthright U.S. rejection of any "condominium" with the Soviet Union and opposition to any Soviet efforts to encircle China diplomatically. In thinking big like this, he must have relied heavily on reports from Pakistani diplomats, which he did not share with State. These suggested a greater Chinese willingness to move than State could have sensed from its sources. In particular, the Pakistani Ambassador in January reported to Kissinger on a talk between the Pakistani Ambassador in Beijing and Zhou Enlai himself:*

---

*I normally employ current usage in the spelling of Chinese names and places, but in citations to statements and some secondary sources, as here, have used the older Wade-Giles spelling. Thus, Mao-Zedong = Mau Tse Tung; Zhou Enlai = Chou En-lai; Qiao Guanhua = Ch'iao Kuan-hua; Jiang Jieshi = Chiang Kai Shek; Lin Biao = Lin Piao; and Beijing = Peking. Familiarity and recognizability are more important than consistency.

The Ambassador found Chou En-lai primarily concerned about the Soviet Union, secondarily about the revival of Japanese militarism. As for
the United States, Chou clearly considered it a lesser threat; he seemed
quite prepared for high-level talks with the United States, provided we
[the United States] took the initiative. In fact, according to this report,
Chou En-lai had mused about our apparent unwillingness "to take a step
like Kosygin"—in other words, to send a high official to Peking.[81]

After considerable pulling and hauling, the U.S. message for the January
20 Warsaw meeting included both Kissinger's ideas—a proposal for high-
level talks in Beijing or Washington and an assurance that the United States
would not "join in any condominium with the Soviet Union directed against
China"—and the points proposed by State. The message stressed that the
United States took no position on the problem of Taiwan, believed that it was
up to the two Chinese regimes to resolve it, and was firm only that force not
be used in doing so. It added that U.S. military forces on Taiwan might be
withdrawn as "tensions in the area diminish," in effect an indication that the
U.S. role in Vietnam would continue to be reduced.[82]

In all probability, both Kissinger's themes and State's resonated favorably
in Beijing: that they would appeal to Zhou was evident, while the assurances
about Taiwan undoubtedly helped keep hard-liners in Beijing from ob-
structing the new dialogue. At a second Warsaw meeting on February 20,
the Chinese representative said that his country was prepared to receive a
U.S. emissary for more extensive exchanges that would include "relaxation
of general Far Eastern tensions," while also insisting that the Taiwan question was fundamental and had to be settled first.[83]

The next American message went further on the Taiwan issue. State
proposed, and Kissinger accepted, a statement that the United States did
not dispute that in the eyes of all Chinese, China, by implication including
Taiwan, was one country. This important icebreaking formula was to find
its way, two years later, into the Shanghai communiqué of February 1972.[84]
Marshall Green recalls that the formula was invented by Paul Kreisberg, in
charge of matters related to the People's Republic in the East Asian Bureau.
Kreisberg was a tireless and imaginative supporter of realistic rapprochement
with China as soon as the Cultural Revolution eased.

At this point, with the Chinese accepting the idea of moving to high-
level talks, the tactical differences between Kissinger and the East Asian
Bureau sharpened. Green urged one more exchange of formal messages, to
forestall the chance of early failure and to devise ways to ease reactions in
East Asia if the new talks should become known. Kissinger, on the other
hand, wanted to move directly to the high-level stage. In his memoirs, Kissinger used harsh and emotional terms in denouncing the State Department
for trying to keep the action for itself and thus earn special credit. The

historian confronted with such an accusation of selfish and discreditable motives in others does well to ask whether it was not in fact the narrator, as often with Nixon as well, who was thinking along those very lines. Kissinger wanted credit and new opportunities, while the principal career officers involved were self-effacing and always discreet.

Meanwhile, Nixon published his first Foreign Policy Report, which had been drafted by Kissinger and his staff. As we have seen, it gave small signals that China "should not remain isolated" and again disavowed U.S. support for any "hostile coalition" against either China or the Soviet Union. The report also emphasized that the United States no longer considered the Soviet Union and China as a single adversary, posing a joint threat that it must be prepared to meet. The reiteration of this view may have been mildly useful, but the view itself had been the basis of U.S. policy for some years and cannot have come as news to Beijing.

The internal Washington debate was resolved by April 1, when the United States proposed April 30 for a third Warsaw meeting: on April 28 the Chinese suggested May 20, which was promptly set. Then came the crisis in Cambodia. For days after the incursion of United States troops into Cambodian territory in early May, following the coup against Prince Sihanouk, the Chinese were silent. Then, on May 18, the New China News Agency denounced the "brazen" act and said it was "no longer suitable" to go ahead with the meeting. It was the end of the Warsaw channel. For the next fourteen months, Kissinger excluded the State Department from China policy and clamped a tight security lid on all significant moves toward China.

What, in historical perspective, had this first phase of Nixon's China policy revealed and accomplished? Nixon's memoir dismissed it: "our tentative approaches to Communist China appeared to have fallen on deaf ears." In direct contrast, Kissinger struck a very upbeat note, saying that the United States had made clear its desire to move forward and "by the end of 1969 it was apparent that China, too, had made a strategic decision to seek rapprochement with us, even while it fended off the Soviet Union by resuming an intermittent dialogue on the border dispute." He goes on that "we were at last in the foothills of a mountain range" and that "it was a moment of extraordinary hope."[85]

This view was more optimistic than the evidence yet warranted. Fragmentary evidence then, with much more to come in 1971, suggested strongly that some of the Chinese leaders, especially Zhou Enlai, were prepared to accept that the United States was indeed reaching out for wider understanding; that it was at least neutral vis-à-vis the Soviet Union; and that it was ready to move rapidly. However, a more hard-line segment of the Chinese leadership, led by Lin Biao, was obsessed with the U.S. position over Taiwan. The new U.S. statements on that subject may well have helped Zhou strengthen his personal position vis-à-vis the Lin Biao group. Things were not yet at the point where either China or the United States could come right out and declare its interest in a new relationship, but underbrush had been cleared away. Finally, both sides had come to an understanding that if and when further progress was possible, there should be direct exchanges through emissaries competent to discuss every aspect.

In all this, the steps the Nixon Administration took were significant, however clumsy. But the real force driving the two nations together was the Soviet buildup along the Chinese frontier. Mainly because of concern about this, China was at least as much the moving party as the United States. What remained to be tested was whether this concern would outweigh new and significant differences among the Chinese leaders over U.S. actions in Southeast Asia, above all in Cambodia.

7. Signs of Change: West Germany

As he worked toward a new American relationship with China, Richard Nixon did not expect or welcome an important change in the foreign policy of the Federal Republic of Germany, the front-line state, pivot, and central focus of the Cold War in Western Europe. Ever since its creation in 1949, West Germany had been not only a dedicated ally in NATO and fully cooperative in various Western economic organizations, but its Christian Democratic government had been extremely stiff and hard-line in its attitudes and policies on any aspect of East-West relations, holding East Germany and all of Eastern Europe at arm's length. In 1969, however, the election of Willy Brandt as Chancellor, the first Social Democrat to hold that post, led rapidly to a new policy toward East Germany and the Eastern European countries, called *Ostpolitik*, which presaged major changes in West Germany's relations with them and also with the Soviet Union.

When the end of World War II in Europe approached in 1944, the Soviet Union, the United States, Britain, and France hammered out in London an agreement to assign four occupation zones of prewar German territory among themselves. But after the German surrender, their inability to make any progress toward a final peace treaty and the onset of the Cold War led to, and in part derived from, increasing differences between the Soviets and the three Western victors over the status and future of Germany and, especially, Berlin. The former capital, surrounded by territory assigned to Soviet occupation, was to be a separate enclave divided into four sectors with a supervising four-power structure.

A defining event was the 1948–49 Soviet blockade of the Western sectors in Berlin, which went on for nearly a year before it was undermined by a resourceful Anglo-American airlift. By then the rift between Soviet and

Western policy objectives was unbridgeable, and the United States took the lead in relaxing the occupation of the three western zones, uniting them in a West German state, the Federal Republic of Germany (FRG). The Marshall Plan for economic aid (1948–52) and the formation of NATO in 1949, which led to a long-term Western troop presence in West Germany, helped to bind the new state to the West.

This process went on with the full cooperation of West Germany's first Chancellor, Konrad Adenauer (1949–63), of the conservative Christian Democratic Party (closely allied with the Bavaria-based Christian Socialists and thus known as the CDU/CSU). The West German government enjoyed wide diplomatic recognition; it became a full member of NATO in early 1955 and developed its own armed forces within the Alliance framework, so that these forces became by 1960 a substantial component in the Western deterrent and defense posture along the East-West dividing line running through Germany.

Initially opposed by the Social Democratic Party (SPD), this *Westpolitik* came to be accepted by a clear majority of West Germans. The country thrived, achieving both political stability and an "economic miracle," in stark contrast to the political and economic stagnation in Communist East Germany. From 1951 on, moreover, West Germany was a leader, one of the original "six," in the successive integrating moves that created the European Economic Community (EEC) in 1957. American policy consistently supported the EEC; American leaders, Democratic and Republican, shared with Adenauer and other European leaders the conviction that embedding West Germany solidly in Western regional structures was the only way to heal the rivalries and expansionist tendencies that had brought on two world wars, as well as to assure the constructive development of a truly democratic German state in at least the western two-thirds of German territory.

Through these years, American prestige in West Germany was high and the relationship extremely close and cooperative on all fronts. Yet there were two underlying differences in West German and American viewpoints.

The one most to the fore in the early and middle 1960s concerned nuclear weapons. An essential condition for West Germany having its own military forces had been its 1954 declaration to the Western allies totally disavowing and rejecting any West German nuclear capability. Yet when "tactical" nuclear weapons were based on German soil from the late 1950s on, excluding the Germans themselves from any participation in nuclear matters came to seem unrealistic as well as offensive to the very West Germans most wedded to the *Westpolitik.*

Half-steps were taken to give West Germany some visible function relating to, but without having or controlling, nuclear weapons. One realistic step was the formation within NATO of a Nuclear Planning Group, where the allies discussed doctrine and strategy on the conceivable use of nuclear weapons, without changing U.S. dominance in this field. Less realistic was an abortive effort to create a sea-based multilateral force (the MLF), in which West Germans would have served alongside nationals of other NATO countries, aboard naval surface craft carrying nuclear delivery systems (still controlled by Americans). Ingenious but cumbersome and extremely hard to explain, the MLF project died a lingering death in 1963–65.

At that point, President Johnson and his strong arms control team started an intensive effort to limit and control the proliferation of nuclear weapons to any countries beyond the five established nuclear powers, the effort that culminated with the signing of the Nuclear Nonproliferation Treaty in July 1968. In that treaty, West Germany was inevitably classified as a nonnuclear power. While few doubted the sincerity of the West German renunciation of nuclear weapons, such a permanent and formal ban grated on West German politicians, especially conservative ones, and successive West German governments sought some kind of escape clause in case of dire need. The Johnson Administration reiterated the firmness of its intent to keep nuclear weapons as a key part of NATO's deterrent posture and to use them if absolutely required, but it declined to write an exception into the treaty.

The second area of underlying difference was less apparent but more fundamental. By deepest instinct, many, probably most, of the West German people longed for the reunification of Germany, which was proclaimed in the Federal Republic's Basic Law as a standing goal, and to which the Western powers consistently paid lip service. In practice, however, the Western powers rejected initiatives that might have gone in this direction, such as expanded economic links between East and West, or treating East Germany as a respectable entity. With this policy Adenauer and his fellow conservatives were in total accord, and particularly firm in pillorying the East German regime (called the German Democratic Republic, or GDR) as a Soviet puppet unworthy of international status or recognition — to the point where, under the so-called Hallstein Doctrine, it was West German policy to break off diplomatic relations with any nation that recognized the GDR.

For their part, the Social Democrats by 1959 had come around to full support of the Western-oriented structures, including NATO and the European Community. But as West Germany became more powerful and less guilt-ridden, many West Germans — especially among those who had past ties to the East — wanted to ease the rigidity of Adenauer's policies. By the late 1960s, similar sentiments were powerfully felt among many other European NATO members. The 1948 Berlin Blockade had been for Western Europe a call to arms and to forging a strong Alliance against Soviet power. A decade later, the easing of a prolonged second crisis over Berlin in 1958–62, the successful outcome of the Cuban Missile Crisis, and the ouster of

Nikita Khrushchev in 1964 were interpreted as showing that the Soviet military threat, particularly in Europe, had receded. The United States still had a clear-cut superiority in nuclear weapons; NATO's conventional forces had been increased under pressure of the second Berlin crisis; and Western Europe was thriving and more self-confident than at any time since the war. At the same time, most NATO leaders saw the Vietnam War as an unfortunate American digression with little importance for Europe; public criticism of the war and anti-American feeling rose to often troublesome levels.

All these factors contributed to a formal NATO pronouncement in December 1967 that was as symbolically significant to the European members of NATO as it was little noticed in the United States. This was the adoption of the so-called Harmel Report (named after its author, Pierre Harmel, then Belgium's Foreign Minister), stating that the objectives of NATO should include not only deterrence of the Soviet military threat but "détente." The word was fuzzy and its scope uncertain, then and later, but the report did clearly convey the idea that henceforth exploration with the Soviet Union of avenues for negotiation and change was approved. Moreover, the report implied that such efforts could be undertaken by individual countries for their own purposes, provided that these were not contrary to NATO's basic deterrence and defense needs. At the same time, the Soviet Union, outmaneuvered time after time on European issues, gradually changed tactics and strategy, but never its objectives. Among these last, the first and foremost was never again to permit the rise of a powerful German state with freedom of action. The defeat and devastation of 1914–17 and the terrible losses of 1941–45 must never be repeated or seriously threatened. A disarmed West Germany, with no allies, would have been ideal from the Soviet standpoint. Thus the formation of NATO in 1948–49, after the Berlin Blockade, was an immense setback to the Soviet Union. Thereafter NATO's firmness and cohesion continued to block the Soviet Union's efforts to expand its influence and power.

Once West Germany had its own armed force, however—even a small one that could not possibly take on the Soviet Army—Soviet policy on NATO became somewhat mixed and conflicting. Having West Germany firmly embedded in NATO, whose members had themselves experienced war with Hitlerite and imperial German states, almost guaranteed that West Germany would not pose a separate threat. Thus while Soviet leaders constantly objected to West German rearmament and opposed NATO, their practical aim became to weaken the Alliance as a whole, not to remove it as a reassurance against an independent West German military force. Likewise, in their inner thinking, the Soviets no longer wanted to get the United States clean out of Western Europe; a substantial American presence helped to restrain the weight and influence of West Germany.

A second basic Soviet objective was to maintain firm control of Eastern Europe. The Soviet-installed satellite regimes in East Germany, Poland, Czechoslovakia, Hungary, Romania, and Bulgaria—some of which were also occupied by Soviet forces and all of whose politics and internal security were dominated by Soviet commissars and agents—had been a major Soviet gain from World War II, both extending the bounds of Soviet power and forming a solid barrier against any threat from the West to Soviet territory.

A special concern was always the East German regime. During the second Berlin crisis, a gigantic hemorrhage of East Germans leaving the country via Berlin forced the Soviets to erect the infamous Wall in August 1961, cutting right through the city, sealing off East Germany, and preventing any further departures. After that the Soviets redoubled their efforts to give the East German regime status and respectability, in part through increasing its share in controlling access to West Berlin.

Despite some ebullient 1950s rhetoric, the West never seriously challenged Soviet control of Eastern Europe. It reached out to the people themselves, through radio broadcasts and other limited efforts, but it went no further even when revolts broke out, as they did in 1953, 1956, and later. But formal Western acceptance of the situation was never given, nor recognition of the redrawn and imposed frontiers, nor explicit renunciation of any attempt to alter the situation by force. It was the Soviet hope that this would change, and that legitimizing the regimes and the whole structure of Soviet domination would make internal disturbances aimed at the regimes (such as those in Hungary in 1956 and Prague in 1968) impossible.

To the same basic end, the Soviet Union wanted recognition of its strategic nuclear parity with the United States, preferably again in some formal manner, as well as Western (particularly American) acceptance of Soviet activity in the Third World as natural and proper. But formal ratification of Soviet domination of Eastern Europe stood at the very top of the list of immediate priorities, just as NATO itself was moving to the Harmel Report.

The specific measure the Soviets proposed, beginning in 1966, was the convening of a Conference on Security and Cooperation in Europe (CSCE). In its original form, this was a Europe-only security system, aimed at dissolving the Atlantic Alliance and at getting ratification of the postwar frontiers as established by Soviet military power in 1944–45. When this made no impression, they fell back by March 1969 to a more modest "Budapest proposal," which did not question the participation of the United States and Canada in any new European security arrangement. The conference was to embrace not only members of NATO and the Soviet-dominated Warsaw Pact, but unaligned other countries of Europe, and was aimed to ratify the status quo through multilateral pledges of noninterference. These would have served in practice as the only feasible substitute for a peace treaty to end World War II.

In NATO, the revised CSCE proposal met with a cool reception. In May 1968, NATO had countered with its own proposal for a multilateral negotiation to reduce conventional military forces on the East-West front; this proposal for Mutual and Balanced Force Reduction (MBFR) was designed to reduce the Soviet-dominated Warsaw Pact military posture through agreement. Less visibly, an agreement on force levels — or even negotiations about them — would provide a political cushion against any effort to reduce Western forces unilaterally. The long-standing 300,000-man level of American forces in Europe had been under special pressure from 1966 on, through a Senate amendment, regularly renewed by Democratic Majority Leader Mike Mansfield, which called for sharp cuts.

In effect, the two multilateral proposals, CSCE and MBFR, lay temporarily to one side in 1969–70. Neither was likely to be accepted without some agreement to do something about the other, and the most advanced of the two, the CSCE, could hardly go ahead without West Germany's formal acceptance of the revised frontiers.

In 1967, the shifting balance of political forces within the Federal Republic had brought together the two major parties in a "Grand Coalition" government that had a conservative Chancellor, Kurt George Kiesinger, and a Social Democratic Foreign Minister, Willy Brandt. This government was instrumental in framing the Harmel Report and getting it accepted, all the while reiterating its firm adherence to NATO. (Kiesinger also initiated an abortive effort to negotiate a treaty with the Soviet Union, which foundered when the conservatives refused to modify their historic policy of not recognizing the East German regime in any way.) But on this and other issues, the Grand Coalition was uneasy by early 1969; and in the election campaign for a new President in February 1969 — by a special Federal Assembly convened by custom in West Berlin — a new coalition emerged between the Social Democrats and the small Free Democratic Party, pro-business and pro–free enterprise but flexible in its foreign policy. The new coalition's candidate, a Social Democrat, won this largely formal post.

The presidential election served also to highlight the unanswered questions about Germany and Berlin. The Soviet Union had consistently objected to the Federal Republic's holding presidential elections in Berlin. The practice was not specifically forbidden under the various patchwork agreements that ended the two major crises over the city, but in Soviet eyes it clearly breached their spirit to assert such an organic connection between West Berlin and the Federal Republic. Thus, apparently serious Soviet and East German threats were made to disrupt the ceremonies.

Although the United States had nothing to do with the decision to hold the election in West Berlin, the fact that Nixon was about to visit West Germany may have been a reason for the Soviets to back off. In one of his early contacts with Kissinger, Dobrynin volunteered that no disruptive action would occur—perhaps seeking credit for restraint—and the inauguration proceeded with the Soviets confining themselves to vigorous formal protests.

From the first, Nixon and Kissinger recognized the crucial and changing role of West Germany in Europe. One indication was the selection as Ambassador to Bonn of Kenneth Rush, a sophisticated and successful business executive with plenty of European experience, who had been a law professor at Duke University when Nixon was a student there. In contrast to many of the ambassadors appointed or held over under Nixon, Rush had Nixon's full confidence and respect.

Kissinger was Nixon's key advisor on European and German policy; Secretary Rogers was rarely in the picture and the experienced professionals in State were relied on for support but not in making the major decisions. Nixon was broadly familiar with the history of U.S. policy in Europe, but Kissinger had made Europe, NATO, and West Germany his central focus over the years. Kissinger had grown up in Germany and still spoke English with a marked accent. In 1945–47, in his early twenties, he was a U.S. Army sergeant in charge of a substantial occupation area there. He frequently visited West Germany during his academic career—and during his brief 1961 stint as a consultant to President Kennedy and National Security Advisor McGeorge Bundy—and had many close contacts among German officials and key observers, mostly in the CDU/CSU establishment.

In his books and articles, Kissinger had often been critical of particular U.S. actions affecting Germany, and had never emphasized West German integration into Europe to the degree that other figures, such as former Under Secretary George Ball, did. But along with Nixon, he completely shared the premise of U.S. postwar policy that German nationalism in the form that had done so much to bring on two world wars must never be allowed to revive, and that keeping the Federal Republic in the Western security and economic structure must remain a cornerstone of American policy.

Thus Kissinger's initial reactions to *Ostpolitik* were sharply negative, and vehemently expressed to his staff. One senior advisor, Robert Osgood, recalled his attitude as one of "great fear and distrust of the Germans, particularly those who wanted closer relations to the East in what he considered a fuzzy-minded and dangerous way." Other staff members caught overtones of outright detestation of Brandt and of Social Democrats generally.[86]

Though the Nixon Administration refrained from public criticism, there can be no doubt that its negative view of *Ostpolitik* registered in Bonn. At the NATO twentieth-anniversary celebration in Washington in April 1969, Nixon spoke out strongly in a semi-private meeting, warning against any NATO member nation getting into a "selective" détente of its own. Foreign Minister Brandt concluded: "Put more plainly, this meant that Washington wanted to have the last word; it was not difficult to recognize Henry Kissinger's handwriting."[87]

Among the major allies, Britain was least critical of Brandt, but France, where Georges Pompidou had succeeded de Gaulle as President, was clearly disturbed, and the government reacted to *Ostpolitik* in an almost classic historical manner, dropping almost at once the objections that had twice led de Gaulle to veto British membership in the European Community. Plainly, France now wanted Britain's participation in order to check any extreme tendencies in the new German policy.[88]

During the summer, and before the far more important Bundestag elections in September, Brandt's position in favor of accepting the East German regime as a fact became more explicit. The Social Democrats were now seen clearly as "the party of recognition," ready to accept the status quo in Eastern Europe and move toward dealing directly with the German Democratic Republic (GDR). That the Soviet Union would be receptive to a new West German approach was evident. In the words of an American historian of German foreign policy:

> By the late 1960s it had become clear to the Soviet Union that a policy aimed at disintegrating NATO could not succeed, but that a policy aimed at stabilizing and legitimizing the European status quo could obtain the consent of the Federal Republic, the indispensable partner in this large diplomatic enterprise.[89]

Forces of change were at work, and tending to converge. But nothing in history is automatic. It remained for a forceful leader to move front and center and take the lead.

At this point in his career, Willy Brandt was a striking but not yet fully proven figure, whose life had been marked by courageous personal conduct, a notable success as mayor of West Berlin, and defeat on the federal political scene. As a young man from a poor background, he had been active in the Socialist opposition to Hitler and forced to flee to Norway in 1933. From there he remained active in anti-Nazi activities through the 1930s, taking Norwegian citizenship and fleeing again, to Sweden, when Hitler occupied Norway in 1940. Returning to Germany after the war, he renewed his German citizenship and was active in Social Democratic politics as a protégé of Ernst Reuter, the heroic Socialist mayor of Berlin during the 1948–49 Blockade. Becoming mayor himself in 1957, Brandt rallied Berliners with a stirring impromptu address in August 1961, when the West's initial failure to respond to the erection of the Berlin Wall momentarily demoralized Berliners and turned them against the West. His party increased in power through the early 1960s, losing the federal elections in 1961 and 1965 by successively narrower margins.

In the 1966 "Grand Coalition," Brandt staked out clear-cut differences from the conservatives over West German policy toward East Germany, the Soviet Union, and the Communist states of Eastern Europe. His long-standing advocacy of an *Ostpolitik* reached the point where he made clear that he was prepared to deal with the East German regime and would go on from there to deal with the Soviets. In effect it was a policy that recognized the East German regime as a reality after nearly twenty-five years, or a full generation, and, more widely, accepted the status quo in Eastern Europe. Necessarily, this meant accepting the permanent loss of the former German territories east of the Oder and Neisse rivers, which had been liberated by the Soviets at the end of the war and given to Poland. Earlier policy had been to promise never to try to recapture these territories by force, but their outright relinquishment remained intensely controversial in Germany and was attacked as an abandonment of any hope of real reunification, which had been stated in the 1949 Basic Law as a fundamental goal. It was also feared that it would lead to a weakening of the immensely successful and productive ties to the West that for twenty years had been the foremost aim and achievement of Adenauer's foreign policy.

Brandt, on the other hand, while fully recognizing how important the Western Alliance, and the United States in particular, was for the Federal Republic, believed fervently that easing relations with the Soviet Union was not inconsistent with either German reunification or strong ties to NATO and the European Community. He was convinced that the Federal Republic was now confident enough to avoid damaging concessions, and even dreamed that the ultimate result of accepting the status quo could be a Germany unified on terms that ensured its genuine independence and its ability to be a leader in a larger, cooperative Europe, which he saw all along as a realistic vision.

Willy Brandt's *Ostpolitik*, a new and imaginative policy for Germany, had evident implications for Europe as a whole that Brandt made no effort to conceal. Other Social Democratic and Free Democratic leaders in West Germany were thinking along similar lines. As if to underline their solidarity, another prominent Social Democrat, Helmut Schmidt, made a well-publicized trip to Moscow in August, where he discussed questions of Germany and Eastern Europe frankly with Soviet Foreign Minister Gromyko. But Brandt was the central and commanding figure.

Nixon and Kissinger followed the German election campaign closely, expecting and hoping for a CDU/CSU victory for Kiesinger that would slow down or abort *Ostpolitik* and leave the way clear for the more traditional European policy they favored. This would have meant continuance of the status quo in Eastern Europe, but no negotiations to ratify it, and a selective reaching out to individual Eastern European nations, enticing them to reduce their Soviet dependence (an early example of which had been Nixon's visit to Ceaușescu in Romania).

The eagerly awaited election on September 29 did not produce a conclusive result: the conservative parties still had the largest percentage of the overall vote (46.1), while the Social Democrats got 42.7 percent and the Free Democrats dropped to 5.8 percent, giving them together only a bare and vulnerable majority. It appeared briefly on election night that the CDU/CSU conservative coalition would have a governing majority, and Nixon was moved to a rare tactical mistake—he telephoned Kiesinger to convey fervent congratulations. Naturally, Brandt soon learned of this telltale gesture, which was hard to explain as a simple error in projecting the returns.[90]

In any case, Willy Brandt and his colleagues moved rapidly, with the full cooperation of the Free Democratic leader Walter Scheel, and by October 21 a new government had been formed and won Bundestag approval. This was due, in the words of one German history, "not to the verdict of the voters, but to the decisive action of Willy Brandt."[91] It was a very strong Cabinet, with Scheel as Foreign Minister and two outstanding Social Democrats, Helmut Schmidt and Kurt Schiller, in charge of defense and economic affairs, all of them known to Americans as convinced supporters of West German ties to the West. A more shadowy figure, not in the Cabinet, was Egon Bahr, who had come with Brandt from the Berlin government after having worked with the American occupation in its early years; a dedicated "Easterner," Bahr was extremely close to Brandt and on his instructions had already worked out a precise program for action.

Brandt moved with extraordinary rapidity and purposefulness, and on October 13, even before the new government was announced, he sent Bahr to Washington to inform Nixon, via Kissinger, of what he proposed to do. In his policy statement on assuming office, Brandt had caused a sensation at home by referring specifically to East and West Germany as "two states," an appealing theme except in conservative circles within the Federal Republic itself. Ten days later, Scheel welcomed a Soviet offer, doubtless prearranged by Bahr, to resume the talks that had broken down under Kiesinger, looking toward the centerpiece of the new policy: a Soviet–West German treaty of non-aggression, border recognition, and mutual renunciation of force.

Egon Bahr's visit to Washington soon showed how different Brandt would be. As Bahr at once made clear, he came not to consult but to disclose a clear-cut and firmly resolved program, the opening to a strikingly new chapter in postwar German-American relations. Under Adenauer, the Federal Republic had never acted on any major issue without the closest advance consultation with the United States; now Brandt was taking a major initiative on his own, keeping the United States fully informed—France and Britain probably more so—but not inviting its advice.

Formally, all three major Western powers took the position of supporting what Brandt was doing. At the December annual meeting of NATO foreign and defense ministers, Walter Scheel won approval and support for a "modus vivendi between the two parts of Germany," to be accompanied by the renunciation of force or the threat of force.[92]

On November 28, moreover, the Brandt government formally adhered to the Nuclear Nonproliferation Treaty, which in his day Konrad Adenauer had attacked as more repugnant than the Versailles Treaty of 1919. It was a break with the standoffish position of the Grand Coalition, and a move well calculated to ease a central Soviet worry and at the same time to reassure the United States.[93]

By January 1970, when it was announced that initial talks were under way over a Soviet treaty, diplomatic *Ostpolitik* was fully launched. There were also significant new economic steps in the form of deals between the West German steel industry and the Bonn government on the one hand and the Soviet government on the other. These called for the Soviet Union to commit itself to assured oil and gas exports to West Germany, using pipelines built with West German steel and technological help. During the 1960s, trade between West Germany and the East had steadily expanded, but the levels were still low. This was a big new development, showing an underlying economic complementarity—Soviet raw materials for Western finished goods and equipment—that had major implications for the future. Shortly, the Federal Republic signed a major agreement for long-term trade with the Soviet Union.[94]

Meanwhile, a significant factor in the settling down of relations between the Federal Republic and its Western allies was the performance and influence of Helmut Schmidt, the new Defense Minister. He had been in the forefront of his party's conversion to support for NATO in 1959 and was a responsible expert on defense strategy. In November 1969, at a meeting of the NATO nuclear planning group in Washington, he had persuaded Nixon to give a frank and unrehearsed talk on the subject, which he found extremely impressive and so reported to Brandt. Almost at once Schmidt formed a close relationship with Melvin Laird, working with him to help hold the Mansfield Amendment at bay by showing that the European allies were doing their part and wanted no change in the U.S. posture.[95]

As the West Germans saw it, Nixon was never as hostile as Kissinger to *Ostpolitik*. The politician in him almost certainly sensed at once that he was up against something he could not alter, at least not right away. Neither his statements then nor his 1978 memoir reveal his inner thinking, but in 1982, in a book assessing his favorite foreign leaders, he went on at length in praise of Konrad Adenauer and gave two revealing judgments of *Ostpolitik* worth quoting:

[I]t is clear that *Ostpolitik* by a West Germany less strong and prosperous than the one Adenauer built through an alliance with the West would have been folly, and that *Ostpolitik* as practiced has not lived up to its architects' overly optimistic hopes.

and two pages later:

Adenauer's reaction to all of this would have been simple. He would deplore the suggestion, implicit in *Ostpolitik*, that the United States presents as great a threat to Europe as the Soviet Union. He would warn that in reaching East, the Europeans are in danger of breaking their lifeline to the West. And he would say that no policy is worth pursuing if it makes you lose those friends you do have while courting those friends you do not have, especially if your new friends turn out to be your deadliest enemies.

Few passages in his writings reflect more clearly Nixon's inner views and tendency to cling to the verities of the 1950s.[96]

Kissinger's memoirs, on the other hand, describe clearly and eloquently how his thinking evolved on this subject, though without admitting the depth of his initial negativism. In this he was affected by his personal judgment of Bahr, whom he saw as "above all a German nationalist who wanted to exploit Germany's central position to bargain with both sides" and "who was not as unquestioningly dedicated to Western unity" as high officials in previous West German governments. Yet Bahr's operating style fitted neatly with his own, and the two established a personal channel similar to the one Kissinger had with Dobrynin, deliberately excluding the State Department from the most important exchanges.[97]

Kissinger spelled out to Nixon the long-term risks of Brandt's policy in a long memorandum in February. This drew on history to argue that Brandt was bound to be disappointed in his high hopes. At some point the Federal Republic would be faced with a dilemma from which it might seek to escape by reverting to a nationalistic policy of playing off East and West for its own selfish advantage.[98] Whatever Nixon thought of this argument, his immediate policy was pragmatic. He arranged successive official visits to Washington by British Prime Minister Harold Wilson, President Pompidou, and finally Brandt—a welcome show of allied consultation. The discussions also clarified policy among the three victors with continued rights in West Germany and Berlin, and between these three and Brandt.

The key to reconciliation and coordination lay in the issues affecting Berlin. These concerned three problems that had never been satisfactorily agreed or worked out in 1944, in the post-Blockade agreements of 1949, or after the erection of the Berlin Wall in 1961:

First, what political ties should be permitted and accepted between West Berlin and the Federal Republic? Here the Federal Republic constantly pressed for ties and the Soviet Union was the prime objector.

Second, access to West Berlin had to be assured both for the Western powers and for inter-German personal and economic traffic. Here the Western powers and the Federal Republic had a common interest in maximum assurances that at the same time kept Soviet responsibility to the fore and minimized the role of East Germany.

Third, least noticed by the occupiers but of great personal importance to West Berliners was their freedom to visit in East Berlin and in at least a limited area of East Germany. This was an issue particularly dear to Brandt himself.

Behind these issues lay the ultimate question — whether the morale and economic well-being of West Berlin, by then under siege for a quarter century, could continue to hold up. Berlin's future hinged less on relative military might than on the gains and losses in constant bitter arm wrestling on the spot, for a little more or a little less that would tell the trend.[99]

Right after the Soviet protest over holding the West German presidential election in Berlin in February 1969, Chancellor Kiesinger had proposed to abandon this practice for the future, in return for getting assurances on access and greater freedom of travel to the East. In April, the three Western nations suggested formal talks with the Soviet Union on Berlin; in July, Gromyko replied favorably; a formal invitation was issued in September and responded to in December, with agreement that the talks should start in January 1970.

After Brandt's election, the idea that the West should connect other negotiations to progress on the Berlin issues came rapidly to the fore. Passages in Kissinger's memoirs suggest that Berlin "linkage" was in some degree an American discovery and initiative, but the record seems to demonstrate conclusively that from the first not only Britain and France but above all Brandt himself considered it essential to create the strongest possible link between Berlin talks and every other actual or pending proposal for negotiations. Thus, as early as December 1969, the NATO Foreign Ministers, making a cautiously favorable reference to a future European security conference, underlined that it was contingent on progress over Berlin. And Brandt reiterated several times that the rights and responsibilities of the three Western powers in Berlin remained fully operative, and that negotiations must in the first instance be among the four occupying powers. From his earlier fruitless efforts, he knew that his side could get results only with the weight of the three Western powers on the scales. He would have concurred with the initial assessment made in the State Department that a "naked" negotiation over Berlin, unconnected to other matters on which the Soviet Union wanted something, would find even the allies in a weak bargaining position.

When Brandt came to Washington in April 1970, right after a dramatic and widely publicized visit to Erfurt, in East Germany, his talks with Nixon went off easily. There was no personal rapport then or later—the two were vastly different in style, and Nixon was always edgy with clear-cut liberals of Brandt's stripe—but there was practical agreement that Brandt would go ahead with his treaty project, that the United States was still crucial to the Berlin negotiations, and that without a Berlin understanding any wider agreement Brandt might reach stood no chance of being accepted by the West German public or the necessary ratifying majority in the Bundestag. It remained only for the Soviet Union to accept the interconnection of the treaties and a new agreement on Berlin.

8. *The Middle East*

When Richard Nixon came into office, concerns in the Middle East centered on the consequences of the 1967 Arab-Israeli War and the continuing effort to move toward peace on this front. Britain had announced in 1968 that it would withdraw its small though crucial military forces in the Arabian Peninsula by the end of 1971, and security in the Gulf region was uncertain—a reason for Nixon's cultivation of the Shah of Iran and for his belief in strong ties to the moderate Arab nations, especially Jordan and Saudi Arabia. Everyone was aware of the importance of Middle East oil, especially to Western Europe and Japan, and Nixon doubtless knew as well that U.S. oil imports from that region were increasing, though the American government was slow to grasp the implications of this.[100]

It was on the Arab-Israeli conflict that Nixon and the State Department focused at the outset. A lasting peace between Israel and its Arab neighbors had been a U.S. objective ever since the creation of Israel in 1948. Its territorial limits were based on a 1947 UN plan to partition British Palestine, and small additions were gained and held when Israel successfully defended itself against the Arabs in 1948–49. Yet the Arab nations had never been willing to recognize or deal with Israel, and beginning in the mid-1950s, organized groups of Arab Palestinians, notably the Palestine Liberation Organization (PLO), founded in 1964, had worked to undermine and threaten Israel. When full-scale war between Israel and its neighbors broke out in the spring of 1967, it was largely due to relentless pressure applied to Israel by Egypt's longtime President, Gamal Abdel Nasser, then at a peak of assertiveness and expansionism. At his request, UN peacekeeping forces were withdrawn from the Sinai Peninsula. He then closed Israel's southern outlet to the Red Sea, the Strait of Tiran, and when the United States and other Western nations were unable to mount a convincing naval response to undo this action, Israel understandably lost patience and went to war. Using Mirage jets bought from France, then its principal military supplier, the highly trained Israeli Air Force quickly dominated the war. Israeli ground forces took over the Sinai (as well as the so-called Gaza Strip), the Golan Heights (on its northeastern border with Syria), East Jerusalem, and the West Bank opposite Jordan, whose King Hussein had unwisely entered the war in a gesture of Arab solidarity.

This crushing and dramatic victory, achieved within six days, transformed everything. Instead of being a small island under constant threat, Israel was now a clear-cut military power and potential threat on its own, holding large areas that had once been parts of Egypt or Syria or under Jordanian rule. (The 1947 UN partition plan for British Palestine had assigned the West Bank to the Arabs, although the rule of Jordan there had never been internationally specified or sanctioned. The division of Jerusalem, with Jordan controlling the east and Israel the west of the city, had also been contrary to the 1947 plan, which called for the whole city's internationalized status.) Egypt and Nasser personally were humiliated, Syria and Jordan were shown to be weak against Israel, and the outcome was also a sharp setback for the Soviet Union. The Soviet equipment and training on which Egypt had relied was far inferior to what crack Israeli forces could do with what the West had furnished to them. Overall, as one good history puts it, the Soviets had lost "most of the credit in the eyes of the Arab publics and third world countries they had painfully accumulated over the previous twelve years."[101]

Israel was briefly ready to return almost all the occupied territories in return for formal recognition and acceptance of its existence and territory. The wartime Cabinet of Prime Minister Levi Eshkol actually adopted a resolution in June 1967 that would have yielded the Sinai and Golan Heights completely and spoken broadly of minor security adjustments along the borders between Israel and the West Bank. A fundamentalist Zionist minority in the Cabinet, led by Menachem Begin of the hard-line Herut Party, prevented the Cabinet from agreeing on a clear-cut position concerning the West Bank.[102]

However, in their humiliation, the Arab nations never made any effort toward peace. Instead they joined with Nasser in the Khartoum Declaration of August 1967, which authorized efforts for a settlement but specified that these must involve no recognition of Israel, no negotiations directly with Israel, and no lasting peace — the "three Noes." Because the United States refused to condemn Israel as an aggressor (and kept the United Nations from even trying to), virtually all the Arab nations save Jordan had broken diplomatic relations with the United States. Communication had to be conducted in the confused setting of the United Nations or through third-country caretaker diplomats.[103]

The General Assembly having proved itself helpless, it fell to the Security

Council to act. After tortuous negotiations in which Britain played a leading role, the Security Council (then with no Arab members) in November adopted Resolution 242, which laid down the principles that should govern a peaceful settlement: in return for withdrawing from "territories occupied in the recent conflict," Israel (along with other nations in the area) should be assured of "secure and recognized borders." To this end, a UN mediator (the Swedish diplomat Gunnar Jarring) was designated.

At the time, Resolution 242 seemed to offer great hope. But its wording was ambiguous: the Arabic language has no definite article and the authoritative English version had not said "the territories," which would clearly have meant all of them. The result was known to be a compromise, with the Arabs insisting that "all" was the intended meaning, the United States for a long time contending that it meant all but a few minor adjustments, and the Israelis progressively taking the position that substantial territory could be withheld for security reasons. Still another bone of contention was that the resolution, again deliberately, did not order direct negotiations with Israel, a matter which the Israelis had emphasized from the first. In short, Security Council Resolution 242 contained ambiguities and omissions that led to constant argument over its interpretation and intent.

With the Khartoum Declaration still fresh, no progress was made for the next year. Nor did the Johnson Administration, in an election year and preoccupied by the Vietnam War, make any serious effort toward peace. However, when the Soviet Union tried to restore its credit with the Arab world by rapidly replacing Egypt's severe losses, especially in combat aircraft, the United States took steps to become Israel's principal military supplier, a role from which General de Gaulle had withdrawn France, in disapproval of the war and in deference to France's interests in the Arab world. Until then the United States had supplied Israel with a fair amount of military training and sold it ground and air defense equipment, but not combat aircraft; a deal to sell A-4 fighter-bombers had been reached in 1966 but then deferred. But in late 1967 Johnson announced that 48 A-4s (called Skyhawks) would now be delivered; the number was shortly raised to 100. Israel had the strong support of a number of senators in pressing for the faster and more powerful F-4 (Phantom), and Johnson agreed in late 1968 to sell 50 of these, with deliveries to start in late 1969.

When Nixon became President, as an objective historian sums it up, "the Arab-Israeli conflict was recognized as dangerous, although hopelessly complex and perhaps less urgent than the other tasks facing the administration."[104] Prior to his Inauguration, Nixon sent former Pennsylvania governor William Scranton to the area. He returned with the suggestion that American policy should be more "evenhanded," apparently meaning that Nixon should move away from what many saw as Johnson's pro-Israeli tilt.

The word also fitted the position taken by most American diplomats with experience in Arab countries, who consistently urged giving great weight to Arab reactions and concerns. It shortly became a buzzword with a negative connotation among Israel's strong supporters in the United States.

Initially, Nixon and Kissinger included the Middle East in their key concept of "linkage" among the diverse issues involving the Soviet Union and the United States. They briefly entertained the idea that some U.S. "concession" over the Arab-Israeli problem (obviously requiring pressure on Israel) might help induce the Soviets to cooperate over Vietnam, but the idea quickly vanished, being impracticable as well as likely to draw fire from Israel's many American supporters. Instead, after the usual extensive staff papers reviewing policy options, Nixon at an NSC meeting in February 1969 approved an intensive negotiating effort by the State Department, to be conducted in two forums—bilateral talks with the Soviet Union, assumed to be in close touch with Nasser, and (at de Gaulle's suggestion) Four-Power talks with representatives of France, Britain, and the Soviet Union, conducted at the United Nations with Ambassador Charles Yost representing the United States.

At this early stage, Nixon deliberately kept Kissinger to one side, telling him frankly that he was concerned lest having a Jewish-American at the forefront might be misunderstood. Nixon's attitude toward Jews in general was ambivalent and at times unpleasant. Up to that point he had had little Jewish support in elections, and professed not to care about such support. Moreover, he was capable—as the Watergate tapes were to show—of nasty and ethnically pointed references to Jewish officials. Yet at the same time he had, in addition to Kissinger, two other valued members of his staff who were Jewish, Leonard Garment and William Safire. Private feelings aside, Kissinger shared Nixon's judgment that early progress on the Arab-Israeli front was unlikely and that this was a good job to give to the State Department. The White House could readily claim credit for any progress, while leaving State visibly responsible for failure.[105]

Accordingly, Assistant Secretary of State Joseph Sisco entered into discussions with Ambassador Dobrynin—an evident exception to Kissinger's proclaimed "linkage." In March, however, just as the two diplomats were starting to discuss general principles for a peace agreement, Nasser launched artillery attacks on Israeli forces on the east bank of the Suez Canal, shortly supplemented by periodic commando raids. His aim, in what became known as the War of Attrition, was to wear down Israel and force it to evacuate the Sinai or to negotiate at a disadvantage. From Nasser's standpoint this grim strategy was promising. With a population of only 2.6 million, a hundred Israeli casualties were numerically in the same proportion to total population as ten thousand Americans would have been, and the effect was magnified by Israel's very limited manpower and its humane tradition. Israel was bound to be highly sensitive to even numerically small losses, while Egypt seemed to be able to go on indefinitely, with its population of 35 million and a continuing flow of expendable military supplies from the Soviet Union.

Efforts at preliminary negotiation through the spring and summer were conducted against a background of low-level hostilities and constant concern in Israel over the military balance, especially in high-performance combat aircraft. With negotiations the province of the State Department and the aircraft balance a matter for the White House, under pressure from Israel's domestic supporters and increasingly from Congress, there was a duality to American policy. By late summer, Sisco and Dobrynin seemed close to agreement on general principles, but Israel was responding to Egypt's actions by carrying out punishing air attacks on the Soviet-installed air defense system near the Suez Canal, and destroying many aircraft in the battle zone there. Events were moving to force at least a choice in emphasis, between the pursuit of a peace settlement and continued or increased arms supplies on both sides, with the risk of expanding hostilities and greater superpower engagement.

In September, the Arab side was agitated by the delivery to Israel of the first of the F-4s Johnson had promised the previous December. At the same time, the United States and the West in general took note of a military coup in Libya that overthrew King Idris, long cooperative with the West and willing to accept American bases on his territory, and brought to power an Army colonel named Muammar al-Qaddafi. Little was known about him, but the change was welcomed by Nasser and was clearly favorable to the growth of Arab radicalism. The danger of Arab radicalism was argued in opposite directions within the American government. The State Department pointed to it constantly as a reason to give top priority to the search for a peaceful settlement. Others countered that only firmness could keep the radicals or would-be radicals in their place and give moderate Arabs the support and confidence to hold to their positions.

A breakpoint in American decision making came with the late September visit to Washington of Golda Meir, installed as Prime Minister of Israel after the death of Levi Eshkol in February. Long prominent in the Labor Party establishment, Mrs. Meir had been born and spent her earliest years in the pogrom-ridden territories of what had become the western Soviet Union, in times of dramatic struggle and repression, and had then moved to Milwaukee, Wisconsin, before migrating to Israel in 1921. The contrasting experiences had left her with friendly feelings for the United States and vehemently anti-Soviet views, both calculated to make her a congenial colleague to Nixon and Kissinger. Her directness, gravelly voice, and businesslike manner were legendary, along with her sharp wit. Nixon, preoccupied as he was by Vietnam War demonstrations and his upcoming

November 3 speech on the war, found her impressive, and his feelings for Israel seem to have become more favorable. Ambassador Yitzhak Rabin, previously Chief of Staff of the Israeli armed forces, was also effective: he had received Nixon at length during a 1967 visit to Israel and the two had found themselves in close agreement on global strategic issues.[106]

For Mrs. Meir's visit, Nixon brought Kissinger in for the first time as a serious participant in Middle East policy. His advisor quickly formed a lasting relationship with Mrs. Meir, part joshingly imitation-filial but serious beneath. Rabin's memoirs make clear that at an early stage Nixon and Meir agreed to handle major matters via Kissinger and Rabin, leaving out Secretary Rogers and Foreign Minister Abba Eban equally. Yet the State Department remained very much involved in the policy process over the Middle East, so that its frequent lack of information on what was passing on the White House circuit was frustrating as well as confusing.[107]

From September on, Rabin urged his government to raise the ante militarily by bombing the interior of Egypt and even the Cairo area, implying strongly that the United States—that is, the two men in the White House who really counted—would not be averse to stronger action of this sort.[108] On the negotiating front, on the other hand, by mid-October Sisco thought he had at least general Soviet and Israeli acceptance for a set of nine principles to serve as a foundation for engaging the parties directly or through the mediation of Jarring. On October 28 Sisco met again with Dobrynin, and the next day Rogers sent Israel, Egypt and Jordan, France, Britain, and the Soviet Union a formal proposal, soon known as the Rogers Plan, which called for acceptance of the international frontier between Israel and Egypt as a "secure and recognized border" within the meaning of Resolution 242; a formal state of peace; and negotiations over the Gaza Strip and the key point at the mouth of the Gulf of Aqaba, Sharm el-Sheikh. In effect, the plan called for a virtually complete return of the Sinai to Egypt. Rogers knew the strong sentiment within the Israeli Cabinet against any concessions on the West Bank, and therefore saved proposals concerning it and the border with Jordan for a separate proposal, which he knew stood little chance of being accepted. In any event, it was on the Sinai front that the War of Attrition was being conducted.

Almost at once, the Rogers Plan met with strong objections from both sides. On November 6 Nasser denounced its proposals root and branch, and the Soviet Union dutifully followed suit, showing that in fact it had never been able to speak for Egypt or accurately appraise its reactions. Israel's response was equally vehement and negative: it particularly objected to deciding the key border issues in advance of any negotiations. Giving back almost all of the Sinai now seemed unacceptable in the face of the military threat Egypt had mounted, and even the moderate and negotiation-minded Abba Eban, in his later memoirs, was moved to call the Rogers Plan "one of the major errors of international diplomacy in the postwar era."[109]

Was this a fair judgment? Attacks on Rogers's impartiality, both in Israel and among its strong supporters in America, would have been inevitable over any serious peace effort. Yet this one did seem inadequately prepared, badly timed, and wide open to the charge that it was dictating key final terms. Its abrupt demise went far to discredit any further attempt at a comprehensive peace settlement, reinforcing the inclination of those who, like Henry Kissinger, were always disposed to favor a step-by-step approach, tackling the fronts around Israel one by one—the Sinai to the south and west, the Golan Heights to the north and east, and in time the areas with large Palestinian populations, the West Bank to the east and the Gaza Strip to the southwest.

In some American quarters Israel was criticized for its negative response, but it had no reason to worry about the reaction in the White House. Even as Nixon let Rogers's effort go forward in October, he authorized members of his staff to convey to the Israelis that he was not in fact behind the plan, thus—as Kissinger himself admits—cutting the ground from under Rogers before he started! It was another example of the confusion of policy and signal that prevailed on this issue through 1969 and much of 1970.[110]

By the end of 1969 Israeli air attacks in the canal zone area had knocked out most of the Egyptian air defense system and inflicted heavy aircraft losses as well. Egypt stood nearly defenseless, yet its forces continued to use their superior artillery to inflict casualties. Satisfied that the Rogers Plan had been aborted, the Israeli Cabinet debated whether to raise the ante and move hostilities away from the canal area by a concerted bombing program deep within Egypt. The last weeks of 1969 and the early days of 1970 saw what Abba Eban later characterized as "one of the most decisive debates in Israel since 1967." Those like him who "feared that this would bring the Soviet Union to Egypt's defense with a consequent disturbance of the strategic balance" lost out. Eban believed that Rabin's strong advocacy was crucial here, including the ambassador's claim "that there were some people in Washington who might react sympathetically to such a course." This can only have meant Nixon and Kissinger. That both were leaning away from the State Department approach by this time is abundantly clear from Kissinger's memoir.[111]

On January 7, 1970, Israeli planes began attacks into the interior of Egypt beyond the canal area, quickly extending to hit targets in a steadily narrowing circle around Cairo itself. These "deep-penetration" raids extended only a modest distance in air-warfare terms, the center of Cairo being only sixty-five miles west of the canal, but hitting the capital area alone meant they

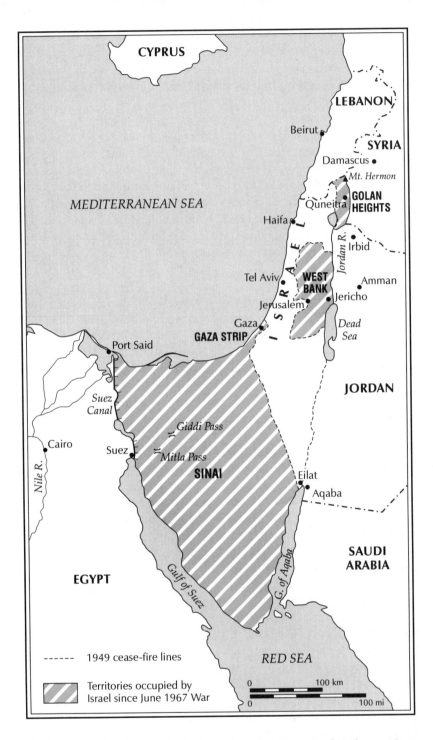

Mediterranean Sea, Egypt, Sinai, Saudi Arabia, Jordan, Israel, Lebanon, Syria
(with territories occupied by Israel since June 1967 War) © 1997 *Chris Brest*

were clearly a major escalation. To amplify their impact and psychological effect, the attacks were conducted daily, with their sonic booms making clear to the Egyptian people their helplessness.

Nasser reacted sharply, departing for Moscow on January 22 to seek additional Soviet aid and support. Almost at once, it appears, the Soviet leadership decided not only to provide advanced types of antiaircraft equipment (the SAM-3 short-range and the SAM-2 intermediate-range missile) but also—since the Egyptians were plainly incapable of effective use of these weapons without long training and direct experience—to send Soviet personnel to set up the equipment and then to operate it themselves, as the Egyptians learned the ropes. This took time: the scale and nature of the Soviet help did not become clear until mid-March. The Soviet Union did not, however, commit itself to sending more combat aircraft, and could therefore claim plausibly that it was acting only for Egypt's defense.

In the meantime the diplomacy was intense and strongly worded. At the end of January a sharp letter from Soviet Premier Kosygin to Nixon warned that if the Israeli attacks continued, the Soviets would be forced to see that the Arab states had "means at their disposal" to give "a due rebuff to the arrogant aggressor." Nixon sent a firm reply, and on February 10 Kissinger, surely on the President's orders, used his channel with Dobrynin (for the first time on a Middle East issue) to convey an informal warning that "the introduction of Soviet combat personnel in the Middle East would be viewed with the greatest concern." In reply, Gromyko simply repeated that Israel must withdraw from all its 1967 gains.[112]

So the pot simmered through February, while the Nixon Administration came to grips with Israel's annual request for arms—this time 25 additional Phantoms (over and above the 50 being delivered under Johnson's pledge of December 1968), 100 additional Skyhawks, and many tanks and armored personnel carriers. The initial reaction to the request was skeptical, notably at the Pentagon, with some arguing that Israel's superiority was already assured for at least the next three to five years. But a new factor was introduced during the state visit of French President Georges Pompidou to America, in February. A month earlier, France had agreed to sell the new Qaddafi regime in Libya 100 Mirage aircraft, originally built with Israel in mind as the recipient. The number was far more than Libya could handle, which suggested that many might go on to Egypt. Obviously the switch in destinations could seriously affect the balance. As a result, demonstrations by supporters of Israel almost cut short Pompidou's visit. Nixon, always partial to France, was chagrined and angry at the demonstrators. He authorized Rogers to announce that Israel's arms request was being held in abeyance. But just as this was done, Rabin, on March 17, came in with firm evidence that 1,500 Soviet military combat personnel had arrived in Egypt with the SAM-3s and additional SAM-2s already flowing in.

Only the week before, Dobrynin had sent Kissinger a proposal for an undeclared cease-fire, with two apparent concessions. A final settlement should establish a state of peace (an Israeli demand, whereas the Arabs wanted only an end to fighting, with Israeli withdrawal to follow before full peace was achieved); and the Arab states would undertake to control the operations of guerrilla forces from their territory.[113] Interpreting this message as a useful gesture, Nixon decided on a two-pronged action. As Rogers announced publicly that the Israeli arms request was under review, Kissinger would tell Rabin privately that America would replace Israel's aircraft losses up to a planned 1970 limit of 8 Phantoms and 20 Skyhawks, and strongly urge that Israel end its raids and accept the undeclared cease-fire.[114]

The revelation that the Soviets were sending arms and combat personnel to man Egypt's air defense system was a sensation, not least because it was the first time that Soviet military forces had been deployed directly and publicly to fight alongside a client state's forces. Altogether the escalation on both sides could only make the situation tenser and harder to resolve. The later evaluation of the remarkably objective Israeli participant and later President, Chaim Herzog, is worth quoting:

> From a short-term point of view, the Israeli deep penetration bombing had contained a certain logic; but, from a long-term point of view, it would appear to have been a major error. . . . Whether or not the natural course of events would have led to increased Sovietization in Egypt, it is difficult to say, but there is no doubt that the Israeli decision to bomb Egypt in depth constituted a major turning-point in the Middle East, and created a situation that encouraged President Nasser to open up Egypt, not only to Soviet advisors, but also to Soviet combat units.[115]

As Rabin told Kissinger of the conclusive evidence of new Soviet aid and personnel in Egypt, he also conveyed the formal Israeli position that it would accept an undeclared cease-fire if the United States doubled the aircraft replacement figure to 16-plus-40, and if Nixon gave a public assurance about maintaining Israel's air strength and the military balance generally. It was a demanding but also cautious response.[116]

In his memoirs, Kissinger noted that the decision-making circle in Washington hesitated, in part because it was "more than half convinced that Israeli belligerence had provoked the Soviet move." His own view, he said, was that regardless of the degree of Israeli provocation, the establishment of a Soviet combat role in Egypt was "overpoweringly dangerous" and should have been met by increasing U.S. aid to Israel at once, making clear that the United States would match anything the Soviet Union did. But at the time, presumably on Nixon's orders, he simply called in Dobrynin for a "tough dressing down," telling him that in light of the Soviet move, further discussion of a cease-fire was off.[117]

In April, Israel entirely suspended its already reduced deep raids, but tension went up another notch when Rabin reported that Soviet pilots were flying combat patrols in Egypt, avoiding the canal area but freeing Egyptian pilots to fly more there. Kissinger was authorized to tell him privately that the United States would supply additional aircraft. The intelligence consensus in Washington, however, still was that the new Soviet effort was primarily defensive.[118]

By this time all four of the principal parties (the Egyptians, the Israelis, the Soviets, and the Americans) were weighing their next moves in a fluid and murky situation. When Nixon decided on April 26 to send U.S. troops into Cambodia, the resulting controversy and distraction caused an intermission of several weeks in U.S. decision making about the Middle East. It was a moment of relative calm before the pace of events again became urgent and rapid in mid-June.

. . .

While the Arab-Israeli problem was the foremost Middle East concern of Nixon and Kissinger in this first year, neither ever lost sight of the importance of Iran, in both regional and global terms. Never directly involved in the Arab-Israeli confrontation, Iran occupied a special place both in the area and in the minds of Richard Nixon and (gradually) Henry Kissinger.

Historically, Iran had been a main theater in the rivalry between Russia and Britain for power and influence, the "Great Game" of the late nineteenth and early twentieth centuries. In 1921 Iran came to an agreement with the Soviet Union, accepting limitations on the activities of outside powers in Iran including Britain and later, by extension, the United States, but Soviet ambitions to dominate Iran continued, and during the period of the Nazi-Soviet Pact, 1939–41, expansion southward to control the Persian Gulf was a stated Soviet objective.

After Hitler attacked the Soviet Union in June 1941, British and Soviet forces joined to depose the pro-German Shah of Iran and install his son, then only twenty-two, who took the name Mohammed Reza Shah Pahlevi. Iran then became the land route for vast quantities of U.S. supplies to Russia shipped via the Persian Gulf. After the war, the Soviets kept large numbers of armed forces in the northern Iranian province of Azerbaijan, violating the wartime understandings that all foreign forces would be withdrawn. Firm U.S. opposition, backed by UN resolutions, forced the Soviets to withdraw in the spring of 1946, and the United States began limited aid programs to Iran. Although Britain remained the principal Western power on the scene, with a monopoly oil concession held by the Anglo-Iranian Oil Company, U.S. influence was strong and increasing.[119]

In 1951, Mohammed Mossadegh, leader of an apparently radical National Front, became Premier of Iran, nationalized Anglo-Iranian Oil, allowed the pro-Soviet Tudeh Party to threaten to take control, and in 1953 forced the Shah to flee for his life. In response the United States, working with Britain but now taking the lead, mounted a small covert operation that gave guidance, tactical advice, and communications equipment to a group of senior military officers who brought back the Shah in a bloodless coup that had the support of much of Teheran's people and also the Shia Islamic clergy, the mullahs. Although the American involvement was secret at the time, sophisticated Iranians were aware of it and within a few years it was written about.[120] As Vice President, Richard Nixon fully supported this covert operation, though he does not appear to have been directly involved. Shortly after, he met with the Shah in Teheran and was impressed: "I sensed an inner strength in him, and I felt that in the years ahead he would become a strong leader."[121]

During the Eisenhower presidency, the U.S.-Iran relationship progressively widened and deepened after the restoration of the Shah: in a new oil consortium arrangement, American companies took a 40 percent interest, matching the British; and when Britain put together the Baghdad Pact in 1955, joining with Turkey, Pakistan, Iran, and Iraq as full members in defense of the Middle East's "northern tier," the United States supported the effort as an "observer." Iraq dropped out when Nuri Said's pro-Western regime was deposed in 1958, and the alliance, now called the Central Treaty Organization (CENTO), continued, with U.S. participation as an observer. In 1959, Eisenhower made a secret executive agreement that in the event of aggression against Iran, the United States would take action, including the use of armed force subject to constitutional restraints—the phrasing used in several parallel treaties. Never debated or noted in the United States, this executive agreement was surely taken as a commitment by the Shah, who did not weigh whether in practice Congress would honor an undertaking reached without its participation.

In all, Eisenhower made the relationship with Iran a virtual alliance. Policy papers of the period spoke of Iran as an ally, and it became axiomatic within the government that its survival and healthy political and economic development were crucial, perhaps vital, to U.S. national interests. As Vice President, Nixon surely shared fully in these judgments and in the sense that U.S. policy toward Iran was a major success story. Then, in his eight years out of office, he kept up contact with the Shah and in November 1967 they spent a whole day in serious conversation, focusing on the security issues that were the intense concern of both men.[122]

The year 1968 saw a major development affecting Iran: the British government of Harold Wilson announced that Britain would withdraw its long-standing security force contingents from the area of the Persian Gulf by

1971. These forces, though small, and Britain's political connections in the area had been a major element in its stability. Now, however, the Shah felt that Iran could become the controlling power in the area — it was firmly established, with growing resources from the Shah's oil revenues, and a moderately effective army.

In the 1960s, with dissent to the Shah's autocracy visible and with the Shah increasingly reliant on personally chosen advisors, President Kennedy took a more critical posture toward him. The American Ambassador in Teheran kept in constant close touch with the Shah, supportive but also offering quiet, often pointed advice, while U.S. officials ranged widely in Iranian circles and regions, accompanying economic aid programs with strong advice and pressure for reform; American military aid was for a time determined unilaterally, at steady and moderate levels designed to keep the Shah focused on his internal problems.[123]

Influenced by these pressures, the Shah did institute major reforms, the so-called White Revolution, which among other things modernized the traditional position of women in ways abhorrent to much of the Shiite clergy. One of its leaders, the Ayatollah Ruhollah Khomeini, the target of a government raid in 1962 in his holy city of Qum, fled into exile. Yet the reforms did appear to help the government, and urban economic conditions at least showed dramatic improvement. With the Shah's rising oil revenues, U.S. official aid was ended by mutual consent and the American Embassy reverted to a more passive mode, going along with the Shah and acknowledging his resentment of its contact with critics or dissenters. To most observers, Iran in the late 1960s seemed stable and increasingly powerful, well along in a transition to self-reliance albeit still dependent on ultimate U.S. security assurances. Such was the situation Nixon inherited.

Nixon's first policy was simple, to treat the Shah, and hence Iran, as an especially favored friend. This was evident in the treatment given the Shah when he came to Washington for President Eisenhower's funeral in March 1969, and in his state visit to Washington that October. No substantive agreements or announcements of consequence were made, but an especially cordial atmosphere was visible to the media. The White House issued a statement saying simply that the meetings between Nixon and the Shah, lasting apparently several hours, had concerned "the military implications of Britain's scheduled withdrawal from the Persian Gulf area in 1971."[124]

What was actually said between the two on this subject? Nixon's and Kissinger's memoirs are silent. Each must have been deeply concerned at the possibilities the British withdrawal would unleash: independence for Kuwait, Oman, Bahrain, Qatar, and the other sheikhdoms in the Gulf, whose new regimes were bound to be vulnerable and unstable, open to tampering or worse from radical Iraq, Nasser's Egypt, or Soviet-backed local Marxists. Yet at least as long as the United States was embroiled in the

Indochina War, it could not explicitly take up, nor would Congress or the public accept, a larger or categorically stated U.S. security commitment in the Gulf. And the fact that the United States was closely linked to Israel made it hard for Arab countries to accept it as an arbiter and protector.

The two may also have discussed the significance of the Nixon Doctrine, announced in June 1969, with its increased reliance on regional powers. For Nixon, Iran was clearly marked out to be such a pillar in the Middle East, but to proclaim this from the housetops would serve no purpose and might easily set off hostile reactions. So it is a safe surmise that the two leaders agreed not to talk in these terms.[125] Given Iran's size and population, geographic position, and dependence on the Gulf for access to the outside world, an enlarged role for Iran would have been almost inevitable in any case. Clearly the Shah welcomed this.[126]

In sum, either before or during this October meeting there was a meeting of minds on the basic proposition that Iran must be a pillar of the Gulf region. The circumstantial evidence is overwhelming that the two also agreed, as a corollary, that Iran's military strength could and should be built up, with the United States the preferred supplier. Between 1950 and 1970, Iran received a total of $1.8 billion worth of U.S. military aid; over the next six years it bought from the United States a total of another $12.1 billion in military-related goods and services, 80 percent of this going to new equipment![127]

Did Nixon and the Shah also discuss oil? Again the record is blank. What is abundantly clear is that the advent of Nixon created an important breakpoint both in Iranian policy and in the U.S. relationship to Iran. The American Embassy in Teheran now became a cheering section for the Shah, discouraging criticism, whether official or private, and making every effort to cooperate with the Shah and meet his desires. In the words of a later scholar:

> When [Nixon and Kissinger] took office in 1969 they inaugurated a turning point in United States policy toward Iran. From its traditional peripheral position, Iran emerged as the key pillar of support for American interests in an increasingly important part of the world. This change did not represent, however, a victory for American over Iranian concerns; rather it marked the triumph of the Shah's own long-held view of a proper role for himself over twenty years of State Department reservations.[128]

9. Japan: The First Phase

By 1969 Japan had achieved an extraordinary recovery from the depths of its defeat in 1945. In the previous decade, it had surged ahead with economic growth, the rates of increase averaging a real 10 percent a year. Its confidence and international acceptance (given a tremendous boost when it successfully hosted the 1964 Olympic Games) grew to the point where it was a respected participant in international economic organizations and in UN activities. At the same time, Japan was still regarded with reserve and underlying suspicion in the vast areas of East Asia where Japanese armies had seized and occupied territory during World War II, and even in industrialized countries of Europe.

Militarily, Japan remained agreeable to the rigid limitations on its armed forces, to self-defense narrowly defined, prescribed in Article 9 of its 1949 Constitution. It was only just starting to consider an air and naval capability in the Pacific (because of concerns about the growth of Soviet military power there). Overall relations with the Soviet Union remained cool, largely because of Japan's steady pressure for the return of the four historically Japanese islands just north of Hokkaido that had been awarded to the Soviet Union under the Yalta Agreements in February 1945.

Relations with the United States were by far the most important part of Japanese foreign policy, though less than in the years of occupation and tutelage. But Japan was also in an advanced stage of transition. In a metaphor that despite its condescending ring was actually used, America was no longer model and almost parent but was still an "elder brother" from whom the Japanese expected a special degree of support and understanding.

Japan never officially engaged with the Vietnam War, reminding everyone of its Constitution and of the U.S.-Japan Treaty of 1960, which bound America to come to the defense of Japan but imposed no parallel obligation on Japan. Japan's leaders in the 1960s did express, repeatedly and with apparent sincerity, their worry about threats from China and the Soviet Union, and accepted that the U.S. efforts in Asia helped to meet these threats. That the Japanese economy got a big lift from war-related spending was also a steadying, though not controlling, factor.

As the United States became visibly bogged down in Vietnam in 1968, a certain reserve emerged, even among Japanese most dedicated to the U.S. tie, along with stepped-up criticism of American policy from opposition quarters. More than most East Asian countries, Japan, while still strongly desiring and depending on a continued major U.S. presence and active involvement in East Asia, was ready for some adjustment.

The most obvious site for change was Okinawa, under American control since the last and bloodiest campaign of the Pacific War. The large island and surrounding area some 350 miles south of the main islands of Japan were run by a military governor, with large contingents of U.S. forces (principally Marines), and two large Air Force bases. The population of nearly a million Japanese had limited powers of self-government, and the island's economy, aided by military expenditures, was in adequate shape by 1969.[129]

Yet, as Ambassador Edwin Reischauer had argued in the early 1960s, and his successor, Alexis Johnson, thereafter, the U.S. occupation was bound to become untenable as Japan regained its footing and national pride. Periodic anti-American incidents on Okinawa itself were reinforced by demonstrations on the main islands, and the issue was kept below the boiling point only by the continued ascendancy of Liberal Democratic governments in Japan, which put pressure for change on the United States.

By late 1967, when Prime Minister Eisaku Sato paid a state visit to Washington, President Johnson had been persuaded by the State Department and the civilian Pentagon, over only mild objections from the JCS, that the time had come to set a date for initiating negotiations to revert the island to Japanese control, with a few American bases remaining. Only the last-minute objections of Senator Richard Russell, then all-powerful in the Senate Appropriations and Armed Services committees, prevented this, but the visit left both sides understanding clearly that negotiations should be an early order of business.[130]

Nixon had visited Japan six times in and out of office, and had close ties with leading conservatives in the Liberal Democratic Party, especially the elder statesman Nobusuke Kishi, Prime Minister from 1957 to 1960, who had guided to completion the U.S.-Japan Treaty of 1960. He also knew Sato, who was Kishi's younger half brother. Nixon was well aware that U.S. control of Okinawa, which had no parallel with any other defeated nation, was a "constant irritant" in the overall relationship. He also kept in the back of his mind that a resolution of the Okinawa issue might clear the way for Japan to become militarily more active and to accelerate its growing participation in the security of East Asia.[131]

After the Inauguration, one of Nixon's first acts was to approve a major study of policy toward Japan. The figures involved were Alexis Johnson, just named No. 3 at State and already well known to Nixon from Eisenhower days; Richard Sneider, briefly on Kissinger's staff and then assigned to Tokyo as deputy chief of mission; the Joint Chiefs; the civil affairs people in the Department of the Army; and military commands at all levels—a rare example in the Nixon era of basic interagency agreement on a course of action and exemplary teamwork in carrying it out.

Japanese Foreign Minister Kiichi Aichi came to Washington in April for quiet discussions primarily about Okinawa, and in late May a full-scale NSC meeting led Nixon to accept reversion of Okinawa if agreement could be reached during 1969 on basic principles, looking to a detailed agreement by 1972. He approved a readiness to yield on one key issue Aichi had emphasized, continued U.S. storage of nuclear weapons on Okinawa. As the target of the only two nuclear attacks in history, Japan had a deep and abiding hostility to any association with such weapons, and since the early 1950s the United States had agreed that it would never station nuclear weapons on the main islands of Japan itself. It was now judged politically impossible for the Japanese to accept a different rule for Okinawa when it again became formally and fully part of Japan. Reluctantly, the Joint Chiefs agreed.[132] At this stage, it was assumed that this nuclear-free concession would be disclosed in the course of discussions leading up to the planned U.S.-Japan summit in the fall. Unfortunately, however, word about it leaked to the press in early June, adding to White House ire already aroused by news reports of the secret bombing of Cambodia.

A second issue concerned "freedom of use." U.S. military planners had always assumed that in a crisis the Americans could use their military bases in Japan in support of conventional operations elsewhere in East Asia. Whether this required formal Japanese consent had never been addressed explicitly, although the practical difficulty of operating without such consent must have been well understood. The Okinawa bases, on the other hand, had always been used with complete freedom, most recently in support of operations in Vietnam. (The first B-52 strikes in South Vietnam were launched from there.) The prospective reversion thus brought into the open the residual uncertainty about a need for formal Japanese consent for any U.S. operations from bases on the main islands of Japan, a potentially thorny issue.

Yet a successful Okinawa agreement seemed clearly within reach, and in August the summit was formally set for November 19–21. While "high policy" was thus proceeding smoothly, however, things had not gone well on the "low policy" issue of restraints on Japanese textile exports to the United States, which had ballooned into a major issue. Protests from the U.S. industry had led first to voluntary restraints, adopted to forestall government action, and to a wider long-term agreement (LTA) about trade in cotton goods, which embraced Japan and other textile-exporting nations. Though Japan chafed under this LTA regime, it held to the line during multilateral trade negotiations for the "Kennedy Round," concluded successfully in 1967. However, the LTA did not cover wool or the newly important category of man-made fiber, in which Japanese exports to the United States had tripled. These became the focus of new demands from U.S. industry, which over the years had cultivated its political connections and become a highly effective pressure group, out of all proportion to its contribution to overall national production.[133]

In the 1968 primaries, as we have seen in Chapter 1, Nixon was under great pressure from textile producers, especially in North and South Carolina, historically strong Republican supporters and major financial contributors. The key man was Senator Strom Thurmond of South Carolina, and it was initially to him that Nixon made a firm pledge in May or June, reaffirmed by a strong public statement at convention time, that as President he would obtain effective quotas on Japanese textile imports, a step Presi-

dent Johnson had consistently rejected. Just what part this pledge played in
Nixon's nomination can only be a matter of guesswork: Wallace did remain
a serious factor until October, although Reagan's last-minute bid at the
convention was surely doomed. In any case, Nixon was never disposed to
take chances. He was hardly one to cavil at taking out a small mortgage on
Japanese-American relations if it would get him crucial Southern support.
As a team of American and Japanese scholars later concluded:

> The primary reason the United States sought restrictions on wool and
> synthetic textile imports, particularly from Japan, is well known. Richard
> Nixon made a strong commitment to do so during the 1968 presidential
> campaign. The commitment was not tied to a broader trade policy ap-
> proach or philosophy, nor was it related to broader U.S.-Japanese rela-
> tions. Rather, it was motivated by electoral politics.[134]

As Nixon took office, the textile producers did not fail to remind him of
the pledge, and one of his first actions was to assign responsibility to Mau-
rice Stans, Secretary of Commerce, a man of little foreign experience —
none with Japan — but dedicated to carrying out to the full any order from
Nixon. Kissinger tried briefly (by his account) to point out the possible
political effects of this, but was swiftly rebuffed.[135]

Stans at once took up the task with zeal and thoroughness, drawing on
key staff members who had shown strong anti-Japanese inclinations in previous negotiations on trade and access issues. The State Department was
only marginally influential on either the tactics or the substance of the
opening U.S. position, which was virtually dictated by the textile industry.
On the Japanese side, responsibility and effective influence mirrored the
American situation: the generally moderate and pro-American Foreign Office was virtually excluded, while the powerful Ministry of International
Trade and Industry (MITI), solidly sympathetic to the industry, and the
industry itself, which had disproportionate political clout with the Liberal
Democratic regime, were actively involved.

Stans, in Japan in May, firmly demanded comprehensive voluntary restraints, and his brusque manner set off a stream of harsh anti-American
comment. Perhaps the Japanese would have been inclined in this direction
in any case: after Japan's extraordinary growth in the world economic arena
in the 1960s, the memory of American generosity and sponsorship had begun to fade. Assertive nationalism became evident, at least on economic
matters — far more dominant in Japan's overall foreign policy outlook than
in the United States at that time. Thus it was typical that the Japanese press
and TV avidly covered Stans's every step and gesture, while in the United
States his visit was scarcely noted, save in the textile-producing areas. This

served only to sharpen the differences between the two sides on textile matters and to raise the political temperature.

In quantitative terms, although the textile industry was a large employer in both countries (2.4 million workers in the United States, 1.8 million in Japan) and had made itself a potent political force, it was already declining substantially relative to other industries. As one American analysis put it, "if overall national economic interests had been decisive, then, the United States would not have placed very high priority on limiting textile imports from Japan, nor would Japan have given very high priority to resisting pressures for limits."[136]

While Japan remained a useful political-military ally and supporter, its large and growing favorable trade balance (though nothing like what it would achieve in the 1980s and 1990s), now made it, in the eyes of many Americans, more an economic adversary. To many Japanese, on the other hand, the American demands about textiles were without foundation in terms of actual injury to American industry, and seemed merely to be ill-tempered reactions to Japan's economic gains. Resistance to them became emotionally necessary, for the sake of national pride, while many Americans, probably including Nixon, considered the Japanese attitude extraordinarily ungrateful for all the America had done in the 1940s and 1950s to help Japan's recovery and for its continued security umbrella. In the phrase of the period, Japan was still getting a "free ride," for which, many were ready to argue, it should compensate on other issues. In short, the dispute was much broader and deeper than the immediate issue of textiles.

Long before Nixon and Kissinger made the use of secret "back channels" almost standard procedure, it had been a habit for Japanese Prime Ministers to resort to them in sensitive dealings with the United States. Sato now did so, designating as his secret emissary a young Japanese scholar whom Kissinger already knew. The link had one striking difference from the Dobrynin and Egon Bahr channels: in this case Kissinger, surely on Nixon's orders, not only told top officials in State and Commerce about it but consulted with both—most of the time. Still, all the threads ran through Kissinger's office, and he did not again set up or recommend any return to the overall NSC evaluation of the spring. This new back channel lent itself readily to the exercise of the deliberate "linkage" so dear to Nixon and Kissinger.

It is not clear who came up with the idea of using an American concession on the Okinawa nuclear storage issue to get a better textile deal, but in early November, Kissinger made such a link clear to the secret emissary at a meeting in Washington.[137] The message was that the abandoning of nuclear storage on Okinawa would be decided after Sato's arrival, so that it would be "his achievement." At the same time, Kissinger presented a detailed formula for limiting Japanese textile exports to the United States. Within a few days, the emissary reported from Tokyo that "the proposed limitations would be acceptable." The deal seemed set and ready for conclusion when Sato and Nixon met.[138]

The Japanese-American summit that ended on November 21 seemed on its face a complete success. In their parting remarks, Nixon said, "A new era begins between the United States and Japan, in our relations not only bilaterally in the Pacific but in the world." And Sato's thank-you letter concluded that the two nations' "mutually cooperative relationship" would rest "upon a far stronger foundation than ever before." Public statements were made that met the Japanese requirement of a "home islands, nuclear-free" status for Okinawa after reversion was completed, and at the same time, the earlier tacit understanding that nuclear weapons could be brought in to deal with a real crisis were left in place. Sato, in a speech to the Press Club in Washington, suggested that the United States could be sure of Japan's consent and approval for use of the bases to support conventional force actions in defense of Korea or Taiwan, which he mentioned as security concerns for Japan itself. This could only be Sato's personal undertaking, but given his strong standing at home and that of the Liberal Democratic regime generally, it carried weight in a situation where a formal or treaty-type commitment would surely have aroused divisive and weakening debate in Japan.[139]

It was a statesmanlike outcome over Okinawa. Working from foundations planned under Kennedy and laid firmly in place by Johnson, Nixon had brought off smoothly — though barely in time — an essential readjustment of the U.S. position in Northeast Asia. With pardonable hyperbole he called it in his first Foreign Policy Report "among the most important foreign policy decisions I have taken as President."[140]

In Japan, the political effect was totally favorable. Diet elections in December 1969 gave the Liberal Democrats a significantly greater majority. Substantial U.S. forces remained in Japan, primarily for its defense, and over time Japan increased its contribution to their expenses.

One cannot leave this subject without noting a curious episode in the meetings between Nixon and Sato. At some point when discussing nuclear weapons storage on Okinawa, Nixon and Kissinger broadly hinted that the United States would "understand" if Japan itself decided to acquire a nuclear weapons capability.[141] Putting out such a feeler was consistent with Nixon's past fretting over Japan's not being a strategic factor, as well as his and Kissinger's strong approval of France's nuclear capability and of national nuclear capabilities generally. Yet such a U.S. position would have been an astounding reversal of all postwar policy toward Japan, as embodied notably in Article 9 of the Japanese Constitution; it would have run up against the very strong opposition in Japanese public opinion to nuclear weapons; and the reaction elsewhere in Asia, especially China, to any suggestion that Japan was even considering "going nuclear" would have been of earthquake proportions.

It certainly appeared extremely risky to State Department officials in Tokyo, to whom the experienced American interpreter confided what his notes recorded. Richard Sneider, deputy to the ambassador, then learned from Japanese officials that they knew of the remark and that it had left Sato and others confused. So Sneider acted. In his words:

> We had to go cleaning up the mess and had to tell the Japanese they'd misunderstood what Nixon and Kissinger were saying. We just quietly sabotaged the whole thing.[142]

In the end, whatever was said or hinted was never brought up again, so far as the record shows, and one may assume that the episode had no effect on U.S.-Japanese relations or on Japanese policy. But it shows the tendency in Nixon and Kissinger to see Japan as not pulling its weight militarily, as well as their bland attitude toward the spread of nuclear capabilities.

All in all, the negotiations over Okinawa reversion were a clear success. Unfortunately, the opposite was true on the textile front. Behind the scenes, and carefully concealed during the Japanese election campaign, the textile problem hit a serious snag during the summit meeting. Two days before the summit started, the secret emissary gave Kissinger a frantic message that Sato could not after all go through with a firm textile deal. He did not spell out the reasons, but apparently Sato's soundings among his ministers, notably in MITI, had discovered a degree of opposition and predicted public outcry that he simply could not deal with at the time. Both sides concluded that the way needed to be prepared and the matter finally handled through regular negotiations in Geneva. He and Kissinger then agreed on a plan: the United States would take an extremely harsh position in Geneva, after which Sato could instruct the Japanese negotiators in Geneva to come up with the privately agreed terms as a Japanese proposal, thus saving face and showing results.

Here one might digress at some length, as Kissinger does in his memoirs, on the collegial or consensus style of decision making in postwar Japan. Over and over, on matters of all sorts, American diplomats encountered extreme difficulty in getting categorical commitments or statements of position from Japanese representatives, and had to wait for a time, even when clear agreement seemed to have been reached, so that the Japanese could get all interested parties in line. Unfortunately, Kissinger was a little late in understanding this basic fact of Japanese organizational behavior. It seems at first glance more surprising that Nixon, surely calling the shots at this point, did not.

Japanese customs aside, linking the reversion of Okinawa, an intensely emotional subject in Japan and one on which Sato simply could not afford to fail, with a secret trade deal was an extraordinarily tricky and risky undertaking in the best of times, doubly so in the atmosphere that Stans had left behind him in Japan. All accounts agree that at their November 20 meeting Nixon stated his "concession" on nuclear storage in Okinawa, and Sato responded with a statement on textiles that Nixon (and others present) took to be a firm commitment to settle the matter. Sato knew that Nixon understood the exchange in this sense, and both expected it to be carried through at Geneva not later than early 1970.[143] However, when Alexis Johnson tried to play out the agreed-on scenario with Ambassador Takeso Shimoda, who was personally close to Sato, the expected compromise proposal from the Japanese side never materialized.[144]

Why did Sato pull back? The most careful study available in English concludes that a key factor was that he felt unable to inform anyone, including his friend Shimoda, of the plan he had worked out with Kissinger.[145] Without such an explanation, his pressures could be resisted by MITI (doubly by the textile industry). Yet he could not explain without arousing even greater criticism and without risking a leak to an already suspicious public that indeed there was a direct link with Okinawa. Why was he put in this position by Nixon? Here the last word belongs to Kissinger, whose criticisms of Nixon in his memoirs were seldom so explicit: "It could be said that the basic mistake was Nixon's campaign pledge of 1968, which cost too high a price in terms of our foreign policy objectives."[146]

On the U.S. side too, secrecy was a handicap. Though the deal was more favorable to the United States than many might have expected, any revelation that it had come via Sato personally would have been so destructive in Japan that Kissinger could not inform either Stans or the negotiators in Geneva, although both eventually suspected what had happened. Thus, the textile negotiations ran into a swamp, with successive failures in mid-1970 and the spring of 1971 before the issue was finally resolved, under strong American pressure, in the fall of 1971. In the intervening period, it cast a dark cloud over the whole official U.S.-Japan relationship. Nixon in particular felt he had been double-crossed and harbored a grudge against Japan and especially the Sato government.

Chapter Three

1970: A Troubled Year

1. *The Cambodian Incursion*

In January 1970 a new North Vietnamese offensive in north-central Laos threatened to produce not only greatly expanded Communist territorial control but the crippling of the Meo forces, who were by now bearing the brunt of the fighting on the non-Communist side.[1] The headquarters of their leader, General Vang Pao, were at Long Thieng, southwest of the Plaine des Jarres, with a substantial airfield hacked from the jungle. This had become the real center for the defense of the core areas of Laos, including the political capital at Vientiane and the royal capital at Luang Prabang to the northwest. Long Thieng was also the focal point for American "covert" support provided to the Meo (or Hmong) by CIA and economic aid personnel, with large-scale contract air transport.

After six years of constant threats and back-and-forth fighting, this improvised defense was still holding up. The key figures in the country remained, as since 1961, Prime Minister Souvanna Phouma, General Vang Pao, and the American Ambassador, who was in effect the U.S. commander. Succeeding William Sullivan in that post in July 1969 was the equally forceful, durable, and decisive McMurtrie Godley, a veteran of other confused conflicts in Congo and Lebanon. Offstage, the main source of air firepower was the U.S. Seventh Air Force, headquartered in Saigon but with its main bases increasingly in Thailand. The defense of Laos worked with remarkable smoothness and resourcefulness. But the effort was at the end of a long line from Washington, Honolulu, and Saigon, and it was under attack at home, where Senator Stuart Symington's charges of a "secret war" had brought the issue to the attention of the media and the Senate.

When the new North Vietnamese offensive got under way, Ambassador Godley cabled a request for B-52 strikes against the buildup area at the eastern end of the Plaine des Jarres. Kissinger was in favor, as was Laird, but Rogers was opposed and Nixon distracted by a dispute with Congress over domestic policy. No action was taken, though all hands were on alert when the offensive exploded on February 12 in the form of a tank-led night attack on the western side of the Plaine des Jarres.[2] The first attack was beaten back, by the Meo particularly, but the situation remained desperate, and on February 13 Souvanna Phouma requested B-52 strikes.[3] These now began on a large scale and were to continue for the next three years.[4] The force of the B-52 operations was terrifying. Without any warning or sighting, each flight of three B-52s could carve out a "box" half a mile square, inflicting almost total destruction. At one moment, calm and peace; at the next, devastation.[5]

Yet even the B-52s could not initially contain the North Vietnamese offensive, and on February 21 Vang Pao gave the order to abandon the Plaine des Jarres and an important forward base there. Predictably, the first B-52 strike was publicized in America, triggering protests from antiwar senators such as Mansfield and precipitating once again the issue of disclosure of Laos operations as a whole.

On Kissinger's recommendation, President Nixon now decided to issue a public statement describing U.S. activities in Laos. In the new situation, Souvanna Phouma gave his reluctant consent. Nixon mentioned ground operations in north-central Laos in general terms, but not the occasional scouting operations in eastern Laos. Nor did he give any idea of the scale of the B-52 strikes in the north-central combat area. Moreover, his statement, prepared by Kissinger's staff, also included a claim that no Americans had been killed in Laos. In fact, about fifty civilians and U.S. military personnel had died in the core areas of Laos, and other military personnel had been lost in secret operations against the Ho Chi Minh Trail. The Defense Department, which had prepared an accurate statement, had to issue a correction, and Nixon's remarks became more suspect than they deserved. It was the kind of error invited by the self-sufficient style of the NSC staff under Kissinger—and a reflection of how little it had followed events in Laos.[6]

The result for informed American opinion was well summarized by a writer covering the war in Laos:

> After years of being overlooked, the secret war in Laos exploded in the U.S. media. . . . Instead of shedding light, the emerging information, often

fragmentary and distorted, bred doubt and fueled the growing domestic voice against the war in Southeast Asia.[7]

In the field, the B-52s were effective in at least slowing the Communist advance. The outnumbered Meo stood and fought, with considerable tactical air support. C-47s of World War II vintage did what helicopter gunships were doing in Vietnam, and light Cessna "Ravens," piloted by Americans from Thailand, served as spotters for air strikes.[8] Yet the North Vietnamese kept coming and by mid-March were threatening Long Thieng.

At this point the government of Thailand, in real alarm, offered to send substantial Thai contingents, under light cover, to aid in the defense of Long Thieng, if Souvanna requested them—as he promptly did. With formal requests in hand from both the Thai and Lao governments, Nixon, again on Kissinger's recommendation, overruled a negative State Department position as well as Pentagon/CIA misgivings and decided to accept this offer. Thai forces did help to drive the North Vietnamese back from a key airfield, and the crisis subsided by early April. The most serious North Vietnamese offensive of the war in Laos had been beaten back. Northern Laos was stabilized for the rest of the 1970 dry season and most of 1971.

· · ·

At this point, attention of the government and media alike shifted to Cambodia. The decisions Nixon had faced in Laos had been difficult but relatively straightforward. U.S. policy was based, as in the past, on a solid relationship with the government and with the Hmong tribesmen, good intelligence, and the ability to bring effective military resources to bear. Not one of these conditions existed in Cambodia. American officials had been kept at arm's length throughout Prince Sihanouk's long rule, then removed entirely when he broke relations with the United States in 1964; there remained almost no one with any "feel" for Cambodia—politically or, for that matter, geographically. A few officers in State, Defense, and CIA kept a watch on what was happening in Phnom Penh, while in Saigon the embassy and military command focused on the border sanctuaries and the sea supply line through the port of Sihanoukville, in southwestern Cambodia. In short, the fog of war that shrouded many U.S. decisions throughout the Indochina wars was especially dense in respect to Cambodia.[9]

Lacking respected sources of information, the policymakers of the Nixon Administration readily judged key Cambodians in terms of simplified labels, as "good guys" or "bad guys"; assessed military forces as though they resembled those in more advanced countries; had little sense of the historic animosity between Cambodians and Vietnamese; and misread the relationships on the Communist side, especially the degree of independence of Khmer Communists.

Still staunchly neutral, Prince Sihanouk was nonetheless trying to have a limited relationship with the United States as a possible protector if North Vietnam became sharply aggressive. In 1969 he had deliberately muted his comments about the B-52 bombing of areas just inside eastern Cambodia, which were surely known to him and senior members of his government.[10] At the same time he tried not to provoke or antagonize North Vietnam and raised no audible objection to the steady expansion of its military presence and use of base areas along Cambodia's eastern border. Moreover, he remained tolerant of the Sihanoukville sea supply route. (Sihanoukville was later renamed Kompong Som.) Set up initially in 1966 at the personal request of Chinese Premier Zhou Enlai, this carried Chinese military supplies, some to the makeshift Cambodian armed forces, but most taken through Cambodia by truck to the South Vietnamese border near the Mekong, to supply the Vietcong forces in the Delta area. China, in constant rivalry with the Soviet Union for credit, was trying to demonstrate that it was effectively helping both North Vietnam and Cambodia. In allowing these operations, Sihanouk was storing up credit with the Chinese, who might intervene on his behalf if the North Vietnamese became really nasty.[11]

The prince's intricate balancing act became steadily more difficult, with North Vietnamese forces in the border areas more numerous and assertive and the secret American bombing program in eastern Cambodia more intense. In fifteen months, it included 3,600 sorties by the B-52 bombers, with more than 100,000 tons of bombs dropped. Although it never succeeded in knocking out the elusive Communist headquarters, it probably did considerable damage to individual small bases and weapons storage areas. North Vietnamese forces and bases gradually moved further west, thus into increased contact with the fledgling Cambodian Army.

Tempers were fraying in Phnom Penh. The North Vietnamese presence was more and more disturbing, anti-Vietnamese sentiment simmered, and within the political establishment an undercurrent increased of criticism and opposition directed at Sihanouk, which he either ignored or badly misjudged. This opposition — rightist, anti-Vietnamese, and anti-Communist — centered on General Lon Nol, since 1955 commander of Cambodia's armed forces, occasionally installed as titular Prime Minister and always closely under Sihanouk's control. In August 1969, Sihanouk had been persuaded or pressured to bring him back again as Prime Minister. With him came Prince Sesawath Sirik Matak, whose family had in the late 1940s lost out to Sihanouk's in a rivalry for the royal succession, but who remained an important political figure, competent and respected, also well known to Americans.

As Prime Minister, Lon Nol became more assertive in military operations, but with an army of only 35,000, ill equipped and totally inexperienced, his efforts were more provocative than effective against the roughly 40,000 Vietnamese Communist forces (Vietcong and North Vietnamese regulars) operating within Cambodia by early 1970.

In short, both sides were increasing their efforts and Cambodia's political structure was starting to rock perceptibly. North Vietnam and the Communist forces it controlled were the original and major violators of Cambodian neutrality, but the United States, too, was upsetting the balance, especially with its B-52 bombings.

When Prince Sihanouk left Phnom Penh in January 1970 for his customary two-month vacation in France, intending then to travel to Moscow and Beijing to appeal for support in getting North Vietnam to reduce its presence, the political pot boiled over. In early March, after a series of anti-Vietnamese riots stimulated by Lon Nol, his argument that a firmer hand was needed persuaded the elite Assembly to oust Sihanouk and vote Lon Nol into supreme power. He became Cambodia's autocratic ruler, with a pliant Assembly and with Sirik Matak and the chairman of the Assembly, Cheng Heng, as his closest colleagues. While there were strong reasons for a rightist coup at this time, there is bound to be a question whether there was a more specific U.S. role than the boat rocking just described. Was Kissinger's repeated claim, "We neither encouraged Sihanouk's overthrow nor knew about it in advance," accurate and candid?[12]

In the main, yes. But U.S. behavior had made Lon Nol and his associates confident that they would have U.S. support if they took power. One factor was the long-standing tie between the United States and a strongly anti-Sihanouk political figure, Son Ngoc Thanh, whose Khmer Serei organization in Cambodia had in the 1950s sought to depose Sihanouk, then moved to South Vietnam, where with substantial CIA help he organized ethnic Khmer to fight and work on the government side. There is no persuasive evidence that the CIA encouraged him to act against Sihanouk in 1970, but the fact that a tie persisted could hardly have failed to impress Lon Nol and political circles in Phnom Penh.[13]

At least equally important, surely, was the reaction to the American B-52 bombing from the people in Phnom Penh who fomented or accepted the coup. This is hard to pin down: few of the relevant people survived the war, and the skeleton U.S. mission was ignorant of the bombing. But it takes little imagination to conclude that word of the bombing reached this small political circle, and that its effect was increased by the secrecy and by the particularly frightening nature of B-52 operations. In South Vietnam and Laos, the governments had known what was happening; in Cambodia no one knew in advance. The shock effect must have been great, and with it the sense that if the Americans would do this much, they must be ready to do more. Thus the secret B-52 bombing was probably the clincher. There can be no doubt that Lon Nol followed American reactions closely, and that the signals he got from Washington were not cautionary or discouraging, but the reverse.

Although the demonstrations leading up to the coup should have warned Sihanouk, who was then in Paris, he stalled for precious days. When the coup came he was in Moscow, where he got only perfunctory support. He then flew to Beijing, where he destroyed any hope of a peaceful return to his country by announcing on March 23 that he was joining forces with the Khmer Communists in a new National United Front, of which he would be the head. Premier Pham Van Dong of North Vietnam was present in Beijing at the time, and although the two apparently never met, the effect was to align Sihanouk firmly not only with Cambodia's Communists, whose movement he himself had christened the Khmer Rouge, and with the Chinese, but also with a new working relationship to the long-hated North Vietnamese. Stung by his repudiation at the hands of his former colleagues and the people he had regarded almost as his children, the prince acted impetuously, cutting himself off from old ties and putting himself in the wrong in the eyes of nationalist Cambodians.

Lon Nol's first statements after the coup reaffirmed the nation's neutrality, but in the border areas the skirmishing between Cambodian and North Vietnamese forces rose to the level of small battles. In Phnom Penh and other cities, where the half million ethnic Vietnamese living in Cambodia were concentrated, harassment of Vietnamese civilians began; by April the authorities had condoned at least one substantial massacre.

At this point Cambodia's traditional patron, France, proposed that a new international conference on the lines of the Geneva Conference of 1954 be convened. Secretary Laird and Assistant Secretary Green in State favored this, but the White House declined to give public support and, with no response from Lon Nol, the effort never got off the ground. Conciliatory noises from the United Nations were also ignored. Though either route toward peace would surely have been vague and unlikely to bear fruit for some time, if ever, the rejection showed which way the wind was blowing in both Washington and Phnom Penh.[14]

There was also an early and apparently serious effort by the Chinese to patch things up with Lon Nol. In return for showing renewed and strengthened respect for Cambodia's neutrality, the Chinese proposed that Lon Nol reaffirm Sihanouk's policy of tolerating some military activity in the border areas, of allowing the sea shipment route through Sihanoukville to operate, and of issuing occasional statements in support of Hanoi's position in South Vietnam.[15] Conceivably Lon Nol might have improved these terms if he had entered into serious negotiations, but he gave them short shrift. The rejection was another step toward military confrontation, while confirming China's enduring hostility to his regime. China's best bet for the future was bound to be strong support for the Khmer Rouge, always preferable to total North Vietnamese control of Cambodia.

By April, then, Lon Nol was aligned solidly against both the North Vietnamese and the Chinese; the fact that the Soviet Union did not break relations was little help to him in power terms. Thieu and the Saigon regime acted to support him, and South Vietnamese forces shortly moved into the Parrot's Beak area of Cambodia (only thirty-five miles from Saigon at its nearest point), where they fought minor pitched battles with the steadily increasing Communist forces.

In Washington, two contrasting attitudes emerged. Rogers and Laird urged caution and diplomacy to get a formal reaffirmation of Cambodian neutrality. Assistant Secretary Green wrote memoranda arguing that a return by Lon Nol to Sihanouk's policies was his best, or least bad, course in the new situation; that active U.S. intervention in Cambodia must inevitably mean a continuing U.S. responsibility to sustain the new government; and that this could not be fulfilled without a large deployment of U.S. forces there, which was politically impossible. Almost all the civilians in the government who knew about East Asia, including those on the NSC staff, broadly agreed.[16]

On the other hand, military leaders, especially in Saigon and Honolulu, were inclined from a very early point to favor active U.S. military intervention. Kissinger's deputy, Alexander Haig (by then a brigadier general), was from the start an ardent interventionist. To the many officers familiar with the secret bombing—as only a handful of civilians were—a limited incursion must have seemed only a small added step that would help to keep the North Vietnamese off balance and thus assist the withdrawal and Vietnamization programs.

On March 30, apparently on his own, General Abrams met with Thieu to persuade him to cease unilateral cross-border operations into Cambodia, arguing that the effort should be to help Lon Nol get the North Vietnamese and Vietcong forces out of the country, but that "this did not mean expanding the war, which could be a risky business." A day later, Abrams got a message from the Joint Chiefs that "higher authority" (the standard label for the White House) wanted a fleshed-out plan for operations in Cambodia, a request that was renewed and reinforced about April 20. Abrams, along with Ambassador Bunker, responded positively: attacks into the Cambodian sanctuaries were "the military move to make at this time . . . both in terms of the security of our own forces and for advancement of the Vietnamization program."[17] This sequence suggests that the military, whose recommendations along these lines had repeatedly been rejected ever since U.S. troops were committed in 1965, at first anticipated more of the same but changed when Nixon's inclination to intervene became evident. Certainly there was accumulated frustration aplenty, especially in Saigon. And in Washington, though Secretaries Laird and Rogers argued against an incursion largely on the ground that it would set off a storm at home, military leaders were never apparently asked whether their views would change if public uproar or some other factor were to mean that U.S. forces would have to be withdrawn promptly and could not be sent back.[18]

Nixon once again kept all the threads in his own hands, consulting frankly only with Kissinger, Haig, and perhaps John Mitchell. In mid-April the Washington Special Actions Group (WSAG) held inconclusive discussions, but from then on the President talked seriously only with General Abrams and Admiral John McCain, the Pacific commander in Hawaii. Even the Joint Chiefs of Staff were unsure how far he was ready to go. As always, he hated confrontation or adversary discussion in his presence, and was content to leave Rogers and Laird in the dark until he had reached a decision.[19]

In mid-April, Lon Nol abandoned the formal neutrality he had proclaimed as he took power, declared himself ready to take on the North Vietnamese, and appealed publicly for outside help from any quarter. Only White House records will show whether Nixon encouraged him to take this stand; probably he had not yet made up his mind.

By this time there was a visible outpouring of popular support for Lon Nol within Cambodia, anti-Vietnamese as much as it was anti-Communist. Some 60,000 volunteers rushed to join the Army and were given rudimentary training in the outskirts of Phnom Penh. As a gesture that surely aroused further expectations, Nixon covertly sent a small consignment of military equipment from CIA stocks.

For the next few days all eyes in America were focused on a near-fatal mishap to a space mission, Apollo 13. When the astronauts eventually came down safely in the mid-Pacific, Nixon was on hand to welcome them back, and took the occasion to stop off in Honolulu to see Admiral John McCain, who, as Commander in Chief, Pacific (CINCPAC), was the nominal theater commander in Southeast Asia (although his role in the war was usually secondary to that of the Saigon command). McCain was an appealing and persuasive figure, the more so as his son (later to become a U.S. senator), a Navy aviator, had been taken prisoner in 1965 and was being held in North Vietnam.

On this occasion, the admiral's staff briefed Nixon in dramatic terms, with lots of "big red arrows," as one observer put it, pointing to Phnom Penh and beyond if the North Vietnamese forces were not checked at once—which could only mean by U.S. forces. It was a far more drastic reading of the situation than was held even in the Pentagon, let alone by Washington intelligence offices. These thought the North Vietnamese were trying to hold their positions in the border areas but not to expand hostilities or overthrow Lon Nol by force—in line with the long-held judgment that

Laos and Cambodia were targets for conquest but only after South Vietnam had been dealt with, so long as neither became a threat in Vietnam.[20]

When Nixon returned to Washington on April 20, he delivered a nationwide TV speech centered on the announcement that a further 150,000 U.S. troops would be withdrawn from Vietnam over the next year. He gave an upbeat picture of progress in the South and noted that the government was watching developments in Cambodia closely and was prepared to react if these threatened the withdrawal program. The public could only be confirmed in believing that the President was still on the course he had spelled out in November.[21]

Over the next ten days, North Vietnamese forces made further attacks in the border areas, and there were reports of military clashes not far from Phnom Penh. Although almost all these reports came from Cambodian sources unverified by any U.S. observer, Nixon's resolve hardened, and he elicited from Abrams a judgment that North Vietnam was indeed threatening the capital. There was no indication that any Washington agency, privy to the same reports and intelligence, shared this view. Richard Helms, CIA Director, went no further than to judge that Hanoi hoped to create so much insecurity in the base areas that the Cambodian government would collapse.[22]

On April 27, Rogers testified before the Senate Foreign Relations Committee, where discussion centered on whether the United States should respond to Lon Nol's appeal for military aid. Sentiment in the committee opposed even this action, and several members, led by the Republican John Sherman Cooper of Kentucky and the Democrat Frank Church of Idaho, stated not only their strong opposition to expanding the war but their resolve, if this happened, to push hard for congressional action denying funds for operations in Cambodia.

The Administration's consultation with members of Congress was at most slight and vague. By Kissinger's account, he met with Senator John Stennis on April 24, at the President's order, indicating that "a U.S.-supported incursion into Cambodia was a military necessity if Vietnamization were to proceed." By prearrangement Nixon phoned Stennis during the conversation, and Stennis told him he would support such action. However, he probably did not think the phrase "U.S.-supported" (Kissinger's careful language) meant that U.S. combat units would participate, an issue not then decided.[23] Nixon was clearly dead set against giving any kind of notice to potential critics. There was no consultation with any member of the Senate Foreign Relations Committee or with any member of the House.

In the Administration's deliberations, the original proposal had called only for a South Vietnamese operation into the Parrot's Beak area. However, after exchanges with Saigon that were almost bound to elicit the judgment that these would not suffice and that only U.S. forces could do enough, the plans were expanded to include a predominantly U.S. incursion about twenty miles farther north, in the area known as the Fish Hook, thought to be the location of the headquarters from which the war in most of South Vietnam was directed.

Worked up to a high emotional pitch, and fortified by almost nightly private showings of a film about the swashbuckling World War II hero General George Patton, Nixon made up his mind tentatively about April 22, then firmly on April 26, to go all the way and include the operation by U.S. forces. On April 28 he told Rogers and Laird. According to John Mitchell's record of the meeting, he also told them that Kissinger was "leaning against" the operation, which Kissinger in his later memoirs denied, saying he had become firm a week earlier in favor of U.S. intervention.[24]

On April 29 the South Vietnamese operation was launched, and on the evening of April 30 Nixon went on national TV to announce his decision to send a U.S. force of 32,000 men into Cambodia. Drafted by Patrick Buchanan of the White House speechwriting staff (later to become a prominent rightist Republican candidate for the presidency in 1992 and 1996), and then reworked for hours by Nixon himself, the speech described the situation and the challenge in the most dramatic terms possible, asserting at its close that failure to respond would reveal the United States as a "pitiful helpless giant," and suggesting in another passage that the United States would be reduced to the status of a second-rate power. Such claims obscured the serious argument that disrupting the sanctuaries could help Vietnamization and American withdrawals in South Vietnam.

Along the way, the President also defended on grounds of military security his not fully consulting with Congress. And, in claiming that American policy until then had been "to scrupulously respect the neutrality of the Cambodian people," Nixon added an important lie. Many among those in the know cringed at this statement, as well as at his exaggerated description of the operation's scope and purpose.[25]

In its emotionalism and divisiveness, this speech of April 30 may have been the most extraordinary presidential speech in a generation, giving to the incursion into Cambodia a far more lurid and drastic coloring than it warranted. As the ever loyal William Safire, a Nixon speechwriter, put it later:

> Nixon had done what only Nixon could do—made a courageous decision and wrapped it in a pious and divisive speech. Appealing effectively to the "silent majority" the President had galvanized the previous November, its tone at the same time outraged the anti-war movement (which had subsided considerably by April) and above all repelled a great many in the large segment of centrist informed opinion that had up to then been giving Nixon support for his announced Vietnam policy.[26]

In the days that followed, President Nixon again and again gave evidence of an extreme emotional state. In the early morning of May 5, on the spur of the moment and taking virtually no one with him, he went to the Lincoln Memorial to mingle and talk with groups of youthful protesters. His whole behavior testified to the degree to which this was his personal decision.

What drove him to it seems clear. Always inclined to take strong military action if it offered any hope of positive results, and to support anti-Communist leaders in almost any setting, he was smarting still from his own failure to move Hanoi or Moscow with his drastic threats in 1969. The Cambodian crisis offered an opportunity to show that he could act decisively and effectively. Cambodia was overwhelmingly his show.[27]

. . .

The jointly executed U.S.-Vietnamese incursion into Cambodia went off smoothly, though South Vietnamese forces encountered some significant resistance. U.S. forces were able to comb a long stretch of the border area and unearth several caches of supplies, duly assembled and portrayed dramatically to Western media. However, the elusive Communist "command center" (COSVN) had moved westward just before the incursion, possibly warned by a night-before B-52 attack in the area. The American intelligence picture of COSVN as a large headquarters, possibly underground and staffed with hundreds of men, was eventually shown to be an illusion. More likely, as some already surmised, it was never more than a handful of communicators with their equipment in a few trucks, attached to a commander with a small staff.[28]

But the border area was, for the moment, cleaned out, and the captured supplies added up to an apparently impressive tonnage. Claims were made that ammunition losses could not be replaced for more than a year, and that the operation had taken the pressure off Lon Nol and sharply reduced the possibility that the sea supply route through Sihanoukville (now renamed Kompong Som) might be revived. (Documents were captured indicating that the past flow of supplies through that sea route had been higher than the CIA had estimated.) In all, a strong impression of overall success was conveyed to the general public. Many were doubtless persuaded that the effect of the operation had been to distract and delay, if not cripple, North Vietnamese plans for an offensive in South Vietnam. As often in the Johnson presidency, strong action of any sort, whether by way of escalation or toward peace, tended to produce an upward "spike" in public support. Nixon's overall approval rating in the Gallup polls, at 53 percent in March, rose by late May to 59 percent.[29]

The reaction among young people and in the media was a different story. Long before success or failure could be assessed, the Cambodian incursion set off a firestorm of protest within the United States, with university campuses the scene of extraordinary demonstrations. Editorials in many newspapers and on television were also sharply critical; key senators protested. These reactions doubtless owed some of their vehemence to the harsh and extreme tone of Nixon's rhetoric. On May 1 he visited the Pentagon and in an aside referred to the demonstrating students as "bums." Then, when on May 4 National Guard troops, called out to deal with demonstrations at Kent State University in Ohio (far from the Ivy League institutions Nixon detested), fired on the students and killed four, including two women, a White House statement failed to express sympathy for the fallen and bereaved and maintained a combative tone. The White House itself was besieged by demonstrators, and in several cities antiwar protesters clashed with "hard-hat" labor supporters of Nixon.

In the Senate, a major move to cut off funds for operations within Cambodia got under way at once, as Senator Cooper had warned, with the threat that it might shortly extend to all Vietnam-related operations. Nixon knew that he retained strong support in the House, so that no immediate cutoff of funds was likely to pass Congress. Yet the demonstrations and clamor unquestionably got to him. In a word, Nixon caved. In his speech he had said that troops would withdraw once the North Vietnamese bases and supplies in Cambodia were dealt with, though those familiar with Southeast Asia knew that the onset of the monsoon season would in any event sharply limit ground operations in Cambodia after about six weeks. Yet when in a press conference on May 8 he pledged categorically that U.S. ground forces would be completely out by June 30 and were not going further than twenty-one miles into Cambodia, it was clear that he was yielding to the pressure of articulate opinion, the very thing he had often said—emotionally in the April 30 speech itself—he would never do.

This apparent retreat distressed his supporters, and Lon Nol especially. The American military were dismayed to learn that the operation would only be a one-shot job, sharply limited in scope and without follow-up, which suggests that their recommendations to charge ahead had been made with little awareness of what might happen on the home front. If so, it was far from the first time during the Vietnam War that such a misunderstanding occurred. Books could be written on the missed communication between military leaders and their Commander in Chief in situations where political clamor, actual or anticipated, limited what Presidents were prepared to accept in the follow-through phase.

As for Lon Nol, who had never been consulted about the operation, what must have been an initial surge of hope and optimism gave way quickly to deep concern and uncertainty. Nixon's response was to send Alexander Haig to Phnom Penh to explain the immediate decisions, but also to carry the bad news that the United States did not plan to give large-scale aid, although it would continue to help by air bombing. The two military men got along, and Haig became the key man in a program of periodic reassurance in which Vice President Agnew also became prominent.

Twenty years later, as perhaps on other less public occasions, Nixon told a British audience that he should have resisted the pressure and carried on in Cambodia. This was latter-day bravado, pure and simple. In 1970 he judged rightly that to hold his ground would lead to continuing harsh disorder, with most informed opinion arrayed against him. As in many other circumstances, Nixon simply could not take this degree of heat. As the prominent columnist Stewart Alsop, generally not unsympathetic to the President, said on several occasions, in the face of public clamor Nixon was often only "semitough."[30]

Was the operation nonetheless a military success? A sympathetic biographer of Nixon has said "that the Cambodian incursion was militarily somewhere between a half-success and a half-failure, but that the political price at home was too costly." Was it in fact even the "half-success" that might have made the decision understandable, even if on balance unwise for domestic reasons?[31]

Visiting South Vietnam at Nixon's request five months after the incursion, Sir Robert Thompson reported that the operation had greatly strengthened the situation in South Vietnam and weakened the Communist side. Noting a sharp drop in weekly American casualties after the incursion, and the closing down of the Sihanoukville supply route, he thought the losses in bases and stocks could not be made up for two years, and that any major Communist offensive would be delayed this long, giving both South Vietnam and Cambodia precious time to prepare.[32] His report was based largely on information supplied by the military command in Saigon (MACV). After the war, he still considered the operation "one of America's truly effective acts."[33]

When Thompson conveyed his conclusions to Kissinger in 1970, however, the latter responded that "everyone" in the Pentagon, State Department, and CIA was telling him that the incursion had only cost the Communists three months! In fact, the Pentagon's civilian research office (Systems Analysis) concluded in August that captured supplies could be reconstituted in about seventy-five days. Others noted that the drop in U.S. casualties came largely from reduced operations, especially offensive ones, as well as from the seasonal decline in hostile contact during the monsoon season. It was also noted that North Vietnamese capabilities within Cambodia itself had not been "substantially reduced."[34]

Probably the most balanced contemporary assessment was that of a CIA draft national intelligence estimate completed at the end of June, just as U.S. forces were being withdrawn from Cambodia. It found that:

- The Communists suffered "a tactical upset," considerable disruption of their supply routes, and dispersal of their forces, but their situation was "by no means critical."
- The claimed Communist manpower losses of 10,000–12,000 were almost certainly exaggerated and in any event could be rapidly made up from replacements.
- The 9,300 tons of Communist supplies captured included 2,000-plus tons of weapons and 317 tons of ammunition; the rest was food. Few of the weapons were new, but the ammunition losses were serious. (Later information showed that the arms were mostly turned over to the South Vietnamese, who in turn offered them to the Cambodian Army, which rejected them!)

Most strikingly, the estimate queried whether the disruption of base areas could continue without U.S. ground action, noting that the supply losses were far less than could readily be moved down via the Ho Chi Minh Trail. Within Cambodia the Communist forces not only were still present in force in the eastern border areas, but had pushed westward to control for the first time a wide area in central and northern Cambodia, all the way to the Mekong River, as well as important rice-producing areas.

The estimate also noted that Hanoi must be well aware of the American uproar and especially of Nixon's pledges of withdrawal, so that they could be expected to resume their former control of supply lines and bases. All in all, "the tactical problems facing the Communists are unlikely to be critical, while the strategic opportunities presented to them could seriously undermine the Allied position and policies in Indochina."[35]

In all this, the key point was that the North Vietnamese were not driven from the sanctuaries. On the contrary, as the incursion ended in late June, their forces controlled not only the northeastern provinces they had effectively occupied for some time but almost all of northern Cambodia. Along the border with South Vietnam, Communist forces were again free to move almost at will, and had to deal only with limited South Vietnamese forces, which continued to move in, out, and around eastern Cambodia for at least another year. Unlike the forces in South Vietnam, these ARVN forces operated without American advisors, and reports through South Vietnamese channels were always notorious for exaggeration and misrepresentation.

Finally, captured invoices showed that a total of about 21,600 tons of military supplies for Communist forces in South Vietnam had come into Cambodia by sea between December 1966 and the last recorded arrival in April 1969. There had been ten substantial shipments, all in named Chinese vessels, and a possible eleventh in July 1969, with none documented or reported thereafter. Since CIA analysts had earlier estimated a total of only 6,000 tons over that same period, these larger figures were for a time treated as a major revelation showing the importance of the route. From the fair conclusion that the Agency had erred, many jumped to the additional conclusion that the sea supply route was perhaps the major channel for supplies moving from North Vietnam to the South, adding greatly to the judgment that Cambodia and the incursion were major successes for Nixon's policy.[36] But later analysis by the distinguished and impartial Vietnam scholar Douglas Pike told a different story. Using North Vietnamese official sources, surely the most reliable of all, he arrived in 1984 at a figure of 5,000 tons a year, for both the Sihanoukville route and the (much smaller) flow over beaches at the southern tip of South Vietnam.[37]

Pike also concluded that the sea route totals were always far less than those over the Ho Chi Minh Trail. This was especially true by 1970, when the North Vietnamese prepared for large-scale offensive operations. On his analysis, in 1965 the trail carried an average of 400 tons a week (20,000 tons a year), but by 1970 this had risen to more than 10,000 tons a week, or more than 500,000 tons a year! In view of the massive U.S. air operations against the trail by that time, as well as the inherent difficulties of terrain and maintenance, Pike estimated that as much as 90 percent of this tonnage may have been needed simply to sustain the trail operation. But this still left 50,000 tons a year going through to the South, ten times more than Pike's final estimate of the annual flow via Sihanoukville!

In short, the Sihanoukville route was insignificant, by no means even a major, let alone *the* major channel sometimes claimed. Finally, there is serious doubt that the Sihanoukville route was still in operation in May 1970. Pike's conclusion was that Sihanouk himself had suspended the sea route in early 1970, and even before that a joint American–South Vietnamese surveillance system had "withered" its use.[38]

In sum, just about every specific aspect of what the incursion supposedly accomplished was challenged and reduced sharply by later intelligence and assessment. Temporarily, there was indeed disruption, but, as Assistant Secretary Green had argued in March, only permanent occupation by U.S. and South Vietnamese forces could prevent the North Vietnamese from using Cambodia as a sanctuary. This fundamental point was ignored by many defenders of the incursion.[39]

By far the most serious result was the effect of the Cambodian action on the public and Congress. In his first fifteen months, Nixon enjoyed a remarkable degree of support for his policies in Indochina. After that emotional month of May 1970, a hawkish third of the public cheered, the doves were outraged, and in the middle the President lost crucial support and confidence. By allowing a new military offensive into a country that had hitherto been only marginally caught up in the war, Nixon distorted the picture he had so successfully created — of orderly U.S. withdrawal, building up the South Vietnamese and turning the war over to them — and alienated critical sectors of public and congressional opinion beyond recovery. In the words of Walter Isaacson, Kissinger's able biographer: "Despite the marginal military gains the U.S. made in Cambodia, the invasion so deepened America's domestic divisions that it destroyed the remaining prospects for a sustained policy in Southeast Asia."[40]

As we have seen, Nixon's overall approval rating actually rose from April to July. Polls about people's underlying views on U.S. withdrawal told an inconsistent story, however. In March, 46 percent favored withdrawal at once or at least by the end of 1971. By June this had risen to 48 percent, by September to 55 percent, and by January 1971 to 73 percent.[41] As had often happened in the Johnson period, once the upbeat effect of a new move wore off, the public's discouragement was greater than it would have been if the move had not been made.

Clearest of all was the effect on articulate opinion. Comment in the written press was predominantly critical, especially among those papers regarded by most of their peers as bellwethers, such as *The New York Times, The Washington Post, The Wall Street Journal,* and the *Los Angeles Times.* To Nixon, such papers were "the enemy," riddled with unthinking liberals. But these "enemies" were not the only opinion makers to become disillusioned with Nixon—he also lost the benefit of the doubt with commentators and key middle-of-the-road individuals. One striking example was Dean Acheson, whom Nixon and Kissinger had gone to great lengths to court and keep informed, and who had contributed useful ideas to the major speech Nixon had given in November 1969. Acheson had urged on Nixon a straightforward policy of withdrawal and Vietnamization and had been skeptical about the usefulness of negotiation. He opposed the Cambodian incursion totally and at once, finding it incomprehensible from any standpoint. While he never made his dissent public, he made it emphatically clear to Kissinger and doubtless to many others, and the press became aware of it.[42]

As for Congress, we have seen that key members of the Senate Foreign Relations Committee, long a center of opposition and criticism, had put Secretary Rogers on notice on April 27 that they would seek to cut off funds for any U.S. military action into Cambodia. This position was now sponsored not only by the liberal Democrat Frank Church but also by a senior and highly respected Republican, John Sherman Cooper of Kentucky, who until this point had publicly supported the war.[43] The Cooper-Church Amendment was attached to the Foreign Military Sales Bill—generally considered "must" legislation for the Administration, since it contained authority for key sales to such countries as Israel. It proposed to deny funds after June 30 not only for American ground combat forces in Cambodia but for U.S. military instructors and supporting personnel, for similar third-country personnel, and for any U.S. combat activity in Cambodia — that is, airpower.

At a strategy conference on May 15, Senator Hugh Scott, the Republican leader, reported that the amendment would command a clear-cut majority in the Senate. On the other hand, in the House only a minority even of Democrats supported it, and the House leadership and key committees were opposed. The Administration's strategy was obvious: to delay a Senate vote by further amendments and then tie up the amendment in a conference between the two chambers, while devising alternate ways to continue essential military sales on a temporary basis. The strategy succeeded. Not until June 30 was the amendment voted on, passing by a vote of 75–20. Even Republican leaders voted in favor, confident that a conference would keep the amendment bottled up. This it did, with the conference group meeting in vain through the summer and fall.[44]

Yet the Cooper-Church Amendment, and the sentiment it represented, continued to hang over the White House. In a major TV address to the nation from San Clemente on June 30, the day of final U.S. withdrawal, Nixon made a calmer and more reasoned case for the incursion. He rejected any idea of "massive" assistance to the Cambodian Army, saying that military aid would be limited to small arms and unsophisticated equipment. "To get drawn into the permanent direct defense of Cambodia" was "inconsistent with the basic premises of our foreign policy" — an apparent reference to the Nixon Doctrine. He also said that U.S. "ground personnel" would be only the regular embassy staff, there would be no U.S. advisors with Cambodian units, and air operations would be confined to interdiction of supplies relevant to the conflict in Vietnam. The "great majority" of the originally 48,000 South Vietnamese forces would be withdrawn, and their operations would be conducted without U.S. advisors or U.S. air or logistic support.

In short, even as he fought on the Hill against the Cooper-Church Amendment, Nixon in practice accepted its terms. By midsummer he gave explicit assurances that U.S. forces would not return to Cambodia under any circumstances. Senior commanders in the field deplored these restrictions. As John Lehman, the member of the NSC staff who was point man on the Hill throughout, later put it: "The impact on executive policies actually ran much deeper. It . . . narrowed the parameters of future options to be considered. Everyone was aware that ground had been yielded and public tolerance eroded."[45]

. . .

The Cooper-Church Amendment was the most prominent and Cambodia-specific Senate initiative in this period. Three other steps to rein in the executive branch were given great impetus from the Cambodian incursion. These were:

- Long-standing efforts by antiwar liberals (the Democrat George Mc-Govern and the Republican Mark Hatfield) to cut off funds for the whole Vietnam War by stated dates;
- A new effort, led initially by the moderate Republican Jacob Javits of New York, to redefine the war powers of the President and the role of the Congress; and
- An ongoing effort to repeal the Tonkin Gulf Resolution, led by moderate Republicans.

Of these, the latter two became running stories over the next three years. To understand their significance, a little background is needed.

Passed by overwhelming margins in both houses of Congress in August 1964, in the wake of apparent North Vietnamese torpedo boat attacks on U.S. destroyers patrolling in the Gulf of Tonkin, the Tonkin Gulf Resolution (TGR) authorized the President to take whatever measures were needed, including the use of force, to combat Communist aggression in Southeast Asia. Almost from the first, there was controversy over whether such a grant of authority was superfluous in light of the President's constitutional powers as Commander in Chief. Controversy also arose over whether the alleged second North Vietnamese attack, on August 4, had in fact taken place or, if it had, whether it had been provoked by U.S.-assisted South Vietnamese covert operations. Most seriously, many senators came to feel that the resolution had never been intended as an open-ended grant of authority for action on the scale that came about by 1966 and 1967. Tentative moves were made in Congress to repeal the resolution, but never pressed to a vote. Johnson himself put out feelers from time to time as to whether it should be replaced by some new grant or acknowledgment of authority, but these were never responded to. So the resolution lingered on, on the books but in limbo, referred to occasionally but never stressed by Johnson in his last year or two, or by Nixon.

In 1969, as much to tidy the situation as to cut short U.S. participation in the war, a moderate Republican senator, Charles Mathias of Maryland, moved to repeal the resolution along with three other similar resolutions (on Formosa in 1955, the Middle East in 1957, and Cuba in early October 1962). In early 1970, the Foreign Relations Committee scheduled hearings on Mathias's joint resolution. After some deliberation Nixon approved an executive branch position that it was up to Congress. The White House regarded all four resolutions as relevant principally to crisis periods long past, and in any case was not relying on the Tonkin Gulf Resolution as authority for its Vietnam policies. Testimony to this effect by Under Secretary of State Richardson in February 1970 was welcomed by Senator Fulbright, and a favorable committee report was prepared and ready for publication in early May. The Administration believed that it was Fulbright's intent to force a spectacular debate in Congress that would go far to get the United States out of Vietnam in fairly short order.[46]

The uproar over the Cambodian incursion then drowned out the committee's action, and in the momentary lull Administration strategists decided to preempt Fulbright by having the Senate Minority Leader, Robert Dole of Kansas, sponsor a repeal amendment to an appropriation bill. This was introduced in mid-June, and though it offended conservative senators who had believed the resolution was in fact the sole basis for the President's authority to carry on the war, the plan worked and the Senate voted for repeal by an overwhelming 81–10 margin, on June 22. The House, however, declined to act. Like the Cooper-Church Amendment, the issue was held over through the summer and fall for eventual decision in early 1971.

Inevitably, however, the Senate action precipitated the question of just what the legal and constitutional basis was for the President to continue carrying on the Vietnam War. In his June 30 speech Nixon had avoided this issue, but the following night, in a television interview with the three major network anchors, ABC's veteran Howard K. Smith asked him point-blank what the basis now was.

The White House staff in Washington had anticipated the question and supplied proposed answers. These would have repeated the February line, stressed historical precedent and inherent authority, and promised careful consultation with Congress. Instead, the President took the bull by the horns: "Yes, Mr. Smith, the legal justification is the one I have given, and that is the right of the President of the United States under the Constitution to protect the lives of American men. That is the legal justification." In effect he was asserting a virtually unlimited power to act so long as American forces were involved, but none if they were withdrawn. It was a response that even at the time dismayed some of his advisors and was to haunt him three years later.[47]

Nixon also argued that the Cambodian operation was not truly "escalation," as other increases in military action had been, because it was "decisive." He compared it to the Battle of Stalingrad on the Eastern Front in World War II, as a turning point that would come to be recognized as time went on.[48] It is doubtful that thoughtful listeners took this boast seriously; Nixon's position in Cambodia was less like that of the heroic Russian defenders at Stalingrad in 1942 than like the plight of the attacking Germans — overextended and increasingly difficult to sustain.

Unquestionably, the North Vietnamese were the true "invaders" of Cambodia and intended its ultimate conquest in the name of the Khmer Communists, whom they surely expected to dominate as completely as they did

the National Liberation Front in South Vietnam and the Pathet Lao in
Laos. It is difficult to imagine any sequence of events or U.S. policy in 1970
that would have offered great hope of preserving an independent and neutral Cambodia, ruled in accordance with its own traditions. Until that
spring, however, fighting on a large scale had been avoided in Cambodia:
that it came then was a direct outgrowth of the U.S.–South Vietnamese
incursion and of U.S. support and encouragement of Lon Nol. One step
led to another: the secret bombing foreshadowed the 1970 incursion, and
the incursion initiated a major U.S. support program. Successive decisions
were of a piece with the mold set in 1970.

It is not premature to put before the reader, at this point, the judgment
of one astute observer, broadly a supporter of the American effort until a
late stage in the Second Indochina War. This was the distinguished journalist and historian Robert Shaplen, who gave his reasons for concluding,
at the time, that the Cambodian venture was a grave error:

> [It was] not only because it laid waste an innocent country trying to
> survive the pressures of the Vietnamese, . . . but because the invasion was
> bound to fail in achieving its aims and would simply widen the war in
> ways that could not conceivably, in military terms alone, help the cause
> of the Americans and the South Vietnamese. . . . [I]t failed to encourage
> Vietnamization in South Vietnam, and instead heightened disillusion and
> disgust back home in the United States, thus helping pave the way for
> the American withdrawal and the North Vietnamese victory. In this sense,
> Cambodia was an Achilles heel.[49]

2. Changing Relationships

The year 1970 was one of ferment in the relationships among major
powers—China and the United States, the United States and the Soviet
Union, and (more dramatically than either) the Soviet Union and the new
government of West Germany. Let us take them up in order.

BEIJING AND WASHINGTON

With the Cambodian crisis in April 1970, the Warsaw channel went dead,
and the White House took over dealings with China entirely. Kissinger now
had the President's full confidence, while Secretary Rogers and Assistant
Secretary Green were discredited—essentially for having been right over
Cambodia, Rogers in predicting the domestic uproar, Green in pointing
out how temporary any gains would be. In mid-June, General Vernon Walters in Paris, who had already arranged the secret talks with Hanoi, was

instructed by Kissinger to convey a message to his Chinese military contact, suggesting a new channel for confidential exchanges. The Chinese contact simply eluded Walters twice during the summer. Meanwhile, Chinese actions did change—from bellicose statements and military gestures to releasing, in mid-July, Bishop James Walsh, convicted on clearly spurious charges of espionage in 1960.[50] His release coincided with the resumption of talks between the Chinese and the Soviets over the navigation rules on rivers along the Sino-Soviet border. Clearly the Chinese leadership was pondering which way to turn, and was almost certainly divided again between Zhou's moderate view and Lin Biao's hard-line position.

The Zhou-Lin struggle was partly over naked power, but basically reflected deep differences about the Soviet Union, with relations with the United States seen largely in terms of how they might affect the Soviet relationship. From long experience, Zhou feared the Soviet Union and was totally hostile to it. The Soviet buildup on the border continued—40 divisions by this time—and an eased relationship with the United States might help to deter the Soviets from renewing their 1969 threats of air attacks on Chinese nuclear installations. Zhou probably also argued that a United States still fully engaged in East Asia might help to restrain a newly powerful and always feared Japan, and that in due course trade with the United States could help the sluggish Chinese economy.[51]

Lin Biao, on the other hand, was eager to make the Sino-Soviet bond even tighter than it had been in the early 1950s. Zhou thought the United States was still a power and a balancer in Asia, but Lin Biao considered it seriously weakened and concluded that the right move was to collaborate with the Soviets to drive America right out of East Asia.[52] The two also had important differences over domestic policy, which divided them as well from the third significant group, the "radicals" led by Mao's young wife, Jiang Qing.

At a climactic Party meeting at Lushan in late August and early September 1970, Zhou's moderate group finally prevailed, and this opened the way for renewed feelers toward America. Lin Biao had overplayed his hand and his struggle now became one with Mao himself, with Zhou emerging as the main beneficiary—as he had so often throughout his career.[53] China's resulting policy was signaled to America in a way that Kissinger concedes he completely failed to detect. Mao invited the American journalist Edgar Snow, a longtime supporter of the Chinese regime, to appear on the platform beside him at the October 1 celebration of the National Day of the People's Republic. In a bizarre comedy of errors, not only did the White House miss the significance of this unprecedented gesture, but it turned down an offer by a thoughtful American academic to go to Switzerland and interrogate Snow at length, on the ground that Snow had often gone to China and been feted there and was in any event so far to the left as to be unreliable. Only in January 1971 was Snow, by then ill, able to convey to the U.S. government his report of interviews with Mao and others, which the Chinese had surely meant to be passed on at once.[54]

The missed signal was partly made up for in late October, when Nixon said in an interview that he wanted to visit China before he died. However vague, this must have been seen in Beijing as an indication of how Nixon hoped things might develop. Then the twenty-fifth anniversary of the United Nations brought to the United States a number of international figures, including Yahya Khan of Pakistan and Nicolae Ceauşescu of Romania. Nixon told Yahya that rapprochement with China was "essential," that the United States would never join a "condominium" with the Soviet Union against China, and that he was willing to send a high-level emissary to China, perhaps Thomas Dewey, Robert Murphy, or Kissinger.[55] When Yahya Khan then visited China in mid-November, he carried not only the memory of this conversation but a formal letter from Nixon raising the question of his visiting Beijing, to be preceded by Kissinger, who would be authorized "to discuss the Taiwan question." Kissinger's account makes no mention of such a letter; perhaps Edgar Snow, the source of this story, misunderstood what he was told.[56]

In any case, the Chinese made no reply for weeks thereafter, as the United States once again blocked their admission to the United Nations, setting off predictable denunciations in the official Chinese press. Finally, on December 8, the response came in dramatic fashion, in the form of a handwritten letter (delivered by Pakistani Ambassador Hilaly in Washington) from Zhou to Nixon, conveying a message from Mao, Zhou himself, and, for good measure, Lin Biao. The key sentence read: "In order to discuss the subject of the vacation [sic] of Chinese territories called Taiwan, a special envoy of President Nixon's will be most welcome in Peking."[57]

The reference to Taiwan in Zhou's message calls for a word of comment. In his memoirs, Kissinger ridicules the State Department for its "pet project" of Taiwan, while setting great store by his own assurances to the Chinese that the United States would not join the Soviet Union in any "condominium" opposing China. The fact was that both elements in the U.S. position were needed, and complementary, as the State Department knew.[58] Without a clear sign of American flexibility over Taiwan, Zhou and other moderates could never have neutralized Lin Biao or perhaps won over Mao himself; it was a "must" issue for most if not all of the Chinese leaders. Kissinger's denigration of the State Department's China experts showed his always latent rivalry and jealousy, and the limitations of his own grasp of the situation.

As Kissinger immediately recognized, Zhou's letter was a major step forward. On that day, December 8, 1970, the corner was firmly turned and the way cleared for a high-level U.S. visit to Beijing. Nixon and Kissinger then moved fast to confirm this, sending a careful reply on December 16 through the Pakistani channel. They were at last on the right road. Had the Cambodian incursion delayed this key step and thus the whole Sino-American rapprochement? In early November 1970, Zhou told Edgar Snow that in the light of the Cambodian operation "the Chinese concluded that Nixon was not to be taken seriously." Unquestionably, the Cambodian incursion was a setback and inspired real doubts.[59] If so, it was responsible for a delay of about seven months. By December the White House's channels, via Pakistan and Romania, had caught up.

As things got straightened out, the Chinese surely grasped two additional points. One was that Nixon himself wanted a large and visible role in reconciliation. Moreover, they could also see the political timing in his desire to be up front. In mid-December, in another interview with the ubiquitous and useful Edgar Snow, Mao let drop a revealing comment (recorded by Snow only in 1973): "Discussing Nixon's possible visit to China, the Chairman casually remarked that the presidential election would be in 1972, would it not? Therefore, he added, Mr. Nixon might send an envoy first, but was not himself likely to come to Peking before early 1972."[60]

Both sides could now sense that rapprochement was inevitable, barring some serious incident or error. And Zhou knew that if he and Mao went along with the schedule the White House probably wanted, the United States would be forthcoming on issues that might arise.

WASHINGTON AND MOSCOW

For the Soviet Union, the year 1969 had been an eventful one. Border clashes with China led to new but unpromising talks; a major *Ostpolitik* initiative came from the key European country, West Germany; a new U.S. President made and then abandoned dire threats, while at the same time starting to withdraw from Vietnam and beginning serious arms control talks; and an uncertain Soviet-American relationship developed over the Middle East, veering from close consultation to outright confrontation.

Yet, while these external uncertainties must have left the Soviet leadership in some doubt about how to proceed on the foreign policy front, they contained many favorable elements and would not in themselves have kept the leadership from agreeing on an overall policy. Rather, the crucial issue confounding and dividing the Politburo was almost certainly the troubled and disappointing state of the Soviet economy, partly a question of domestic policy, but loaded with implications for foreign policy as well. Should the Soviet Union reach out for much increased external ties in order to speed up its economic growth and deal with serious and growing domestic problems?

The most striking feature of the Soviet situation, to foreign observers and surely even more to politically sensitive Soviet citizens, was the failure of the leadership to produce a Five-Year Plan. This compelled successive postponements of the Twenty-fourth Soviet Party Congress, which had never before happened in peacetime to this most important conclave. That the Soviet economy was in real difficulty is clearer in hindsight than it was at the time to all but a few serious observers. A major factor was the cost of the big military buildup in conventional as well as strategic nuclear forces, under way at least since 1965. But this was only part of a wider picture of technological, qualitative, and managerial backwardness all along the line: in research and development, in the emerging use of computers and all that went with the new information age, and in providing the consumer goods increasingly important to national morale.[61]

Nixon and Kissinger seem to have given little weight to these indicators of economic trouble, emphasizing rather the threat posed by the Soviet military buildup. Many observers at the time shared the view that the only thing that worked well in the Soviet Union was the military-industrial complex, but that the nation could stand the strain of a poorly functioning economy.[62]

Historically, Russian governments had always gone to great lengths to conceal defects, often by steering outsiders to showcase villages. But in this case, the defects were sufficiently evident for Leonid Brezhnev himself to give a blunt and critical analysis at a special meeting of the Soviet Central Committee in December 1969. By July 1970 the ensuing struggle was still unresolved, and no new Five-Year Plan could be agreed on. There were two plenums of the Central Committee that month (the first time this had happened since the October Revolution of 1917). The first wrestled with the key problem of agriculture. The Politburo then thrashed out the issues, and at a second plenum it was announced that the Party Congress (supposed to have been held in March or April 1970) would take place in March 1971.[63]

Linked to these central disputes was an ongoing battle for position and influence between Brezhnev and Alexei Kosygin, who, as Premier, had been principally responsible for the economy. In July, Kosygin's influence was dropping steadily, as the Nixon Administration sensed. In hindsight, we can ask whether Soviet policy in 1970 was under any systematic control or guidance, with the large exception of dealings with West Germany. The evidence strongly suggests that decisions were taken impulsively at the urging of one or another special interest or vocal segment, but with no coherent strategy, especially for dealing with the United States.

American policy was also in flux, with an experimental and tentative flavor. This was visible above all in an extraordinary gambit, conceived by Nixon and executed by Kissinger without the knowledge of Cabinet members or supporting staffs even in the White House, and not made public until Kissinger's memoirs in 1978. This was a serious effort to bring about a U.S.-Soviet summit by the fall of 1970—in time to affect the congressional elections.

As both Nixon and Kissinger were well aware, U.S.-Soviet summit meetings had been rare and without lasting results. Truman had had none, with Dean Acheson insisting always that forward-looking negotiations would be fruitless until they could be conducted from Western "situations of strength." Eisenhower had three: a 1955 "Spirit of Geneva" meeting whose gains quickly dissipated when the U.S.S.R. sent military aid to Egypt; a 1959 meeting that was modestly useful in easing tensions over Berlin; and a 1960 summit aborted at the last minute by the famous U-2 incident, leaving only acrimony. Kennedy had his May 1961 meeting in Vienna, at which he was bullied by Khrushchev, with results still debated by historians but certainly not constructive. And Johnson had only a single impromptu one-day session with Kosygin in 1967, which had little effect on Soviet arms control policy. The conventional wisdom among professional diplomats was that a summit meeting should be proposed only when substantial agreement on one or more major issues was virtually certain to be achieved.

According to Kissinger, Nixon "entered office convinced that summits could succeed only if they were well prepared. His original intention was to use the prospect of a summit only when it could be a means to extract important Soviet concessions."[64] If concessions were to be extracted, this could only happen because the other side was eager for the summit itself.

Nixon and Kissinger must have considered these factors often in the first fifteen months. Indeed, a long report by Dobrynin on a conversation with Kissinger in July 1969, which we have noted earlier, showed Kissinger musing aloud at length about the desirability of summits becoming a regular, perhaps annual, means of discussion. But whatever expectations Kissinger's remarks may have kindled, they were vague.[65]

What happened in 1970 was much more specific. In early April, according to Kissinger's memoir account:

> Nixon threw sober calculations to the winds and pressed for a summit. Tormented by anti-war agitators, he thought he could paralyze them by a dramatic peace move. Meeting the Soviet leaders in the wake of Cambodia might show Hanoi that it could prove expendable in a larger game;

this indeed is what happened in 1972. He foresaw benefits for the congressional elections in the fall as well. Thus, as the year proceeded, Nixon grew increasingly eager for a Moscow summit. What started as a maneuver reached a point of near obsession until only the eternal Soviet eagerness to squeeze one-sided gains from negotiations saved us from serious difficulties.

Kissinger claims that he argued strenuously against this move, noting that no situation or negotiation was ripe for progress or agreement, also that a Soviet summit would sit very badly with China. It seems reasonable to conclude that the wish to probe for a summit at that time was Nixon's own. It is telling evidence of the high priority of election considerations in his thought and planning, even at the expense of sound foreign policy.[66]

On April 7 Kissinger put the basic proposal to Ambassador Dobrynin, who soon suggested that a first summit be linked to the UN anniversary that fall. Kissinger rejected this, and indicated that SALT could be the primary topic. During the uproar over the Cambodian incursion, neither this nor any other part of U.S.-Soviet relations seems to have been affected. In June, Nixon had Kissinger step up the urging. At once it became clear that the Soviets had a price. The first general suggestion, spurned at once, concerned the Middle East. The Soviets then made what amounted to a twofold proposal for SALT: that early agreement be reached on ABM limitation, and that this be combined with an agreement to cooperate in reducing the danger of "accidental war" caused by the "provocation" of a third country.

Spelled out in a memorandum conveyed to Gerard Smith in early July by the head of the Soviet SALT delegation in Vienna, the "accidental war" idea, innocuous on its face, was in fact far-reaching. Put simply, if China made any move involving or even hinting at the use of nuclear weapons, the two superpowers would collaborate against her. Nixon promptly rejected this proposal, via Dobrynin, and Kissinger at the same time conveyed intense displeasure at using Ambassador Smith for such an initiative. The Soviets then made an equally unacceptable suggestion that the United States accept forthwith a European Security Conference.[67]

Finally, in September, Dobrynin brought the real reply, suggesting exchanges to prepare the way for a possible summit in 1971. Nixon's 1970 idea was definitely laid to rest. As a relieved Kissinger saw it, Nixon had made an unwise proposal but then resisted Soviet moves to capitalize on it.[68] As a 1970 summit became out of the question, the Soviets must have seen 1972 as Nixon's probable target date for dramatic agreements and a meeting or meetings with Brezhnev. It was the same conclusion Mao in China had drawn. Both were now aware that Nixon's eagerness gave them negotiating leverage.

As we have seen, the scope of the SALT sessions held in 1970—from April to August in Vienna, and in Helsinki at the end of the year—had been defined so as effectively to exclude any attempt at agreement on MIRV warheads. Equally important, Kissinger indicated to Dobrynin in April (apparently on his own and certainly without the knowledge of the American negotiating team) that the United States had no firm position on whether a final agreement should cover only antiballistic missiles or must also embrace offensive missiles! This extraordinary message left the way open for the Soviets to press for the ABM limitation they desperately wanted, while at the same time doing everything they could to talk to death any limitation on offensive missiles.

By this time, both sides had come to recognize that any agreement on totals of offensive missiles would have to be in the form of a freeze as of some stated date. Unilateral (or "national") verification measures—U.S. aerial reconnaissance and Soviet perusal of open American sources, including disclosures to Congress and the press—were not thought adequate to verify the contents of new installations, only to confirm that existing installations were unchanged. The prospect that an offensive missile agreement would take the form of a freeze highlighted the situations of the two sides, which were entirely different. On the Soviet side, a rapid buildup in numbers of missiles had continued, producing a total of 1,300 ICBMs and 280 SLBMs by mid-1970. On the U.S. side, the number of strategic missiles had been constant since mid-1967 at 1,054 ICBMs and 656 SLBMs. In terms of overall *missile* totals, the Soviets had almost drawn even and would shortly move ahead.[69] On the other hand, final MIRV tests in the United States were completed rapidly and MIRVed U.S. Minuteman missiles began to be deployed in June 1970 and sea-based Poseidon missiles in January 1971. The balance in terms of independently deliverable nuclear *warheads* was then certain to move rapidly in the United States' favor, at least until the Soviets had their own MIRV capability.

These trends were readily observable and calculable by Soviet and American military officials. In round numbers, while the total of Soviet missiles (hence deliverable warheads) would rise slowly to about 2,000 by the end of 1972, the United States would by that time have more than 4,000 MIRVed warheads that could reach the U.S.S.R.[70] It is not hard to see why the Joint Chiefs were, however shortsightedly, adamant for deployment of MIRV—or why the Soviets were bound to go all out to master the MIRV technology.

At the same time, as the balance in numbers of strategic missiles moved rapidly to parity by 1972 and then to a numerical Soviet lead, there should have been a strong incentive for the United States to try for an early freeze on strategic missiles and an offensive missile agreement as soon as possible. Conversely, there was a clear incentive for the Soviets to resist any early offensive missile agreement. In this effort, the fact that Kissinger, unknown to Ambassador Smith and his team, had essentially told Dobrynin that the United States would not insist on linking an ABM deal to one on offensive missiles can only have encouraged the Soviet negotiators. As both Gerard Smith and Paul Nitze were later to note, it was an extraordinarily sloppy negotiating performance, with Kissinger to blame.[71]

Against this background, the U.S. negotiators at Vienna duly tabled the options Nixon had authorized. By June the Soviet team had decisively rejected them, and Smith recommended to Washington that the United States move to a new position that would withdraw the two clearly objectionable elements in Options C and D (MIRV with on-site inspection in C, progressive reduction in missile numbers in D). The result was a so-called Vienna option, proposing ceilings of 1,900 launching vehicles on each side (that is, taking into account bombers on the U.S. side as well as ICBMs and SLBMs on both sides), with a subceiling of 1,710 in missile launchers and 250 in modern large strategic missiles. The last was an effort to limit the Soviet SS-9, a heavy missile potentially able to carry many MIRVs. In early August the Vienna option was tabled but not pursued, in the absence of clear instructions from Washington.[72]

Instead, through most of the 1970 SALT sessions the U.S. negotiators had to cope with Soviet stalling tactics, which centered on their perennial argument that any agreed ceilings in offensive weapons must take into account the so-called Forward-Based Systems (FBS) on the U.S. side: medium-range missiles and aircraft in Europe or on aircraft carriers, with ranges that could reach Soviet territory. The Americans knew that any limitation on them would be very damaging to U.S. relations with its allies, so they continued to resist the effort to include FBS.

The attempt to divide NATO thus failed. Its members were held together firmly throughout by the U.S. position and by constant and full briefings from Smith and Nitze, both highly respected and trusted in Europe. In fact, the NATO allies were considerably better informed than the U.S. Congress, where neither the leadership nor the relevant committees were given any systematic briefing between March 1970 and the conclusion of the agreements in May 1972. In the area of arms control, members of Congress were prepared to trust the executive branch, at least during the first years of the Nixon Administration.

The two 1970 sessions did make substantial headway on limiting ABMs, ironing out all sorts of difficult problems and producing a draft ban on "exotic" future technologies. Firm agreement was still not possible, mostly because the U.S. position wavered between permitting none or only one installation, finally coming down for two on each side.[73] Meanwhile, it appeared that Congress might scuttle the whole ABM program, leaving the

United States with sharply reduced negotiating leverage. Intense efforts to save it included a message to congressional leaders direct from Gerard Smith to the effect that the ongoing Safeguard program was important to his success in negotiating really low ABM limits. This finally held the line, and a program calling for four installations was approved.

On offensive missiles, however, the FBS impasse persisted throughout the year. The Helsinki session at year's end was, as one participant put it, "the nadir" of the whole negotiation. An understanding that final agreements should include offensive missiles as well as ABM had been essential all along, but Kissinger's evasion in April held up progress and left the delegation trying in vain to make bricks without straw.

It was hardly the way to conduct a major negotiation: a President not really interested, his principal assistant intervening without the knowledge or concurrence of the negotiating team, and the team left to fend for itself. True, any arms control negotiation was pioneering, and not likely to move rapidly in the best of circumstances, but with better handling the morass of 1970 might well have been avoided, and more progress made in ways favorable to U.S. interests. As it was, the SALT atmosphere both mirrored and influenced the wariness and rigidity still evident on both sides.

MOSCOW AND BONN

Having tidied his relations with his Western allies, Willy Brandt sent his special emissary, Egon Bahr, to Moscow in May 1970 for ten days of intense and comprehensive secret talks. These eventuated, as leaks at the time made clear, in agreement on basic principles. First and foremost, a treaty would formalize West German recognition of the borders created by Stalin in 1945 — the Oder and Neisse rivers as the eastern border of Germany (giving large territories to Poland on this front), a Czech-German border that restored the Sudetenland to Czechoslovakia, and a Polish-Soviet border several hundred miles west of where it had been between 1921 and 1939. Since the Allies had for practical purposes accepted these borders at Yalta in 1945, the effect of a treaty would be to ratify and legalize the whole Soviet position in Eastern Europe. Second, West Germany would renounce any use of force to change borders or for any other offensive purpose. Third, the Federal Republic would in short order recognize the Communist regime in East Germany, the German Democratic Republic, on terms to be agreed.

These features were to be key parts of a treaty. In addition, West Germany would make several additional pledges: full support for the Soviet proposal for its long-desired European Security Conference; permanent re-

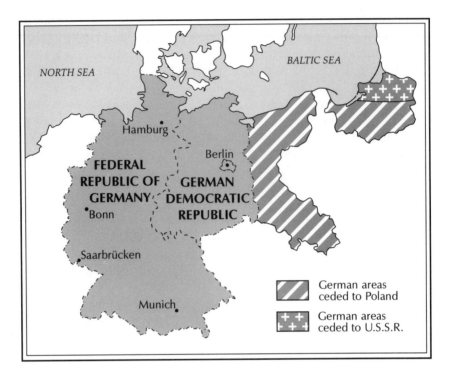

Federal Republic of Germany, German Democratic Republic, with German areas ceded to Poland and the U.S.S.R. © *1997 Chris Brest*

nunciation of nuclear weapons; and continued readiness to engage in loans, economic deals, and trade with the Soviet Union, especially in energy (such as the agreement for large steel pipe from West Germany in return for Soviet oil).

None of these basic elements can have surprised knowledgeable West Germans. All had been foreshadowed by Brandt before the 1969 election. Nonetheless, the prospect that they were about to be codified in international agreements inevitably raised the temperature of the political debate. Here it is important to note that the West German Basic Law deliberately did not adopt a key feature of the U.S. Constitution — namely, the requirement that any treaty with a foreign nation or group of nations be ratified by a two-thirds vote of the upper legislative chamber. In the Basic Law, essentially parliamentary in nature, power was weighted heavily in favor of the lower house, the Bundestag, elected (like the U.S. House) from individual districts of comparable population. The upper chamber, the Bundesrat, resembled the U.S. Senate only in that its members were chosen within the individual provinces (*Länder*); it had only limited power, with no veto over any legislation. In the case of treaties, Bundesrat disapproval meant only that a treaty vote in the Bundestag required an absolute majority of all members rather than a simple one of those voting.

Thus by July 1970 Brandt was in a position to go right ahead on a treaty, provided he could hold together his slim Social Democratic and Free Democratic majority. He also had to take careful account not only of party discipline in both coalition parties but of the special influence of groups such as the so-called expellees—Germans who in 1945 had been evicted from lands to the east of the Oder-Neisse line, though often their families had lived there for centuries. He was asking his countrymen to take a truly enormous leap, accepting the permanence of several unpleasant realities in return for what were only a few serious concessions from the Soviets, and—as he eloquently argued—the longer-term prospect of lasting peace.[74] The leaked gossip about Bahr's talks in Moscow brought all these issues into the open. It also highlighted the importance of a new agreement on Berlin. Berlin was not to be covered in the treaty itself, but would be left for negotiation among the four occupying powers and then, in detail, between the two Germanys.

In late July, open and formal talks began, with the Bonn government represented by Walter Scheel, Foreign Minister and head of the Free Democratic Party, a man of great political and diplomatic skill. With Soviet Foreign Minister Andrei Gromyko, he hammered out the final treaty terms. Very important in political terms was the Soviet acquiescence to West Germany's accompanying statements reiterating that the eventual unity of Germany was a key objective and underlining the importance of a new agreement over Berlin, which everyone now understood was a condition for West German ratification of the treaty.[75]

In early August, Brandt himself came to Moscow, and on August 12 the West German–Soviet Treaty was concluded in a dramatic and highly publicized ceremony. The reaction throughout the world was one of immense acclaim, with the exception only of the most hard-line Communist nations and, most important, the opposition conservative coalition of Christian Democrats and Christian Socialists within West Germany itself. As Europeans could readily see, the treaty, once ratified, would not only resolve the central issues about Germany but form the basis for a de facto European peace settlement. In effect, as many noted, this treaty and its companion agreements would take the place of the formal peace treaties for Europe that had been discussed but never remotely achieved in 1945–47.

The opposition of the West German conservative parties was itself a measure of how sweeping and fundamental the treaty was. At one level, they argued that it was too one-sided, that the West German negotiators had made too many major concessions. But though the CDU/CSU leaders railed against Brandt for alleged haste and carelessness, the root of their objections was their simple unwillingness to accept the permanent loss of large chunks of territory that had historically been German before the Nazi era. It was to this point that Brandt directed himself especially when he spoke on radio and TV from Moscow after the signing.

> The time has come to found our relationship with the East anew—that is, on unconditional mutual renunciation of force on the basis of the political situation as it exists in Europe. . . . *[W]ith this treaty nothing is lost that had not long since been gambled away.*

It was the bitter truth, brought home with memorable eloquence, and the end of illusions concerning Germany's borders that many Germans had harbored for too long.

Yet the conservative opposition fought on, as Brandt in the fall turned his attention to a companion treaty with Poland. This complex undertaking involved a host of attempts to atone for the past in ways bearable in the present, but its core issue had already been decided. The Poles had no choice but to accept the reaffirmed loss of enormous territories along their eastern borders with the Soviet Union (principally in the Ukraine), losses for which the Oder-Neisse line to the west, giving them territories historically far more German than Polish, could hardly compensate in patriotic, economic, or human terms.

Finally, with the details ironed out, Brandt went to Warsaw in December for the final touches. Once again his flair for the dramatic was in evidence. As he was laying a wreath at a memorial to Polish Jews who had died in a heroic struggle against the German occupiers for the ghetto in December 1943—while Soviet troops stayed on the far side of the Vistula River and made no move to help—Brandt suddenly and spontaneously fell to his knees in a gesture of contrition that registered throughout the world. It was one of the great historic photographs of the Cold War period. As one journalist wrote: "Then he who does not need to kneel knelt, on behalf of all who do need to kneel but do not—because they dare not, or cannot, or cannot dare to kneel."[76]

Americans generally joined in the worldwide chorus of approval for the two treaties and what they represented. But in official statements from the State Department and, especially the White House, a note of reserve could be detected. Brandt was moving in a direction the United States had approved at least since 1967, and it was hard for Americans to object that he was acting too quickly. Still, both Nixon and Kissinger chafed at what Brandt had done, seeing it as giving the Soviets an opening for a "selective détente" that would isolate the United States diplomatically while appealing tremendously to allied publics, including the American one. Brandt has recorded that at some point in the 1970 sequence of events, Kissinger "told [a colleague of Brandt] that any détente with the Soviet Union would be America's doing." In saying this, Kissinger was betraying a trace of jealousy, but also his sense of American power. As Nixon and Kissinger saw things, it was all very well for a revived West German government, representing a truncated Germany, to go ahead with this diplomatic gambit. But it would always be America that counted, in Soviet eyes, and America had the power to rein in an overly adventuresome ally through a combination of reasoned argument, security dependence, and economic interdependence.

This inner confidence that Kissinger and Nixon had in ultimate American power and control of its allies is a theme that will recur frequently in this book. One feature of it, at this stage, was that Americans (including Nixon and Kissinger in their memoirs) slighted the economic aspect of the new Soviet–West German relationship. Only a few observers pointed to the enormous possibilities arising from the complementary character of the Soviet and West German economies, or noted that with oil supplies becoming tighter worldwide, the exchange of West German help in materials and finance, in return for Soviet oil and natural gas, could readily bond the two in ways no American economic tie could match.

The United States was not in fact in a strong position to bring about future trade and economic ties with the Soviet Union. So far as the record shows, not until 1972 did Nixon and Kissinger give serious thought to what they might offer the Soviet Union by way of economic incentives to détente. Their overall approach mixed gestures toward détente with acute rivalry and near-confrontation in arms buildups and in the Third World, and a low priority to economic relations. The result was to leave West Germany to assume a pioneering role with Eastern Europe and especially with the Soviet Union itself.

In the last months of 1970, the West German conservative parties carried their fight against Brandt's *Ostpolitik* to Washington and New York. Prominent conservatives, notably the CDU leader, Rainer Barzel, came to the United States to assess and stir up American criticism. For an opposition party to act in this way—in effect undercutting the policy of its nation's government—was rare and risked backfiring. In many situations an American government would have quietly discouraged it: that it did not do so in this instance showed Nixon's and Kissinger's long-standing sympathy for the Christian Democratic Party and its allies. Barzel's meetings with senior U.S. officials, including a meeting with Nixon in September at his San Clemente home in California, were handled with almost ostentatious correctness, and statements to the press were anodyne, the normal practice for visits by opposition leaders from any country. In addition, though, a major target of the West German group was the Old Guard of now retired American officials who had been at the forefront of American foreign policy in the 1940s and 1950s and now, as elder statesmen, retained considerable credibility on issues concerning Europe, NATO, and Germany.

Notable among these were Dean Acheson, Secretary of State in 1949–53, and John J. McCloy, High Commissioner in West Germany at the same critical time. To them, any step that even hinted at weakening West Germany's ties to the West and to the United States—ties they had done much to create—was at best suspicious, at worst rank heresy. They saw *Ostpolitik* as a serious danger to the entire relationship between America and Western Europe, which, they believed, should be the cornerstone of America's global foreign policy. Four key members of this group, Acheson, McCloy, former governor and presidential candidate Thomas E. Dewey, and retired general Lucius D. Clay, met with Nixon and Kissinger on December 7. Acheson's account of the meeting leaves no doubt that the visitors fired both barrels, vehemently criticizing Brandt personally and *Ostpolitik*. Three days later the seventy-seven-year-old Acheson told a group of reporters that Brandt "should be cooled off" and "the mad race to Moscow" slowed down. He was also concerned lest West Germany be left in control of the promised talks over Berlin. His remarks set off a minor storm in West Germany, where they were widely seen as condoned if not approved by the White House.[77] The White House had no comment. However, when a few days later Acheson carried his argument a step further, accusing Brandt of acting for domestic political reasons and viewing his course "with great alarm," the State Department (though not the White House) mildly demurred. In all probability the effect of the episode was minor and short-lived, even with Nixon and Kissinger and certainly with the American public. But it highlighted how revolutionary Brandt's policy was in relation to American and German policy in the Adenauer era.

Partly in response to such American concerns, Brandt's government, through Defense Minister Helmut Schmidt, took a lead in pledging additional defense efforts at the December NATO ministers meeting. At the same time, Schmidt and other European leaders pointed out what they saw as the dangers in Senator Mike Mansfield's perennial amendment to reduce U.S. forces in Europe sharply, an amendment that was picking up support in the Senate.

As 1970 ended, with the feelers back and forth between China and America totally concealed, the SALT talks becalmed, and Soviet-American relations friction-laden, the striking success of Brandt's *Ostpolitik* stood out, in the United States and throughout the world, as the foremost international development of 1970. *Time* magazine called his Warsaw gesture a dramatic "turning point in the history of Europe—and of the world" and went on in terms that well expressed the dominant reaction of informed American opinion:

> While most political leaders in 1970 were reacting to events rather than shaping them, Brandt stood out as an innovator. He has projected the most exciting and hopeful vision for Europe since the Iron Curtain crashed down. Using West Germany's considerable strategic and economic leverage, he is trying to bring about an enlarged and united Western Europe, which would remain closely allied with the U.S. but would also have sufficient self-confidence and independence to form close ties with the Communist nations. It is a daring vision, full of opportunity and danger . . . [which] may not be realized for a long time, if ever. But in holding it up as a goal for all Europeans, Willy Brandt emerged as 1970's Man of the Year.[78]

3. September 1970

September 1970 was a testing time for Nixon and Kissinger. In rapid succession, often overlapping and competing for attention, three situations became acute, one in Jordan, one over a possible Soviet submarine base in Cuba, and a third arising from the election plurality and apparent victory of a Soviet-leaning Socialist, Salvador Allende Gossens, as President of Chile. The crisis in Jordan was played out in the full glare of public attention. The confrontation over Cuba was known to the public but kept low-key. And the Allende election was handled by covert actions kept totally secret from the public or Congress. Three more different situations it would be hard to imagine. To Henry Kissinger, however, they appeared to be simultaneous tests contrived by the Soviet Union.

By far the most important was the crisis in Jordan. We have seen that the Soviets, in response to Israel's deep-penetration air raids into Egypt, were sending Egypt not only antiaircraft missiles and electronic gear but also Soviet personnel to man these and thus in effect participate directly in combat. Moreover, Soviet pilots had been detected flying combat missions in the rear, thus freeing Egyptian pilots to concentrate on operations over the Suez Canal. President Nixon authorized increments of new aircraft to replace Israeli losses, but he declined to provide the full list Israel presented for 25 Phantoms and 125 Skyhawks, over and above the number President Johnson had agreed to, some of which remained to be delivered. Israel was better protected, but far from satisfied.

Among Washington policymakers distracted by Cambodia, a tug-of-war went on between Secretary Rogers and the State Department, on the one hand, and Kissinger, who favored giving large-scale help to Israel, on the other. Faced with this division among his advisors on the only major issue where he had given the State Department a strong role from the beginning, Nixon found it difficult to make a categorical decision. What finally persuaded him to give State another shot was almost certainly the intense controversy that continued to rage over the Cambodian incursion. He did not relish the prospect of uncertain, possibly increased battle in the Middle East but, rather, wished to reiterate the note of peace and negotiation he had stressed in his first Foreign Policy Report.

In mid-June he surprised Kissinger and others by accepting Rogers's arguments that something should be done to ease the situation in the area of the Suez Canal. He proposed that Egypt and Israel should agree to a ninety-day cease-fire and a complete military standstill in a zone fifty kilometers wide on each side of the canal. During the ninety days, they would negotiate indirectly, through the UN-designated Ambassador Gunnar Jarring, to see if general principles to carry out the still basic Security Council Resolution 242 could be agreed on. Jordan was also mentioned as a potential negotiating party, and Rogers added, with Palestinian activity in mind, that every nation, including Egypt, should prevent the use of its territory as a base for guerrilla activities against one another. This "Rogers Initiative" (to distinguish it from the plan that already bore his name) was a more modest and realistic effort to get serious talks under way and to stop the fighting at a time of dangerously rising tension. Through May and June, air combat and Israeli attacks on the Egyptian missile sites near the canal had been intense, with high continuing damage and casualties, especially on the Egyptian side.

For a few days neither Nasser nor the Israelis reacted. Then Nixon made a series of moves to persuade Israel to accept: the United States would provide new electronic countermeasure equipment for possible use against the Egyptian air defense systems, speed delivery of the last items in Johnson's package, and give assurance that more would be forthcoming if the cease-fire went into effect and Egypt violated it.

Nasser was the first to respond. (His close associate and confidant, the newspaper editor Mohammed Hassanein Heikal, claims that he made up his mind almost at once to accept.) On June 29 he went to Moscow, ostensibly to seek medical care from Soviet doctors for an increasingly serious heart condition, but the visit looked like a replay of his January excursion, when he had sought new Soviet aid. His stay extended to July 17, far longer than any other such visit. Heikal is persuasive, however, that in the only substantive discussions, Nasser brought the Soviets around to his viewpoint by saying that he actually saw little hope of movement toward a settlement from the Rogers Initiative, but that the Soviet and Egyptian forces could use the time to good effect to make the missile complex a true wall against Israeli air attacks.[79] Whatever position the Soviets took, it seems clear that they did not seek to dissuade Nasser from accepting the Rogers Initiative. By this time they could see that the fire had not been put out, as they must have hoped, but threatened to spread, and might even lead to some sort of superpower confrontation with the United States. Another factor may conceivably have been the ongoing debate over the internal Soviet economic situation.[80]

On July 22, five days after his return from Moscow, Nasser announced, to general surprise, that he would accept the Rogers Initiative. King Hussein of Jordan followed suit on July 26. In Israel, many senior officials surmised that Nasser was planning simply to use the ninety days to master the new air defense system, perhaps also to move it right up to the west bank of the Suez Canal, so that it could be used to support a ground crossing into the Sinai Peninsula. Yet Israeli forces, too, were in need of a respite; Israel was also aware that agitated Americans were not in the mood for more fighting. In the days after Egypt's acceptance, Nixon assured Mrs. Meir about the U.S. position and agreed to sell Israel additional Phantoms as well as air-to-ground missiles that could be used against missile sites.[81] With obvious reluctance, Israel accepted the Rogers Initiative on July 31. It was probably coincidence that only the day before, Israeli fighters had shot down at least four Soviet-piloted MiGs near the canal, which had the useful effect of showing that Israel was not acting from weakness but, instead, got credit for a forthcoming and helpful action.

When the State Department moved fast to firm up the deal and put the cease-fire into effect, it neglected to take certain obvious precautions. One should have been last-minute reconnaissance to produce photographs of just where the Soviet-Egyptian missile sites were, and in what condition, at the moment the cease-fire went into effect. Another omission was detailed agreement on what sorts of changes would violate the cease-fire. The United States and Israel reached an understanding on this, but conveyed it to Egypt and the Soviet Union only after the cease-fire went into effect, and they never agreed to it.[82]

It did not help that State rejected last-minute wording changes proposed by Mrs. Meir. Moreover, with American opinion in mind, she had taken the important step of announcing that Israel accepted Resolution 242 "in all its aspects." Since this necessarily meant that Israel might have to give up West Bank territories in a final peace agreement, it was anathema to Menachem Begin and the far-right groups which had joined the government to demonstrate national unity just before the June 1967 War. On August 4 these groups pulled out of the government and broke up what had always been an uneasy coalition.

The cease-fire went formally into effect on August 7. In time it was to bring a lasting end to the "war of attrition." But before then, reactions to it made the situation even more confused and dangerous. Within a few days, both Israeli and American intelligence sources reported that Egyptian missile sites were being moved closer to the canal and others were being completed. Given the short range of the key Soviet SAM-3 missiles, the moves enlarged their area of operation considerably, and in theory could assist in covering a future crossing of the canal by amphibious forces.

Israel complained at once, and vigorously, as did its vocal supporters in America. Kissinger was ready to protest, even to risk aborting the cease-fire, while the State Department downplayed the changes and for a time refused to concede that they were in fact clear violations. Nixon himself was in San Clemente for his annual long stay, half work half relaxation, and at this point was not constantly engaged. The resulting audible debate did nothing to slow down Egypt. By September 1, the State Department conceded the violations, and on the 5th the Israelis announced that they would not attend the Jarring-mediated talks. Collapse of the whole Rogers Initiative seemed imminent.

On the next day, however, September 6, a radical Palestinian group spectacularly hijacked three large commercial aircraft (two American and one Swiss) and took them to a desert airstrip in Jordan. For the next three weeks the crisis there commanded everyone's attention.

Why were large organized groups of Palestinians in Jordan, and what had brought about their hostility to their fellow Arab King Hussein? To what extent were Syria and the Soviet Union, or Egypt itself, implicated in Palestinian actions or, if not strictly party to them, nonetheless involved as suppliers and encouragers?

From very shortly after the creation of Israel in 1948–49, Arabs who had lived in British Mandate Palestine (essentially the area west of the Jordan River, including the territory that became Israel), as well as those who through earlier residence or other connections considered themselves Palestinians, rejected Israel's very legitimacy. After the 1967 War, the former group comprised roughly 1.6 million people, many still in the refugee camps set up in 1949, while an almost equal number of those who thought of themselves as Palestinian, about 1.5 million, lived in communities scattered through the Arab world, with over a million clustered in the four Arab states bordering on Israel. By far the largest concentration was in Jordan—644,000—while Lebanon and Syria were hosts to 288,000 and 183,000, respectively.[83]

From these ranks had sprung, in the 1950s, the irregular fedayeen whose raids into Israel from Gaza, administered by Egypt, helped to bring on the 1956 Suez War. Finding these irregulars disruptive and hard to control, Nasser formed regular Palestinian brigades within his army out of some of them and suppressed others. Syria then became the principal supporter of Palestinian groups, but at the same time denied them sanctuary in Syrian territory, for fear of Israel's retaliation—insisting rather that they have their bases in Jordan and Lebanon. The natural effect was to make the Palestinians threats to the internal security and stability first of Jordan, where they became for a time virtually a state within a state, and later, tragically, of Lebanon.

To identify and classify all the active Palestinian groups, and their often shifting ties, would be an uncertain business at best and is not necessary to understand the fundamentals. The Palestine Liberation Organization itself (the PLO), set up with Nasser's backing in 1964, was at first conservative, and confined itself to propaganda of limited appeal. Only after the 1967 War did it attract wide attention and loyalty, mainly through the colorful figure of Yasser Arafat, whose personal organization, Fatah, in effect took over the leadership of the PLO. At that point Fatah was considered moderate in the Palestinian spectrum.

Arafat was to stride the Middle East stage for the next generation as the Palestinians' most visible leader. An occasionally brilliant tactician and opportunistic arranger of support, he was capable also of monumental blunders. For a time after 1967 he tried to put together a serious guerrilla movement within the West Bank territories occupied by Israel. When this failed, he turned to working mainly with Syria, seeking always to enhance the status of the PLO and give it international legitimacy. To Western eyes raffish and crude in appearance and manner, with his trademark Arab headgear and a scraggly growth of beard, he appealed to many Arabs, particularly among the downtrodden. Most Arab national political leaders viewed him skeptically.

Jordan and King Hussein were from any standpoint natural targets for the Palestinian cause. Hussein, a remarkable character, heir to the Hashemite dynasty originally installed by British arms in World War I, as a young man had been with his grandfather, King Abdullah, in 1951 when Abdullah was assassinated on the steps of the Al Aqsa Mosque in Jerusalem. He succeeded to the throne at the age of eighteen and came through several crises. In 1967, however, out of loyalty to an Arab cause, he joined with Nasser of Egypt in the war against Israel and paid the penalty of defeat by seeing Jordan evicted from the whole of the West Bank as well as from East Jerusalem, shortly thereafter taken over by Israel.

A British military education and a naturally gentle manner helped his relationships with Westerners. His army was supported by Britain and then by the United States, both of whom made up his war losses rapidly after 1967 — with Israel's tacit consent, since its leaders perceived Hussein as a moderate barrier to radical Arab elements, as well as a serious potential negotiator ready for compromise. The small Jordanian Army had well-equipped core tank forces composed almost entirely of desert-based Bedouins loyal to the Hashemite dynasty. It was perennially at odds with the city-based Palestinians who moved into Jordan in large numbers after 1967.

By 1970 Hussein and his regime, the embodiment of the moderate Arab tendency, were suspect to radical rulers and popular elements, on an edgy basis with Nasser, and close to outright hostility with the radical Ba'ath regimes in Syria and Iraq.

The Palestinian movement weakened Hussein politically, and his control became shaky when its efforts increased in the summer of 1970. Armed Palestinian bands roamed the streets of Amman with impunity, and in June an attempt was made on Hussein's life. When Nasser and Hussein accepted the cease-fire in late July, the PLO thought they had betrayed the Palestinian cause at just the time when it appeared to be gaining. PLO criticism was so sharp that Nasser closed down its broadcasting facility in Egypt.

In early September, the situation in Jordan was close to civil war, and the match was lit not by Arafat or Fatah but by an extreme radical group, the Popular Front for the Liberation of Palestine (PFLP), led by a notorious character, George Habash, actually a Christian. Habash was always a maverick, whom the central PLO barely put up with and certainly did not control. On September 4, a second failed attempt was made on Hussein's life, and two days later the TV screens of the world lit up with the successive hijackings of the three Western planes (followed shortly by a fourth, British, one). Non-Arab passengers were made hostage under trying conditions, and the planes were destroyed. The PFLP at once took responsibility, and submitted a list of demands for sweeping political concessions and actions, above all the freeing of Palestinian terrorists held in several countries, notably Israel. From September 9 to September 14, the PFLP tried to achieve its demands: three European nations agreed to free fedayeen prisoners, but only if all the hostages were let go. With Nixon's strong support, Israel rejected the most important demand, for the release of key Palestinian terrorists held there. Outraged reactions in Europe and the United States persuaded the hijackers to release most of the hostages, leaving only fifty-four, with alleged connections to Israel. These were dispersed to unknown locations. Arafat seemed to be playing a moderate role in furthering these releases, but at the same time he made it a general Palestinian cause to force Hussein to abdicate. The king had his back to the wall.

Meanwhile Nasser told the United States that he was still accepting the Rogers Initiative and preserving the cease-fire on his front. Nixon put a U.S.-based airborne division on semi-alert, sent transport aircraft to help evacuate the hostages, and deployed the Mediterranean Sixth Fleet eastward. None of these moves was immediately threatening or enabled U.S. forces to intervene on the ground.

On September 15, Hussein finally turned on his enemies. Major fighting broke out as the Jordanian Army tried to drive the Palestinians out of Amman and defeat them totally. After three days it appeared that the Army was gaining the upper hand. At this point all parties faced important choices.

Nixon had encouraged King Hussein to stand firm, and clearly wished to see him crush the fedayeen. At the same time, he did not want the fighting to spread beyond Jordan. The need was to deter or rapidly end any outside intervention. Strong Syrian forces were massed on Jordan's northern border, and Iraq had had a force of 17,000 men in the desert areas of eastern Jordan since after the 1967 War. Complete American and Israeli restraint might invite Arab overreaching, but strong intervention might bring on not only direct hostilities with Arab countries but the kind of Soviet-American confrontation Nixon had sought to avoid on the Egyptian-Israeli front at the canal. The situation called for constant reassessment and decisions, and for close contact with the king on the one hand and Israeli leaders on the other.

Fortunately, by this time a new and resourceful American Ambassador, career officer Dean Brown, had arrived in Amman and managed to establish close communication with Hussein. With the palace and the embassy cut off from each other by the fighting, the two resorted to walkie-talkies, in the clear (using code words and allusions that may have protected their messages).[84]

In Washington, most officials and observers at first discounted the possibility that Syria or Iraq might intervene, but not Nixon. On September 17 he used the occasion of an off-the-record meeting with newspaper editors in Chicago to convey a strong message, which in the circumstances was sure to leak. Its gist was that Hussein's survival was essential for every reason, including the peace settlement effort; that Israeli intervention would be dangerous; but that the United States itself was "prepared to intervene directly . . . should Syria and Iraq enter the conflict and tip the military balance." The warning was probably made more effective by being a leak of supposedly private remarks. This remarkable action was vintage Nixon in form and substance.

On September 18, Mrs. Meir arrived in Washington on a long-planned visit. Just before she arrived, Nixon announced a new $500 million military aid program containing the requested aircraft and much else. For this he had a new tool provided by Congress in early September, an amendment authorizing military aid to Israel, without limit and at the discretion of the Administration—an almost unprecedented grant of authority. With this bone of contention removed, the Nixon-Meir talks went well. There was little discussion of Jordan, and they did not get into what might be done if Syria did move. By this time reports of Nixon's Chicago remarks suggesting U.S. intervention had aroused much negative comment, including one from Senator Russell, strongly opposing the use of U.S. forces. Instead, Kissinger now urged, Israel should be encouraged to act.[85]

On the evening of September 18 (Friday), Washington time, came word that Syrian tanks had moved into Jordan. By the next morning (evening in

Jordan, Egypt, and the Soviet Union), the Soviets had warned against outside intervention, joined with Nasser in an appeal for an immediate cease-fire, and sent word to the State Department that they were urging restraint on the Syrians and that no Soviet forces were involved. Nixon received these assurances skeptically, when he learned not only that the Syrian tanks had been repainted with Palestinian markings but that Soviet advisors had actually accompanied them as far as the border.[86]

The Washington Special Actions Group (WSAG), chaired by Kissinger, met almost continuously that day; Nixon ordered a high alert for the 82nd Airborne Division and sent the Sixth Fleet farther east toward the Lebanon coast. These preparatory measures, involving about 20,000 men in addition to the large Sixth Fleet forces, gave the United States an immediate intervention capability substantially greater than what the Soviet Union could muster short of a week or more.

At that point the ominous possibility of a Syrian invasion of Jordan seemed very likely. Late in the evening Amman time, King Hussein appealed via Ambassador Brown for help from any quarter, and a similar message went to Britain. Israel's Air Force was mentioned as a possible intervenor.

The message reached Washington almost simultaneously with word that Syrian forces had captured the town of Irbid, in northern Jordan. Kissinger, on Nixon's orders, contacted Ambassador Rabin at a New York dinner for Mrs. Meir, and put the question whether Israel would be prepared to send in its Air Force.[87] After a night of intense consultation, Rabin returned to Washington early the next day and told Kissinger his country would be prepared to act, but asked whether the United States would take responsibility for deterring any Soviet intervention. Kissinger gave no immediate reply, but contingency plans were drawn up for joint U.S.-Israel action. (Rabin had earlier been Chief of Staff of the Israeli Army.) Meanwhile the British rejected King Hussein's request, in marked contrast to the great help they had given him in an earlier crisis in 1958. They and other European nations counseled against U.S. intervention, plainly fearing that anti-Western Arab reactions would not be confined to American targets.

By late afternoon the Jordanian Army appeared at least to be holding its own against the Syrians. When the latter sent in a small additional reinforcement, Nixon told his associates that if Egypt or the Soviet Union intervened, he would take action (unspecified) against both.[88] However, the United States was not in a position to put strong forces on the ground against Syria. Nixon in fact continued to rely for deterring Syria on the threat now mounted and made visible by Israel, which moved tank forces close to its borders and flew aircraft close to the scene of action.

Did those aircraft also go into action against the Syrians? Almost all accounts say that Israel never went this far, but Alexander Haig's memoirs suggest otherwise. He relates persuasively that Nixon on the evening of September 20 approved Israeli air strikes, which Haig promptly relayed to Rabin, and that on the next morning, when Rabin called, Haig told him the President had not made up his mind about ground force action but urged air strikes at once. He maintains that in fact such air strikes were made — presumably on September 21 and 22 — and were devastatingly effective, "breaking the back of the Syrian invasion."[89]

One can see strong reasons for not revealing earlier that Israel played this part. Throughout the crisis, Nixon argued that for King Hussein and Jordan to be seen as being rescued by Israel could be devastating for their standing in the Arab world. As for Israel, it had no need to boast again of its prowess in the air, so long as American and Jordanian leaders understood the debt they owed.

During the climactic day of September 22, a reassured Hussein threw his forces unreservedly into battle against a Syrian command that was probably under Israeli air attack and certainly well aware of the Israeli forces' ominous moves nearby and of the American threats and Sixth Fleet within reach. There was a third factor, too, little noted at the time. Hafez al-Assad, commander of Syria's Air Force, was engaged in an acute struggle for power with Syria's tank commander and chief of all forces; in this extremity he declined to commit his Air Force, for the reason that it would almost certainly have been chewed up by the Israelis, but also with an eye to discrediting his rival and laying on him the burden of the defeat he saw coming in any event. For whatever reason, Syrian tanks started to pull back across the border in the late afternoon, and when the retreat continued the next day, King Hussein was able to commit his whole force against the Palestinian guerrillas, wiping them up in short order. Soon all the hostages from the hijackings were released, with no concession from Israel or any other nation.

. . .

While the results of the Syrian invasion were still not clear, Nasser convened in Cairo a meeting of the so-called confrontation states: Syria, Jordan, and Iraq, with the Sudan also invited. With the repulse of the Syrian forces, however, the task of this group turned into one of conciliation and damage limitation. Hussein came to Cairo, Arafat was spirited out of Jordan, and Nasser set out to mediate between them, with Syria and Iraq not represented. By September 27, Hussein and Arafat agreed on an immediate ceasefire within Jordan and the withdrawal of Army and guerrilla forces from all its cities. This apparent evenhandedness hardly concealed that the ceasefire was a ratification of the king's victory and the total defeat and humiliation of all Palestinians, the PLO and Arafat foremost.

At this point, strained by the previous months and now by this arduous and emotional mediation, Nasser's health gave way. He died abruptly on September 28 from his long-standing heart condition. It was a shocking end to what quickly became known in much of the Arab world, especially among Palestinians, as "Black September." The mourning in Egypt and in most of the Arab world was intense. Only fifty-two, Nasser had ruled his country with a firm hand since 1954, when it had just emerged from British colonial control, giving it a renewed sense of its past greatness and potential present stature as the leading symbol and promoter of pan-Arab sentiment. His prestige, at its peak after the 1956 Suez War, had been tarnished by failure in the Yemen and the debacle of the 1967 War, yet he had remained a commanding and charismatic figure.

How Egypt would respond to his death and what would happen to its relationships were in doubt as the leadership scrambled to produce a successor. Shortly the mantle settled on Anwar el-Sadat, who had been at Nasser's right hand from the start but was relatively unknown to outsiders and even to his countrymen.

. . .

In contrast to the disarray and disagreement that characterized American decision making in the Cambodian crisis in the spring, the American government functioned as a smoothly operating team in the Jordanian crisis, producing a series of wise judgments and effective actions. These included recognition that this was indeed a major crisis with high stakes, calling for the fullest effective U.S. role; firm but cautious handling of the hijackings and taking of hostages so that they could come to reasonable conclusions without interfering with the far more important struggle for control of Jordan; close consultation with and constant encouragement to King Hussein, despite extraordinary difficulties of communication; planning for and responding at once to Syria's intervention; equally close consultation with Israel, with the United States as the only channel of communication between Jordan and Israel; and constant and effective warnings to the Soviet Union against becoming directly involved.

The conflict could be seen in the form of three concentric circles: Hussein and the Palestinians in the center; Syria and Israel in an intermediate ring; and the superpowers on the outside. In the center, the Jordanian Army (estimated to have 50,000–52,000 effectives) greatly outnumbered the ill-armed and trained Palestinians (with only 10,000 troops in units, of which only 7,500 were capable of standing up to conventional forces). Such a ratio might not have been decisive in favor of defenders against sophisticated guerrilla tactics in favorable terrain, but the Palestinians were neither sophisticated nor well organized, and once the king unleashed his Army he was almost bound to get the upper hand.[90] Syria's intervention could have changed this balance, however. Its tanks were superior to those of the Jordanian Army and if unopposed would certainly have turned the tide—as Haig and Rabin agreed. However, Israel had shown its decisive superiority over Syrian forces in 1967 and was very close to the Jordanian battlefield. Thus, the local power relationships were heavily in favor of the side backed by the United States, provided that Syria was deterred or forestalled.

It does not follow that the outcome was inevitable. A less than firm and resourceful American policy might well have led a beleaguered King Hussein to compromise or even abandon the struggle. Conversely, if the United States had tried to take charge and use its own forces, the political consequences might well have included dangerous hostile reactions. A middle path between these dangers was not easy or automatic. While U.S. policy was indeed of great importance and brilliantly handled, other central actors were crucial. The foremost hero was unquestionably King Hussein: under enormous pressure from all sides, and in grave personal danger, he kept his head and showed great qualities of leadership and courage. Had his Jordanian Army been less effective, the rest would have been impossible. Also, whether or not Israeli airpower was actually used, the threat it posed to Syria was surely a key factor. Lastly, Assad's refusal to commit the Syrian Air Force helped to limit the battle.

As for the outer circle with the Soviet Union and the United States, the Soviets seem to have dithered throughout, never making up their minds, and as in many other Middle East situations, being lame and ineffectual. This brings us back to the question of whether the Soviet Union really set off the crisis. What influence did it have, and how was it exerted?

Senior American officials had persistently different views. The State Department, all along, saw the crisis as primarily a regional one, stressing the rivalry between radical Arab states and the moderate Hussein, along with the Palestinians' frustrations and their ability to bring pressure to bear on radical Arab states. In this view, the Soviet Union, badly burned in the 1967 War, cautiously assisted both Egypt and Syria—enough to retain credit and give them protection, but not to trigger another Arab confrontation with Israel. Soviet relations with the Palestinians were largely a matter of preserving appearances.

At an opposite extreme was the view Kissinger expressed to Nixon early in the crisis: "It looks like the Soviets are pushing the Syrians and the Syrians are pushing the Palestinians. The Palestinians don't need much pushing." Alexander Haig was more forthright: it was an "attempt to take over Jordan that Moscow had conceived, encouraged, advised and equipped." The Soviet Union was closely linked to both Egypt and Syria, and Palestinian groups were armed with Soviet equipment. Yet, as example after example throughout the Cold War amply demonstrated, even the closest kind of relationship between superpower and client did not necessarily mean that the superpower could restrain the client from pursuing its own objectives. Probably no aspect of the Cold War was more subject to mis-interpretation and miscalculation than this one. Broadly speaking, later scholars have tended to stress the degree of independence of these Arab powers from Soviet policy and the extent to which they pressured the Soviets to go along with provocative moves, rather than the reverse.[91]

In the summer of 1970, there were many crosscurrents. Nasser had opted for a three-month cease-fire, and the Soviet Union had gone along. Both then clearly planned to use the interval to improve their missile system along the Suez Canal, and both connived in violating the cease-fire in minor ways. Yet this hardly showed that they wanted the cease-fire to fail or break down completely, or that they wanted a new crisis.

Certainly the Palestinians saw the cease-fire as an abject act of appease-ment, and it was this that triggered their stepped-up attacks on Hussein in August, which in turn led directly to the hijackings, creating an internal crisis within Jordan that might well have occurred in any event. The cir-cumstantial case is strong that the tail was wagging the dog.

Yet this hardly weakened the case for a strong American reaction. All American policymakers saw the ouster of King Hussein by force as a disaster that must be prevented at almost any cost. In believing this, one could put different weights on various factors: his warm relationship with the United States (except briefly in the 1967 War); his standing as a moderate; his potential effectiveness in the peace process; the impetus his ouster would give to Arab and Palestinian radicalism; and the lift it would give to Soviet prestige in the Middle East.

But had the United States done all it might have done to head off the crisis? Nixon's policy during the War of Attrition had tacked back and forth between the State Department and Kissinger approaches. Kissinger's con-stant urging of greater military aid to Israel (occasionally, as in the previous spring, moderated by Nixon) produced a measured policy. It did not give Israel the free hand it wanted, but it seems likely that Israel would have acted as it did without U.S. advice.

Although the Rogers Plan had been mishandled all the way through, the well-timed Rogers Initiative, in contrast, eased a dangerous Egypt-Israel con-frontation that could readily have drawn in both the United States and the Soviet Union. Nixon gave Rogers and Sisco deserved praise for that effort.[92] In sum, Nixon's policy and its execution deserved high praise. But to a later observer it is surprising that some in the White House did not see that, in a situation where U.S. control over events and actions was never great, the Soviet Union was roughly in the same position.

The outcome of the Jordan crisis not only averted disaster but changed the Middle East situation in respects reaching well beyond Jordan itself. Hussein's triumph was an enormous gain for Arab moderates generally, as well as for American prestige and standing in the Arab world.

Israel, too, emerged from the crisis with enhanced prestige, which had a great effect on both official and popular American views of Israel. Ever since 1948, Americans in and out of government had debated whether a close American relationship with Israel adversely affected other U.S. interests and objectives in the Middle East: stability, good relations with Arab states, access to oil at reasonable prices, and containing Soviet influence. Did U.S. support for Israel rest mainly on some combination of humanitarian concerns, respect for its democratic institutions, and shared history and religious ideals, or was it also the strengthening of a strategic asset?

Part of the answer had been provided by Israel's incredibly successful retaliatory attack on Egypt in 1967 — proof positive of discipline, resolve, and technological prowess in its own defense. The events of September 1970 took this a step further. Israel's performance showed that even in what was largely an inter-Arab struggle, it was capable of measured and sophisticated action, both political and military. Israel's strong backers in Congress, notably Senator Henry Jackson, appeared to be confirmed, and sentiment in Congress as a whole shifted markedly. Within the Nixon Administration as well, there was a significant shift. As his memoirs make vividly clear, Kissinger had always argued that trying to work with the Soviet Union in any way was a delusion, that the Arabs had to realize that the Soviets could not help them mitigate Israel's gains from the 1967 War, and that in the meantime "no war/no peace" was not favorable to increases in Soviet influence. From these arguments it followed that the best course was to lie low, not take negotiations seriously, arm Israel to the teeth so that the Arab states would not be tempted to take military action, and wait until they turned to the United States for help toward a reasonable settlement. More and more, U.S. policy moved in this direction. The earlier restraint on arms for Israel was gone.

. . .

The Jordan crisis, with its threat of war in the Middle East, coincided with the apparent construction of a Soviet submarine base in the port of Cienfuegos, on the southern coast of Cuba. In this episode, the United States dealt solely and directly with the Soviet Union.

On August 4, the Soviet No. 2 in Washington, Yuli Vorontsov, in Ambassador Dobrynin's absence, visited Kissinger to express a Soviet desire to confirm the understandings reached between President Kennedy and Soviet Party Chairman Nikita Khrushchev after the Cuban Missile Crisis of 1962. Remarking on news reports of training in subversive activities by Cuban exiles in Florida and American plans to strengthen the defense of its base at Guantánamo Bay, Vorontsov asked for a reaffirmation of that part of the understandings which, in the Soviet view, pledged that the United States would not invade Cuba or seek to overthrow Castro by force. He made no mention of the other half of the understandings, which concerned Soviet military activities in Cuba.

For his response to Vorontsov, in consultation with Nixon, Kissinger got the 1962 record from the State Department, but did not seek its help or advice. In the confused ending of the 1962 crisis, with the focus on immediate removal of missiles and bombers, there had been extensive exchanges both at the top level and between the appointed negotiators, John J. McCloy for the United States and Vassily Kuznetsov for the Soviet Union. But on the key issue of getting the missiles out for good and for sure, the Soviets had refused to agree to an adequate inspection system (to which Castro objected), and in response the United States declined to make a formal and unconditional no-invasion pledge, although U.S. assurances to this effect had been a key breakthrough in the crisis. The negotiations ended without a formal agreement, but the thrust of what had been agreed was clear.[93]

Kissinger concluded that despite the absence of a final document, the exchanges were detailed and specific enough "to constitute mutual assurances." On August 7, with Nixon's authority, he told Vorontsov that the United States considered the 1962 understandings to be in full force and construed them to mean that "the Soviets were forbidden from the emplacement on Cuban territory of any offensive weapon of any kind or any offensive delivery system; and, in return, the United States would not use military force to bring about a change in the political structure of Cuba."

Kissinger did not reveal this exchange to any other part of the government. He and Nixon speculated that Vorontsov's message "might be a token of Soviet goodwill to improve the atmosphere for a summit in the fall," a possibility which then absorbed them both. (That no one in State or Defense was aware of the summit project may have been one reason they were not consulted on the reply to Vorontsov.)[94] But had there been the usual wider consultation, it would surely have suggested the possible relevance of some recent developments.

Relations between the Castro regime and the Soviet Union, poor and distant since 1962, had begun to improve in early 1969, with a resumption of Soviet military aid; also, seven Soviet ships paid a port call in Cuba, and in November, Marshal Andrei Grechko, chief of the Soviet armed forces and a key figure in the dramatic growth of the Soviet Navy's size and range, paid a highly publicized visit to Cuba. In April 1970 another Soviet naval task force visited Cuba, and in June, as Kissinger noted in a memo to Nixon, Soviet air and naval activity steadily increased. He speculated that the Soviets might be seeking to establish a pattern that could move gradually to Soviet naval units operating "in the Caribbean–South Atlantic on a more or less permanent basis, refueling and resupplying out of Cuba." Later in June, Kissinger was informed of a CIA study suggesting that the Soviet

Union might have in mind a new facility in Cuba to service either ships or reconnaissance aircraft.[95]

Why did Kissinger not warn the Soviet Union about the effect of any such activity? Part of the reason may have been that the 1962 understandings were not well known within the American government; more important, in 1962 the Soviet Union had no significant submarine-launched missile capability. Still, Khrushchev had orally assured U.S. Ambassador Foy Kohler that there would be no Soviet submarine base in Cuba, and President Kennedy had noted this assurance and declared that he attached the "greatest importance" to it. McCloy had told Kuznetsov that the United States objected to the presence of any Soviet military base in Cuba and Kuznetsov had replied that he understood. And the Soviets never objected to several later U.S. public statements that the understandings precluded any military base in Cuba.[96]

Two weeks later, U.S. air photography noted new construction on a small island just off Cienfuegos. Shortly after, the same source detected a Soviet flotilla headed toward Cuba, including not only a guided-missile cruiser, destroyer, and oceangoing salvage ships but a submarine tender and special large barges associated with taking in waste from nuclear-powered submarines. At the time, the White House and State were preoccupied with the cease-fire violations near the Suez Canal and the brewing Jordan crisis, but when the flotilla reached Cienfuegos on September 9, alarm bells went off.

Daily U-2 reconnaissance was then instituted, disclosing by September 16 the construction within the previous month of a substantial installation on the island, including barracks and recreation facilities and, on the mainland, an apparent dock, fuel storage depot, and communications facility. The evidence strongly suggested that the Soviet Union was engaged full-speed in a project to set up and equip a new base capable of handling nuclear-powered submarines. By this time, many such submarines carried strategic nuclear missiles, though others did not and were of the attack type. Uncertainty over just what a "nuclear submarine base" meant was to confuse later exchanges. There were other confusions: Kissinger made much of photos showing a soccer field, telling Nixon that from his experience as a soccer player and fan, this surely proved that the base was for Soviet occupancy, since Cubans did not play soccer. He was wrong: the sport was common in Cuba.

Accompanying Nixon in Chicago, Kissinger used a background briefing with news editors on September 16 to say that any possibility that the Soviets were to start operating strategic forces out of Cuba would have to be studied "very carefully." This alerted the editors, whether or not it reached the Soviets. Earlier that day, talking to Cyrus Sulzberger of *The New York Times*, Kissinger had referred to "Soviet horsing around in Cuba" and hinted at a base for nuclear-armed submarines. The veteran Sulzberger, especially trusted by the Administration to time and frame disclosures help-fully, extracted the whole picture from Richard Helms two days later, then held his fire.[97]

On September 19, WSAG, already in daily session over the Jordan crisis, discussed the evidence from Cuba. Kissinger made the point that whatever the 1962 understandings covered, the question should be whether a new base could be tolerated now, given U.S. national interests. It was as yet only a marginal challenge, but it should be nipped in the bud.[98] Nixon, however, wished to play down the problem.

A paper from the State Department for the next NSC meeting, on September 23, argued that the Soviet action was largely symbolic and should be dealt with between Rogers and Gromyko when they met in a few weeks. The Defense Department, on the other hand, noting that a facility on Cuba would greatly extend the cruising time of Soviet naval vessels, especially nuclear-powered submarines (the estimate was that it would lengthen this time by a third), argued for a dramatic response, even to the point of calling up reserves.[99] At the NSC meeting, Rogers urged postponement of any discussion until November, and the President told all hands to keep it quiet. He had always felt that Kennedy's dramatic presentation to the public of the 1962 Cuban Missile Crisis weakened his bargaining position and had contributed to unwise concessions.[100]

In fact, this observation was itself faulty. The idea that the Cuban Missile Crisis could have been played in a low key was and is totally unrealistic. The various contingency U.S. actions alone guaranteed that the situation would become known at about the time Kennedy made his speech, and in the absence of such a speech, speculation would surely have been both confused and even more alarming than the naked truth. Nixon's critical view is another example of his instinct to conceal. Also, from both 1960 and 1962, he tended to view a combination of Cuba and an imminent election as a bad mix. In 1962, he had been at the climactic phase of his disastrous campaign for the California governorship. Being at a distance must have distorted his perspective: several colleagues have noted that he always harbored the bizarre notion that Kennedy staged that crisis for political advantage.

The leak to Sulzberger, in any event, resulted in a major story on September 25, speedily confirmed and amplified by the Pentagon, so that the Associated Press reported that the United States had "firm indications the Soviet Union may be establishing a permanent submarine base in Cuba." Comment on this was mixed, with such normally dovish voices as Mike Mansfield and James Reston raising an alarm, while others remained skeptical and critical.[101] With the issue thus forced, Kissinger gave another press background briefing that the Soviet Union should be in no doubt that the United States would regard a "strategic base" in the Caribbean "with the utmost seriousness." That afternoon, he was more explicit to Ambassador Dobrynin, who had just returned from Moscow with a long-delayed response about a summit, to the effect that the Soviets welcomed the idea but believed it would be better to wait until 1971. Already irritated by Soviet foot-dragging and now by this response, Kissinger told Dobrynin that the United States saw the Cienfuegos project as unmistakably a new submarine base and wanted withdrawal before there was any public confrontation.[102]

Nixon, with Kissinger in tow, then set off on a nine-day trip to Italy and thence to Yugoslavia, Spain, and Ireland. During the trip, Kissinger prodded Haig in Washington to repeat the message to Dobrynin more strongly, which Haig did in such threatening terms that Kissinger was worried that Moscow might react too sharply.[103]

Dobrynin was ready with a reply on October 6: The Soviet Union had not created, and would not create, any facility in violation of the 1962 understanding, "on the assumption that the American side, as President Nixon has reaffirmed, will also strictly observe its part of the understanding." Photography of the island promptly showed some dismantling in progress and no new work. Kissinger then drafted with his JCS liaison officer, Admiral Rembrandt Robinson (again without consultation with State or the Pentagon), what he styled a "President's Note," designed to be slightly less weighty than a state message. This was approved by Nixon, and it read:

> The U.S. government understands that the U.S.S.R. will not establish, utilize, or permit the establishment of any facility in Cuba that can be employed to support or repair Soviet naval ships capable of carrying offensive weapons: i.e., submarines or surface ships armed with nuclear-capable, surface-to-surface missiles.

The paper went on to list five examples of activities not to be undertaken. It was handed on October 9 to Dobrynin, who accepted it and said there would soon be a public statement from Moscow, which duly appeared on October 13.[104]

Since Rogers had never been told of either the recent Kissinger-Dobrynin exchanges or the earlier one with Vorontsov, Nixon did not mention Cuba when he and Rogers met with Gromyko in New York on October 22, but the next day Kissinger extracted from a puzzled Dobrynin the formal message Gromyko had been prepared to give him. This said that the Soviets were not building either a submarine base or a military naval facility in Cuba, and did not intend to do so. The Soviet Union would "abide strictly by our understandings of 1962. We are also making the exchanges *from August onward* part of the understanding of 1962" (emphasis added). The effect of this was to accept the "President's Note" as the definition of a forbidden base, thus extending the 1962 understandings to cover explicitly not only land-based missiles but facilities supporting sea-based nuclear missiles. But in its reference to the August exchanges, the message also subtly ratified the assurance Kissinger had given that the United States would not use force "to bring about a change in the political structure of Cuba." It was a significant addition.

This Gromyko message effectively wrapped up the affair. Both sides were content to depict the outcome simply as a reaffirmation of the 1962 understandings, thus stifling discussion of whether there had been concessions on either side. Yet there remained ambiguities in the private exchanges, some of them noted at the time by Admiral Elmo Zumwalt, U.S. chief of naval operations, whom Admiral Robinson had (unknown to Kissinger) consulted. Did the note cover nuclear-*powered* submarines carrying no strategic missiles or, conversely, conventionally powered submarines carrying nuclear-*armed* missiles with short ranges but still capable of hitting U.S. territory? Did it adequately define what constituted a base?[105]

Over the next six months many vessels arrived at Cienfuegos, and tenders from the base there were also used to service submarines at sea. Each time the United States objected, and the activity stopped fairly promptly. Yet a limited facility remained in operation at Cienfuegos, and in later years was visited by both kinds of "nuclear submarine." Thus, in effect, the new understanding came to cover solely the "double nuclear" case, nuclear-powered submarines carrying strategic nuclear missiles. These had been the main worry all along, so that ruling out bases for them was a gain for the United States, as Kissinger and Nixon later claimed, though Soviet naval access to Cuba continued.

If Soviet actions were assessed solely as an attempt to shade and extend the limits of tolerated naval support operations in Cuba, obviously the probe was a failure. The same was true if, as some have argued, their main objective was to show that the new nuclear "parity" meant that it could match all that the United States had by way of support facilities near the other side's borders.[106] But it is possible that the Soviet Union's most important aim was to gain a much clearer U.S. commitment not to interfere with Castro's rule. This would be useful for its own sake and also — a completely overlooked point — reassuring to Castro if he cooperated with the Soviet Union in other countries. If this was part of the Soviet purpose, Vorontsov's inquiry may have been primarily an effort to ensure that the Nixon Administration adhered to the 1962 understandings.

In 1970, informed Americans assumed that the United States in 1962 had pledged unconditionally not to invade Cuba; conservatives such as William F. Buckley, Jr., repeatedly assailed the Kennedy Administration's handling of the crisis on just this ground, and it was a view shared by such political figures as Ronald Reagan and almost certainly Richard Nixon himself. In fact, however, as we have seen, the "pledge" was never written down in specific terms, and in many of the surrounding discussions it was linked to Soviet acceptance of adequate inspection, which never materialized.[107]

Against this background, Kissinger's undertaking that the United States would do nothing to change the "political structure" of Cuba by force was actually more sweeping than a simple "no invasion" pledge. The formulation on its face covered not only invasion but forceful subversive efforts—with which Castro and his colleagues had had a lot of experience. Was this what the Soviets were aiming at, as their ultimate purpose?

Richard Nixon's strong feelings about Castro and Cuba were evident on many occasions over the years. When he became President, one of his early orders was for the CIA to step up anti-Castro harassing operations, reversing the trend to phase these out that had prevailed for several years under Johnson.[108] In the nether world of the Cuban exiles in Miami and their well-penetrated contacts in Cuba, impressions could have been formed of a serious renewed U.S. intent to go after Castro. Americans who knew how very small the covert effort was may have misjudged its effect on Castro and his colleagues, who in turn may have exaggerated the danger to the Soviets.

Vorontsov's inquiry may therefore have had as its main objective simply to confirm the 1962 pledge, if possible with the wider interpretation Kissinger provided. But there was also, surely, the objective Nixon and Kissinger perceived—namely, a restatement of the U.S. view on the restraints on Soviet military activities, especially those related to missiles. The two were probably not wrong in judging that this was a deliberate, highest-level attempt to establish an interpretation from which the envelope of tolerated Soviet activities could be expanded.

On this subject, Kissinger's reply—focusing on "emplacement" of missile-related capabilities—left the way open for testing the limits of U.S. tolerance on the naval front. The Soviet Navy, carrying great weight and prestige in the Soviet structure by this time, must have chafed under its cruising-time limitations, one of its biggest handicaps vis-à-vis the U.S. Navy. It is not implausible that it pressured the leadership to make this try. If it worked, the gain would be substantial, narrowing at a single stroke the gap in real capabilities; if it was turned back, no ground was really lost.

It is noteworthy that Kissinger urged, and in effect carried out, a stronger and more rapid response to the Cienfuegos crisis than Nixon was initially inclined to. The outcome, coming at the same time as that of the Jordan crisis, did much to enhance his status both in the public eye and with Nixon. Moreover, it seemed to vindicate firmness as a keystone of success in dealing with the Soviet Union. What it did not vindicate, however, was the practice of handling key negotiations solely within the White House.

. . .

Alongside the hijackings that launched the Jordan crisis and the reconnaissance photos that set off alarms about a submarine base in Cuba, another event in the busy first week of September took place at the other end of Latin America. This was the election for a new President of Chile, held every six years in a nation with a unique and almost unbroken record of democracy since its independence in 1818. The candidate of the left, Salvador Allende Gossens, got 36.2 percent of the total, a bare 39,000 votes more than the conservative, Jorge Alessandri (at 35 percent), with the candidate of the incumbent and historically moderate Christian Democratic Party, Radomiro Tomic, well behind at 27.8 percent. Under the Chilean Constitution, if no candidate had more than half of the vote, the final selection passed to the two chambers of parliament, meeting jointly some weeks later. In the past the parliament had always gone along with the popular vote, however small the plurality, so that it was at once widely accepted that Allende would soon take office. He had been a perennial presidential candidate and, in the intervals, a vocal member of parliament. In 1958 he had lost only very narrowly to Alessandri, but in the especially hard-fought and polarized election of 1964, with conservatives and moderate reformers uniting behind Eduardo Frei of the Christian Democrats, Allende had held only his core base of support and been soundly beaten by Frei.

After that, Frei, while still much admired, had to deal with adverse economic trends, a fall in copper prices, and a rise in inflation. His promised "revolution" stalled after he had initiated a number of politically divisive reforms (including partial nationalization of U.S. copper and telephone interests), which aroused conservatives while not going far enough to satisfy much of his own party. Barred by the Constitution from running again, Frei in 1970 stayed on the sidelines while his party moved toward the left and the conservatives surged ahead.

Most of Latin America took the result calmly, relating it to Chile's underlying problems and special circumstances. In Washington, the State Department and CIA analysts also reacted with only moderate concern. Nixon and Kissinger, on the other hand, were at once aroused to fever pitch and, unknown to Congress or the public (until 1975), they undertook an extraordinary covert operation to undo the results of the election.[109]

In the 1960s Chile had been a special focus of U.S. policy toward Latin America. The Alliance for Progress, begun under Eisenhower, renamed and expanded under Kennedy, provided Chile more economic aid per capita than any other Latin American country; its political and economic success came to be seen as a model for the continent as a whole. In the 1964 election, Allende, a proclaimed Socialist and often at odds with the local Communist Party, had received substantial financial help and other forms of support from Communist and Communist-front organizations with ties to Moscow. Partly in response to these efforts and partly for more specific reasons including the welfare of U.S. corporations operating in Chile, a large semi-covert U.S. operation was mounted. Its main propaganda focused on the dangers of a Communist-leaning regime, but local anti-Allende organizations were also given support, notably the *El Mercurio* newspaper chain and a number of Catholic groups. Some funds were also provided to the Christian Democratic Party (through channels unknown to Frei). Sophisticated Chileans were generally aware of what was going on, on both sides, and had come to take such outside intervention almost for granted.

In the United States, while some liberals and leftists were critical of any U.S. intervention, many informed observers saw Chile as warranting an exception to the general trend under Kennedy and Johnson to lessen or cease such covert operations. Foreign observers agreed that the 1964 outcome reflected the will of the Chilean people, as well as a success for the basic U.S. policy of supporting Frei and the moderate center, mostly through the Alliance.[110]

The 1970 election in Chile was another test of the power of the left in circumstances more favorable for an Allende victory. Within the U.S. government, opinion was divided and centralized coordination weak and indecisive on the issue of what to do in Chile. Ambassador Edward Korry, originally brought into government under Kennedy, was a longtime political reporter with experience in Eastern Europe. He was vehemently anti-Allende, but his liberal reformist views made him reluctant to back the conservative candidate, Alessandri. His CIA chief of station, Henry Hecksher, was a hard-line anti-Communist who advocated no-holds-barred support for Alessandri.[111]

Ironing out the differences in such a situation should have been imperative. The National Security Advisor had long chaired the committee responsible for policy on covert operations, making decisions on some and recommendations to the President in other major cases. Strong White House control and direction had been the tradition. In early 1969, that committee had been renamed "the Forty Committee," with the same members as before: Deputy Secretaries from State and Defense, the Director of Central Intelligence, the JCS Chairman, and Attorney General John Mitchell. The statutory authority for covert operations was a catchall clause in the National Security Act of 1947, which authorized the Director and the Agency to undertake such other activities as the President might direct. In 1947–48, at the urging of the State Department (including George Kennan), this authority was the legal basis for an extensive U.S. involvement in support of anti-Communist parties in Italy and France. Then, during the Korean War, virtually every conceivable form of covert operation came to be embraced and accepted as within the CIA's charter.

In the spring of 1969, CIA Director Richard Helms duly brought before the Forty Committee the issue of Chile, noting that an effort on the 1964 scale would need at least a year of preparation. However, the committee put off action. In June, a group of Latin American Foreign Ministers, in Washington for a meeting of the Organization of American States (OAS), were received by President Nixon at the White House. The Foreign Minister of Chile, Gabriel Valdéz, took the occasion to give a lecture on how beneficial U.S. aid was to the United States itself, that it was hardly merely altruistic, as most official comment suggested. Nixon, already critical of President Frei—he thought him too close to the Kennedy legacy—was angered by these remarks, and a lunch between Valdéz and Kissinger the following day only aggravated the tension. Kissinger lectured the Chilean to the effect that nothing important ever happened in "the South" and that it was of no consequence in world power terms.[112] Throughout its first year the Nixon Administration downgraded the Alliance for Progress, and in the case of Chile, where economic grant aid had ended in 1968, only a moderate military aid program continued. Most important, the level of official U.S. loans to Chile for economic purposes fell from $57.9 million in 1968 to $18 million in 1970, further complicating the growing problems linked to a substantial drop in the price of copper. All along the line, the U.S.-Chile relationship cooled. Neither Kissinger nor Nixon paid real attention to Chile, and in their scheme of things, little could be properly debated, still less decided, in the absence of a push from the White House.

By March 1970, when the Forty Committee again discussed the election in Chile, the left had managed to forge a broad coalition in support of Allende, so that his chances of winning were good. With Korry and the State Department leery of large-scale operations, which they believed would be much more heavily criticized than in 1964, and Korry particularly opposed to outright backing of Alessandri, the committee adopted a small ($125,000) program for generalized anti-Allende propaganda and information activities. But by summer, with the election only two months away and the Cambodian crisis over, concern over Chile rose, and the Forty Committee approved an additional $300,000, again for generalized anti-Allende activities. Alessandri, now seventy-four years old, had lost ground, but a CIA-commissioned poll still put him comfortably ahead of Allende, with Tomic out of the running. Ambassador Korry argued in vain that the CIA's polls were using outdated demographic and residence data.[113]

In this situation of growing unease, three major U.S. corporations with large Chilean interests got into the act. Senior officials of Anaconda Copper, General Telephone and Electronics (GTE), and Pepsi-Cola offered to put up substantial sums to supplement the CIA's effort, provided that the government would also devote part of its effort to direct support for Alessandri. A compromise was struck: the CIA would advise the companies what organizations to go through in support of Alessandri, without itself participating. The cost of the total U.S. efforts, public and private, remained a small fraction of the 1964 operation. Hastily mounted without much local base, it was nonetheless conspicuous enough to be noted and identified within Chile. As Helms repeatedly pointed out, it suffered from the defect of trying to defeat somebody with nobody; the fundamental problem was that the center and right, united in 1964, had been driven apart by Frei's policies.[114]

When the results of the 1970 election became clear, a high-level meeting in Washington on September 8 focused on ways that Chile might hold a new election in which Frei would again be eligible. Alessandri himself publicly proposed that, if elected President, he would rule only long enough to set up such an election; in the United States others devised far-out schemes to the same end, some involving interim military rule. Frei himself lent no support to such ideas, however, and the general sentiment in Chile was that parliament should ratify the election result when it met on October 24, with the new President taking over on November 1.

In the chorus of alarmist predictions that reached the White House in these weeks, Nixon's later recollection singled out one from an Italian businessman, who roundly declared that with Allende in Chile and Castro in Cuba, "you will have in Latin America a red sandwich. And eventually it will all be red." Given the geographic separation alone, this was an extreme conjecture. Nixon also claimed that several senior Latin American statesmen conveyed to him deep concerns. State Department personnel had very different reports and reactions, but they were not consulted.[115] The "worst case" scenarios became dominant for Nixon, Kissinger, and Mitchell.

The Forty Committee's project to get a new election, called Track I, was set in motion, though with scant expectation that it could succeed. Instead, the decision-making trio turned to a much stronger alternative, dubbed Track II, knowledge of which was confined to them and to the CIA personnel directly involved, remaining unknown then and for years thereafter to anyone in State or Defense, to the Joint Chiefs, and to Ambassador Korry and his non-CIA colleagues. This Track II became Nixon's real hope and the heart of his policy toward Chile.

On September 15, Nixon personally gave Richard Helms the widest possible authority ("a marshal's baton," Helms later called it) to prevent Allende's presidency by any means whatever, at whatever cost or risk of failure. Whether or not the instructions carried at least a hint of presidential willingness to accept assassination of Allende himself as one option—a later claim that Helms denied—some violence was implicitly authorized and was reflected in much of what the CIA did.

From mid-September to mid-October a small task force, working only through the CIA station in Santiago and the military attaché, made plans that focused on military intervention and particularly on the removal of Chile's Army Chief of Staff, General René Schneider, who was known to be a staunch upholder of the Constitution and adamantly opposed to any military intervention. Contact was made with two lesser military men: General Roberto Viaux, an extreme rightist already thrown out of the Army for disruptive activities the year before, and General Camilo Valenzuela, a local commander of less extreme views but with little weight or following. To deal with these men without detection, the CIA sent various Latin Americans not previously familiar with Chile to Santiago under deep cover; the military attaché was the channel for limited shipments of small arms and for payments to the two generals. Despite all this effort, both the attaché and the CIA station chief made clear their view that the plan had no realistic chance of success.

Ambassador Korry came to Washington on October 14 to present once more his negative judgment on Track I. Alerted by a series of bombings in Santiago that had been traced to associates of Viaux, but still ignorant of Track II, he argued strongly once more against any notion of a military coup. He got to see Nixon himself, and also presented his views to the Forty Committee. He emerged convinced that all attempts to upset the election of Allende were dead. The next day, though, with the Chilean parliament set to meet on October 24, Nixon and Kissinger had to decide whether to continue dealing with military groups intent on first removing General Schneider from the picture, then preventing Allende's accession to power. Later, Nixon was to claim that he had no knowledge of Chilean developments at that time, while Kissinger claimed repeatedly that the operation was called off at that meeting, and that Thomas Karamassines, Helms's deputy, was instructed to that effect.[116] To the contrary, Karamassines, an experienced professional, understood that his instructions from Kissinger and Haig were to avoid further contacts only with the extremist General Viaux; General Valenzuela was still to be encouraged, and the whole effort to forestall or hamper Allende's presidency was to continue indefinitely. His evidence is convincing, and the denials of Nixon and Kissinger unpersuasive. The most charitable interpretation is that both men underestimated the ongoing momentum and did not see that only the most categorical instructions to the military groups would turn them off. A more realistic judgment may be that Kissinger hoped against hope that somehow they would pull something off, believing that the CIA would ensure that no U.S. connection could be proved.[117]

Just what was conveyed to the two generals has never been clear. But small-scale arms deliveries did continue, and U.S. officials in Chile did not protest or object when two botched attempts to kidnap Schneider were made on October 19 and 20. Finally, on October 22, a group of military conspirators ambushed Schneider's car and wounded him fatally. He died three days later.

The almost universal reaction in Chile to this killing was outrage, directed at the individual generals and at the extreme right, not at the United

States, whose role had been well concealed. In due course Chile's courts convicted General Viaux and found General Valenzeula responsible for the murder but in lesser degree. The effect was to strengthen Allende's position and to affirm public support for maintaining constitutional measures. Between his election and inauguration he had already accepted protective laws proposed by his opposition and designed to make the Constitution more secure.

From any standpoint, Track II was a miserable undertaking. In the list of U.S. political covert operations to affect the leadership of other countries during the Cold War, Track II was at the outer extreme both in its objective — overturning a clear-cut election result — and in the lack of any solid connection to a viable alternative or to the popular will. Thomas Powers's conclusion is convincing: "The CIA's intervention in Chile was a spoiling operation of the purest sort. . . . [Its] role was pervasive, it violated the spirit of the American political tradition, and it was undertaken at Nixon's explicit order, for reasons which seem shallow, cursory and offhand at best."[118] In 1975, when the Senate's Church Committee on intelligence activities studied the case, it reached the legalistic conclusion that since the actual killing of General Schneider was done with guns not supplied by the CIA, and since the Chilean courts focused on Viaux, from whom the United States had disengaged before Schneider was killed, the CIA had not been implicated directly in Schneider's death. But as Powers pointed out, "both Viaux and Valenzuela were actively encouraged to proceed with their plan for kidnapping Schneider, were promised a substantial sum of money if successful, and very likely would have done nothing at all without American encouragement to move. If the CIA did not actually shoot General Schneider, it is probably fair to say that he would not have been shot without the CIA."[119] In legal terms, a U.S. judicial proceeding would surely have concluded that U.S. agents (acting on presidential authority) had been at least accessories before the fact and co-conspirators in the kidnapping, and thus in the killing that resulted from it.

More broadly, the Agency had handled the preelection operations badly, and may also be blamed, as it was by Nixon, for its failure to foresee the outcome. Korry emerged as idealistic but ambivalent. Finally, Nixon and Kissinger never gave Chile the attention required under their own decision-making system, and acted impulsively, with inadequate reflection. Their actions were not only morally repugnant but ran grave risks of the eventual exposure that damaged the United States in Latin American eyes.

. . .

Nixon's handling of the Cienfuegos base issue and his secret attempt to prevent Allende from taking office in Chile were defining events in his overall Latin American policy. It had two preeminent objectives: to keep

any Latin American country, Cuba in particular, from becoming a base for
Soviet military power; and to deal as harshly as possible with any emergent
leftist regime judged likely to cooperate with worldwide Communist organizations, Cuba, and the Soviet Union. Beyond that, he almost certainly
shared the view that Kissinger had expressed to the Chilean Foreign Minister: that "the South" — at least the Western Hemisphere "South" — simply
did not count in the geopolitical global balance. Neither man took an
interest in the possibilities of constructive U.S. government action to further
democracy and economic welfare in Latin America. Nixon's views on this
had pretty well hardened before he took office. In early 1967, he wrote:

> I found that Kennedy's Alliance for Progress had raised expectations too
> high. The leaders I met with expressed their disappointment and urged
> that the United States develop a new approach to attract the private invest-
> ment from both the United States and Europe that the Latin American
> economies desperately needed in order to make any meaningful progress.

By 1967 there was indeed disappointment in Latin America, and the U.S.
government effort had started to decline, in the face of the cost of the
Vietnam War and budgetary pressures generally. But whereas President
Johnson (or Hubert Humphrey) would have wished to resume a serious,
substantial effort as soon as possible — after all, the Alliance stemmed from
seeds planted in the Eisenhower Administration — Nixon did not think in
those terms, or hold much faith in economic development support generally. Nor did he much care whether Latin America turned to dictatorship
or on occasion made a travesty of democratic institutions. There and elsewhere, such concerns were secondary if any significant geopolitical factor
pointed in another direction.

4. The Midterm Elections

For the first two years of Nixon's presidency, the Democratic Party had a
majority of 58–42 in the Senate and 243–192 in the House. But as we have
seen, deep divisions over both the Vietnam War and domestic policy made
party lines exceptionally fuzzy, and Nixon had been able to get a working
majority on the Vietnam issues by finding allies and supporters among
House Democrats. In the Senate, on the other hand, several moderate and
liberal Republicans were critical of U.S. involvement in the war (Charles
Goodell of New York, for example). In the 1970 congressional elections
Nixon, taking account of these differences, directed his most energetic campaign efforts against antiwar Democrats like Albert Gore, Sr., of Tennessee,
and gave only backhanded support to antiwar Republicans.[120] Yet he re-

mained acutely aware that, as he told Ambassador Rabin, the country was in a "peace mood."

Early in the fall, the Senate rejected by a vote of only 55–39 the McGovern-Hatfield Amendment setting a deadline of December 31, 1971, for the withdrawal of all U.S. forces from South Vietnam—the closest such vote yet. Even some of the senators who staunchly supported the war were urging the President to end it quickly. Casting around for a new proposal, a group of fourteen senators from both parties, led by Senator Jackson of Washington, came to focus on the idea of "an internationally supervised standstill cease-fire throughout Vietnam." Their public letter to that effect was shortly endorsed by another sixteen senators. Meanwhile, a major citizens organization led by President Clark Kerr of the University of California favored a similar cease-fire. Nixon had repeatedly rejected such suggestions, and Hanoi had insisted that a cease-fire could come only after a fully agreed settlement.

The year before, the American Embassy and military command in Saigon had judged that a cease-fire would demoralize the South Vietnamese and lead rapidly to collapse, but by the fall of 1970, the situation in South Vietnam seemed more hopeful. Sentiment grew within the Administration to give a cease-fire proposal a try. From Paris, the elder statesman David Bruce (who had taken Lodge's place early in the year) and his deputy, the highly respected Philip Habib, argued strongly for trying to break the logjam in this way. The unstated but inevitable corollary was that the United States no longer insisted on mutual total withdrawals. With a cease-fire, it would have no pressure or leverage to get North Vietnam to withdraw, while Hanoi had made it clear that it would never release its American prisoners without a total U.S. withdrawal. Yet Nixon had no wish to make it clear, either to the American public or to President Thieu in Saigon, that he was no longer demanding total North Vietnamese withdrawal as part of a peace deal.[121]

Nixon understood and accepted these harsh realities. He sent Kissinger to Paris on September 7 and again on September 27, for the sixth and seventh secret sessions with the North Vietnamese. The authoritative Le Duc Tho did not attend, but his stand-in, Xuan Thuy, was obdurately hostile to Kissinger's feelers about a cease-fire.

When Nixon met with Rogers, Kissinger, and Bruce at a castle in Ireland on October 4, at the end of his European trip, all agreed that a cease-fire in place should be the centerpiece of a major Vietnam speech that the President would give that week. William Safire quickly grasped that its main purpose was to help the congressional election and to win applause from editorial writers and war critics. His instructions were to fudge key elements, so that they would not be too prominent, especially the abandoning of the oft-repeated demand for total North Vietnamese withdrawal.[122]

Accordingly, Nixon's national television and radio speech on October 7 was delivered in a careful, almost dry tone, far from the combative emotionalism of his remarks in the spring about the Cambodian incursion. The cease-fire proposal was very popular, and drew approving comment even from Averell Harriman. As predicted, Hanoi at once rejected it, so that when Nixon took to the campaign trail, he was able to refer again and again to his offer's being on the table and Hanoi's spurning it. This was enough to cool off the issue of Vietnam policy throughout the remainder of the election campaign.[123]

Few noted that Nixon was no longer demanding total North Vietnamese withdrawal, though sophisticated observers could see it clearly as an important and inevitable concession, and Hanoi could be in no doubt that it would be allowed to leave forces in the South under a peace agreement when American forces departed.[124] In effect, this political speech resolved one of the two key negotiating issues. On the second one, Hanoi's negotiators continued to insist that Thieu and his regime should be replaced and the way opened for a Communist government in the South, and on this issue the "true believer" never wavered.

With Vietnam and foreign policy playing only a secondary part in the election, domestic issues bulked large. Inflation was building up and so was the unemployment rate, partly because of the reduced war effort. (On election day, the inflation and unemployment percentages — what later came to be called "the misery index" — were each above 5 percent, considered at that time a disturbing level.) It was seared in the experience of Nixon and his chief economic advisor, Arthur Burns, that in 1958–60 Eisenhower's stubborn refusal to depart from economic orthodoxy in order to counter or end a recession had been important, perhaps decisive, in Nixon's defeat in 1960. Yet in 1969 and 1970, with the strongly anti-inflation William McChesney Martin as Chairman of the Federal Reserve Board, succeeded by the initially like-minded Burns in early 1970, Nixon took no strong measure to lift the economy, hoping that things would improve by election time and he could stress other issues.

To Nixon, domestic policy was always of far less interest than foreign policy and, where necessary, subordinated to it. His foremost domestic aim was not to stir up controversy or expend political capital, so he made no serious effort to cut back Johnson's Great Society programs, most of which had strong supporting constituencies.[125] Only a very few, like the experimental Model Cities program, were discarded, and major programs such as health insurance for senior citizens and the poor (Medicare and Medicaid) grew in size and expense beyond earlier predictions, so that social programs as a whole rose steadily as a proportion of the total budget. A really hardheaded conservative, such as Nixon portrayed himself in Republican settings, might have tried to head off or limit this upward trend. But to the quiet distress of many staunch supporters, Nixon did not do so. Indeed, at the end of 1970 the percentage of the federal budget going to meet domestic needs actually crawled ahead of that for defense, for the first time since the start of Truman's military buildup of 1950, and Nixon's budget message to Congress in January 1971 pointed to this with pride in its lead sentence. In later years his domestic policies were remembered as almost liberal — "The Last Liberal" was the title of an essay about him written in the mid-1990s. But the evidence suggests that most of Nixon's actions of this sort were taken not on their own merits but to pacify potential opponents of his Vietnam policies.

In other respects, too, Nixon did not challenge the prevailing climate. In addition to sponsoring changes in the draft law that limited the exposure of young men to a single period after they turned nineteen, he also appealed to the young by supporting a reduction in the voting age to eighteen, which was enacted in 1970 to take effect in 1972. Moreover, he backed the creation of an Environmental Protection Agency (EPA) (first headed by the moderate Republican Russell Train), and did not oppose the Clean Air laws enacted in 1970. He also steadily increased appropriations for the National Endowments for the Arts and for the Humanities, causes in which Leonard Garment of the White House staff took a particular interest.[126]

Much of this was reactive, but Nixon also launched two important initiatives of his own. The first, urged by Burns in particular, was "revenue sharing" between the states and the federal government. With the federal fiscal system having by far the largest tax base of resources and range of measures to tap them, state and local governments habitually appealed for aid to Congress, which tended to respond with substantial grants, conditioned by closely defined objectives and tight federal control and supervision. Nixon now proposed to substitute a system of outright federal grants to be expended by the states largely at their own discretion, a sound and appealing concept — except to those with vested stakes in the status quo, above all key committee chairmen in Congress and the interests they served, who had enough weight to delay enactment.

The second big domestic initiative was truly original, and heterodox coming from a Republican President; it concerned the federal welfare program, which from idealistic beginnings in the 1930s had grown over the years into a huge and untidy monster, inequitable and debilitating even to many of its recipients. Among its many defects, two stood out: its aid to dependent children tended to encourage single parentage and weaken family ties; and there was little incentive, or help provided, for recipients to get out of welfare and into the workforce. These defects were forcefully pointed out by Daniel Patrick Moynihan, a courageous young thinker who was then working on Nixon's White House staff, where he tried fervently to persuade Nixon of the virtues of the model of Benjamin Disraeli's "Tory democracy" in Britain. He thus got the President to accept a new Family Assistance

Plan, which would provide substantial guaranteed stipends to needy families but require that recipients in a position to work accept jobs and train for them within a certain time, on pain of losing the money. In Congress, FAP was opposed by conservatives because of its cost and by liberals who resisted the work emphasis and wanted bigger stipends with fewer conditions. A modified version of the program squeaked through the House in early 1970 but then stalled in the Senate.

More important during the 1970 campaign than any of these issues, however, were what came to be called "the social issues," notably school integration. Earlier in the year, in a case initially advanced during the Johnson Administration, the Supreme Court had ruled that segregated schools must be integrated without further delay—a decision that was a ready handle for schools located within reach of both black and white families but created problems for schools in areas where the races lived apart and the schools were geographically segregated. Many urged that court-ordered integration programs, with busing of students back and forth, were essential to produce a genuinely integrated public school system.

Nixon's cherished "Southern strategy" had already embroiled him in two bitter fights in the Senate over nominations to the Supreme Court, although he was not ready to carry the strategy to the point of opposing the Supreme Court's famous *Brown* v. *Board of Education* decision ending school segregation. But the controversy over busing revealed the considerable backlash occurring against the liberalism of the Johnson era and the whole mood of the 1960s.

The task of exploiting "the social issues" to the maximum for the 1970 campaign, and at the same time pillorying the antiwar media and college demonstrators, fell to Vice President Spiro Agnew. Armed by White House speechwriters with headline-catching phrases—"nattering nabobs of negativism" was one contributed by Safire—Agnew roamed the land in September giving tough and controversial speeches that appealed to patriotism, national pride, the work ethic, above all law and order, and accused the Democrats of being "soft" on these central subjects. The immediate political effect of this blistering and well-remembered effort was mixed. Nixon returned from Europe to find that the polls indicated substantial Democratic gains; as he saw it, Agnew's offensive had peaked too early, the Democrats had been able to blunt it and had shifted the focus to their strong suit, the economy.[127]

Nixon's response was to pitch in himself: he gave no fewer than forty speeches in twenty-two states over the last three weeks of the campaign. At the end, in his native California, where his combative instincts were often at their strongest, he courted a confrontation in San Jose with a large group of demonstrators against the Vietnam War when, as he emerged after a speech to a screened audience, he got up on his limousine and made his habitual V sign with his arms. Objects, including rocks, were then thrown and the limousine itself dented before the Secret Service could make a hasty getaway. Nixon may have recalled that his handling of hostile demonstrations in Caracas in 1958 had produced public reactions favorable to him, and this was again the case. Two nights later, in Phoenix, Arizona, he was warmly received when he proclaimed that he would not be silenced and that this kind of disruptive behavior, along with other threats to law and order, must be brought under control.

Then he made the kind of mistake that had dogged him before: he decided to use a recorded tape of his Phoenix speech and of the crowd's response as his closing campaign address to the nation on election eve. Unfortunately, the tape was static-laden and came over very poorly, whereas the spokesman for the Democrats, Senator Edmund Muskie of Maine, seated in a fireside setting, delivered a restrained and dignified defense of the Democrats' record and of their approach to the social issues Nixon had raised.

The election next day gave the Democrats a gain of nine in the House, against a two-seat gain for the Republicans in the heavily Democratic Senate. Only three longtime Senate critics of the Vietnam War either lost or retired; the swing in House seats was considerably less than the average for midterm elections. Like almost all observers, Nixon knew that the election was a setback for him, and that he would need new accomplishments to win in 1972.

One immediate reaction was to soft-pedal any plans for domestic reform or innovation. Nixon let the Family Assistance Plan go down the drain, and a disappointed but still loyal Daniel Patrick Moynihan returned to Harvard. (In 1973, he accepted Nixon's offer to become ambassador to India, and went to the United Nations a year later. In 1977, returning to the Democratic fold, he was elected to the Senate from New York.) Nixon also looked hard at a favorite project, reorganizing the executive branch. A citizens commission, to that end, created in early 1969 and headed by Roy Ash of Litton Industries, was by now ready to report. Its main proposals, pressed by Nixon, were for a domestic policy structure that would enable the President to exercise much tighter control of the executive through the creation of three supercabinet positions with defined areas of responsibility. Nixon wanted machinery that normally ran without his direct intervention, so that he could keep himself apart, think in broad, long-range terms, and come into view only when it was necessary to put a case to the country.

Congress, always a graveyard for ambitious plans to reorganize the executive branch, handled the Ash Commission's recommendations during the next year in its usual fashion, so that no significant part of them was adopted. But the exercise did bring to Nixon's close attention an outstanding personality on the Ash Commission. This was the Democrat John Connally, just ending eight successful and well-publicized years as governor of Texas. Fresh from playing a decisive part in the nomination and election of Lloyd Bentsen to the Senate, over George Bush, he was going back to law practice, ambitious without limits, hankering for a shot at the national scene, but torn between residual loyalty to the Democratic Party and vigorous dissent from its liberal wing and recent behavior.[128] A few years before, hardly anyone would have dreamed that "Big Jawn" Connally would ever serve in a Republican Administration. He had come to Washington in the late 1930s as a protégé of Lyndon Johnson, and had remained very close to Johnson. Elected governor of Texas in 1962, he was riding in President Kennedy's car in Dallas on November 21, 1963, and was wounded by the same series of shots that killed JFK. This made him more of a national figure (and glamorous object of sympathy) and he continued to dominate Texas politics through outstanding qualities of decisiveness and voter appeal, a mastery of politics at all levels, and a commanding personality and appearance.

Nixon knew a political professional when he saw one, admired political skills more than any others, and was drawn to Connally temperamentally. When the Ash Commission briefed Nixon and key members of Congress in mid-November 1970, Ash became confused explaining its recommendations. Connally stepped forward and did a masterful job of simplification and advocacy. Nixon was sold. Though Connally had few credentials as a financial thinker, Nixon wanted him to replace David Kennedy as Secretary of the Treasury, not least because, as he told close colleagues, his Cabinet lacked a potential successor as President. From the first, Nixon saw Connally as his heir in 1976. The Texan quickly mastered the essentials and the politics of the Treasury's wide range of problems. In January he sailed through hearings on the Hill, and was confirmed and installed in early February.

At once the new Secretary made it clear that he looked only to President Nixon for guidance. He quickly became an important voice on issues beyond his immediate sphere, including the Vietnam War. Altogether, he made an enormous difference in both style and substance to the Administration's domestic and international policies, in a conservative and hard-line direction.

5. Oil and the Dollar

The advent of John Connally in Nixon's Administration came at the simmering stage of two crises that bulked large in the next years. One, in which Connally played a leading part, concerned the value and role of the dollar in the international economy. The other, over the price and supply of oil, did not come to a dramatic head until the fall of 1973, but well before that had threatened a major shift in the balance of international power—in favor of oil-producing countries and at the expense of consumer nations, especially the United States.

Wrenching change in both areas was virtually inevitable, or at least could have been headed off earlier only by remarkable foresight and imagination, combined with candor, courage, and great skill in devising and selling to the American people changes in policy and lifestyle that ran strongly against ingrained habits of thought and behavior. In the years since World War II, Americans at all levels had come to take for granted the solidity and primacy of the dollar and the ready availability of cheap oil. (It was symptomatic that a 1960 report on "national goals" for the next decade included no chapter on oil or energy, while the international economic chapter dealt only with questions of trade and aid.[129]) No U.S. Administration from 1945 to 1969 had gotten down to basics on the role of the dollar and the question of an adequate energy supply at fair prices. Now the Nixon Administration was forced to do so.[130]

What the ordinary voter could see in the summer before the 1970 elections was a mild recession, with unemployment and inflation both up. To professional economists and observers, the international aspects of this situation were especially worrisome. For many years the U.S. balance of payments with foreign nations had shown a deficit, largely due to the expense of keeping U.S. forces stationed abroad and maintaining what were still, under Nixon, a substantial number of overseas bases. By late 1970 there was also a substantial trade deficit, in part with a resurgent Japan. Concern over this situation was not new, including doubts whether the United States could go on acting as kingpin of the Bretton Woods system (named for the resort in New England where a 1944 conference of the wartime Allies had produced agreement on it). Under that system the dollar was the lead currency by which all others were measured, with the United States undertaking to keep a fixed-price gold supply adequate to meet demands from other nations and to act as a banker of last resort when others might be in difficulties. For twenty years the United States had been the Atlas supporting the system. Coming before the Marshall Plan or NATO, Bretton Woods stood as perhaps the foremost example and symbol of U.S. leadership in the postwar world. Initially a "First World" grouping embracing only industrialized non-Communist countries, the structure—especially through its offshoots, the World Bank and the International Monetary Fund—came in the next twenty-five years to have a great effect on the "Third World" of less developed nations. Only the Communist great powers, the Soviet Union and China, along with their dependent Communist regimes in the "Second World," remained outside it.

Concerns about the inability of the Bretton Woods system to maintain an adequate supply of funds for a rapidly growing trading system—"liquidity" in the jargon — led to the creation in 1967 by the International Monetary Fund of a new financial source, called Special Drawing Rights, to which nations could turn for funds in tight times. SDRs were a novelty and it was not clear whether they were truly an international money or more like a line of credit. At any rate they had not become a strong stabilizing force. As Paul Volcker, Nixon's Under Secretary of the Treasury for Monetary Affairs, later wrote:

> [E]conomic performance during the 1960s had been enormously encouraging. . . . European economic recovery was complete, with enormous growth in Germany and most European countries. . . . International investment revived and trade expanded steadily. Economists developed new confidence in their ability to manage the economy. But by the end of the decade, there was no disguising the fact that, SDRs or not, the very monetary system that had helped make it all possible had fallen into jeopardy.[131]

One early tremor had come in the spring of 1968, when President Johnson, trying to sort out Vietnam policy after the setback of the Tet offensive, found himself constrained by the fact that gold was under pressure from private buyers at the low official price. Almost certainly his decision not to order a significant force increase in Vietnam at that time would have been the same in any case, but the financial situation was a clinching factor. The policy response was limited: sales of gold to private buyers were suspended, creating a two-tier gold market with official transactions separate from private ones. The private market came rapidly to reflect and dramatize underlying confidence in the system and in individual nations, above all the United States. Then, concerned about continuing high budget deficits, Johnson reluctantly agreed to a substantial tax increase. This fiscal effort to stabilize the economy was joined by a tight monetary policy guided by Chairman William McChesney Martin of the Federal Reserve, a policy that continued when Martin's fourteen-year term ended in December 1969 and Arthur Burns took his place.[132]

Under Nixon, with the costs of the war declining and domestic program costs rising, the policy of restraining inflation led to continued monetary austerity. The rate of inflation did slow down in 1970, from 6 percent to 5.5 percent, and was still going down in early 1971. Yet even though inflation had not been experienced seriously since World War II, fear of it remained high in the business community and elsewhere. Significant support grew for an outright "incomes policy" — that is, for government action to freeze wages and prices in some fashion or to limit the scale of increases.[133]

John Connally quickly showed himself able to speak authoritatively to high-level gatherings of bankers and businessmen on these and other issues.

(Particularly reassuring to this key audience was that he had retained all the top professionals in his department upon taking office.) But behind the scenes, Volcker in particular was becoming deeply concerned by the steady drop in U.S. gold stocks, to less than half what they had been in 1960, and by continuing adverse trends in the U.S. trade and liquidity positions. Knowing that any formal paper might leak, with devastating consequences, he set down his concerns in a draft private memorandum to Connally early in 1971, saying that if these trends continued, as he thought likely, a change in the parity rate of the dollar would become necessary. However, this could be done only in the wider context of negotiating a major currency realignment, which in turn would be possible only if the "gold window," official sales from U.S. gold stocks, was closed. Lastly, he favored concurrent major anti-inflationary moves, a temporary wage/price freeze, and complementary restraints in fiscal and monetary policy.

The draft memorandum was prophetic, and surely influential. But there is no indication that it reached Nixon, or that in early 1971 he or Kissinger was much concerned over economic problems. In Volcker's words: "Those responsible for security affairs, typically beginning with the president, were inclined to view the dollar problem as something we [the experts] should make go away, presumably painlessly."[134] But events were taking over. The foundations of the postwar economic system were under threat as they had not been for nearly twenty-seven years.

Oil, the subject of the second budding crisis, had been since the late 1930s the most critical raw material for all industrial societies, hence an important source of international friction and national power.[135] In any survey of twentieth-century America, two features would always stand out— the rise of the automobile and the availability of cheap oil. At first the main source of oil supplies was right at home, with large discoveries and strikes in the American South and Southwest coinciding from the 1920s on with the spreading use of automobiles and trucks. After World War II, federal and state government policy continued to promote domestic oil production, especially through favorable tax provisions. New discoveries continued, and for two decades the United States remained the largest producing nation in the world, satisfying domestic oil consumption while retaining a substantial reserve capacity to serve allies and friendly countries in crisis.

Between 1948 and 1972, however, the use of oil and the national and geographic distribution of oil production capacity and proven oil reserves changed with great speed. Global crude oil production increased fivefold, from 8.7 million barrels a day (mbd) to 42 mbd, while the U.S. share, though rising at a healthy rate from 5.5 to 9.5 mbd, shrank as a percentage of total world production from a dominant 64 percent to 22 percent. The distribution of oil reserves changed even more, with the Middle East becoming the new center of gravity. Proven reserves in the United States increased from 21 to 38 billion barrels, but this now represented only 7 percent of total world reserves, as compared with 34 percent in 1948. In the same period, proven reserves in the Middle East went from 28 to 367 billion barrels, 68.7 percent of the world total and rising! The oil industry and oil experts took all this in, though many thought that new discoveries in Alaska and elsewhere would hold the line of American predominance for some time. The general public hardly grasped it at all and continued to think of the United States as assuredly self-sufficient.

Almost all this expansion in oil production and discoveries came through the efforts of private interests, the old international oil companies, long dominated by a few major American, British, and Anglo-Dutch corporations, the famous Seven Sisters. These were intensely competitive in production and sales but quietly collaborative in sharing their experiences, in not undercutting each other in dealing with oil-producing nations, and in maintaining parallel prices. It was only a slight exaggeration to call them a cartel.

At the gas pump and on the trade highways of the world, the Seven Sisters were conspicuous. Their American members, especially Standard Oil of New Jersey (later Exxon), were household names everywhere. In the halls of Congress, on the other hand, the "internationals" had little influence as compared with domestic oil interests, with their local bases, their employees who could lobby members of Congress, and their patriotic aura, as opposed to the slightly alien and mysterious image of the internationals.

The result, under Eisenhower, was that strong pressure from the "domestics" to limit oil imports prevailed over his free-trade instincts, leading to the creation in 1959 of a system of oil import quotas administered by a federal entity, the interagency Oil Import Board, which set total imports at levels designed to protect the domestic industry's sales and prices at all times. Prices for foreign crude oil were far lower than those in the United States, and there was lively competition among U.S. refineries for shares in the quotas. With their sales to the U.S. market limited, the internationals developed markets in Europe, Japan, and elsewhere. They became immensely powerful — magnets for stock-market investors but also for suspicion among liberals in their own countries, as well as resentment in the regimes of the oil-producing countries.

Then, in quick succession, came a measure of competition from the Soviet Union, with vast reserves but only a moderate capacity to develop and transport them, and the discovery of large deposits in Libya. (In addition to its "west of Suez" geographic advantage, Libyan oil was low in sulfur.) Overall, there was an oil glut by 1959–60. Forced to lower their own sale prices in the resulting intense competition, the old internationals — first British Petroleum, later Standard Oil of New Jersey — imposed two successive unilateral cuts in the so-called posted price, the amount per barrel that determined what they paid, at an agreed percentage, to the oil-producing nations.

These fateful moves were taken with no consultation with the producers. The second price cut led to the national governments creating an Organization of Petroleum Exporting Countries (OPEC), which included almost all the principal producing countries in the Middle East, Latin America, and Africa. Under the leadership principally of the oil ministers of Saudi Arabia, Venezuela, Iran, and, at times, Iraq, OPEC shortly demonstrated considerable cohesion, but in a still glutted market could only head off further drops in the posted price. As one oil executive put it later, it was a sideshow: "The reality of the oil world was U.S. import quotas, Russian oil exports, and competition. This was what filled the columns of the trade press, the minds of oil executives and the memos of government policy makers."[136] Along the way, few took account of the "new internationals," with their own concessions and links to supply, notably two companies active in Libya, Conoco and Occidental, the latter headed by the legendary Armand Hammer, veteran of early trade with the Soviet Union and a natural loner and bucker of systems.

The old internationals and their parent governments were still in control of the market when the Six-Day War between Egypt and Israel broke out in 1967. The Arab oil producers wanted desperately to demonstrate their power by a concerted embargo of, principally, the United States and Britain, but the threatened countries and Seven Sisters quickly organized a system to divert oil to the embargoed countries. It became clear that the maximum cutoff of 1.5 mbd could be made up by a surge of a million barrels a day from the United States and lesser increases from Venezuela, Iran, and Indonesia. By July, six weeks after the war ended, the Arab embargo had been defeated, with the countries that had instigated it the biggest losers.

Then came the crucial turnaround, triggered by simple arithmetic — growing American demand rapidly exceeding the maximum attainable U.S. rate of production, which was by then leveling off. By the time Nixon was elected, a State Department officer reported publicly that American production would shortly be unable to serve again as a reserve in crisis. With help from high prices and the protectionist import quota system, domestic oil production had increased substantially in the 1950s, but diminishing returns now set in with no favorable offset in sight — not, at least, in the lower forty-eight states. Still, there was hope — centered on a major strike in the Prudhoe Bay area of northern Alaska in December 1967, which in the first blush of optimism was forecast to produce 2 mbd within three years, with a chance of additional strikes nearby. If this level had been attained, the balance might perhaps have held for another five years;

but the attempt to build a pipeline ran into major problems of climate and terrain, then into objections from groups concerned with its effect on the environment.

In the fall of 1969 the aged King Idris of Libya, who had permitted important American air bases on his territory and, later, oil exploration, was deposed in a quick coup by Colonel Muammar al-Qaddafi. At one point a protégé and disciple of Nasser in Egypt, Qaddafi was an ardent Pan-Arab and a zealous Muslim, hostile not only to Italy, once Libya's colonial master, but to the West in general. From the first, he saw clearly that his country could bring great pressure to bear on the oil companies operating in it, the "new internationals" that lacked the alternative capacity in other countries that gave the Seven Sisters such power.[137] In August 1970, the premium value of Libyan oil in the European market—of which it already had a 30 percent share—was enhanced by an accidental break in the pipeline that carried Saudi oil to the Mediterranean coast (avoiding the still closed Suez Canal). Qaddafi made his move: after an intense and dramatic negotiation with Armand Hammer, who vainly appealed to Standard Oil of New Jersey for supplies to help his bargaining position, Occidental accepted a large increase in the posted price and an increase in Libya's share of the company's profit from 50 to 55 percent. As Daniel Yergin wrote: "The Libyan agreements decisively changed the balance of power between the governments of the producing countries and the oil companies. For the oil-exporting countries the Libyan victory was emboldening. It not only abruptly reversed the decline in the real price of oil, but also reopened the exporters' campaign for sovereignty and longer control over their oil resources."[138]

After Qaddafi's triumph, the next producer to move was Iran; the Shah insisted on the same 55 percent of profits and got it in November from the nation's operating consortium. The companies were being whipsawed between the producers in the Persian Gulf on the one hand and those west of Suez (or with pipeline terminals on the Mediterranean) on the other.

In December, a full OPEC meeting concurred that 55 percent should hereafter be the minimum producer share. The participant nations also closed ranks to agree that they would not allow any company negotiating with a single member to fortify its bargaining position by increasing its take in another country. In effect, this put all the companies in the same position Hammer had been in, with no alternative source to turn to if a host country was difficult. The companies therefore reversed their field, accepted group negotiation, and tried to make it OPEC-wide, to avoid leapfrogging between Gulf and Mediterranean-access producers. On cue, Libya made new demands in January 1971. In response, a total of two dozen companies, representing 80 percent of world oil production, asked OPEC for a global settlement. At once the Shah dug in against an OPEC-wide forum, offering a deal with the Gulf countries only and claiming that with his influence on the other Gulf producers he could ensure an agreement that would be stable for five years.

At this point the Nixon Administration got involved. In preparing for a hoped-for conference with OPEC nations, America's oil companies had again sought a waiver of the antitrust laws, which they had been granted in 1956 and 1967 for their cooperative allocation of oil among consuming countries. This time, too, the Justice Department (presumably in consultation with the White House) agreed; it was a routine and natural move. Then, in early January 1971, it was decided to bring U.S. government influence to bear directly. Previous dealings with Iran had often been top-level and personal—in 1969 the Shah had asked Nixon for greater import allowances in the U.S. market than the quota system permitted, and Nixon had demurred. This time, Under Secretary of State John Irwin was sent to Teheran to back up the companies' case for OPEC-wide negotiation. Whether this decision was made in the White House or at the State Department is not recorded, nor whether the companies asked for such an intervention. What does seem clear is that an Administration already beset by problems with Congress over Cambodia and Laos, during the normally let-down holiday season (with the President at San Clemente and Kissinger not engaged on oil matters), simply did not get its act together.

The result was a fiasco. With some fanfare, and plenty of notice in business and government circles, Irwin—in private life an experienced New York lawyer—went out to Teheran, found the Shah totally adamant, and within two days yielded and accepted a Gulf-only negotiation. The two senior Seven Sisters executives waiting in the wings were horrified, especially since there had been little sharing of thoughts before Irwin went out.[139]

To what extent was the President involved? Did he or anyone else invoke his long-standing relationship with the Shah, or Iran's reliance on the United States for its security? Probably the President did not play any real part, though he may have formally approved Irwin's mission. After all, we know that he hated confrontation or difficult negotiations, especially with a warm personal friend. And, with his limited grasp of economics and of oil, he probably did not consider the stakes in this case very high, certainly not high enough to warrant the risk of unsettling the relationship with the ruler he counted on as a twin pillar of security in the Persian Gulf. In effect, relations between Iran and the United States thereafter proceeded on two tracks, with security collaboration kept quite separate from decisions about oil.[140]

After the failure of the Irwin mission, it was inevitable that the companies would collapse. After a month of intense negotiation, they and the Gulf producing countries signed a final agreement in Teheran on February 14, 1971: the 55 percent profit share was given to all nations in the group, along with an immediate increase in the posted price, with further increases to follow over the next four years, by small but cumulatively important amounts (eleven cents a year). In return, the producers accepted the Shah's promise that the agreement would hold for the five-year period.

In the spring, Qaddafi took another bite, demanding and getting a further large increase in the posted price, with a similar escalation clause running through 1975. This second agreement underlined the precariousness of the Shah's promise at Teheran. Dismayed as they were, the oil companies tried to downplay the agreement; some believed that cries of alarm would not only upset the market further, but make the producers all the more aware of their power.

In the U.S. market, the effect on gasoline prices at the pump at first was only slight. Thus, for some time the significance of the change symbolized by the Teheran and Tripoli agreements was grasped only in small circles. One of the few Westerners to sound an alarm was the highly respected oil expert Walter J. Levy, who assessed the situation in downright terms:

> The balance among oil-producing and exporting countries and oil-consuming and importing countries, and among oil companies themselves appears, at least as of now, to have shifted decisively in favor of the producing countries. . . .
>
> For their part, consuming countries are faced with appreciably higher prices for their oil imports, which for most constitute by far the major share of their total energy supplies and energy costs. Foreign exchange outlays are thus mounting rapidly. And the traumatic experience of confrontation between the industry and the producing governments raises new questions as to the security of essential oil flows against interruption. Clearly, a very real challenge to the historical structure and operation of the internationally integrated oil industry is emerging—at a time when demand for oil is increasing swiftly.[141]

Europe and Japan depended heavily on OPEC oil, he noted, and with the United States' surplus capacity nearly gone, it would have to increase its OPEC imports perhaps "appreciably."[142]

Levy's tocsin for greater government attention and coordinated action among the principal consuming countries was well ahead of its time. Yet even his apparently alarmist projections much underestimated the pace of events, while his broad policy suggestions kept to the issues of increasing oil production and generating new non-oil energy sources. Like almost all other observers, he made no mention of steps to reduce oil consumption. Even the best minds were always behind the events, and thought about necessary change too narrowly.

. . .

The threat to the dollar, like the change in the oil business, suggested to serious observers a drastic transformation in the structure of free world economies. And it, too, represented a downward step in the role and importance of the United States in the world economy. The extent of the changes was often understated at the time, by the U.S. government particularly, but it was to become very great indeed. Moreover, the two changes fed on each other. More expensive foreign oil from abroad made the difficulties that the dollar encountered in the 1970s all the harder to solve, and when the dollar declined, the oil producers inevitably demanded compensatory increases in the dollar-denominated price of oil. A third problem had to do with the effect of dollar and oil trends on countries that were outside the mainstream, or free world, economic system, specifically the Soviet Union. To say that the power and influence of the United States were reduced is not of course to say that the situation or status of the Soviet Union improved in equal or balancing measure. Even in security matters during the most acute phases of the Cold War, the concept of a "zero-sum" game, with every gain for one side an equally serious loss for the other, was highly suspect and often overdrawn, and in economics it rarely applied. Yet in this instance the unsettled dollar tending downward and oil prices tending upward worked almost at once to the benefit of the Soviet Union, since it was a major producer of gold and oil. In the unofficial free market in which Soviet gold was traded, the price trend was almost always the reverse of the trend in the dollar's exchange rate, even when the official gold price remained constant. By 1970 Soviet sales of gold were a principal source of hard currency, which the Soviet Union perennially needed. At the same time, Soviet oil sales in the world market immediately benefited from any increase in the market price arising from new oil agreements. In 1970, these oil sales were another substantial contribution to Soviet hard currency levels.

6. Cambodia Again and Laos[143]

When the last American forces and advisors were withdrawn from Cambodia in the summer of 1970, the American government had only its small mission in Phnom Penh to provide information. For a time, journalists gave the country a high priority. Without the usual protection from U.S. forces, several were taken prisoner, and some were killed or missing. Three — Richard Dudman of the *St. Louis Post-Dispatch*, Elizabeth Pond of *The Christian Science Monitor*, and Michael Morrow of Dispatch News Service — were captured in May by a mixed Vietcong/Khmer Rouge force under North Vietnamese military command. Their accounts painted a striking picture of Communist forces operating with real concern for rural Cambodians, in contrast to what the people saw as harsh and indiscriminate shelling and bombing from its government, linked directly to U.S. support. Dudman wrote:

> . . . the bombing and the shooting was radicalizing the people of rural Cambodia and was turning the countryside into a massive, dedicated and effective rural base. American shells and bombs are proving to the Cambodians beyond doubt that the United States is waging unprovoked colonialist war against the Cambodian people.[144]

This stark conclusion made clear the acute dilemmas that confronted any American attempt to assist Lon Nol. To approach the situation in conventional military ways alienated the Cambodians and stunted the development of an effective indigenous military force. The Cambodian Army was a ragtag lot that had grown from its original 35,000 to now more than 100,000 (eventually to more than 200,000), its offensive capabilities were nil, and it was kept under steady and shifting pressures by the North Vietnamese and Vietcong.

By the fall of 1970, Communist forces controlled almost all of northern and northeastern Cambodia, and were strong enough in the central and southern parts to threaten the main roads connecting Phnom Penh to other towns and to the seaport of Kompong Som (formerly Sihanoukville). The sea line of communication and supply was never truly opened up, and Phnom Penh had to rely on supplies coming up the Mekong from South Vietnam by boat, a route vulnerable to sporadic harassment. In this situation of perpetual siege of a constricted area around the capital, Lon Nol pressed constantly for greater assistance to make his army a viable force. Buoyed by an initial surge in morale and patriotism, volunteers had flocked to enlist in the spring and the tide continued to flow through the summer. Alexander Haig, the first important visitor in May, and a succession of military visitors from Saigon and Honolulu readily persuaded President Nixon that it was unconscionable not to do as much for Lon Nol as Congress would allow. The result was an initial program of about $40 million in Army equipment, chiefly small arms.

From the first, this aid effort had to confront enormous obstacles, starting with the personality of Lon Nol. Out from under the shadow of Sihanouk and on his own for the first time, Lon Nol, who had been imagined by many Americans, including Nixon, as a "strong man," soon showed himself mercurial, mystical, indecisive, and in no real touch with his people. His only close allies were mediocre officers from the old Army, and his relationship with the one civilian who was a leader, Prince Sirik Matak, was uncertain. His grasp of social and economic issues was never more than rudimentary, and the pool of talent on which he could draw for help in governing was extremely small.[145]

Moreover, dislocation inevitably strengthened a latent tendency to corruption. The familiar East Asian pattern for troubled regimes — military pay-
rolls padded to line the pockets of commanders, favoritism and "squeeze"
at every turn — soon took hold and grew steadily. Phnom Penh ballooned
to several times its prewar size as refugees streamed in from the countryside, and shortly came to embody just about every defect and weakness that
had developed in South Vietnam over years of warfare, and added a few of
its own.

Another problem was the eruption of the always latent hostility between
Cambodians and Vietnamese (whether non-Communist or Communist).
Basically, no Cambodian ever forgot that it was Vietnamese who had taken
the last big bites, in the south, out of the once vast area of the Khmer
Kingdom. When Lon Nol took power in March, he had appealed to
nationalist feeling by encouraging not only attacks on Communist Vietnamese, including the North Vietnamese Embassy, but harassment of
Cambodia's half million ethnic Vietnamese, most of whom had lived there
for long periods and were politically neutral, or in many cases supporters
of Thieu in Saigon. So the continued presence of South Vietnamese
forces, filling in with American blessing as the U.S. forces departed, was
a dubious asset. These ARVN troops, about 15,000 of them at this point,
made no effort to cooperate with the Cambodian Army. Roaming the
countryside on their own, as one later description said, "Thieu's troops
looted their way across the country to Phnom Penh," stealing automotive
equipment and much else as they went. When they "finally reached
Phnom Penh in September, fighting broke out between Cambodian and
Vietnamese soldiers."[146]

Yet giving reassurance to Lon Nol — stroking, as some called it — was a
primary feature of American policy. Vice President Agnew visited in August
1970 with much fanfare, struck up a relationship with Lon Nol, and came
at intervals thereafter. Nixon himself sent Lon Nol frequent personal letters
of support and encouragement, which the general proudly displayed to all
and sundry. From the first, he saw Lon Nol as a special charge, a leader
who had gone out on a limb to change his country's policy and align
himself with America; it was typical of Nixon's strong tendency to person-
alize relationships.

Although Henry Kissinger was to become the chief target of at least one
influential account of the war in Cambodia (William Shawcross's *Side-
show*), the evidence is persuasive that except for Haig, the NSC staff and
Kissinger himself played little part in guiding American policy in Cambodia
or even in following developments there. By his strong advocacy of the
Cambodian incursion when others, including Kissinger, were doubters,
Haig had made his mark with Nixon and greatly increased his influence.
Kissinger made only one fleeting visit to Phnom Penh between 1970 and

1973, but Haig went repeatedly and at key points, as in May and December 1970 and the spring of 1971. The American officer talked with Lon Nol as one military man to another, probably doing little to discourage his flights of military fancy. The result was that U.S. policy in Cambodia was from the first dominated by military advice, far more so than was the case in South Vietnam.

This military predominance was established before the American Embassy in Phnom Penh became a truly functioning outpost. Only in the late summer of 1970 did it get a building of its own, and in September an ambassador, Emory Swank, a Foreign Service officer of considerable experience and capacity, who was joined in January 1971 by Thomas Enders, also a Foreign Service officer, as deputy. Swank's career had been concerned primarily with the Soviet Union and Eastern Europe, but he had done well in Laos as deputy to William Sullivan in 1964–66 and was a sensitive reporter with good policy judgment. However, his past career little prepared him for the kibitzing he had to deal with from the White House for the next three years. Enders was more adaptable and assertive. He was a neophyte on Southeast Asia, but a quick study. Soon, many key matters were dealt with by a back-channel to him personally from Haig and Kissinger. Swank and Enders could have been in other circumstances a strong team. Certainly their selection reflected the State Department's loyal support for the Cambodian policy that Secretary Rogers and Assistant Secretary Green had advised against before May 1.

By the summer, Rogers and Green were charged with the task of enlisting third-country aid in Cambodia. Although the Cooper-Church Amendment was rejected by House conferees right through the summer and fall, in practice the Administration did not dare challenge its dictates, and the Senate, especially the Foreign Relations Committee, was cool to any sort of American aid program. Moreover, the SEATO alliance was becoming a dead letter. In Britain, France, the Philippines, even Australia and New Zealand, there was only support enough for the American effort in Indochina to permit some aid to South Vietnam, but not Cambodia. Elsewhere, attitudes were at best neutral. Cambodia, under Sihanouk, had never been a participant in any Southeast Asian group, and the increasingly important Association of Southeast Asian Nations (ASEAN) was willing only to urge that both sides withdraw from Cambodia.

The only potential exception was Thailand, which generally welcomed the U.S. incursion into Cambodia as a deterrent to the feared North Vietnamese, and for similar reasons willingly collaborated with the United States in northern and central Laos. In 1970, the problem was, or was said to be, one of cost. The Thai, through their feisty Foreign Minister, Thanat Khoman, professed a willingness to send equipment and trainers, but the United States would have to pay for resupplying their forces and (directly or indirectly) paying those in Cambodia. In effect the Thai leaders were suggesting a modest repeat of the deal that in the 1960s had led to Thailand's sending a combat division to South Vietnam itself. With these discussions well publicized, the American Congress moved in. Senator Symington's hearings in 1969 had given a bad name to the idea of any U.S. recompense for Asian nations supplying forces in Indochina, and the Senate Armed Services Committee, normally responsive to Nixon, voted unanimously in July to oppose any support arrangement whatever, with Thailand plainly in mind.

By September the Administration was in a bind, partly of its own making. Nixon had said publicly that "to get drawn into the permanent direct defense of Cambodia" was "inconsistent with the basic premise of our foreign policy." Now he had to choose between eating his words and letting Lon Nol languish unaided.

Nixon often hesitated when faced with such choices, but this time he had no doubt. In late October, he had Kissinger push through a decision to seek from Congress a substantial military aid program for the Lon Nol regime, with accompanying economic aid. The $100 million already diverted from other programs would be repaid, and a new $150 million provided. There was no significant chance for debate among the policymakers, and the decision was kept secret from Congress and the public until after the elections. The program was finally announced in November, as Congress was reconvening for the first lame-duck session in years.

Nixon had to convene this session because Congress had been unable to agree on the necessary actions to complete a budget for fiscal 1971 (ending in July 1971). But he also had to confront the still pending Cooper-Church Amendment and, of lesser importance, the formal repeal of the Tonkin Gulf Resolution, to which he had, in effect, already agreed in June.[147]

The Administration's plan for aid for Cambodia was put in a supplemental foreign aid package that also included the $500 million military aid program for Israel which Nixon had promised Mrs. Meir in September and which had almost universal support. While it was generally known that Secretary Rogers had initially opposed involvement in Cambodia, he now was the one to present the case for this aid, arguing essentially that the United States simply could not let it collapse into Communism.

A key man was the able Assistant Secretary of State for Congressional Relations, David Abshire. A graduate of West Point, he had left the Army to work first with the Republican Senate minority and then in a conservative think tank. Under his guidance at daily meetings, the Administration spoke with one voice, and missed no trick during the two months of intense struggle.[148] The battle lines were clearly drawn from the start. The House Foreign Affairs Committee, which had to authorize foreign aid programs, had with a few exceptions strongly supported the Vietnam War policies of successive Presidents. True to form, it convened promptly to hear Rogers and then voted to recommend approval to the House as a whole, which passed the supplemental authorization bill on December 10 by an overwhelming 344–21 margin. The aid to Israel was doubtless a factor in the size of the majority. With the House Appropriations Committee equally favorable and sure to approve, the action moved to the Senate.

Majority Leader Mansfield and Foreign Relations Committee Chairman Fulbright had both opposed U.S. involvement in the whole Indochina War for at least a half decade, and had spoken out with special vigor against the Cambodian incursion. Both now did all they could to block the bill. Yet, with the link to aid to Israel and the many other pending budget items that were popular, and with the fiscal year already half over, they could not tie up the remaining budget requests. Those in favor of the aid to Cambodia, on the other hand, could hardly oppose the restraints in the Cooper-Church Amendment, which were drawn almost literally from what Nixon had promised on several occasions he would not do. There was room for compromise on both sides, and it was achieved between Secretary Rogers and Senator Cooper. He and Church agreed to modify their amendment's total ban on U.S. combat air activity in favor of wording that permitted such action if directed at North Vietnamese supply or force buildups in Cambodia. It was a frail distinction at best, especially since there were no Americans in Cambodia to provide the necessary information. From the first, Nixon and his air commanders operated virtually without restraint.

Finally, in the second week of January, the key bills were passed, including, for good measure, the formal repeal of the Tonkin Gulf Resolution. All in all, the outcome surely exceeded Nixon's hopes, as well as the initial expectations of those who had worked so hard and effectively for him. As a bitter Senator Fulbright said shortly after, "providing money to finance the war in Cambodia was in fact a commitment whether we called it that or not." He was right. Congress had crossed the Rubicon, and knew it. For the next two years it approved appropriations to support Lon Nol's Cambodia, and basically went along with Nixon's policy.

The law enacted by Congress in January 1971 did contain one key restraint. A year earlier, Nixon had readily accepted a ban on the introduction of U.S. "combat forces" into Laos. At that point, all parties were thinking primarily in terms of the continued fighting in northern and central Laos, well away from the Ho Chi Minh Trail, and "combat forces" were understood to mean organized ground forces. (In central Laos, U.S. military and paramilitary personnel were active only on a very small scale.) In the January 1971 law, however, a significant change was made: not only "combat forces" but "advisors" were barred from both Cambodia and Laos. Just how this change came about is impossible to extract from the written record.

But the stiffening of the ground rules shortly had great consequences in Laos.

As the campaign season began in early 1971, Nixon and his civilian and military advisors had no doubt that the North Vietnamese were building up for a climactic offensive, in either 1971 or 1972. By late 1970, intelligence reports of a greatly increased flow of men and matériel down the Ho Chi Minh Trail underlined the possibility of a 1971 offensive. All hands recognized that North Vietnam was likely to hit particularly hard, as it had in the Tet offensive of 1968, not only at the two northern provinces along the coast but in the central highlands and farther south, areas for which the trail was the only supply route.

So it was natural for both General Abrams and Henry Kissinger's staff to consider a dry-season push against those supply routes. Initially, Kissinger recommended a safe but limited second offensive into Cambodia, but Haig, in Saigon in December to look into the possibilities, reported that Abrams, Thieu, and Bunker favored a much bolder effort, aimed at cutting the trail at its northern end, near or alongside the demilitarized zone.[149]

The trail had long been under constant air attack, now including many B-52 strikes, and by this time the North Vietnamese had developed not only respectable antiaircraft defenses (against all except the B-52s) but also a whole network of routes to be used when one was knocked out. Only a ground operation could really cut off the flow or cause prolonged disruption. And it had been long recognized that the ideal target would be Tchepone, a small town in Laos that was at the intersection of north-south supply routes and those that ran east-west to serve the northernmost parts of South Vietnam. Tchepone was in rough country, but it could be reached by main roads from the south and southeast. Being an obvious target, it was bound to be well defended and vigorously contested.

Abrams proposed a moderate South Vietnamese operation aimed primarily at inflicting severe damage on trail installations and dumps and at capturing supplies. He knew that the North Vietnamese would put up a stiff fight with regular forces, but he judged that with U.S. air support and helicopters, the South Vietnamese could hold their own or at least, if really pressed, conduct an orderly retreat. He looked on the operation as a solid test from which Thieu, his generals, and ARVN as a whole might emerge with more confidence and experience. Moreover, it was a last clear chance to have such a test while U.S. forces were still around in strength — 344,000 at the start of 1971, of whom 60,000 were ticketed for withdrawal by spring, sharply reducing combat capability.[150]

When Haig returned from Saigon and Phnom Penh, he brought Abrams's recommendation for this offensive. It seems probable that Nixon was already three-quarters persuaded. First, he had Haig report to him with only Admiral Moorer present; then Haig repeated his briefing for Secretary Laird, with Moorer present and supporting it (without indicating he had already been informed). Impressed, Laird then went to Vietnam; on his return the circle was expanded to include Secretary Rogers and CIA Director Helms. The Secretary of State agreed with the plan—perhaps to Nixon's surprise, in light of his earlier opposition to a Cambodian incursion—but Helms pointedly recalled that a similar operation, considered in 1967 under Johnson, had been rejected when General Westmoreland estimated that he would need two army corps of American troops (several divisions) to be confident of success.

At the very least, this comment should have led to cross-examination of the Pentagon's plans, and a careful study of North Vietnamese strength in the area and likely reactions. No such study in depth was done, however. Only after the firm decision had been made, about January 18, did Kissinger raise with Admiral Moorer some obvious questions about North Vietnamese forces in the area, likely casualty rates, and—most important of all—the ability of the South Vietnamese to handle themselves without American advisors or an American-operated system of forward air controllers. Communication between ground troops and supporting airpower and helicopters would depend on South Vietnamese whose English and experience with such key elements as map coordinates were sketchy at best. To cover these points, Nixon met with Moorer and Kissinger on January 26, and the admiral stoutly reassured him. The following day, Rogers, reconsidering his position after consulting with his East Asian Bureau, argued strongly that the enemy had clearly been forewarned, that the force was inadequate, and that a setback would risk the gains made on Vietnamization.

Nixon was unmoved. In the next few days, he brought in Agnew, Connally, and Mitchell, his hard-line Greek chorus, who predictably favored going ahead, and brushed off a last-minute memo from Kissinger noting that surprise had been lost and that the government was "clearly divided." On February 3 the President gave the final go-ahead for the operation, which was given the name Lam Son 719.

The strung-out series of meetings in Washington lost precious time, for an operation that depended on some degree of surprise and on rapid movement. It left the field headquarters with only a week or two to complete the plans, which for the inexperienced South Vietnamese was much too short a time to work out the details. Help from an American corps headquarters could not pick up the slack.[151]

At least as serious a problem was the quality of the top South Vietnamese commanders. In charge at the outset was General Hoang Xuan Lam, a loyal officer with a combat record that senior Americans considered "only mediocre," even with much smaller forces than the one he now commanded. This included virtually all the best units in ARVN, totaling about three divisions of regular troops (Rangers, Airborne forces, and Marines), but almost none of these had operated together. President Thieu, in constant touch with Lam, interjected his own orders and restraints, including a sharp admonition against taking substantial casualties.[152]

Lastly, North Vietnamese capabilities were seriously underestimated. Their antiaircraft capability against low-flying aircraft had been greatly strengthened by the introduction of the Russian Strela shoulder-fired missile, and other weapons were positioned to command most of the few good landing zones in the rough terrain.[153] In all, the handicaps were enormous.

From the start, on February 8, nothing went right. U.S. helicopters were subjected to by far the most effective fire they had yet experienced — in all more than 100 helicopters were destroyed and more than 600 seriously damaged, with heavy casualties among their American crews.[154] A series of sharp engagements against the new bases set up to protect the flanks of the attack resulted in steady casualties, slowing the advance to a halt. Heavy rains added to the delay, so that the main force was less than halfway to Tchepone in the five days Abrams had planned for it to get there.

Abrams prodded the South Vietnamese without success. When the advance finally resumed, it did not reach Tchepone, by now a mere shell, until March 8, nearly a month late, and then probably only because the North Vietnamese stood aside to let the force become trapped. Dismayed by the ARVN casualties, Thieu then ordered an immediate withdrawal.

The ensuing retreat quickly turned into a rout. Forces returning by road were mercilessly strafed and shelled, and many had to be taken out on U.S. helicopters. The exhausted South Vietnamese often panicked, forcing their way onto helicopters or clinging to their skids. As these landed at the American base at Khe Sanh, in South Vietnam, journalists and photographers could see and depict vivid pictures of demoralization and defeat.

Later estimates claimed that the North Vietnamese had suffered 12,000 killed in action, against admitted South Vietnamese losses of roughly 8,000.[155] From Nixon down, American officers and officials tried to show that the operation had achieved worthwhile results. In his memoir, Nixon still called it "a military success" which forestalled any Communist offensive in the spring of 1971 and reduced casualties for the rest of the year. At the time, it was asserted that the operation had destroyed a large quantity of supplies and disrupted the trail complex at least for some months, but field reports indicated within weeks that the flow of vehicles over the trail appeared to have returned to pre-operation levels.

Whatever its net military effect, Nixon later admitted that the outcome was "a psychological defeat." To almost all observers on the ground, the dominant impression was one of defeat, even disaster. In Saigon, Thieu rigorously controlled what Vietnamese sources published, and banned the publication of accounts from outside sources, almost all of which were critical and negative. Even more revealing, he ordered the badly mauled elite Airborne and Marine forces to stay where they were, lest their condition become evident to the people.

The 1970–71 operations in Laos and Cambodia also led to particularly damaging losses among the senior South Vietnamese military leadership. Over the years, especially in the embattled year 1968, two general officers in ARVN had performed outstandingly well, General Nguyen Viet Thanh in the IV Corps area, the Mekong Delta, and General Do Cao Tri in the crucial III Corps area, west and northwest of Saigon. General Thanh was killed in a helicopter accident during the Cambodian incursion in the spring of 1970. In the offensive of early 1971, according to one reliable account, Thieu—though leery of Tri's popularity and somewhat glamorous image—was on the point of sending him to Laos in late February to take over from the indecisive General Lam, when he was killed in a helicopter crash in Cambodia. The two losses were devastating for an army almost totally lacking in senior officers capable of inspiring their troops.[156]

"Defeat is an orphan" was an old saying recalled by President Kennedy after the disastrous Bay of Pigs effort in 1961. Inevitably the handling of the Lam Son 719 offensive was subject to sharp criticism at the time, and the debate on responsibility and blame went on in later years. General Abrams never spoke out, although others defended him, noting particularly the difficulty he had with interference from Washington.[157] Kissinger and Haig later blamed the Saigon command for slowness and lack of adequate prodding, and Kissinger also blamed Washington civilians (presumably Rogers and Laird) for insisting on modifications to the plans. Conversely, General Bruce Palmer, then Deputy Chief of Staff of the Army, criticized Kissinger and his staff (meaning Haig) for excessive kibitzing. For his part, Nixon asserted that the operation had fallen short for lack of adequate air support as the going got rough. In fact, a tremendous air and helicopter effort had been made. The real defect was the lack of adequate target guidance, since no U.S. advisors or forward air controllers accompanied the force.

The greatest causes of the debacle were at the strategic level—underestimation of the North Vietnamese and overconfidence in the performance of the South Vietnamese—and for these the responsibility was multiple. Thieu's personal intervention was a major negative; the outcome showed again his reliance on senior officers for their personal loyalty rather than performance.

Haig in his memoirs asserted that the original plan always envisaged that if the South Vietnamese force ran into serious difficulty, U.S. troops would be sent into Laos "despite congressional restrictions." He blamed the Saigon command for not using American forces as early as the third day. By his account, he also handled repeated messages from Nixon to the Pentagon and the command to this effect, and Nixon went into a rage over this, even briefly proposing to send Haig himself to replace Abrams as top com-mander.[158] Neither the written record nor any other available recollection supports these statements about using U.S. forces. To have done so in the face of the emphatic ban that Congress had just enacted would surely have set off a tremendous public and congressional outcry in America. Haig could not accept, apparently, that Congress, through its constitutional power of the purse, could set conditions for military operations. That a senior military officer might be so far wrong on a central constitutional point is striking (and disturbing) even at a distance of time.

Chapter Four

1971: PROGRESS AND

PREPARATION

1. The Opening to China

At 7:30 p.m. Pacific Time, July 15, 1971, Richard Nixon appeared on all national television networks for a short statement, in which he announced that Henry Kissinger, who had just come back from a round-the-world trip, had detoured to Beijing to meet with Premier Zhou Enlai. A simultaneous announcement was being made in Beijing, the President went on, which said:

> Knowing of President Nixon's expressed desire to visit the People's Republic of China, Premier Chou En-lai, on behalf of the Government of the People's Republic of China, has extended an invitation to President Nixon to visit China at an appropriate date before May 1972. President Nixon has accepted the invitation with pleasure.
>
> The meeting is to seek the normalization of relations between the two countries and also to exchange views on questions of concern to the two sides.

This "new relationship," Nixon added, would not be "at the expense of our old friends." He had acted out of a "profound conviction that all nations will benefit from a reduction of tensions and a better relationship" between the two countries.[1]

The White House had put out an alert five hours before that an important announcement would be made on "a secret subject," so the audience was exceptionally large. And for most thoughtful Americans, except perhaps for a small segment of die-hard conservatives, the news gave a shock of pleasure. It was the signature event of Nixon's first term, and even Democrats who had long urged movement in this direction "could not forbear to cheer." Around the world the applause was loud and almost universal. The notable exception was the Soviet Union, notified only fifteen minutes before the announcement and taken completely by surprise.

Comment in the following days was filled with praise not only for the result but for the skill with which it had been accomplished. Pakistan, it emerged, had been a key actor. Stopping there in an apparently routine way, Kissinger had been reported to be indisposed at a remote hill station, but in fact he had flown in a Pakistani aircraft with three staff members all the way to Beijing, been received there without publicity, and returned the same way.

How had this all come about? As we have seen, on December 8, 1970, the Pakistani Ambassador in Washington had delivered Zhou's handwritten letter to Nixon suggesting a high-level American visit for discussions about Taiwan. On December 16, Nixon suggested discussion on a number of issues, "including the issue of Taiwan," and remarked: "With respect to the U.S. military presence on Taiwan, however, the policy of the United States Government is to reduce its military presence in the region of East Asia and the Pacific as tensions in this region diminish."[2]

It was easy to surmise that Zhou emphasized Taiwan in order to placate Lin Biao and his faction, while being himself wholly ready for wider discussions that would address the Soviet threat in the area, to which Lin Biao was blind. The next message, from Zhou alone, came via the Romanians on January 11, 1971, referring to Taiwan as the "one outstanding issue," but not objecting to a further range of subjects urged by Nixon. Most strikingly, Zhou noted that Nixon, who had already visited Bucharest and Belgrade, would also be welcome in Beijing. It was the first explicit suggestion of a visit by the President himself. Again the White House replied at once, in a receptive tone. Rightly, Kissinger considered this "a major step."[3]

Then the line went dead for three months, with no messages either way, obviously because of the South Vietnamese offensive into Laos. Although the border between Laos and China was well to the northwest of the battle zone, the extensive deployment of U.S. forces in the upper corner of South Vietnam and feints of an American attack along the North Vietnamese coast were bound to alarm the Chinese.[4] They must also have wondered, as many Americans did, whether the new U.S. involvement in Cambodia and Laos lessened the likelihood of a definite U.S. withdrawal from South Vietnam itself. At the time of the early Sino-American exchanges, the Chinese must have assumed that this withdrawal would occur, and when Zhou carried the day against the radicals and the Lin Biao faction in the fall of 1970, he could well have argued that the U.S. pullout from Cambodia proved it.

The White House watched the Chinese reaction to the Laos operation closely. Though Beijing denounced it on February 4, at the same time the Deputy Foreign Minister told the Norwegian Ambassador that China was aware of a new trend in American policy. At a press conference on February 17, Nixon was at pains to say that the Laos offensive was not directed against "Communist China"; a week later his second Foreign Policy Report corrected this outdated label, referring to the People's Republic of China by that name. Then, on March 15, drawing from the State Department's long-standing list of appropriate conciliatory moves, Nixon authorized it to announce the end to all restrictions on the use of U.S. passports for travel to China.[5]

By then the ignominious South Vietnamese retreat from Laos, with U.S. forces assisting the evacuation but making no move to get directly involved on the ground, must have helped persuade the Chinese leaders that the United States was indeed sticking to a course of withdrawal. Any remaining doubts were surely laid to rest when Nixon, in April, announced that a further 100,000 U.S. troops would be withdrawn from Vietnam between May 1 and December. The 150,000-man reduction announced a year before was about to be completed, bringing total strength down to 284,000. The new announcement meant a drop to 184,000 by December, with combat units reduced even more proportionately.[6]

That spring, the World Table Tennis Championship in Nagoya, Japan, included teams from both China and America. On April 6 the Chinese team invited the Americans to visit China. Given a green light by an alert officer at the American Embassy in Tokyo, the team accepted. "Ping-Pong diplomacy" became an instant rage in the media, and ears pricked up all over the world when the team was warmly received in China. Nixon then drew again from the list of possible conciliatory actions, modifying the long-standing embargo on trade with mainland China, for example.

On April 27 Ambassador Hilaly delivered another handwritten note from Zhou to Nixon. Any fundamental restoration of Sino-American relations required the complete withdrawal of U.S. forces from Taiwan and the Straits area, Zhou wrote, a subject that required direct discussion, for which China would be prepared to receive a special envoy "(for instance Mr. Kissinger)" or the Secretary of State "or even the President." All arrangements could be worked out through the Pakistani President, Yahya Khan. Within a day Nixon picked Kissinger for the mission, and Kissinger promptly instructed the American Ambassador to Pakistan, Joseph Farland, to start detailed planning, using a special communication link to the White House. On May 10, Nixon's reply to Zhou stressed that the first meeting should be secret. Once again, he said that each side must be free to raise any subject it wished.[7]

Kissinger has argued that any announcement or even hint of his trip would have set off a barrage of speculation as well as requests for information and reassurance, especially from allied countries in East Asia. This was a valid argument, and secrecy, as both Nixon and Kissinger knew, was also some protection against the possibility, by now very slight, that the trip would end in failure. But above all, Nixon did not want to detract from the drama of his eventual announcement.[8]

In a note delivered on June 2 by Ambassador Hilaly, Zhou accepted and suggested a late June date; Nixon responded with July 9–11, and on June 11 Zhou agreed to those dates. The next weeks were spent arranging a plausible schedule for Kissinger's trip, and working out all the details with the Pakistani government and the Chinese.

. . .

This secret process was in full swing when *The New York Times*, on June 13, began to publish excerpts from what came to be called the Pentagon Papers, a massive compilation of documents (many of them top secret) concerning U.S. policy in Vietnam from 1945 to 1967–68, prepared secretly in the last year of the Johnson Administration at the direction of Secretary of Defense Robert McNamara. The documents, almost all drawn from Defense Department files, were accompanied by narrative chapters written by individual participants in the study. In each installment, the *Times* drew on the documents and chapters but set the tone with new lead stories by its own staff to highlight and expound on their meaning. The first of these lead stories, by Neil Sheehan, a veteran reporter of the Vietnam War, to whom the Papers had been given, focused on the early summer of 1964, prior to the Gulf of Tonkin incident. It put the documents in a harsh light, suggesting a high degree of deception, which quickly became the keynote of comment about the Papers as a whole.

At once Nixon saw that the release and commentary were damaging to the Kennedy Administration and especially the Johnson Administration, but left no stain on his own Administration, indeed tended to put it in a good light by comparison. There was thus a first inclination in the White House to stand aside and let the Democrats take the heat. Not so with Kissinger. It quickly emerged that the Papers had been turned over to Sheehan and the *Times* by Daniel Ellsberg, an extremely bright and zealous man who had been in the Defense Department in 1964 and on a special mission in South Vietnam in 1965–66. At that time Ellsberg was very hard-line in his views, but by 1968 (after he participated in the compilation of the Pentagon Papers), he was a sharp critic of the war and favored early withdrawal.

Kissinger had known and briefly taught Ellsberg at Harvard, and also seen him in Vietnam in 1965–66. In early 1969 Kissinger chose Ellsberg to participate in his overall review of the Vietnam situation. Ellsberg soon joined the staff of the Rand Corporation and had access to the copy of the Papers that resided there. He became convinced that the record should be made public, and he first offered the Papers to Senator Fulbright of the Senate Foreign Relations Committee. When Fulbright refused to be the channel, Ellsberg gave the Papers to his friend Neil Sheehan, in the spring of 1971.[9]

At just that juncture, Kissinger was consumed by the need for secrecy about his China dealings. He therefore urged that such breaches of secrecy within government be dealt with harshly: he feared, not unreasonably, that the Chinese might conclude that the American government was too harassed and insecure to be a useful partner.[10] His own past ties to Ellsberg must also have been embarrassing. At Kissinger's urging, Nixon took a very tough line. In quick succession the Justice Department tried (unsuccessfully) to get a pre-publication injunction but did obtain an indictment of Ellsberg for theft of government materials. The stage was set for further White House efforts to discredit Ellsberg.

On June 30, the White House announced that Kissinger was shortly to leave on a fact-finding trip to Vietnam, that he would wind up by consulting Ambassador David Bruce in Paris on the state of the peace talks, and that along the way he would stop in Thailand, India, and Pakistan. This neat design, putting the Pakistan stop in low key, went off exactly as planned. It was Kissinger's first solo trip abroad. His purposes seemed straightforward, and the American press gave him only routine coverage and was completely taken in by the security scenario worked out with Yahya Khan in Pakistan.

Four hours after his arrival in Beijing, Kissinger met with Zhou for nearly seven hours, and the talks continued for two more days. From the first, the two men hit it off, a big step forward in itself. Both were most at home discussing issues in broad strategic terms, and each enjoyed the other's cut and thrust. This personal rapport was to continue for three years. Its only disadvantage was that the new Sino-American relationship became heavily dependent on it.[11]

A quarter century later, the record of these talks is still kept secret, but it is possible to develop a reasonably full picture on the basis of fragments of direct evidence and later comments by Kissinger. Apparently Taiwan was discussed only briefly at the outset. One American participant recalls that Kissinger's opening statement said that the United States did not support any notion of two Chinas, or one China and one Taiwan, but recognized that there was only a single China. This seemed to break the ice almost at once.[12] Both Zhou and Kissinger, then, treated Taiwan as a topic to be got out of the way. Zhou left the clear impression that China was in no hurry to take it over, and that as long as the United States was honestly moving in the direction of withdrawal from Taiwan and formal recognition of Beijing, the Taiwan issue — and a continued absence of formal relations — need not interfere with the two governments coming closer together. Contrary to what many China watchers had supposed, resolution of the Taiwan problem was not a prior condition to progress on other issues.

Along the way, Zhou volunteered a lengthy comment on the recent Cultural Revolution, with hints on how bad it had been for him and other moderates. Discussing China's internal turmoil was another sign of confidence and intimacy. Obviously he meant to emphasize that he spoke for what was now a stable Chinese leadership.[13]

On Indochina, Kissinger explained U.S. policy and discussed at some length his talks with Le Duc Tho. (In his memoirs he noted that Zhou was a rare Asian statesman who understood clearly by early 1970 that the United States was indeed getting out of Indochina. This must surely have been based on their first talks.)[14] Kissinger must also have suggested that China might exert influence on Hanoi to be more reasonable in peace talks, but in his report to Nixon he "doubted that the Chinese leaders could or would do much to help directly." This probably also meant that Zhou gave no hint that China would reduce its material and military aid to North Vietnam. In fact, this flow continued at a high rate for more than a year.[15]

Whereas Zhou wanted America out of Indochina as soon as possible, elsewhere in East Asia he saw, or came to see, that a continued large American role and presence could be in China's national interest. The East Asian problem most on his mind was the latent threat of a more activist and nationalist Japan. No Chinese mindful of Japan's behavior toward China in World War II could possibly not have had this worry when Japan re-emerged as a major regional power in the 1970s.[16] Just before Kissinger's visit, in a long conversation with Ross Terrill, an Australian expert on China, the Premier had become very agitated about the possibility of the United States working with reactionaries to revive "Japanese militarism," perhaps even giving the Japanese tactical nuclear weapons.[17] It was a fear to which Secretary Laird contributed when on July 8, in Tokyo, he "helpfully declared" (as Kissinger wryly put it) "that he was not opposed to an independent Japanese nuclear capability and that the SALT talks would confirm a strategic parity that might provide an incentive for a Japanese nuclear program."[18] Zhou had surely also studied Nixon's own strong statements about Japan's increased importance in East Asia.

Although U.S. policymakers had rarely worried about the reactions of a distant and alienated People's Republic to the postwar relationship between America and Japan, that alliance must have been an additional irritant to the Chinese. Certainly there was in Beijing a bedrock of concern and potential antagonism about it. Kissinger met the problem head-on:

On my first visit to Peking Chou En-lai accused us of tempting Japan into traditional nationalist paths. It took me some time to convince him that the U.S.-Japan alliance was not directed against China; indeed that the surest way to tempt Japanese nationalism would be to set off a competition for Tokyo's favor between China and the United States.[19]

Clearly, the original U.S.-Japan Treaty of 1951, revised and reaffirmed in 1960, *had* been directed in large part at China. Kissinger must have explained how the sharp American concerns of the 1950s had eased after the mid-1960s and were no longer acute, and that as of 1971 the U.S.-Japan alliance was really directed against a potential *Soviet* threat. Furthermore, Kissinger must have argued that the effect of the alliance was to tamp down and tightly control the nationalistic tendencies in Japan that had been so devastating in the 1930s and 1940s. Through Article 9 of the Japanese Constitution, imposed by the United States in the MacArthur era, America had consistently insisted that Japan renounce offensive military capabilities. The military posture America had helped Japan to develop and maintain was suited only for defense of the home islands and surrounding areas. Japan's tie to the United States should therefore be seen not as a menace but as a reassurance. Only if it were broken or disturbed would Japan be likely to threaten the peace of East Asia or the security of China.[20]

In the end Kissinger apparently succeeded not only in persuading Zhou to see the U.S.-Japan alliance in a favorable light but also in moving him to be more receptive to Japanese overtures toward China. Observers noted an easing of Chinese critical comment about Japan in the fall of 1971, and a year later Prime Minister Sato's successor, Kakuei Tanaka, managed to establish formal diplomatic relations between Tokyo and Beijing—a step for which the United States was not ready for many more years (till 1979).

In effect, Nixon and especially Kissinger helped to create a new and balanced triangular situation, easing Sino-Japanese enmity, leaving the United States in the position of having good relations with both the great Asian nations, and removing any chance of unhealthy competition for a favored position among the three capitals. The result also showed that an alliance with the United States could be a reassurance to other powers, even those against whom the alliance had once been directed. In all, the hours Zhou and Kissinger devoted to the Japan issue were extremely important, perhaps historic in themselves.

Their most crucial discussions, however, revolved around the Soviet Union. In the two years since the Ussuri River incident of March 1969 and the threat that summer of preemptive Soviet air attacks on China's key nuclear installations, a tense situation had continued along the northern border of China, Soviet deployment had risen to an estimated 44 divisions, and attempts to negotiate a border settlement had gone nowhere. The

Brezhnev Doctrine, which justified Soviet intervention against heretic Communist states, continued in force, and the Soviet leader had also been trying to whip up an anti-Chinese front of other Asian nations. In this situation, the Kissinger visit was an extremely important event for the atmosphere it created. That China and America were now seriously communicating, and that in response to Soviet queries they were not revealing what was discussed with any semblance of candor—these changes in themselves can only have been extremely disturbing to Moscow. Right away, Zhou had what he probably most wanted—namely, a relationship with the United States sufficiently meaningful to add a major deterrent to Soviet adventurism along the border. At the same time both Zhou and the Americans knew that anything in the nature of a formal U.S. commitment was out of the question. All that was needed, in the first instance, was a meeting of minds about the Soviet threat.

To this end, Kissinger brought with him an unusual gift. In his memoirs, he refers to giving Zhou "internal studies that supported our conclusions" about the Soviet Union. The reporter and historian Seymour Hersh has turned up persuasive evidence that Kissinger went much further than this bland description would suggest—that on this first visit he gave Zhou information on Soviet activities derived from electronic intercepts of Soviet communications and from high-resolution satellite photography, intelligence sources protected within the American government by the most stringent security measures.[21]

Nixon and Kissinger hardly needed convincing that the Soviet threat was worldwide. In 1970, both had seen the Soviet hand at work in the Middle East, Chile, and Cuba. Zhou and Kissinger now agreed that the Indian threat to East Pakistan, which had emerged that spring, was part and parcel of the same offensive thrust. Did the conversations go to the point of suggesting that the United States give direct military aid or equipment to China? It seems most unlikely that the always proud Zhou even suggested it might be wanted, or that Kissinger would have answered if he had. For the time being at least, the security part of the new relationship rested primarily on reaching common views and on sharing intelligence information.

Likewise there was probably no discussion of economic relations or the possibility of trade. (At least, there is no hint of this in the memoirs of either Kissinger or Nixon.) But one passage in Kissinger's memoirs does throw light on another subject—namely, Chinese reactions to American arms control negotiations with the Soviet Union:

[T]he possession of vast arsenals of weapons of mass destruction imposed on us a fiduciary responsibility for hundreds of millions of lives. We had a moral and political obligation to strive for co-existence if it was possible;

we would not shrink from confrontation if challenged but the thermo-
nuclear age evokes the imperative of mutual restraint. Critics—some in
Peking—might sneer at this quest and proclaim its futility; but, paradoxically, only by pursuing it would we be able to rally our people when we
needed to face up to military pressures.[22]

The argument is strong evidence of Kissinger's own underlying views:
whether it persuaded Zhou and his colleagues is doubtful. Later evidence
suggests that they remained disturbed by the SALT talks, both because they
were too intimate and because they could lead to reductions in Soviet forces
in other theaters and thus permit greater force concentrations on the China
front.

Finally, Kissinger gave Zhou a remarkable undertaking about future
communication and consultation:

> From my first visit I told Chou that we would continue to deal with
> Moscow, but that we would inform Peking *in detail* of any understanding
> affecting Chinese interests that we might *consider* with the Soviets, and
> we would take Chinese views into account.[23]

In diplomacy, this is about as far as one nation can go toward another.
Nixon and Kissinger were promising to treat Zhou and the Chinese leaders
on essentially the same basis as America's closest allies, in fact more candidly than with several. Moreover, they were establishing a double standard
between the two great Communist powers. With the Soviet Union, Nixon
and Kissinger almost never disclosed even the broad outlines of their dealings with the Chinese. In fact, Kissinger delighted in baiting and teasing
Dobrynin whenever the latter put out feelers about China.

In short, from the very beginning the new U.S.-China-Soviet triangle was
unbalanced. It was based not on equal treatment of the Communist powers
but on a pronounced favoring of China. In the report to Nixon that Kissinger drafted with his staff on the long flight back from Pakistan to Paris, two
key sentences were: "The beneficial impact on the U.S.S.R. is perhaps the
single biggest plus that we get from the China initiative. . . . We have already achieved this." He was right that the change registered at once. His
visit created a new reality in international affairs.

In the euphoria that surrounded the July 15 announcement, however,
one serious error was hardly known in America. This was the failure to give
Japan more than a very few minutes of advance notice. After World War
II, it was natural that Japan had no relations with China, the nation it had
recently invaded, terribly damaged, and deeply wronged. When the Japanese Peace Conference was prepared in 1949 and the Peace Treaty was

signed at San Francisco in September 1951, the newly emerged People's Republic of China had no part.

By the late 1960s, Japan was bound to reconsider its policy of not dealing with China. However, given its dependence on the American alliance and loyalty to U.S. policy, the Japanese leadership made no move toward the People's Republic. By 1971, there was a rising sense that it was time to end this paralysis. In January 1971, Prime Minister Sato had announced that Japan wished for better bilateral relations with China and offered to begin governmental contacts.

In this delicate transitional period, the Japanese government and informed public were more sensitive than ever about changes in U.S. policy on China. As the veteran diplomat Alexis Johnson put it in his memoirs:

> Few thoughts aroused more trepidation in the Japanese government over the years than the possibility that the United States would suddenly reverse its policy toward Peking, leaving Tokyo, which had loyally kept Peking at arm's length despite many reasons not to, red-facedly bobbing in our wake. Asakai, one of the first Japanese Ambassadors to Washington and a very competent diplomat, once said he had had a dream that we abruptly switched policy toward China without even informing Japan, and this scenario became known in the Japanese Foreign Office as the "Asakai nightmare." Given the extraordinarily strong relations of trust and confidence that we had carefully built up with the Foreign Office, however, I and everyone else involved in American policy toward Asia scoffed at the nightmare and assured them that such a thing would be impossible. They accepted our assurances at face value.[24]

In the State Department, the "Asakai nightmare" was known to everyone who worked on Japan or China; it was a constant reminder to inform the Japanese in advance of any crucial move affecting their interests, above all of any easing of U.S. relations with the People's Republic. Over and over again, when there were critical developments in American policy (for example, President Johnson's speech of March 31, 1968), the State Department gave several hours' advance notice to Tokyo, with no trace of a leak. What mattered was that the Prime Minister and senior officials had time to devise a response for their own public. For them to appear flustered or taken by surprise could only mean that the United States was neglecting Japan, which was for Japan even more than for other societies a humiliation of the deepest personal and national sort.

Unfortunately, neither Nixon nor Kissinger thought of this. In the State Department, only Secretary Rogers was informed (on July 8) about Kissinger's trip. On July 13 in San Clemente, Rogers was told the outcome and given the job, solo, of notifying affected governments. He had Japan at the head of the list, but Nixon so insisted on security that he would allow only an hour's notice before the announcement. Rogers managed to reach Ambassador Ushiba in the late evening Washington time of July 15, giving him a bare outline of what Nixon was about to announce, but this gave the Japanese leaders no time to prepare their public reaction. Alexis Johnson himself, the senior State Department officer who habitually supervised informing key nations of important developments, was alerted on July 14 by Alexander Haig to fly to the West Coast for an undisclosed purpose, but the trip was then postponed, so that he arrived in San Clemente only in the late afternoon of July 15. Learning from Winston Lord, on Kissinger's staff, what was to be announced, he shortly received a frantic call from Ushiba: "Alex, the Asakai nightmare has happened!" Johnson later learned that there had briefly been a plan to fly him to Tokyo to tell Prime Minister Sato, but this had been dropped, and apparently no one on the White House or NSC staffs gave a thought to alternative methods of notification.

Sato therefore got the word only as the President was going on television. Inevitably, his delayed and flustered reaction revealed to all Japan that its great ally had given it no notice of the one action that most clearly and seriously affected Japan's interests and concerns. The result was turmoil and dismay. The event rapidly acquired a name, the "Nixon shokku," which for at least the next decade was a household phrase in informed and influential Japanese circles. To this day it survives in Japanese history and commentary. As Alexis Johnson said in the mid-1980s, "there has never again been the same trust and confidence between our two governments."

It is useless to consider whose fault it may have been. Kissinger's regard for Japan at this stage of his career was limited, and both he and Nixon were totally preoccupied with how the news would be received in America. While tight secrecy served important purposes in the handling of the trip generally, as the moment for disclosure approached there was a great need for professional staff work and experience and no serious excuse for neglecting it.

The response in America was all that Nixon could have hoped for. In the media and in Congress, the only skeptical or even mildly dissenting voices came from the extreme right, from those still influenced by the old China Lobby, and from a few liberals and others worried about the Soviet reaction. The trip to China and its outcome made Henry Kissinger a national figure overnight, rather than just a celebrity in the Washington area ("within the Beltway"). Moreover, it fundamentally altered Nixon's reputation not just for skill and foresight but for being much more ready for basic change than he had seemed before. The breakthrough also boosted his candidacy for reelection: in June a Gallup poll had shown 39 percent for Nixon and 41 percent for his assumed rival, Senator Muskie, but in late August the count was 42–36 in favor of Nixon![25]

Nixon's first act after the July 15 announcement was to send off a personal message to Zhou confirming the communication channel on which they had agreed. This was their respective military attachés in Paris, where the redoubtable General Walters had already distinguished himself for resourcefulness and exact following of orders. Nixon's first message, delivered on July 19, was followed by a steady stream of notes drafted by Kissinger, approved by Nixon, and then hand-carried to Paris by the White House staff. Kissinger also used three secret visits to Paris for negotiations over Vietnam to meet separately with a senior Chinese diplomat close to Zhou.[26] Agreement was quickly reached that he would go again to Beijing in October.

While the Soviet leaders tried to shrug off the Kissinger trip in their public statements, there could be no doubt that they were deeply perturbed. On July 19 Ambassador Dobrynin asked Kissinger, almost plaintively, whether a cool Soviet message of July 5 about a Soviet-U.S. summit had contributed to the arranging of the U.S.-China summit, and went on to suggest a meeting in Moscow in early 1972. Kissinger crisply replied that the summits would have to be held in the order of their announcement, and the one with China would come first. It was the kind of one-upmanship in which Nixon and Kissinger delighted.

A more dramatic reaction came in China itself. The success of Kissinger's visit gave a big boost to Zhou Enlai's standing in the running battle with the radicals on the one hand and, on the other, Marshal Lin Biao, who had minimized the Soviet threat to China and opposed any move to ease relations with the United States. Zhou put a very close watch on Lin Biao in August, including precautions against his getting any means of transportation, but Lin eluded the net and took off to fly to the Soviet Union. On September 13 his plane crashed in Mongolia, killing all aboard. Zhou must have learned of this the next day, but for almost a year Lin's death was kept secret. All the American government knew at the time was that he was not being heard from, but Zhou's communications with Kissinger must have made it clear that the Premier was totally confident of his position.[27]

The second Kissinger trip to Beijing, announced on October 5, turned out to take place just before the United Nations came to a vote on the perennial issue of which Chinese regime should be recognized there as "China." It was an issue on which the Nixon Administration had acted in contradictory ways. During the spring, the State Department kept hinting about "two Chinas," and even after Kissinger's trip in July, the American Ambassador at the UN, George Bush, remained under orders to stick to this position, which meant conceding that the People's Republic would take the Security Council seat, but supporting the Nationalist government's membership in the General Assembly. Bush was a dedicated Republican who had been defeated for the Senate in 1970 in Texas by the Democrat Lloyd Bentsen. His consolation prize, at his own request, was the UN post, which he handled capably and energetically. He now went all out to keep the General Assembly seat for the Nationalist Chinese.

In the end, predictably, the new rapport between the United States and the People's Republic made this rearguard action a hopeless cause. When the decisive votes came on October 25, the People's Republic was confirmed as the "China" member of the Security Council and equally in the General Assembly seat. Kissinger's return from Beijing was deliberately delayed so as not to fall on the very same day as the decisive vote, but it was plain to all that his diplomacy, under Nixon's orders, had been the decisive factor.

To trim ship with pro-Taiwan conservatives at home and to cushion the blow to the Nationalist regime itself, Nixon put out a statement that the United States would continue to have formal diplomatic relations only with the latter. This was not easy to reconcile with the statement in the July 15 announcement that Nixon would go to China in part to "seek the normalization of relations" with the People's Republic. It must have taken some effort and verbal ingenuity to persuade Zhou Enlai that the new relationship was still on track. Probably Kissinger, in messages via Paris, fell back on the political factors in America, saying that Nixon needed time to turn these around. Perhaps it was at this point that Nixon and Kissinger conveyed to the Chinese leaders an assurance that outright recognition would be achieved, if not in 1972, at least in Nixon's second term. Or perhaps this assurance awaited a clearer picture of Nixon's election prospects. What is certain is that such an undertaking was at least informally conveyed in the 1971–73 heyday of relations with China and Zhou.

Kissinger's October visit to Beijing was open and widely reported from start to finish, though no communiqué was issued. The line put out was that he devoted himself to making arrangements for Nixon's trip, and this was indeed a major topic. But Zhou and Kissinger also worked long hours to frame the formal communiqué to be issued on that occasion, and continued their broad-ranging strategic talks.

As the Chinese quickly discovered, Nixon had in mind an absolute maximum of publicity and exposure about his trip. The Americans produced lists of literally hundreds of people who would have to be in the official party, not to mention equally large numbers of media representatives both American and international. Yet different backgrounds and perceptions among Americans and Chinese dovetailed neatly to produce agreement on the plans to give maximum dramatic impact to Nixon's visit to China. The July 15 announcement had referred to "President Nixon's expressed desire to visit the People's Republic of China." To the Chinese, this amounted to saying that the foreigner had asked to come, in the long tradition that

China received official visitors as a matter of grace and favor, from the inherently superior position of the Middle Kingdom. For Americans (and most others) a top-level visit had no such significance. It did not bother Americans that Nixon was going to China and not the Chinese coming to the United States. On the contrary, most were thrilled, as was much of the world, to see that China was at last opening up, and that the United States was the nation that had achieved this.

Over the formal communiqué to be issued at the end of the Nixon visit, the discussion was of a totally different order. Both sides had much at stake and much to lose if its formulations were not carefully drawn. China had to take account of its standing in the Communist world and in Third World countries where it vied with the Soviet Union for influence. Kissinger and his staff had to consider American public opinion, especially on the Right, and the attitudes and feelings of East Asian allies who for a generation had relied on U.S. leadership and the U.S. presence to hold China's potential ambitions in check.

When the American side submitted a possible draft communiqué in the customary joint form, Zhou promptly rejected it as far too vague and meaningless (which it probably was) and proposed instead that on the most difficult issues (Taiwan above all) the two sides should simply "agree to differ" — that is, each side should state its position without attacking the other's parallel statement. There would then be a customary joint text on the points where a high degree of agreement was possible. This was the breakthrough. Kissinger still pleaded that Nixon could not accept extreme formulations even in the Chinese-only section, and Zhou obliged by changing the wording here and there. In the end, after arduous negotiations conducted apparently without reference to Washington, the two produced a virtually complete proposed text, subject to the final approval of Mao and Nixon.

The really difficult issue was, of course, the future of Taiwan. Here Kissinger found the best formula in a planning document drafted in the State Department in the 1950s. The sentence he proposed read: "The United States acknowledges that all Chinese on either side of the Taiwan Strait maintain there is but one China. The United States government does not challenge that position." This recognized that both Beijing and Taipei laid claim to being the sole government of all of China, and implied that the claims should be resolved between them. Other passages stated the U.S. position that force should not be used, which Kissinger also emphasized privately. In all, the draft communiqué on this subject was classic diplomacy, producing the only position that could pass muster in both countries.

Kissinger's October visit was clearly a success. By the end of the year there was even a perceptible change in the Chinese position on Vietnam — though this was only revealed years later and was probably unknown to the American government at the time. When the North Vietnamese Premier,

Pham Van Dong, went to Beijing in November, he was urged, presumably by Zhou, to make concessions on the future political structure in South Vietnam. Although these might have helped toward a settlement, Pham Van Dong rejected the Chinese advice, and relations between the two Communist nations cooled.[28]

The renewal of serious diplomacy between the United States and the government of mainland China—always called "the opening to China"—was hailed then and later as the foremost achievement of Nixon's Administration. On his death in 1994, it was the accomplishment most widely rated at the top of his record. A historical judgment, at the distance of a quarter century, must confirm the importance of the change, at the time it took place and for some time thereafter. In 1971 and 1972 its impact was especially great, in public opinion and for a time in great-power relationships.

Might another American President have achieved such a renewal of serious dealings? Even partisans of Nixon have admitted that in the early 1970s some sort of rapprochement between America and China was inevitable, sooner or later. China's armies had stayed at home since the Korean War nearly twenty years before. The notion of a "Sino-Soviet bloc," discarded by most informed Americans after the early 1960s, had faded also in the popular mind. And the convulsions of China's Cultural Revolution had eased. Moreover, in 1969, the American government, from intelligence sources not available to the general public, knew how seriously Soviet nuclear forces were threatening the Chinese. This threat was almost certainly the precipitating factor driving Mao and Zhou to seek a new relationship with America.

Kissinger's own 1994 summation was: "For both sides [America and China], necessity dictated that a rapprochement occur, and the attempt would have had to be made no matter who governed in either country."[29] This is surely correct. As we have seen, Nixon's Cambodian incursion of May 1970 and the Lam Son 719 operation into Laos in early 1971 delayed the opening to China for many months. For some time, the war in Vietnam had a decidedly higher priority for Nixon, and although Zhou might have been ready to move ahead in the spring of 1970, the power struggle he faced was still an obstacle. Breaking the trail would have taken time in any event.

What about the effect of the Nixon-Kissinger style, approach, and objectives? Again in 1994, Kissinger concluded:

> The smoothness and speed with which it developed and the scope it assumed owed a great deal to the subtlety and single-mindedness of the leaders on both sides who brought it about and, on the American side in particular, to the unprecedented emphasis on the analysis of the national interest.[30]

Smoothness and speed there certainly were, once the Cambodia and Laos incursions were over. In policy terms as well as in public relations, the achievement of instant high drama was important. This kind of change was best taken at a gulp. Kissinger was right that if news of it had leaked or if it had come about in stages, caviling in many quarters might readily have knocked the project off course. Secrecy was correct in the circumstances, and might have been hard for a more orthodox Administration to sustain.

Secrecy did, however, have costs. That it discomfited the professionals in the State Department was hardly a serious matter: the effect was momentary, their staff work had visibly been used to advantage, and they wholly supported the objective of renewed serious relations with China.[31] What mattered far more was the secret debt that the United States incurred to Yahya Khan and his regime in Pakistan, without whose resourceful help—especially the delivery (and possibly stimulation) of key messages and the arrangements for Kissinger's first trip—the desired smoothness, speed, and secrecy could not have been achieved. Nixon had picked well, and his long-standing friendship with Pakistan was an asset; it is hard to think of any other national government that could have done the job. Yet to a degree that the public did not perceive, Pakistan earned not simply favorable mention but concrete help. Kissinger was later at pains to praise the Pakistani leaders for not suggesting a specific reward, but the obligation needed no underlining. When Yahya Khan sought help, Nixon and Kissinger, always sensitive to personal ties, were bound to respond.

2. Relations with the Soviet Union Before and After the China Opening

The year 1971 was an extremely important one in Soviet-U.S. relations, far more decisive and meaningful than the probing and tentative exchanges and semi-confrontations of 1969 and 1970. A May agreement in principle over the SALT talks freed up those negotiations and brought agreement in 1972 within reach. In July the two sides agreed that, with a SALT agreement as its anchor, there should be a summit in Moscow in May 1972. And in August a four-power agreement over Berlin was concluded, leaving only the administrative arrangements to be worked out between the two Germanys before the whole "German package" could be submitted for ratification to the West German Bundestag. It was in 1971 that détente between the United States and the Soviet Union took shape and moved toward realization. This was also the first year to test the thesis that Richard Nixon and Henry Kissinger urged then and later, that the best explanation for the progress achieved in their era was America's opening to China and the resultant "triangular diplomacy."

1971 was also a time when individual leaders stood out in key countries. In a democracy it is possible for an individual, or a closely coordinated pair such as Nixon and Kissinger, to put a strong stamp on a nation's foreign policy. But that power is usually shared with the legislature and conditioned constantly by public opinion. Even in a dictatorship, sharply competing views are likely to be unresolved, as was the case in China before August 1970. Rarely do domestic political forces in several countries permit their leaders to exert real control simultaneously over foreign affairs. From 1971 to 1974, however, this was the case in the four most important countries at the time. This short period was an age of personalities, comparable roughly to the period in the nineteenth century during and after the Congress of Vienna in 1815. Whether its results were equally lasting is another question.

Already in 1969 and 1970, Willy Brandt, Zhou Enlai, and Richard Nixon (advised by Henry Kissinger) had emerged as such individuals. The policy and personal control of the fourth key personality, Leonid Brezhnev, became clear only in 1971. Most practitioners of the murky discipline of Sovietology would agree that Brezhnev was at least first among equals from 1964 on, holding as he did the traditionally supreme position of Party Chairman, and that he took the lead in 1968, laying out, in the wake of the rape of Prague, his doctrine that the Soviet Union had the right and duty to discipline heretic Communist regimes by any measures necessary. On many fronts, however, actions and statements by other members of the Soviet Politburo, especially Alexei Kosygin, premier and head of government, suggested that Brezhnev's control was still limited, and that other Politburo members had weight he could not ignore and occasionally had to accede to.

By 1969–70, the influence of the doctrinaire ideologist Mikhail Suslov appeared to have declined, and the struggle lay between Kosygin and Brezhnev. Kosygin was primarily responsible for the economy, hence weakened by its faltering performance. Brezhnev, having once opposed extensive foreign ties, emerged as their advocate because of the nation's manifest need for advanced technology and hard currency, both of which could only be had by greatly expanded dealings with the West. As we have seen, the disagreement was so acute as to compel the almost unprecedented step of delaying publication of the next Five-Year Plan, and postponing the Twenty-fourth Party Congress.

Over the next six to nine months, the debate was resolved, partly by backstage maneuvers and secret debates in key meetings. Yet it is hard to imagine that the major external events—the Soviet–West German Treaty in August and the West German–Polish Treaty in December 1970—did not have influence. Greatest of all, surely, was the prospect that with West

Germany lined up, the long-standing Soviet proposal for a European Security and Cooperation Conference (CSCE) would not only be realized but achieve its maximum desired result—namely, full ratification and legitimization of Soviet control of the Eastern European countries, the recognized "sphere of influence" for which Stalin had striven in the war and immediate postwar years.

If the importance of this historic Soviet objective needed underlining at the end of 1970, this was provided by a third key event, following on the two treaties. When the labor force in Poland rose in massive protest over a host of accumulated grievances, the regime, headed by Wladyslaw Gomulka, tried to be tough, then temporized, and was finally, after making a number of concessions to the strikers and their supporters, forced out of office. The Polish flare-up, expressing in part the hopes raised by the new Polish treaty, showed once again how difficult it was for any Communist regime to meet the material needs of its people so long as the Soviet Union was clearly the controlling power. As in the earlier succession of crises behind the Iron Curtain—Berlin in 1953, Warsaw and Budapest in 1956, Prague in 1968—the root cause of ferment and dissension was the iron heel of the military victor in 1945, which had no claim to legitimacy.

More than ever, therefore, the Soviet Union wanted a European Security and Cooperation Conference to give at least a color of legitimacy and international acceptance to its continued domination of Eastern Europe. Yet as Brandt made clear in August and NATO reaffirmed in December, the West would never agree to a CSCE unless the "Germany package" went through—agreement on Berlin in addition to the two Eastern treaties.

As with the Lushan conference among the Chinese leaders in August, the best evidence of what the inner Soviet councils decided is what was done. As Zhou left Lushan with a mandate to pursue reconciliation with the United States, debates within the Politburo—probably in December 1970 and January 1971—established the primacy of Brezhnev over Kosygin and the Politburo, and laid down an overall foreign policy in which completion and ratification of the German package was a cardinal objective. That very objective had an inevitable corollary. Not only was the United States a key party to any four-power Berlin agreement, but it was hopeless to expect any West German parliament to ratify new treaties or agreements if the Soviet Union was at evident odds with the leader of the West, the United States. In short, if Brezhnev was to get what he wanted from Brandt and the Bundestag, he had to ease relations with Nixon and Kissinger. All Soviet policy roads ran through Berlin. A vital case of linkage had been created, by Brandt in the first instance, and then by the Western powers in NATO. Usually inclined to downplay the Soviet-German front, Henry Kissinger perceived the connection clearly in his memoirs. "[T]he Soviets could not risk a crisis with us if they wanted the Berlin agreement concluded or the German treaties ratified. . . . And there was no possibility that the German Parliament would ratify Brandt's Eastern treaties under Cold War conditions."[32]

Thus Brezhnev had overwhelming reasons in early 1971 to want an agreement on Berlin and to be willing to compromise there, also to conduct the SALT negotiations in a forthcoming manner, at least to avoid a deadlock. A SALT agreement would ratify the strategic nuclear parity that had been reached by then and, perhaps most important, establish the Soviet Union as a recognized superpower on a level with the United States.

In all probability, the decision to pursue at least for the next two years a policy of eased relations with the West and the United States had been worked out before the postponed Twenty-fourth Party Congress convened in late March and early April 1971: the lack of visible conflict at the Congress bespeaks an earlier understanding. Although it was not until a few months later that Dobrynin gently told Kissinger that formal communications from Nixon, thus far addressed to Kosygin, should go to Brezhnev, his growth in power was already evident in a host of ways. In short, at this critical juncture the Soviet Union had not only a new policy but revamped leadership. It was no longer merely in opportunistic readiness for new agreements with the West, but an ardent seeker of them. Brezhnev's new policy, brought on in large part by the initiatives of Willy Brandt, had laid the basis for new agreements with Nixon and Kissinger, and with the core nations in the Western Alliance, first over Berlin.

Negotiations over Berlin did not start from scratch in January 1971. In February 1970, as we have seen, shortly after Egon Bahr began his talks with Soviet leaders, Britain, France, and the United States accepted the Soviet proposal for quadripartite talks on Berlin. All sides agreed that the status of the four occupying powers would remain unchanged and that basic adjustments had in the first instance to be worked out among them; only after that could the two Germanys take on the details of administration, border controls, and the like.

Yet a four-power Berlin agreement could not be reached on its own, for both procedural and substantive reasons. For one thing, while the Federal Republic could not be a direct party to the negotiations, only an initial basic agreement between it and the Soviet Union could set the framework. Second, differences among the three Western occupying powers had to be resolved. Accumulated and encrusted over the years, sometimes with almost theological overtones, these differences were not trivial. Each party had its sore points, and reconciliation was bound to take time. Third, and most important, the allies alone could not alter the unacceptable Soviet and East German practices that had been imposed over the previous decade. Over and over, the East Germans — usually with explicit Soviet backing — had made superficially small changes in border procedures, in granting permission for West Berliners to travel in East Germany or to the West, for example, and in all the other encumbering aspects of Berlin's unique status and its position as an island surrounded by East German territory. Hence, the State Department's assessment in the early months of the Nixon Administration of the chances for progress in renewed Berlin negotiations was gloomy.[33] But by January 1971, these obstacles had changed shape or been removed.

In this process, the experts on Berlin in all three Western governments played crucial parts. Berlin was not, at any time after World War II, an ordinary diplomatic assignment. Those who worked there were necessarily deeply involved in the governance of the city's Western zones, in constant and wearing sessions ironing out difficulties with the Soviets, and in daily liaison with the mayor's office in West Berlin and with the commanders of the allied military units. French, British, and American diplomats were usually assigned to Berlin for long periods and rotated back to their home offices for policy assignments related to Berlin. In his memoirs, Henry Kissinger belittled the State Department's Berlin experts as sterile theologians so immersed in their specialty that they could not see the larger picture. It was a ridiculous charge. The Berlin experts were front-line soldiers in the Cold War, at the most exposed and vulnerable salient of the Western position in Europe, and in daily touch with the Berliners, whose morale and capacity to carry on were the ultimate decisive factor.

In a situation where every incident had special significance—sometimes in terms of legal rights, always in psychological effect—the experts' grasp of Berlin's recent history was the foundation stone for any Western diplomatic effort. Kissinger does not seem to have understood this, but Ambassador Kenneth Rush, in Bonn, did. He made it his business to travel to Berlin frequently and to stay in the closest possible touch with the American mission there, which was under his overall command. With past private experience as a lawyer and top executive of an international business, and eighteen months on the job in Bonn, he was highly qualified as the American and chief Western negotiator.

As always, Kissinger took a hand. He stayed in direct touch not only with Dobrynin but with Egon Bahr and therefore with Brandt (through a special Navy communications link to Bonn), and, at Rush's initiative, set up a similar back channel to him (in sharp contrast to his exclusion of Gerard Smith and Paul Nitze from the back channel on SALT). In his memoirs Kissinger boasted of his command of German matters, but in this case he left things largely to Rush and the Berlin experts, working from basic positions Nixon had approved in early 1970. They—Assistant Secretary Martin Hillenbrand, James Sutterlin from the Berlin desk, Jonathan Dean, and others—along with their British and French colleagues, were well aware that back channels were being used, since they could not otherwise account for sudden shifts in emphasis and tactics. Their teamwork was excellent. Yet Britain and France — always sensitive to undue American dominance — came to resent methods of operation that kept the West German government constantly in the picture, but often did not include genuine allied consultation. There were unnecessary strains, with hidden costs to allied relations and little evidence of offsetting gain in increased wisdom at the White House.

On the allied side, the first objective was to assure access to West Berlin without interference. The unremitting Soviet effort to build up East Germany as the responsible party had been a great irritant for years, and Kissinger underlined that the United States considered the Soviet Union beyond doubt responsible on this matter. The second allied objective, a particular concern of West Germany, was to broaden greatly the freedom of West Berliners to travel to and from West Germany and to visit in East Germany, and to gain and assure freedom of movement of people and goods between West Germany and West Berlin. This meant removing the network of arbitrary bans and requirements imposed since 1962.

The original 1944 agreements had clearly specified that neither the whole of Berlin nor any part of it should form part of any of the zones of occupation of Germany assigned to the Soviet Union, the United States, Britain, and (shortly) France. However, when Germany was split in two in 1949, the Soviets made East Berlin the capital of East Germany. The Western allies and the West Germans could not respond in parallel, but the Bonn government did establish visible links between West Berlin and the Federal Republic, a gray area not specifically defined under the 1944 agreements. Conspicuous branches of several federal offices were opened, and it became the custom to hold the formal election of a President in Berlin, with the Bundestag and Bundesrat meeting together as provided by the West German Basic Law. Although these actions were not expressly forbidden under the 1944 agreements, they were clearly open to challenge as contrary to its spirit. In March 1969 the Soviets had not pursued their protest to the point of physical action, but the threat was always there.

The negotiations proceeded by moving back and forth between the two sets of issues, in effect matching concessions and new arrangements in a rough balance of importance. Working in this way, the negotiators made steady progress and by June had narrowed the unresolved issues to only a few, one of which was a Soviet demand for the right to have a consulate in West Berlin.

Here we come to the issue, whether the announcement of Kissinger's visit to Beijing and Nixon's forthcoming visit there influenced the Berlin negotiations. Both Nixon and Kissinger have claimed that it did, Nixon to the point of asserting (erroneously) that until then there had been no significant progress. We do not yet have the full written record, but all the American direct participants in the negotiations, from Ambassador Rush down, reject the express or implied claim that the Kissinger trip made any significant difference. On the contrary, their testimony is that in early July the only unresolved issue was whether the Soviets would be allowed to open a consulate in West Berlin. Either before his departure or immediately on his return, Kissinger concluded that this American concession should be made, but for a time the State Department objected, on various grounds including both precedent and the danger that such an installation would help Soviet intelligence. But every other key point had been resolved by the time of Kissinger's trip. Rush has testified that to him the real "linkage" came entirely from Brandt's *Ostpolitik*.[34]

Both direct evidence and a reasonable judgment support this conclusion. As French President Pompidou said (more dubiously) to Kissinger about his Vietnam negotiations, this negotiation was "condemned to succeed."

The other major negotiating front in 1971 was, of course, SALT, which as we have seen had languished during 1970 in the wake of Kissinger's failure, in a talk with Dobrynin that spring, to insist on a parallel firm agreement on offensive strategic weapons to go along with one on defensive ABM limitations. By the end of the year, the necessity of such an agreement was so evident that the Soviets themselves broached the subject. Gerard Smith reported that they were interested in "an ABM agreement accompanied by some less formal understanding on offensive limitation measures."[35] Though vague, this appeared to be a return to the position the Soviet negotiators had taken at the outset. As Smith put it, the feeling in both delegations was that "something had to give."[36]

Kissinger gave no instructions in response to Smith's report, but instead resolved to take over the negotiations himself again, direct with Dobrynin. For five months he continued in this way, not informing State or Smith or the Pentagon, while the SALT delegation went back to Vienna for a second session there (the fourth session overall). This lasted from March to May 1971 and was predictably sterile and frustrating, although some marginal headway was made.

Meanwhile, Nixon finally made the crucial decision that there had to be a firm link between offensive and defensive limitations, and this was expressed in his second Foreign Policy Report, of February 25, 1971. Ironically, a major reason for taking this position, at last, was that pressure was building for an ABM-only agreement among the very groups the President and Kissinger most detested, liberal senators and outside university experts.[37]

At the same time, the question of a separate limit, or sublimit, on heavy missiles loomed larger. All along, U.S. intelligence had followed with particular care the Soviet program for such missiles, which could in time carry many MIRVed warheads and multiply the Soviet offensive capacity enormously. When in early 1971 the Soviets suspended further deployment of their then-key large missile, called the SS-9 by Americans, there was a flicker of hope that they might be limiting their heavy missile program, but by early spring reconnaissance picked up new large holes and the hope flickered out. (It became clear in 1974 that the Soviet Union had been taking its first steps toward a new-generation heavy missile, the SS-18, which became its principal carrier of MIRVs.) Kissinger's negotiating objective with Dobrynin was thus clear. He had to get out of the hole he himself had dug a year before, and he had to go further to define just what the offensive/defensive link should be.

In February, Dobrynin was ready to join an ABM agreement for a freeze on offensive missile deployments, but in mid-March he went back on this, insisting on an early agreement that each side would have ABMs at national capitals only, with offensive limitations to be discussed only afterward and "in principle."[38] The sequence and dates lend support to the view that SALT had been one of the issues the Soviet leaders debated before and during the Twenty-fourth Party Congress. Probably the Soviet generals wanted to be dead sure they could go ahead with their heavy missiles, and Gromyko was always inclined to bargain hard and slowly. On March 25, Kissinger finally laid it on the line in an "oral" note to Dobrynin — in his summary: "The terms of an ABM agreement and the freeze on offensive weapons would have to be negotiated simultaneously and completed at the same time." Dobrynin took this message to the Party Congress in Moscow.

Dobrynin returned to Washington on April 23 with the crucial Soviet concession. They accepted simultaneous negotiations on offensive and defensive weapons, and simultaneous final agreements in each area, if the United States accepted that ABMs should be limited to one complex on each side protecting the national capital (a position called NCA for short). On this point, the U.S. negotiators and Kissinger had been on the spot for months, since the United States had offered NCA as an option in its formal proposal at Vienna a year before and had never withdrawn it. Yet when Congress finally approved a continued ABM program in late 1970, it allowed for only four ABM complexes protecting offensive missile sites in remote Western areas. The allergy to ABM installations near big cities was overpowering, especially in regard to Washington. The actual U.S. program was now sharply at variance with the U.S. position in the SALT talks, and Kissinger had to (in his phrase) "slide off" the 1970 proposal, telling Dobrynin that NCA was now out of the question as an agreed common posture. On the Soviet side, in contrast, the defensive missile complex protecting Moscow, however backward, had become a sacred cow, to be preserved at all costs.

Kissinger and Dobrynin went back and forth for weeks over the details. Finally, on May 12, full agreement was reached and the stage set for a formal announcement on May 20, which the Soviets drafted and Kissinger accepted. The announcement, put out with considerable fanfare in Washington, read:

> [The two governments] have agreed to concentrate this year on working out an agreement for the limitation of the deployment of [ABMs]. They have also agreed that together with concluding an agreement to limit ABMs, they will agree on certain measures with respect to the limitation of offensive strategic weapons.

In his memoirs, Kissinger made extravagant claims for this result, asserting that it implied (1) a freeze on new starts of strategic missiles; (2) a sublimit on heavy missiles (as proposed in the "Vienna option" of August 1970); (3) that the Soviets had dropped their demand that forward-based systems should be counted; and (4) that the Soviets were on notice that submarine-launched ballistic missiles (SLBMs) would have to be limited or accounted for. Of these claims only the first and third were accurate.

With the firm acceptance of the freeze approach, it was obviously advantageous for the Soviets to set the latest possible date for a freeze and to forge ahead meanwhile on their missile programs. If agreement came within a few months, the Soviets would have a distinct numerical edge in the key category of land-based strategic missiles (ICBMs) — 1,510 to 1,054 — and the disparity would grow. On the other hand, in terms of a better measure of capability, deliverable *warheads*, the United States' MIRV program gave it undeniable advantages.[39] For the rest, Kissinger had left many loose ends, in another sloppy negotiating performance. The May 1971 agreement was indeed a turning point; a triumph of negotiating skill it was not.

In the days before the announcement was made, Gerard Smith had come back from Vienna, at his own request, to see how progress might be resumed. Informed for the first time of Kissinger's talks with Dobrynin, he was allowed to read what he was told was the whole record of those talks, which, however, the NSC staff had edited on Kissinger's orders.[40] Smith's first reaction — apart from understandable feelings of hurt and resentment — was to note at once that submarine-launched missiles had not been dealt with, though they were steadily more important, as the Soviet missile-submarine-building program had produced 160 new launchers in the last year alone. (Apparently parts of the record could actually be read to exclude SLBMs, although Kissinger claimed it was "ambiguous.") This major omission showed how risky it was to have any one man, especially one as pressed as Kissinger, handle a complex matter without full expert support. With good reason, Smith believed that the May 20 "understanding" could have been reached sooner and more solidly by the SALT delegation, whose trust in Washington, further shaken, was never to be restored.[41]

It is easy enough to ascribe Kissinger's action that spring to his love of negotiating and to his usual zeal to get credit (for Nixon as well as himself) at the expense of the professionals. An added reason in this instance — entirely omitted in Kissinger's memoir — may have been that Nixon and Kissinger had sweetened the pot by suggesting the possibility of future U.S. economic dealings with the Soviet Union, though when and how this was mentioned is unclear from available evidence. A useful step, in early 1971, was surely the appointment to Kissinger's staff of an extremely able businessman, Peter G. Peterson, a large part of whose assignment was to assess the Soviet economy and its potential for dealings with the West. One early result, announced in May, was a U.S. undertaking to supply equipment for a large Soviet truck plant, a one-shot, toe-in-the-water effort.

Peterson's overall assessment, conveyed to Nixon as well as Kissinger, was that the Soviet Union in fact had very little potential for commercial exports to the West. Soviet products simply could not compete in cost or quality, and the United States hardly needed oil or gold, the two raw materials that made up a large part of Soviet exports. Any idea of large-scale industrial exports to the Soviet Union held little promise, and Nixon readily agreed that the United States should go slowly.[42] But agricultural exports were a very different prospect. Perennially subject to fluctuations and shortfalls in their grain output, the Soviets had also just seen a warning signal in Poland. The scarcity and high price of meat there, directly traceable to shortages of feed grains, had caused riots. In early June, Kissinger (never until that point engaged in economic matters) set about to lay the groundwork for large-scale future U.S. grain shipments to the Soviet Union. The main obstacle was that in 1963 President Kennedy had been persuaded by the American maritime unions to issue an Executive Order requiring that half of all food shipments to the Soviet Union or any other Communist country should go on U.S. vessels. Given the extremely low state of the American merchant marine, the practical effect was to limit grain exports to the U.S.S.R. to a trickle.

In all probability Kissinger used hints of future grain sales as an argument to get the Soviets to accept an initial SALT agreement; after May 20, he had to follow through to show good faith. Seymour Hersh is probably on the mark in concluding, "Nixon had accomplished his back-channel SALT breakthrough only after assuring Moscow that he would end the grain embargo and once again sell American wheat to the Soviet Union."[43] For on June 10, the White House made a neat, two-target announcement. Export controls were lifted on a wide variety of nonstrategic items, including metals, electronic and communications equipment, and agricultural products. This could be, and was, depicted as aimed in large part at China. But tucked away in the decision was the repeal of the 1963 Executive Order. The maritime unions and the leadership of the AFL-CIO objected, but the

Soviets went into action, apparently confident that in due course they could get large quantities of grain. Contacts in July were followed by orders amounting to $200 million in October. By the end of 1971 additional large orders for hard goods were placed. Shipment, though, awaited clearance from the maritime unions, which retained the practical and political leverage of simply refusing to load.[44]

The Twenty-fourth Party Congress was a landmark both in Soviet foreign policy and in the ultimately unsuccessful effort to adjust the Soviet political system to the needs of the late twentieth century. The subsequent concessions over SALT and the beginnings of Soviet economic negotiation with the United States were only a part of the change that flowed from the Party Congress. Soviet policy thereafter reflected a wide-ranging "Peace Program" reaching into almost every facet of Soviet foreign and domestic policy.

It was not so perceived at the time. Indeed, the Soviet leaders went to great lengths to mask the importance of their shift. To have explained it candidly, especially the reaching out to the West for economic relief that could only come in a more relaxed general atmosphere, would have been to admit backwardness and weakness, which Russian leaders—famous for the invention of the phony showcase "Potemkin Village"—always avoided like the plague. Yet Western observers could see, from what was said in the Congress and around it in the Soviet media, new notes. These included a strong emphasis on the theme of "peaceful coexistence," differing in degree from past uses of this ambiguous slogan; considerably less emphasis on Soviet support for national liberation movements in the Third World, and on ideology generally; more emphasis on dealing with the West and a slightly gentler tone toward the United States; and a general willingness to consider negotiations on conventional military force levels in the European area.[45] Most Western comment focused on the implications of the Congress for the Soviet Union's domestic economic policies and on the perennial question of who stood out among the leaders. However, the willingness to talk about force levels in Europe should also have been salient. It was a hint that the Soviets might be on the way to accepting NATO's insistence that there could be no security conference on Europe without a reduction in conventional force levels or at least negotiation about it.

This hint was soon tested over an issue the Soviets can hardly have foreseen, with startling results. The issue was the fate in the Senate of the Mansfield Amendment, calling for a major reduction in U.S. forces in NATO. It was decided, probably coincidentally, in the same week as the May 20 SALT announcement. As we have seen, Senator Mike Mansfield of Montana, Majority Leader of the Senate throughout the Nixon years, was a rock of integrity, respected on all sides for his fairness and patriotism. In the Senate Foreign Relations Committee he was active on all fronts, a moderate liberal with a strong vein of idealism, never petty or vindictive, and so low-key that many who shared his viewpoint thought he was less telling and effective than he might have been. When he did speak out, his colleagues listened. So, often, did the country. (I knew Mansfield well through shared friends. In 1953 we had joined in an effort to save the career of a friend who had worked for him on an early UN delegation and was being attacked by Senator McCarthy and his minion, the infamous Roy Cohn. Our purely official encounters during the Kennedy and Johnson Administrations were always easy and direct, even when we disagreed. Later, in the Carter and Reagan Administrations he served with distinction as Ambassador to Japan, probably the only man to occupy senior "political" positions under such disparate Presidents.)

Over the years, Mansfield had come to believe strongly in cutting U.S. force strength assigned to NATO, not so much on the ground that the dangers there had eased — though he tended generally to take a dovish view of Soviet behavior — as on the basis that the European NATO members, now solid and prosperous, and after all the ones most affected, should carry much more of the burden. Since they would never do so voluntarily, he favored simply cutting the U.S. effort and forcing them to act.

The result was a series of "Mansfield Amendments" in this direction, usually expressing the "sense of the Senate," hence not binding. In mid-May 1971, after several times coming to the edge of calling up his amendment in a more emphatic form, Mansfield attached to "must" legislation (for draft reform) a version that categorically denied funds "for the maintenance or support in Europe of any military personnel of the United States in excess of 150,000 after December 31, 1971." It was a straight 50 percent cut, which he rightly judged would have maximum appeal to his colleagues. The defense budget was still high, despite reductions in Vietnam-related allocations, and the new treaties that Willy Brandt had signed with the Soviet Union and Poland suggested that the situation in Europe was indeed easing. The word "détente" had not been used by Nixon or his colleagues to that point, but change was in the air.

When Mansfield called up his amendment on Wednesday, May 12, setting a vote for a week hence, May 19, the odds looked at least even that a majority of the Senate would pass it. Few thought that the House would go along, but in a conference between the two chambers some compromise reduction was likely to emerge. So it certainly appeared to Nixon and Kissinger, also to Laird and Rogers, though they all recognized that their influence on liberal and moderate senators in the majority was limited. At once these top officials, on behalf of Nixon, responded to an offer of help from Dean Acheson in rallying the Old Guard. On May 13, at Nixon's invitation, a group of about ten former senior officials came to the White House to meet with him, with Rogers and Kissinger in attendance. Some of the group favored a compromise that would consider a reexamination, or definite phased reduction, of the force level, but Acheson advocated total resistance, without compromise, and it was his view that dominated the press release after the meeting. At the same time, official cables to Europe hummed with requests for support from current leaders in the key Western European countries.[46]

On Saturday, May 15, Nixon issued a ringing statement opposing the amendment without reservation. It was endorsed by a longer list of former senior officials and military commanders. Although this was an impressive rallying of elite sentiment, the reaction was mixed: on the floor of the Senate, and in public comment, some belittled the Old Guard as predictably wedded to the past in a new situation.

What did really change minds was a voice from a totally unexpected quarter. In a major scheduled speech in Tula on May 14, Leonid Brezhnev went out of his way to say that the Soviet Union was ready to enter at once into serious negotiations with NATO about conventional force levels in Europe. It was a much stronger statement than the vague one that had come out of the Twenty-fourth Party Congress, and the effect in the Senate was immediate and electric. On the floor that day, several senators referred to it and argued that with agreed reductions on both sides now a possibility, it would be (in the words of Republican senator Gordon Allott) "drastically wrong for the United States to make unilateral reductions at this time." Mansfield had no real reply other than to say that reduction made sense "with or without negotiations."[47]

On Monday, May 17, Andrei Gromyko threw another log on the fire, summoning U.S. Ambassador Jacob Beam for discussions and having him in again the following day—both sides taking care to publicize the talks. This made the hard-line Foreign Minister a clear party to the Soviet initiative. On the floor of the Senate that day, the strongly liberal Senator Gaylord Nelson of Wisconsin and at least a dozen others suggested that their thinking had altered. It was a rare case where one could readily trace a sharp reversal of sentiment, stemming from the Brezhnev statement.[48] When the vote came on May 19, the amendment was rejected by a vote of 61–36, a decisive margin. Conspicuous in the majority to reject were the veteran liberal Hubert Humphrey and Edmund Muskie, the foremost candidate for the Democratic presidential nomination in 1972.

Brezhnev had gone out of his way to pull Nixon's chestnuts out of the fire and to maintain the strength of the U.S. forces assigned to NATO for the purpose of deterring Soviet attack. On its face, the paradox seemed enormous. In his memoirs, Kissinger expressed puzzlement about "what possessed Brezhnev" to speak as he did on that particular day. His interpretation was that the speech had been prepared as an effort to move the Berlin negotiations along and that Brezhnev had simply stuck to it after the Mansfield Amendment emerged on May 12. "Nothing illustrates better the inflexibility of the Soviets' cumbersome policymaking machinery than their decision to stick to their game plan even when confronted with the Mansfield windfall."[49]

If, however, the Soviet Union had genuine reasons to dislike the Mansfield Amendment, Brezhnev's speech took on an entirely different coloration. And in fact, one senator suggested just such a reason. In the floor debate, Senator Chan Gurney of North Dakota quoted a speech made a year or two earlier, in which Elliot Richardson, then Under Secretary of State, had noted that if the American forces in Europe were reduced, the loss would have to be made up mostly by an increase in West German forces, and that this would damage Brandt's *Ostpolitik* and be very troubling to the Soviet Union. This was a consideration seldom advanced within the American government, but commonplace in the analyses of the British Foreign Office in particular. The Soviet Union was only moderately concerned by the existence of a new German Army *within NATO and under U.S. leadership*, but if the U.S. presence was lessened, it feared a resurgent German nationalism. The Soviets would have liked to see a weaker NATO in general, but a strong NATO dominated by the United States was decidedly better, or less bad, than a somewhat weaker NATO with the West Germans in a major position. If this was indeed Soviet thinking, then Brezhnev's Tula speech took on a totally different aspect than that suggested by Kissinger. Written on the basis of a solid policy, it was a resourceful response by a leader truly in charge.

Once again, as on many other occasions in 1970–72, Kissinger underestimated the part played in Soviet policy by concern about the future of Germany. The Soviet leaders had responded with breathtaking speed (for orthodox diplomacy) to Brandt's *Ostpolitik*, and after the Moscow and Warsaw treaties of 1970, a new Berlin agreement was their top priority. The last thing Brezhnev wanted was an American action that would throw NATO into confusion and destabilize the West German role within NATO.

In other contexts, however, as in his initial strong objections to *Ostpolitik*, Kissinger emphasized the danger of a new German assertive nationalism. In 1971, in China, he had rebutted Zhou's concerns over a resurgent Japan by stressing the moderating effect of the U.S. alliance with Japan—an essentially equivalent case. On both fronts, the United States was acting as a force restraining the emergence of new aggressive nationalist elements.

Was part of Kissinger's reaction a simple resentment that the Soviet leaders considered their relationship to West Germany as important as their relationship to the United States? Most American diplomats and commentators on international affairs in the late twentieth century have tended to put the United States at the center of other nations' thinking—America-centric, so to speak—and Kissinger carried this tendency to an extreme. That Brandt's *Ostpolitik* had an enormous influence and momentum of its own was a thesis that cut across this. Perhaps there was also, in some official minds, an underlying distaste for Germany.

. . .

The SALT negotiators reconvened in Helsinki in July to September, and then met again in Vienna from November to January 1972. Yet during these fifth and sixth sessions, the Administration never discussed the issues with the relevant Senate and House committees, which in due course would have to deal with the proposed ABM treaty and with any executive agreement. This omission, particularly in contrast to the frequent and detailed briefings of NATO ambassadors in Brussels, was a striking feature of Nixon's process. (That a few individual members of Congress visited the delegation during the negotiations hardly amounted to serious consultation.) Yet it did have great advantages. Briefings on Capitol Hill were notorious for their leaks, and public discussion might easily have led to distorted impressions and irresistible new pressures. In the end, as Nixon and his colleagues saw it, any set of agreements would have to be seen and accepted as a whole. Its parts were individually almost bound to be open to challenge, understandable only in an overall context that reflected Soviet concessions in other areas. The secrecy also kept any special interests (such as missile, aircraft, and submarine makers) from exerting influence through their friends on Capitol Hill. All in all, it was a case where secrecy may have been, on balance, the better course, not simply because it was always the preference of Nixon and Kissinger. Inevitably, however, it imposed a particularly acute need for full and candid information once agreements were reached.

As it was, the summer Helsinki session got off to a bad start, with a massive leak to *The New York Times* on July 23 about the U.S. instructions. Predictably, the leak enraged Nixon and Kissinger and intensified their wish to discredit the leaker of the Pentagon Papers, Daniel Ellsberg.[50] Still, the Helsinki session managed to finish off agreements to handle the danger of accidental missile launches and to provide, for this and other purposes, a "hot line" between Washington and Moscow. The joint announcement on September 30 showed that the talks were making progress and held off potential critics from both directions.

A lot was also done, both in Helsinki and later in Vienna, to arrive at an ironclad understanding not only on ABM controls but especially on controls of future technology. Strong and apparently total bans on exotic future weapons were agreed on. On the other hand, the negotiators made little progress on the number and location of ABM complexes. Smith had the impression that his lack of instructions from Washington meant that the White House, believing that the differences were now minimal, wanted to reserve the issue for resolution at the summit, which would give the credit to Nixon and Kissinger.[51]

The biggest obstacles were lack of guidance on how to handle submarine-launched ballistic missiles (SLBMs) and the problem of adding a separate numerical, or freeze-type, sublimit on heavy land-based missiles to the agreed-on freeze limits on land-based ICBMs. Neither issue had been covered on May 20, and the opening U.S. position at Helsinki—to freeze ICBMs and SLBMs as of the end of July 1971, and heavy missiles at the level of those "externally completed" by the end of the year—was quickly rejected by the Soviets, who naturally wanted the latest possible freeze dates. On these main fronts, Helsinki accomplished much less than the White House had hoped and expected. In Gerard Smith's later summation: "SALT agreements that had seemed relatively simple in the spring looked complex in the fall."[52] Along the way, Smith privately urged that the United States advocate a complete ban on ABMs, which intensely irritated Kissinger. Nixon turned this down in August in a long personal letter to Smith, presumably drafted by Kissinger. Smith found the whole exchange very revealing about the President's—and Kissinger's—general attitudes toward SALT.[53]

At Vienna the Soviets still refused to talk about limits on SLBM numbers and types, but finally began to negotiate seriously on land-based offensive weapons and seemed agreeable in principle to separate control arrangements on heavy missiles. Yet little headway was made on what an agreement on the limits of future missile stocks might look like. There was also an important provision that expressly permitted the United States to withdraw from the ABM treaty if the follow-on talks about offensive missiles failed. Thus, by the end of January 1972 an ABM deal was pretty well set, but the U.S. delegation was disturbed at the shortness of time remaining. The final Helsinki session was due to start in March, before a summit meeting in May.

Anticipating the process of congressional debate, Smith, in a talk with the President during the Christmas break, had renewed his earlier suggestion that a small number of responsible senators be made observers to the delegation. He had in mind Senator John Stennis and Senator John Sherman Cooper, but nothing came of this.[54] Meanwhile, the President's defense budget proposals for fiscal 1973 (to be approved in late 1972) called for an overall 16 percent increase, with an even larger proportional jump in funding for the Trident program of giant missile-carrying submarines with long cruising ranges, which Nixon considered the core of future U.S. missile strength.

Nixon's concern to assuage Pentagon fears that under a SALT agreement the United States might fall behind was more than matched on the Soviet side. The Soviet military leaders were determined to avoid any SALT outcome that could tie their hands with respect to the promising MIRV-laden future. Both defense establishments, especially the Soviet one, had put brakes on the SALT process, and neither visualized that a SALT agreement would do more than limit the strategic arms race.

3. The End of the Bretton Woods System

In the first six months of 1971 the fears that Paul Volcker of the Treasury had conveyed to his new Secretary, John Connally, were amply realized. Over the years the favorable balance of trade had been a crucial positive factor for U.S. international accounts, partially offsetting the outflows for security and other purposes. As the country dug out of the recession of 1969–70, the trade balance turned negative; that with Japan, already negative, worsened especially rapidly. The overall balance of payments—always seen around the world as the key index of a currency's health—was in a large and growing deficit.[55]

As a result, foreign nations increased their holdings of dollars—from $23.8 billion to $36.2 billion by July 30, 1971. By early August, official dollar holdings eligible for conversion to Fort Knox gold totaled $40 billion, more than three times the $12 billion value of the gold at the official price of $35 an ounce. While it was most unlikely that all the holders would seek conversion at once, the possibility of a large withdrawal, further increasing the ratio of claims to stock, was plain to all.[56]

It was inevitable that searching questions would be directed at Connally about what the United States proposed to do. In May, at a monetary conference in Munich, the Secretary responded that there would be no devaluation and no change in the gold price. The international financial community was used to such denials by finance ministers in countries whose currencies were under threat, but the Texas-style vehemence of Connally's response held the line for a time.

Meanwhile, as the American economy recovered, wages and prices started to move upward. Inflation, though reduced from 1968 levels, still stood at about 4 percent, an alarming figure at that time. Sentiment grew among businessmen and politicians in favor of freezing prices and wages for a few months. Some industrial prices were raised to get under the wire before controls were imposed. Always politically appealing, freezes were viewed very skeptically by orthodox economists, and had had a mixed record when tried abroad. Yet they remained a topic of discussion, and in August 1970 a small group in Congress had pushed through a grant of authority to the President to impose wage and price controls, thus putting the ball squarely in Nixon's court.

In early 1971 Arthur Burns, the respected Chairman of the Federal Reserve Board, called publicly for strong wage and price controls—giving greater respectability to the idea of an "incomes policy" of this sort. He stated his case in terms of the domestic economy, while Paul Volcker had already thought of wage and price controls as an effective way of offsetting the inflationary effect of devaluing the dollar in the international setting. In simplified terms, a devalued dollar would raise the dollar price of imported goods and materials, raising costs and permitting prices of competing domestic products also to rise. The issue of wage and price controls was therefore a hot topic both in its own right and because of its potential link to measures to devalue the dollar. During the spring, Nixon and Connally agreed that wage and price controls should accompany action on the dollar, informing only George Shultz at the Office of Management and Budget (OMB) and Paul McCracken, Chairman of the Council of Economic Advisors (CEA). True to form, at the end of June, Connally responded to questions by proclaiming vigorously that there would be no price controls and no wage and price review board, and for good measure no tax cut or increased federal spending.[57]

At that point the trade data for the second quarter of the year came out, showing an alarming further deterioration. Peter Peterson, as director of an interdepartmental Committee on International Economic Policy (CIEP), dramatized the effect of the overvalued dollar on U.S. exports and on the U.S. competitive position.[58] And in July, Connally put more pressure on Nixon to act, filling out a proposed program with a bargaining chip in the form of a temporary import surcharge.

In the absence of other factors, major nations could offset any U.S. devaluation by simply devaluing their own currencies to the same extent; a senior official of the European Community had told a member of the Council of Economic Advisors that the European countries would do just that. The belief ran deep in many quarters that since the Bretton Woods agreement of 1944 the United States, as the dominant country in the system, simply could not change the value of its currency. Although an import surcharge ran counter to long-standing U.S. positions favoring free trade, Connally argued persuasively that only such a sharp and painful knock on the head would persuade other nations to cooperate in revising the exchange-rate structure and, in cases such as Japan, in opening up their markets.[59]

Connally's new program thus came to include "closing the gold window" as its central feature—that is, refusing to honor the requests of foreign countries to convert their gold holdings into dollars. There would be subsequent action to devalue the dollar and, if possible, to set new exchange relationships among the major hard currencies. More immediately, there should be an import surcharge, a bargaining tool privately intended to be temporary if the key nations responded on the dollar and trade fronts. Finally, there would be the immediate imposition of a three-month freeze on U.S. wages and prices.

These first three key measures were considered simple necessities once pressure on the U.S. gold holdings became irresistible, which everyone expected would be soon. As for the wage and price freeze, debatable on pure economic grounds, it also had an underlying domestic political purpose of which Nixon and Arthur Burns were particularly aware. Both had experienced the 1958–60 period when Eisenhower and his economic advisors (including Burns) held to an orthodox anti-inflationary program of restrictive trade and monetary policies, so that the 1958 recession lingered on into the election year, hurting Nixon's presidential candidacy badly. Both men now believed it crucial to put an apparently painless method of controlling inflation in place for the coming 1972 election year.[60]

In addition, Connally's plan included raising the level of the investment tax credit (always popular with business), easing financial controls, and looking for a stimulative net increase in government expenditures. There were also sweeteners for especially influential segments of industry, notably lifting the excise tax on automobiles. In all, it was an astute mix, designed to adjust the value of the dollar and at the same time depict this action in a positive way. It bore the special stamp of its author, always highly sensitive to political factors and by this time — as we have noted — Nixon's prime favorite to succeed him in due course.[61] (In July 1971, Nixon as much as offered the vice presidential nomination in 1972 to Connally.)

On August 2, Nixon and Connally had a long talk, which Haldeman attended in order to record their conclusions and the supporting case they would make to the American public. The key features, Connally believed, should be "self-balancing measures to control the economy, both the inflationary side and on the import side, as well as to meet the international monetary situation, and get us away from being the victims of the foreign governments that are arbitrarily floating their currency and leaving us hanging." Haldeman added that this was becoming a "rather momentous decision." Shultz was trying to "put some brakes on," but Haldeman doubted he would be effective.[62] Shultz's job at the Office of Management and Budget might normally have limited his influence here, but by this time he had earned Nixon's great respect. In tune with his University of Chicago background, he was a strong believer in relying on market forces, leading him to urge floating exchange rates but to oppose wage and price controls strongly.[63]

The triggering event came ten days later, when Britain asked to draw $3 billion in gold, or at least to have its holdings guaranteed in value. A meeting was set at Camp David starting the next day, Friday, August 13, with elaborate security precautions taken to avoid leaks. The participants were chosen rigorously, but with Kissinger in Paris for secret talks with North Vietnam, Rogers away, and the Economic Under Secretary of State, Nathaniel Samuels, on leave, neither the NSC staff nor the department was present to offer political judgment.

At Camp David, Nixon presided over the plenary sessions at which Connally laid out the program. Working groups were then assigned to write supporting papers. The final decisions were reached on Sunday, and a presidential speech was drafted by William Safire. A three-month wage and price freeze was quickly approved and not seriously contested. The principal bone of contention was, curiously, the central action of "closing the gold window." Burns argued vigorously that the financial markets might explode, and Nixon gave him a special hearing, but he was overruled in the face of the judgments of Volcker and others that decisive action was imperative and would be well received. In the end, Connally's program was adopted in its entirety.

Connally also made a major contribution to the tone of Nixon's announcement, which came on Sunday evening, August 15 — before the global financial markets reopened for the week. Volcker had brought with him a draft in the mode of other countries' announcements of currency devaluations, apologetic and with earnest promises of sound behavior henceforth. It was a revelation to hear Nixon transform the key points into an upbeat picture of the United States taking charge and asserting itself to maintain its competitive position. The fact that the United States was abandoning its postwar role as the keystone nation in the international monetary system was obscured to the point of invisibility.

Striking this note, the speech was a complete success in terms of the domestic reaction. As summed up by Herbert Stein, a man of measured words:

> The imposition of the controls was the most popular move in economic policy that anyone could remember. The President had been concerned that the closing of the gold window might be interpreted as a confession of national bankruptcy. But he had presented the move as an attack by the United States on international speculators, and the public cheered him on. The DJ [Dow-Jones index of stock prices] went up by the biggest increase ever up to that point the day after. The man in the street felt great satisfaction and relief.[64]

In Congress the reaction was also favorable. As in the diplomacy with China, the reasons for tight secrecy were persuasive. Legislators recognized that advance public discussion or congressional hearings would have roiled the situation and raised speculation to damaging levels. And soon thereafter the Administration began to consult with leaders in Congress on the broad outlines of the next steps.[65]

Abroad, reactions were mixed at first, with an element of shock especially at the import surcharge, but it was slowly accepted that strong action had been the only course possible in light of the gold situation alone. The Japanese in particular were badly upset. The August 15 announcement, on top of the surprise news of Kissinger's visit to China a month earlier, was a second "shokku," although this time Volcker had given the Finance Ministry a little advance notice.[66]

In themselves, the decisions announced after Camp David were obviously incomplete. What would happen after the three-month wage and price freeze ended was left up in the air, and the shape and nature of a new international exchange-rate regime had not yet emerged. All that was clear was that the Bretton Woods system was dead, after twenty-seven years as the centerpiece of the international economy outside the closed Communist world.

The first U.S. goal had to be to stop the outflow of dollars that had brought on the crisis. This meant that the major European nations and Japan would have to accept a big shift in exchange rates, trade liberalization, and more help on U.S. overseas defense costs as well. It was a large order, and the key nations resisted strongly. Connally's tactics, in response, were to the longtime professional Volcker "a fast lesson in big-league negotiation." In the Finance Ministries and reserve banks that were the Secretary's targets, doubtless stronger and more critical expressions were used, especially as the U.S. goal turned out to be a much larger change in exchange rates than had been expected.

Early in September, Volcker gave his opposite numbers in the so-called G-10 grouping of major nations—the major Western European nations plus Japan and Canada—an idea of how much change in the U.S. accounts the Administration considered essential over the next year. The figure, $13 billion, was initially much higher than the other nations were prepared to accept or contribute, but the American calculations had the general support of the International Monetary Fund. At the regular IMF meeting at the end of the month, Connally offered to remove the import surcharge if the major nations would agree to a short-term free float of currencies as a transition toward a new agreed-on level for the dollar. This offer was not picked up, but currency negotiations slowly gained momentum in October and November, as Connally continued to play his cards very closely, which worried many in the American government. In preparation for a G-10 ministers' meeting convened for the end of November in Rome, Volcker wrote a memorandum, which promptly leaked, that set the U.S. target as an 11 percent change in trade-weighted relative exchange rates: if this was accepted, the import surcharge would be dropped, but the United States would still insist on good faith negotiations over trade liberalization and sharing of security burdens. ("Trade-weighted" meant that each currency's adjustment was weighted by its total trade accounts—a more meaningful index of change than a simple arithmetical averaging.)[67]

From the first, Japan, with its large trade surplus, had special problems. Moreover, one aftermath of the Camp David meeting had been a decision to force Japan to agree on the vexing issue of "voluntary" textile quotas, by taking the harsh step of threatening to invoke the Trading with the Enemy Act, passed in World War II. It was an especially insensitive step to take toward a country that had ceased to be an "enemy" twenty-six years earlier and had been exceptionally supportive and cooperative with America. Volcker rightly noted that Nixon seemed to feel more strongly about meeting his 1968 campaign pledge to Senator Thurmond than he did about gold! On October 15, Japan finally yielded, accepting export restraints "with a strong sense of defeat."[68] To a small extent, the damage was offset when the Senate soon ratified a treaty giving Okinawa back to Japan. Reversion duly took place in 1972.

In November, Connally visited Japan, and his modest public manner somewhat countered the harsh image that had preceded him. He pressed key officials hard to accept a major change in the yen's exchange rate, 24 percent, suggesting that the West German mark might go up by 18 percent while the dollar remained unchanged.

At that point the United States was resisting appeals to devalue the dollar by accepting an increase in the gold price. Over the years $35 an ounce had been a symbol of American rectitude and steadiness, but the psychological barrier to change was out of tune with what the United States now had to do and recognize. Finally, at a principals-only session of the G-10 meeting in Rome in late November—which Volcker later described as "the most interesting international meeting of my career"—Connally, in the chair, confronted several Finance Ministers who insisted that there was nothing to discuss unless the United States was prepared to make a "contribution" by raising its official gold price. In a whisper Connally authorized Volcker, speaking for the United States, to suggest a 10–15 percent increase, which the Secretary quickly modified to a straight 10 percent.

There ensued a silence for almost an hour, before the West German Finance Minister, Karl Schiller, accepted, saying that his country would revalue the mark upward by two points to make a 12 percent realignment. None of the other major Europeans joined in, but the ice had been broken and the form of a final agreement outlined: a U.S. devaluation joined with upward revaluations of other currencies.[69]

By this time Kissinger was warning Nixon and the Treasury that these intense, strung-out negotiations were damaging NATO cohesion. With big issues pending—what to do about a European security conference, and conventional arms negotiations — Kissinger persuaded Nixon to get into direct contact with several heads of government to resolve the key issues. France was the principal holdout, demanding that the value of gold and new exchange rates remain fixed even if at new levels, rather than moving to a system of floating exchange rates as others were suggesting.

With the next G-10 meeting scheduled to open in Washington on December 15, Nixon journeyed to the Azores, with Connally and Kissinger, to meet with French President Pompidou on December 13 and 14. The French agreed to accept a new gold price of $38 an ounce, and the United States agreed that exchange rates would at least initially be fixed. Tentative new figures for each nation were discussed, with France invited in effect to lead in bringing the European nations into line, a role always congenial to proud French statesmen.

After a memorable final session, the meetings, held at the Smithsonian Institution, produced agreement. The Japanese yen was to be revalued upward by 16.9 percent, the West German mark by 14 percent, other currencies by lesser percentages (except that Canada, America's largest trading partner, refused to abandon its floating posture and so remained unchanged). Together with the U.S. devaluation of 8.25 percent through the increased gold price, the total trade-weighted realignment of currencies among the G-10 came to just under 8 percent, below the target of 10–15 percent the Treasury had indicated would truly bring the U.S. international account into equilibrium. A key condition of the agreement was that the United States give up the import surcharge.

Although financial experts and markets were skeptical that the new agreement would hold indefinitely, it was a considerable achievement to have reached an agreement. A top Japanese official later called Connally "a superb negotiator" and "magnificent deal maker," but at the time, Nixon's claim that this was "the greatest monetary agreement in the history of the world" seemed to experts a political leader's boasting. Ordinary Americans, however, considered that the Smithsonian agreement demonstrated successful international leadership by their President once again.

In the event, the Smithsonian parities held for only fourteen months, but they gave an impression of steadiness throughout the election year 1972, which may have been what counted most to Nixon as well as Connally. In hindsight, Volcker thought Connally had actually been too gentle in the last phase, especially with the Europeans, and Shultz judged that without Kissinger's moderating intervention the dollar devaluation would have been larger and more realistic, much reducing later problems in 1973 and 1974.[70]

Yet if the Smithsonian agreement turned out to be only temporary in its effect, the whole negotiation did break new ground. For the first time an American government had conferred publicly with its closest partners and allies about issues of great domestic and international importance, and in the negotiations all sides had made concessions. The result was an important benchmark of reduced U.S. power and influence, brought about in large part by the strains of what came later to be called "imperial overstretch"—above all the heavy overseas costs of the Vietnam War. On the plus side, an enormous change had been achieved with bearable strain and little ultimate confusion. On the other hand, Nixon's sugarcoating of the outcome served to conceal from the American public that in a deep sense this was, or symbolized, a setback for the United States and its role in the world. The U.S. actions made the way easier not only for later devaluations but for irresponsible fiscal and monetary policies.

President Nixon had grasped the issues, presided ably over serious deliberations with a highly capable team of advisors, and given the final product a strong presidential stamp. As crisis management, it was a bravura performance, and Americans generally could sense, even if they understood only dimly, the details and even the effect of what was agreed. The final Smithsonian agreement might have made a still stronger impression had it not coincided with the Administration's lamentable performance in dealing with the war between India and Pakistan.

Looking back on the Camp David discussions, the conservative and cautious Herbert Stein noted years later how few of the key decisions had been thought through. The gold window was closed without its being clear whether the dollar would float or be fixed at a new level, a choice that was then made only in response to the views of foreign nations, notably France. The future of the wage and price freeze was even more uncertain—in Stein's words "a jump off the diving board without any clear idea of what lay below."[71]

Along with George Shultz, Stein had opposed an incomes policy. Like Nixon himself, he had served in the wartime Office of Price Administration and found it a negative and confused experience that demonstrated how ineffective the bureaucracy's methods were in interfering with the market. Again like Nixon and Shultz, he was resolved that controls should be as brief as possible, with as small a structure as possible.

Thus, when the three months of the first freeze elapsed in November, with less effect on inflationary assumptions and psychology than some had hoped, the new bureaucracy was far smaller than the wartime Office of Price Administration. Moreover, it sought initially to discriminate less among sectors of the economy and be less concerned with the problems of particular companies. In the short term, this simplification undoubtedly had great advantages, since politically and psychologically a "no exceptions" program was easier both to administer and to gain acceptance for.

One sector, however, was dramatically in flux, and a different policy for it should have been at least considered. This was oil. By 1970 the system of quotas on oil imports was being relaxed, and foreign oil supplies increased in the U.S. market as demand (chiefly for transportation) steadily rose and domestic oil production leveled off. Oil imports rose from a pre-1969 level of 2.5 million barrels a day to 6.7 million in 1973, with most of the increase coming in 1971 and 1972.

Under the terms of the Teheran and Tripoli agreements of early 1971, the devalued dollar meant that the price of Middle Eastern oil went up 5 percent immediately, with provision for further increases to match new devaluations of the dollar (in which oil prices and producer payments were denominated). In practice, OPEC was granted two further significant rises in price by the end of 1972. The result was that whereas for years the price of domestic oil had been controlling in the U.S. market, and almost always exceeded that of imported oil, the imported price came to dominate. To this situation, the Camp David price freeze narrowed the profit margins of the major oil-importing companies, so that it was partly in self-interest that some of the Seven Sisters began, in 1972, to reduce their sales efforts and even to urge economy in the use of oil. But as we have noted earlier, pain in that quarter had little political or popular effect. What mattered much more, both to economic and to foreign policy, was the continued surge in U.S. oil consumption, to which controlled prices greatly contributed. In a normal market, oil prices at the pump should have increased greatly, slowing down a rise in consumption. But under the price freeze U.S. oil consumption ran wild, so that by early 1973 the level of oil imports—above all from the Middle East—had reached a point where both economic and political power were flowing rapidly to the oil-producing states of the Middle East. Together with other elements, this added up to what became the most critical set of problems the Nixon Administration faced in the President's last year in office.

4. Fiasco: U.S. Policy in the Indo-Pakistan Crisis

Handling the international monetary crisis and attendant domestic policies showed Nixon at his best, working with careful and well-argued advice to arrive at considered decisions and effective public presentation. The reactions of Nixon and Kissinger to the nine-month crisis between India and Pakistan that erupted into war in December 1971, however, showed both men at their worst. They lurched to highly doubtful conclusions on the basis of fragmentary intelligence, little understood the decisive regional elements, and misjudged the conduct of both the Soviet Union and China at key junctures.

From the very beginning of Pakistan's existence as the Muslim state created by Britain when it withdrew from the Indian subcontinent in 1947, there was a vast gulf between East and West Pakistan—in culture, attitudes,

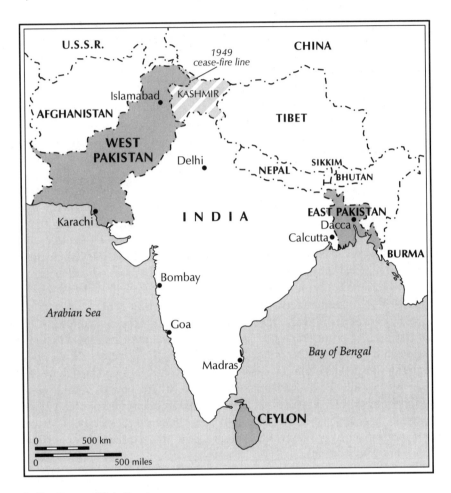

India © 1997 *Chris Brest*

economic welfare, and simple geographic distance. The western part of
Pakistan held the country's center of government and dominated its civil
service (especially its armed forces) and until 1970 its electoral politics.
Pakistani of the West, in image and largely in reality, were austere and stiff,
while the Bengali of East Pakistan were volatile and poor, considering themselves with reason to be second-class citizens.

In 1965, a badly misjudged military attack on India in the West (the
Punjab) had led to Pakistan's humiliating defeat in a brief but decisive war
that left India clearly the dominant power on the subcontinent. The rift
between East and West Pakistan deepened, as the West made considerable
economic progress while the East stagnated.

In the fall of 1970 an unprecedented cyclone brought terrible floods to East Bengal, and the regime in Islamabad badly botched the response. In the December elections for a new National Assembly, the strongly regional and anti–West Pakistan Awami League took 167 out of the 169 seats in the East, which made it the majority party in the overall Assembly. But the regime of General Yahya Khan simply refused to convene the Assembly, retaining his hold on power by plain force. This brought to fever pitch the sentiment in East Pakistan for autonomy and an end to Western domination. In March 1971, Yahya sent 40,000 regular army forces into East Pakistan to quell riots. As the troops moved in, the head of the Awami League and spearhead of its overwhelming victory in the 1970 elections, Sheikh Mujibur Rahman (known to all as Mujib) was peremptorily arrested and detained, though no charges were brought against him. This arrest, the heavy-handed and brutal behavior of the Pakistani troops, and the many atrocities set off an outcry of protest in the world press. At least some expression of disapproval and concern by an American government seemed called for, since the United States had frequently spoken out in similar situations over the years and under Presidents of both parties.

Not so the Nixon Administration. Even the State Department spokesman was silent. Alexis Johnson suggested another possibility, private suggestions to Yahya to avoid or limit the use of force, but Kissinger said that the President had a "special relationship" with Yahya and would be reluctant to intervene himself, while any representation by the U.S. Ambassador would simply be brushed off. This response puzzled his listeners, none of whom knew of Yahya's intermediary work on the China front.[72]

At that point, Nixon's Pakistani channel to China was actually dormant. When it resumed in April, culminating with the crucial meeting in Beijing, Nixon and Kissinger were even more adamantly opposed to giving advice to Yahya on what was on its face a domestic issue, albeit already becoming international. At the same time, Kissinger agreed with the professionals that Yahya could not ultimately hold East Pakistan by force, and that American policy should be noninvolvement—the policy adopted and maintained, for example, by Great Britain and virtually every other outside nation. However, not only Ambassador Kenneth Keating in New Delhi (a former Republican senator) but virtually the entire staff of the U.S. Consulate General in Dacca were cabling vigorous protests at the absence of any public U.S. statement deploring what was widely, and reasonably, seen as the use of brute force to oust an elected majority. The consulate officials, whose cable promptly leaked to the press, thought that U.S. policy "serves neither our moral interests, broadly defined, nor our national interests, narrowly defined."[73]

U.S. military grant aid to Pakistan had ceased after the disastrous 1965 war with India, but a substantial military sale had been made in 1970. Now the State Department moved to deny new licenses for such sales and put a hold on current shipments, unfortunately overlooking a small number of already licensed shipments en route, which came to light in June. Informed promptly of the hold action, Kissinger agreed to get firm guidance from President Nixon, but never did so.[74]

Almost at once, the Pakistani crackdown led to a massive outflow of refugees, both Hindu and Muslim, from East Pakistan to West Bengal in India, next door—rough estimates were 2.8 million by the end of May, 7 million by June, and by fall as many as 10 million. The numbers and desperate state of the refugees far exceeded India's capacity to care for them, and their presence was also politically threatening in an often turbulent and disaffected area. Prime Minister Indira Gandhi, who had been reelected in March with a strong majority, protested vigorously at the effect of these burdens. In response, the economic aid agencies of the U.S. government, long familiar with these problems, flexibly and resourcefully allocated and transported relief supplies, and a special fund of $250 million was proposed and quickly accepted by Congress. In addition to its humanitarian purposes, the effort aimed to keep the situation within bearable limits and to reduce India's incentives to take military action.

In mid-July, right after Kissinger's return from Beijing, Nixon convened an NSC meeting in San Clemente, at which the whole situation was a main topic. Kissinger did most of the talking, reporting the impression he had gotten in New Delhi that Mrs. Gandhi was bent on war, and from his talks with Yahya that he did not have the imagination to "solve the political problems" in time to prevent an Indian assault.

> Our objective had to be an evolution that would lead to independence for East Pakistan. Unfortunately, this was not likely to happen in time to head off an Indian attack. Therefore immediate efforts were needed to arrest and reverse the flow of refugees and thereby remove the pretext for war.[75]

To State and the aid agencies, a logical corollary would have been to suggest to Yahya that he reduce the government's military presence in East Pakistan and lower the level of brutality, so that civilian supplies could be more effectively handled and distributed. However, in two interagency meetings in late July, Kissinger rejected even this idea with the revealing comment: "Why is it our business how they govern themselves? . . . The President always says to tilt toward Pakistan, but every proposal I get is in the opposite direction. Sometimes I think I am in a nut house."[76]

In these meetings, both Assistant Secretary Joseph Sisco of State and CIA Director Richard Helms judged that although India had made contingency plans for war and Mrs. Gandhi was under political pressure to act, she had not definitely decided to go to war. Kissinger and Nixon still resisted urging Yahya to release Mujib and negotiate with him, the only course that offered any promise of a peaceful outcome. Those working on the problem perceived that the White House was backing generous aid to India largely in the hope that it would lessen congressional and public clamor to apply pressure to Pakistan.[77]

The differences of view in Washington only deepened with the signing of the Indo-Soviet Friendship Treaty in early August, to which Kissinger at once gave the darkest possible interpretation. In his view, "for all practical purposes [it] gave India a Soviet guarantee against Chinese intervention if India went to war with Pakistan. By this action the Soviet Union deliberately opened the door to war on the subcontinent." The Soviet experts on the NSC staff were categorical in their reading: the Indo-Pakistan conflict had now became "a sort of Sino-Soviet clash by proxy."[78]

Such judgments flew in the face of abundant continuing evidence that the Soviet Union still wanted good relations with Pakistan. Soviet leaders had seen their mediation role after the 1965 war as a tremendous boost to their prestige. In the overall pattern of Soviet policy, moreover, to alienate a principal Muslim state, Pakistan, would badly undercut important Soviet efforts to gain favor in the largely Muslim Middle East.[79]

Likewise, China's policy in South Asia never deviated from support for Pakistan's "independence and sovereignty," never using the formula Yahya repeatedly urged, support for Pakistan's "territorial integrity." In effect, China was committed only to support the survival of a West Pakistan.[80]

Nixon and Kissinger—with their strong tendency to see great-power ties as the key to regional situations—judged the positions of both China and the Soviet Union to be far stronger and more committed to the opposing sides than was probably ever the case. The differences between State and the White House were great. Kissinger's memoir is blunt and revealing about both those differences and Nixon's failure to face up to them.

On no issue—except perhaps Cambodia—was the split between the White House and the departments as profound as on the India-Pakistan crisis in the summer of 1971. On no other problem was there such flagrant disregard of unambiguous Presidential directives. The State Department controlled the machinery of execution. . . . [There was] a constant infighting over seemingly trivial issues . . . whose accumulation would define the course of national policy. Nixon was not prepared to overrule his Secretary of State on what appeared to him minor operational matters; this freed the State Department to interpret Nixon's directives in accordance with its own preferences, thereby vitiating the course Nixon had set.

No one could speak for five minutes with Nixon without hearing of his profound distrust of Indian motives, his concern over Soviet meddling, and above all his desire not to risk the opening to China by ill-considered posturing.[81]

So far as the available record, or Kissinger's memoir, shows, however, there were never any "directives" from the President, "unambiguous" or otherwise, except to move forward at full speed on the refugee relief program, which was never in dispute. That State (and others, including CIA analysts) saw the situation differently only makes it doubly hard to explain why Nixon never provided explicit policy guidance, or moved, through Kissinger, to keep track of those "minor operational matters" that often amounted to setting policy. This failure to manage, in part a failure of nerve, reflected the curious quality in Nixon's character that made it terribly difficult, even impossible, for him to tell any but his small inner circle what he really thought of their ideas or proposals. It was only natural that when the policy objectives were never made clear, confused and discordant actions resulted.[82]

As the summer went on, the monsoon season in South Asia put a damper on military activity. The East Pakistan rebels, now strongly established in India with headquarters in Calcutta, changed their aim from autonomy to outright independence as "Bangla Desh." Concurrently, guerrilla forces in India, under the name of the Mukhti Bahini, began to infiltrate in small groups into East Pakistan to attack communications systems, notably the avenues for export of jute and tea, and to harass the Pakistani Army. With semi-covert support from the Indian government, these operations were increasingly successful. With the several million refugees ever more agitated and burdensome, pressures toward war were building and the chances of a peaceful resolution steadily receding.[83]

With an eye also to the upcoming session of the United Nations, Yahya did make some concessions in August and September, appointing a civilian governor in East Pakistan and granting an amnesty for some of the rebels. But he remained adamant against negotiating with Mujib and still threatened to try him for treason. This snail's-pace progress could not alter the drift to war, although Kissinger, who was on good terms with the highly capable Indian Ambassador in Washington, L. K. Jha, repeatedly tried to reassure him that an evolutionary process, "with our support," would surely lead to self-determination for East Pakistan.[84]

In August, according to Kissinger, Washington got "incontrovertible" evidence that the Soviet Union had agreed to use its veto in the Security Council if India were charged there with aggression against Pakistan, and to airlift military supplies to India if she were attacked by Pakistan or China. Once again, Kissinger failed to note the limited and defensive character of these assurances, even if they were reliably reported.[85] In September and early October, the White House obsession with Soviet policy increased when top-level visits between Moscow and New Delhi were exchanged, though the Soviet statements on both occasions were reserved. Both India and Pakistan moved their forces close to the borders, and Secretary-General U Thant at the United Nations made a brief, vain effort to persuade both to pull back.[86]

Mrs. Gandhi then took her case to a succession of Western capitals, ending with a visit to Washington on November 4 and 5. Kissinger had extended an invitation to her during his July stopover in New Delhi, to balance Yahya's visit of October 1970, but now the visit came at a most difficult time. Usually Nixon liked direct talks with heads of state or government. He prided himself on his careful preparation, avoidance of set-piece remarks, and his shrewd assessments of his interlocutors. As President, he probably set a record in the number of such contacts, both formal and informal, and in most cases he enjoyed and profited from them.

India was a conspicuous exception. Nixon had gone there in mid-1953, just as Eisenhower and John Foster Dulles were forging the first strong U.S. ties with Pakistan. He himself shared Dulles's view that Nehru's nonalignment in the East-West struggle was "immoral." He had no visible part in the improvement in U.S.-Indian relations in Eisenhower's last years, culminating in Ike's extraordinarily successful and popular visit to India in 1959. Neither then nor later did he appear to shed his first unfavorable impressions and reactions. Now, with his friendship with Pakistan's leaders at a peak, he had to confront Nehru's daughter, like her father a proud and prickly character not easy to deal with at the best of times.

Little wonder that the talks with Mrs. Gandhi on this occasion were, in Kissinger's judgment, "without a doubt the two most unfortunate meetings Nixon had with any foreign leader." With Kissinger doing much of the talking, the main American pitch was that the outcome of any negotiation would surely be autonomy leading to independence for Bangladesh. Yahya had now expressed a willingness to talk to leaders of the Bangladesh movement. He himself expected to turn over power in Pakistan in late December to a civilian, Z. A. Bhutto, leader of the Pakistan People's Party, which had done well in the 1970 election, and Bhutto would then be prepared to talk directly to Mujib. It should be possible to arrange an agreement by March 1972 that would give early independence to Bangladesh, so that India should not consider resorting to force.[87] But the obvious weakness was that Nixon could not say that Yahya was prepared to talk directly with Mujib in the very near future. Given this stubborn fact, Kissinger's latter-day claim in his memoirs—that Yahya's concessions had created a "near-certainty" of a successful outcome—is ridiculous. Yahya's adamant refusal to talk with Mujib was only part of the problem: the central fact was that Mujib would never settle for less than outright independence, and Pakistan with Yahya and its powerful military establishment would never agree.

The highly uncertain possibility of a deal by March was simply not acceptable to Mrs. Gandhi; pressures in West Bengal and in the Indian parliament fortified her resolve to settle the issue soon.[88] She received Nixon's message with "aloof indifference." When it came her turn, she "gave a little lecture" on the history of Pakistan, arguing that Pakistan was an artificial creation rather than, like India, the result of a genuine independence movement; that it was held together mainly by hatred of India; and that parts of West Pakistan such as Baluchistan and the North-West Frontier deserved autonomy as much as East Bengal did. She denied that she was opposed to the very existence of Pakistan, but her presentation — at least as described by Kissinger — supported such an interpretation.

Americans and others familiar with South Asia would have seen at once that this was probably a reflexive repetition of old grievances rather than a statement of present intent. Yet Kissinger at least was apparently affected by Mrs. Gandhi's lecture. Convinced that India had decided to go to war over East Pakistan, and that the Soviet Union was aiding and abetting the effort, it was for him a short step to believing that India's designs extended to West Pakistan as well.

Two days after Mrs. Gandhi's visit to Washington a Pakistani delegation led by Bhutto went to China to obtain a firmer Chinese commitment to help. The results were disappointing, however, with the Chinese in the end simply repeating their readiness to support Pakistan's "state sovereignty and national independence." In November, Pakistan made gestures as if to receive heavy military traffic from China, but the Indians were unimpressed, and went ahead with the movement of several divisions, then stationed in the Himalayas, into position for operations in East Pakistan.[89]

In late November, regular Indian forces supporting the insurgent Mukti Bahini crossed into East Pakistan for short distances, creating an ambiguous situation just short of outright war. The Pakistani Ambassador in Washington approached the State Department with the claim that a bilateral 1959 Executive Agreement, concluded under Eisenhower — though never submitted to Congress, let alone ratified — amounted to a U.S. commitment to come to Pakistan's aid in such a situation, at least with supplies and even with combat forces. Once again Kissinger and the State Department clashed, the department sticking to the long-standing U.S. position that the agreement was not a binding commitment, whereas Kissinger tended to see any such assurance — by the United States or other nations — as binding, and to reject any argument to the contrary as legalistic quibbling. Nixon made no move to resolve the dispute. In response to a predictable press question, the State Department's view was stated as the position of the Nixon Administration, while in private Kissinger assured the Pakistani Ambassador that he and the President regarded the exchanges with Pakistan as amounting to a commitment![90]

On December 3, Pakistan sent ground forces across the border into western India and across the 1948 cease-fire line into Kashmir, and it used its Air Force against Indian air bases. India responded by making deeper and bigger incursions into East Pakistan, while taking up defensive positions in the West. War had begun in earnest. As everyone in Washington perceived, it was a desperation move by Yahya, motivated in part by pressure from his military colleagues. Kissinger later commented that Yahya "must have known [that it] was suicidal." To the extent that there was any rational hope behind it, it was that Pakistani forces might take significant Indian territory in the West and in Indian-controlled areas of Kashmir. Indian attacks in the East might be contained for a time, and the United Nations might then bring about a cease-fire, opening the way for Pakistan to yield back conquered territory in the West in return for reassertion of control over East Pakistan.[91]

Within the first two days, it became apparent that any such hopes were totally unrealistic. Indian forces were driven back in Kashmir and the Punjab, but only for short distances, while in the East they swept all before them, advancing steadily. It was apparent that they would control the whole of East Bengal in a matter of days. Headlines emphasized Pakistani operations in Indian territory, with less stress on what India was doing in the West. Nixon directed that the United States, through Ambassador Bush at the UN, should strongly support a Security Council resolution calling for an immediate cease-fire and a withdrawal of forces to the border. Bush in New York and the White House in Washington blamed India for the crisis. On December 6, Bush said on TV that India was guilty of "clear-cut aggression." The cease-fire resolution was debated on December 4 and vetoed by the Soviet Union on two successive days. A flurry of other resolutions also failed, and on December 6 the United States took the case to the General Assembly under the "Uniting for Peace" procedure established in 1950 for use when the Security Council was crippled by veto. In the General Assembly, an Argentinian resolution similar to the American one was debated at length. There was no consensus, but the call for a cease-fire was approved on December 8 by a vote of 104–11, with the Soviet bloc and India opposed.[92]

More concretely, on the same day, the United States suspended economic aid to India, and Nixon, in a letter to Brezhnev, took a strong line, invoking the "spirit in which we agreed" to a summit and saying that an "accomplished fact" in India would adversely affect other issues. The Soviet reply was that a political solution—meaning a commitment for independence for Bangladesh—should be the precondition for a cease-fire.

The next day, with Yahya cabling Nixon to warn that East Pakistan was disintegrating, Kissinger held a lengthy press backgrounder, responding to vehement media comment that Nixon and he had been anti-Indian and pro-Pakistan. In it he rejected charges of anti-Indian bias as "totally inaccurate," alluded to Nixon's past support for aid to India, and expounded the same line as Nixon's to Mrs. Gandhi the month before.[93]

On this same day, Kissinger received a CIA report from India that became central. As he summarized it in his memoir, a source "whose reliability we had never had any reason to doubt" reported that in Indian Cabinet deliberations it had been agreed that India would not accept a cease-fire until Bangladesh had been liberated. After this was achieved, Mrs. Gandhi

> was determined to reduce even West Pakistan to impotence. . . . Indian forces would proceed with the "liberation" of the southern part of Azad Kashmir—the Pakistani part of Kashmir—and continue fighting until the Pakistani army and air force were wiped out. In other words, *West* Pakistan was to be dismembered and rendered defenseless. Mrs. Gandhi also told colleagues that if the Chinese "rattled the sword," the Soviets had promised to take appropriate counteraction.[94]

The text of this report has never been revealed, but Kissinger's alarm was not shared by others present. The JCS representative, General John D. Ryan, Air Force Chief of Staff, thought that India would be content for a time with a holding action in the West. Answering Kissinger's question, Ryan judged that while an Indian airborne brigade could be moved to the western front within five or six days, it would take "a reasonably long time to move all the forces." Joseph Sisco agreed with Kissinger that if in fact Pakistan's armor and air forces were eliminated in the literal sense, the viability of West Pakistan would be at serious risk, but he did not believe that this was India's objective.[95] Despite these reservations and differences of interpretation, the CIA report had a great impact on Nixon, who said it was the first time he had got really timely intelligence from the CIA.

With the creation of Bangladesh now seen as inevitable, the focus switched to West Pakistan, and the crisis entered a new phase about December 9. Even if Indian forces took over only the Pakistani-held areas of Kashmir, Kissinger believed that "there was no way Pakistan could survive the simultaneous loss of Bengal and Kashmir"—that in short the survival of Pakistan as an independent state was at stake.[96] At this point, the White House took over policy totally. There were no further WSAG meetings and no serious consultation with the Defense or State Department. As often, Nixon and Kissinger focused on the Soviet Union as the key—"our only card left was to raise the risks for the Soviets to a level where Moscow would see larger interests jeopardized."[97]

In quick succession:

On December 9, Nixon used a visit from the Soviet Minister of Agriculture, Vladimir Matskevich, with Chargé Vorontsov also present, as the occasion for telling the surprised minister that relations were bound to be seriously affected if the Soviet Union did not cooperate over the South Asia crisis. He added, "The Soviet Union has a treaty with India; we have one with Pakistan." (The former claim was probably exaggerated, the latter downright misleading, as we have just seen.) Privately, Nixon also mentioned to Kissinger the possibility of canceling or postponing the May 1972 summit.

Kissinger worked out with Yahya a new UN proposal that in effect abandoned the demand for India's immediate withdrawal from East Pakistan, calling instead for a cease-fire in both East and West, to be followed by negotiations for "the satisfaction of Bengali aspirations"—which was bound to mean an independent Bangladesh. In presenting this to Vorontsov the next day, Kissinger added a note of threat, referring specifically to a 1962 message concerning U.S. assistance to Pakistan against India as a "pledge" the United States would honor.[98]

After exchanges between Washington and the Pakistani government in which Kissinger warned strongly that a cease-fire would only release Indian forces to go to the West, a proposal by the Pakistani commander in the East for an immediate cease-fire there was abruptly withdrawn on orders from Islamabad. It was an extraordinary act of intervention.

On December 10, Kissinger conveyed directly to the Chief of Naval Operations, Admiral Elmo Zumwalt, an order by Nixon to assemble an impressive naval task force and start it into the Strait of Malacca on the route to the Bay of Bengal and the Indian Ocean. Neither Secretary Laird nor the JCS was consulted about this, though Laird supported the action when informed. This Task Group 74 centered on the largest aircraft carrier in the Navy, the nuclear-powered *Enterprise*, with appropriate escort ships. (*Enterprise* was off South Vietnam at the time, as part of a general airpower buildup.)

That evening Kissinger went to New York to meet with the Chinese UN Ambassador, Huang Hua, who had become an accepted channel to Zhou Enlai. Kissinger "told him of our reliable information of Indian plans to destroy West Pakistan's armed forces," of the plan for a standstill cease-fire, and that U.S. naval forces were moving to the Strait of Malacca. Huang Hua expressed fear that Indian-Soviet collusion to dismember Pakistan would set an example elsewhere. Kissinger responded that the United States would not be indifferent in such cases. Huang Hua left a strong impression that China would intervene militarily if things worsened, raising the possibility that in response the Soviet Union would take diversionary action against China in the border area of Sinkiang. A nightmare scenario of great-power war took shape in Kissinger's mind. More than ever, he saw the crisis as a key test of U.S. reliability in the eyes of Zhou and the Chinese leadership.[99]

On the morning of December 11, Kissinger met in New York with Z. A. Bhutto, who had just been named Pakistan's Deputy Prime Minister as well as Foreign Minister, and was Yahya's presumptive early successor. Kissinger was much impressed by the articulate and forceful Bhutto and in the end the two agreed that the new U.S. proposal for a standstill cease-fire should be pursued in the Security Council if the Soviet Union did not agree within the next day to cooperate. One may surmise that Kissinger at least mentioned the naval movement as evidence of U.S. firmness. Later that day a Pakistani spokesman in Islamabad stated that Pakistan had invoked "understandings" with friendly powers to come to its assistance.[100] On the other hand, Vorontsov told Kissinger that Deputy Foreign Minister Vasily Kuznetsov had been sent to New Delhi to further a peaceful outcome.

On Sunday morning, December 12, with Nixon and Kissinger due to fly to the Azores that afternoon to meet with Pompidou, Kissinger and Haig sent a "hot line" message to Moscow. Just at that point, Huang Hua called from New York to say that he had an urgent message that could only be delivered face to face to a White House person known to him. Nixon, Kissinger, and Haig, with no others present, immediately concluded that the message would be that China was coming to the military assistance of Pakistan. The three concurred that in that event, based on what Kissinger described as "all our information," the Soviet Union was committed to use force against China (presumably in Sinkiang) and would do so. Nixon decided that, if it did, "we would not stand idly by," and issued an order for Task Group 74 to proceed through the Strait of Malacca into the Bay of Bengal. Vorontsov was promptly informed of the fleet move.[101]

That evening, Bush presented the U.S. cease-fire proposal to the Security Council, which adjourned early Monday morning without reaching a vote. In the debate, Bush pressed hard for a "clear and unequivocal assurance" that India did not intend to annex Pakistani territory or "change the status quo in Kashmir." In response, the Indian Foreign Minister repeated that India had no designs on "West Pakistan." When Haig and Winston Lord, of the NSC staff, arrived in New York to receive the Chinese message, they learned to their great surprise that the message did not say that China was taking military moves of any sort, but rather that China would support the standstill cease-fire proposal!

Tension in the White House over a possible great-power conflict subsided, but concern over the threat to West Pakistan and the Pakistani-controlled area of Kashmir continued. The naval force (TG 74) was held up for twenty-four hours, then sent through the strait in broad daylight, as conspicuously as possible, to emphasize the intended message to the Soviet

Union to put pressure on India to accept the cease-fire. However, there was a significant change in its destination. Admiral Zumwalt, arguing that the Bay of Bengal was too close to Indian Bengal and to the fighting area, got the order amended so that the task group in fact went to waters south of Ceylon, more than a thousand miles farther from East Bengal![102]

On December 13, the Soviet Union vetoed the new U.S. cease-fire proposal at the United Nations, but reports from New Delhi were that Kuznetsov was meeting with Indian leaders. On December 14, a long Soviet note delivered in Washington still stopped short of the necessary assurances, while Indian forces continued to drive toward Dacca, the capital of East Pakistan, with the prospect of surrounding it completely within a day or so. Returning with Nixon from the Azores on the presidential plane, Kissinger took it upon himself to tell the press pool, "on background," that if Soviet conduct concerning South Asia continued on its present course, the United States would have to reconsider holding the May summit.

Predictably, this threat at once became a lead story. Kissinger writhed to discover that Nixon attached far too much importance to the summit to support such a threat—even though he himself had mentioned it a few days before and, by one account, seen and approved a summary of Kissinger's remarks. As the first bulletins went out, the White House quickly put out disclaimers, and shortly issued a statement that was definitely soothing toward the Soviet Union:

> If the Soviets continue to support Indian military action and the Indians should move into West Pakistan, this could very well affect future relations with the Soviet Union. But we have no reason to suspect this will occur. We have every expectation that fighting will stop in South Asia.[103]

On December 15, Vorontsov conveyed repeated messages that India was coming around, and these were confirmed the next day when, with Indian forces by then moving into Dacca and the western front calm, India accepted a renewed cease-fire offer from the Pakistani commander in the East. Most important, Mrs. Gandhi offered an unconditional cease-fire in the West, thus at last meeting the principal U.S. concern. With the surrender of the Pakistani forces in the East, the "two-week war" ended on December 17. There was a newly established Bangladesh state, India's dominance in South Asia was reinforced and confirmed, and Soviet prestige in the area increased at the expense of China.

As for the *Enterprise* and its Task Group, there was already one smaller Soviet task force in the Bay of Bengal area and another known to be en route from the Soviet east coast. When Admiral Zumwalt succeeded in changing the locale to the waters south of Ceylon, the rival superpower forces, in his words, "circled around each other warily, much as their counterparts had been doing in the Mediterranean for years. Finally, in early January 1972, TG 74 was ordered out of the Indian Ocean as mysteriously as it had been ordered in."[104]

With the crisis over, Nixon moved rapidly to undo the effect on the Soviet leadership of Kissinger's threat and to ease remaining tensions, saying in an interview published in *Time*: "We had differences at the beginning of the war, although not at the end, when both sides urged restraint. [The Soviets helped to bring about] the cease-fire that stopped what would inevitably have been the conquest of West Pakistan as well." In the same interview, Nixon gave his view of Indian intentions:

> I would not like to contend that the Indians had a definite plan to [conquer West Pakistan]. But once these passions of war and success in war are let loose they tend to run their course. . . . It is my conviction based on our intelligence reports as to the forces that were working on the Indian government, that they would have gone on to reduce once and for all the danger that they had consistently seen in Pakistan.[105]

Kissinger defended himself by telling friendly reporters, again on background, that his own warning about the summit had been decisive in getting the Soviet Union to lean on India. But most officials, notably Joseph Sisco, continued to doubt that India had ever seriously intended to move on the western front or that Soviet influence had been crucial.[106]

At this point, no one apparently sought to judge what the effect of the *Enterprise* naval movement might have been. Nixon conspicuously did not mention it in his *Time* interview or in his 1978 memoirs. In the media, it was reported but not emphasized, and faded away in the face of another sensation.

In the very last days of the war, Nixon and Kissinger—already under heavy editorial fire for the pro-Pakistan thrust of their policy—suffered another blow. On December 14, the nationally syndicated columnist Jack Anderson published in *The Washington Post* and many other papers a report that in policy meetings, contrary to the Administration's claim that it was impartial between India and Pakistan, Kissinger had several times stressed the President's strong wish to "tilt" in favor of Pakistan. The "tilt" theme was picked up at once. It further damaged the credibility of Nixon and Kissinger, adding to the confusion about the real purposes of U.S. policy in South Asia. The startling leak included verbatim quotations from what were obviously a participant's notes of the meetings. Anderson also reported, as did many others, the first accounts of the *Enterprise* task group moving toward the Indian Ocean.

In the White House, these revelations almost overshadowed the actual conclusion of the war. Always upset about leaks, Nixon turned loose his so-called "plumbers," an in-house investigating unit he had formed after the publication of the Pentagon Papers the previous June. Under the supervision of his two senior staff members, Haldeman and Ehrlichman, these started to question everyone who had access to the leaked records.

The answer was not long in coming. A Navy enlisted man, Yeoman Charles Radford, assigned to the JCS liaison officer to the NSC staff, Admiral Robert Welander, had previously served in India and developed great affection for the country and its people. As the reports of successive WSAG meetings passed through his hands, he could see the President's and Kissinger's strong anti-Indian views repeated again and again. Apparently he was brought to boiling point by the publication, first in the *Congressional Record* and then in *The Washington Post*, of Kissinger's statement on December 7 that claims of bias against India were "totally inaccurate."

As chance would have it, Radford had met Jack Anderson in India, and later got back in touch with him in Washington. The fact that both were Mormons strengthened the tie. When the sleuths discovered that Radford had lunched with Anderson on December 13, the evidence seemed conclusive.[107] Radford's role had not yet been publicly revealed, however, when Anderson went ahead on December 31 to publish further excerpts from the notes of policy meetings. Kissinger recklessly challenged these for being taken out of context, and on January 5 Anderson responded by publishing the verbatim notes of four WSAG meetings in December. These and other materials skewered Kissinger's claims and branded him and Nixon as parties to deceit and untruth.

At least as serious, in the eyes of many, was another scandal involving Yeoman Radford, known at the time to only a few. Under renewed questioning by the White House staff after he had revealed his tie to Anderson, Radford acknowledged that since 1970, in his post at the National Security Council, he had been making copies of important and sensitive documents that were not intended for the Joint Chiefs of Staff. These were then conveyed by the JCS liaison officer to the Chairman of the JCS, Admiral Moorer. Nixon and his core staff were informed at once of this new revelation, and there was a tense period while the President considered what action to take. He finally decided to keep his knowledge of the unauthorized flow of NSC materials to Admiral Moorer totally secret; Radford was simply reassigned to a routine job at an Oregon naval installation. In his memoirs, Nixon was to explain that he allowed the matter to drop because of the danger of further disclosures if Radford were brought to trial. Admiral Moorer, then and later, claimed that in the mass of his daily reading material he never noted that these particular items were special and, in any event, had known through other sources the gist of what they contained. On reflection Nixon chose not to confront Moorer, gave him no sign of dissatisfaction or concern, and appointed him to a second two-year term as

Chairman beginning in July 1972. This second scandal, in which Anderson was not involved, became known to the public only in January 1974, when one of Nixon's White House plumbers spilled the beans in an effort to justify his operations, which had become linked to the Watergate scandal.[108]

Radford's leaks to Anderson were a clear-cut breach of standing practices in keeping policy discussions confidential, and it could be claimed that the material affected national security. Probably the leaks made Nixon and Kissinger still more secretive, to the detriment of good policymaking. Certainly Nixon took them seriously, while shrugging off the unauthorized flow of information to Moorer as not all that surprising. Others took a harsher view on both counts. Few could deny that the atmosphere Nixon created lay at the root of the problem. Perhaps the last word belonged to Admiral Zumwalt. In his memoir, he concluded his discussion of the events of 1971: "It wasn't easy to keep hold of your integrity or honor or pride when you worked for Richard Nixon."[109]

. . .

Let us turn back to the substance of U.S. policy. What was its effect at the successive stages of the Indo-Pakistani crisis, what lay behind it, and how should it be judged?

From March to December the central problem was the behavior of Yahya Khan, a man proud, stubborn, politically insensitive, and inept. Yahya turned the maintenance of law and order in East Pakistan into the most provocative type of military operation with the least control of excesses. He arrested a bona fide political leader, Mujib, who had just shown prowess at the polls, and then for months kept alive a threat to try him, while refusing steadfastly to consider a possible compromise. He delayed the transfer of power to Bhutto, a man of far greater political capacity. Finally, as tensions with India built to an almost inevitable clash of arms, he put Pakistan in the wrong, in the eyes of key outside nations, by authorizing the large-scale attacks of December 3. Along the way, he never developed a plausible political program for the future of East Pakistan or a realistic military or political objective.

In short, Yahya was about as hopeless a partner-client as could be imagined. The case was far from unique in American experience at the height of the Cold War. Not to exert influence could mean the situation going from bad to worse. But if the influence and advice became evident, political intervention tended to deepen the perceived U.S. responsibility. In the case of Yahya, Nixon never seriously offered advice in the early stages, when it might have counted. The fact that there was a genuine debt for Yahya's help on the opening to China was of course a factor: apparently neither Nixon nor Kissinger ever stopped to consider that he had hardly been acting altruistically or without a shrewd eye to his own and his country's interests.

All along, Pakistan needed Nixon's support against India, in a quarrel where the average American or member of Congress would have seen hardly any U.S. national interest.

In this key first period, Nixon's and Kissinger's repeated private remarks that the United States had a binding commitment to come to Pakistan's aid against India encouraged Yahya to believe that whatever he did would have strong American support. The effect was not to moderate his stand, but rather to make him more rigid. While the State Department continued, uncorrected, to assert publicly the historic (and much sounder) view that there was no such commitment, Yahya surely believed Nixon and Kissinger.

Kissinger saw almost from the outset that at least autonomy for East Bengal was virtually inevitable. But the influence he exerted, with Nixon's concurrence, on Yahya stimulated the latter to a series of unwise actions. These simply deepened the crisis and made the final outcome more decisive and humiliating for Yahya, for Pakistan, and, in lesser degree, for the United States itself.

In the last stage of the war, however, as it became clear that East Pakistan was doomed and the creation of Bangladesh inevitable, Nixon and Kissinger's attempt to deter and forestall India's move against West Pakistan or Azad Kashmir was coherent and, on the diplomatic front, helpful. Their collateral nondiplomatic moves were less constructive. U.S. advice was apparently decisive in the joint decision on December 9, with Pakistan, to postpone an eastern cease-fire and go for one embracing the West Pakistan area as well. In the final week, as we have seen, Nixon and Kissinger pulled out all the stops to keep India from attacking West Pakistan, or trying to retake all or part of the areas of Kashmir controlled by Pakistan.

But did India seriously intend to attack West Pakistan, and if so, did U.S. actions play a crucial or decisive role in deterring and forestalling her? Can Nixon and Kissinger, for all their failures in other respects, reasonably claim to have "saved" West Pakistan? The CIA report so much emphasized (and embellished) by Kissinger was the only evidence of such an intent the American government appears to have had at the time. Given the lack of evidence (such as, for example, satellite reconnaissance of major troop movements), it seems highly probable that the discussion reported by the CIA was about contingency plans. For India to "straighten out the line" would have been a natural and feasible undertaking, requiring the defeat of the local Pakistani armor and air forces that had made the incursion into Indian-held Kashmir. It seems much more likely that the Indian high councils had discussed this than that they truly envisaged an all-out engagement to "eliminate" all of Pakistan's armor and air.[110]

Later evidence, from an Indian source, suggests that Mrs. Gandhi did briefly contemplate a move on the western front to retake some part of Azad Kashmir, but that her advisors recommended against it, arguing that it would damage India's reputation for peaceful behavior (which was of great practical value to India) and that any territorial gains would not be worth the damage to that reputation from rejecting a Western cease-fire. According to this source, the Soviet Union was party to these discussions and was of the same view.[111]

This account is highly persuasive. The actual outcome—a further weakened Pakistan and a weak and independent Bangladesh—was a major gain for India, with no offsetting negatives. For India to have renewed the fighting in the West would surely have set off a tidal wave of disapproval, and though Mrs. Gandhi was, like most leaders of all nationalities, not without a strain of hypocrisy—as Nixon and Kissinger kept pointing out then and later—defiance of international opinion would have lost not only generalized goodwill for her country but enormous tangible benefits. For one thing, the U.S. Congress would surely have cut off, perhaps for good, billions of dollars of U.S. economic aid and (equally important) the U.S. help on agricultural techniques (the so-called Green Revolution) that was soon to make India nearly self-sufficient in food. Also, it is hard to imagine that Mrs. Gandhi would have tried to take over parts of Pakistan that, before 1947, had been part of India. Any such effort would have been an enormous undertaking, not only bloody but internally disruptive of relations with India's still substantial Muslim population.

The most reasonable conclusion is that Mrs. Gandhi was in full charge throughout the crisis, welcoming limited Soviet support but never influenced by Soviet advice. In fact, available evidence also points to a restrained Soviet posture throughout, at pains always to keep up communications with Pakistan and not to offend Muslim opinion, and sending only small amounts of arms to India. Similarly, while the Soviet use of the veto in the Security Council on December 5 and 6 helped to give India time to complete the investiture of East Pakistan, it was hardly unprecedented to act in that way.

This conclusion does not mean that Nixon and Kissinger should be denied credit for their diplomatic activities in the last phase. These were consistent, well orchestrated, and useful—with two exceptions: Kissinger's short-lived threat to cancel the summit meeting, and the sending of the *Enterprise* naval force into the Indian Ocean. About the first, there is little more to say. Clearly Nixon and his top aides at once saw this as a serious mistake, and in the next weeks made their displeasure clear, cutting Kissinger off from Nixon and making him suffer other indignities, to his intense chagrin. Nixon's own conciliatory statements surely cleared the air, and reminded both Kissinger and the Soviet leaders how much he valued the Moscow summit.[112]

What then of the sending of the *Enterprise* task group? The first thing to note is that this action did not come out of the blue. Prior to the crisis,

Admiral Zumwalt and others had consistently impressed on a receptive White House their concerns about the Soviet Union becoming truly a global power threat, especially through its rapidly growing Navy.[113] In 1970 Zumwalt presented his arguments to Kissinger, a number of NSC studies were commissioned, and the Navy began the contingency planning that was later to flower in the creation of a major American base on the island of Diego Garcia, west of India.[114]

Yet, when Task Group 74 was deployed, Zumwalt lamented that it had no clearly defined mission and found the whole operation extremely dubious. In his later memoir, he concluded that it was probably "untimely and futile," since there was no clear-cut evidence that Mrs. Gandhi intended to move on West Pakistan or Kashmir. Similarly, a later scholarly study considered this case at length and concluded that the dispatch of TG 74 had not been a significant persuasive factor.[115]

What of its effect on U.S.-India relations? This was not the first time the *Enterprise* had been in the Indian Ocean. In 1962, with a military aid program to India in place, President Kennedy sent the *Enterprise* into the Bay of Bengal, with India's full consent, to underscore American support *for India against China* during the conclusion of the brief Sino-Indian war. Indian leaders had long memories; many must have noted the stark contrast.

In 1971, the Indian reaction to U.S. policy as a whole was naturally very critical, to the point where Marvin and Bernard Kalb, normally admirers of Kissinger, concluded: "The turn of developments was catastrophic for American policy in the area. The United States . . . found itself siding with a corrupt Pakistani military dictatorship against the world's most populous democracy. Moreover, the dictatorship lost and the democracy won."[116]

Yet victory did ease Indian criticism of America. Official discussions of economic aid programs resumed in early 1972 and the programs themselves never really lapsed. In later years, economic aid appropriations were sharply cut by the American Congress; indeed, there had been one drastic cut just before the war. But Congress for the most part did not share Nixon's interpretation of the crisis and the war. It seems unlikely that ill will to India had any part in these actions. As the Indians must have known, not only the media but most informed Americans disagreed with the Nixon-Kissinger policy (by a 2–1 margin according to a Harris poll), and Congress supported the rapid restoration of friendly and cooperative relations. Kissinger even seized on this to tease Dobrynin that India would set records for ingratitude to his country.

A more serious question about the *Enterprise* foray, however, especially in the light of later developments and concerns, is whether it affected India's attitudes and actions toward nuclear weapons. The "nuclear factor" does not appear to have been taken into account at all in the hasty decision to dispatch the *Enterprise*. Though she was nuclear-powered, carried air squadrons capable of handling nuclear weapons, and had stores of such weapons aboard, American civilian and military leaders, from Nixon down, never contemplated the use of nuclear weapons in the mission. By this time a clear-cut separation existed in the minds of military planners and top civilians: only in the event of all-out war with the Soviet Union was the use of nuclear weapons, however or wherever based, contemplated as a possibility. All other operations were regarded as "conventional."

Yet this was hardly the way other nations, especially those remote from the front lines of the Cold War, could be expected to see U.S. policy. The *Enterprise* task group was a truly imposing force: giant aircraft carriers make a very deep impression in any setting. The nuclear factor may have sunk in with special force among the ruling circles as well as the people of India. If any nation could be expected to resent perceived nuclear bullying, it would be India. (Indeed, in codifying the Nixon Doctrine, Nixon had a special category for threats made by a nuclear power against a nonnuclear nation. In effect, he said that whereas the United States would expect threatened nations to provide their own military manpower, for nations under threat *by a nuclear power* the United States would "provide a shield." Implicit was the sense that military pressure by a nuclear nation on a nonnuclear nation was a particularly disturbing form of bullying which the United States should oppose.)

In the following year, 1972, a major debate took place in India over whether to proceed with its nuclear research program, which was active and well manned, to the point of testing a device. In 1973–74, a firm decision to do so was made, and in May 1974, the first test explosion took place. Although India has since then consistently been silent as to whether it has actually made nuclear weapons, it is assumed in informed quarters that it must have done so soon thereafter.

The reaction in Pakistan was foreseeable, indeed inevitable. In later years, intensive Pakistani efforts to match the Indian program led to an accumulation of nuclear material in both countries, and then some diffusion of the material, and know-how, from Pakistan to other Muslim nations. By the 1980s South Asia was the most worrisome case of actual and potential nuclear proliferation, and has remained so into the 1990s.

Might this have happened in any event? The answer can only be "not proven." On this as on all else at the time, the decisive voice was that of Mrs. Gandhi herself, and she appears to have left no record for the benefit of history. But a connection seems plausible. Certainly it was a risk Nixon took—part of his extraordinarily carefree view of nuclear proliferation, a view even harder to understand in the 1990s than it was in the 1970s.

From any standpoint, Nixon and Kissinger's policy on the Indo-Pakistan war was replete with error, misjudgment, emotionalism, and unnecessary risk taking. The alternative, the cool and correct stance urged by the State Department, through Joseph Sisco, and the Defense Department, through Deputy Secretary David Packard, would not have affected the inevitable outcome, in the form of an independent Bangladesh, but it might have led to greater moderation on Yahya's part and less humiliation in the outcome. It certainly would have avoided the clear errors of the *Enterprise* mission and Kissinger's brief effort to threaten the Soviet Union. Only Zhou Enlai, apparently, was pleased with American behavior. China itself had hedged its bets all along, avoiding commitment and backing off in December, but the United States stepped into the breach and, as Zhou was apparently persuaded, "saved" West Pakistan — or so Bhutto told Kissinger.[117]

What lay behind Nixon's policy? Why the "tilt" to Pakistan? Why the intense involvement in December? First was Nixon's debt to Pakistan for its help vis-à-vis China, which at the time was considered a reason for Nixon's posture. Yet it hardly seems enough to account for his behavior. Second was the attitude of Nixon and Kissinger toward China and, specifically, the new bond between Kissinger and Zhou Enlai. Here there is a large evidence gap, for we do not have the full record of the many hours of discussion the two had together, especially in 1971. Clearly claims of Soviet perfidy bulked large in these talks, and the India-Pakistan crisis must have been extensively covered. It became, as Kissinger and members of his staff saw it, the test case of the new relationship with China. America had to measure up to Zhou's expectations, or China might not go through with the 1972 Beijing summit that was a cornerstone of Nixon's calculations for that make-or-break election year.

There is still a third explanation, concealed at the time — by Kissinger in particular — for the sake of promoting his favorite picture of "triangular diplomacy," in which the United States was friendly to both China and the Soviet Union and therefore in a position to get concessions from each by the threat of moving closer to the other. The fact is that, if the relationships between the Nixon Administration and the two great Communist powers were ever truly balanced, this ceased to be the case at the time of the Indo-Pakistan crisis. Writing a long diplomatic history in 1994, Henry Kissinger was much franker than he had been at the time. In it he described the agreements announced in the Shanghai communiqué of February 1972 — agreements that had been worked out in October 1971 and then tested during the Indo-Pakistan war — in these terms:

> These agreements meant, at a minimum, that China would do nothing to exacerbate the situation in Indochina or Korea, that neither China nor the United States would cooperate with the Soviet bloc, and that *both*

would oppose any attempt by any country to achieve domination of Asia. Since the Soviet Union was the only country capable of dominating Asia, a tacit alliance to block Soviet expansionism in Asia was coming into being (not unlike the Entente Cordiale between Great Britain and France in 1904, and between Great Britain and Russia in 1907).[118]

So the third explanation was Kissinger and Nixon's overriding emphasis on balance-of-power factors, more than at any other point during the Nixon presidency. Perceiving that India and the Soviet Union together might predominate in the vast area from Aden to the Strait of Malacca, Nixon and above all Kissinger sought to set up a rival alignment of Pakistan, China, and the United States. Reaffirming and reinforcing those ties was the guiding star for their policy.

This was balance-of-power diplomacy at its most naked and extreme. By the time roughly of his second visit to Beijing in October 1971, Kissinger had come to regard China as a tacit ally of the United States against Soviet expansionism. It followed that because Pakistan was a friend to China, it must not be humiliated by India, a client of the Soviet Union. The United States must act to prevent, not a humiliation of China itself but a humiliation of *a friend of China*. Nixon himself summed up the point in earthy terms in his memoir, quoting Kissinger with approval:

If we failed to help Pakistan, then Iran or any other country within the reach of Soviet influence might begin to question the dependability of American support. As Kissinger put it, "We don't really have any choice. *We can't allow a friend of ours and China to get screwed in a conflict with a friend of Russia's.*"[119]

This surely was the core of the argument. At the time, few observers saw how close Nixon and Kissinger had drawn to China and to Zhou, or that Kissinger had come to think of the new relationship in the terms he eventually described as equivalent to an alliance against the Soviet Union. But that view of the relationship, concealed at the time, unlocks the puzzle. Demonstrating that the United States could be relied on was more than an ordinary requirement for any close relationship. The United States, as Kissinger certainly saw it and probably Nixon as well, had to show that even in a highly unprofitable situation, remote from any normal calculation of U.S. national interest, the United States would rally to the side supported by China. If a commonplace metaphor may be used, it was like an eager young man courting a lady and showing her his devotion by undertaking some otherwise absurd task.

Kissinger himself, writing later as a historian of the pre-1914 situation in Europe, well described where such a process could lead:

Each Great Power was suddenly seized by panic that a conciliatory stance would make it appear weak and unreliable and cause its partners to leave it facing a hostile coalition all alone. Countries began to assume levels of risk unwarranted by their historic national interests or by any rational long-term strategic objective. . . . Germany accepted the risk of world war in order to be seen as supportive of Vienna's South Slav policy, in which it had no national interest. Russia was willing to risk a fight to the death with Germany in order to be viewed as Serbia's steadfast ally. Germany and Russia had no major conflicts with each other; their confrontation was by proxy.[120]

Yet this was exactly the situation into which Kissinger helped to thrust the United States in 1971. No national interest remotely warranted the risks he and Nixon ran, not to mention the intense domestic controversy that would surely have ensued if there had been a direct confrontation with the Soviet Union. American public and congressional opinion could not conceivably have approved putting major ships into the area (let alone actual combat), for the reasons that lay behind this action.

The fundamental point is that a naked balance-of-power policy, going beyond recognized and accepted U.S. national interests, was (and is) simply not possible under the American system, which compels concern for public opinion, for the separation of powers, and for the role of Congress. In the Indo-Pakistan crisis and war of 1971, the policy pursued by Nixon and Kissinger was not merely contrary to these American principles or misjudged at almost every turn: it was an excellent example of the weakness of any American policy that is based heavily on balance-of-power considerations without proper weight to other factors.

In the same history, his 1994 *Diplomacy*, Kissinger was to divide American leaders in the twentieth century into realists (Theodore Roosevelt) and idealists (Woodrow Wilson), with the former setting great store by the balance of power and the latter more visionary. This was at best an oversimplification, at worst a serious distortion. A concern for the balance of power has almost always been present in the policies of *every* American President faced with continuing decisions on foreign policy. Before World War II, Franklin Roosevelt was thinking at every turn about a power balance, in both Europe and Asia, to restrain Hitler and Japan's military regime. Only when the end of the war approached did he become "Wilsonian" in seeking to create and develop the United Nations, and even there the hopes he held out for it were far short of what Wilson had envisaged from the League of Nations.

Again, in the early stages of the Cold War, American efforts to maximize cooperation among the nations threatened by Stalinist expansion—most of all, to create the North Atlantic Alliance—rested squarely on having a solid balance of power or, in the phrase of the period, "situations of strength." Such efforts, based on the participants' shared values and national interests, have been fundamental to creating and preserving a climate in which free (or relatively free) nations can survive and flourish. They contribute enormously to stability and peace. But balance-of-power thinking broke down, during the Cold War, precisely where concrete American interests and shared values were not present. In some cases — Northeast Asia, for example — the need to have a solid front on a clear-cut geographic line was decisive for enlisting as allies such a frail and immature nation as South Korea then was. In other cases, however — Southeast Asia comes at once to mind — protecting similar nations and becoming committed to them by pact or deed, in the hope that they would find themselves, ran the risks all too vividly demonstrated in the Indochina Wars. The commitments could not be fulfilled without a better local performance than the United States could manage to stimulate. The American commitment in Indochina, created under Eisenhower (with Nixon closely involved), and briefly tenable and useful, brought in the end great tragedy.

Pakistan, by these measures, was a most unwise candidate for enlistment in an alliance. Economic and military aid to Pakistan, deliberately stopping short of any commitment, might have been a useful, limited-liability step, enabling that country to focus on its domestic problems — as happened for a time in the 1950s and early 1960s. But Pakistan's preoccupation with its relation to India was always a complicating element that was almost certain to create situations where no U.S. national interest was involved, as happened in 1965 and again in 1971. To impress on such situations a mold of balance-of-power relations was bound to lead to trouble.

This more than anything else was the fundamental error of Nixon and Kissinger's policy in South Asia. Within a very short time, the Indo-Pakistan war of 1971 faded from the public mind of America. But as a continuing example of the fallacies and dangers of the Nixon-Kissinger approach, it continues to deserve careful analysis and reflection.

5. Vietnam: Girding for a Showdown

Let us now turn back to developments on the Indochina front during 1971. Important as the opening to China and the other dramatic developments of the year were, Nixon never lost sight of the Vietnam War or ceased to plan ahead for what he saw all along as the climactic year, 1972. The same was clearly true of the North Vietnamese. After the Laos operation ended in March 1971, both sides prepared for the showdown that loomed in the spring of 1972, when U.S. combat forces would be almost all gone and the burden of defending against a North Vietnamese offensive would fall squarely on the South Vietnamese Army.

During the year, the reduction in the American military role that had started in 1969 continued. American forces, by then engaged only in local security operations, suffered 1,380 combat deaths in 1971, down from 4,200 in 1970, 9,400 in 1969 (mostly in the first six months), and the high of 20,600 in 1968. By contrast, the estimated number of South Vietnamese military killed in action went from a high of 28,000 in 1968 to 22,000 in 1969, 23,000 in 1970, and 24,000 in 1971 (many in the Laos operation).[121]

Three tasks dominated Nixon's Vietnam War policy in 1971. The first was to advance Vietnamization of the war to the utmost. Pacification, the effort to extend and deepen the South Vietnamese government's control of the countryside and towns, was important for its own sake and also to ensure that there could be no repetition of the multipronged Communist offensive at Tet in 1968, predominantly by Vietcong guerrilla forces. Inherently unglamorous and out of the limelight, pacification had been a dirty job all along, a grinding process of moving into disputed areas, fighting off the Vietcong, and gaining the confidence of the peasants and town dwellers in the face of unrelenting Vietcong terrorism aimed at local leaders and disruption of the economy. So long as American forces were present in large numbers and focused their major emphasis on seeking out the enemy for large-scale engagements, with the hope that attrition would bring progress and eventually victory, pacification had been secondary, and lacked a real concentration of effort. With the shift in emphasis in 1969, making the security of the population a primary military objective, those concerned with pacification got the resources and support they needed. Civilian and military efforts went hand in hand.

Results were evident in 1970 and 1971. Statistical hamlet-by-hamlet assessments had long been suspect and unconvincing, especially to the press, but as these improved, observers could point to more convincing pragmatic tests. Could one move from point X to point Y unmolested? Were Americans or, especially, South Vietnamese able to go about their business in the villages, tending crops, sending them to market, and living a near-normal life? By such tests, some progress could be demonstrated. There remained impregnable Vietcong strongholds northwest of Saigon and in the foothills of the narrow northern coastal plain. But in the populous Delta provinces, where from 1968 on the senior American was the legendary John Paul Vann, a former military officer now turned civilian, the main communications were open and crops moved unmolested to the Saigon market. William Colby was probably accurate in concluding that by late 1970 "the war in the Delta essentially had been won."[122]

By 1971, therefore, the Communist threat centered on the North Vietnamese regular army, the NVA. The war would be decided in major combat. Improving the South Vietnamese forces was therefore the main focus of Vietnamization. Under the guidance of Secretary Laird in Washington and General Abrams in Saigon, the supply of arms and other equipment to ARVN was kept steady and substantial, down to the irregular units such as the Village Self-Defense Forces, who for the first time got top-grade rifles. As this was done, ARVN itself was slightly expanded, so that combat-capable forces grew to just over a million men. South Vietnam was as fully mobilized as its population and economy permitted.

In the expansion, ARVN remained the main element, with the Air Force and Navy small and limited in capability. Yet all but two of ARVN's twelve divisions continued to be stationed in fixed areas, where their personnel lived (and in most cases came from). The elite Airborne and Ranger divisions, by this time kept within ready range of the northern area, known as Military Region 1, had both been hard hit in the Laos operation, but were brought back to full capability by the end of 1971. The front line in the north, however, was now entrusted to a new division, the 3rd, made up of troops with no experience of working together. By the end of the year this unit was stationed at the very front line, across from the demilitarized zone (DMZ). This was in part because Thieu and his advisors believed that North Vietnam would continue to adhere (as it had done for three years) to one of the clear understandings that accompanied the stopping of the bombing of the North in October 1968—namely, that there should be no North Vietnamese violation of the DMZ.

As the Laos campaign had shown, the presence of U.S. advisors could make a crucial difference. While the total number of American officers acting as advisors was reduced by late 1971, with few assignments below the level of a division or province, they and their staffs were handpicked, highly motivated, and experienced, usually on their second or third tours of duty in Vietnam.[123] But in the last analysis, as Abrams and his staff knew well, the performance of ARVN depended most of all on the quality of its leaders, which unfortunately remained inadequate. All along, as we have seen, Thieu, like his predecessors, had made loyalty to himself a key factor in senior appointments. Critics were kept on the sidelines or fobbed off into noncombatant jobs. Bunker, Abrams, and perhaps most of all Bunker's deputy, Samuel Berger, from his Korean experience, were well aware of the problem. Abrams teamed frequently with Berger to give Thieu their evaluations, sometimes with specific recommendations for relief or reassignments. Few of these were acted on, however. As we have noted before, the situation in this key respect might have been different if Nixon had ever intervened personally.

The most basic factor of all was the underlying morale and cohesion of the people of South Vietnam. Bunker and Abrams had seen them rally remarkably after the Tet onslaught in 1968. And if Thieu had seized that wave and truly taken hold—as Ramon Magsaysay did in the Philippines in 1951–53—there might have been a lasting lift in morale and performance, but he simply was not up to it. In effect, the years from 1967 to 1971 had seen a mediocre South Vietnamese regime under an uninspiring leader. Now, in 1971, the quadrennial election of a President was to take place, under the Constitution approved in 1966–67. What shape could an election take under these circumstances?

When Lyndon Johnson had pressed the South Vietnamese in 1966–67 to frame and adopt a Constitution, and hold elections, he well knew that he was going against the grain of a long cultural tradition of mandarin-type rule, at its best benevolent authoritarianism, at worst repressive and dictatorial. Never, as those involved in that effort perceived his plans, did Johnson suppose that South Vietnam could become overnight a working democracy. But the hope was that some sense of political accountability might take root, and that the process might give new legitimacy to the South Vietnamese government after a revolving-door succession of military coups.

In the 1967 election, Thieu had gotten only a plurality, with 35 percent of the total vote—hardly a mandate or firm proof of legitimacy. He had made his biggest gain in personal standing by refusing in 1968 to participate in Johnson's plan for a bombing halt and the immediate opening of serious negotiations. Since then, he had consolidated his position in political terms. Yet, when faced with a test of leadership in the Laos operation, he once again failed to lead, faltering under pressure and blaming the defeat on American advice and shortcomings.

As election preparations began in the spring of 1971, he had no special accomplishments to point to, only a generally better national situation and the obvious support and approval of the Americans, starting with Nixon. Most of all, he had the political alliances formed over five years of picking people and backing them, with the ability to extend favors including financial rewards to the faithful. The National Assembly in particular was his rubber stamp: in early 1971, 22 of its 25 officer posts and chairmanships were held by pro-Thieu deputies.[124]

These assets were far greater than those that any opposition group or potential challenger could command. In the spring and early summer, discussion in Saigon political circles centered on two perennial candidates. One was Duong Van Minh, a professional soldier with a physique imposing by Vietnamese standards, who for a time in his younger days had been a hero for his resistance to the Japanese under torture. "Big" Minh's main asset was name recognition. Given every chance for leadership after the overthrow of Diem in 1963, he had failed miserably. He then spent several years in Bangkok with a high-sounding title in the Southeast Asia Treaty Organization, before returning to South Vietnam. All along, he had a brother in the Vietcong's political showcase, the National Liberation Front, which made him suspect to some, but to others suggested the hope that somehow all this violence could be worked out among South Vietnamese of all views. The other perennial candidate was Nguyen Cao Ky, the flamboyant air marshal who had briefly been in charge before Thieu took over in 1967 and he was made Vice President. He was an uneasy partner to Thieu, still ambitious and with some support from former Northerners and Catholics, but no wide base.

Comparing the three in early 1971, Bunker told Washington in no uncertain terms that "the current incumbent is far more qualified . . . than any other candidate on the scene."[125] Bunker aired his views only to his senior commanders and advisors, but to South Vietnamese accustomed to studying him, the way he went on dealing calmly and confidently with Thieu carried its own unmistakable message.

It appears from Nixon's behavior at the time that he never thought of supporting an alternative candidate or making more than a show of a truly open and fair election. As for Kissinger, all evidence suggests that in 1971 he chafed at the election as an annoying distraction, totally unrealistic in an untried country under siege. He never lost an opportunity in his later writings to blame Lyndon Johnson for trying to move South Vietnam toward democracy. With these judgments and attitudes, the only policy decision Nixon and Kissinger saw themselves facing was whether they should seek to make the election at least appear honest and genuine by covertly helping to launch a rival candidacy. The record contains tantalizing hints that this was briefly considered, but nothing was done. The election on October 3, 1971, became a walkover for Thieu, with some grumbling, a few demonstrations, but mostly resigned acceptance among South Vietnamese. In the American media, the outcome was met with dismay and some derision. It certainly added to negative feelings about Thieu and American policy.

. . .

Meanwhile, the negotiating front had an important burst of activity during the late spring and summer of 1971. As we have seen, Nixon's speech of October 5, 1970, had included a major concession, by omitting his previous insistence that any withdrawal of U.S. forces must be matched by a parallel and eventually complete North Vietnamese withdrawal. The change can hardly have passed unnoticed by the North Vietnamese. But it was simply accepting the inevitable. The ongoing unilateral American withdrawals left the United States with no leverage to press North Vietnam to follow suit.

Moreover, the American forces in South Vietnam were deteriorating, in the static but still painful role they now played. The major 150,000-man withdrawal announced by Nixon just before the Cambodian incursion in the spring of 1970 was to have been spaced out so that only 60,000 men left during that year. But this was accelerated to 90,000, in part a response to budget tightness, but probably also reflecting the growing difficulties the American Army was having with drugs and other problems. The flow of drugs into South Vietnam increased markedly after the Cambodian incursion, perhaps because the borders became more porous. Drugs then became a truly serious problem for American forces in South Vietnam, and progressively, as men were transferred, for the Army elsewhere. This was a major factor in the weakening of the prime U.S. force in West Germany, the Seventh Army, which had long been in the front line of the Cold War. In the words of General Bruce Palmer, former deputy commander in South Vietnam and then Deputy Chief of Staff in Washington, the Seventh Army experienced "a drastic drop in combat readiness, lowered morale, and deteriorating discipline . . . [and] was in effect, over time, destroyed as a fighting force."[126]

Through the winter and spring of 1970–71, both sides were preoccupied with the conflict in Laos, and there was no move to reopen the secret Paris talks. In May 1971, demonstrations against the war peaked once more, with ugly behavior on both sides, and there were a spate of congressional attempts to fix a date for U.S. withdrawal. The most formidable of these, by Senator Mansfield, finally passed the Senate on June 22 as a sense-of-the-Senate resolution, declaring that "it is the policy of the U.S. to terminate at the earliest practicable date all military operations in Indochina and to provide for the prompt and early withdrawal of all U.S. forces not more than nine months after the bill's enactment subject to the release of American POWs."[127] As had happened regularly with similar proposals, this one died in the House of Representatives, but the idea of a withdrawal-for-prisoners deal had taken hold and for some time dominated congressional initiatives and public debate, with such important papers as *The New York Times* coming out squarely in favor of such a deal. To Nixon and Kissinger, its prominence in American debate became another reason to explore the possibilities for peace more intensively.

In early May, General Walters conveyed to the North Vietnamese in Paris a proposal to renew the talks "on the basis of new approaches," and May 31 was fixed for the first in this series of talks, which were far more serious from the start than the intermittent discussions of 1970. At the May 31 meeting, Kissinger tabled a new seven-point plan with these key elements: setting a date for total U.S. withdrawal (not mentioning a parallel North Vietnamese withdrawal, though speaking of a ban on reinforcement, which could hardly be enforced); a cease-fire throughout Indochina when withdrawals began; guarantees for the future neutral status of Laos and Cambodia; release of all POWs; and the political future of South Vietnam to be settled among South Vietnamese.[128] Kissinger's memoirs call this proposal "a turning point." It had been reviewed with Thieu and accepted, and was to form the skeleton of the eventual 1973 agreement.

As the negotiators slogged through the seven points and a reply nine-point proposal by the North Vietnamese, with frequent detours for Le Duc Tho to taunt Kissinger with the weaknesses of South Vietnam and the ongoing U.S. withdrawals, it became clear that agreement might be possible on every point save that concerning the political future of the South. Le Duc Tho never wavered in his insistence that Thieu be removed from power. Again and again he suggested that the upcoming South Vietnamese elections would be an excellent occasion for the United States to dump Thieu, either by rigging the election for a peace candidate or by "direct action," meaning unmistakably physical removal or assassination. Kissinger summarily rejected the suggestion. As the North Vietnamese followed election developments in Saigon closely and Thieu's victory became certain in mid-August, Le Duc Tho effectively brought the round of negotiations to a close.

Though they failed, the 1971 talks were important in clarifying positions on both sides, while underlining the remaining key point of contention. Kissinger must have been disappointed that the American opening to China in July 1971 had no apparent effect on Hanoi's leaders, who were, in the end, dug in as before. Years later it was revealed that the Chinese did make a serious effort in November to persuade the North Vietnamese to accept a compromise peace in Vietnam. North Vietnamese Premier Pham Van Dong, visiting Beijing, tried hard to get Chinese support for all of the North Vietnamese positions, but the Chinese urged compromise. It was probably on this occasion that Mao himself allegedly summarized the Chinese advice by saying that the North Vietnamese did not have a broom long enough to sweep away all the unacceptable features of the Saigon regime. To which the North Vietnamese indignantly responded that their "broom" of power was indeed long enough to clean out the South. The session ended in acrimony.

But North Vietnam's leaders were soon reassured that China's military support of their war was not affected. On the contrary, rivalry between China and the Soviet Union for influence with the Communist regimes of Indochina, North Vietnam above all, was more intense than ever. In the late fall and early winter, the steady flow of men and equipment down the Ho Chi Minh Trail appears to have come from both the major Communist powers.

For their part, the South Vietnamese used American support to replace the losses from the Laos operation and to improve their equipment levels and types significantly. Abrams and his generals continued to judge that they were vulnerable in the First and Second Combat Zones (the northern and north-central areas); the only available South Vietnamese strategic reserve was still the usual two divisions (the Airborne and Marines) and a few other units. Neither the commanders nor Washington contemplated using American ground forces.

General Abrams's real strategic reserve was American airpower. By the end of 1971, the American Seventh Air Force, with bases in Thailand and a few in South Vietnam, was hitting the Ho Chi Minh Trail harder than ever. In late December it announced five raids into North Vietnam, as a "protective reaction" to North Vietnamese antiaircraft fire directed at American reconnaissance aircraft, which under the October 1968 deal were permitted to continue reconnaissance operations up to the 20th parallel. The attacks were nonetheless criticized by the antiwar movement and in the Senate, but Congress was not in session and the White House rode out the storm.

Later, however, it emerged—when an Air Force enlisted man wrote to a senator on the Armed Services Committee—that the raids had been much more extensive, prolonged, and systematic than they had been depicted, and that they had taken place at times and in places where there was no sign of hostile enemy activity against the reconnaissance aircraft. When the deception was revealed in March 1972, the Seventh Air Force commander, General John Lavelle, was immediately relieved and replaced. He admitted the attacks and defended himself by saying he had thought he was doing what the White House wanted, which may well have been true. His successor was General John Vogt, an experienced Southeast Asia hand fresh from heading the Joint Staff in the Pentagon and long familiar with contingency plans for the use of airpower.

American military planners had long assumed that even if a cease-fire and peace arrangement were reached, U.S. airpower would be left within reaching distance and used if needed against a Communist offensive. The American Navy and Air Force, on Nixon's orders, started in late 1971 a massive buildup of airpower in Southeast Asia, hoping to deter a North Vietnamese offensive but in any case to meet it head-on. The number of aircraft carriers in Vietnamese waters was substantially increased—the assignment of the *Enterprise* was an example—and special emphasis was given to the deployment of the awesome B-52 bombers, about 100 of which were sent to South Vietnam, Thailand, and Guam in the early months of 1972. Nixon was determined that American forces should be ready in every possible way, as they had not been for the Tet offensive of February and March 1968. Always drawn to the maximum use of airpower, especially the B-52s, the President was putting into Southeast Asia the means for air attacks at a level never previously approached.

As 1971 ended, Nixon's position had strengths and weaknesses. The public and Congress welcomed the prospect of summit meetings in both Beijing and Moscow, and the opening to China had given the President several months of reduced controversy. At the same time, the Democrats had become remarkably united in support of the presidential candidacy of Senator Edmund Muskie of Maine, who by the end of the year was almost dead level with Nixon in the trial-heat polls. As always, Nixon left no stone unturned. At the end of 1971 he set up a new organization, the Committee to Re-elect the President, quickly called by its initials, CREEP or CRP, and headed by John Mitchell. Behind the scenes, a young group of operatives recruited by the White House and CREEP were starting to dig deep into their bag of dirty tricks, seeking especially to discredit Muskie, whose moderate views made him by far the most formidable of the Democratic aspirants.

Most of all, Nixon now needed a new and impressive foreign policy move. He had seen how the element of surprise and revelation multiplied the impact of Kissinger's visit to China, and had stored up Kissinger's secret talks with the North Vietnamese so that their dramatic disclosure could have maximum impact on the public at the right moment. In January 1972 he concluded that the moment had come, both from the standpoint of his presidential candidacy and in terms of setting the stage for possible drastic air action against North Vietnam, perhaps also because he wanted the public to forget his inglorious handling of the Indo-Pakistan war.

Accordingly, he made a major TV speech to the country on January 25. In it, without excess rhetoric, Nixon referred to the just announced further reduction of 70,000 American soldiers in South Vietnam, which would bring the total down to 69,000 by May 1, 1972, a precipitous drop from the level of 284,000 men on May 1, 1971. But the sensational part of the speech was his disclosure of the twelve secret Paris meetings between Kissinger and Le Duc Tho, going back to July 1969. In addition to the glamour and startling character of this revelation, Nixon matched or outdid most of the pending Senate proposals for an end to the war. He offered to link withdrawal of U.S. forces to the release of all prisoners and to carry out such a deal, right down to zero forces in units, within six months of agreement and the initiation of a cease-fire. In effect, he and Kissinger, knowing that the continued unilateral withdrawals left them no bargaining power, were prepared to have a rapid and complete withdrawal linked to prisoner release and a cease-fire. They, and most critics, must have been well aware that a North Vietnamese withdrawal could not be verified, though the proposal contained a ban on sending new forces, which again could not be monitored. On the withdrawal front, inevitably, the negotiating struggle had been decided in favor of Hanoi.

Nixon was also forthcoming on several other points. He suggested (as he

President-elect Nixon and his National Security Advisor–designate, Henry Kissinger,
meet with Israeli Ambassador Yitzhak Rabin (left) and Israeli Defense Minister
Moshe Dayan, New York, December 14, 1968.

UPI/Corbis-Bettmann

Anna Chennault with Nixon at a campaign occasion, 1968.
Courtesy of Mrs. Anna Chennault

President Johnson receiving President-elect Nixon at the White House,
November 11, 1968.

Courtesy of the Lyndon Baines Johnson Library

President Nixon with Henry Kissinger in the Oval Office during the South
Vietnamese offensive into Laos, February 10, 1971.

Courtesy of the Nixon Library

President Nixon with President Thieu in Saigon, July 30, 1969.
Courtesy of the Nixon Library

West German Chancellor Willy Brandt kneels at the Warsaw Ghetto Memorial to
victims of the Hitler regime, December 1970.

Courtesy of the German Information Center

Premier Zhou Enlai of China greets National Security Advisor Henry Kissinger,
Beijing, July 1971.

President and Mrs. Nixon touring the Great Wall of China,
February 24, 1972.

Courtesy of the Nixon Library

Soviet Party Chairman Leonid Brezhnev and Nixon at the signing of the SALT I
Arms Control Treaty, Moscow, May 26, 1972.

Courtesy of the Nixon Library

Henry Kissinger and North Vietnamese negotiator Le Duc Tho (right)
conduct private talks at a villa in Paris.

UPI/Corbis-Bettmann

Nixon and Kissinger confer at a crucial point in the Paris peace talks,
December 2, 1972.

UPI/Corbis-Bettmann

President Nixon meets with General Alexander Haig and National Security Advisor
Henry Kissinger before Haig flies to Saigon to discuss the nearly completed Paris
peace negotiations, January 14, 1973.

UPI/Corbis-Bettmann

Soviet Foreign Minister Andrei Gromyko (right), with Ambassador Anatoly Dobrynin, greets Secretary Kissinger on arrival in Moscow for cease-fire talks on the Middle East war, October 20, 1973.

UPI/Corbis-Bettmann

Egyptian President Anwar el-Sadat (left) and Egyptian Foreign Minister Ismail Fahmy (right) after a three-hour talk with Henry Kissinger. This was a breakthrough meeting at which progress was made and a lasting relationship of trust achieved between the two principals, November 7, 1973.

UPI/Corbis-Bettmann

Outgoing Prime Minister Golda Meir of Israel greets Henry Kissinger for a working lunch, May 2, 1974.

UPI/Corbis-Bettmann

Gerald and Betty Ford say goodbye to the Nixon family as they take off
to go to California, August 9, 1974.

Courtesy of the Nixon Library

had in a secret October 1971 draft proposal that never got to be discussed with Hanoi) that, if new elections were agreed on and scheduled, the Thieu government would step down a month before, in favor of an "independent body to organize and run the election, representing all political forces in South Vietnam, including the National Liberation Front." Alternatively, the political future of South Vietnam matters would be left to the Vietnamese alone following U.S. and allied withdrawals, a cease-fire, and release of all prisoners. And he observed that a cease-fire should cover all of Indochina. Finally, he emphasized an important offer, already put forward privately by Kissinger to Le Duc Tho the previous July. This was that when the war was over, the United States was "prepared to undertake a major reconstruction program throughout Indochina, including North Vietnam." Perhaps because Lyndon Johnson had spoken in similar terms as far back as 1965, the proposal did not attract the comment its substance might have warranted, but was surely noted by the North Vietnamese.

The speech went far to paint a picture of American reasonableness and desire for peace. But on the issue of whether the Thieu regime should be removed, Nixon was adamant.

> The only thing this plan does not do is to join our enemy to overthrow our ally, which the United States will never do. . . .
> This has been a long and agonizing struggle. But it is difficult to see how anyone, regardless of his past position on the war, could now say that we have not gone the extra mile in offering a settlement that is fair, fair to everybody concerned.

If the offer was refused, he said, the program of Vietnamization and withdrawal would simply continue. If the other side stepped up its attacks, however, "I shall fully meet my responsibility as Commander in Chief of our Armed Forces to protect our remaining troops." This compelling speech was warmly received by most of the American public. Nixon's approval rating went back up beyond the levels before the Indo-Pakistan war, with 53 percent approval and only 36 percent disapproval generally, and a 52–39 count in favor of his handling of Vietnam.[129]

. . .

Reviewing American policy on the Vietnam War from mid-1970 to early 1972, Kissinger entitled a long chapter in his memoirs "Forcing Hanoi's Hand," as though the combination of developments in this period actually exerted pressure on Hanoi to change its plans. This claim hardly stands up under examination, in light of the mixed results of the Cambodian incursion, the failure of the Laos offensive, the new restraints enacted by Congress, and the fact that the opening to China had produced no real change in either Chinese or Soviet support for North Vietnam. The simple truth is that Nixon's strategy in this period amounted to a managed retreat, avoiding demoralization of U.S. forces in South Vietnam by only a small margin, inflicting damage and losses on North Vietnamese forces that were no greater than those suffered by the South Vietnamese, and leaving the balance of forces within Vietnam at least as favorable to the Communist side as before.

On the other hand, the opening to China (July 1971) and the revelation of the secret Paris talks (January 1972) had a crucial effect on American public opinion, while the planned Nixon visits to China and the Soviet Union promised to further improve his standing and his image as a seeker of peace. Most Americans were now persuaded that their President had launched hopeful diplomatic initiatives that might eventually bring results in a reduction of Communist support for North Vietnam, and that on the negotiating front he had indeed "gone the extra mile." Nixon was no longer under compelling congressional pressure for early unilateral American withdrawal. Congress and a majority of the public were prepared to see what the President might get by way of agreement. If Hanoi continued obdurate and again went on the offensive, Congress and a majority of the public might also be ready to accept a drastic American response. Nixon and Kissinger could face the prospect of a military showdown in the Vietnam War with some chance of being able to handle it.

Chapter Five

THE TRIUMPHS OF 1972

1. *The China Summit*

In January 1972, Nixon dispatched Alexander Haig to Beijing to iron out the last details of the arrangements for his visit to the Chinese capital. In their first encounter, Zhou received Haig in a very formal manner, surrounded by senior Party leaders—something that had not happened on either of Kissinger's visits—and subjected him to a bitter harangue about U.S. colonialism and imperialism. On the spur of the moment Haig replied that he had not come to hear his country insulted and if that was why he was there he would take his party to the airport and depart at once. Zhou then clapped his hands, almost everyone left, and Zhou sat down and changed his tone completely, giving Haig a very warm welcome. Thereafter, all conversations were courteous and businesslike.

This remarkable piece of theater may have been intended to demonstrate to residual hard-liners among the leadership that he could still be tough and that his country had not forgotten past acute differences with the United States. But more important, Zhou was conveying to American leaders that he had to take into account the continuing opposition to the two nations' new relationship.[1]

Besides Haig's visit, there were many exchanges via the Chinese delegation at the United Nations. For good measure, the President's third annual report to the Congress, carefully drafted under Kissinger's supervision, contained a substantial discussion of China and indicated in broad terms what the United States looked for from the summit.[2]

When Nixon landed in Beijing on the morning of February 21, there was no firm appointment arranged with Mao Tse Tung, who—as later testimony confirmed—was suffering serious physical problems and had to be specially medicated to take any part at all in this historic encounter. He was equal only to a single brief meeting, which was held on short notice the very first afternoon. This encounter was nonetheless significant, for it put the stamp of Mao's supreme authority on everything that followed. Mao also revealed what Nixon had already surmised, that Lin Biao, at the head of "a reactionary group which is opposed to our contact with you," had died while fleeing the country. Mao clearly indicated that differences over Taiwan were secondary to firming up the new American relationship and, equally clearly, that China wanted increased trade and economic ties. He also gave an elliptical assurance that China would not intervene militarily in Vietnam.[3] Very likely, Zhou made a summary of the meeting and circulated it to the top Chinese officials, using Mao's authority to fend off critics and set down a clear policy line.

The next days were consumed by no less than fifteen hours of talks between Nixon and Zhou, with Kissinger in attendance, another twenty hours of evening negotiations over the communiqué between Kissinger and Deputy Foreign Minister Qiao Guanhua, four formal banquets, a concert of Chinese music, and a politically loaded ballet performance under the auspices of Mao's radical wife, Jiang Qing—indicating, in effect, her acceptance of the visit—and sightseeing expeditions to the Great Wall and other notable places. Visually, China was being shown to the world as never before, and Americans, glued to their TV sets, were proud that their President had made this possible. Kissinger was right to say, "In the mind of the American public, television established the reality of the People's Republic and the grandeur of China as no series of diplomatic notes possibly could have."

In his talks with Zhou, the President expressed the hope that a full normalization of Sino-American relations could be achieved in his second term—he seemed to take for granted that he would be reelected—but (contrary to some accounts) apparently did not make a commitment to this effect. As to Vietnam, Zhou said frankly that as long as the North Vietnamese went on fighting, China was bound to support them with military aid— in part, he claimed, to atone for the historical debt of Sino-Vietnamese antagonism.

On Taiwan, despite Mao's disclaimer, the negotiations were exceptionally intense. In the end Nixon drew on the twin formulas that had already been discussed, which could be traced back to State Department texts of 1970: that the United States did not challenge the position of "all Chinese on either side of the Taiwan Strait," that "there is but one China and Taiwan is a part of China"; and that U.S. forces and installations on Taiwan would be progressively reduced "as the tension in the area diminishes," with the ultimate objective of complete withdrawal.

The American alliance with Japan, naturally, figured heavily in these talks. But the principal subject was, as it had been previously with Kissinger, the Soviet Union. The communiqué never mentioned that country by name and said only that neither China nor the United States "should seek hegemony in the Asia-Pacific region and each is opposed to efforts by any other country or group of countries to establish such hegemony." But this was well-understood code language for their "tacit alliance" or "near-entente" relationship against the Soviet Union. In his discussions with Qiao, Kissinger was at pains to describe exactly what agreements the United States foresaw in the upcoming Moscow summit, thus fulfilling the always important American commitment to keep China closely informed on this front.

In sum, the highly successful discussions in Beijing staked out no new diplomatic ground, but brought Mao and Nixon fully and firmly into the picture. In Kissinger's words:

> [O]nly the President could confer final authority and conviction. Much would depend on the Chinese leaders' assessment of Nixon's ability to execute, parallel with them, a global policy designed to maintain the balance of power which was the real purpose of their opening to us.[4]

In Beijing, Secretary Rogers had a separate schedule with Foreign Minister Chi P'eng-fei on collateral subjects such as trade, technology, and cultural exchanges. He had never been told of Kissinger's October discussions with Zhou, nor was he informed now about the negotiations between Kissinger and Qiao over the communiqué. Not until the flight from Beijing to Hangzhou, where the schedule was meant to provide the Americans with a moment of relaxation in a beautiful city, did Rogers and Green get the text of the draft communiqué for review. They immediately saw a few minor and correctable problems, but also one that seemed more serious.

In the statement of U.S. positions, there was a sentence to the effect that the United States reaffirmed its alliance relationships with a list of named Asian and Pacific countries (Japan, Korea, ANZUS, etc.) — an obvious enough reassurance to the allies — but there was no mention of Taiwan. As Green pointed out, this omission was bound to be spotted at once and interpreted as a declaration of America's intent to drop the long-standing defense treaty with the Nationalist Chinese government, which would surely trigger not only a strong protest from the Nationalist Chinese but an outcry in America from conservatives and others sympathetic to the China Lobby, who included many of Nixon's old associates and allies in both parties and in Congress.

Kissinger flew into a rage, in habitual fashion, denouncing the State Department. Nixon, too, was at first angry, but after talking with Rogers he agreed that the text had to be revised. The remedy was to omit the entire sentence about American defense commitments, though he felt that the Chinese Nationalists needed to be specifically reassured. It was decided that this should be done by a planted question at Kissinger's final briefing, to which he would respond briefly by saying that the Taiwan defense treaty still stood, referring to a statement to that effect in the just published President's Foreign Policy Report.

It was a sensible and inevitable decision, yet it was naturally aggravating to Kissinger to be caught making a clear error, to be forced to get Qiao to agree to drop the sentence, and then to have to carry out the press conference gambit. Qiao accepted the deletion, somewhat quizzically, along with many of the smaller drafting suggestions, in an arduous night session with Kissinger.

The episode may seem trivial, but it showed that Nixon believed (if Kissinger did not) that it was not then possible even to suggest, in public, disengaging from the Nationalist Chinese and normalizing relations with the People's Republic. Nixon and Kissinger both noted in their memoirs that Mao and Zhou repeatedly referred to the need to get the new relationship onto a firm basis. Each spoke about not living long, but the joking tone of these references obviously concealed deep worries. On the Chinese side the problem of the possible succession to Mao hung like a cloud over the visit, and Mao and Zhou needed prompt movement. Yet even Nixon— while personally ready to go ahead—did not dare to risk the controversy that fully normalized relations would have caused.

On Sunday, February 27, in Shanghai, Kissinger and Qiao ironed out the communiqué, and it was presented to the press in the afternoon—with the planted question on the Taiwan treaty and Kissinger's response accepted without further comment. This was followed by a farewell banquet at which Nixon, speaking emotionally and without notes, used language that was apparently not recorded exactly but that, as Kissinger heard it, "edged up to an American military guarantee of China." This was a valid expression of how Nixon felt at the moment—that the relationship was in fact similar to an entente, an understood commitment. This was very different from the arm's-length Soviet-American relationship.[5]

Nixon flew home the next day on a high note. His final statement at the farewell banquet—"This was the week that changed the world"—seemed only a slight exaggeration. The visit was almost universally applauded as an immensely important foreign policy act. Of course, Nixon also saw it as very helpful in domestic political terms. This feeling can hardly have been diminished by an incident in America that occurred on Nixon's last day in China, and ran alongside it in many newspapers at home. Senator Muskie, still the front-runner for the Democratic nomination and exhausted from hard campaigning, was confronted in a press conference by a particularly nasty story, reflecting on his wife, that had appeared in the New Hampshire papers. When he was asked to comment, tears welled in his eyes, and he was widely televised as if he had broken down. In the harsh ways of politics, this was considered seriously damaging, so that in the crucial New Hampshire primary nine days later he won by a much smaller margin than had been expected and never recovered his momentum. Later it was learned that the offensive story had been planted by the dirty tricks crew brought together by Nixon's campaign organization, the Committee to Re-elect the President.

2. The Two Decisive Months

In the history of the Cold War, the months of April and May 1972 were crucially important. By coincidence rather than design, the strongest North Vietnamese offensive of the war threatened the collapse of South Vietnam; the United States and the Soviet Union conducted final preparatory negotiations for a Moscow summit; and West Germany went through an intense parliamentary battle over the ratification of the Eastern treaties with the Soviet Union and Poland. In their memoirs, Richard Nixon and Henry Kissinger link the first two but scant the third. In fact, all three became closely intertwined.

VIETNAM

Nixon and General Abrams had expected the long-awaited North Vietnamese all-out offensive to start in February, like the Tet offensive of 1968. Yet the North Vietnamese delayed—perhaps for the greatest possible amount of training and practice with their new weapons, perhaps to coordinate the several fronts of the offensive, just possibly because they calculated that a late-starting offensive might come to a head just before the Moscow summit, limiting the American response. When the attack finally came on March 30—Thursday of Easter Week, hence known as the Easter offensive—it hit hard on three fronts. First, a major move against the northernmost area of South Vietnam, with a frontal thrust through the demilitarized zone and a left hook from Laos south and then east toward Hue on the coast. Second, a two-division attack from Cambodia, which quickly surrounded the province capital of An Loc, only sixty-five miles northwest of

Saigon. And third, ten days later, an attack on the highland province capitals of Kontum and Pleiku, aiming to open the way for a drive to the coast that would cut off all the area to the north.

This was overwhelmingly a North Vietnamese regular army operation. In the end all its thirteen divisions were committed, most of them equipped with new long-range artillery and antiaircraft weapons from the Soviet Union. Over the preceding two years, 25,000 North Vietnamese had received intensive training in these weapons in the Soviet Union. For their part, the Chinese contributed large quantities of clothing, food, and small arms.

Almost at once, the offensive scored a major success. As we have noted, Thieu and his generals had been lulled into believing that North Vietnam would continue to abide by the understandings of October 1968, and especially that the DMZ along the border would not be violated. They left the defense of that sector to their recently assembled 3rd Division. Now, against a determined attack with new 130 mm guns and other equipment not seen before, one regiment of the 3rd surrendered within the first two days. The remnant went on fighting, but confusion reigned, with the politically well-connected but incompetent General Hoang Xuan Lam in overall charge.[6]

Nixon ordered a maximum bombing effort, moving shortly up to the 20th parallel in North Vietnam, and especially heavy in Quang Tri province and other threatened areas in the South. The weight of the bombing was substantially greater than ever before, also vastly more effective, since the attacking North Vietnamese units offered ready targets. The lessons of the disastrous Laos operation a year before had been well learned. English-speaking officers, mostly American, were at every important point in the communications net, identifying targets for air attack. The American air forces, both from ground bases and from aircraft carriers, were well located and ready, with nearly 200 B-52s shortly committed, and naval gunfire could be used on key targets near the coast.

Quang Tri city, capital of the northernmost province of South Vietnam with the same name, only just held on even with the help of many American air attacks. The related push from Laos and east toward Hue at first made only slow headway, and the threats to Kontum and Pleiku and to An Loc were initially arrested. Within South Vietnam, American aircraft and helicopters were crucial, both as strike weapons and for the mobility they provided. Electronic intelligence also played a major part.[7] And on all three fronts American advisors were active, since the congressional restraints that had sharply limited the role of American advisors in the 1971 Laos campaign did not apply to South Vietnam. By this time there were American advisors only at senior levels, but these were experienced from past tours of duty and carefully selected. For practical purposes, many effectively took charge, reporting directly to Abrams's headquarters.

On April 15 and 16, despite reservations expressed by both Laird and Rogers, Nixon ordered two days of heavy bombing by B-52s of the oil-storage depots on the outskirts of Hanoi and Haiphong. (The North Vietnamese needed oil much more than they had before, with their new equipment.) The attacks were successful, but the offensive continued. On the 15th Hanoi put off the next secret meeting with Henry Kissinger in Paris, which had been set for the 24th. Probably the North Vietnamese expected to be in a winning position by then.[8]

On April 26, Nixon felt sufficiently confident to give a report to the nation on TV, highlighted by the announcement of a further U.S. troop withdrawal of 20,000 men, which would shortly bring the total of U.S. forces in South Vietnam down to 49,000. He felt a constant need to satisfy Americans that he was working hard for peace, so that he would have support if stronger measures became necessary. The President quoted Abrams as predicting that there would be several more hard weeks of fighting, but that with continued U.S. air and naval support the South Vietnamese would show they could defend themselves, and the offensive would be blunted and defeated. Many noted that Nixon made no prediction of his own.[9]

MOSCOW

Nixon knew that large-scale Soviet aid to North Vietnam had made the Easter offensive possible, but he still thought that the Soviet Union could exert strong influence on Hanoi to accept a compromise peace settlement. Getting help over the Vietnam War still headed his agenda with the Soviets. Kissinger, on the other hand, held little hope that at this point he could do more than outline to the Soviets the positions he was preparing to take at the reopened Paris talks with Le Duc Tho. When agreement was finally reached for Kissinger to make a short secret trip to Moscow on April 20 to complete preparations for the summit, Nixon insisted right up to his departure that Vietnam must be the lead topic. Only if Hanoi made a helpful gesture on that subject should Kissinger go on to the summit-related issues.

Yet a refusal by Kissinger to discuss the summit would leave at least three issues dangling and almost impossible to handle there. These were: in the SALT treaty, the number of ABM sites on each side; in the agreement on offensive weapons, the inclusion of submarine-launched missiles and the numbers of SLBMs on each side; and the final text of a general statement of principles to govern the Soviet-American relationship in the future. (An additional important area for possible discussion, future economic relations, was by this time tacitly excluded, with Kissinger making the familiar argument that progress on political issues should come first. Linked with trade expansion was the tricky issue of token Soviet repayment for the massive Lend-Lease shipments the United States had sent to its then ally during World War II. Future agricultural exports to the Soviet Union, mostly grain, had been explored by the ministers for agriculture on both sides, but no proposals had yet emerged.)

Arriving secretly in Moscow after a particularly ingenious disappearing act, Kissinger talked with Brezhnev for a day and a half about the Vietnam War, explaining the new positions the United States would be taking in the renewed Paris talks. These called for withdrawal from South Vietnam of forces on both sides introduced after March 29; an immediate exchange of prisoners held for more than four years; respect for the DMZ; and setting an agreed time period for the conclusion of an overall settlement. While he gave these points a dramatic ring, they were simply a reconfiguration of already stated positions. Even as a sample to get Moscow engaged, the "new" proposals had little appeal.[10]

Brezhnev showed himself unfamiliar with the negotiating situation— itself a sign of Soviet powerlessness—and agreed simply to submit the proposals to Hanoi. Kissinger saw that there could be no real progress over Vietnam, as he had probably expected. From Moscow, with Nixon's concurrence, he proposed to the North Vietnamese a secret meeting in Paris on May 2, which Hanoi promptly accepted, and left it at that.

Kissinger then had to make a difficult decision, whether to comply with Nixon's order to end the visit, or to push forward on summit issues. When Brezhnev indicated that he had new SALT positions to offer, Kissinger decided to risk Nixon's wrath and continue. The new positions turned out to be worth exploring. First, Brezhnev suggested a compromise on the number of ABM sites—two for each side, one for the capital and one elsewhere. Although the Administration was still asking Congress to approve and fund four sites, two would surely be acceptable. The ABM treaty was now a sure thing, subject only to a few minor points.

Second and most important, Brezhnev presented as his own idea a proposal that the Interim Agreement on offensive missiles set a ceiling on future submarine-launched ballistic missile deployment of 950 missiles, carried by 62 submarines. Behind this SLBM proposal lay a revealing story of intrigue and ingenuity. During 1971, the Pentagon had not been able to reach a firm decision on what type of missile-carrying submarine to adopt for the long term. The choice lay between a great many more Poseidons, using existing technology and a proven sub design, and a much smaller number of the new, very large Trident, carrying many more missiles but not likely to be available before 1978. If the former, the Pentagon believed that an agreed limit on future numbers of submarines would be an unwise restraint; only if the United States went with the Trident would an agreed numerical ceiling on SLBMs and SLBM-carrying submarines be in the U.S. interest. The struggle over this issue, within the Navy and up to Secretary Laird, was intense. Admiral Zumwalt was inclined to back Poseidon, whereas the famous Admiral Hyman Rickover, the father of nuclear submarines, still active at seventy-two, strongly favored Trident. Only in early January did Laird, presumably with Nixon's approval, decide in favor of the Trident. Getting acceptable future ceilings for SLBMs then became an urgent SALT issue, with very little time left before the summit.

Kissinger took over the problem, knowing that the Navy and Admiral Moorer were regularly estimating future Soviet SLBM totals. He connived with Moorer so that the current estimate set a very high number, 1,150 SLBMs within five years, as the likely Soviet program in the absence of agreement. From that basis, he was able to get Moorer's formal concurrence in proposing to the Soviets a 950 figure, which could be made to seem a significant limitation. Meanwhile, Laird contributed the idea of having the Soviets trade in older land-based missiles for a generous SLBM ceiling.[11]

In one of his regular talks with Dobrynin, on March 18, Kissinger, saying he was "thinking out loud," put forward the combined proposal, 950 and trade-ins. Dobrynin did not respond, but his cable must have gone straight to Brezhnev, who promptly took the hint. When the discussion in Moscow reached the subject of SLBMs, therefore, Brezhnev's "new proposal" was exactly what Kissinger had outlined to Dobrynin a month before! The Soviets knew in advance that the United States would agree to these terms, and Kissinger thought they were the best to be had and would be accepted by the American government, provided Moorer continued to agree. There is no indication that the proposal was aired with any part of the Congress before it was submitted to the U.S.S.R. It was, to say the least, a remarkable way of negotiating. By getting the Soviet Union to propose his own idea, Kissinger avoided the suspicions and controversy that, in light of his past high-handedness, would surely have been aroused if the proposal had come from him.

Third, the Soviets readily accepted Kissinger's proposal that the offensive missile agreement last for five years instead of three. This, too, could be depicted as an important Soviet concession, both in giving the agreement more weight and because it would last until the Trident became available on the U.S. side. And fourth, Brezhnev responded to a draft Statement of Basic Principles which Kissinger had forwarded in late March through Dobrynin, by submitting his own proposed text. As the two texts were worked over during the visit, it was apparent that only minor differences remained, which Nixon and Brezhnev could readily resolve (and get credit for) at the summit. By the time Kissinger returned to Washington, Nixon had calmed down over what at one point he called rank insubordination. In his memoir he was to concede that the summit "undoubtedly owed a large measure of its success to Kissinger's negotiations during this secret visit to Moscow."[12]

A hectic round of meetings ensued in Washington to nail down SALT positions. Confronted with the proposed SLBM figures, Gerard Smith objected that the proposed ICBM freeze (set to take effect in mid-1972) would already allow the Soviets over 1,500 such missiles, against the constant U.S. total of 1,056. He argued that to agree to a ceiling as high as 950 Soviet SLBMs, against a projected 656 American ones and 144 in allied navies, meant far too great a Soviet numerical edge in the two categories combined! He and Secretary Rogers both urged lower SLBM ceilings, first in working group meetings and then at a climactic meeting of the National Security Council on May 1. When Smith and Rogers made their objections, however, Nixon reacted sharply, at one point rejecting one of Smith's suggestions in barnyard language, and made the decision to accept the "Brezhnev proposal" on SLBMs. The meeting also agreed on the proposed five-year period for the interim agreement on offensive missiles and on a two-site ABM position. The President, Smith finally realized, had settled the issues before the meeting.[13]

It was another in the long list of slights of Smith and the negotiators. As it turned out (and as might have been foreseen), the points Rogers and Smith raised also occurred to members of Congress and later caused serious difficulty. The Soviet leaders were entitled to the conclusion they probably drew, that Nixon wanted a SALT agreement badly and that the White House was a softer touch in negotiations than the experienced SALT delegation.

BONN

At the end of 1971, Willy Brandt stood at a peak of prestige and power, dramatized when he was awarded the Nobel Peace Prize in October. In December he came to the Crimea at Brezhnev's invitation for a private meeting. Brezhnev probed him hard on the chances that the treaties would be ratified by the Bundestag, and Brandt responded frankly that it would be close. As both knew, the Social Democratic–Free Democratic coalition had only a fragile majority.

At this point, Nixon and Kissinger were still cool toward Brandt's Eastern policy, despite the much improved Berlin agreement it had made possible. When Brandt visited Nixon in Key Biscayne on December 27–28 — part of the tidying up with the major European allies after the Smithsonian agreement on future exchange rates — and expressed gratitude for NATO's support for the *Ostpolitik* policy, Nixon replied coldly that NATO had only indicated that it did not *object*.[14]

As planned, the two Germanys managed to negotiate almost all the detailed modalities on Berlin by the end of 1971. The remaining bits were ironed out in early 1972, and the Soviet and Polish treaties were tabled before the Bundestag on February 27, with all parties understanding that the Berlin agreements could not go into force unless the treaties were ratified. In effect, there was now an inseparable "German package"—all or nothing.

Under the West German Basic Law, a treaty came before both houses in the West German parliament. If the upper house, the Bundesrat, voted against ratification, the more powerful Bundestag could still ratify, but only by an absolute majority. In the early months of 1972, Brandt's coalition, with several conservatives won over by the gains from the Berlin four-power agreement, appeared to have such a clear-cut Bundestag majority, but as the months went by, it shrank to only one or two votes.[15]

On April 7, Brandt's government reached a new trade agreement with the Soviet Union, looking to a substantial expansion from the 1971 level of $750 million and containing a new Soviet concession, the inclusion of West Berlin. The effort was intended to win over the many West German industrialists (and their workers) who had tasted the fruits of earlier dealings with the Soviet Union. On April 17, Mikhail Suslov, perennial hard-liner in the Politburo, added an admonitory note, that if the Eastern treaties were not ratified, West Germany would lose Moscow's "political trust" and the hoped-for trade would not materialize. It was a hint that the Soviet leadership, too, had differences of opinion and could not be relied on indefinitely.[16]

Attention then centered on bellwether elections in the West German province of Baden-Württemberg, set for April 23. In Moscow, Gromyko showed how worried the Soviet leadership was by pressing Kissinger to exert American influence in support of the Brandt coalition's candidates, but Kissinger (for what he later claimed were separate bargaining reasons) rejected the plea.[17] The elections confirmed the fears of Brandt and the Soviets: the conservative (CDU) vote went up dramatically, from 43 to 53 percent, and Brandt lost seats in both the Bundestag and the Bundesrat, leaving him without a clear majority in either chamber![18]

Emboldened, CDU leader Rainer Barzel on April 25 tabled in the Bundestag a motion of no confidence. It was a sensational development, the first time a West German opposition leader had tabled such a motion (which has no parallel in American practice) since the Federal Republic was established in 1949. In almost all parliamentary systems, such votes are taken on a simple majority basis. If the vote goes against "confidence" in the government, it falls and a leader from the opposition takes on the task of forming a coalition that can govern. However, in Weimar Germany between the wars, as well as in France both before and after World War II, opposition forces could often find enough "dissenters" to throw out a government, but not enough "doers" to put together a new one. The result was revolving-door governments and near-paralysis. To avoid such outcomes, the West German Basic Law deliberately provided that the government would not fall unless those voting in favor of a "no confidence" motion were also able to demonstrate that they held a "constructive" (i.e., absolute) majority of the total membership in support of a designated individual (and party) as the new Chancellor and government. This made the process so difficult and uncertain that no postwar opposition had yet dared to attempt it.

On all sides, the confidence vote was seen as a test for Brandt's Eastern policy. The battle lines were drawn with exceptional clarity, and both sides went all out to round up votes. In a dramatic session on April 27, Barzel got a simple majority in favor of his motion, but his 247 votes fell short by three votes of the 250 "constructive" majority he needed in the total membership of 498.[19] The Brandt government had survived, but it remained in deep trouble. A day later, in a tie 247–247 vote, the Bundestag refused to adopt its proposed budget. The government's position was beset also by reports that decisive pro-government votes in the confidence showdown had been obtained by improper pressures or even outright bribery.[20]

Yet Barzel, too, had serious problems. He was inclined to favor ratification of at least one of the treaties, as were a minority in his CDU/CSU coalition, including members of wide standing and appeal, such as Richard Weizsäcker. The result was that backstage discussions began, in which the Brandt coalition, represented chiefly by Walter Scheel, and members of this CDU/CSU minority sought to produce a draft resolution interpreting points in the treaties that had caused difficulty. The plan was then to get informal endorsement of the resolution by the Soviet Union, which would reassure enough of Barzel's followers to give a majority in favor of ratification. The final vote was postponed from May 4 to May 10.

VIETNAM

In the last week of April, the situation in Vietnam turned sharply worse, and on May 1 General Abrams sent a very gloomy assessment. By then the city of Quang Tri was being subjected to the heaviest artillery barrage of the war in support of an attack by large numbers of tanks. The city and citadel of Hue, Vietnam's ancient capital, were in grave danger, as were Kontum and Pleiku. Abrams again emphasized that American and Vietnamese airpower could not contain the offensive; additional measures were needed. His recital of the losses incurred by the South Vietnamese forces in April was chilling—65 out of 74 medium (M-48) tanks, also 60 light tanks and more than 100 armored personnel carriers; of 190 ARVN battalions in the field, 16 were now totally ineffective and 27 others partially so. Above all, Abrams stressed that "the senior military leadership has begun to bend and in some cases to break. . . . In light of this there is no basis for confidence that Hue or Kontum will be held."[21]

Reaching Washington on May 1, the report was put before Nixon by Kissinger late that afternoon, right after the strenuous NSC meeting over SALT. Kissinger commented, "The pattern seems to be that they can hold for about a month, and then they fold up." Both thought that the fall of Hue would be practically and psychologically devastating. Sitting in on the meeting, Haldeman saw Nixon "obviously facing the very real possibility now that we have had it in Vietnam." Nixon himself mused that if the South Vietnamese Army collapsed no action would be possible except a blockade and a settlement for the return of prisoners.[22]

That evening (Washington time) Quang Tri fell and Thieu was at last persuaded to replace the inept General Lam by the commander of the southern IV Corps (previously commander of the 1st ARVN Division in the north), General Ngo Quang Truong, whom Abrams had named as one of two exceptions to his negative picture of South Vietnam's military leaders. In a manner reminiscent of the advent of General Matthew Ridgway in January 1951 in the Korean War, after General MacArthur had been thrown into headlong retreat from the Yalu River, the energetic Truong moved rapidly to rally the army.[23]

The next day Kissinger met with Le Duc Tho in Paris and found him "unbelievably arrogant and insulting," not even pretending to negotiate, and gloating that North Vietnam's prospects were now "good." The meeting was "brutal." Clearly, the North Vietnamese considered themselves on the verge of victory. Recounting the session to Nixon and Haig on his return to Washington, Kissinger summed up: "Le Duc Tho's disdain of any stratagem indicated that in Hanoi's judgment the rout had begun, beyond our capacity to reverse by retaliation. Our action had to provide a shock that would give the North pause and rally the South."[24]

What action could do this? Nixon's first instinct was to order a three-day program of B-52 strikes in the Hanoi-Haiphong area. Believing that such attacks would incite the Soviets to call off the summit, he thought of preempting this action by canceling the summit himself. His views changed rapidly, however, after Kissinger, on his orders, consulted with John Connally on May 4 and found him strongly opposed to any American initiative to cancel, which he saw as politically damaging at home. Connally's advice was to take the most effective military action possible to stop the rot in Vietnam, and leave it to the Soviets whether to cancel the summit. He thought it by no means sure that they would do so.

Kissinger himself judged that the military effect of a short, sharp bombing program on Hanoi would wear off rapidly, while it would be vigorously attacked in Congress and by the antiwar movement. Casting about for an action that would both have lasting effect and be easier to explain to the American public, he turned to the idea of mining the port of Haiphong, by far the largest seaport in North Vietnam. A quick check found Admiral Moorer enthusiastic.[25]

Proposed several times before, this action had hitherto been rejected for several reasons. Under international law, only a complete cutoff of an enemy's maritime imports had the standing of a legitimate blockade; without that status, neutral or ostensibly neutral trading nations were bound to object strongly. (Historically, as in 1914–17, the United States itself had fervently defended the trading rights of neutrals and criticized partial "blockades.") Far more important was the balance of practical factors. In earlier years, the equipment moving through Haiphong had been limited, with little promise that its reduction would sharply affect events. And there was always concern over Soviet and Chinese retaliatory measures, and over the possibility of strong negative reactions at home.

By May 1972, each of these factors had changed. Haiphong was by far the largest entry point for Hanoi's military supplies, especially the bulky, sophisticated weapons now coming in massive quantities from the Soviet Union, as well as their replenishment ammunition. Mining the harbor, as opposed to bombing it, ran less risk of leading to an outright military confrontation with the Soviet Union. Above all, mining would be a novel approach, probably involving no military combat or American casualties. Moreover, Admiral Moorer and the Navy planners could time the mines to allow for shipping to leave.

What would the Soviets do? That was the crucial question. By this late date, Soviet cancellation of the summit, even a postponement, would be a heavy blow to Nixon, not only for his foreign policy but for his momentum in the American presidential race. Most of his advisors, including Kissinger, thought that the Soviets would cancel the summit or at least postpone it for several months. But Nixon concluded that Moscow might not care all that much about letting North Vietnam down, and did care a great deal about the material and psychological benefits it would gain from the summit—above all, the dramatic recognition of nuclear parity and the Soviet Union's status as an equal superpower. He came to think that the odds were good that the summit would not be affected. And (as he was to argue strongly in his memoirs) he believed that failure to deal effectively with the North Vietnamese offensive would seriously harm American prestige and negotiating power. He simply could not visualize talking to Brezhnev while Soviet weapons carried North Vietnam to victory, and judged that the American people would accept losing the summit rather than losing Vietnam in this way.

Accordingly, Nixon decided late in the afternoon of May 4 to mine Haiphong, and at the same time to step up the bombing of the North substantially. It took three days to complete the preparations for the mining, which had to be carried out by aircraft flying precise patterns so that the location of the mines would be known if Nixon later decided to disarm or withdraw them. In the interval, General Truong rallied the defenders of Hue, so that it seemed less likely to fall.

After an intense weekend of preparation, Nixon convened an NSC meeting on Monday, May 8, seeking the views of his advisors, as he often did, after he had actually made his decision. Rogers asked whether the operation could not be postponed until after the summit, while both Laird and Helms observed that since land routes could handle most of what was then coming through Haiphong, the mining operation would not stop or even seriously limit the offensive. Helms thought the Soviets would "almost certainly" cancel the summit and might put pressure on Berlin, and that the Chinese would strongly support North Vietnam—perhaps by an effort as large as the 90,000 Chinese support troops they had supplied to Hanoi years before and then withdrawn when the U.S. bombing was suspended. In reply, Kissinger challenged the argument that land routes could handle the estimated 2.1 million tons of imports now arriving annually by sea. He supported the mining and bombing, though he thought the chances better than even that the Soviets would cancel the summit.[26] The most influential voice may have been that of Connally. Rejecting Rogers's surmise that the American public would accept the "loss" of Vietnam, he asserted that a collapse there would discredit Nixon's whole foreign policy.[27]

At the end of the meeting Nixon simply restated his decision to go ahead. The State Department prepared a full-scale program of notifying and explaining the action to important foreign countries, while Nixon himself sent emollient messages to the Soviet Union and China that the action should not damage or threaten the interests of either power. At the usual last-minute session with congressional leaders (none of whom had, apparently, been consulted beforehand), the response, according to Haig, was "stony silence," but Nixon went right ahead with the announcement on national television at the very moment the mining was starting—nine in the evening Washington time.[28] He particularly stressed that the Communist offensive now threatened the 60,000 American forces still in South Vietnam and that the mining action was aimed to reduce its supplies and thus the level of fighting, not step it up. He also announced what he had already conveyed to Brezhnev, that in the Vietnam peace talks the United States now called for a standstill cease-fire (meaning that North Vietnamese forces need not withdraw), the release of the POWs, and a total withdrawal of U.S. forces four months later. In effect, these were the terms that the Administration had resisted a year before when Congress had proposed them.[29]

Finally, Nixon included messages aimed straight at Moscow. The Soviet Union was responsible, he said, for supplying the arms that made the North Vietnamese offensive possible. Yet he ended the speech (in Dobrynin's later words) with "something like an appeal to Moscow to put its relations with Washington ahead of those with Hanoi."[30] An hour before the speech was delivered, Dobrynin had been given an advance copy at the White House — a remarkable gesture in itself. Even more remarkably, when Dobrynin objected to the wording of one point, Kissinger consulted with Nixon and changed it!

On the morning of May 9 (Vietnam time), the Navy completed the mining operation within an hour, suffering no losses. Most shipping nations had been told that the mines had delayed fuzes, so that ships in Haiphong Harbor had time to leave, and there were no immediate losses. Perhaps the crispness of the action helped to hold American opposition within bounds; there were no substantial demonstrations on the 1970 or even the 1971 scale, though the mining was sharply criticized in much editorial and congressional comment. Everywhere, people held their breath. If the Soviet Union had its ships challenge the mining by entering the harbor or moving about in it, there might be a nasty confrontation. If it canceled the summit, it would be construed by many both at home and abroad as a major setback, far outweighing any favorable effects.[31]

On the same day, in Washington, Kissinger again called in Dobrynin, ostensibly to tell him that Willy Brandt and the West German opposition leader, Rainer Barzel, had just reached an agreement that should facilitate Bundestag ratification of the Eastern treaties. Since the Soviet Union was following developments in Bonn much more closely than the Americans were, the information can hardly have come as news. Kissinger's real purpose must have been to indicate that the United States now supported the Eastern treaties, and to appraise Dobrynin's response to the actions in Vietnam. At that point, Dobrynin gave no hint what the response might be. May 9 was the Soviet V-E Day, celebrating Germany's surrender of 1945, with extensive ceremonies and appearances by top officials at celebrations throughout the nation making it difficult to come to decisions.

The next day, May 10, Dobrynin personally delivered to Kissinger a strong protest note over the deaths of nine seamen and damage to Soviet ships by American *air* bombing in Haiphong. According to Dobrynin, Kissinger took the note directly to Nixon and returned in ten minutes with a message that the President expressed to Brezhnev his "deep personal regrets," offered to pay damages, and assured him that he "was ordering the military command to prevent any recurrence." It was another conciliatory gesture.³² Both men noted that the protest did not refer to the mining, and Dobrynin gave his "personal view" that this was an encouraging sign that plans for the summit were still on track. Finally, he remarked that following up on the earlier trade negotiations, the Soviet Minister of Commerce, Nikolai Patolichev, was in Washington: might Nixon receive him? Nixon promptly agreed to do so the next morning.

The first official Soviet statement about the Haiphong mining, issued by the Tass news agency on May 11, was mild in tone. In Washington, when Patolichev called on Nixon, the Soviet minister responded to shouted press questions that he had never doubted the summit would go on. Brezhnev's reply to Nixon's letter reached Kissinger as he lunched with Dobrynin, Kissinger saw quickly that the blustery protest said not a word about the summit. Should the American note have mentioned the summit? Kissinger asked. "No," said Dobrynin, "you have handled a difficult situation uncommonly well."³³ It was the moment of truth: no more needed to be said. The Soviet leadership had had three days to call off the summit meeting and had not done so.

Later, Georgi Arbatov, a prominent Soviet expert on America, told of participating in a high-level Moscow meeting on the morning of May 10 that included Gromyko and Yuri Andropov, then head of the KGB. Arbatov himself recommended that the summit not be canceled, because "it won't help Vietnam, and our main concern should be Germany and relations with the United States." Brezhnev, he said, with the support of "most of the Politburo," tentatively decided not to cancel plans for the summit. But since many local Party officials disagreed, he decided to convene a Central Committee meeting for May 19, when the decision was formally ratified.

BONN

After Rainer Barzel's "no confidence" motion narrowly failed to carry on April 27, backstage discussions began, with the CDU and SPD negotiators in regular touch with Soviet Ambassador Valentin Falin, the foremost Soviet expert on Germany. For the next ten days, the German negotiators wrestled with the terms of the resolution, in effect rearguing the issues of 1970. Did the treaties establish the new frontiers forever? Did they affect the chances of Germany's ultimate reunification, or impair West Germany's freedom of action?

By the morning of May 9, the conferees had managed to reach agreement on a draft resolution, which then went to Falin. (This must have been the "agreement" Kissinger reported to Dobrynin that day.) As *The New York Times* reported the following morning, Falin challenged two of its points, particularly one that suggested that the Polish treaty did not create a legal basis for the Polish-German boundary (in effect since 1945) well to the west of the 1937 line.[34]

This was the height of the crisis, the moment of greatest uncertainty. That evening, Falin and Horst Ehmke, an SPD foreign policy expert, met for three hours. Finally (surely on instructions), Falin made a major concession: the agreed resolution interpreting the treaties need *not* say that the borders were legally established and permanent; a side pledge that West Germany would never seek to change the new frontiers by force would suffice. This was the final turning point.

On May 10, the final Bundestag vote was postponed until May 17 to enable members to examine the resolution. In the interval, as Brandt and Scheel had hoped, the doubts of many in the opposition and the general public were eased and the tide started running strongly in favor of the Brandt government. Barzel's own somewhat equivocal position became clearer, and several CDU members decided not to oppose the treaties as now interpreted. When the final Bundestag vote was taken on May 17, Brandt had 247 votes; with most of the CDU/CSU abstaining, ratification was approved. When the Bundesrat followed suit on May 19, the ratification was complete, after the most difficult and prolonged parliamentary crisis in West Germany's history.

Why did the Soviet Union decide not to cancel or postpone the summit? In the history of the latter part of the Cold War, there may have been equally important decisions, but none more dramatic. It made a new atmosphere of détente possible and gave Nixon a great boost with the American public. The spectacle of American bombing of North Vietnam going on while the Soviet leadership sat down calmly with Nixon lifted morale in South Vietnam and lowered it in the North. And in the Communist world, the decision stamped the Soviet Union as a traitor to "international solidarity," letting down its most beleaguered and dependent Communist regime for its own wider purposes.

In his memoirs, Kissinger concluded that "with hindsight it is possible to see why the Soviets chose not to confront us." He listed four possible factors: that cancellation would increase Soviet-American tensions and, specifically, that an aroused United States was "likely to prevail in a real arms race"; that it "would bring about the Soviets' worst nightmare, an American relationship with Peking not balanced by equal ties with Moscow"; that "it would have undermined the Soviet Union's entire European policy," since renewed Soviet-American hostilities "would almost certainly have upset the apple cart of Brandt's policy; the Soviet Union's carefully nurtured strategy for Europe would have collapsed"; and, lastly, cancellation "would also have jeopardized the Soviet Union's economic prospects: Brezhnev had made a strategic decision to seek Western, and particularly American, trade and technology; that hope would vanish without a summit."[35]

In their retrospective analyses, Arbatov and Dobrynin made no mention of the prospects of an arms race if the summit were canceled. Rather, the factor both singled out and emphasized was the Soviet need to get West German ratification of the Eastern treaties.[36] As Arbatov concluded:

> Kissinger thinks it was China that played the decisive role in getting us to feel the need to preserve our relationship with the U.S.A. . . . But Berlin actually played a much bigger role, almost a decisive one. Having the East German situation settled was most important to us, and we did not want to jeopardize that.[37]

Ambassador Dobrynin was not in Moscow to participate in the discussions, but must have learned of them from Gromyko. His summary is that Marshal Grechko and President Podgorny opposed the summit, Kosygin and Gromyko favored going ahead, and others, including the usually hardline Suslov, were undecided. His account emphasizes the Soviet resentment of North Vietnam for repeatedly getting into scrapes without consultation and then asking for help, and the Soviet refusal to allow Hanoi to have a veto over Soviet-American relations. This was in effect a defensive argument. At the top of the list of affirmative reasons for going ahead with a summit meeting was the effect on the German situation: "[C]ancellation of the summit could exacerbate relations and block the ratification." Dobrynin does not mention China as a factor.

Statesmen make most critical decisions for more than one reason, and that was probably true here. But the evidence of the central importance of Germany is solid. Nixon and Kissinger acted wisely, but in the end Brandt's carefully developed policy and its coming up for final Bundestag approval at that crucial moment saved the summit. At the moment of truth, stabilizing the situation in Germany, completing a new European order, and ensuring Soviet control of the Eastern European nations for as far ahead as the eye could see were more important to the Soviet Union than "international solidarity." In Dobrynin's words: "That was probably the first time that ideological considerations gave way to common sense on so important a subject."[38]

By May 22 North Vietnam's Easter offensive had been checked. The American public was focused on the summit, accepting the mining of Haiphong and Nixon's bombing of the North more calmly than in the past and taking note of the Bonn ratification only in informed circles. It is not hard to imagine a disastrous sequence of events, if the Soviet leadership had canceled the summit and gone all out to help North Vietnam. Nixon had made a courageous decision and won his gamble. As the Moscow summit got under way, he was in a strong position to bargain hard for the best possible results.

3. The Moscow Summit

For Henry Kissinger and Andrei Gromyko, the week of the Moscow summit was a marathon test of endurance. But for Nixon and Brezhnev, who made the key decisions and bore the weight of final responsibility, it was equally demanding.[39] Nixon and his working party were installed in the Kremlin complex, which was convenient but not secure from Soviet detection devices, so that their internal consultation was significantly hampered. The American SALT delegation, which had been working in Helsinki in its seventh session, did not arrive in Moscow until after the final SALT texts had been completed—a deliberate decision by Kissinger, "not uninfluenced by vanity and the desire to control the final negotiation," as he himself later admitted. On SALT matters, he and Nixon had only the immediate advice of two nonexpert members of Kissinger's staff, and could check key points only via Washington or Helsinki.[40]

On the Soviet side, great deference was shown to Nikolai Podgorny as President, Alexei Kosygin as Premier, and Andrei Gromyko as Foreign Minister. But it was clear all along that Brezhnev was the key figure. Important new decisions had to be referred to the Politburo for review, which twice consumed long periods of time.

After short introductory meetings on Monday, May 22, Brezhnev and Nixon met for a general discussion on Tuesday, with important exchanges over SALT issues. The first of several ceremonies for signing subsidiary agreements on bilateral cooperation took place that afternoon; others followed in the next two days. Then, on May 24, Brezhnev staged a dramatic unscheduled event, whisking Nixon to his dacha outside Moscow (with Kissinger giving frantic chase), and there joining with Podgorny and Kosygin in a long harangue about the Vietnam War. Nixon responded calmly by restating the latest U.S. positions in Paris, and the Soviet leaders finally subsided and turned to other subjects. Plainly, Kissinger concluded, they were making a record of their firmness to show to the North Vietnamese. The subject of the war in Vietnam came up again only on the last day, when Brezhnev out of a clear sky asked what Nixon thought of having Podgorny go to Hanoi in the near future. Nixon naturally said he would welcome any effort toward peace, and that evening Kissinger filled Gromyko in on the status of the Paris secret talks and suggested points that Podgorny might usefully make in Hanoi. It was the first time the Soviet Union had offered to be an intermediary over the war.

The 24th, 25th, and 26th were consumed with SALT; the agreements were announced late on the 26th. On Sunday, May 28, Nixon spoke on Soviet television and there was a closing reception. The following morning the communiqué was issued along with the Statement of Basic Principles. With the subsidiary agreements, the SALT agreements, and these final documents issued in sequence, the media had been given a constant flow of materials and events that produced steady headline and TV coverage all over the world. Two subjects were not on the summit agenda: trade agreements, which were endorsed in principle but referred to a new joint commission to be convened later in the year; and American agricultural exports, on which Secretary Earl Butz had held preliminary discussions in Moscow in April.

The subsidiary agreements included one that sought to prevent incidents between the two navies at sea or in airspace over the sea; another called for cooperation in space activities. Others concerned more general cooperation in science and technology, education, health, and environmental matters.

Far more striking, at least to the public around the world, was the statement of "Basic Principles of Mutual Relations between the United States of America and the Union of Soviet Socialist Republics." This had been almost completely negotiated ahead of time, and only a few small changes were made in the texts exchanged on Kissinger's April visit.[41] The statement provided that mutual relations were to be conducted "on the basis of peaceful coexistence. Differences of ideology . . . are not obstacles to the bilateral development of normal relations based on the principles of sovereignty, equality, non-interference in internal affairs and mutual advantage. . . . The prerequisites [for improved relations] are the recognition of the security interests of the Parties based on the principle of equality and the renunciation of the use or threat of force."

In this statement, the key words were "equality" and "peaceful coexistence." As Soviet watchers were well aware, the latter was a code phrase meaning that the relationship with the United States would still be intensely competitive. The U.S.S.R. would not abandon any form of pressure, threats, or covert action by intelligence agencies; it merely implied that it would not engage in the outright use of force against the United States. Kissinger knew the significance and long history of the phrase, which the Soviet negotiators had insisted on, and had given in for the sake of having an agreed statement of some sort. To expert eyes all over the world, the phrase rendered the statement almost meaningless as a real move toward peace, although most nonexperts took it seriously. "Equality" was less loaded: it simply confirmed the Soviet Union's claim to be a superpower alongside the United States—a major Soviet objective. Yet the statement did convey a significant change in the atmosphere of the Soviet-American relationship: a party seen to be acting contrary to its spirit would suffer pain and difficulty at the hands of elements of international opinion.

For the pivotal SALT discussions, the negotiating delegations had already reached full agreement on a treaty text covering antiballistic missiles for an unlimited period, but subject to review at least every five years. On the key remaining issue, the number of ABM installations, the Soviets had agreed with Kissinger in April on the obvious compromise figure of two complexes on each side, one of which could protect the capital.[42] The negotiators had also agreed on most of a companion Interim Agreement on offensive missiles, to run for five years.

Two issues remained: the permitted size of new land-based missiles and the numbers of submarine-launched missiles and how these might be calculated. The first issue became more pressing when American intelligence detected, on April 23, a Soviet test of a new and apparently heavy long-range missile, presumed to be a successor to the existing SS-9.[43] Such a missile could be a vehicle for large numbers of MIRVed warheads, making imminent the Soviet capability for a first strike against U.S. land-based missile installations. Within the executive branch, pressure grew to come up with a workable control regime covering the characteristics as well as the number of future strategic offensive missiles, as older land-based missiles were converted to or superseded by newer ones — in effect, "conversion controls."[44]

The draft agreement prohibited the conversion of launchers for "light" ICBMs or heavier old ICBMs into launchers for "modern heavy" ICBMs. This could be made more precise and binding by agreed definitions for "light" and "heavy." The alternative was to agree to limits on the future size of launching silos, which the United States could measure precisely with satellite reconnaissance and the Soviets through open sources. In the Helsinki seventh round, the U.S. delegation had tried for the first, but the Soviet delegation had been adamant: evidently, the Soviet leaders were reluctant to give any hint of their future plans. This impasse continued in Moscow, and Kissinger was forced to settle for a unilateral U.S. statement giving the American definitions of "light" and "heavy" missiles. As he wryly noted in his memoirs: "We overestimated the restraining effect of such a unilateral statement."[45]

On future silo dimensions, the Pentagon's initial advice had been that the next land-based American missile, Minuteman III, required a slightly larger silo than the existing Minuteman II, so the American negotiators at Helsinki had got a tentative agreement that existing silos could be enlarged but not more than "significantly" — which the U.S. side stated to mean anything more than a 10–15 percent increase in diameter.

The result was a comedy of errors. On May 23, Brezhnev almost casually agreed with Nixon that silo sizes could be frozen, with no size increase, an unexpected concession that aroused some concern in the Pentagon but, on the Soviet side, must have triggered explosive reactions. Brezhnev had simply made a mistake, and it fell to Gromyko to restore the situation. Eventually the Soviets accepted the "significant" 10–15 percent formula, but at that point, the Pentagon told Kissinger that Minuteman III could, after all, fit into existing silos! Yet it now seemed too late to get back to a straight freeze on size. More seriously, the Pentagon pointed out that a 15 percent increase in diameter actually enlarged the surface size of a missile by 32 percent, while calculating in the silo depth, or missile length, would produce a still greater volume increase.[46] There being no way to detect depth from the air, Kissinger was left with the diameter measure, misleading as it was. In the end he succeeded in getting Soviet agreement to the "significant" formula, the understanding being that new silos could not be more than 10–15 percent greater than present "dimensions," an obvious ambiguity. The U.S. negotiators were convinced that the Soviets would never have accepted any tighter control.[47]

As for submarine-launched ballistic missiles (SLBMs), as we have seen, Kissinger on his secret visit to Moscow had achieved essential agreement on the "Brezhnev proposal," which was in fact his own idea. Unlike the ICBM part of the agreement, a *freeze* at the point each side was about to reach, the SLBM agreement had to be in terms of a future *ceiling*, because of the large ongoing Soviet construction program. (Nonetheless, many diplomats, including Kissinger, kept on referring to an SLBM "freeze.") As Rogers and Smith had argued in the NSC meeting on May 1, a Soviet SLBM ceiling in the 900s, with the United States staying at 656, would simply add to the aggregate Soviet edge.[48] Many in Congress were to share his concern over such a Soviet numerical edge, but there were in fact many offsetting factors. The United States was well ahead in numbers of deliverable *warheads* (by the end of 1971 the U.S. total was 3,082 to the Soviets' 1,763, and by the end of 1972 the totals were 4,146 to 1,971). The Soviets no longer sought to count U.S. Forward-Based Systems (FBS), nor did the draft agreement cover intercontinental bombers, of which the United States had 450 to the Soviets' 155. And whereas the Soviet Union had considerably greater total explosive power (megatonnage) on its missiles, the United States was still substantially ahead in accuracy. Counting in terms of missile numbers alone was thus misleading. On an overall basis, the United States was probably ahead still in the ability to hit Soviet targets.[49]

The thorniest problem lay in the second half of the position worked out by the American government and presented in principle on Kissinger's April visit, but not yet refined in detail. Secretary Laird had suggested a complex formula for allowing more SLBMs, in step with reductions in existing missile types (land- or sea-based) that were taken out of service and destroyed. Part of Laird's intent was to move more of the Soviet arsenal to sea, where both it and its U.S. counterpart could not be targets of a destabilizing first strike. A related purpose was to retire outmoded heavy missiles that could be useful only in a first strike.[50] These were sensible purposes, but the Soviets could see only that they would have to destroy missiles above an agreed baseline figure. They therefore pressed hard for the highest possible "baseline" and got a modest increase. Making this alternative computation clear to Congress (even perhaps to Nixon) would be difficult in any event, and the problem was made harder by a separate decision. To get the Soviets to go along, Kissinger secretly told the Soviet negotiators that while the formula gave the United States the right to withdraw 56 outmoded Titan missiles (dinosaurs dating back to the late 1950s) and to enlarge the modern SLBM force to 710 missiles, it would not try to exercise that right.[51]

As all this was being negotiated in Moscow, *The New York Times* on May 24 published the basic numbers being discussed in Helsinki and Moscow. Senators Goldwater and Jackson promptly raised an alarm, and the Joint Chiefs too were upset and "restless" about positions they had accepted prior to the negotiations. At almost the same time, Gerard Smith in Helsinki concluded (once more) that the draft SLBM provisions gave the Soviet Union such substantial numbers that it "could sour the whole SALT outcome," and cabled Kissinger and Nixon to urge leaving out SLBMs for later negotiation.[52] It fell to Kissinger, at one in the morning of May 25, to put Smith's proposal to Nixon, along with word that the JCS were wavering. Relaxing on a massage table in the Kremlin, Nixon decided to reject Smith's advice and not be affected by the JCS worries. In Kissinger's words, it was "a heroic position from a decidedly unheroic posture."[53]

Kissinger then went to the Soviet Foreign Ministry to negotiate with Gromyko until four in the morning. With the Politburo in session all the next day checking the Soviet positions, Kissinger and Gromyko were not able to resume their SALT talks till five in the afternoon. They recessed for a ballet performance and resumed at 11:30 p.m. for an hour. Only on May 26, with the Politburo meeting again, did the breakthrough come. Gromyko accepted the U.S. position on ICBM silos and the last element in the submarine counts—and then insisted that the whole package had to be signed that night!

Smith and the delegation in Helsinki had to finish agreed texts of the agreements—an arduous task in itself—and go with the Soviet delegation (on an American plane) to Moscow. Smith and Paul Nitze, arriving at dinnertime, had to scramble madly to get into the Kremlin for the signing ceremonies at eleven that evening, and on Nixon's order, Smith had to detour to brief the press. When the White House staff, especially Kissinger, got word that the journalists were initially critical about the disparity in numbers of strategic missiles for the future, Kissinger himself went to the Intourist Hotel bar for a dramatic early morning supplemental press conference in which he put the agreements in a rosy light, with apparent success.

Not so with the Joint Chiefs in Washington. When the texts were reported via Haig in Washington, including the SLBM compromise, the JCS concurred only on the basis that the President would take "action necessary to ensure acceleration of our ongoing offensive programs as well as improvements to existing systems." This JCS position, though not disclosed at the time, was bound to influence Congress when it inevitably became known.[54]

In harsh hindsight, the handling of the SALT issues in Moscow was certainly sloppy. The inefficient arrangements and working conditions played a part, and the decision not to bring the SALT delegation to Moscow a bigger one. Kissinger's perennial urge to keep control and credit once again ran away with him. A more basic failure was not coming to grips sooner with the SLBM issue. This was ultimately Nixon's fault, for not insisting on an earlier decision about the future U.S. missile-carrying submarine, but partly also Kissinger's fault for not attending to the issue before March and April.

Despite all these defects, the 1972 Moscow summit was a big forward step in American foreign policy. It was a "first" in the formal sense that an American President and a Soviet Party General Secretary had worked together for nearly a week, along with their staffs. But it was also a first in terms of atmosphere and concrete results, although (as we have seen) the showcase Statement of Basic Principles was decidedly ambiguous through its use of the Soviet code words "peaceful coexistence." The centerpiece, of course, was the SALT I Treaty and Interim Agreement, whose value would have to be tested in the years to come.

Of the political benefits to Nixon there could be no doubt. With strengthened ties to both China and the Soviet Union, he was in a much stronger position to resort to drastic military measures in the Vietnam War without fear of a convulsion at home. And while he hardly needed a boost in his bid for reelection, this accomplishment made victory certain and likely to be overwhelming. If he had called off all marginal political activity in early June 1972, the rest of his career might have been very different.

THE TRIP HOME

Leaving Moscow on May 29 and Kiev on May 30, Nixon stopped for twenty-four hours in Teheran and then in Warsaw, arriving back in Washington on June 1 in time to report to Congress that evening. That Nixon could visit Iran and Poland right after being in Moscow, without visible offense to the Soviet Union, was in itself a measure of a distinctly new, more relaxed stage in the Cold War. After all, in the spring of 1945, the Soviets' heavy-handed behavior in Poland, violating the Yalta Agreement, had been the first clear sign that all would not be well in the postwar period, and in 1946, their refusal to evacuate Azerbaijan, in Iran, led to the first diplomatic confrontation of the Cold War. Times had indeed changed by 1972.

Nixon's visit to Warsaw was intended mostly to demonstrate once again his concern for the increasing liberty of Eastern Europe, as his visits to Bucharest and Budapest in 1969 had been. The President evaded his hosts momentarily to mingle with a large crowd at the Tomb of the Unknown Soldier and to show sympathy for all that Poland had gone through in World War II.

His conversations with Edward Gierek, who had been installed as leader after food riots in December 1970, were also more for atmosphere than to deal with specific bilateral problems. Gierek made it clear that he approved strongly of the "Basic Principles" statement as a help for the weak against the strong, which perhaps contributed to Kissinger's favorable judgment of him. He also implied clearly that his nationalist feelings were at least as strong as his adherence to Communist ideology.

It all usefully demonstrated American concern—and also played well with Polish-American voters in the United States. Nixon could hardly have expected more.

. . .

The Teheran visit, on the other hand, had great policy importance. Nixon made a new commitment that both deepened the relationship between the United States and Iran and contributed greatly to future problems in Iran.[55]

In early 1971, as we have seen, the Shah presided over the meeting in Teheran between the OPEC oil-producing countries and the principal oil-consuming countries that ended with a substantial increase in basic oil prices. As the dollar was devalued, oil prices were adjusted further upward. Meanwhile, global demand for oil continued to grow rapidly, and by 1972 the market was tight. Though Saudi Arabia was starting to think of using oil as a weapon against the United States, the Shah consistently rejected such action and Iran continued to produce at full capacity.

Iran's oil revenues increased dramatically, from an earlier annual norm of about $500 million in 1964 to $4.4 billion in 1973. Much of this money was used for domestic programs, but a great deal was available for increased purchases of military equipment. Security was always uppermost in the Shah's mind. Over the years, he had regarded the Soviet Union as the serious threat, and the U.S. military aid program had aimed to provide arms that would at least enable Iran to hold up any Soviet attack until help could come: the American nuclear deterrent remained the basic guarantor of Iran's security. Iran was not a member of any alliance with the United States, but high-level policy statements had created what amounted to a security commitment, which was certainly so regarded by Nixon and Kissinger.

As long as the United States supplied equipment on a grant aid basis, it effectively controlled Iran's military program, subject to some discussion and negotiation. But the Shah chafed under this arrangement, and when his country's finances improved so dramatically, he shifted willingly to straight purchases, on which he personally made the final decisions. This was the situation in 1972.

By that time also, the Shah, Nixon, and Kissinger had all embraced an important change in the role of Iran in the Middle East. The Soviets were supplying arms in large quantities to Syria and had entered, in April, into a Friendship Treaty (in this case, genuinely a virtual alliance) with Iraq, Iran's close and usually hostile neighbor. The Soviet Navy was also an intermittent visitor to the Persian Gulf. Moreover, Britain's withdrawal from the Gulf area had led to the creation of the United Arab Emirates and an independent Bahrain, which, with Kuwait, Qatar, and Oman, were new and vulnerable states. A Marxist government ruled in South Yemen and a small guerrilla war was being waged in Oman. Finally, the Shah was upset by what he saw as the ineffectiveness of U.S. support for Pakistan in the 1971 Indo-Pakistan crisis.[56]

In this disturbed situation, Nixon and Kissinger regarded Iran and Saudi Arabia as the "twin pillars" of stability and security in the Gulf area. The Nixon Doctrine had come to have an extended meaning—that the United States would depend heavily on anti-Soviet regional surrogates, powerful nations within a region, with Iran the foremost example and prototype. Moreover, since Saudi military capabilities were limited, both the Shah and Nixon considered that Iran was the principal pillar in terms of actual power. They wanted it to have forces capable of facing down and defeating any Gulf state or combination of Gulf states, if possible on their own.[57] By May 1972, therefore, the Shah had a lot more money and a new and bigger job to do. He and Nixon saw eye to eye on this, so that the stage was set for substantial increases in his purchases of military equipment. In addition, Nixon was eager for the United States to have as large a share of the orders as possible.

The immediate issue was the Shah's request to buy a new high-performance fighter aircraft to replace 1960s-model F-4s and F-5s. Some in the Pentagon worried about sending such advanced technology to an exposed nation; there was also doubt whether the aircraft should be the already available F-14, or the F-15, not yet in service. The State Department also had reservations about the effect such a sale might have on other states in the area, specifically that it might lead to the Soviet Union tightening its ties to Iraq and Syria.

Sorting out these conflicting issues in a real internal debate was never Nixon's style. In this case, he cut through it all by deciding simply that the Shah should get what he wanted. Immediately, this decision became accepted as an order applying to all Iranian requests for arms. Nixon was thought to have made his position so clear that to go back to him and ask about later instances would be fruitless and would likely incur a sharp reprimand. In effect, Nixon had handed the Shah the keys to the store. The whole American inventory of equipment, produced or planned, was at his disposal.

Kissinger in his memoirs was to claim that no clear-cut policy was laid down in this Teheran visit to the Shah, and that in any case Iran's military purchases did not substantially increase until the Ford and Carter Administrations. But this is wrong on both counts. Within days, all American policymakers treated Nixon's decision on the aircraft as the governing rule about Iran. Sales contracts picked up rapidly, and when James Schlesinger became Secretary of Defense in mid-1973, he designated a single officer as liaison to the Shah, bypassing the review mechanisms for military sales in the Pentagon and the State Department. Between mid-1969 and mid-1976 Iran entered into agreements to buy the fantastic total of $11.95 *billion* of American equipment. In the same period, it received deliveries worth $3.45 billion, reflecting long lead times for equipment not yet produced.[58] At the time, no announcement was made of the new understanding, although any careful observer could see that Iran's military sales were increasing greatly and that many American technicians were helping to instruct and participate in the care and use of the equipment. The political effect of this intertwining was soon to become evident.

Finally, the meeting between Nixon and the Shah produced, a month later, another American decision, to join Iran, through the CIA, in aiding the Kurdish autonomy movement, then principally directed against Iraq. This decision, confirmed in June by John Connally on a separate visit, was wholly secret, and not revealed to Congress or the American public until congressional hearings in 1975 about covert intelligence operations. It was not a pretty story at any time.

The Kurds, numbering perhaps 10 million altogether in the early 1970s, were (and are) a hardy tribal people inhabiting substantial areas of Iraq, Iran, Turkey, and the former Soviet Union — the largest communities being in Iraq and Turkey. Never able to establish their own state, they continued to have great cohesion and to battle as hard as they could, at least for autonomy within the four host nations. In 1972, their armed struggle against Iraq was tying down substantial Iraqi forces. Israel at that point was giving them some help, as was Iran.

The Shah now suggested to Nixon that the United States make a substantial financial contribution to the Iranian forces helping the Kurds in the Kurdish border area of Iraq. To the Kurds, this common effort was depicted as assisting their struggle for autonomy. But in fact autonomy was remote. Iran's real aim was simply to tie down and weaken Iraqi forces, especially in light of the new Soviet-Iraqi treaty.

The American funds involved were not large, an estimated $16 million from mid-1972 to mid-1975. But the fact that the aid came from the United States gave it exceptional importance in the eyes of the Kurdish leader, General Mustafa al-Barzani. In 1973 and 1974, his forces were to fight the Iraqi Army to a standstill, one consequence being (as Kissinger later pointed out) that Iraq could spare only a single division to fight against Israel in the October 1973 War.[59]

In March 1975, however, after Nixon had left office, there was a reconciliation between Saddam Hussein of Iraq and the Shah. Their representatives met in Algiers and worked out the framework of a new agreement, formally signed in June. Its main feature was an agreement over the long-disputed boundary between the two in the Shatt-al-Arab waterway connecting to the Gulf. In addition, each side promised to cease supporting Kurdish operations in the territory of the other. The deal was, naturally, a heavy blow to the Kurds. Barzani was given sanctuary in Iran for a time, then wound up his life as a CIA pensioner living outside Washington.

The whole episode was power politics at its most naked. For a time it drew Nixon and the Shah closer, but the denouement left only a bitter taste for President Ford and, when they learned of it, the American people. Not to have given aid to the Kurds in the first place would have been understandable. But to give it, build up expectations, make the Kurds bolder and more vulnerable, and then abruptly cut off the aid was hardly admirable behavior or — on a point Kissinger in other situations was wont to argue — a good signal to others in similar cases. It showed once more the two-sided nature of the strategic cooperation between the United States and the Shah. He was more than a surrogate for U.S. power; he often called the tune.

4. High Tide and Undertow

The four months from June through September 1972 were a personal and political high point for Richard Nixon. A Gallup poll taken at the end of May, in the last days of the summit meeting in Moscow, gave him an approval rating of 61 percent, up from the 48–50 percent ratings of 1971. Equally important, groups of informed voters and commentators who had earlier been critical swung strongly in his favor.[60]

Nixon returned to the United States on June 1, and reported on television that evening to Congress and the nation. A feeling of optimism, of a new kind of future within reach, permeated the reactions to his report at home and abroad. Even hard-line anti-Soviet opinion makers were reassured: Richard Nixon, of all people, could not have sold out the American side or weakened its strategic military posture.

In political terms, Nixon knew at once that he had scored an unbeatable coup, that from then on the Democrats would wallow in his wake unless something extraordinary and unexpected happened. For the summer, certainly, he enjoyed the kind of political and public honeymoon that occasionally comes to Presidents at the start of a new Administration but seldom at other times. The prognosis was that Congress would shortly approve the agreements he had reached and, where necessary, give the authority to put them into effect. He was riding high.

Developments on the domestic political front also helped his political standing. On May 15, just before the summit, George Wallace of Alabama was shot and severely wounded by an apparently deranged assailant, and could not continue his run for the presidency. With memories of how Wallace had siphoned off support in 1968, leaving Nixon with only 43 percent of the vote, the President was reassured by polls that seemed to confirm that voters who had backed Wallace would turn mostly to him rather than to the Democrats. The Southern strategy that Nixon had pursued relentlessly had paid off again.

Then, on June 6, the always important California primary gave Senator George McGovern a clear-cut win over Hubert Humphrey. This and other primaries showed the effect of important rule changes the Democrats had adopted since 1968. Drafted by a party commission headed by McGovern himself, these applied great pressure on state organizations to come up with delegate slates with substantial representation from women and minorities, the groups most opposed to Humphrey for having supported Lyndon Johnson so long over the Vietnam War. The following week, the New York Democratic primary drew only 15 percent of eligible voters, a measure of apathy and disunion, and produced a new-style slate of delegates. It was symptomatic that Averell Harriman, veteran diplomat, intimate of Presidents, and onetime governor of the state, was defeated by a nineteen-year-old college sophomore! Every media pundit concluded that McGovern would be the Democratic candidate and that Nixon's foreign policy performance and political skill, combined with the near-collapse of the riven Democratic Party, would make Nixon an easy winner in November.

In this atmosphere, the news, on June 18, that a group of five men had been caught attempting a burglary of the Democratic Party headquarters in the Watergate building complex in Washington—even the disclosure two days later that one of the five had been a security officer for Nixon's Committee to Re-elect the President (CRP)—caused little sensation. The White House quickly labeled it "a third-rate burglary" and denied any involvement in emphatic tones. Most Americans accepted the denial.

The Democratic convention in Miami Beach, in July, ordinarily the occasion for some coming together and for gains in the polls, instead gave television audiences a picture of disarray and confusion—from interminable challenges to delegations under the new rules, to a final night when McGovern's acceptance speech had to be delayed till the early hours of the morning, well after all but the most faithful had tuned out. From start to finish, the convention was a shambles. In mid-July, a Gallup poll on presidential preference showed 56–37 for the Republicans, the same spread as at the end of May.[61]

To add to the party's troubles, at the end of July the Democratic nominee for Vice President, Senator Thomas Eagleton, a respected middle-of-the-roader from Missouri, admitted having been three times, in years past, treated by psychiatrists and hospitalized for mental strain from exhaustion and fatigue. The media went after Eagleton at full cry and he was forced to retire from the ticket. Eagleton was replaced by Sargent Shriver, first director of the Peace Corps and John Kennedy's brother-in-law, a capable man who had, however, never been elected to any office. At this point, Gallup's poll figures were at 57–31 and by the end of August, after a smoothly run Republican convention and a statesmanlike acceptance speech by Nixon, 64–30.[62]

At least from that point on, Richard Nixon can never have had a serious worry about winning the election. Rather, his thoughts and energies focused on achieving the highest percentage victory in history, topping Lyndon Johnson's 61.1 percent win in 1964. By this time, incidentally, Nixon had talked to Johnson several times and been assured of his quiet support. This was predictable, given McGovern's repudiation of the Vietnam War and declared readiness to withdraw American troops from Indochina unconditionally and at once. With the tide running so strongly in his favor, Nixon had no reason to campaign, issue statements, or comment on McGovern. Rather, he relied on his image of foreign policy wisdom and success, kept a low profile right through the summer, and made no major statement or speech between his appearance in Congress on June 1 and his acceptance speech at the Republican convention in late August.

As Nixon and John Connally had planned and hoped, the economic situation was (or seemed) extraordinarily favorable throughout the election year. In the election-critical third quarter, the nation's economic growth rate was 6.3 percent, the highest since 1965. At the same time, the Dow-Jones index for common stocks on the New York Stock Exchange went shooting up on its way to the 1,000-point mark in November. Income-tax levels for low-income Americans had been reduced, while at the same time Nixon could boast of having increased federal spending for the arts (five-fold) and for mass transit, and of having introduced the first serious environment program and contributed greatly to a pioneer United Nations conference on environmental issues in Stockholm in June 1972. In all, the federal budget, which in fiscal 1968 had allocated 45 percent to defense and 32 percent for "human resources," had by fiscal 1973 reversed these percentages. Nixon did not stress, or even note, that most of the turnaround was due to the increased cost of already established domestic programs like

Social Security, Medicaid, Medicare, and the School Lunch and Head Start programs—the latter four all initiated by Lyndon Johnson.[63]

It was a banner year for the world economy as a whole, too. In Europe, Japan, and the rest of the industrialized countries grouped in the Organization for Economic Cooperation and Development (OECD), the total growth for 1972 was uniformly high. World trade surged to record levels, and the currency exchange rates set by the Smithsonian agreement of December 1971 held firm through the year. Moreover, George Shultz, who replaced John Connally as Secretary of the Treasury in June, when he resigned to campaign for Nixon, came up with important proposals in September for moving the international currency system in the direction of floating rates, a big step forward that was welcomed in many countries.

To the experts, the economic picture was not nearly as rosy as these events and figures suggested. With all the major countries surging ahead together, the threat of inflation was bound to increase. Moreover, as they could see but the general public did not, demand for oil was especially strong. In America, with domestic output unable to grow and with prices controlled, demand surged, along with import levels, mainly from the Middle East. Foreseeing an approaching bind, the big American companies cut back sharply on advertising and in a few cases published cautionary messages urging consumers to limit their buying.

During the summer, the Vietnam War continued to go well for South Vietnam and the United States. The fighting moved back and forth in the killing grounds of Quang Tri province and to the south, but the South Vietnamese forces, with the immense help of U.S. airpower, were slowly gaining ground, while the port of Haiphong remained closed by the mines laid in early May. In the so-called Linebacker operation, American bombers continued to hit North Vietnam hard and often; several raids were made on Hanoi and Haiphong without significant losses. Remarkably, this bombing of North Vietnam did not arouse much serious controversy in the United States. For the time being, Nixon's striking success in easing relations with both China and the Soviet Union had damped the fires of protest; the legislative initiatives to set a firm and early date for the withdrawal of U.S. forces from Indochina lost momentum. In August another 10,000 men went home, leaving only a residual force of about 39,000.

There was a lively hope that a real move toward peace might now become possible, along with trust that the Administration was taking action to bring this about, including its "triangular diplomacy" to take advantage of the split between China and the U.S.S.R. When the American hero General John Paul Vann, fresh from success in the highlands, was killed in a helicopter accident, the circles of grief and appreciation went far beyond the phalanx of officials and officers who attended his funeral at Arlington on June 16.[64]

As both Washington and Moscow were aware, the picture of a new Soviet-American détente—which Nixon painted a shade rosier than reality for American voters—was bound to arouse concern among the allies and clients of each superpower. For the Nixon Administration this meant primarily China; the European allies were generally sympathetic and approving—"détente" had, after all, been an agreed NATO objective for years. Mindful of his repeated promises to Zhou Enlai that the United States would keep the People's Republic of China fully informed of all the Administration's dealings with the Soviet Union, Kissinger headed for Beijing on June 16, the day after he gave members of Congress a briefing on the SALT I agreements.

The trip was all business, with minimum staff, no formalities, and little press coverage. In contrast to his long and flowing descriptions of other visits to the Chinese capital, Kissinger was very sparing in his memoir account about this one, and the reason is not hard to surmise. The main topic, which he does not mention, was surely what had been said and agreed on in Moscow. Always edgy over American emphasis on arms control, Zhou must have been concerned that the two parties could arrive at an agreement of such breadth and importance, and especially that the agreement might permit the Soviet Union to reduce its emphasis on strategic weapons and hence have more men and money to deploy on the Chinese border.

To American and European audiences, Kissinger's emphasis was on showing this first arms control agreement as a major landmark and forward step. To the Armed Services Committees in Congress, he stressed (in deference to the Joint Chiefs of Staff) that to keep abreast of the Soviet Union in strategic forces would require continuing major cost and effort. To the Chinese, the probable explanation was that the agreements constrained the Soviets more than the United States (which was debatable), and above all that not one ruble or Soviet soldier would be released for the China front as a result of SALT I (which was probably true). As at every meeting with the Chinese leaders, Kissinger and Zhou surely gave full play to the Soviet threat and Soviet perfidy. Whatever was disclosed can only have been designed to keep the Sino-Soviet rift at least as acute as it had been for the past three or four years.

A second substantial topic was Indochina. Zhou apparently made clear that he regarded Communist control of all of Vietnam as inevitable. On the other hand, according to a later account by Kissinger: "As early as June 22, 1972, Zhou Enlai had told me that he did not favor Hanoi's conquest of either Laos or Cambodia or of [sic] a Communist takeover in either country. A negotiated settlement was the right course." In an apparently verbatim quotation from the exchange, Zhou had said that Cambodia and Laos should be "comparatively easier" to deal with than Vietnam:

No matter what happens we can say for certain that elements of the national bourgeoisie will take part in such a government; and we can be sure in Cambodia Prince Sihanouk will be the head of state. . . . So if it can be solved through negotiations such an outcome would be a matter of certainty.[65]

It was a comforting prognosis, suggesting that China would make some effort to achieve it.

Here it is useful to note other East Asian reactions to the Nixon visit to China, the Moscow summit, and the new thrust of U.S. policy. After the Nixon visit, Marshall Green of the State Department and John Holdridge of the NSC staff had visited all the key East Asian countries with close U.S. ties to reassure them that the United States would continue its East Asian presence and basic Asian policies. In itself, the Moscow summit probably required no further reiteration of this intent. By fall, however, many of the more hard-line or dependent East Asian leaders saw the clear signs that the United States, one way or another, was moving toward disengaging from Indochina—and that this, in turn, might reduce the American security arrangements in East Asia generally. The sense of change in the air led to, or was the excuse for, some diverse reactions.

In the Philippines, the reaction to the Nixon visit to China in February had been dramatic and confused. Within a week, the flamboyant Imelda Marcos had taken off for Beijing, telling Filipinos that going to China at the head of an expected queue would give the Philippines better deals than others. The Chinese were too astounded by such behavior to say much in response. In the fall, Ferdinand Marcos himself moved in a different direction, imposing martial law and imprisoning key political opponents on the flimsy excuse that a strong hand was needed to guide the country in the new situation. As the State Department and other observers saw it, the coup came from Marcos's own ambitions, the "new situation" being simply a pretext for doing what he had long planned.

October saw another coup from the top, in South Korea by President Park Chung Hee, who dissolved the parliament and imposed martial law. In his case, the concern about a reduced U.S. presence and less firm policy may have had a shred of reality—South Korea, after all, had been invaded in 1950, and North Korea remained threatening and armed to the teeth. As with Marcos, however, the urge to take control and rule unchallenged was probably the dominant motive.

The U.S. response in both instances showed the habitual instinct of Nixon and Kissinger to stand by their "friends" and not to let the flouting of human rights or the end of democratic practices outweigh the perceived security need to keep America's alliances firm. Washington and the American Ambassador in Manila went along with the Marcos coup without an audible murmur; in Seoul, Ambassador Philip Habib urged at least a serious statement in protest, but was quickly overruled from Washington.[66] By ditching democracy, Marcos and Park were buying short-term gains in stability and personal control at the expense of later trouble.

Japan presented a different problem. The twin American "shokkus" of the previous summer had done much to undermine Prime Minister Eisaku Sato's position; he left office in June 1972. His successor, the unconventional and assertive Kakuei Tanaka, was convinced that a new relationship with China should be his first task. To restore some semblance of confidence and closeness, Nixon and Kissinger made a special effort to meet with him in Honolulu at the end of August. The new Prime Minister then went to China in October and in short order reached agreement for mutual diplomatic recognition and extended economic and other dealings. In effect, Japan—with no need to take account of reactions in Nationalist China—leapfrogged over the United States and moved directly to complete recognition of China.

Yet, for all these changes, East Asia was much more stable in the fall of 1972 than it had been in 1964–65, when the United States first sent large-scale forces to South Vietnam. The most striking case of this was the firmly planted Suharto regime in Indonesia, which was now stable and growing economically, and had reached a peace agreement with Malaysia, ending the confrontation, the so-called Konfrontasi, that had seemed so threatening in 1964 and 1965.

There was a very different reaction to the Moscow summit in Anwar el-Sadat's Egypt. Since taking over after Nasser's death in September 1970, Sadat had been preoccupied with establishing his power, hence slow to show his intentions. Then, in May 1971, he had made two striking and apparently contradictory moves: a purge of leftist and pro-Soviet political figures such as Ali Sabri; and the completion of a Friendship Treaty with the Soviet Union, negotiated in two weeks at Soviet initiative. Which of these showed where Sadat was really headed? Washington tended to take the treaty seriously, and certainly Kissinger saw it as a sign of a new Soviet boldness, whereas the State Department thought it would permit Sadat to be more flexible.[67] For a year, Sadat had kept up a barrage of threatening statements about how 1971 would be the "Year of Decision" with Israel, but the Soviet Union neither gave him strong verbal support nor sent new military aid.

In February 1972, Sadat paid a long visit to Moscow. Washington learned that he had come with a long list of armaments requests and a demand for total Soviet diplomatic support, but had got assurances only on some of the military equipment. Very soon Sadat was back in Moscow, shortly before the Moscow summit. At the same time, an Egyptian military officer in Cairo relayed through an American contact a proposal, apparently authorized by

Sadat, that Kissinger have a special channel with Egypt. Kissinger responded sympathetically but suggested waiting until after the summit. He could sense that the Soviet-Egyptian relationship was cooling, but not to what extent.

At the Moscow summit, the only discussion of the Middle East came late on the last night, when Kissinger was negotiating with an exhausted Gromyko over the communiqué. In contrast to the separate strong statements the Soviets had insisted on over Vietnam, Gromyko acquiesced in a brief, bland joint statement of objectives, which merely invoked Security Council Resolution 242. No demand was made for Israel's complete withdrawal, which Egypt had long insisted was the intended meaning of Resolution 242. For Sadat, this was the last straw. In his memoirs he was to describe his reaction as one of "violent shock." On July 18, to the surprise of the Nixon Administration and virtually everyone else, he announced the immediate end of the arrangements under which more than 15,000 Soviet armed forces were in Egypt. For good measure, all the military installations and property the Soviets had set up in Egypt since 1967 now became Egyptian property.[68]

This dramatic and unexpected development was immensely popular with the Egyptian people. Few then guessed what Sadat later confirmed, that the main factor in his decision had been a growing sense among Egypt's leaders that the Soviet Union was not a reliable friend, and that the Soviet presence made it harder for their country to take steps to unfreeze the situation.[69] On July 20 the head of Egyptian intelligence sent a message in the new "secret channel," stressing Sadat's genuine interest in new ideas that might be pursued at a high-level meeting, and reporting that Egypt was "especially interested in an interim agreement along the Suez Canal."[70] Kissinger's reply, a week later, turned aside the notion of sweeping "new ideas" and urged instead preliminary discussions focused on "what is realistically achievable." There ensued in September an exchange of long messages, but when the Egyptians proposed secret bilateral talks in late October, Kissinger begged off because of his total involvement in Vietnam negotiations. Thus nothing was done until February 1973, a noteworthy lag at a potentially critical time. Discussions with the Soviet Union about the Middle East also lapsed. As Kissinger explained in his memoirs: "The seminal opportunity to bring about a reversal of alliances in the Arab world would have to wait until we had put the war in Vietnam behind us."

.   .   .

Sadat's expulsion of the Soviet Union could only further the strongly favorable reaction that the American public and Congress had had to the summit meeting and to the new détente policy announced and exemplified there. Yet as beachgoers in tidal waters know, a high tide is often accompanied or followed by a strong undertow drawing a bather downward and outward. Other developments during the summer attracted less notice but hampered the détente policy as Nixon and Kissinger envisaged it. One was the progress of grain sales, a subject that had not been discussed in Moscow but was very high in Soviet priorities. Developments on this front utterly confounded the expectations of the Nixon Administration and in the end seriously set back its reputation for astute management and negotiation. What came to be known as the Great Grain Robbery was a striking example of flaws in Nixon's foreign and domestic policy structures.[71]

Soviet agriculture since 1945, though still extremely backward by American standards, had managed in most years to meet basic domestic needs for grain, both for human consumption and for animal feed (a principal weakness was in corn, where the American crop vastly exceeded Soviet production). After the Polish uprising of December 1970, brought on largely by meat shortages and exorbitant prices, Soviet plans increased the emphasis on feed grains substantially, which meant buying much more corn and soybeans from the United States.

Wheat was a different story. The U.S. harvest ran usually at about 40 million tons, against a Soviet output averaging 90 million tons at the time. (Three-quarters of the American wheat crop was planted in the fall and harvested in the spring; in the colder Soviet climate, this kind of winter wheat generally accounted for only a third of the output.) In a normal year, the bulk of the crop went to domestic consumption, leaving about 6 million tons for export. The United States, with different food habits, needed only about 14 million tons for human consumption and another 6–7 million for feed, hence regularly sought to export roughly 20 million tons.

Normally, then, the Soviet Union and the United States were competitors in the world wheat export market and thought of each other that way rather than as consumers of imported wheat. The year 1963 had been an exception, when the Soviet Union had a serious grain shortage, to which President Kennedy had responded by authorizing substantial purchases— over the fervent protests of the Republican "Mr. Agriculture," Ezra Taft Benson, in which Richard Nixon joined on the ground that selling grain to the Soviet Union would increase its security threat. Nixon went so far as to say that the sales could "turn out to be the major foreign policy mistake of this administration," arguing that they were subsidizing Khrushchev at a time when he was in deep economic trouble, and would enable him "to divert the Russian economy into space and into military activities."[72]

By 1972, however, Nixon's view had changed. The main White House interest in the grain market was that it be used to increase income to American farmers, a sensitive and restive political bloc with the presidential election coming up. The new Secretary of Agriculture, Earl Butz, was told to give top priority to increased food exports, and in January 1972 Henry Kissinger issued a directive to the State, Commerce, and Agriculture Departments (unmentioned in his memoirs), the effect of which was to give the main action responsibility to Agriculture. White House supervision was only limited.[73]

Butz made an exploratory trip to Moscow in April, with a view to concluding a grain sales agreement after the summit. On this visit, Matskevich took him on a tour that included the Crimea, in the heart of the Soviet food-producing areas. It appeared that the winter wheat crop would be meager, but the much more important summer crop seemed to be in good shape.[74] Soviet officials gave no hint of wanting to import grain, although they hinted that there might be some need for soybeans and corn, as Butz had anticipated.

At the summit, Nixon himself promoted the idea of grain sales, telling his hosts several times that they would be very helpful to him politically. The Soviets responded by suggesting that they might wish to buy $150 million worth, a sum so small that Kissinger left it out of the various announcements.[75] But in June, hot dry weather persisted in the wheat-growing zone. Butz had come up with a formula for extending credits, and at the end of the month a Soviet official came to Washington to work out a broad arrangement supporting Soviet purchases of American grain by a line of credit totaling $750 million over the next three years. He was quickly granted a waiver of long-standing laws that barred making loans to countries in default on previous credit. (In the Soviet case, the chief item here was the remaining Lend-Lease advances left over from the early years of World War II, which the Soviets always argued should be written off in view of their enormous contribution to victory in World War II.)

At this point, official contacts lapsed and the private wheat market took over. The major wheat trading companies, one by one, worked out substantial contracts with Soviet officials, which it was enormously in the Soviet interest to conceal, lest the market price jump upward. Contracts for a first wave of sales, totaling some 7 million tons of wheat as well as some corn and soybeans, were completed by July 10.

By then the Soviet government was cutting estimates of the summer wheat crop almost daily. On July 5, the U.S. Agricultural Attaché in Moscow sent a long cable describing conditions and estimating that the Soviets might need as much as 10 million tons of wheat alone — but the cable seems to have been overlooked or discounted.[76] In August, as Soviet buyers rounded up another several million tons of wheat, alarm signals went off about the continued granting of export subsidies on such a high volume of exports.[77] In the Department of Agriculture, such subsidies, authorized by statute, had come to be taken for granted and approved without serious reflection. But now, since subsidies and credits affected the federal budget, the situation came to the notice of the new Secretary of the Treasury, George Shultz, who was concerned, though not to the point of intervening—one of many indications that Nixon had given his Cabinet the strong impression that the sales had a special priority and importance.[78]

In all, by the end of the harvest season the Soviets had bought the astronomical total of 20 million tons of wheat from trading companies, filling their orders from the U.S. crop. The companies started to ship this grain in the fall, which meant it was necessary to revise the regulations to allow for the participation of U.S. ships in carrying it to Russia. Nixon authorized a large new government-financed shipbuilding program, which induced the unions to go along in October with a revised agreement that gave American shipping a third of the business, the most it could handle in its depleted state.[79]

Because of Soviet secrecy and the self-interested cooperation of the American and European grain trading companies, the story of all these grain sales began to leak out to the public and Congress only in late August. It was briefly regarded, especially in food-growing states and the food industry generally, as a master stroke for the United States. But as the full picture emerged, with hints of special favors given and taken and even of outright corruption, it became clear that the Nixon Administration had been outsmarted. The "robbery" tag caught on, and by election day the issue of the Soviets getting American grain on the cheap was being discussed everywhere. The Senate's Government Operations Committee, chaired by Senator Henry Jackson, learned a lot about it but did not get into a full-scale investigation. (Jackson had other concerns in the summer of 1972.) In his memoirs, Henry Kissinger ducked major responsibility: "Fundamentally, the Soviet purchase of grain in our markets was seen as a domestic matter, an element of our agricultural policy; the NSC staff was kept informed only in general terms." But this dodges the question whether he and his staff had a duty to stay on top of a matter he had considered important in U.S.-Soviet relations. Kissinger went on to note also that Butz would have been difficult to control; in view of Nixon's extraordinary reluctance to give his Cabinet members categorical orders, this may have been true. Certainly the ultimate responsibility lay as always with the President. On the overall performance, Kissinger's later conclusion was stark:

It was painful to realize that we had been outmaneuvered, even more difficult to admit that the methods which gained that edge were those of a sharp trader skillfully using our free market system. We had no one to blame but ourselves. Our intelligence about Soviet needs was appalling. Our knowledge of what was happening in our markets was skimpy. The U.S. government was simply not organized at that time to supervise or even monitor private grain sales as a foreign policy matter. The Soviets beat us at our own game.[80]

One consequence of the sales was that the Soviet Union got the wheat at subsidized prices, with Agriculture paying the traders about $140 million in unnecessary subsidies, amounting in effect to a giveaway to the Soviet government. The lower subsidized price also undoubtedly increased the size of the Soviet purchases, which must have eased the situation of the Soviet farming sector as well as the hard currency balance. Brezhnev's crucially important policy change at the Twenty-fourth Party Congress the year before had been due in large part to the need for hard currency; easing this in 1972 must have been a special help.

Even more important was the eventual damage to American consumers and to the American economy as a whole. In effect, Nixon had the best of both worlds politically through the election season, with agricultural producers looking forward to higher prices and the consuming public not yet aware what was coming. After the election, food prices indeed began to rise. The increase in calendar 1972, mostly at the very end, amounted to 5 percent, but in 1973 prices took off, increasing 20 percent overall. But most immediately significant was the effect of the grain sales on the Nixon Administration's credibility, which had been sky-high after the Moscow summit. By the fall of 1972, an undertow of critical comment was building up.

. . .

In two other major policy areas, the Administration ran into trouble during the summer of 1972, and in both the key actor was Senator Henry M. Jackson, Democrat of Washington. Jackson never came close to winning his party's nomination for the presidency. Yet his effect on events and attitudes must rank him among the top American public figures concerned with foreign policy in the 1970s.

Born in 1912, Henry Jackson picked up the lifelong nickname of "Scoop" as a boy delivering newspapers in Washington State. He was elected to the House of Representatives in 1940 at the age of twenty-eight, when he was already a successful lawyer and prosecutor, and to the Senate in 1952. There he quickly managed to get important committee assignments dealing with atomic weapons, national defense, the Interior Department (including energy policy), and government operations. In 1960 John Kennedy made overtures toward him as a possible running mate on the presidential ticket, but ended by giving him only the visible but powerless job of chairman of the Democratic National Committee. As time went on, he drew apart from Kennedy and became privately critical of many of his Administration's actions and policy positions, particularly those of Secretary of Defense McNamara.

By 1968 he had staked out a position as the prominent Democrat who most clearly combined firmness on defense issues with liberal positions on domestic matters. As we have seen, Nixon asked him to be Secretary of Defense—an unusual reaching across party lines—but Jackson declined after some reflection. By then his political standing in his home state was impregnable. His reelection in 1970 with 84 percent of the vote established him in the top rank of possible Democratic candidates for the presidency in 1972. He played a key role in winning Senate approval in 1969 and again in 1970, by knife-edge votes, for the funds to develop and deploy antiballistic missiles; he also strongly backed the proposed defense budgets and increases, as well as Nixon's Vietnam policies. He was by this time not only the second senior member of the Democratic majority on the Senate Armed Services Committee but chairman of its subcommittee on arms control. Yet, perhaps because he was considered such a reliable supporter, Nixon and Kissinger did not, it appears, consult him in any depth during the SALT I negotiations.[81]

In 1972 Jackson mounted a serious campaign for the Democratic presidential nomination but lost ground by not entering the early and always much publicized New Hampshire primary. He then foundered in the Florida primary, which he had chosen as a major test, and withdrew formally in May. Apart from tactical errors and a dull speaking style, he never developed a consistent theme, perhaps because his real views were well to the right of the dominant sentiment among Democratic primary voters that year. He was sharply critical of George McGovern, and although he allowed his name to be placed before the Democratic convention in July, in the fall campaign he supported the national Democratic ticket only nominally.

Jackson was a skeptic and critic of Nixon's Soviet policy, not only of specific agreements but of the whole concept of détente. He had come to believe that the Soviet Union was implacably and incurably evil, deceitful and aggressive, bent literally on world domination in a fairly short time frame. In this view, any agreement would probably be violated and used to take advantage, while the idea that Soviet behavior might be modified over time by enlarged trade and other contacts was a dangerous illusion. Moreover, Jackson was convinced that the overall power relationship with the Soviet Union depended predominantly on the balance of military forces in being, especially the balance in strategic nuclear weapons. In the 1950s, he had been acutely responsive to assessments suggesting that there were successive bomber and missile "gaps" in the Soviets' favor, and advocated large U.S. buildups and civil defense programs. Critics noted not only that the alleged gaps failed to materialize but, less fairly, that Jackson's position coincided with the economic interests of his state and specifically of its largest employer, Boeing Aircraft. He came to be known in some liberal circles as the senator from Boeing.

But most people thought his convictions were sincere. In support of them, Jackson marshaled a formidable set of arguments, with frequently replenished examples of Soviet statements and behavior. Among thinkers on foreign policy to whom he was particularly close were Paul Nitze, Albert Wohlstetter of the Rand Corporation and later the University of Chicago, and James Schlesinger, also from Rand originally, who was to become director of the CIA and then Secretary of Defense in 1973.[82] Finally, Jackson had a dedicated and brilliant staff, including Dorothy Fosdick (who in the Truman Administration had worked on the State Department's Policy Planning Staff with Nitze) and a rising junior, Richard Perle.

Asked to describe Jackson, his colleagues and those who saw him in action would have agreed that he was purposeful, disciplined, capable, and articulate. Beyond that point, judgments differed, at least in degree. His mind was attuned more to weighing ascertainable "facts" than to intangible factors, which he tended to see in black and white. He was a man of principle but also of consuming personal ambition, tinged with jealousy of others whom he considered to have risen beyond their deserts. Exceptionally sure of where he stood, he was courageous and forthright, and at the same time tended to see opponents as foolish, lazy, or even malevolent. Politicians doubted his popularity with the American public beyond his home territory in Washington State, for his speeches tended to be hectoring and he had almost no sense of humor or lightness of touch. But none could doubt that, in the halls of Congress, Jackson was a formidable figure, especially redoubtable in marshaling opposition to specific measures, where both command of the issue and mastery of legislative technique could come into play. Such was the man who took up the cudgels in the summer of 1972 to criticize Nixon's summit agreements on arms control and to consider brewing problems about agreements with the Soviets on future trade.

Only a few members of the Foreign Relations Committee had been kept abreast of what was happening in the SALT negotiations, as Senators Fulbright and Cooper made clear during the briefing sessions and in the final floor debates. Members of the Senate and House Armed Services committees also had no early briefings, notably on the SLBM and missile conversion parts of the Interim Agreement, two matters on which there was bound to be controversy.

And the Administration had a procedural problem. The senior official best equipped to testify, because he was most familiar with all aspects of the agreements and above all with the desired line of explanation, was Henry Kissinger. But as National Security Advisor he was regarded as a member of the President's personal staff, who by long custom, under the doctrine of executive privilege, could not be called before congressional committees. Ordinarily the work of defending the agreements would have fallen to the Secretaries of State and Defense, with the Joint Chiefs of Staff, again by long custom, giving their independent judgment. In this case, Nixon was so eager to have the first word that a new strategy was used— Kissinger briefed members of Congress at length, at the White House, prior to the opening of formal hearings.

As in Moscow, Kissinger's arguments, and his command of the subject, were impressive, though he skirted some points and was less than candid on others. But the briefing was well received and held the line until formal hearings began in mid-July. By that time, the Administration had decided to increase the size of its ongoing strategic missile programs, the Trident submarine in particular, along with the B-1 bomber and a new land-based missile called the MX. These decisions reflected the position the Joint Chiefs had taken on the SALT agreements, that they could support them only if accompanied by stepped-up U.S. programs.

From the start, it was clear that the ABM treaty did not present a problem. But at the Armed Services Committee hearings Senator Jackson came to the fore as a critic of the Interim Agreement on offensive weapons. He picked away steadily at some of its weak or ambiguous provisions, making the valid point that the negotiations on offensive weapons had been rather loose, so that there were openings the Soviets could take advantage of if they chose. But his main point was that the agreement allowed for a Soviet numerical superiority in offensive missiles for the next five years. In particular, he harped on the freeze of land-based ICBMs at mid-1972 levels (1,618 land-based missile launchers for the Soviets against 1,054 for the United States) and on the SLBM provisions that permitted the Soviets to build up to a total of 950 missiles on 62 submarines, versus 656 and 44 on the U.S. side. At the May 1 meeting of the NSC, Nixon had summarily dismissed similar concerns expressed by Secretary Rogers and Gerard Smith, although as an experienced politician he should have seen that a determined critic could make much of the numbers.

Although Jackson believed that the whole SALT package was "a bad one," President Nixon's prestige stood so high that summer that the senator knew he had scant chance of persuading his congressional colleagues to reject the Interim Agreement. In mid-August, he opted instead for adding a sense-of-the-Senate amendment telling the President to seek in future negotiations a full-scale treaty that "would not limit the United States to levels of intercontinental strategic forces inferior to the limits provided for the Soviet Union."[83]

This Jackson Amendment was adroitly drafted: how could any senator vote to have a future treaty that left the United States "inferior"? It was also ambiguous: "forces inferior to" those of the Soviets could mean inferior on an overall evaluation, taking all factors into account and using a criterion like the total ability to hit key targets—a test the Interim Agreement would surely have passed. Or it could mean inferior simply in numbers of launchers and delivery vehicles. As an astute parliamentarian who knew that the legislative history of a congressional action could be decisive in its interpretation, Jackson made a strong verbal record that the words meant that there had to be downright "equal aggregates" in numbers of ICBMs, SLBMs, and strategic bombers, or, in some phrasings, "essential equivalence."

When the bill to approve the Interim Agreement came to the floor of the Senate in mid-September, an alternative amendment was proposed, but its backers — chiefly Senator Cooper and Senator Charles Mathias of Maryland — were outgunned by the stolid and patient Jackson. On September 14, the Jackson Amendment was adopted by a 56–35 majority.[84]

Whether President Nixon made any serious effort to defeat or alter the amendment is not clear. Never comfortable in dealing with Congress, he was also away in San Clemente for most of the time that Congress was debating this issue. As we have seen, his grasp of SALT issues, especially numerical and technical ones, was never sure or full. Moreover, he was still in some respects a 1950s-style hard-liner, and definitely did not like people in State or the Arms Control and Disarmament Agency (ACDA) who steadily pushed for substantial arms control, starting with Gerard Smith himself.

But above all he wanted SALT I approved by an overwhelming majority, partly for his personal prestige, partly to add to his majority in the presidential election. This was Jackson's principal bargaining lever, and he used it to the full. It would not be surprising, therefore, if records not yet disclosed show the President acquiescing in the Jackson Amendment.

So it went through. Among those who opposed it, the one most realistic in his prediction of its effect was Senator Cooper, who not incidentally was the member of Congress who had been most assiduous in talking with the negotiators. Cooper argued in vain that the Soviet and American strategic arsenals were in fact so asymmetrical that the only realistic standard should be overall effectiveness rather than equality defined solely by numbers.[85]

The Jackson Amendment was a formidable hurdle for future arms control negotiations. Another action Jackson took had its own substantial effect on future strategic arms negotiations. When the SALT I agreements were signed formally by Nixon on September 30, with a large ceremony at the White House, Jackson afterward walked in the Rose Garden with Nixon for forty minutes, during which they talked about the trade agreement with the Soviets and about arms control personnel. In their talk, Jackson asked for, and got, nothing less than the removal of the senior members of Smith's negotiating team and a veto on their successors! The only exception was Paul Nitze.

These personnel changes strongly affected arms control policy for the rest of Nixon's time in office and beyond. As Jackson bored in relentlessly, not only the whole top echelon of the Arms Control and Disarmament Agency but the future negotiating team took on a distinct hard-line coloration, and Jackson himself gained an unprecedented degree of influence and control on arms control matters. Throughout SALT I, the ACDA had generally advocated flexible positions, tending to balance the occasional rigidity of the Joint Chiefs of Staff and enabling Nixon and Kissinger to take compromise positions. But for the rest of Nixon's tenure the ACDA was at least as rigid as the JCS, so that the debate within the executive branch became more one-sided and limited in initiative and imagination.

Did Nixon really have to make such a concession? On the eve of an overwhelming victory in November, Nixon certainly had no overriding political reason for handing over such power to a single senator, whose zealot tendencies had long been evident. But having got the SALT I agreements as the centerpiece of his détente policy, Nixon had apparently given little thought to the future of arms control, and perhaps had even turned against it in his inmost thoughts.

The other issue on which Senator Jackson focused, and which the two discussed in the Rose Garden, concerned the President's goal of working out an agreement on the conditions for U.S.-Soviet trade. Nixon had gone slowly on this front, giving no encouragement to the kind of large-scale private projects that, for example, had gone ahead between West Germany and the U.S.S.R. even before the Eastern treaties were signed, and been sustained since. Part of this delay was due to simple hesitation and uncertainty, but also no major U.S. industry had recent experience dealing with the Soviets or was advocating the trade. And there was no large potential area where the United States had special resources that fitted Soviet needs.

The larger cause for slowness, however, was deliberate policy. As we have seen, Nixon and Kissinger believed that only when progress had been made in reducing political differences and areas of friction should efforts be made to develop economic ties. Trade was a reward that could be withdrawn, not an initial appetizer or a stabilizer deserving high continuing priority. It was a crucial difference between the American and West German versions of détente.

From the beginning of Nixon's first term, he and Kissinger had linked trade expansion to Soviet international behavior. And they continued to hope for the linked Soviet action they most wanted, pressure on North Vietnam to arrive at a reasonable conclusion to the Vietnam War. Even at the summit, they told Soviet leaders that a trade agreement might not be concluded unless the Soviet Union showed it had done its utmost to move Hanoi toward a peace settlement. Podgorny's visit to Hanoi in June was at least a token response, whatever its effect on the North Vietnamese. So the decks were cleared and the trade agreement could be negotiated in late summer. It was signed in early October.

In the meantime, however, Senator Jackson had developed his own idea of linkage, which neatly combined his instinctive opposition to expanded trade with a deep concern that the Soviet Union should allow many more of its citizens, especially Jews, to emigrate.

The situation of the roughly three million Jews in the Soviet Union had long been known to be precarious, with much discrimination and occasional bouts of persecution, though less than in some past periods of Russian history. However, there was little communication between Soviet Jewry and the main Jewish organizations in the United States, and pressures for improvement were limited. This began to change in 1967, when Israel's quick victory in the Six-Day War aroused a new degree of Jewish identification among Soviet Jews, gave Israel's image a great boost, and stimulated the urge to leave.[86] In September 1968, the Soviet Union had started to accept applications for exit visas; about 3,000 people took advantage of this move and emigrated to Israel. Then, in late 1969, Golda Meir's government, which like its predecessors had not encouraged Soviet emigration, changed its policy, seeing in Soviet Jewry an important reservoir of new Israeli citizens.

On this as on other fronts, the Twenty-fourth Party Congress in 1971 was a turning point. To further the new Soviet policy of seeking Western imports, and also in response to Jewish pressures, the authorities began to permit departures at a rate of about 2,500 a month. Most of the emigrants went to Israel via Vienna. The new arrivals, many of them trained professionals, were settled rapidly and on the whole successfully.[87]

Nixon's and Kissinger's memoirs do not suggest that they raised the issue of Soviet Jews, either directly or indirectly, at the 1972 Moscow summit. One historian has speculated that a Soviet participant may have been asked what the dimensions of the flow were and replied with an annual projection of somewhat more than 30,000, which was relayed to American Jews. (A later study suggested an actual emigration of 32,000 Jews in 1972.)[88] From the Soviet standpoint, allowing any flow at all was a major concession. Jewish communities in the West, on the other hand, saw the freedom to emigrate as a right that the U.S.S.R. had denied and abridged for too long. While the Israeli government wanted the flow to continue and increase, it feared that overt pressure might lead the Soviet Union to cut it off or to renew large-scale aid to Arab nations.

Nixon and Kissinger professed sympathy with the objective of increased emigration, no doubt sincerely, and claimed that their "quiet diplomacy" had much to do with the new outflow. Yet they also made clear that improvement in U.S.-Soviet relations and more moderate Soviet international behavior were their first priorities. American diplomacy should concentrate on these goals rather than seek to modify Soviet practices in an area the

Soviets had always regarded as one of internal policy, and an especially sensitive one at that. Such an effort was likely to be counterproductive, they argued, and it was in any event contrary to their own conception of the nature of interstate relations. (What if the Soviets made an issue of U.S. treatment of blacks or other minorities, they were fond of arguing, or of the restraints, including ideological tests, then contained in U.S. immigration laws?) Thus, Nixon and Kissinger came back from Moscow with no clear record of having pressed the Soviet leaders over this issue.

Senator Jackson, on the other hand, was receptive to the American Jews who "were disappointed by an apparent reluctance of the Republican administration to broach the issue with Soviet officials forcefully." Not only was he "basically skeptical of détente with the Soviet Union" but "he was picking up advice at the same time from activists . . . about the oppressive domestic conditions inside the Soviet Union."[89] Jackson therefore went to work hard on the issue, well before the Jewish lobby in Washington did so. He and others thought that the Administration was pursuing trade negotiations too flexibly, and even in June he had thought of slowing down the pace by introducing condition-setting amendments. He also co-sponsored bills to give Israel extra financial help for the purpose of resettling Soviet immigrants.

At this point, an unexpected event greatly changed the picture. On August 3, the Soviet Union announced that henceforth it would impose a substantial tax on every departing emigrant. In practice this fell most heavily on Jews, by then far the largest group seeking emigration. In addition to the question of principle, the amount of money was a significant obstacle to would-be emigrants. Jackson saw that freedom of emigration could now be a much more appealing issue for Jews and liberals in America and elsewhere.[90] Why Soviet decision makers chose to impose the exit tax was a matter of conjecture at the time. Only in 1995, in Ambassador Dobrynin's memoir, was there solid evidence of how it came about. When it was announced, Dobrynin was surprised and disturbed. When he next went to Moscow and asked, he learned that the Minister of Education had proposed the tax as a repayment for having educated the emigrants at state expense. This proposal came to the Politburo for decision at a time when Brezhnev and Gromyko were both away on the long summer vacations habitually taken by Soviet leaders, so that the longtime hard-liner, Mikhail Suslov, was in charge. Under his guidance the tax was promptly approved and put into effect. Dobrynin described Gromyko's reaction: "he realized what a stupid move it was. Gradually we convinced Brezhnev and the Politburo to annul it. But the harm had been done."[91]

The effect of the exit tax was to focus the Jewish community in America much harder on the issue of freedom of emigration from the Soviet Union.

The mainline Jewish organizations got together with organizations already working on the problem to create a National Conference on Soviet Jewry, which coordinated its efforts with those of other Jewish lobbies.[92]

Yet none of these — nor, for that matter, the state of Israel, often leery of incurring Soviet anger — turned out to be the effective center of opposition to the exit tax. That role was earned and taken over by Senator Jackson. Politically, Jackson had always made a special point of reaching out to Jewish leaders and staying closely in touch with their organizations, and he had a deserved reputation as a solid friend of Israel. His other main source of support was the mainline labor movement. He was always close to the veteran George Meany, leader of the AFL-CIO, whose hard-line views of the Soviet Union corresponded closely with Jackson's. Appealing to liberals as a case about freedom to emigrate and to conservatives who were worried about too much new Soviet trade, Senator Jackson by the end of September had assembled no fewer than seventy-two senators as co-sponsors of a draft amendment categorically linking trade arrangements with the U.S.S.R. to its progress on improving emigration. On October 4, the amendment was introduced in the Senate, while in the House Congressman Charles Vanik introduced a closely similar one. By then it was too late in the 1972 session for Congress to take up trade legislation, but the way had been prepared for a major fight.

Four days after adjournment, on October 18, with Soviet Minister of Commerce Patolichev on hand, Nixon and Peter Peterson initialed a comprehensive trade agreement, in which the United States agreed to seek congressional approval for granting most-favored-nation tariff status to the Soviet Union, and the Soviet Union promised to pay $722 million to settle the Lend-Lease debt. (Probably the most misleading label ever invented, most-favored-nation [MFN] status merely meant that a nation's goods could enter the United States on the same tariff and other terms that already applied to goods from other nations. By 1972, almost every trading nation outside the Communist world had such status with the United States.) On the same day, Nixon authorized the extension of Export-Import Bank credits to the Soviet Union, stating that such a move was in the country's national interest. The lines had been drawn for renewed debate in 1973.

Chapter Six

"PEACE" COMES TO

INDOCHINA

1. *Hammering Out a Deal*

The military situation in South Vietnam had turned around in May 1972, as we have seen, and the Soviets had gone through with the Moscow summit despite the mining of Haiphong and the heavy bombing of North Vietnam. During the summer, the North Vietnamese abandoned the harsh position they had taken in Paris in early May, and reopened serious private negotiations. Now it was they who were losing on the battlefield. The likelihood that the United States could negotiate a bearable outcome to the war was far greater than at any previous time.

The basic truth was that an overconfident leadership in Hanoi, fortified by new Soviet equipment, had initiated a campaign for which the South Vietnamese and Americans were well prepared. U.S. airpower came into play more fully than ever before, by tactical bombing in the combat area just north and south of the 17th parallel, and with occasional devastating strikes against communication lines and installations in North Vietnam. The mining of Haiphong, at a stroke, cut off the main supply route for Soviet equipment to get to North Vietnam, and the land routes were plastered from the air with much greater accuracy and sophistication than in the past. Part of this was new technology: for example, the long "Dragon's Jaw" railroad bridge, a key link in and out of the Hanoi-Haiphong area, had been attacked over and over in past years with conventional bombs, but always only partially damaged and able to be rebuilt. On May 13 it was hit by new laser-guided bombs and collapsed beyond possibility of repair.[1]

For the only time in the course of the war, air bombing was able both to contribute to a defensive military action in the border areas and to inflict severe yet discriminating damage on North Vietnam. The bombing applied relentless pressure, causing great damage to key installations, particularly power stations and oil storage, while at the same time the unswept mines in their harbors forced the North Vietnamese to use Chinese ports and rail connections, and then off-load onto trucks. At a time when North Vietnamese forces needed far more supplies than in the past to fight what was essentially a conventional campaign, their supply flow was sharply reduced. The losses in men and equipment far exceeded Hanoi's expectations and could not possibly be recouped quickly.[2]

Equally important, the fact that the bombing had been resumed to check an all-out offensive across the 17th parallel made it much more acceptable to the American public than bombing had been in earlier periods of the war. By July, Hanoi could see that Nixon had won back public confidence in his Vietnam policy. A handful of North Vietnamese leaders apparently held some faint hope that he might lose the election, but most sensed that he was certain to be reelected.[3] The behavior of China and the Soviet Union was an important additional factor. In previous bombing periods, they had never seriously threatened to intervene. Now they barely protested and North Vietnam must have concluded that neither Communist great power would lift a finger to stop the United States from bombing as it chose, or even try to stir up world opinion in more than a routine way. Yet it is also important to note that, contrary to much speculation in the United States at the time, there is little evidence that either power tried to pressure Hanoi by reducing or threatening to reduce its aid. On the contrary, the balance of evidence is that during the summer and fall both China and Russia continued to send substantial amounts of military aid, though somewhat less for civilian needs.[4]

As they looked at the prospects before them in negotiations, the North Vietnamese must have noted that the U.S. position did not require them to give up anything except the hope of complete and early political victory. In return for simply dropping their demand that Thieu be removed or that some political process begin prior to a cease-fire, they would get not only a cease-fire in place that would leave their forces in the South but also some sort of accepted status for the Vietcong. Above all, they could use the leverage of their American POWs to get U.S. forces promptly and completely out of Vietnam. Perhaps the United States would go on helping the South, but there would be equal freedom for them to resupply their forces there. As they had seen over and over since 1954, it was easy to create a "double standard," where U.S. actions would be public and visible while theirs would be largely under jungle canopies remote from observation or interference. As for any supervisory commission, they had long experience in frustrating such a group, and could count on the full cooperation of any Communist members.

The question, in short, was whether to accept two-thirds of a loaf and strive patiently for the rest, or go on with the war at a high tempo. In 1954 and again in 1968, the North Vietnamese leaders had been prepared to wait; this time, they stood to get much more than had been achieved before. The chances must have appeared good that the South Vietnamese political, military, and economic structure would weaken and in at most a few years make possible a complete North Vietnamese victory. One shrewd observer, Gareth Porter, a vehement critic of American policy in the war who visited North Vietnam frequently, concluded at about this time that "Hanoi regarded a settlement in 1972 as being in the interests of the revolution," capable of producing "a net gain for the struggle in the South rather than a defeat." His judgment seems altogether plausible.[5] On the other hand, Thieu and most political leaders in Saigon were far from reconciled to any kind of cease-fire or agreement.

On June 12 Nixon proposed resuming the private talks, and after some maneuvering, the public Paris meetings (which never counted in the slightest, except marginally as a propaganda forum) began again in early July; far more important, the private talks between Kissinger and Le Duc Tho resumed on July 19, continuing on August 1 and 14. Two big issues remained. Hanoi had not agreed on a cease-fire *before* negotiations began among the Vietnamese on the nation's future political structure. Nor was it ready to accept political terms that left Thieu in power while those negotiations went on. But Hanoi had now come a long way to accepting the separation of military and political issues, which Kissinger himself had urged as far back as 1968.

At this point, attention turned to Thieu in Saigon. In early July, Haig found him confident and assertive; Kissinger decided he himself should go to Saigon in mid-August, where they reviewed the existing texts of proposals, including one that clearly rejected any coalition government. As Kissinger went over points long agreed with Hanoi and reported to Saigon without objection, it became clear to him that beneath the surface calm and courtesy, Thieu was actually rejecting all that had been agreed and discussed to that point, and would much prefer fighting to a finish whatever this cost the South Vietnamese people.[6] Most of all, he objected to the absence of any provision requiring North Vietnamese forces to withdraw from the South. As Nixon well knew and Kissinger tried again to explain, there was no hope that the American public would support the greatly stepped-up military campaign that this would entail. Kissinger made little headway, and there was apparently no message from Nixon, which might have had an effect.[7]

The breakthrough came in mid-September, after General Truong's South Vietnamese forces recaptured the key city of Quang Tri, the initial prize of the North's Easter offensive. Hanoi now had almost no territorial gains to show for an enormous effort. Morale was low, and from every standpoint it needed a breather, although it was not so hard hit that it had to make basic military concessions, such as withdrawing its troops from the South.[8] At the Paris negotiations, Kissinger found a changed atmosphere.

In this session, Le Duc Tho in effect abandoned his insistence that agreement on political issues precede agreement on the military issues. He also showed he was in a hurry, setting the next session for September 26 and agreeing in principle that North Vietnam would withdraw its forces from Laos and Cambodia. He promised an early cease-fire in Laos, but evaded Kissinger's repeated attempts to get a similarly firm agreement on Cambodia, saying frankly that Hanoi's influence there was "not decisive." According to Kissinger: "We were skeptical. As subsequent events have made clear, it turned out to be one occasion when Tho was telling the truth."[9] Neither Kissinger nor (apparently) American intelligence agencies had grasped that a far-reaching change in Cambodia was now having its full effect.

All along, the Nixon Administration, in keeping with its general habit of seeing Communist nations or organizations as controlled from above in a hierarchic structure, assumed that the Communist forces in Cambodia were effectively under Hanoi's control. Actually, a bitter fight had gone on almost continuously between the radical Khmer Rouge, supported but not controlled by China, and a smaller and less extreme organization of those Cambodian Communists who had been supported by Hanoi ever since 1954 but who by 1972 had no power within their own country.[10] As long as North Vietnam had roughly 40,000 regular forces in Cambodia, there was no doubt that it controlled Communist actions both on the war front and on the peace front there. However, when Hanoi launched its 1972 Easter offensive in Vietnam, it took its forces out of Cambodia to bolster those fighting in South Vietnam. Lon Nol was too weak to take advantage of the resulting vacuum, but the Khmer Rouge did so and promptly established themselves as the dominant military force. Through the spring and summer, Khmer Rouge strength, prestige, and fanaticism grew by leaps and bounds, so that by September they controlled the countryside and no longer had to defer to Hanoi.

Reading between the lines of Kissinger's memoir, one gets the sense that he had some inkling of the new situation and Hanoi's lack of control. However, he acted on the old view that Hanoi was in control, and this misjudgment was to prove a serious weakness in the agreement hammered out in Paris.

One other provision in the draft agreement deserves special mention. This was Kissinger's undertaking that once peace was established the United States would provide North Vietnam with massive economic aid to help with its reconstruction after the war. Over the years, President Nixon, like President Johnson before him, had implied such a program; now it was made explicit, ostensibly unconditional but clearly dependent on North Vietnam's future behavior, an obvious inducement to Hanoi to keep the peace.

Observers and historians have been tempted to discount this offer as never seriously meant. Nixon's strong support for the Marshall Plan in Europe throughout its life, however, and his later occasional outbursts of evangelical goodwill and support for massive aid to Communist countries (provided they behaved) indicate that he was sincere. In 1965 President Johnson, and in 1969 President Nixon, had spoken of possible postwar aid to North Vietnam; in Paris, Kissinger had made similar suggestions. In public, moreover, Nixon's annual Foreign Policy Report of February 1972 affirmed America's readiness to undertake a massive reconstruction program for Indochina in which North Vietnam "could" share to the tune of $2.5 billion over five years.[11] As Nixon wrote later about inserting the aid promise into the agreement,

> I considered [the economic aid provision] to be potentially the most significant part of the entire agreement. . . . [T]aking money from the United States represented a collapse of Communist principle. More important, our aid would inevitably give us increasing leverage with Hanoi as the North Vietnamese people began to taste the fruits of peace for the first time in twenty-five years.[12]

There is no indication, however, that he ever discussed such a project with members of Congress, which would have had to appropriate the money to support it. Nixon seems to have thought that general public statements would be enough to prepare the way.

These useful September meetings led up to a climactic four days beginning on October 8. At the first day's session, Le Duc Tho made several important concessions: agreeing to a cease-fire as the starting point, to the release of all American and South Vietnamese prisoners when the last remaining U.S. forces were withdrawn, and to provisions barring further infiltration of military personnel on either side. He also agreed that each side could replace military equipment already in South Vietnam, but not go above the replacement level. And then he made the key concession: the military provisions were to be carried out by the United States and North Vietnam; and the political provisions, for which only general principles were laid down, were left to the two Vietnamese parties. In effect, Thieu's government was left in place.

Detailed bargaining followed, much of it over wording significant to the Vietnamese in ways not always evident to the Americans. Finally, in the early morning hours of October 12, the text was accepted on both sides. It had no specifications for a North Vietnamese withdrawal from the South, and only called for North Vietnam's "best efforts" to obtain a cease-fire in Cambodia.

Thieu was now the problem. All along, he and his colleagues had chafed at the United States' being in the driver's seat. Ambassador Bunker had only sketchily informed him of the content and tenor of the 1969–71 private meetings. In January 1972 he had been carefully briefed on the proposals that Nixon made in his speech that month, but he learned only in August what Kissinger had put forward in Moscow in April. This limited disclosure has to have been deliberate on Nixon's and Kissinger's part, and done for sound reasons going beyond their usual tendencies toward secrecy for its own sake. They were acting in accordance with precedent, for one thing: American negotiation of the cease-fire in Korea in 1951–53 was done without South Korea's Syngman Rhee, who would have vehemently opposed any deal. Both had also accepted the judgment of their predecessors in the Johnson Administration that any attempt to involve the South Vietnamese government as a true partner would produce at best confusion and at worst acute disagreement and paralysis.

The blunt truth was that the United States had to make a deal with Hanoi that would sit badly with Thieu, almost regardless of its specific terms. The South Vietnamese leaders disliked the idea of a cease-fire and of any serious internal political discussions, and they were frightened by the prospect of a complete U.S. force withdrawal. In 1969, Thieu had told Nixon face to face that the United States must leave something behind to show his people that it was still with them.[13] Events since then had left a mixed legacy. The American public's outcry over Thieu's walkover reelection in 1971 had died down and the political situation seemed stable, but cronyism and corruption were still widespread. The pacification program was making headway, and there was a general lift in morale and in the government's standing when South Vietnamese forces met the Easter offensive and recaptured Quang Tri. However, the evident truth was that only U.S. airpower had saved Thieu's forces from defeat, and he had the searing memory of his own failed Laos offensive in early 1971, perhaps also an underlying sense of his own limitations as a political leader. He was bound to accept any agreement negotiated by the United States only with the greatest reluctance, and was capable of mulelike stubbornness and of nitpicking any proposed agreement to death. This capacity had been amply demonstrated in the fall of 1968, when he resisted the pleas of President Johnson while doing what he knew candidate

Nixon wanted. Now history had come full circle, and it was President Nixon he was resisting.

Part of what Thieu objected to was a bedrock feature of the agreement, complete United States withdrawal. Although he should have seen this as inevitable for a long time, he feigned surprise and dismay, doing all he could to get more from Nixon by way of support and pledges. Another objection, concerned with the political provisions, was peculiarly Vietnamese. For nearly twenty years both Hanoi and Saigon had disputed whether they were two countries or one and, for a decade, had argued about the status of the NLF and its successor Vietcong organization. Every nuance of wording had come to count in ways that only the most sophisticated Americans could grasp. All this Nixon and Kissinger knew, at least in their heads. Yet Kissinger was less than thorough in working over Hanoi's draft, which was riddled with verbal booby traps designed to tilt future issues and put South Vietnam in the weakest possible position to assert that it was a separate entity and a legitimate government.[14] He was impatient, and in a big hurry to get the agreement completed before the election on November 7. Certainly Thieu considered that the American negotiator was being far too hasty, and this belief contributed to his coming to have intense personal distrust of Kissinger.

In all probability neither Vietnamese side believed that the draft agreement's elaborate provisions for Committees of Reconciliation and the like, intended ostensibly to lead to an agreed compromise government, would ever be carried out as written. Long before this could possibly happen, the issue of who held real power would be decided by military force or by a collapse of government in Saigon. While political labels and boundaries probably had no ultimate concrete meaning, they did have enormous symbolic significance, particularly to the side that had a semblance of genuine public opinion, the South Vietnamese. Nixon and Kissinger should have known how sensitive these wording matters were.

After returning briefly to Washington, Kissinger brought the draft agreement (which he had not sent ahead) to Saigon on October 19. There ensued four anguished days in which Kissinger and Ambassador Bunker pulled out all the stops, but Thieu was totally dug in. On October 24, in a stinging speech, he made public his very negative interpretation of the draft agreement and firmly rejected it as it stood. North Vietnam then put pressure on the United States by publishing the October 11 text as it had been agreed in Paris. For the first time the American public, and the world, could see the likely shape of a final agreement.

This move put the Americans, and Kissinger personally, on the spot. His response was to hold a long and dramatic press conference in Washington on October 26, in which he summarized and commented on the key provisions. He predicted that the remaining difficulties could be handled in another session of only a few days, and wound up with the unforgettable phrase "Peace is at hand." Partly he was trying to reassure the North Vietnamese and, even more, the American public, that he had acted sincerely and that things could be brought around; partly he wanted to elicit a favorable public reaction that would show Saigon how strong was the sentiment for an agreement. But the effect was certainly to raise hopes for an early peace agreement far more than was warranted.[15]

The press conference made Kissinger even more a central figure. Many Americans who were opposed to the war argued, then and later, that essentially the same terms could have been obtained three or four years earlier: Averell Harriman, Johnson's chief negotiator, made this claim, and George McGovern repeated it. McGovern himself went further, saying that while the draft agreement preserved the right of the United States to send further aid to Saigon, he as President would oppose aid if the Thieu regime remained in power and continued its repressive ways.

Less predictable was the response from those who had been supporters of U.S. policy in Vietnam. No significant voice was raised to argue against the key provision that North Vietnamese forces could remain in South Vietnam, or to question the efficacy of the supervisory provisions. Astutely briefed by Kissinger and his team, such key columnists as Joseph Alsop, Rowland Evans, and Robert Novak acclaimed the terms as considerably better than had been thought possible, stressing that Thieu would remain in power and that the United States would be free to go on helping him. Alsop even accepted Kissinger's claim that North Vietnam's forces in the South would die on the vine since Hanoi could no longer use Laos and Cambodia to supply them. By contrast, the more detached Chalmers Roberts of *The Washington Post* had grave doubts that the agreement could hold up, either in bringing peace or in preserving a non-Communist regime in the South.[16]

Congress was of course out of session and its members preoccupied by the election campaign, so congressional reaction was delayed and when it came was limited. These final negotiations, from August on, do not appear to have been discussed in any way with congressional leaders, certainly not before the election. After it, Nixon retreated to Camp David and (according to John Ehrlichman) "had no personal contact with the Congress until he delivered his State of the Union message in late January 1973."[17]

As the likely terms became known, therefore, there was little public or congressional pressure to improve this or that feature. This absence of comment was itself the strongest possible evidence of where the nation stood. On all sides, the overwhelming sentiment was that U.S. participation in the war should end and that a new Administration should start with Vietnam no longer the obsessive concern it had been for at least nine years.

On November 7, the voters reelected Nixon by a 61–38 percentage margin, with the largest numerical plurality up to that time in American history. Unquestionably his handling of the war played a big part in the size of his victory. In October, McGovern had framed the issues even more clearly in a major speech where he promised that he would effect the immediate withdrawal of U.S. forces, with no condition even that prisoners be released and with no clear plan to achieve this. The speech only added to Nixon's huge lead.

Whatever mandate Nixon got on Vietnam policy was confined, however, to approval of just the kind of terms Kissinger had made public — getting the prisoners back and American forces out, while giving Thieu a fair chance to survive. In the congressional elections, not only did the Democrats retain their House majority handily, losing fewer seats than normal in a losing presidential year, but in the Senate they added two seats to their majority, bringing it to 57–43. Most striking of all, and surely most noted by Nixon, only one senator clearly opposed to the war (Fred Harris, Democrat from Oklahoma) lost his seat, while six of those who had voted with Senator Stennis in September against a firm four-month withdrawal deadline either retired or were defeated. The makeup of the new Senate showed conclusively that, in a renewed test on similar lines, advocates of immediate withdrawal would win provided only that prisoners of war were also released.

In short, while the election results gave Nixon a great psychological lift and the public an impression of enormous personal power for him, the voting picture on Capitol Hill over getting out of the war was if anything more adamant. In the minds of Nixon and Kissinger, as their writings abundantly attest, all doubt had been removed; a negotiated final agreement had to be reached before the new Congress took hold.

2. Bringing Thieu Around:
Pledges and the Christmas Bombing

To persuade Thieu to accept a settlement, Nixon sent him an extraordinary series of letters, altogether twenty-one from December 31, 1971, to late January 1973.[18] These letters, from a powerful ally to an unwilling but dependent leader, consist overwhelmingly of reassurance and encouragement. Thieu treasured them and kept them together in a very private file. He must have read them in large part for their tone. But he looked also for what they said on two key points: future military aid from the United States and a clear intent to use U.S. airpower massively if the agreement was violated on a large scale by Hanoi.

Nixon had fully grasped the first point well before Kissinger went to Saigon in late October. During the summer he had ordered, in the so-called Enhance program, a large-scale replacement from U.S. stocks of South Vietnamese military equipment lost or consumed in the spring and summer fighting. This was a reasonable measure, and most of the equipment was probably soon put to good use.

In October, he went much further. The additional program, called Enhance Plus, was conveyed to Thieu by General Abrams on October 19, the day of Kissinger's arrival in Saigon. Within days, massive deliveries were under way by airlift into the airport at Saigon. Key items delivered before December 1 included 266 transport and fighter aircraft, 277 helicopters, and two squadrons of C-130 transports. In testimony to Congress in January 1973, Admiral Moorer, JCS Chairman, gave the figures for total U.S. deliveries to South Vietnam as 107 million tons (sic) between September 15 and October 14, and 152.6 million tons from October 15 to November 14! Even if these totals contained some civilian items, they represented an extraordinary effort.[19]

Moreover, since the draft peace agreement provided that future external military supplies could only replace items already on hand at the date of final signing (originally set for October 31), the effect of the new shipments was to raise the future ceiling substantially.[20] At the same time, orders were given to sign over to South Vietnam vast quantities of U.S. property on military bases in South Vietnam — making a dead letter of the provision in the draft agreement that called for the United States to remove the equipment at these bases. Hanoi could hardly fail to note both these actions.[21] Both may have stimulated Hanoi's own resupply effort, which in November and December focused especially on antiaircraft equipment — even though the United States, pursuant to Kissinger's talks, had suspended the bombing of the North on October 23.[22] Both sides were preparing for new battles.

Although these enormous new supplies were welcome, what Thieu wanted most was a categorical assurance that the United States would again resort to drastic action if the North Vietnamese violated the cease-fire. In early November, Haig went to Saigon for long and earnest discussions with Thieu. On his return, and probably at his suggestion, Nixon took a major step that he kept totally secret from Congress and the American public. It was known at the time, even within the executive, to no senior official save Kissinger, Haig, and Ambassador Bunker, who handled delivery of the correspondence.[23] Possibly, in keeping with Nixon's inclinations, the idea had been brewing in his mind for months, as a card to be played at the right time. By mid-November, savoring his election triumph, he may have been confident that he could carry out any threat without interference from Congress or the American public.

Accordingly, in a letter to Thieu dated November 14, Nixon wrote: "You have my absolute assurance that if Hanoi fails to abide by the terms of this agreement it is my intention to take swift and severe retaliatory action."

And, at the end of the letter: "I repeat my personal assurance to you that the United States will react very strongly and rapidly to any violation of the agreement."[24] This was a powerful pledge indeed, especially given the vivid memory of how its author had acted in April and May. However, it was phrased in terms that were indefensible—and without binding effect or authority—under the American Constitution, in that it purported to be a categorical promise of military action by the U.S. government, *without any mention of constitutional processes or consent by Congress.* Inevitably, however, especially given his frail grasp of the American system of government, Thieu took it at face value.

Not surprisingly, this secret pledge only stiffened Thieu's objections to the draft agreement. When the Paris talks reconvened in early December, he had marshaled no fewer than sixty proposed changes in the text. Partly in response, Hanoi too became very tough, not only rejecting the changes that Kissinger sought in order to propitiate Saigon but reneging on some of its own earlier positions. By December 15 the talks were stalemated.

There was a slightly surreal quality to events at this point, and particularly to the atmosphere within the White House. Nixon had been enraged by Thieu's behavior, but still wanted to get him aboard in support of the draft agreement. He also wanted to frighten the North Vietnamese into submission, and get them to drop the new points Le Duc Tho was making in Paris. For these dual purposes, Nixon now turned to his favorite weapon, giving the order for intensive bombing of North Vietnam, particularly of military targets within the city limits of Hanoi and Haiphong, many of which had been spared during the spring and summer air offensive. B-52 attacks, unprecedented in both scale and objective, began on December 18. In what came to be called the Christmas bombing (Linebacker II was its military label), nearly 20,000 tons of bombs were dropped on North Vietnam, about 15,000 by B-52s, in the space of eleven days!

For the only time in the war, this was genuine strategic bombing as the U.S. Air Force conceived it, and the responsibility was first given to the Strategic Air Command headquartered in Omaha. In the first three days, SAC's unimaginative tactics led to serious losses, after which the operation was put in the hands of the Eighth Air Force, based on Guam, which had extensive experience of North Vietnamese defenses. The losses then fell off, but altogether the North Vietnamese succeeded in destroying fifteen B-52s and heavily damaging many more aircraft. U.S. aircrew losses were substantial, including about eighty crew members captured by the North Vietnamese.[25]

Although the targeting was carefully confined to military-related installations, the physical damage was vast and some errors were inevitable. In one case a major hospital was partly destroyed. The North Vietnamese themselves finally estimated the casualties at slightly more than two thousand people killed, although initial reports had suggested much higher figures. It may well be that the North Vietnamese leadership, to keep up morale at home and maintain a firm front, deliberately understated the casualties by a considerable margin. But even if the total was only a fraction of those killed in Tokyo or Dresden in World War II, it was surely substantial. By standards applicable to bombing in large part for the political purpose of reassuring one's ally, it should be judged harshly.[26] In the United States, there was intense criticism in many quarters, though the holiday season tended to dampen the reaction. An incomplete poll of available senators taken on December 21 showed only 19 of 73 favoring the bombing, and a 45–25 majority now advocating legislation to end U.S. involvement in South Vietnam.[27] Abroad, the condemnation of U.S. policy reached new heights. Many national leaders denounced the bombing as sheer bullying; almost none defended it.

Yet the attacks were militarily effective, especially against North Vietnamese antiaircraft capabilities. By December 29 the North Vietnamese had almost no surface-to-air missiles left and were at the mercy of further attacks. That day they sent a message saying they were prepared to resume negotiations, on the basis of the October text, withdrawing the changes they had sought in November and early December. Nixon at once accepted and the bombing was stopped. The Christmas bombing, for all its negatives, did the two things it set out to do: Hanoi came back to the table in a mood to settle and Saigon was persuaded that the United States under Nixon could indeed be tough. But had the public known that a principal purpose of the bombing had been to give substance to Nixon's secret pledge of November 14, the outcry against it would surely have been even greater than it was.

Thieu, however, still hung back, and on January 5, 1973, Nixon went a step further. At the end of a letter that was otherwise very firm in tone, devoted to how the United States proposed to proceed in the renewed Paris talks and why South Vietnam should agree, he concluded with these words:

> Should you decide, as I trust you will, to go with us, you have my assurance of continued assistance in the post-settlement period and that we will respond with full force should the settlement be violated by North Vietnam.

The sentence was underlined by Thieu and shared at once with key members of his Cabinet.[28] In the light of the Christmas bombing, the phrase "full force" clearly strengthened the earlier general promise, implying unmistakably that U.S. military action would be on a similar scale and for whatever length of time might be needed.

. . .

In the reconvened Paris talks, Kissinger obtained one modestly significant change sought by President Thieu. This was explicit mention of the demilitarized zone at the 17th parallel as a border, in the terms used in the Geneva Accords of 1954. There was also a sentence calling for the withdrawal of "foreign" forces and forbidding the introduction of new ones. Kissinger could claim that this covered North Vietnamese forces — or at least that Hanoi would be compelled to see its forces in the South reduced, as some of them went home. Hanoi, however, could continue to argue that its forces were not "foreign." Kissinger's interpretation was not accepted even at the time by Hanoi, nor could it even be supported by his own legal advisor. Above all, it was not remotely backed by credible provisions for identifying violations of the agreements or doing anything effective about them. If Hanoi set out once more to rebuild its posture and reinforce the troops it had in the South, the only recourse for the United States would be some sort of military threat or action.

Outside the framework of the agreement, Kissinger was able to get a firm oral commitment from Le Duc Tho that a cease-fire in Laos would come within fifteen days of that in Vietnam. But when Kissinger renewed his attempts to commit Tho similarly to an early cease-fire in Cambodia, Tho referred again to Hanoi's difficulties with the Khmer Rouge and went no further than to say orally that peace in Vietnam and Laos "would create favorable conditions for the restoration of peace in Cambodia." Thus, Kissinger had to fall back on reiterating his previous statements. If Lon Nol proposed a cease-fire and the Communists did not respond, this would be "contrary to the assumptions" on which the United States had entered the agreement; and it might well continue military action.[29] He was painting Nixon and himself into a corner, as events were to demonstrate.

In fact, the Christmas bombing extracted no significant concession from Hanoi. The shock effect of the bombing may have been severe, even traumatic. At least one of Kissinger's staff argued that if the bombing had been kept up, or even threatened once more, Hanoi would have had to yield on the crucial point of withdrawing its forces from the South.[30] But as Kissinger well knew and Nixon explicitly ordered, the United States needed an agreement in hand by January 20, Inauguration Day, or the new Congress, in tune with public opinion, would deny funds for continuing the U.S. role in the war.[31] For practical purposes the United States had no leverage: the fuse of public support, already short, had been further burned down by the Christmas bombing and barely lasted another month.

Meanwhile, blunt exchanges between Nixon and Thieu continued, and in Paris, Kissinger repeated to South Vietnamese representatives a claim he had made to Thieu in October, that the United States had "secret assurances" from both the Soviet Union and China that they would not supply North Vietnam with large quantities of weapons for offensive purposes.[32] As far as one can tell from Kissinger's memoirs, the only basis for this claim was a few remarks made to him in Beijing and Moscow in May and June. This was apparently a case of simple deception—though hardly unique in the annals of alliance diplomacy during endgame situations.

There was, however, considerably more reality to the offer now extended formally to Hanoi, of reconstruction aid in large amounts.[33] In the draft agreement, the subject had been referred to only in a general statement of intent in Article 21, although Le Duc Tho occasionally sought a more explicit commitment.[34] When he did so again in January, Kissinger's team worked out with Tho's colleagues a formula. This promised that, shortly after the final signing, there would be a supplemental message from President Nixon undertaking to consider aid "in the range of" $3.25 billion over five years, and providing for a special commission to work out the details. From Hanoi's standpoint, this undertaking was surely a key part of the final deal.[35]

Such were the main inducements used by Nixon and Kissinger to get the agreement accepted by both North and South Vietnam. They knew well that the agreement was a bitter pill for Thieu to swallow and that it posed great risks for the future of South Vietnam. But they did not believe they could have gotten better terms, and they were prepared to go to great lengths to reassure Thieu for the future. In the process, they apparently never thought of discussing seriously with him what policies his government would follow thereafter—when the United States would remain critically involved and when Thieu's actions could make or break the agreement.[36]

In effect, North Vietnam had been bludgeoned into accepting the final form of the deal, and South Vietnam compelled to accept it. The negotiating process had thus made even more acute what would in any case have been, on both sides, intense suspicion and a desire to evade the agreement. Arnold Isaacs's conclusion is not too strong:

> By any fair standard, Nixon and Kissinger had treated their Vietnamese ally with contemptuous disregard, and their Vietnamese enemies with bad faith and brutality. In doing so, they had almost certainly magnified the enormous difficulties of enforcing the peace they had finally succeeded in negotiating.[37]

At the time, little of this background was known, especially not the secret pledges to Thieu of "full force" U.S. retaliation for "any" breach of the agreement by Hanoi. The tortuous three-way negotiating process seemed to have reached a triumphant conclusion on January 23, when Kissinger and

Le Duc Tho initialed the Paris Agreement. On January 27, Secretary of State Rogers signed for the United States in a formal ceremony.

3. What Was Agreed and What Was Expected

It took no great insight to see how full of holes the final Paris Agreement was.[38] A rare exception was the very precise terms for withdrawal of U.S. forces within sixty days and for release of U.S. and South Vietnamese military prisoners, with parallel releases of prisoners held by South Vietnam and the United States. On a related provision important to the United States then and later, however—promising cooperation in locating military personnel killed or missing—North Vietnam dragged its feet for years, saying it would comply only if the United States followed through on the promise of special economic aid.

As to the political process to be followed in South Vietnam, the provisions were deceptively concrete and detailed. The two South Vietnamese parties, the government and the Vietcong, were to negotiate arrangements for a three-headed council, bringing in "third force" political elements, and this council in turn was to set up elections for a new government. The practical levers, however, remained under Thieu's control. He was as unlikely to negotiate seriously to effect a compromise as North Vietnam was to let the Vietcong yield on any point of consequence. Thus, this provision was nearly 100 percent fake—which favored Saigon, since there was no way for Hanoi to press for carrying out the process.

Another key provision, also deceptively detailed, called for a cease-fire to be supervised by the four signers of the agreement. However, neither then nor later was there any delineation of which areas were controlled by which side or even where military units were located. With the two sides equally balanced in the supervisory commission, both sides could cheat as much as they thought they could get away with. As usual, South Vietnamese (or American) actions were likely to be more visible and reported by observers and the press than those of North Vietnam and the Vietcong.[39]

Another major example of deceptive detail was the provision forbidding the introduction and limiting the resupply of forces external to South Vietnam, meaning primarily American and North Vietnamese forces. Resupply could be replacement items only, with supervision by a new International Commission for Control and Supervision, which was evenly balanced between Communist and non-Communist members—Poland, Hungary, Canada, and Indonesia. (The three-nation International Control Commission, after the 1954 Geneva Accords, had had neutral India to break ties.) Apart from the impossibility of a working majority on any issue of violation, the new commission lacked mobility, communications, and everything else it needed to do the job. Nor was there agreement on entry points, or, most important, any head count of outside forces or inventory of externally supplied equipment in South Vietnam, such as had been done in 1954. In short, the provisions under this heading were another charade, this time in Hanoi's favor. One can readily surmise that the two charades were an important trade-off between Kissinger and Le Duc Tho. Each side got totally loose supervision in the area it cared most about.

The most controversial part of the agreement was Article 20, covering Laos and Cambodia. On its face, this bound all parties to respect the neutrality of both countries and refrain from using their own territory to "encroach" on other countries, while "foreign countries" (so defined as to include North Vietnam as well as the United States) were to end all military activities, withdraw their forces totally, and refrain from bringing back troops, military advisors, or military equipment. The fatal flaw, however, was that—on any reasonable reading—these obligations did not apply until a cease-fire was achieved. Whether this could be done was simply left to the local contending forces. As we have just seen, the North Vietnamese had given persuasive assurances that there would be a cease-fire in Laos, but refused to go beyond general predictions about one in Cambodia. Kissinger later claimed a "private understanding" with Tho that Hanoi would "contribute actively" to producing a cease-fire in Cambodia.[40] Only in 1986 was real light shed on what happened. On the basis of interviews with North Vietnamese and perhaps also Khmer Rouge sources, Nayan Chanda of *The Far Eastern Economic Review* recorded that several clandestine meetings were held in late 1972, coming to a climax in a two-day encounter on January 24–26, 1973 (just as the Paris Agreement was being signed), between Pol Pot, leader of the Khmer Rouge, and a member of Hanoi's Politburo. The North Vietnamese strongly urged accepting a cease-fire and warned that failure to do so would bring heavy punishment from America. Pol Pot rejected the idea "scornfully," arguing that victory was in sight and that the Lon Nol regime was "on its last legs." This convincing report not only shows that Hanoi made a real effort, but throws light on the state of mind that propelled the Khmer Rouge into their reckless offensive in the next six months. If the Khmer Rouge saw victory within reach, as Chanda reported, the desire to achieve it for themselves and not to be beholden to North Vietnam would also have become stronger.[41] Once again, the view that higher Communist states or organizations could control lower ones was shown up as false.

After the Paris Agreement, Kissinger and other Americans repeatedly asserted that the obligation of the North Vietnamese to withdraw from Cambodia was unconditional and not dependent on a cease-fire having been agreed. On its face, this contradicted Kissinger's own repeated statements to Le Duc Tho, that if a cease-fire offered by Lon Nol were not accepted, the United States would feel free to resume its own military actions in Cambodia. It was also contrary to the interpretation of the agreement by Kissinger's lawyer during the negotiations, to which we shall return.[42]

The basic situation in South Vietnam under the Paris Agreement must have been unique in the history of armistice agreements, and not only because of the tenuous character of these detailed provisions. One side (North Vietnam) retained a large military force within the territory of the other, and there were not even general descriptions, let alone defined boundaries, of the areas where that force was entitled to operate, or of the areas that were to be under the control of the legalized Communist political entity. To any serious observer familiar with the history of past armistice or "peace" agreements in Indochina, it must have seemed most unlikely that this one could hold together. The 1954 Geneva Accords in particular had been much more tightly constructed and effectively supported by outside nations, yet their political provisions had become a dead letter within two years, and from 1961 on, increasing hostilities eroded all barriers and restraints, destroying what had been a moderately useful International Control Commission.

The supervisory structure created in the 1973 agreement was not only far weaker than that of the 1954 Accords, but weaker even than the structure laid down in the 1962 Geneva Accords on Laos, which had quickly proved to be only a sounding board for protests. The four nations persuaded to serve on the new International Commission for Control and Supervision (ICCS) in early 1973 were not ill-chosen; Canada especially was acting in a spirit of public service, knowing well from earlier experience how difficult and thankless the task was likely to be. But the group lacked the international approval that had given the earlier post-1954 commission some semblance of legitimacy and stature, and it had neither the will nor the capacity even to identify violations of the agreement, let alone do anything about them.

Most important, neither of the contending Vietnamese parties intended to take more than a short tactical breather. North Vietnam meant to protect its substantial foothold in the South and in due course enlarge it toward complete control, while South Vietnam was determined to oust the North Vietnamese altogether and establish itself solidly as an independent nation. To neither party did the ineffectuality of the Paris Agreement come as a surprise — both assumed that the war would go on and that the agreement would be used mainly to pillory the other side while doing all one could for oneself.

On a larger scale, neither Hanoi nor, it is fair to say, Washington planned to interpret narrowly the provisions on equipment resupply. The North Vietnamese knew they could bring down to South Vietnam whatever they wanted. At once they set about creating a new supply route to run through remote South Vietnamese areas they could claim to control—and from which they could readily exclude the international commission. On the U.S. side, the visibility of U.S. points of access—mostly around Saigon—to the press, to the ICCS, and to the legitimized Communist missions meant that the United States would be hard put to violate the "replacement only" requirement on military supplies, at least for some time. On the other hand, as we have noted, the massive last-minute Enhance and Enhance Plus programs, together with the transfer to the South Vietnamese of U.S. equipment on existing military bases, were bound to appear to the North Vietnamese as willful evasions of the pending agreement, inviting a response.

Finally, to repeat, the most crucial element of all in the agreement—allowing North Vietnamese forces already in South Vietnam to remain (in numbers then estimated by U.S. intelligence at 140,000 men)—but not allowing new forces to be introduced, was simply and obviously unenforceable. Thieu had been right to make this the centerpiece of his objections since October, and the Americans knew it. In explaining the agreement to the press right after it was signed, Kissinger put a brave face on the matter, insisting that the agreement meant that the North Vietnamese contingent would be gradually reduced by attrition, as men had to return home. It was a wholly spurious argument. Both he and Nixon knew better. They simply felt they had no choice, given the state of American opinion.

On any reading, therefore, the Paris Agreement was weak, with key provisions transparently toothless. Those who negotiated it, and the Americans who accepted its completion with relief, may have supposed that sheer exhaustion would leave the situation in some sort of shape for a considerable time. Serious observers of the Second Indochina War were much less hopeful.

. . .

Was the agreement, all this being said, nonetheless as good as was reasonably attainable? How did South Vietnam's prospects for survival appear under it? How much did it owe to the improved U.S. relationships with China and the Soviet Union and to influence exerted by those nations on North Vietnam? And what was the realistic chance of future help from these quarters in keeping the peace?

Almost certainly, no better terms could have been secured. In the manifold writings about the war, few have attempted to assess how well the job was done. Some have asserted that Le Duc Tho outnegotiated Kissinger in getting permission for the North Vietnamese forces to remain in the South. To the contrary, one experienced American diplomat later judged that Kissinger "really distinguished himself" in the final negotiations by getting political provisions that were vague and favorable to Thieu, as well as a clear-cut U.S. right to continue economic and military aid.[43]

Both judgments are wide of the mark. Tho and Kissinger were sophisticated and well-prepared negotiators, and in the closing stages Kissinger had with him an able staff with a lot of experience of previous agreements in Indochina. If the agreement was crafted with a considerable degree of cynicism, even hypocrisy, on both sides, it was also done competently. Each side understood the other—all too well, one might say. The important exception was Kissinger's failure to grasp that the North Vietnamese genuinely could neither speak for nor pressure the Khmer Rouge about a Cambodian cease-fire. While this made an important difference in terms of expectations, the provision itself would not have been different.

It was, rather, in Nixon and Kissinger's dealings with their South Vietnamese ally that major errors were made. Thieu repeated his objections to leaving North Vietnamese forces in the South for months, but only in August was he told this was inescapable, and then by the already distrusted Kissinger rather than by Nixon. At no stage did either man really thrash out the subject with him. Nor was it, apparently, ever made clear and categorical to him that the American force withdrawal had to be total. Moreover, Kissinger in September and early October was much too insensitive to wording problems that helped to inflame Thieu. Other difficulties could not have been avoided, but this carelessness contributed substantially to Thieu's loss of confidence not only in Kissinger but to some degree in American good faith and resolve.

This is not to contend that major disagreements between Thieu and the top Americans could have been avoided. Nineteen sixty-eight had given a foretaste of Thieu's stubbornness and tactics, when much less had been at stake. He was bound to put up a big show of objecting to what he knew he could not prevent and would have to accept, and a measure of responsive obduracy by the North Vietnamese was also likely. With Nixon facing a January deadline, he might well have been driven to some sort of threat of renewed bombing, but hardly to the smashing Christmas attacks designed largely to reassure Thieu that his secret pledges would be carried out.

Errors by both Nixon and Kissinger made the last phase more difficult and painful than it need have been, perhaps with important consequences then and for the future. In the last analysis, however, the terms of the final Paris Agreement reflected accurately the bargaining leverage of the principal parties. Kissinger himself was fond of quoting what General Walter Bedell Smith, then Under Secretary of State, had said in 1954 of the first Geneva Accords: "Diplomacy has rarely been able to gain at the conference table what cannot be held on the battlefield." The United States had not lost, but the American public and Congress insisted that American forces and prisoners be brought home at once, which for bargaining purposes came to the same thing as losing. With almost no leverage except the threat of renewed bombing, Nixon and Kissinger managed to work out a nominally balanced set of provisions that did not appear to sentence South Vietnam to an early takeover if it performed adequately in its own defense.

As of January 27, 1973, as the remaining American forces prepared to withdraw, it was hard to judge South Vietnam's prospects objectively. It is symptomatic of the mood of the times that few in the United States attempted to guess, at least in public or on the record, just what its chances were. The overwhelming sentiment was one of relief, applause for Nixon and Kissinger — set against substantial moderate-to-vehement disapproval of the Christmas bombing — and, as to the future, suspended judgment. In a Gallup poll taken on January 26, the tally was 58–26 that this was "peace with honor," but 35–41 that the peace agreement was likely to last and 27–54 that South Vietnam would prove strong enough to hold out even against what the poll stated only as "political pressures." At the same time, the respondents were convinced (70–16) that Hanoi would try again to take over the South, presumably using military as well as political measures.[44] These were hardly optimistic expectations; experienced observers of the war and the two Vietnams would probably have been even more pessimistic about South Vietnam's chances of survival.

Yet Nixon and Kissinger can be excused for claiming otherwise at the time. Being upbeat was the only possible basis for future policy. What Kissinger really thought may have been a different matter, though. One of Nixon's two top personal aides, John Ehrlichman, recalled in his 1982 memoir that on January 24, he found himself next to Kissinger at a White House function and asked him casually how long he thought the South Vietnamese regime could survive and that Kissinger replied, "I think that if they're lucky they can hold out for a year and a half."[45] To be sure, Ehrlichman was often critical of Kissinger. This would not have been true of Marvin and Bernard Kalb, journalists who knew Kissinger and were sympathetic to him. Writing in 1974, they described a candid conversation a few months after the agreement, in which Kissinger said Nixon had been tougher than he himself wished to be in the concluding stages. From this and presumably other conversations over the years, the Kalbs recorded this clear impression:

> Kissinger had a bleaker vision of Saigon's future than Nixon. He believed that the most that could be salvaged from the U.S. involvement in Vietnam was a "decent interval" between an American pullout and the possibility of a Communist take-over. In the best of all Vietnamese worlds, nothing could be ensured for more than three or four years.[46]

It was a realistic appraisal, even as the situation stood at the time the agreement was signed.

Both at the time and later, Nixon, Kissinger, and their associates claimed that the Paris Agreement was in effect the third act in a magnificent 1972 sequence—that the opening to Beijing and the détente with Moscow led straight to North Vietnam's making the necessary concessions. On the contrary, the defeat of the Easter offensive, the American bombing of the North, and general exhaustion were almost certainly more powerful causes. In any case, once negotiations got under way, evidence of any kind of Soviet or Chinese influence is virtually nonexistent. In his memoirs, Nixon wrote of jogging Foreign Minister Gromyko in October and Ambassador Dobrynin in December, the latter assuring him that the Soviet Union was indeed pressing North Vietnam to accept the draft agreement as it then stood.[47] Nixon went on to make the revealing statement that in January "we continued to play the Soviet and Chinese strategies *for whatever they might turn out to be worth.*"[48] But neither American ever claimed that there was any significant Soviet or Chinese influence in the last phase. Finally, there is Kissinger's January 1973 claim, to assorted South Vietnamese in conversations in Paris, that he had some sort of assurance that Moscow and Beijing would reduce their military support for Hanoi after the Paris Agreement went into force. From every standpoint, such a claim—unsupported by other evidence—seems implausible. Certainly it was not borne out by Soviet and Chinese behavior in later years.

To sum up, the best reading of the evidence is that after about July 1972 both Moscow and Beijing simply stood aside, neither wishing to lose any part of its new relationship to the United States, least of all in favor of the other, but neither, equally, wishing to lose influence with North Vietnam. Neither the Chinese nor the Soviet leaders envisaged or favored the survival of an independent, non-Communist South Vietnam. Whether they were prepared even to try to restrain North Vietnam after the Paris Agreement remained to be seen, but the record of their past competition for Hanoi's favor would have suggested grave doubt that either would make such an effort or, even more, that either of them could.

4. The First Two Months of the Second Term

For the American public, February and March 1973 were dominated, almost to the exclusion of other events, by the return from Vietnam of the last 25,000 American troops and the release, at long last, of the nearly 600 prisoners of war who came home in four batches ending on March 28.[49] The troops, like their predecessors, were welcomed with relief, but with few demonstrations of gratitude for a thankless job carried out to the end. The

POWs were a different story. Mostly officer fliers in the Navy and Air Force, their periods of captivity dated back in some cases to mid-1964 and early 1965. They had been kept in various locations, at first scattered around North Vietnam. After a failed rescue attempt aimed at the remote Son Tay prison camp in late 1970 alarmed the North Vietnamese, they were brought together at the infamous "Hanoi Hilton" central prison. The prisoners had never been permitted visits from the International Red Cross, monitor of the Geneva Conventions on the treatment of prisoners, since North Vietnam refused to accept the Conventions as applicable to what it consistently asserted to be a Vietnamese civil conflict. A few had been paraded to visiting antiwar Americans or done propaganda broadcasts. Their behavior on these occasions had unmistakably indicated coercion.

As they now returned, to receptions both somber and joyous, the Administration sought initially to restrain their accounts of how they had been treated, lest these risk interrupting the release process. But enough leaked out to establish almost at once that they had all been subjected to a pattern of hardship, deprivation, isolation, and psychological pressure, with a great many cases of torture and sustained physical ill treatment that crippled and maimed their victims. Several hero leaders had displayed extraordinary fortitude; hardly any prisoners had flinched or caved in.

The reports and pictures of these POWs aroused intense national pride and equally intense outrage over the behavior of their captors. Previous government disclosures, based on the little that could then be learned, had been seen through a glass darkly. Now the country was face to face, often on television, with a stark and ugly picture. People were angry with the North Vietnamese as never before. The shock and indignation, however, did not translate into a firming of national resolve for the United States to continue to support South Vietnam under new conditions and without the use of U.S. forces. Rather, Americans were exhausted and fed up, with a heightened sense that America was well rid of the whole experience.

As Nixon and Kissinger should have foreseen, but apparently did not, the increased hostility toward North Vietnam unleashed by the POWs' stories very shortly came to affect sentiment toward plans for reconstruction aid there. In a memorandum handed over shortly after the main Paris Agreement, the United States had offered—subject to the consent of Congress and by implication to Hanoi's complying with the agreement—a tentative figure of $3.25 billion over five years. Although this idea had long been brewing, the record does not show that either Nixon or Kissinger had discussed it with leaders in Congress. Like all else in their plans for preserving the agreement, this project depended on Nixon's having, at the crucial time, such great prestige that he could override opposition or reservations.

In those first weeks it seemed to most observers that he did have that kind of power. A 68 percent approval rating in a Gallup poll at the beginning of February was the highest he had ever attained, reflecting general acceptance of his claim that the Paris Agreement represented "peace with honor." Kissinger's articulate press conference after the signing, explaining and interpreting the agreement, at first persuaded many that the United States had obtained more concessions than Hanoi. The Christmas bombing seemed at least partly vindicated. Few stopped to ask whether the terms achieved in January were really all that different from those available in October, still less to assess the reactions in Saigon and the complex three-way relationships that had compelled Nixon to resort to the bombing. Only the outcome counted, for the moment. When asked how the United States should react if Hanoi again attacked South Vietnam, the sample showed 50–38 against sending even military aid and 71–17 against renewed U.S. bombing operations in Vietnam.[50]

After working on the reconstruction aid memorandum in Paris, Kissinger set off on a round of visits in East Asia, leaving out Phnom Penh, where there was no cease-fire, and Saigon, where Thieu, as he knew, had come to hate and distrust him. He went successively to Bangkok, to Vientiane in Laos, then to Hanoi (for the first time), with Beijing as the climax. As his account of this trip made clear, only the last was a pleasant stop.[51]

In Thailand, never a battle zone but now home to the U.S. Seventh Air Force, and the last country where the SEATO alliance still had meaning, he could sound a believable note of reassurance that the United States would continue with past policy and relationships. He could hardly do the same in Laos, where the cease-fire was about to be agreed on. This set off political negotiations that were to drag on until they produced a weak coalition government in September. Hanoi did not even pretend to withdraw its troops in Laos. Plainly it meant not only to keep the Ho Chi Minh Trail in full operation but to exert constant pressure in the rest of Laos, so that the eventual outcome would be a Communist government controlling the whole country. Kissinger's toast to the gallant Souvanna Phouma — telling him that the United States had not come this far to let its friends down — was at best extravagantly optimistic, at worst faintly cynical. The inescapable fact was that the withdrawal of U.S. ground forces from Indochina left Souvanna, always at the end of the line, in a hopeless position. Worn out by the years of warfare, he made no effort to resist the cease-fire or to continue the fight by asking for continued U.S. bombing, although he was prepared to wink at sporadic U.S. air attacks on the trail areas in eastern Laos.

In Cambodia, Lon Nol at once complied with U.S. urging and put out a formal appeal for a cease-fire, but did so on terms so one-sided toward immediate Communist surrender that the Khmer Rouge had an excuse for not responding. In the nearly three years since the incursion and then the withdrawal of American ground forces, every trend had favored the KR.

They were by now much larger and better armed, with 40,000 to 50,000 fighting men, while North Vietnamese forces operating against Lon Nol had been reduced to a few thousand. Lon Nol now controlled only Phnom Penh, a few provincial towns, and the southwestern part of the country. The rest was in the hands of the Khmer Rouge, except for slightly enlarged North Vietnamese base and supply areas along the Vietnamese border. They had no reason to accept a cease-fire, and every reason to keep up and even increase the pressure. The surprise and indignation expressed by Nixon and Kissinger, then and later, smacked of a false front, or at best self-deception. Once again, as in their long failure to understand the limited influence of Moscow or Beijing on Hanoi itself, they found it hard to grasp that the Khmer Rouge were not under Hanoi's control.

As in 1970 President Nixon was not prepared to stand aside and let matters take their course. Thieu argued that a quick Communist takeover of Cambodia would complicate the problem of defending South Vietnam, for psychological reasons alone, and to Nixon, Kissinger, and Alexander Haig, still a key advisor on Cambodian matters from his new position as Vice Chief of Staff of the Army, the stakes were personal as well as practical. It was clearly hopeless to reduce North Vietnamese use of their base areas, or to engage their forces, but the American objective must still be, they believed, to keep Lon Nol afloat somehow just as long as possible. And for this the tool was ready at hand, with the Seventh Air Force and part of the Eighth in Thailand, able to bring to bear the formidable force of B-52s and tactical bombers assembled there for the Christmas bombing.[52] Nixon's last resort weapon, his hole card in preserving the Paris Agreement, remained the threat of renewed bombing of North Vietnam itself, as he had done the previous May and December. Only if he kept airpower at full and visible capacity would this threat be real to Hanoi, especially during the testing first months.

The bombing of Cambodia was therefore resumed in early February without any formal announcement and with deliberately low-key justifications given in response to inquiries. The intended impression was that this was simply a minor bit of unfinished business that would soon result in a cease-fire similar to those in Laos and South Vietnam. With no cease-fire yet agreed and with the United States acting in Cambodia at the request of its official government, the action had at least a color of justification under international law: without an armistice, both sides in a conflict normally continue to fight. Nor did the Paris Agreement make the obligation to withdraw foreign forces firm and unconditional.

More important than international law, however, there should have been larger questions within Nixon's circle of advisors. Could the bombing have any useful effect to justify the damage done and the inevitable casualties, including civilians? Finally, was there any basis, under the American Constitution and in light of Nixon's own statement after the Cambodian incursion, for the President on his own to resume bombing there?

For a time the American public paid almost no attention to what was happening in Cambodia, where media reporting had long been sparse. More and more, the dispirited, inept, and corrupt Cambodian Army was giving ground, while Lon Nol himself, with a severe physical ailment, was less and less in control.[53] In this situation a few press reports did arouse concern over civilian casualties and control of the bombing. The Senate Foreign Relations Committee in late March ordered two veteran members of its staff, James Lowenstein and Richard Moose, to visit the area, with the situation in Cambodia a top priority.

As always, however, it was on Vietnam that the public, as well as Nixon and Kissinger, focused — when its attention was not on the returning POWs. When Thieu spoke to the South Vietnamese people on the day the agreement was signed, his words could hardly have been in greater contrast to what was being said that day in Washington. He made no pretense of satisfaction and said bluntly that to believe that the Communists would respect the cease-fire was simply "naive and erroneous." He was right. The shooting did not stop, even for a day. The tempo of war in fact picked up, in large part through actions by the South Vietnamese forces. In the weeks before the cease-fire, it was the North Vietnamese who had been more active, trying to grab as much territory as possible, which they could then claim to control when the cease-fire went into effect. Thieu had a lot of justification for redressing the balance, but he quickly went beyond recapturing areas the Communists had just seized. Seeing his military position at a high point — and feeling insured against sharp counterattack by Nixon's secret pledge of renewed United States bombing — he set out to reap all the gains he could. It was a strategy that during the year was to produce some expansion of the areas under government control. But it also seemed to the press in Saigon that South Vietnam was the principal initial violator of the cease-fire.

On the record now available, the United States did nothing to discourage this strategy. While the American public thus got a picture of South Vietnam on the offensive, U.S. intelligence piled up convincing evidence, most of it from air photography in Laos and Cambodia, that North Vietnam was sending a great deal of equipment to the South. Much of the flow may have entered South Vietnam before the Paris Agreement. To a large extent the North Vietnamese were only doing what the United States had done with its Enhance airlift programs, stocking up and setting up high ceilings for future replacement levels. U.S. airlift capacity had permitted quick and large anticipatory equipment transfers, while Hanoi's capacity for concealment allowed it to get away with grabbing territory on the quiet at the last moment. As it supported Thieu's land grabs, the United States was in a weak position to argue that Hanoi's supply actions (on a much smaller scale than the Enhance programs) were serious violations.

No such refined analysis hampered Kissinger. He quickly concluded, with Nixon, that the North Vietnamese had decided to test the United States right away. During his visit to Hanoi in mid-February, he presented an initial compilation of violations to North Vietnamese leaders, but got only evasive replies.[54] Meanwhile, the machinery envisaged under the Paris Agreement began to move creakily. By early March, a formal international conference had convened in Paris to push ahead with support for the various multilateral supervisory commissions, and on March 15 there was a first meeting of the U.S.–North Vietnam working group to refine estimates of reconstruction needs as a basis for the projected U.S. aid program. But in South Vietnam itself the ICCS was already hamstrung by its two-to-two structure, with Poland and Hungary refusing to certify any Communist violations. In particular, the ban on sending more forces or equipment save on a replacement basis was, predictably, a farce from the start. The two sides could not agree even on entry points, much less on policing them or supplying inventories of what was already in the country. Moreover, when the commission's staff did seek to visit the scene of disputed military actions, they were given little help by the Saigon government and were fired on by the Communist side. When two helicopters were downed with many casualties in early April, Canada gave vent to understandable feelings of frustration and disillusionment, suggesting that it might soon withdraw.

By early March hundreds of North Vietnamese tanks and trucks were observed moving into South Vietnam. In Washington, James Schlesinger, the new Director of Central Intelligence, estimated that at this rate of resupply the North Vietnamese forces would be as well equipped by fall as they had been before the 1972 Easter offensive.[55] The possibility of some sharp U.S. response moved to the fore. Kissinger later recorded that four warning notes were sent to Hanoi in the first two weeks of March: if its actions continued, the notes said, the consequences would be "most grave." On March 8 he tackled Ambassador Dobrynin, who was evasive, suggesting that the Chinese had hijacked Soviet equipment and were now sending it in and seeking to blame Moscow! A similar warning to the Chinese elicited only an ambiguous response.[56] By then, Kissinger and Nixon should have realized that their hopes that China and the Soviet Union would limit their flow of supplies to Hanoi after the Paris Agreement—hopes that Kissinger had raised to the level of assurances in his appeals to the South Vietnamese to go along with the agreement—were made of dust and paper. Hanoi was not about to let up in playing its two suppliers off against each other, and the deep hostility between the two only made each more forthcoming. One more asserted prop for the survival of South Vietnam was shown to be a delusion.

On March 14, the crisis management group chaired by Kissinger, WSAG, formally recommended to Nixon a strong two- to three-day bombing program aimed directly at the routes in Laos and North Vietnam over which the supplies and new forces were moving. The next day, Nixon at a press conference charged Hanoi with serious violations and recalled the Easter and Christmas bombings, but he never hinted that he had made promises to Thieu or revealed the nature of those promises.[57] One Nixon watcher noted a "palpable chill" in the pressroom after the President's remarks:

> Did he mean it this time? I think he did, although questions would arise in the next few days about his authority to act on his own. . . . But I suspect that Mr. Nixon, despite the furies certain to be aroused in Congress and in the country, would again prove himself capable of taking the kind of retaliatory action he has taken before if he thought it necessary.[58]

Editorials in *The New York Times* and *The Washington Post* soon opposed such action in strong terms.[59] Tension rose sharply.

Within the Administration, Kissinger kept pushing, even from a vacation in Mexico, for a short demonstrative set of strikes against the supply lines in Laos. However, the President kept putting him off. In any event, Kissinger believed that diplomacy should go on concurrently with renewed bombing. Seizing on a suggestion from Hanoi, he formally proposed a meeting with Le Duc Tho in Paris, which was set for May.[60] Kissinger, it should be noted, was at this point frenetically active on every front except contact with members of Congress. His White House position precluded his testifying before congressional committees, but it is striking that he never joined in any consultation with Congress and apparently made little if any effort to understand where its members stood and how they were likely to react.

Meanwhile, the departure of the last American prisoners and forces from South Vietnam on March 28 had foreseeably raised the question of Nixon's authority to bomb without some form of consent or acquiescence from Congress. As many editorials noted, Nixon himself had said, on July 1, 1970, that the protection of American forces was the sole remaining basis for his authority to conduct military operations in Indochina. Though that justification no longer existed, the bombing in Cambodia continued.

On Thursday evening, March 29, after welcoming the last group of released prisoners, Nixon went on national television to sound a note of achievement, which many Americans accepted. But beneath the surface, his policy toward Indochina was in a confused and uncertain state. The sixty days since the Paris Agreement had seen a marked change in the mood in America. New and serious problems and doubts had arisen; only the troop withdrawal and release of the prisoners had been accomplished as the Paris Agreement prescribed. It was hardly the opening act of the new term that Nixon had planned and visualized. Nor had he foreseen that on the very next day, the 30th, the Watergate burglary he had monitored and worried about for months would break open for all to see.

5. *Watergate Becomes a Crisis*

On June 17, 1972, James McCord was one of five burglars arrested in the act of breaking into the headquarters of the Democratic National Committee in the Watergate building complex in Washington. A former CIA officer concerned only with security, McCord seemed somewhat different from the hardened covert operators caught with him — especially the ringleaders, E. Howard Hunt and G. Gordon Liddy. To investigate the burglary, Federal District Judge John Sirica convened a grand jury, which in mid-September indicted the five, all of whom denied that any other persons were involved. Finding this unlikely, Sirica maintained the grand jury, waiting for trial and sentencing to put pressure on the burglars to come clean. A Republican appointed to the bench by President Eisenhower, Sirica had a reputation as an especially upright and tough judge, known in the District of Columbia as "Maximum John" for the severity of his sentences.

At their trial in January 1973, the five were quickly convicted. All again said that no others were involved, and Judge Sirica set their sentencing for March 23, aiming again to put pressure on the men. That day, four of the five accepted their sentences, which were severe. McCord instead handed the judge a letter, which attracted attention as a possible break in the case. Sirica gave the letter as relevant evidence to the Ervin Committee staff, and on March 30 headlines proclaimed that McCord had identified senior officials in the White House and in the President's personal campaign organization, the Committee to Re-elect the President (CRP, or CREEP), as having had advance knowledge of the break-ins. It was the first in a series of revelations that turned "Watergate" into a full-fledged crisis.

. . .

Let us wind the reel back to June 1972. After the burglary, money found on the burglars was quickly traced to funds held by CRP. Still, the prevailing view through the summer and fall was that the burglars' actions had not been authorized by the President or any senior official in the White House. This supposition seemed confirmed on September 15, when Sirica's grand jury handed down indictments of the burglars without implicating any higher-ups.

In October, however, *The Washington Post* published a series of stories revealing campaign "dirty tricks" concocted by men with links to CRP and the White House, and the use of campaign funds to pay the lawyers for the burglars, linking these actions explicitly to H. R. Haldeman, Nixon's top personal assistant. Walter Cronkite, oracle of CBS News, with enormous public credibility, played up the *Post* stories in two October newscasts, focusing primarily on prodigal Republican spending and loose rules for campaign contributions. Both the *Post* and Cronkite acted with great courage and in the highest traditions of journalism, in the face of nasty pressures from Nixon people to lay off. But the later legend that the *Post* stories were mainly, even solely, responsible for the exposure of the Watergate burglary and cover-up is not supported by the record.

This legend was consolidated and apparently confirmed by *All the President's Men*, a book written by the two principal *Post* reporters, Bob Woodward and Carl Bernstein, and by the motion picture based on the book. These gave a dramatic account of the reporters' work, including clandestine meetings with a never identified government source christened "Deep Throat." The actual disclosures were not spelled out in the film, but a strong impression was left that these included the background and responsibility for the Watergate burglary. This apparent claim was erroneous. In fact, the *Post*'s articles throughout the election period of 1972 covered other "dirty tricks" extensively, but had only glancing references to the burglary. The *Post*'s enterprise kept the pot stirring, but the issue of dirty tricks attracted only moderate public attention outside of Washington, and the Watergate burglary still less. When the *Post*'s well-known cartoonist, Herbert Block, later published a small book of his contemporary cartoons, which were savage and right on target, he included as an appendix a report by Haynes Johnson, a top political reporter at the *Post*, on travels around the country in the last months of 1972 and the first months of 1973. Johnson reported that during this period the people he talked with did not even mention the Watergate burglary.[61] It appears, therefore, that the *Post* stories reached informed opinion, certainly the Washington audience, but not the public at large. This fits with the conclusion of Theodore White, historian of presidential campaigns, that revelations about Republican campaign behavior did not have a major effect on the 1972 election.

Nor was the issue of campaign behavior pressed by Democratic candidates or leaders — with one crucial exception. Senator Mike Mansfield, the Democratic Majority Leader, declared in Montana in September that the Watergate burglary was beyond the pale and needed to be investigated further. After the election, Mansfield quickly moved to set up a Select Committee, chaired by Senator Sam Ervin of North Carolina, with a broad mandate to look into dubious campaign activities in 1972 and recommend appropriate legislation. The Ervin Committee was formally established by the Senate in February 1973, and it was to its chief lawyer, Samuel Dash, that Sirica sent a copy of McCord's letter, triggering the March 30 disclosure.

Post publisher Katharine Graham (who incurred Nixon's special wrath), managing editor Benjamin Bradlee, the two reporters, and all concerned at the paper deserved immense credit for courage and enterprise. The legend is a good one, but in the end it was not the *Post* (or the Ervin Committee) but rather Sirica's pressure on McCord that produced the first crucial disclosures.[62]

. . .

How was Richard Nixon affected by all this? Through the last six months of 1972 and into the new year, he handled the Vietnam negotiations, the Christmas bombing, and the completion of the Paris Agreement—then the only major foreign policy problem on his plate—with little apparent distraction or other effect from the Watergate affair. He seems to have been able to put it to one side. His confidence in his future power was reflected in his secret pledges to Thieu.

Beginning in January, however, there was (according to Kissinger's later memoir) a falling off in the President's decisiveness and grasp. Later evidence confirmed that he had a series of worry sessions with Charles Colson and others of his staff. Only in mid-March, however, did the full gravity of the situation hit home. A series of talks between Nixon and John Dean, the White House counsel who was secretly in charge of the cover-up, came to a head on March 21, when Dean told the President (on a recorded tape) that the burglars were no longer prepared to accept the prison sentences and other hardships that they and their families faced, and that it would take large sums to keep them from talking. Nixon waffled in the face of this ugly choice, not appearing to rule out such payments while telling Dean that of course they would be illegal.

But he knew how serious it now was, and McCord's statement cannot have come as a great surprise. Only then did congressional and public concern heat up. Over the next two weeks a series of news stories reported that first McCord and then Dean and Jeb Magruder, deputy to John Mitchell, the former Attorney General who had become head of CRP the year before, were revealing a great deal to the Justice Department and the Ervin Committee staff. Smoldering became flame in mid-April. With a compliant Justice Department official keeping him abreast of what his subordinates were disclosing, Nixon then learned that they had implicated not only Mitchell but also Haldeman and Ehrlichman. On April 17 he made his first public statement, trying to stall by claiming that the White House itself had been looking for "the truth" since March 21. Thereafter, in quick succession:

This line of defense collapsed, and on April 30 Nixon was forced to announce the resignations of Haldeman and Ehrlichman and, for some reassurance, the appointment of the upright Elliot Richardson as Attorney General in place of the marginally implicated Richard Kleindienst. Alexander Haig, by this time a four-star general, was brought back to the White House as the new Chief of Staff, and John Connally and Melvin Laird were brought in as part-time White House advisors.

William Ruckelshaus became Acting Director of the FBI, succeeding the unfortunate Patrick Gray, who had "cracked" in his March confirmation hearings and disclosed the destruction of Watergate-related evidence. Ruckelshaus shortly learned of, and in May made public, the fact that from 1969 to 1971 there had been illegal White House wiretaps on officials and journalists suspected of having leaked the May 1969 *New York Times* story about the secret bombing of Cambodia.

One of John Dean's early disclosures to the Justice Department was that in August 1971 a burglary team set up from the White House had broken into the Los Angeles offices of a Dr. Fielding, psychiatrist to Daniel Ellsberg, the leaker of the Pentagon Papers, seeking evidence to discredit him. When the Justice Department conveyed this information to Judge Matthew Byrne, presiding at Ellsberg's trial in Los Angeles on the charge of theft of the Papers, Judge Byrne revealed the burglary and its purposes and dismissed the case.

With the clamor rapidly rising, by mid-May Nixon was under irresistible public and congressional pressure to appoint a Special Prosecutor independent of his control. Given the task of nominating a lawyer for the post (there being at that time no legislation on the subject, as was later enacted), Attorney General designate Richardson sounded out a number of senior trial lawyers of different political tendencies and encountered considerable reluctance to take on the job. He finally proposed Professor Archibald Cox of the Harvard Law School, a Democrat and former Solicitor General under President Kennedy, with an exceptional reputation for integrity and thoroughness.[63] Nixon felt compelled to accept the nomination, unpalatable as he probably found it. Though the choice of Cox as Special Prosecutor was not subject to Senate confirmation, the Senate Judiciary Committee, when it acted to confirm Richardson as Attorney General, extracted from him a categorical understanding (presumably with Nixon's authority) that Cox would not be dismissed for any reason short of extreme misconduct.

On May 17, the Ervin Committee began televised hearings, first with the small fish and then dramatically, in June, with the testimony of Jeb Magruder and John Dean. The latter's revelations dominated national attention during the last week of June, as he described the measures taken to cover up CRP and White House involvement in the burglary. In July, separate confirmation hearings for a new Air Force Chief of Staff elicited the story of the secret bombing of Cambodia in 1969–71, along with the falsification of records to conceal it. The secret bombing would probably have come to light regardless of Watergate, but the disclosure had special impact coming when it did.[64]

Even more dramatically, a member of the White House staff, Alexander Butterfield, testified to the Ervin Committee in mid-July that since February 1971, President Nixon had maintained a voice-activated taping system in his offices. This had produced voluminous tapes of conversations, indexed in a master log showing entries on crucial dates in the Watergate chronology. Both the Ervin Committee and the Cox office at once requested all the tapes and were abruptly turned down by the White House on grounds of executive privilege — a long-accepted doctrine that the White House could withhold information on the details of high-level official deliberations. Cox then asked Judge Sirica to compel disclosure of specified tapes, on the ground that they might bear on wrongdoing or criminal acts. Meanwhile, John Ehrlichman testified for several intense days at the end of July, and H. R. Haldeman more briefly. Both confirmed that most of the inner circle in the White House staff had been deeply involved in the cover-up, but denied that Nixon himself had been.

Finally, in mid-August, as Judge Sirica considered Cox's request for tapes, and the Ervin Committee recessed to let its staff work on a draft report, the nation's television sets clicked off in daytime, after more than two months of the most intense public exposure and attention any matter has received in American history. Polls showed that 98 percent of the public now knew of the scandal. Opinion was divided over Nixon's involvement. In a Gallup poll taken in August, 9 percent thought he had been in on the planning of the burglary and another 28 percent that he had known of it in advance, while 36 percent believed he had not known of it, but had been in on the cover-up; only 15 percent thought he had been candid about his own role or had acted promptly to bring the facts to light. Yet the same poll showed strong public opposition, 61–26, to any move to impeach the President on the basis of what was then known. Badly wounded, Nixon did not seem beyond recovery or in danger of total destruction.[65]

During this first traumatic period, from April to August 1973, Nixon's public approval rating dropped from 68 percent in early February to 40 percent in late July.[66] At least as important, as the White House tapes later showed, he was distracted by his own efforts to devise successive evasions, each of which promptly broke down, and then by a steady barrage of revelations that made him look worse and worse and to which he had no response. As Theodore White noted, Washington became a terrible place to him. He was there for only thirteen days in May, ten in June, twelve in July (seven of these in the hospital with pneumonia), and five in August. On most of the days he was present, he was greeting high-level foreign visitors who had been invited in the confident days of January and February.

. . .

Congress had been out of play during the fall because of the election campaign, and in the new year reconvened just as the Paris Agreement was being concluded. Despite the Democratic majorities in both houses, many in Washington felt at the time that Nixon had so much prestige that the Nixon presidency was now more powerful than any since Johnson's 1965 honeymoon or Eisenhower's first years. Above all, the President and Kissinger, jointly named by *Time* magazine as "Men of the Year" in its New Year's edition, seemed so skilled and successful in foreign policy that in this area, at least, the President would be in near-total control.

It was this power, apparently confirmed and on display in his March 29 speech welcoming home the prisoners, that was now to be tested, much sooner and more seriously than he had anticipated. In early April, Nixon and Kissinger were preparing for Leonid Brezhnev's return visit to America for a June summit; Kissinger was planning a major speech to kick off a "Year of Europe," designed to restore and reshape Atlantic relations; and Senator Henry Jackson was pressing for Soviet concessions on Jewish emigration, linked to Nixon's planned expansion of Soviet-American economic exchanges and thus to his whole détente policy. But by far the most pressing foreign policy problem was getting the situation in Indochina settled down.

6. Congress Asserts Its Will

As the North Vietnamese buildup became clear in March, the bombing program recommended to Nixon called for only a few days of bombing of the supply lines in Laos and southern North Vietnam. By April, Kissinger was thinking in stronger terms. His meeting with Le Duc Tho now set, he proposed to bring Hanoi to heel by at least a week, perhaps even a month, of concentrated moderate-scale bombing.

On April 2, President Thieu came to San Clemente, the Western White House, for two days of private talks with Nixon. Reporters thought the visit went well, and Thieu seemed satisfied with a bland communiqué. It was a correct reading, for Nixon privately reiterated the undertaking Thieu cared most about, the secret pledge of "full force" reaction to serious violations by Hanoi.[67] The President took the occasion to state his intention to ask Congress to approve $1.6 billion in continued military aid to South Vietnam after June 30, the same level as in the 1973 fiscal year (exclusive of the very large Enhance programs). In doing so, Nixon made no effort to influence a public sentiment now visibly dubious of, if not hostile toward, such action.[68]

Thieu's personal confidence in Nixon was doubtless reaffirmed. Yet he cannot have helped noting that when he moved on to Washington for the formal part of his visit, with Vice President Spiro Agnew serving as host, his reception was extraordinarily subdued. A state dinner at the White House attracted few distinguished private citizens, a mere handful of members of Congress, and almost no Cabinet members or senior officials from the Nixon Administration itself! It was a clear indication of turning away from Vietnam, as well as how little regard there was for Thieu himself. To Kissinger it was "a shaming experience."[69]

In a Washington press conference, Thieu put a damper on talk of a U.S. commitment to future military action, by a categorical statement that he would never again ask for U.S. troops, and by expressing confidence in his government's ability to handle any foreseeable situation. This and the mood of the Thieu visit led the astute James Reston to conclude on April 8 that Nixon's March 15 threats had been a bluff.[70] Certainly, by April 17, when Nixon made his first public statement about Watergate, any thought of bombing North Vietnam had evaporated.

Kissinger later contended that the "normal Nixon would have been enraged" by North Vietnam's actions, but by early April "Watergate Nixon" (his phrase) was unable to concentrate, dithered, and lost the opportunity to respond.[71] Nixon's recollection was different. Agreeing that the failure to attack North Vietnam itself or its forces moving south through Laos was "a major mistake," he wrote in 1985:

It was not a failure of presidential will—I was willing to act—but an erosion of congressional support. Whenever I had spoken of retaliation, a tremor of opposition rippled through Congress, and with each recurrence it had grown more intense.[72]

After mid-April no threat of bombing was uttered in Washington save as a theoretical possibility. There were two days of bombing of the Ho Chi Minh Trail in Laos, and in another gesture the United States suspended the clearing of mines in North Vietnamese harbors called for under the Paris Agreement. By April 23 Kissinger was reduced, on a public occasion, to complaining of the difficulty "if we can neither threaten nor offer incentives." Murrey Marder of *The Washington Post* concluded that "three months after coming into force, the vaunted Indochina accord is disintegrating."[73]

Meanwhile Congress had begun to go beyond restiveness, first on issues related to the President's fiscal power and then on both the wisdom and presidential authority in the bombing of Cambodia. As part of his plan for centralized and more conservative government in his second term, Nixon had set out in the new year not only to present a greatly revised budget for fiscal year 1974, with much less spending for social programs, but to seek the same ends at once by impounding funds already voted for the current fiscal year 1973. By March he had announced impoundments totaling several hundred million dollars, affecting domestic programs highly valued by many in Congress of both parties. Other Presidents had delayed or withheld spending on a limited scale; none had acted so provocatively and with so little consultation. The Senate reacted promptly and vehemently. After several days of vigorous debate, on April 4 it approved, by a 70–24 vote, an amendment providing that presidential impoundments could not stand unless affirmatively approved by Congress. It was the beginning of a major confrontation that in 1974 produced new legal rules on the subject, with the House eventually moving in the same direction.

The following day, in what was really a consecutive debate, the Senate voted to assert its power of the purse on the Administration's proposal for reconstruction aid to North Vietnam—a crucial part of Nixon's plans to preserve the Paris Agreement. By that time the bilateral North Vietnamese–American Commission in Paris had reached virtual agreement on the outlines of a reconstruction program. But on April 5, the Senate voted, by an overwhelming 88–3 margin, that no funds from any source could be applied to this purpose without Congress's specific approval! The debate, in which the treatment of American prisoners figured heavily, made it abundantly clear that for the foreseeable future congressional approval was out of the question. In the debate, also, Senator Mansfield asked how the President could expect Congress to allow money to be spent to attack North Vietnamese forces with one hand, while being asked to approve or accept economic aid to the North with the other. It was a stumbling block that should have been foreseen by Nixon or Kissinger. These demonstrations of a much more assertive attitude on Capitol Hill were bipartisan, and came before Watergate revelations had major public impact.

. . .

Congressional concern now focused on the bombing in Cambodia. In February and March, most of the attacks had been against the North Vietnamese base areas in the east and northeast, where they attracted little notice and only a faint groundswell of protest. But in April, with the Khmer Rouge gaining ground and closing in on Phnom Penh, the weight of attacks was greatly increased and most of the bombs fell on central Cambodia. All told, in the four months after the Paris Agreement, over 80,000 tons of bombs were dropped in Cambodia. Arnold Isaacs later told how it seemed from Phnom Penh:

> As government troops kept giving ground, the sounds of the bombing drew closer to the capital. On days and nights when action was heavy on

one or another of the fronts around the city, the drumroll of B-52 bombloads erupting on the torn earth seemed never to stop.[74]

To what end? Isaacs noted that few observers in Cambodia "could see any purpose in the air offensive" — no chance that the Khmer Rouge would relent and accept a cease-fire, or that the attacks would expel the North Vietnamese or do anything but slow down slightly the pace of the Khmer Rouge gains.[75]

By April, media reports were more and more disturbing to members of Congress. Editorial comment began to focus on the question of legal authority as well as on the whole policy in Cambodia. Both were challenged by *The Washington Post* in strong editorials on March 30 and April 3, the first concluding that "Nixon bombs to save a policy which, in its Cambodian aspect, was bankrupt from the start" and the second that "The Constitution does not authorize the President to bomb foreign countries at his own discretion."[76]

On a field trip, Lowenstein and Moose of the Senate Foreign Relations Committee staff soon learned of the new emphasis on bombing in central Cambodia, unrelated to North Vietnamese activities against South Vietnam, and found evidence of substantial involvement by the American Embassy in operational matters — both apparently in violation of the Cooper-Church Amendment of 1970 governing U.S. support operations in Cambodia. They cabled a summary of their observations to the committee.[77]

In Congress, questions had already been raised about the President's legal authority to conduct military operations in Indochina now that American forces had been withdrawn. On April 3, Elliot Richardson, at that point still Secretary of Defense, was strongly pressed by the House Appropriations Committee. His argument that Cambodian operations were "only a residual carryover" of the war met with a skeptical reaction from the powerful (and conservative) committee chairman, George Mahon of Texas, who drily noted that the only basis for presidential authority in Indochina since 1970 had been the safety of U.S. forces, which no longer applied.[78]

The Senate Foreign Relations Committee pressed hardest for a full statement of the Administration's legal case for continuing the bombing. After stalling for three weeks, Secretary Rogers testified on April 30.[79] His defense was essentially similar to Richardson's, relying heavily also on the claim that under Article 20 of the Paris Agreement the North Vietnamese had no right to retain forces in Cambodia. This argument was demolished by Senator Symington, who quoted from a memorandum by George Aldrich, Kissinger's own legal advisor in the final negotiations; this stated the common-sense view that the Article 20 obligation to withdraw foreign forces and cease military activities did not take effect until a cease-fire was agreed, and that reaching a cease-fire was left to the Cambodian parties, with no recorded undertaking or obligation on the part of North Vietnam.[80] Faced with this rebuttal, Rogers fell back on a new claim, that there had been an implied obligation for North Vietnam to do its best to achieve a cease-fire and that it had not made an appropriate effort.[81] Even if an outsider could tell what had passed between Hanoi and the Khmer Rouge, this was the weakest possible legal basis for military action, as he must have known.[82]

A preliminary report by Lowenstein and Moose, published on April 27, again raised these legal questions. Observers in Phnom Penh, they said, believed that only U.S. air support was keeping the Cambodian government alive, but that even continued air operations (and government reforms) had only a slim chance of stabilizing the situation. Most Cambodians now felt it was "beyond the government's ability to do more than get out of the war," which could only be done through a deal admitting the Khmer Rouge to a share in power, a step plainly likely to mean ultimate Communist control in Cambodia.[83]

In short, the United States was raining bombs on a small country with little prospect of a good outcome. It was a particularly hard operation to defend in terms of the defense of South Vietnam. Since late 1970, North Vietnam had been unimpeded in its use of eastern Cambodia in support of the main South Vietnamese theater. The stakes in Cambodia came down, then, almost entirely to the asserted psychological impact in South Vietnam if Cambodia fell and to Nixon's sense of personal commitment to Lon Nol.

Both wisdom and legal authority had another intensive airing on May 7, when Richardson made a farewell appearance as Defense Secretary, before the powerful Senate Appropriations Committee chaired by the conservative Democrat John McClellan of Arkansas. In a series of intense and sometimes emotional exchanges, senator after senator attacked Richardson's legal theory, and discussion came to focus on the effect of an outright congressional ban on the use of funds for operations in Cambodia. Toward the close, McClellan, who had been a consistent hard-liner on Indochina for a generation, declared that while it would be "bad" for the United States to "walk away" at this point, "I am convinced that the American people will want no more of it, and I am persuaded that the Congress may be in the same mood."[84] Senator Norris Cotton of New Hampshire, a conservative Republican who had consistently supported the war, made an emotional statement. With the prisoners home and the Cambodians clearly not ready to fight, he said,

> speaking as a dyed-in-the-wool, moss-backed administration Republican, I do not want to go on record to authorize one red cent to continue hostilities in Southeast Asia. . . . [Other senators] have been doves all the time. I have just been a dove since we got our prisoners home.

He went on to make a telling point:

> I recognize the moral obligation that you [Richardson] and the President
> and the administration feel, having made these agreements, to enforce
> them. . . . On the other hand, some of us may feel rather strongly that no
> matter what have been the terms of these agreements, Congress wasn't
> party to them, they weren't a treaty of peace, they were executive agree-
> ments. The only thing that can possibly happen if we stay over there [will
> be that] we are just getting back into another conflict over there.[85]

Three days after this hearing, on May 10, the first congressional action
came from an unexpected quarter. All along, the House had rejected Senate
resolutions and amendments aimed at ending American participation in the
war by specified dates; in August 1972 it had defeated such an amendment
by a 50-vote margin. Now, however, after lengthy and passionate debate it
approved an amendment to the military appropriation bill, by Congressman
Clarence Long of Maryland, cutting off funds for combat activities in
Cambodia after June 30. The margin was 224–172, with 35 Republicans
in the majority and 45 Democrats still with the Administration. In the debate, Congressman Robert Leggett of California made telling use of
the Lowenstein-Moose report and the Aldrich memorandum; the few Republicans who defended the Administration position, notably Jack Kemp of
New York, fell back mainly to the argument that repudiating the President
on any issue would be damaging to his prestige on other fronts.[86]

This landmark May 10 vote deserves a closer look, both for itself and to
see how much of it might have been traceable to the growing impact of
Watergate. On the Democratic side, as compared with the January vote of
the Democratic House caucus—154–75 to withdraw forces if the prisoners
were released—there had been a switch of an additional 30 votes by May
in the direction of ending U.S. participation in the war. More striking still
(especially to a historian familiar with the House of this era) was the list of
those who had voted with the Administration in August 1972 but turned
against it in May 1973. This included many members close to Speaker Carl
Albert, moderates from Southern and border states who had consistently
given successive Administrations the benefit of the doubt over Vietnam
issues, almost all of them House veterans. With them were a few moderate
Republicans of the same stripe and past voting records.[87] The switchers were
emphatically not the sort of congressmen who were likely either to act
vindictively toward Nixon or to be affected by the emotions of the moment
over Watergate. Rather, as the debate abundantly showed, they and those
who followed their lead, which came partly from the Speaker himself, did
so on the merits and as a matter of conviction and conscience. It was a
genuine revolt.

In the Senate a majority was already in place. After long debate on May 29 and 31, it voted to ban funds for operations in both Cambodia and Laos in the new fiscal year, by a decisive 63–19 margin (20–16 even among Republicans). Senator Mansfield promptly urged that the Senate should insert similar bans in every key financial bill for the new fiscal year beginning June 30, holding appropriations hostage until the White House compromised or gave in.

Meanwhile, from mid-May to mid-June, Kissinger went back and forth between Washington and Paris, facing an obdurate Le Duc Tho and with the South Vietnamese clamoring to change wording in the Paris Agreement on which he had already used up his arguments. The meeting ended with a mere reiteration of the agreement. Concerning Kissinger's main purpose, to enlist Hanoi toward a cease-fire in Cambodia, he made no headway whatever.[88]

In late June, the amendment denying further funding for military operations in Cambodia, by then extended to North and South Vietnam and to Laos, was approved by both houses in Congress. The Administration could only urge delay on the basis of what it vaguely described as hopeful negotiating signs toward a compromise regime in Cambodia, but Kissinger declined to give any specifics, on the ground that this would queer the effort. On June 25, as his summit meeting with Leonid Brezhnev ended, Nixon received the first appropriation bill with the Indochina ban amendment in it. He vetoed it on June 26, and the next day his veto was narrowly sustained by the House (241–173 to override, 35 votes short of the necessary two-thirds).[89] By then, however, the Democratic leadership in both houses, with substantial Republican support, had reached the point where Senator Mansfield could carry out his plan. He now announced that he would not permit the passage of any major appropriations bill for the next fiscal year — in effect, closing down the government after June 30 — unless the President agreed to a ban.

This use of Congress's ultimate power could not be resisted, and on June 29 a "compromise" was reached. In return for Congress agreeing to extend the starting date for the new ban by six weeks, to August 15, Nixon accepted having the ban apply to North and South Vietnam as well as Cambodia and Laos. In a dramatic scene on the floor of the House, Minority Leader Gerald Ford went still further, conveying to the House Nixon's personal pledge, from California, that he would not, after August 15, initiate any military action in "Southeast Asia" without the authority of Congress.[90]

In deciding to yield, over Kissinger's fervent protests, Nixon acted largely on the advice of Melvin Laird, his main contact with Congress, who told him that resistance was hopeless. In this last phase, the President's position lost the support of additional conservative senators who had been supporters of policy in Indochina all along. At the very end, one of these, Senator

John Stennis of Mississippi, turned against the Administration in part because of rumors that some kind of secret promise of U.S. bombing had been made to the South Vietnamese, allegedly by Alexander Haig—which was essentially true, but still kept totally secret.[91]

Basically, Congress had simply lost confidence in Nixon's Indochina policy. Moreover, the extension of the new ban not only to all of Indochina but to renewed military action anywhere in Southeast Asia was a natural outcome. Sentiment to go the whole way had built up in both houses of Congress ever since March 29, when the last POWs and American forces left South Vietnam. In effect, Congress was now saying that it had understood that after the Paris Agreement was carried out in these respects, there would be a complete and final end to the direct American military role in Southeast Asia; that understanding, in view of Nixon's attempts to evade it, must now be written into law. On all available evidence, the American people had reached the same conclusion. The dominant reaction was a widespread sense of relief that American participation was truly and finally over.

At the time, the importance of what Congress had done in terms of institutional power, the balance between the executive and Congress, was almost eclipsed by public preoccupation with the Ervin Committee hearings on Watergate. From a historical perspective, this assertion of congressional power was a landmark of great importance, brought about in small part by Watergate, in much greater part by Nixon's maladroit policy after the Paris Agreement and his consistent failure to consult with Congress, and to some degree by an ongoing revolt in the Senate, to which we shall return. In the overconfidence brought on by his reelection and then the Paris Agreement, Nixon simply did not grasp how sick the American people were of the war (including the use of airpower), or foresee the effect of the POWs' stories in dooming the always precarious project for reconstruction aid to North Vietnam.

Looking back in 1985, in one of the most reflective passages in his writings, Nixon summed up his own view of this period:

> Our growing difficulties in Congress were rooted in a profound backlash against our involvement in the war, which antedated our Watergate problems. . . .
>
> Without Watergate we would have faced the same opposition to our use of military power to enforce an agreement that would bring peace to Vietnam. I was caught off-guard by the intensity of this backlash. . . . I did not foresee any major difficulty in raising support to enforce the peace agreement, which would require actions involving relatively little expense or risk to American lives compared to those during the war. We could not find strong support for our policy in any quarter.[92]

. . .

Congress's action cutting off funds for military operations in Southeast Asia after August 15 turned out to mark the end of direct American participation in the Second Indochina War. It was not, as many senators pointed out in the hearings and debates, a total forswearing of any future U.S. action. All it forbade was the undertaking of such action without further specific authorization by Congress. If North Vietnam had acted in some drastic way which Congress and the public thought warranted a response, Nixon or a successor President might have sought to enlist congressional support for retaliatory measures. In practice, however, the fact that the issue had been carried to a showdown tended to reduce that possibility. No longer, in any event, could Nixon threaten air bombing on his own, as he had done in March.

In Cambodia, the bombing ended on the prescribed date. In the last days, a tragic error led to bombs falling in the center of a large government-held town just down the Mekong River from Phnom Penh. It was a one-time error, not typical of the operation, but perhaps a fitting epitaph. American commanders, notably the experienced General John Vogt, commander of the Seventh Air Force, were convinced that their efforts were generally well targeted at military concentrations; the official claim was that in the May–July period the air attacks may have killed as many as 16,000 of the best Khmer Rouge troops—all with no loss of aircraft or U.S. casualties. Whether these claims were exaggerated or not, the evidence of later observers was also persuasive that there was a great deal of damage to civilians and civilian targets.[93]

General Vogt and most of the senior civilians involved (including Ambassador Swank) believed that the bombing kept Lon Nol afloat in the face of the 1973 Khmer Rouge offensive. It may have been crucial in enabling the government forces, using artillery, to hold their central enclave, including Phnom Penh, into 1974 and eventually until the early spring of 1975. Massive airpower used against a lightly armed attacking force with no antiaircraft capability could be effective in preventing victory for the opposing force.

On the other hand, the intensity of the bombing—as a matter of common-sense judgment shared by many objective observers—drove the Khmer Rouge to greater military efforts. It also made them more self-reliant, more separate from North Vietnam, more alienated from Sihanouk, and altogether less subject to influence from any of their Communist supporters. The bombing surely made it more rather than less difficult for any party to persuade the Khmer Rouge to accept a cease-fire and negotiate a political compromise—which was the stated objective.

The chances of such a change of course by the Khmer Rouge were

almost certainly slim already. A determined negotiating effort to enlist Sihanouk, begun not later than December, combined with a much more
limited program of bombing to keep the threat alive, might just have stood
a chance. As it was, intense bombing with no negotiating effort, until the
Khmer Rouge were even more embittered, was the worst of all worlds. As
throughout the American involvement in Cambodia, the policy miscalcu-
lations alone—apart from eventual congressional reactions—were monumental. They must be laid squarely at the door of Nixon and his two
principal advisors, Alexander Haig and Henry Kissinger.

When Ambassador Swank left Phnom Penh in September 1973, exhausted after three strenuous and frustrating years, he told a farewell press
conference that the war "is losing more and more of its point and has less
and less meaning for any of the parties concerned." Time had been "bought
for the success of the program in Vietnam" and for this "some measure of
gratitude is owed to the Khmers." The statements were as accurate as they
were unwelcome at the top in Washington.⁹⁴

By the fall of 1973, Thieu's offensive in the South Vietnamese countryside was slackening. By this time, all could see that the Paris Agreement
was essentially inoperative. There was no pretense of a cease-fire, the international supervisory commission had been shown to be an empty shell,
with Canada finally withdrawing on August 1 to be replaced by Iran, and
the desultory political discussions between the government and the Communist Vietcong were getting nowhere—as Thieu surely intended. On both
sides, expectation had hardened into certainty that the future of the South
would be decided by a trial of arms. Many serious observers, including the
principal U.S. intelligence agencies, thought that South Vietnam still had
a good chance to maintain its independence, although it seemed only a
question of time before Cambodia would go the way of Laos and come
under Communist control.

To Nixon and Kissinger, however, the future looked considerably darker.
Alexander Haig recalled that after Congress acted on June 29 he remarked
to the President: "We've lost Southeast Asia, Mr. President," and Nixon
replied: "Al, I'm afraid you're right."⁹⁵

. . .

It remains to consider, in one piece, the negotiating effort that bulks large
in Kissinger's 1982 account of these events. Congress's ban, he argued,
aborted a promising secret approach he had made to Prince Sihanouk, via
the Chinese. This was aimed at tacitly coordinated actions by China and
the United States that would have dumped the principals each was supporting in Cambodia, the Khmer Rouge and the Lon Nol regime, respectively, in favor of a political compromise that restored Sihanouk to power
after a few months of maneuver.

In June 1972, Zhou Enlai had told Kissinger in Beijing that Communist control was the inevitable outcome in Vietnam and Laos, but that in Cambodia the prince was the right answer. Kissinger apparently did not pursue this lead with any vigor, although he mentioned Sihanouk to one Chinese in late 1972. In early 1973, on his visit to Beijing, the discussion of Cambodia was in terms of talks between the Lon Nol government and the Khmer Rouge, even then the dimmest of hopes, and although Sihanouk was then pointedly present in Beijing, Kissinger made no effort to get into direct communication with him.

Why was the idea of dealing directly with Sihanouk resurrected in April 1973? Kissinger has described a renewed series of hints from Zhou Enlai, which were then cautiously probed with Chinese in both Washington and Beijing. It may be, also, that Nixon, with his old prejudice against Sihanouk, was out of play and prepared to leave the running to Kissinger. At any rate, on May 27—with the handwriting in Congress already on the wall and Le Duc Tho in Paris offering no help toward a Cambodian cease-fire—Kissinger conveyed via the Chinese Ambassador to the United Nations a U.S. offer to stop the bombing in Cambodia and get Lon Nol to leave the country for medical reasons, if there could be a temporary cease-fire and talks between the Lon Nol people and Sihanouk (not the Khmer Rouge). The United States would then have no objection if these produced agreement, after some months, for a new Sihanouk regime incorporating some elements of both the Khmer Rouge and the Lon Nol regime.[96]

Kissinger later wrote that he based his hope of success on indications that the Khmer Rouge were becoming discouraged by the bombing and might be ready to negotiate if a stalemate were achieved—for which continued bombing was essential. He also argued that by agreeing to pass on the proposal to Sihanouk, the Chinese were indicating that they in effect supported it and would be prepared to help bring about the result. During June, Kissinger talked several more times with Chinese representatives, eliciting no confirmation of his hopes.[97]

Sihanouk was traveling during June, but surely not beyond the reach of a determined Chinese effort to reach him. He did not return to Beijing until July 5. By then the ban imposed by Congress on June 29 meant, as Kissinger (and he claims Zhou) saw it, that the Chinese could no longer offer the Khmer Rouge a stop to the bombing. Thus the Chinese no longer had any influence with the Khmer Rouge, and on July 18 informed Kissinger's office that (in his words) "China was no longer willing even to communicate the American negotiating proposal to Sihanouk"—implying unmistakably that it had never in fact done so![98]

These diplomatic exchanges were surely, on their face, thin stuff. If one looks at the judgments on which Kissinger was acting, the effort appears still more farfetched and unrealistic. His basic premise that the war in Cambodia was stalemated (so that the Khmer Rouge might be less rigid) is contradicted by massive evidence. Every indication on the ground that spring and early summer was that the Khmer Rouge were going all out for victory, taking immense costs in casualties but making striking gains and driving the government forces right back to within ten miles of Phnom Penh. Moreover, as later evidence made clear, the Khmer Rouge were not only freeing themselves almost totally of North Vietnamese influence but initiating truly radical measures that foreshadowed their fanatical post-1975 regime.[99]

Finally, later evidence also showed dramatically how Sihanouk, the linchpin of Kissinger's attempt, stood with the Khmer Rouge at this time. In the spring of 1973, the prince wangled his way to Cambodia for a month's stay, his first visit since he was deposed three years earlier. In that month he learned on all sides how deep the frictions had become between Cambodians and Vietnamese. At the same time, although his Khmer Rouge hosts kept him under tight restraints, his very presence rekindled intense loyalty and devotion from the people.[100] Frightened by this visible appeal, the Khmer Rouge leaders redoubled their harsh measures after the prince left, obviously aiming to establish solidly their own form of rule. In such a mood, the last thing they would have accepted was the kind of deal Kissinger was trying to promote.

In sum, on all the evidence then and later, Kissinger's project was hopeless. He was grasping at straws to try to keep Congress from acting. Arnold Isaacs's verdict is irrefutable:

Henry Kissinger's claim that a Cambodian settlement was within reach, only to be obstructed by the American Congress, is based on a proposal that was never presented to any Cambodian on either side, that was premised on a military stalemate that did not exist, that led to no negotiations of any kind, and whose principles were violently rejected then and later not just by one but by both Cambodian sides—hardly, it seems, a plan that would warrant any description of American diplomacy as "promising."[101]

7. Behind the Congressional Revolt

The congressional ban on further American military operations in Southeast Asia was brought about in large part by Nixon's misjudged and reckless action, after the Paris Agreement, in initiating heavy bombing in Cambodia. The first phase of Watergate also weakened Nixon's power. But there was a third major cause. Many in Congress, especially in the Senate, had come to believe that there should be a fundamental readjustment in the respective powers of the President and Congress in situations where American military forces might be committed to action.

This view became significant at the time of the original controversy involving Cambodia in May 1970, when Nixon ordered the incursion of American forces there. Congress intervened, first by setting a June 30 time limit for the withdrawal of the ground forces taking part in the incursion and then, in January 1971, by passage of the Cooper-Church Amendment barring the use of ground forces in Cambodia or Laos for the future. But the power balance on the Hill, after that, rejected any tighter restraint. Congress appropriated money for military aid to Cambodia and, in Vietnam, confined itself to time-limit amendments calling for the withdrawal of American forces, but without teeth or operative force.

Thus, many congressional opponents of the war felt, after mid-1970, powerless over the war itself. To give vent to their strong feelings, a group of centrist senators turned to the possibility of institutional reform. One such effort, by Senator Clifford Case of New Jersey, a moderate Republican, focused on the frequent failure of successive Administrations to inform Congress of important executive agreements. The Case bill to require such disclosures finally passed the Senate unanimously in 1972, and the House shortly thereafter, with Nixon giving way and in the end not opposing it. It was a significant and sensible change, owing much of its impetus to disclosures in 1969 hearings of various agreements by the executive with countries sending forces to Vietnam.[102]

The main effort in the Senate, however, aimed higher. It sought to change the balance between Congress and the President, not only in actually going to war but in the making of initial decisions to use American forces abroad where hostilities might ensue. The reasoning was simple. History had shown, and the Vietnam experience confirmed, that Congress, once forces were in the field, would be under enormous pressure not to limit or seek to control them. Yet Vietnam had also demonstrated that the executive, in what Senator McGovern had called "secret wars, secretly arrived at," was capable of grave error. Finally, if one looked back at the original intent of the framers of the Constitution, a strong case could be made that a much more active congressional role had been envisaged than the accepted norm in twentieth-century American practice.

In this effort the principal figure was Senator Jacob Javits, a moderate Republican from New York. Up to the spring of 1970 he had gone along with the war. Then, however, as he met with waves of students and other protesters from his state—a hotbed of dissent from the Cambodian incursion and increasingly from the whole war—he felt the need to offer a serious proposal for future war-threatening situations. His staff put together the basic ideas for a bill, which he introduced in the Senate Foreign Relations Committee that July.[103] Its three original features were: a long list of defined contingencies in which the President was entitled to order U.S. forces into combat or potential combat (for example, protection of U.S. nationals, attack of any sort, or following a resolution or treaty); a requirement that the President promptly report to Congress the actions taken and their justification in terms of the defined list; and a stipulation that the deployment or action might continue for 30 days solely on the President's authority as defined, but could not continue beyond that time unless specifically approved by both houses of Congress.

Contingency list, reporting requirement, time limit — these became the checklist on the subject. The first in particular raised fundamental questions about the President's power as Commander in Chief under Article II, Section 2, of the Constitution — the power successive Presidents had invoked as they sent U.S. forces into action on a great many occasions, most recently and notably in the Korean and Vietnam wars. The competing provisions in the Constitution were those parts of Article I, Section 8, giving to Congress alone the power to "declare war," and the more general "power of the purse," to grant or withhold appropriations for any government activity.

The balance between these necessarily imprecise provisions had been vigorously argued when the Constitution was adopted and recurrently thereafter, with the pendulum in the twentieth century swinging markedly in favor of the President. Only twice in history had Congress actually declared war. Never had it denied funds for a military operation initiated by the President, or in recent times even used the power of the purse to put great pressure on him.[104] In effect, it had come to be taken for granted that in modern times the rapidity with which threatening situations arose, and the need for maximum flexibility and decisive action, required that the President take the lead. Congress would then, necessarily, be asked to provide funding, but it was almost always the case that a denial of funds would appear to imperil Americans risking their lives for their country.

Crucial to Javits's thinking and drafting was his vivid recollection of the way the key Vietnam decisions had been made. In sharp contrast to the abrupt way Truman had committed U.S. forces in Korea, the commitment of American forces in Vietnam was gradual and in its first stages ambiguous, with no formal statement of the constitutional power relied on. From a legal standpoint, a pivotal event came in August 1964 when President Lyndon Johnson, following precedents under Eisenhower and Kennedy, sought and obtained the famous Tonkin Gulf Resolution authorizing actions up to and including the use of American forces in response to the North Vietnamese threat in Indochina. Even then, the President treated the resolution as merely affirming, for the sake of national unity, his power as Commander in Chief. Members of Congress, on the other hand, tended to regard it as a particular-case *delegation* flowing from powers held fundamentally by Congress. It was a crucial and enduring difference of view.

President Johnson then invoked the resolution for years to justify successive decisions to deploy air and shortly afterward large ground forces in the Vietnam War. Critics and skeptics of the war, and those concerned with the issue of constitutional power, finally obtained the repeal of the Tonkin Gulf Resolution in early 1971. The decks were cleared for the consideration of new arrangements.

. . .

In 1970 the Javits bill languished in committee, to be reintroduced in 1971 with three other sponsors. This time, the effort picked up new and formidable support from Senator Stennis, the conservative Democrat from Mississippi who was then chairman of the Armed Services Committee and had enormous influence in military-related matters, and had also been a public supporter of the war from the outset. Stennis submitted his own bill in May.

The Senate Foreign Relations Committee proceeded with hearings on the two bills (and others), with the Nixon Administration, in the person of Secretary Rogers, a former Attorney General, strongly opposing all legislation of this sort. His learned brief argued that the presidential power to initiate military action could not be limited, especially not to contingencies defined by Congress, but his adamant posture aroused the institutional loyalty of wavering senators, especially moderate Republicans. By summer the bill had picked up support from several of these, including Senator Hugh Scott, the Republican Minority Leader.

In October 1971, further Senate hearings produced new supporting testimony, notably a strong statement from Stennis summing up his reasoning:

> Vietnam has shown us that by trying to fight a war without the clearcut prior support of the American people, we not only risk military effectiveness but we also strain the very structure of the republic.[105]

Stennis's position was all the more weighty because he emphasized that he was speaking strictly in terms of principle. On the current issues of withdrawing troops from Vietnam more rapidly or in return only for release of American prisoners, he had voted with the Administration in June 1971 and was to do so on other occasions until May 1973.

By the end of 1971 the Senate was moving toward strong war powers legislation. In late November, key senators agreed on compromise language still based primarily on Javits's ideas, and in December this new bill was approved unanimously by the Senate Foreign Relations Committee. It was, however, no more than a shot across the Administration's bow, since the House was much less concerned over the issue. Its own bill on the subject, passed in August 1971, had gone no further than to require the President to report any military action and its background promptly to Congress.

As 1972 began, the Senate bill had plainly become a serious proposal that might well pass. At this stage it drew fire from several prominent liberals, notably the historian Arthur Schlesinger, Jr., who particularly attacked the contingency list for not covering many past cases where action had been, in his view, rightly taken by Presidents without congressional authority and where Congress might not have endorsed the action even retrospectively.[106] Despite this considered objection, liberal and moderate senators rallied to the bill, and it was debated by the Senate in March 1972 and passed on April 13 by a decisive 68–16 margin. Substantial conservative support was ensured, however, only by an understanding, insisted upon by Stennis, that the bill should not affect Nixon's powers in the conduct of the Vietnam War itself. Yet, as *The New York Times* report of the Senate passage noted, the bill was "a direct outgrowth of the Vietnam war."[107]

Throughout 1972 the House was not prepared to move beyond the weak reporting-only bill it had passed in 1971. There were, however, signs of a shift in opinion there. The Republican Minority Leader, Gerald Ford, for example, indicated that he favored some specific check on the President's power and a definition of the role of Congress. But only in 1973 did the House finally take action, as part of the same change of views that led it to vote an end to the bombing of Cambodia. In May a House subcommittee came up with its own bill, featuring a 120-day time limit on presidential use of military forces if Congress did not expressly approve such use. By this time, however, some in the Senate, notably Senators Fulbright and Eagleton, had developed reservations about the Senate bill on the ground that it conceded too great an inherent right in the President to resort to the use of force on his own.

The controversy hung fire during the early summer, as attention was focused on Watergate and the bill to end funding for military operations in Southeast Asia. Once that was passed, the House approved its war powers bill on July 18, but only by a vote of 244–170, well short of the two-thirds needed to override the presidential veto to which Nixon was committed. The Senate again acted decisively on July 20, and by early October a conference committee had worked out a compromise bill. This set a time limit of 60 days for any presidential use of force not approved by Congress, with an additional 30 days to withdraw forces. Notably, this final version of the bill dropped the prolonged attempt to define the contingencies in which the President was entitled to act, a list attacked from both sides as either too limiting or too permissive.

The stage was set for a showdown. Both Senate and House approved the compromise in mid-October, with the House majority short of the required two-thirds by only three votes. At this point, the Middle East war intervened, causing Nixon to delay sending his veto message. On October 20 came the Saturday Night Massacre, a crucial event in the second stage of Watergate.

Up to that point, it had appeared unlikely that a two-thirds majority to override his veto could be obtained. With Nixon's position severely weakened, though, the veto was overridden on November 7, 1973, by 75–18 in the Senate and by a close 284–135, five votes to spare, in the House.

Without Watergate the House would probably not have swung into line in May, and only the Saturday Night Massacre made it possible to override the Nixon veto in November. Yet the struggle had taken on so much momentum that it would surely have continued. The real impetus came from the Vietnam War, from origin to final passage. Well before Watergate broke, polls had indicated popular majority support for some version of the bill, and by the time of final passage, public support was at 80 percent.[108]

In its final form, the resolution was simpler in substance than some of the early versions. The list of specific contingencies in which the President might act was now replaced by a broad statement of principles that lacked any sanction or teeth. But at the same time the procedural requirements were detailed, and the basic provisions extended to any case in which U.S. forces were in danger of being drawn into combat, even if their intended purpose was only to make a show of force. Thus, its potential effect was far-reaching, and the debate about it was bound to revive, on issues of constitutional principle alone. Moreover, there were serious practical questions about its impact on the range of measures a President might employ, not necessarily to get into a military conflict, but perhaps for the opposite purpose of dealing with a crisis without having to take the final step.

The War Powers Act was an important move, bound to have substantial relevance in future crises. Whether congressional approval was required for a proposed military action or deployment did not become an acute issue in the remainder of Nixon's presidency. In 1990–91, when President George Bush had to deal with the crisis arising from Iraq's invasion of Kuwait, it was touch and go whether he would seek congressional approval before going to war. In the event, he did so at the last moment, getting a thin majority, but enough to give him clear constitutional sanction.

On the other hand, there were many cases under both Ronald Reagan and Bush when congressional approval was not sought. The passage of the War Powers Act was not a lasting solution to a perennial problem, but it was a significant change in the balance. No legislation can anticipate all contingencies, but the burdens of proof, consultation, and approval for a President ordering American military forces into action were undoubtedly made greater than they had been for Richard Nixon, Lyndon Johnson, or John F. Kennedy.

Chapter Seven

UNDER PRESSURE

1. U.S.-China Relations in 1973

When Henry Kissinger visited Beijing in February 1973, his conversations with Zhou Enlai were both wide-ranging on present problems and suggestive for the future.[1] Zhou was plainly delighted that America had held on to get the Paris Agreement, and was extraordinarily candid, informal, and forthcoming. At the end of the visit Kissinger was accorded a private talk with Mao himself, typically in the middle of the night on short notice.

By then, China had normalized its relations with Japan, in a dramatic visit by Prime Minister Kakuei Tanaka in the fall of 1972. This move to full official relations, beyond where Nixon was politically prepared to go, went far to undo Japan's sense of shock, humiliation, and isolation over the twin "shokkus" of 1971 (first, not being informed before the announcement of the secret Kissinger trip to Beijing, and second, the Camp David economic measures). In his first talks with Kissinger in July 1971, as we have seen, Zhou Enlai had started by denouncing the U.S.-Japanese security treaty and even accused the United States of helping to revive Japanese militarism. Now he applauded the treaty as an important restraint on any Japanese tendency to aggression and supported the closest possible cooperation between the United States and Japan. Similarly, he lectured Kissinger on the importance of strong NATO defenses. In discussions ranging around the whole periphery of the Soviet empire from Western Europe to Japan, via Turkey, Iran, and Pakistan, Zhou and Mao urged that the United States lead a solid anti-Soviet coalition, with which China herself would cooperate, largely by exposing "Soviet motivation." At the same time, Zhou derided "the very thought of negotiating with the Soviet Union"; his ideas, as Kissinger noted, had much in common with the views of "American conservatives" — meaning no doubt the likes of Senator Jackson, who became an ardent supporter of the closest possible ties and consultations with China. Kissinger's own response, however, was that, while he believed that it was "correct" to resist Soviet threats, a measure of "flexibility" (i.e., détente) was necessary to preserve U.S. leadership and prevent the United States from being denounced as "the cause of tensions."[2]

Much of what Zhou and Kissinger discussed related specifically to Indochina. It is not clear whether they reverted to their discussion of June 1972, in which Zhou had suggested that while Communist control was inevitable in Laos, "we can be sure in Cambodia Prince Sihanouk will be the head of state . . . if it can be solved through negotiations," but Kissinger was struck by Zhou's revelations of China's long-standing suspicions of Hanoi and of an "emerging split" with North Vietnam. Even at this late date, Kissinger did not seem to understand this deep historical antipathy, though it was by then evident, especially in Cambodia.

Kissinger's account is peculiarly elliptical and guarded on the issue of the Soviet threat to China. By 1973 the Soviets had increased their forces along the northern borders of China to 43 divisions (from 16 in 1969). While there had been no recurrence of the clashes or veiled Soviet nuclear threats of 1969, the situation remained tense and was bound to be uppermost in Chinese concerns. In the 1972 Shanghai communiqué, Nixon had accepted a Chinese formulation that both nations shared the "common goal of opposing the hegemonic aims of others in Asia."[3] With this well-understood code phrase, the formula in effect moved the United States from its earlier policy of deep but outwardly impartial "concern" at least partway to China's side, though well short of any commitment to act. Zhou and Kissinger did not, apparently, go beyond this general formula or put forward the idea of the United States giving weapons or any other military help to China; proposing such a thing while China continued to aid North Vietnam in the war and support its cause verbally would have been out of the question, as everyone knew.

By now, both Kissinger and Zhou talked as though the Vietnam War was over, at least for America, and came more frankly to grips with where the United States stood and how far it might be prepared to go to support China. According to Kissinger's later account, he spoke at some length about the American policy style and tradition, and why it required flexibility with public opinion always in mind. He went on to describe his and Nixon's own belief that American national interests included the territorial integrity of China.

Should the Soviet Union succeed in reducing China to impotence, the impact on the world balance of power would be scarcely less catastrophic than a Soviet conquest of Europe. . . . Japan would begin to dissociate from us . . . Europe would lose confidence and all its neutralist tendencies would accelerate. Southeast Asia would bend to the dominant trend; the radical forces in the Middle East, South Asia, Africa, and even the Americas would gain the upper hand. Thus we could not possibly wish to encourage a Soviet assault on China. We would have, in my view, no choice except to help China resist.

Kissinger added, however:

But I also knew that in the early 1970s such a proposition was as yet unfamiliar and uncongenial to most public and leadership opinion in America. Thus it was crucial, first, to strengthen the tangible links between our two countries.[4]

He put "these considerations" before Zhou "in one of the most candid and comprehensive accounts of our foreign policy that I ever made to any foreign leader." In effect, Kissinger was saying that Nixon and he were prepared to come to China's aid in a conflict with the Soviet Union, but they could not say so now, nor could they be sure of the necessary public support. It was another important indicator of just how warm and frank Sino-American relations had become, but at the same time of what the United States could and could not do. Kissinger does not suggest that the question of U.S. military aid to China came up in this February 1973 meeting. Four months later, during Brezhnev's visit to America, when the Soviet leader denounced China and proposed a secret exchange of views with the United States on the subject, Kissinger supplemented Nixon's noncommittal response by volunteering that (in his words) "we had never had any military discussions with China."[5] The assertion seems credible from every standpoint.

Kissinger's February visit to Beijing had one immediate result: agreement, on China's initiative, to open "liaison offices" in Beijing and Washington—"embassies in all but name," as Kissinger proclaimed it. Soon, the distinguished senior diplomat David Bruce was appointed to the post in China, and with the release in March of the last American still held in China as a prisoner (from the Korean War) the past did seem to be buried and the way cleared for a new relationship.[6]

Then, however, came the onset of the Watergate crisis and, in May and June, Kissinger's attempt to get China's cooperation in an effort to have Prince Sihanouk installed as a compromise ruler in Cambodia. The murky Chinese role in that effort must have left doubts both in Zhou's mind and in Kissinger's. Certainly the outcome was a failure for both, whether of understanding or possibility is not clear. Kissinger naturally blamed Congress, which had stopped the bombing there, and judged that Zhou must have been "politically wounded at home by our failure." In his memoirs, Kissinger recounts that he had planned to return to Beijing in July for "regular consultations" (presumably including an account of the 1973 summit with Brezhnev), but that after the congressional action Zhou "pointedly" postponed the visit.[7] But perhaps Zhou never set much store by the Sihanouk project; he probably had a much surer grasp than Kissinger of Cambodian realities and the toughness of the Khmer Rouge. In any event, Watergate and the congressional ban on all U.S. military action in Southeast Asia confirmed a general picture that neither the United States nor Nixon personally was now so powerful as in February.

As far as the available evidence shows, Kissinger did not report to the Chinese on the June Brezhnev summit, either directly or indirectly, though the declaration about nuclear war clearly concerned Chinese interests. Both the declaration and the failure to explain it must have hit hard at Chinese confidence in the United States and even in Kissinger personally. The mission in Beijing, which opened in May 1973, never got beyond an apparently cordial initial conversation between Zhou and Bruce. Indeed, the mission found itself subject to minor harassments (probably instigated by the radical faction in the Chinese leadership), which Zhou was apparently powerless to prevent. Nor did it even serve as a communications channel: Kissinger continued to reach Zhou through China's UN delegation.[8]

From May until October, therefore, a gap opened between Kissinger and Zhou, and also an accumulation of negative developments of the kind that always fed Zhou's radical hard-line critics. Finally, in November, Kissinger (by then Secretary of State) paid his sixth visit to China, part of a breakneck schedule of visits to a number of major nations; this fact alone must have registered negatively in Beijing.

By this time the seventy-five-year-old Zhou was known to be ill (it later emerged that incurable cancer had been diagnosed as early as March 1972), and his position was under continuing attack from radicals close to Mao.[9] Once again, however, he talked for several hours with Kissinger, who again defended American détente with the Soviet Union as essential. Zhou urged more active support of Pakistan because of the threat from Iraq and Afghanistan, both of which had just taken a radical turn. In the wake of the Indo-Pakistan war of 1971, Kissinger replied that renewed U.S. military aid to Pakistan was politically impossible, but emphasized U.S. help to Iran, which in turn might help Pakistan. (More than ever, Iran was the key country in the area in the eyes of Nixon and Kissinger.)

In all, Kissinger thought that the conversations with Zhou were of the same high order as on previous visits, but "something was missing" and his perceptive colleague Winston Lord noted the absence of Zhou's "old bite and sparkle." While parallel discussions on increased trade and cultural exchanges went exceptionally well, Kissinger was puzzled that Zhou seemed anxious to "get things settled."[10]

Once again, a talk with Mao was added on short notice, and this time turned out to be the substantive high point. For a full three hours, Mao ranged all over the world, filling in and giving his personal imprint to the global parallelism of thought and action Zhou and Kissinger had worked out since July 1971. Nudging Kissinger to pay greater attention to Japan, Mao said frankly that China did not see itself as competing with the United States to be the country closest to Japan; he supported the U.S.-Japan alliance even more fervently than Zhou had done in February. He also stressed the importance of Turkey, Iran, and Pakistan as barriers to Soviet expansion, applauded the reduction of Soviet influence in the Middle East, and discussed European attitudes at length. As Kissinger noted, Mao's lengthy remarks were probably meant to be circulated throughout the top levels of the Chinese government, in an effort to put a solid floor under the American relationship, as China went through an inevitable change of leaders. David Bruce, with long experience, considered the solo performance masterly.[11]

Mao also questioned whether there were secret U.S.-Soviet understandings that had not been disclosed to the Chinese. Kissinger's denial, repeated in his memoirs, was probably accurate, but may not have convinced the Chinese. By this time, Zhou's radical opponents in China, led by Mao's wife, Jiang Qing, were surely arguing that America's web of agreements with the Soviet Union was much more extensive than with China, and that Nixon and Kissinger had simply used the Chinese relationship for leverage with the Soviets.

In other respects, the November 1973 visit went smoothly — Kissinger was to call it the "most cordial" of any. The functions of the liaison offices were expanded. The Chinese hinted that normalization of Sino-American relations might be possible even if the United States did not drop its recognition of Taiwan. And a number of technical issues seemed near resolution. Yet, despite Mao's performance on this occasion, it is hard to avoid the conclusion that 1973 saw a significant decline in Sino-American relations. In part this was perhaps inevitable, but a large factor was certainly the declining health of Mao and the retirement of Zhou, who, as Kissinger notes, was never referred to thereafter by Chinese officials.[12] And with Kissinger's attention devoted almost entirely to the Middle East war and the oil crisis, China clearly and visibly no longer had the same importance and priority in U.S. policy.

2. *Snags in U.S.-Soviet Relations*

Nixon was still riding high at the time of his second inaugural in January 1973, but the public mood about the Soviet Union had changed. In the heady days of 1972, the American people had been caught up in the novelty of détente, welcomed the apparent easing of tensions, and were ready to give Nixon's vaunted "triangular diplomacy" with China and the Soviet Union the credit he and Kissinger claimed for it in getting North Vietnam to accept the Paris Agreement. As the American prisoners came home in March, along with the last of the military forces, the Vietnam War was no longer the obsessive concern it had been. Equally, though, it was no longer a supporting justification for détente with the Soviets; that policy had to stand on its own merits. Moreover, with the first Watergate revelations, beginning in March, as well as Nixon's intense and eventually losing confrontation with Congress over renewed bombing of Cambodia, both he and Kissinger were hard pressed and unable to give the forthcoming Soviet summit the same kind of personal attention as in 1972.

Still, in the months since the May 1972 summit, relations with the Soviet Union had seemed on a level course, and there was hope that substantial progress would be made toward a new arms control agreement on offensive missiles, envisaged for completion by 1974. It was also hoped that the trade agreement of October 1972 would be confirmed, and that called for dealing with the issue of emigration from the Soviet Union, made more acute by the Soviet imposition of an exit tax and the substantial protest in the United States against the whole idea of expanded trade under these conditions. The arms control front was, of course, familiar territory. Although the successful SALT I agreements seemed to promise early further progress on strategic weapons, a closer examination of the situation would have revealed serious difficulties. SALT I had avoided the issue of multiple warheads (MIRVs), which the United States had and the Soviet Union did not. Instead, SALT I had dealt in terms of numbers of missiles and missile launchers. If Soviet scientists mastered the MIRV technology fairly soon, every measure of capability on both sides would have to be rethought and new formulas devised. In early 1973, the Soviets had not yet tested MIRVs, and Americans had given little thought to arms control when they had it.

In this situation, Gerard Smith was succeeded as chief negotiator by U. Alexis Johnson, the senior U.S. diplomat at the time, not previously involved with SALT but long familiar with the Pentagon and with many political-military issues; Paul Nitze stayed in place as the Defense Department representative on the negotiating team. But in Washington, where issues were thrashed out and instructions issued, only Henry Kissinger remained. The new Secretary of Defense (succeeding Elliot Richardson in the first post-Watergate shuffle) was James Schlesinger, who had long been close to Senator Jackson. He had been briefly Director of the CIA and before that the head of the Office of Management and Budget, and had spent many years at the Rand Corporation, where intensive analysis of public programs was mixed with a tendency to black-and-white thinking on East-West issues. He had also been a contemporary and occasional rival of Kissinger's at Harvard; the two were in many ways antithetical and disliked each other.

At the Arms Control and Disarmament Agency, Gerard Smith was succeeded by Fred Iklé, also from the Rand Corporation, an unabashed critic of the doctrine of "mutual assured destruction" and supporter of "counterforce targeting" and seeking nuclear superiority.[13] The same views were held by the new JCS member of the negotiating group, General Edward Rowny, a hard-liner of deepest dye, with implacable convictions about Soviet perfidy. Still another senior Pentagon official concerned with arms control was the new Deputy Secretary of Defense, William Clements, a prominent Texas oil executive with no previous government experience, whose inclinations were likewise conservative and skeptical of arms control.

With this largely new cast, there was a sharp drop-off in teamwork. By his own account, Kissinger was "bureaucratically isolated"—perhaps in no small part because of resentments aroused by his high-handed conduct in SALT I.[14] So, while the issues were argued within the government during the winter and heatedly in late spring, no agreement had been reached by the time Kissinger went to Moscow in May to prepare for the second summit. He tried out on the Soviets a scheme for limiting the MIRVing of Soviet missiles in return for the United States not developing long-range air-launched cruise missiles (the possibility of developing and deploying such missiles had just arisen, but was being opposed by the Air Force for diverse reasons), but the Soviet leaders were not responsive. On his return to America he worked with Clements to revive the cruise missile effort and give it a high priority, so that he could use it as a "bargaining chip." The military importance of such missiles was never great, but the difficulty of verifying their numbers and characteristics made them a constant stumbling block.[15]

By mid-June, with Schlesinger fully involved, the impasse in the executive branch had become unbreakable. Every meeting only deepened the divisions among the agencies, and Alexis Johnson in Geneva had very little to go on. Nixon himself remained aloof, as Watergate distracted him more and more, but also because he was inwardly convinced that until the Soviet Union had proved it could develop its own MIRVs, no deal could even be sketched out. There were other problems. The Jackson Amendment of September 1972 had called for "essential equivalence" in any new agreement, which the JCS especially insisted had to mean "equal aggregates"—that is, equal ceilings in total numbers of weapons launchers. Moreover, Nitze continued to press for agreed limitations on throw weight, where the Soviet experience in developing heavy missiles gave the Russians a continuing edge that was bound to become more important when they mastered the not too difficult technology of MIRVs.

Because of these difficulties nothing substantial was said or done at the 1973 summit, and shortly after, the MIRV shoe dropped. In Kissinger's words:

> Two new Soviet MIRVed ICBMs were identified in the testing process in the summer of 1973, namely the new "light" SS-17, which would re-place the SS-11, and carry three to four warheads; and the huge SS-18, to be the replacement for the SS-9 and to carry an estimated nine MIRVed warheads (in the end eight). . . . Later in 1973, yet another missile ap-peared—the SS-19—which . . . turned out to be the most formidable of the new weapons.[16]

For the rest of the year, the agencies in Washington concerned with arms control wrestled inconclusively with the new situation.

Meanwhile Jackson's other issue, linking emigration from the Soviet Union to trade and credit concessions, picked up where it had left off. When the new Congress convened in January 1973, Jackson and his staff consoli-dated their support in the Senate and then focused on the House, the initiat-ing chamber for legislation bearing on trade and tariffs. Congressman Vanik took the lead in rounding up an impressive 235 co-sponsors of what had now become generally known as the Jackson-Vanik Amendment, and after much hesitation, the Administration decided to include most-favored-nation (MFN) treatment for the Soviet Union in a broader Trade Reform Act, whose primary purpose was to authorize renewed multilateral negotiations to lower tariffs and other trade obstacles generally. This act was already strongly op-posed by leaders of the AFL-CIO, whose crusty president, George Meany, shared Jackson's negative view of trade and détente with the U.S.S.R. and his deep concern for Jewish causes and Israel. Thus the move to put MFN into a Trade Reform Act tended to strengthen Jackson's position.

By February, Nixon and Kissinger (along with Soviet Ambassador Do-brynin) finally grasped the seriousness of the situation, and a White House emissary, followed by Treasury Secretary Shultz, told the Soviets in Moscow that the exit tax must be withdrawn. About March 15 they privately agreed to do so, but the following week Jackson said this alone would not be enough, that there had to be continuous monitoring to ensure adequate levels of emigration.

Along the way, both the Administration and the Jackson camp pressed the Israeli government to move off its neutral position on Jackson's proposed

legislation. Although the stout Golda Meir resisted making a public statement, it eventually came to be known that Israel favored the Jackson-Vanik
Amendment; even more important, the American-Israel Political Action
Committee (AIPAC), agreed in January to work closely with Jackson. In
response, Nixon courted Jewish leaders hard, arguing that his record should
make them trust him to achieve continued large-scale emigration his way.

In early April the Soviet Union went a step further. In what it must have
considered an enormous concession, it not only agreed that for an indefinite
future period the exit tax would not be enforced, but allowed Nixon to
convey a formal statement of this position to congressional leaders (it was
actually drafted by Kissinger and approved by Dobrynin).[17] In effect, the
Soviet government was now negotiating with Congress via the Administration, a process unusual, almost unprecedented, for any foreign government.
For Soviet leaders, to whose way of thinking the importance of Congress
was alien and unfamiliar, it was doubly painful. And that it should be
deemed necessary, after years of counting on Nixon's making decisions on
his own, must have come as a practical and psychological blow, shaking
Soviet confidence in the firmness of détente.

The formal text of the proposed Trade Reform Act, including most-
favored-nation status for the Soviet Union, went to Congress on April 10.
Nixon moved promptly to convey the new Soviet assurance to key senators
on April 18 at a White House meeting. As it happened, the meeting came
the day after the White House had been forced to yield important ground
in Watergate by announcing that previous denials of any White House staff
involvement were now (in one of the stilted words that dot the Watergate
record) "inoperative." This was another blow to Nixon's power.

Yet Nixon and Kissinger both thought that since the exit tax had seemed
to be the main reason for inflamed feelings since August 1972, there would
now be ready agreement with members of Congress. Instead, Senator Jackson responded coolly that this was not enough: the Soviet Union must
guarantee a minimum number of exit visas and ease emigration not just
for Jews but for all nationalities. Not for the first or last time, he simply
pocketed a concession and demanded more. His colleagues sat silent.[18]

Kissinger's summary of the Soviet reaction is fair: "For the Soviet Union
to alter its domestic practices in response to a frontal public assault by a
foreign nation would be perceived by its already nearly paranoid rulers as
a direct impairment of their authority."[19] Almost all other nations would
have felt the same way. If the United States itself had ever been subject to
such a demand, the reaction would surely have been volcanic. (In arguing
their case, both Nixon and Kissinger on several occasions drew a parallel
to a foreign nation demanding changes in U.S. civil rights policies.)

As word of the Soviet move and Jackson's response leaked out, a brief
struggle ensued for the support of key Jewish leaders on the one hand and

of Congressman Wilbur Mills, the powerful chairman of the House Ways and Means Committee, on the other. Under well-orchestrated pressure, Mills finally agreed to remain a sponsor of the amendment and the Jewish leaders came back into line. This success was at one level a triumph of bare-knuckles lobbying by the amendment's promoters; at another it expressed the strong emotional support that had built up. In effect, the Jackson-Vanik Amendment not only united Jews with other ethnic groups and with organized labor but it enlisted, under the banner of human rights, liberals and conservatives in a broad and almost unique coalition. The main affected group had special influence in American politics, but the principle was one that people considered that Nixon and Kissinger's realpolitik had unduly downgraded. Among conservatives, there were also many for whom, as for Jackson himself, concern for human rights was paired with deep reservations about easing relations with the Soviet Union.

Kissinger later claimed that the onset of Watergate weakened Nixon's position on this issue (and on others), but as one looks at the force of the arguments and the firmness of the positions taken, as well as the basic difference between Americans and Soviets on emigration as a right, one must conclude that, Watergate or no, Nixon and Kissinger had their work cut out for them. Jackson was onto a very strong and appealing issue, and not about to let go of it.

For the time being, the lack of MFN had little impact on Soviet-American trade. Much more important was the question of export credits, and for these the Administration then needed no new legislative authority. From February onward, at Nixon's direction, the Export-Import Bank granted modest credits for exports to the Soviet Union. As the June summit approached, the trade front was in trouble but not totally crippled, and Soviet-American relations seemed good on the whole.

. . .

During Leonid Brezhnev's eight days of talks with Nixon (June 17–25), first in Washington and then in San Clemente, Senator Ervin's committee declared a short recess in its televised Watergate hearings, but the scandal hovered inescapably over the visit.

With nothing new to say about trade or arms control, the principal public statement that emerged from the summit was a high-sounding declaration of common resolve to prevent nuclear war. This was a Soviet initiative launched just before the previous year's summit, on which the U.S. side then stalled for months.[20] The original Soviet draft was patently designed to get the United States to agree to something that would appear to weaken and discredit the threat of use of nuclear weapons in any crisis involving another nation. In many areas, notably NATO but also by this time China, the threat that America might use nuclear weapons in the event of a Soviet attack—"extended deterrence," it was called—was basic to U.S. policy and to its relationship to the countries involved. In proposing an agreed statement on the subject, the Soviet leadership was making a shrewd effort to undermine America's position and policy.

Among the NATO allies, it had always been accepted that only prompt use of nuclear weapons could deter a threatened Soviet attack, given the U.S.S.R.'s marked superiority in conventional forces. This alliance policy of "first use"—well known to informed circles in the United States, perhaps not fully grasped by the American public—was always potentially sensitive, but in Europe it was an old and familiar story. Soviet leaders feared that the United States might develop and apply a similar "first use" policy in support of China, which had some nuclear capability of its own. A Soviet-American deal denigrating nuclear weapons would thus be a heavy blow to China, both strategically and psychologically, and a gain for the Soviets.

So the American leaders stalled. Kissinger later claimed that the United States' major allies were informed, but in what detail is not clear. He enlisted the advice and drafting help of Thomas Brimelow of the British Foreign Office (rather than Soviet experts in the State Department), but did not keep other allies abreast of what he was doing.[21] Kissinger aimed to reduce any draft declaration on this subject to as near meaninglessness as possible.

Cannily, Kissinger waited until May to negotiate seriously. By that time, whatever leverage the Soviets had had in 1972 to get the Americans to entertain the project was minimal. In fairly short order the declaration was revised to provide that both sides should make every effort to avoid conflict at any level, and should agree to consult urgently in any situation where the use of nuclear weapons seemed conceivable. This revised draft was then shown hastily to the European allies and the Chinese, who liked it little but were powerless to stop it.[22] When it was approved at the summit, few observers saw any great meaning or purpose in it. Kissinger's claim at the time that it had been "a significant landmark" showed his desire to dramatize new events in foreign policy as an antidote to the damaging Watergate news—a motive he admitted in his memoirs. At best it had been an exercise in defensive American diplomacy, with results that did little harm to strategic postures and assumptions.[23]

By contrast, the conclusion of ten new agreements on transportation and commercial air services, agriculture, the peaceful uses of atomic energy, expanded exchange of scientific, technical, educational, and cultural visits, and enlarged commercial offices was significant.[24] These agreements had ground their way through the rival bureaucracies with apparently minimal attention at the top of the American government, but in the future they deeply affected the exposure of Americans to Soviet citizens and of Soviets to American people and ways of doing things.

Another principal area of discussion was European security. Under an agreement reached in principle in May 1972, two projects were under way, implicitly linked. One was the perennial Soviet proposal for a Conference on Security and Cooperation in Europe (CSCE), involving all the European nations plus America and Canada, the other the long-discussed negotiation between NATO and Warsaw Pact members on "mutual and balanced force reductions" (MBFR), affecting conventional forces in the European theater.

On the CSCE project, a preparatory conference had been held in December 1972, and by June 1973 agreement had been reached on the terms of reference: the West was pressing to include human-rights issues alongside those of economics and borders. Conventional force reduction talks, on the other hand, were lagging. Few in any NATO capital were hopeful that such talks could produce early agreement, or perhaps any deal at all, but their initiation and conduct permitted the Administration to argue that with negotiations pending it would be a great mistake to make unilateral force reductions. The MBFR project thus became central to holding the line against renewal of the Mansfield proposal for force cuts, which Nixon and Kissinger, along with many moderate and conservative Democrats, continued to see as a serious threat to NATO cohesion and U.S. leadership.

In effect, these two projects were being traded against each other and were now proceeding in rough parallel in their opening stages. The discussion at the June 1973 summit gave them a boost, so that formal CSCE negotiations started in September 1973 and those on MBFR late in the year.

Perhaps the most important exchanges at the summit, however, were in private and not discussed in the communiqué or any published agreement. These were on two subjects, both at Soviet initiative: China and the Middle East. On China, the Soviets made clear their acute concern lest the United States enter into some kind of military arrangement with China, either helping China if threatened or giving specific military supplies or help. Nixon declined to say just what the Americans had discussed with China, but assured Brezhnev that the United States would make no arrangement inconsistent with the declaration on preventing nuclear war just concluded—a sweeping but vague assurance. In his memoirs, Nixon later said: "I could not be in the position of agreeing to establish a reporting relationship with him on our relations with the Chinese."[25] Yet, as he surely knew, Kissinger had by this time established with Zhou Enlai just such a reporting habit with China on all points of Chinese concern in U.S. dealings with the Soviet Union. As the Soviets probably surmised, a double standard had already been created.

In this same discussion of China, Kissinger went further than Nixon by telling a top Soviet official categorically that military matters had not been discussed with the Chinese.[26] If the Soviets had been given any picture of the wide-ranging strategic surveys that were by then habitual between Kissinger and Zhou, they would hardly have seen these as lacking in present and future military implications. But holding back was the right and indeed inevitable American policy. In later years, the temptation to form military links with China was handled in less sophisticated ways, notably by Zbigniew Brzezinski in 1978 and Alexander Haig in 1981. Its pitfalls were then all too clear. To wander into the minefield in 1972–73, even by mentioning the subject, would have been very unwise.

The other subject of private discussion, the Middle East, was broached in a startling way, late at night on Brezhnev's last day as Nixon's guest at San Clemente. The two had retired early, with the communiqué set and the discussions apparently complete, when Brezhnev summoned Nixon from bed by a message relayed through Kissinger. He then launched into a two-hour harangue on the dangers in the Middle East, trying to get Nixon to subscribe to a joint Soviet-American statement defining the principles that should govern a peaceful settlement. These included total Israeli withdrawal from occupied territories and in several other respects were tilted in a pro-Arab way that was obviously unacceptable. Even if the substance had been neutral, the idea would surely have been impractical, as some at least on the Soviet side must have known. Yet Brezhnev pushed relentlessly, to the point of saying that if hostilities were to break out in the area in the near future the United States would be largely to blame for having refused to take this joint step. Nixon declined the proposal, as courteously as he could in the strange circumstances, and the next day the communiqué simply said that the parties had discussed the Middle East and expressed their respective positions, diplomatic language for disagreement that was welcome news to Arabs concerned about Soviet support.

The Americans tended to suppose that Brezhnev's aim had been to undo, or at least avoid repeating, his mistake of failing to raise the subject at the 1972 Moscow summit. But while making a record for disclosure to Sadat was probably one Brezhnev purpose, there may well have been another and more important one, which apparently did not occur to Nixon or Kissinger. This was that Brezhnev was trying to distance himself, in devious fashion, from what he must already have known was a likely military thrust by Egypt within a few months. Since January, as he well knew but the top Americans may not have taken in, the Soviets had changed course with Sadat and were making major arms shipments to Egypt. While Soviet leaders surely had no direct word of Sadat's thinking, they may well have sensed that there was now a serious possibility of his going to war in some fashion.

If this was the case, the Soviets may have hoped that the discussion would jog the Americans to do something to forestall the outbreak of hostilities. On its face this idea may seem bizarre, but the Soviet Union had been badly damaged by the quick and overwhelming Israeli victory in 1967 and the exposure of Soviet arms as completely ineffectual. Now Israel was even better prepared, and the odds must have seemed high that history would repeat itself; if so, the Soviet Union's military reputation in the Arab world would be not merely damaged but shattered.

Brezhnev (and the Soviet military) probably saw any resort to arms by Sadat as a harebrained idea likely to lead only to quick defeat and humiliation. But since they had been expelled from Egypt, they had little influence or leverage with Sadat. In this remarkable situation, it is entirely possible that Brezhnev's appeal for the United States to act was in fact sincere! He was scared enough of the prospect of renewed war on this front to turn even to the archrival Americans.

Overall, despite its limited accomplishments, the 1973 summit produced more frank and searching exchanges between the two government heads than had been possible under the pressures for specific agreement at Moscow in 1972. Much of the détente structure envisaged in 1972 was thus falling into place, even without progress on Soviet-American trade or a SALT II agreement. To the public, the second summit could persuasively be presented as a success, albeit a far less dramatic one than in 1972. The communiqué and specific announcements were greeted with worldwide approval. At home, the applause was quickly drowned out by the next Watergate revelations in the Ervin Committee hearings.

On substantive matters the summit was not the big step forward both sides had hoped for at the start of the year. It was surely brought home to the Soviets, if it had not already been, how much Nixon's power was being affected by Watergate — it was on the day after Brezhnev's departure that the House and Senate first passed the ban on future military action in Indochina. But even this was partly offset by the obvious Soviet sympathy for Nixon's position and low regard for his critics. The Soviets still wanted to do business with him and with Kissinger, and had every hope that the squall would pass.

3. *Europe and Economics*

It was natural for the Nixon Administration to give a high priority in the first year of its second term to its relations with Europe — the core of the alliance system on which overall U.S. policy relied. And by 1973, the European Community had changed significantly in two respects. Three new members took their places in January 1973: Britain, Ireland, and Denmark, the first additions to the original membership of six dating from the Rome Treaty of 1957. (The original six were France, West Germany, Italy, Belgium, the Netherlands, and Luxembourg.) In anticipation, the Community in October 1972 voted to commit itself to the objective of political unity, with the first step expected to be starting to speak with one voice on selected international issues through its Council of Ministers.

The expansion and strengthening of the Community had long been supported by the United States. Moreover, *Ostpolitik* had proceeded in parallel with the American negotiations leading to détente. Yet Nixon and Kissinger continued to be skeptical of the West Germans' *Ostpolitik* and of Chancellor Brandt personally—for going too fast and with uncertain ultimate aims. They feared specifically that West Germany's devotion to NATO might lessen and its defense effort flag and, on the economic front, that the expanded European Community might evolve in ways that would set up barriers to trade with America. Already, the Europeans had embarked on several special relationships with former colonies in Africa.

For their part, the Europeans, notably West German Finance Minister Helmut Schmidt and his French counterpart, Valéry Giscard d'Estaing, were troubled by continued inflation, budget deficits, and trade imbalances in the United States, believing that these put special burdens on Europe and slowed overall growth. France in particular strongly favored fixing exchange rates as firmly as possible. When the American balance of payments once again worsened at the end of the boom year of 1972, in January 1973 a dollar crisis led, after costly and ineffective European efforts to hold the line, to the emergence by March, without formal agreement, of a floating rate system. A second dollar crisis caused the dollar to slip still further in early July.

As these differences and concerns over American fiscal and monetary policy worsened, the situation in the oil market was becoming steadily more disturbing. Europeans were well aware that American per capita energy use, consumption of oil in particular, was two or three times as great as theirs, and that heavy American demand for Middle East oil might lead to further price increases, which would fall hardest on Europeans because of their limited domestic oil supplies. (North Sea oil had not yet come on stream.) As Europeans saw more clearly than the leaders of the Nixon Administration, the oil situation was building rapidly toward a crisis, in their eyes largely brought on by American profligacy over the years.[27]

To these economic and energy concerns were added frictions over security matters and a felt need to redefine the Alliance's military aims and posture. In effect, the SALT I accords had ratified a condition of strategic nuclear parity between the United States and the Soviet Union, and this was bound to affect Europe, accustomed to rely on the American nuclear deterrent. The repeated American position—that the basic deterrent still held, but that NATO's European members should do more to build up conventional forces and thus raise the threshold of possible nuclear response—had never been fully accepted in practice by most European governments. By 1973 it grated for two additional reasons. The European powers, especially West Germany, had in fact significantly increased their efforts; and American forces stationed in Germany, while nominally at full strength, were in fact riddled by the demoralizing effects of the Vietnam War (including drug use), so that in the early 1970s their effectiveness was in grave doubt—as their hosts were acutely aware from seeing them every day at close quarters.[28]

Finally, the United States had an uneven record of consulting with its allies, notably over the Soviet-American Statement of Basic Principles signed in Moscow in May 1972. While the Europeans generally welcomed the whole panoply of détente agreements, there was considerable suppressed resentment that they had not been kept more fully in the picture. This fed an always latent fear that the superpowers might negotiate over their heads on matters that affected them profoundly. The periodic meetings of NATO Foreign Ministers seemed inadequate to deal with these frictions, and on matters concerning the European Community, there was no accepted way for the United States to talk with its members. Moreover, senior officials in the working organization, the European Commission in Brussels, were more assertive and felt entitled to a role and status of their own.

Against this background, a conversation between Kissinger and French President Georges Pompidou in December 1972, followed by an interview in which Pompidou suggested to James Reston of *The New York Times* the possibility of consultations "at the highest level," led the American leaders to think in terms of a dramatic initiative.[29] Nixon and Kissinger decided there should be a new declaration on the model of the wartime "Atlantic Charter." The new declaration would be worked out in the spring and summer, and Nixon would visit Europe to sign it and to reaffirm Alliance sentiment and ties.[30] This plan provided appealing public roles for its two authors, Kissinger to kick off the idea and negotiate the Charter, Nixon to supervise the whole and preside over the final stages. Once again, as with the opening to China and the decisive dealings with the Soviet Union, the State Department and the rest of the government would play only minimal parts. There is no record that Nixon and Kissinger discussed any of this with members of Congress.

Whether such a plan could ever have succeeded is open to grave doubt. Dealing with several sensitive allies, each with its own interests and public opinion to consider, was not remotely the same as dealing with a handful of leaders controlling totalitarian governments. In his memoirs, Kissinger later admitted as much—in terms not favorable to democracies:

> [R]elations with Europe did not lend themselves to secret diplomacy followed by spectacular pronouncements. There were too many nations involved to permit the use of backchannels.... Had I been Secretary of State at the beginning, instead of national security adviser, I might well

have been more sensitive to the need to engage allied foreign offices. But from the White House it was easier to deal with heads of government, and this antagonized the experts in the ministries whose goodwill was essential for the kind of detailed negotiations required by our initiative.[31]

Errors began with the formal announcement of the American project, christened "the Year of Europe," in a speech Kissinger gave to the annual meeting of Associated Press Editors on April 23. It was his first formal policy pronouncement, delivered at the height of his popularity and, as it happened, as Watergate reached fever pitch. The State Department was left out of all the planning and preparation and was indeed not even informed about the speech, which was the product solely of the speaker and his personal staff.[32]

Kissinger's ideas seemed to put Europe on the same plane with the Soviet Union and China, where such techniques had been used as part of dramatic transformations in relationships. Yet NATO and the European Community considered themselves "family" and resented being treated in this lordly way; it was like a father saying he would reserve Sunday for communication with his children. But this point was trivial alongside the tone of Kissinger's speech — didactic, occasionally scolding and petulant, and free of any suggestion that the United States might have neglected some of its own obligations, or might have erred in some of its economic policies or energy practices. This was the ex-Harvard professor laying down the law, not a senior American thoughtfully outlining a crisis, offering American help, and appealing for cooperation — as Secretary of State George Marshall had done in June 1947 in launching the plan named for him. Much of the discussion was conceptual and theoretical, with little to meet the growing list of European concerns.

Above all, in linking security and economic matters, Kissinger was all but saying: You Europeans depend on us for your protection, and therefore you must follow our lead unquestioningly on economic issues. Such a link was hardly news to thoughtful Europeans. It had existed from the inception of NATO, and not reduced when members of NATO became also the core of the European Community. It formed essential background to discussions in both areas, especially economics, right through the Cold War. Yet for Europe to know that the two were inevitably linked was one thing, to have the link thrown publicly in their faces something else again.

Moreover, the speech included one particularly stark passage: "The United States has global interests and responsibilities. Our European allies have regional interests." To a large extent, again, this was true. Since World War II, the interests of European countries outside their continent had indeed narrowed, with only occasional willingness to act even in areas where there were old connections. But to imply that Western Europe was no longer concerned with global issues was wide of the mark, especially in economic terms, and was certainly tactless and unlikely to help persuade Europeans to take wider perspectives.

Such were the main flaws in a speech that had few redeeming virtues — and was in all probability a lasting lesson to its perpetrator. Along the way, Kissinger included several vague passages on how Japan should be brought into the proposed exercise, but reactions quickly showed that neither the Japanese nor the Europeans were ready for such a three-sided framework of cooperation.

The follow-up diplomacy was equally clumsy. To be sure, the constellation of political leaders in Europe was not favorable in early 1973. In France, an aging Pompidou had just made the nationalistic Michel Jobert his Foreign Minister. Willy Brandt was preoccupied with projects for further easing in East-West relationships; and in Britain, Edward Heath, the most Europe-minded British leader of the postwar era, was noticeably cool to the United States. Heath had good personal relations with Nixon and had been the only major European leader to defend the Christmas bombing of Hanoi (Nixon was explosively critical of the others). But the British Prime Minister had almost an allergy to even concealed use of the often unwisely emphasized "special relationship" between Britain and America. Far from being willing to act as a bridge or explainer of American positions, he was drawn, both by his own instincts and by the need to prove himself a good European, to go out of his way to demonstrate that he was not going to act in the old ways. In practice this meant that Heath deferred to the French from the outset.

Finally, the smaller members of the fledgling European Community, especially Belgium and the Netherlands, were at this transitional time more than usually sensitive to the larger nations hogging the show. And France, historically the most disruptive member of the Community, was now asserting itself as if leadership were its natural due.

Into this minefield Kissinger blithely stumbled that spring and summer, trying to move forward almost exclusively through personal meetings sandwiched between his many other commitments, leaving himself wide open to misunderstanding on all sides as he dealt primarily with Michel Jobert. While Nixon and Kissinger prided themselves on having warmed up Franco-American relations a great deal since the chilly eleven years of Charles de Gaulle (1958–69), Jobert was by instinct a proud Frenchman in the Gaullist tradition. He proceeded to tie Kissinger into bowknots, and the project was soon mired down. The French spurned two initial American drafts, and the Community refused to let Americans discuss drafts with its members individually until it had framed a Community position. (It proposed then to speak with a single voice through the temporary chairman of its Council of Ministers, the Foreign Minister of Denmark.) By fall Kissinger was intensely irritated not only at Jobert but at almost every European leader, while they in turn believed that Nixon had tuned out and a distracted Kissinger was being crude.

Not all was sour, fortunately. At the Treasury, George Shultz quickly developed good working relations with his key European counterparts, Helmut Schmidt and Valéry Giscard d'Estaing. Always in style a tortoise to Kissinger's hare, Shultz welcomed the participation of colleagues, worked through counterparts in foreign governments, drew in the career specialists at every stage, and maintained steady and extensive contacts with Congress. His first task on taking over in June 1972 was to work out and sell a new monetary system to replace the bargaining and politics of the Smithsonian agreement. What he proposed, on the advice of a "heavyweight" team of experts, was, in his own words, "a novel proposal, having the appearance of a traditional par-value system, in which currency values were formally stated, but with automatic and symmetrical changes in par values triggered by changes in reserves." In effect, a floating rate system with rules, obligations, and penalties.[33]

At an early stage, Shultz brought in the key European colleagues, Schmidt, Giscard, and Tony Barber of Britain. By the summer of 1973, a series of preparatory meetings with this group—the first one actually held in the library of the White House (in Nixon's absence)—bonded them closely, and the transition to the new floating exchange rate system was accomplished. The adjustments were inevitably painful in the short run, but the gain in teamwork among top economic officials was great. In the fall, on Shultz's initiative, the Japanese were brought into the "library group," which was to become the foundation stone for later summit meetings on economic issues. It was a masterful performance, at a time when teamwork was badly needed.[34]

Moreover, Shultz also worked closely with William Eberle, the Special Trade Representative, to organize a new multilateral negotiation on trade, which the major nations had agreed on in principle in 1972. Its chief objective, at least in American eyes, was to reduce the nontariff barriers that had spread rapidly, notably in Japan, after the significant tariff reductions achieved in the Kennedy Round of the 1960s. In the summer of 1973, a successful organizing meeting was held in Tokyo. The process then became known as the "Tokyo Round," instead of the "Nixon Round" as it had started out, a change probably due partly to the Watergate cloud. Likewise, the long-paired CSCE and MBFR negotiations got under way in 1973, with a first working session on European security in Helsinki in July and on mutual force reduction talks in Vienna in late October. The traditional cumbersome methods of multilateral diplomacy went forward that spring and summer almost unaffected by Watergate or Kissinger's publicized efforts to declare the Year of Europe.

A benevolent observer might argue that without the horrible example of Kissinger's ill-judged venture, neither the Americans nor the key Europeans would have made the adjustments that led, by 1975–76, to the institution of seven-nation summits. As it was, American relations with Western Europe and Japan were still strained in October 1973, especially over the oil situation. In all, the reservoir of goodwill, on which both sides had drawn when they got into trouble, was still well below its normal level, and this may have made a serious difference in European reactions to the events in the Middle East that followed.

4. Kissinger Becomes Secretary of State

After the 1972 election and the Paris Agreement, Kissinger and others in the White House assumed that he would retire as National Security Advisor at some point in 1973. William Rogers was also expected to leave as Secretary of State, to be replaced, most assumed, by a new face. Kissinger himself supposed that the choice at State would fall on Kenneth Rush, by then Deputy Secretary of Defense, whose ties with Nixon went back to the days when he had taught at the Duke University Law School while Nixon was a student there. As Ambassador to West Germany, Rush had done yeoman service in orchestrating the 1971 four-power agreement on Berlin. When he moved over to be Deputy Secretary of State right after Nixon's second Inauguration, the supposition that he would take over the top spot gained momentum.

The principal rival candidate appeared to be John Connally, who had backed Nixon solidly and openly in 1972, organizing a group called Democrats for Nixon. Nixon considered putting him on the Republican ticket as Vice President, but Connally demurred, fearing that Republicans would see him as a Johnny-come-lately. In early 1973 he moved formally to the Republican Party. In his memoirs, Nixon gave his opinion of Connally at that time:

> I believed that John Connally was the only man in either party who clearly had the potential to be a great president. He had the necessary "fire in the belly," the energy to win, and the vision to lead.[35]

In January 1973 a senior political observer close to Connally told this author that the script was set. Kissinger would carry through the return-engagement summit with Brezhnev, finish tidying other jobs, and depart along with Rogers; Connally would become Secretary of State by the fall of 1973. If he was to succeed Nixon, he needed a top job and the only position not too small for him was at State.[36]

It seemed certain that the choice lay between Rush and Connally, and that Kissinger was not in contention. He had affronted the White House staff mightily in late 1972 by appearing to dissociate himself from unpopular decisions, notably the Christmas bombing of Hanoi, and by what they saw as personal publicity-seeking. He had also become altogether too popular for Nixon's ego or personal comfort—it can hardly have sat well that *Time* magazine's year-end issue paired the two as joint "Men of the Year" for 1972.

With the advent of the Watergate crisis, the odds began to shift. In an April 1973 Gallup poll, Kissinger was viewed favorably by an impressive 62 percent of those polled.[37] Meanwhile, Rush had little occasion to shine nor, apparently, was he brought into the salvage crew helping Nixon handle Watergate. Connally, on the other hand, was invited to the White House in early May as a special advisor on that front, and stayed on intermittently at least into July. According to one report he told the President that he faced a "disaster" and should clean house completely.[38] Then, when the taping system became known, Connally advised Nixon bluntly to destroy the tapes publicly (and presumably claim that he had acted on national security grounds). Such advice would have been pure Connally, and might just have worked.[39] Whatever he urged the President to do, his advice was not accepted. He was shortly caught up in troubles of his own, but Nixon continued to have a very high opinion of him and supported him for Vice President in 1976 and for President in 1980.[40]

As Watergate became more threatening, Kissinger became important in a new dimension—not only for what he was doing but for the respectability he gave the Administration and the President. He had apparently been planning to return to Harvard that fall or early in 1974, but by June he sensed that he might be asked to become Secretary of State. He was right. When Nixon eased Rogers out in August (in typically graceless fashion) he turned at once to Kissinger. The appointment was announced on August 22. That Kissinger also continued to serve as National Security Advisor underlined the extent of his power.

After the Labor Day holiday, the Senate Foreign Relations Committee held confirmation hearings from September 7 to September 21. The reason for their length was not the members' hostility to Kissinger; on the contrary, its liberal and moderate members were the only congressional group with which Kissinger had long been on friendly terms, thanks to informal private meetings arranged by Chairman Fulbright. With Vietnam now effectively in the past as a divisive issue, the chairman and leading committee members such as Hubert Humphrey and Jacob Javits were (and remained) outspoken Kissinger supporters on almost every important issue, notably détente with the Soviet Union.[41]

Yet the committee felt compelled to air thoroughly the questions that had been raised about Kissinger's role in 1969 wiretaps on NSC staff members suspected of having leaked the secret bombing of Cambodia. It finally concluded that Kissinger was essentially correct in claiming that he had done no more than complain vigorously about the impact on policy of the leaks, and had then supplied at Nixon's request the names of people with knowledge of the leaked information, but had not been involved in the decision to resort to wiretaps. The matter appeared to have been laid to rest.[42]

The senators spent considerable time on détente and arms control, in a sympathetic vein, while the Middle East and oil price problems came in for only fragmentary mention at the close of the committee's last session with Kissinger on September 17. Four days later it voted 16–1 to confirm the nominee, and on September 22 he was sworn in, to wide acclaim.

. . .

While the hearings were being held, with Kissinger still only National Security Advisor, there was a dramatic change in Chile. On September 11, a military coup ousted and killed President Salvador Allende Gossens, installing in power a junta headed by General Augusto Pinochet. In his hearings, Kissinger was asked only whether the United States had been involved in any way in the coup, and said that it had not been. This reply was accepted and the issue did not affect his confirmation. It did, however, become progressively more controversial in the next few months, and a year later became a major issue, when CIA political activity in the 1970–73 period was revealed. (The plot to upset the 1970 elections in Chile by violent means did not become known till the Church Committee hearings on intelligence activities in 1975.)

The Nixon Administration had pursued a mixed policy toward Allende after he was installed, professing a correct posture and continuing some forms of U.S. aid to Chile, while opposing several loans from multilateral agencies. Allende proceeded to nationalize American and other foreign companies, triggering negotiations from which no adequate compensation emerged. His domestic economic policies were recklessly populist, leading quickly to currency devaluation, very high inflation, and steadily growing economic difficulty for all classes. As opposition to him grew, Allende turned in early 1973 to moves that seemed to many to be clearly aimed at installing a dictatorial regime and suppressing opposition. (One key action, for example, was to deny any newsprint supplies to the main opposition paper.) Certainly this alarmist view was strongly held by Eduardo Frei, the former President, who was still much admired by many Americans (though not by Nixon) and whose judgments reached many American observers.

The issue of CIA involvement in Chile had been aired in Washington earlier in 1973, as a result of documents leaked to the press from the files of the giant American multinational corporation International Telephone and Telegraph. These indicated that in 1970 ITT had contributed large sums of money to Alessandri's campaign, with the cooperation and connivance of CIA officers in Chile. Questions about this were directed at Richard Helms when he came before the Senate Foreign Relations Committee in early February for confirmation as Ambassador to Iran. Director of Central Intelligence since 1965 and a career intelligence officer since World War II, Helms was never a Nixon favorite. Most crucially, in June 1972 he had failed to carry out an order that he head off FBI investigation of the funds found on the Watergate burglars. (Nixon wanted him to claim that such FBI activity would interfere with CIA operations.)[43] He was replaced at the CIA by James Schlesinger in December 1972, and named to the Iran post partly so that he would not feel aggrieved, but probably also so that he would be far away from prying inquiry.

At Helms's public confirmation hearing, Senator Symington asked him, out of the blue, whether the CIA had tried "to overthrow the government of Chile" or had caused money to be "passed to opponents of Allende." Helms responded with a categorical negative to both questions, and also denied that the CIA had been involved at all in "the war" (meaning the political struggles) in Chile since 1970.[44] Here he was adhering instinctively to conventions about discussing covert operations that had been accepted by key congressional committees and the CIA for many years. Under these conventions, set up and made firm by Senator Richard Russell in particular, questions concerning any sort of covert operation were not to be raised or answered except in executive (private) sessions before designated members of the Armed Services and Appropriations committees. (At that time there were no separate congressional intelligence committees such as were created after 1975.) In the March hearing, Helms was also under express orders from the White House to reveal nothing about the Agency's actions in Chile.[45] At the time, his responses were accepted in most quarters, although the testimony did show close connections between CIA and ITT personnel, and the controversy was soon overshadowed by the first revelations of the Watergate scandal. In later years, CIA activities in Chile and Helms's testimony were to become significant parts of an intense debate over CIA covert operations.[46]

In the summer of 1973, riots broke out in Chile, engaging the middle class especially and creating a sense of impending showdown. In early September, Ambassador Nathaniel Davis reported to Kissinger (then still at the White House) that a crisis might erupt at any moment and that the embassy, following standing instructions, was staying scrupulously neutral.

In his memoirs, as in his testimony to the Senate Foreign Relations Committee in September, Kissinger stoutly denied that there was any American involvement in the 1973 coup.[47] It was a denial that seemed credible at the time and has essentially stood up since, insofar as it relates to the planning and execution of the coup. That the United States would not oppose a coup, however, had clearly been the dominant impression both in Chile and among Chile watchers, and was confirmed when the Administration moved rapidly not only to recognize the Pinochet regime but to start talks on renewed financial help. The new regime was imprisoning thousands of Allende adherents and embarking on other acts of repression, so this Administration posture—a "policy of silence" toward abuse of human rights, as it was seen—was criticized by many Americans and sharply attacked by liberals in Congress.[48] Pinochet's regime was from the first particularly stiff and unwilling to explain or justify its actions. Thus, in the forum of world and above all Latin American and U.S. public opinion, what stood out was not Allende's behavior but the military character of the new regime and its initial repressive acts, including the arrest and detention of several U.S. citizens. Leftists were joined by liberals and many moderates in seeing the murdered Allende as a martyr for having pursued progressive policies after having been democratically elected. In the battle for public opinion, this view won hands down, despite the statement by ex-President Frei in early October that "a civil war was being well prepared by the Marxists" and that only the action of Chile's armed forces had saved his life and those of many other liberals and moderates.[49]

Much of the debate centered on whether the cool Nixon policy toward loans and other help, the "invisible blockade," had undermined Allende, a charge later largely rejected by one centrist scholar.[50] Chile went off the front pages rapidly that fall, and remained off for almost all of the next year. Nixon doubtless saw the overthrow of Allende as a significant gain for U.S. policy. In his view it removed a regime that was already crypto-Communist and headed all the way, which in time might by both example and action have moved other Latin American countries to the extreme left and to strongly anti-American positions.

Yet if Nixon drew back to look broadly at how the world situation had evolved in the first nine months of his seond term, a time for which he had held high hopes when he was reelected, he can hardly have been pleased. Kissinger's "Year of Europe" project continued to go nowhere. Relations with China were stable on the surface, but not of great import. Détente with the Soviet Union continued, but there was no sign of progress in removing the impasse created by the pending Jackson-Vanik Amendment. (In August the eminent Soviet scientist and well-known dissident Andrei Sakharov publicly urged Americans to hold firm for conditions on emigration policy, and The New York Times and influential liberals shortly switched to support the amendment. On September 26 it was approved by the powerful House Ways and Means Committee.)

Moreover, Nixon's relations with Congress remained cool and friction-laden. An attempt to cut back domestic spending by impounding funds already appropriated was rejected in March, before Watergate broke, and by fall Congress was on the verge of passing legislation that would forbid the practice in the future. Another significant Nixon effort, to raise the defense budget by a small percentage, ran into heavy weather. Much of the country had expected that the end of American involvement in Vietnam would produce a "peace dividend," not realizing that the decline in funds for the Vietnam War was more than offset by the steady rise in the cost of domestic programs. By this time the defense budget was down to 6 percent of the gross national product, while social spending continued to rise inexorably, much of it in the form of "entitlements" whose level was largely independent of any explicit decision by Congress or the President.

Nixon wanted to check both trends, particularly the downward trend in defense appropriations. Yet during the summer, Congress came close to denying funds for the Trident SLBM-carrying submarine, the first strategic missile program since the ICBM and SLBM programs were closed down in 1965, and considered essential to keeping some balance with the now clearly fast-moving Soviet MIRV program. The country as a whole was not disposed to raise defense spending, and leading Democrats were more and more vocal in questioning both totals and particular projects.[51]

· · ·

Taking office on September 22 as Secretary of State, Kissinger lost no time in making his voice heard. Two days later, on an annual occasion that Presidents had often attended themselves, he delivered the main American speech at the opening session of the United Nations General Assembly, followed on October 8 by a major speech to an international gathering, "Pacem in Orbis," convened in Washington.[52] Both speeches were on a high plane, suitable for the first major speeches by a new Secretary of State and considerably more eloquent than anything that had come from Nixon or Secretary Rogers for many years past. Kissinger devoted much of his UN remarks to areas of common action by the "world community," stressing particularly "the quality of life." As one of five guiding principles to this end, he said, "A world community cannot remain divided between the permanently rich and the permanently poor," and pledged full American cooperation toward "new and imaginative solutions to the problems of development." His most specific proposal, carrying out a promise made to Senator Humphrey in his confirmation hearings, called for the convening in 1974 of a World Food Conference "to discuss ways to maintain adequate food supplies." He noted that stocks of cereals had been depleted steadily since 1969 and were by then "at the lowest levels in years," with the possibility that reserves could not be rebuilt within the 1970s. The speech reflected the hopes then held by many, in and out of government, that with détente stabilizing the superpower relationship, attention could now move increasingly to this type of problem.

The Secretary of State's second speech likewise spoke in terms of global hopes, but was at the same time a strong argument for moderation and realism in dealing with the Soviet Union, arguing the case specifically against the Jackson-Vanik Amendment. Kissinger eloquently defended the role of the statesman charged with action responsibility, as opposed to the pure idealist anxious for immediate results, an argument that probably went down well with a sophisticated international audience but had little effect on Senator Jackson and his allies.

At this critical point in Kissinger's fight to preserve the momentum of Nixon's détente program, the country's and the world's attention moved to the Middle East, where war broke out between Egypt and Israel on October 6. At the same time, Nixon had to cope with a new top-level scandal and with major Watergate developments. For a time, domestic and international crises ran side by side.

5. Watergate and Another Scandal

The Watergate scandal was often likened, then and later, to a cancer, moving from apparent remission to virulence and back again, weakening the patient progressively. When the Senate's Ervin Committee went into recess in July 1973 (never to resume its hearings), there was a short remission while the country digested the revelation of Nixon's taping system. The White House still withheld the tapes themselves, but when Special Prosecutor Archibald Cox went to court to obtain selected ones, Judge Sirica granted his motion. The White House promptly appealed the order to the Court of Appeals for the District of Columbia, as it was of course entitled to do.

Then, in September, a major new scandal broke open. Attorney General Richardson disclosed in court (as he had privately to Nixon in August) that there was conclusive evidence that Vice President Spiro Agnew had accepted bribes from people with government interests, both as governor of Maryland and after assuming his present office. Though totally independent of Watergate in its origins, this new charge inevitably added a big smudge to the Administration's image. After an intensive personal review of the file by Nixon himself, Richardson worked out with Agnew's lawyers a deal for the Vice President to plead "no contest" (nolo contendere) to the charges. Having thus preserved a semblance of dignity in what was for practical purposes a confession of guilt, Agnew resigned on October 10.

Foreseeing this outcome, Nixon had ready the nomination of Gerald Ford, Minority Leader of the House, as Agnew's successor. (He had considered John Connally and others, but in his canvassing of congressional leaders had become convinced that only Ford could be readily confirmed.) Many noted that with the honest, experienced, and respected Ford in line to succeed, rather than the erratic and fiercely partisan Agnew, it was less difficult to contemplate the removal of Nixon.

On October 12, as the Ford nomination went forward (the result was never in doubt, but he was not confirmed till early December), the Court of Appeals for the District of Columbia upheld Judge Sirica's August order to produce selected tapes. This triggered several days of intense negotiation between Alexander Haig, acting for Nixon, and Richardson, consulting with Special Prosecutor Cox. Finally, Richardson (but not Cox) agreed to a procedure for submitting these tapes to Senator Stennis, who was to decide on the relevance of particular tapes and passages and what should be made public. But Cox stoutly resisted Haig's demand that he refrain thereafter from seeking any more tapes, a demand Richardson also considered improper. Both men were mindful that in Richardson's confirmation hearings in May before the Senate Judiciary Committee, he had pledged that Cox (whom he had personally selected) would be removed only for extreme misconduct, which the subpoena seeking the tapes obviously was not. The disagreement came to a head on Saturday, October 20. Sticking to his position and pledge, Richardson resigned rather than carry out Nixon's order to fire Cox. His deputy, William Ruckelshaus, also resigned, and it fell to Solicitor General Robert Bork to carry out the order—while at the same time joining with many others in pressing Nixon strongly to appoint a new Special Prosecutor.

Nixon may have thought that the October War between Egypt and Israel, which, as we shall see, was at its most critical point that same weekend, would limit the public response to his actions. On the contrary, what was quickly labeled "the Saturday Night Massacre" set off a vast national outpouring of protest and disapproval. Nixon's power and standing never recovered from the damage that weekend. That he had gone to such extremes to prevent release of key tapes could only mean that he was much more implicated personally than most of the public had supposed up to that point. Moreover, the firing of his highest legal officers—for doing their duty and adhering to pledges given to the Senate—hit a national nerve to which he was extraordinarily insensitive, as to most questions that involved the concept of the rule of law, throughout the crisis.

In face of the clamor, Nixon reversed course, released the contested tapes to Sirica unconditionally, and shortly appointed a top trial lawyer, Leon Jaworski of Houston, to succeed Cox, with a guarantee to Jaworski that he could go after more tapes and even bring the President to court. Right away came the revelation that one of the key tapes had a missing segment of eighteen and a half minutes, which set off a new mini-storm, with unconvincing explanations. With rising belief that Nixon had been personally involved in the cover-up, his impeachment became a serious possibility. Under the Constitution it was for the House to vote "articles of impeachment" and for the Senate then to sit as a court to take final action. On Speaker Carl Albert's advice, the chairman of the House Judiciary Committee, Peter Rodino of New Jersey, began gearing up for a committee investigation looking to possible impeachment articles. John Doar, a lawyer formerly in the Justice Department under Robert Kennedy, was appointed in December to serve as chief counsel.

Chapter Eight

THE MIDDLE EAST WAR

AND THE OIL CRISIS

1. *The Run-up to War*

In his memoirs, Henry Kissinger says flatly that Anwar el-Sadat decided as early as the summer of 1972 to go to war with Israel; his source was almost certainly Sadat himself at a later time.[1] But for Nixon and Kissinger at the time, the situation was dominated by the expulsion of the Soviet military presence, which, as we have seen, they considered evidence of Sadat's being resigned to passivity against Israel.

In fact, the expulsion freed Sadat's hand, and in the next fifteen months he made remarkable improvements in the Egyptian military posture. He went right back to the Soviet Union for much more massive weapons supplies than it had provided while it had a presence in Egypt. He turned to private sources in the Federal Republic of Germany for one especially crucial piece of equipment—high-powered water hoses to blast holes in the enormous sand wall that was a key part of Israel's defenses along the Suez Canal. Most important of all, he formed a firm compact to attack Israel jointly with Syria, which also got large-scale new help from the Soviet Union.

The story of this secret Egyptian buildup and deception is fascinating for military historians, but for purposes of understanding U.S. policy needs only this listing. For early warning of a possible attack on Israel, U.S. intelligence agencies depended overwhelmingly on Israel's renowned secret intelligence organization, Mossad. There must have been some sharing of material from especially sensitive sources. But it is clear from the record that U.S. intelligence agencies veered back and forth during the spring and summer, and gave no warning in early October, even after the skeleton Soviet civilian contingent in Egypt was visibly evacuated by air, two days before the attack came.

By these measures, Sadat achieved what to most observers had seemed impossible, tactical surprise. His reputation soared at home and abroad. Israelis and Americans, including top officials and especially Kissinger, now knew for sure that they were dealing with a remarkably able and resourceful Egyptian leader.

Yet Sadat knew all along that even if he greatly improved his forces and was able to get across the canal in the first phase of a war, the odds were still great that a fully mobilized Israeli Army and Air Force, resupplied from the United States, would wear down and in fairly short order defeat the Egyptian Army and Air Force, which had been trained and organized overwhelmingly for the initial battle. He needed some form of pressure, direct and indirect through third nations, to keep U.S. help to Israel to bearable levels and to make life sufficiently difficult so that the United States would assist a compromise armistice in which Egypt might retain some of its gains and would in any case not be humiliated. For this purpose, he put together an extraordinarily sophisticated plan to achieve strategic surprise. Its key was enlisting Saudi Arabia, the bellwether Arab oil-producing state, to frame and unleash an "oil weapon" — major embargoes and cutbacks in oil shipments — that would threaten and damage the Western oil-consuming nations and cause them to press Israel and the United States strongly for a compromise outcome.

During the era of Gamal Abdel Nasser, from 1954 to his death in September 1970, few relationships among nations were more bitterly antagonistic than that between his radical, sprawling, modernizing, pan-Arab Egypt, with its 35 million people, and the conservative, traditional, and vastly less populous Saudi kingdom across the Red Sea, with perhaps 6 million. Only over Israel was there agreement, on a posture of unremitting hostility. For the rest, the two were always at odds. When Nasser was at his most assertive in 1962, he stirred up and supported radical South Yemen in a five-year war against North Yemen, which for a time threatened Saudi dominance of the Arabian Peninsula. In almost every respect the two nations were antagonists, and on no issue did they differ more than over their relationships with the United States.

What had drawn Saudi Arabia and the United States together, in the first instance, was that American geologists had been key players in the discovery of the country's vast oil deposits in the 1930s. By World War II these were already very important to America, and President Roosevelt went to great effort to cultivate the longtime Saudi ruler, the legendary Ibn Saud.

In the late 1930s Ibn Saud granted substantial concessions for oil discovery to Standard Oil of California and Texaco, which combined their operations through a joint company, Caltex. Roosevelt approved a major program of aid and support to Saudi Arabia in 1943, with a formal declaration that the kingdom was vital to the defense of the United States, and in 1944 Caltex split off its Arabian operations into a new entity, the Arabian-American Oil Company (Aramco), which rapidly became a large American presence in the country.[2]

In 1957, Ibn Saud's first son and successor, Prince Saud, paid a state visit to Washington. In 1962 Prince Saud stepped down in favor of his brother Faisal, who by 1964 had consolidated his position as clear-cut ruler of the kingdom, continuing in the conservative traditions of his father. When Britain in 1968 announced that it would withdraw all its forces and presence from the Gulf region by the end of 1971, Saudi Arabia took on added importance as a "twin pillar" of future security there, alongside Iran.[3] But relations between the two countries were never close. In addition to historical legacies of rivalry, the Iranians were Shiite Muslims and the Saudi were adherents of the Wahhabi sect, an austere branch of Sunni Islam. Culturally, the differences were also acute, Iran under the Shah open to Western influences, the Saudi zealously excluding them.

The two dominant themes in postwar Saudi Arabian foreign policy were always fervent anti-Communism and anti-Zionism. It rejected the legitimacy of the state of Israel and adhered strongly to the Arab boycott of companies trading with Israel. Faisal also remained determinedly opposed to secular radical Arab states. When Sadat succeeded Nasser in the fall of 1970, Faisal was at first suspicious, but decided in short order that this new man was worth dealing with. In reaching this judgment, Faisal appears to have been much influenced by his brother-in-law, Kamal Adham. "A man of great intelligence and infinite cunning," Adham had occupied for years a special place in Faisal's regime. An active international businessman, he was also, for practical purposes, the head of Saudi intelligence, with extensive liaison links to other intelligence services including the CIA (and Britain's MI6 counterpart). He moved freely even in Arab countries on edgy terms with Saudi Arabia and had a business relationship with Sadat's wife. From these contacts he assured Faisal that he could get along with Sadat, and the link rapidly became an unproclaimed entente.[4]

According to one knowledgeable account, as early as November 1970 the idea took form in Faisal's mind that if Egypt were to expel the Soviet military forces, the United States might take a "more positive" (that is, more pro-Arab) position over Arab-Israel problems. He sent Adham to Cairo, where Sadat allegedly countered with the suggestion that he would ask the Soviets to leave if Israel withdrew its forces from the east bank of the Suez Canal and allowed the canal to be cleared for all shipping. In 1971 Sadat did negotiate (in vain) for a deal with Israel over the opening of the canal, and Adham became pivotal in Saudi-Egyptian collaboration from then on.[5]

By 1972, the dominant position of the Arab oil-producing countries, Saudi Arabia in particular, made evident the possibility of their using oil as a political weapon. Sadat himself spoke of its use for political purposes, as did a number of other Arab leaders. In September the Harvard-trained Saudi Oil Minister, Zaki Yamani, told a Washington audience that oil could be in the picture, but stopped short of an outright threat. At that point, however, Faisal himself was not persuaded, and even publicly stated that it was "dangerous even to think of this." Seeing his U.S. tie as central to Saudi security against the radicals, he was then opposed to any kind of confrontation with the United States.[6] Among Americans who followed Middle East matters, some argued that the vaunted new power of the OPEC countries was an illusion, that if the consumer nations would only stand firm and act in concert, the producers could not raise prices or limit production without suffering too severely for the action to be sustained. These quarters also objected strenuously to the idea that U.S. policy might be dictated by repressive foreign governments, at the potential expense of America's virtual ally, Israel.[7]

A different view was stated by a State Department official, James E. Akins, in an article published in the April 1973 issue of *Foreign Affairs*, "The Oil Crisis: This Time the Wolf Is Here." Akins was a Foreign Service officer who had become immersed in the oil situation at his job at State. (As he completed the article, he was detailed temporarily to the White House to work with Peter Flanigan, Nixon's aide on economic affairs, to help frame an energy policy.) The main point of Akins's article, as its title suggested, was that oil production, as well as proven and probable oil reserves, were now so concentrated in the Middle East, above all in Saudi Arabia, that it was naive to suppose that price and output adjustments could be warded off, or that such great and concentrated power might not be used at some point in support of Arab objectives. This would inevitably be to the detriment of the main oil-consuming countries, with the United States about to become as dependent on Middle East oil as Western Europe and Japan already were.[8]

Akins's policy recommendations were general: cooperation with other nations, developing alternative energy sources, and "controlling our consumption reasonably," along with a suggestion (never pursued) that Saudi Arabia might be persuaded to increase its output to meet the supply crisis. None of this was novel to anyone who worked on energy problems, but the article did spread to a wider circle of readers, including policymakers all over the world, the picture of the situation that was shared in broad terms by most, though not all, oil experts. It appears that it did reach this wider audience, especially in Japan.[9]

By the spring of 1973, the managements of the top international oil companies were expressing their strong concerns both privately to government officials and in a few cases in public.[10] But with the general public, and especially among strong supporters of Israel, their warnings had little credibility. Until the fall of 1973, the American public and Congress simply did not focus on the underlying situation and pace of change.[11]

Nevertheless, by then King Faisal had changed his mind about using oil as a political weapon, in part at the urging of Sadat and in part because radical Arabs, including the Palestinians, were making threats of disruptive action and were angry at Saudi Arabia for refusing to enlist fully in the Arab cause against Israel. These threats were made concrete by two acts of sabotage against the pipeline to the Mediterranean (called Tapline) that carried much of the Saudi oil to market. In May, Faisal used an interview with top officials of Aramco to send an urgent message to Washington and the American public, that it was "absolutely mandatory" and a matter of "extreme urgency" for the United States to act "to change the direction that events are taking in the Middle East today," pointedly suggesting "a simple disavowal of Israeli policies and actions." In a second interview a few weeks later, Faisal—fresh from a trip to Cairo—specifically threatened loss of the American oil concessions if the United States did not give "positive support" to Saudi Arabia and, by implication, to the Arab position vis-à-vis Israel.

In late August, Sadat made a secret trip to Riyadh, where he informed Faisal that he intended to go to war with Israel, beginning with a surprise attack at the end of September or in early October, and asked for Saudi Arabia's support. In response, Faisal pledged a half-billion dollars toward the cost of the war, and, above all, promised to lead in using the oil weapon. At the same time, the king stressed that he did not want this to be on a one-shot basis. Rather, he pleaded, "Give us time. We don't want to use our oil as a weapon in a battle that goes on for two or three days, and then stops. We want to see a battle which goes on for a long enough time for world opinion to be mobilized."[12] Given the disastrous experience of 1967, Sadat might have had difficulty promising to sustain the war for as long as Faisal demanded, but by then his new military measures had made him confident that he could hang on long enough. Sadat envisaged that his surprise attack, already arranged to take place jointly with a Syrian attack in the Golan Heights, would have at least initial successes. Arab influence would hold the line against effective UN intervention, and the oil weapon would be brandished, unleashed if necessary, against the United States and especially against its vulnerable major allies in Europe and Japan, thus restraining American support for Israel. A negotiating framework would then emerge from which Egypt and its Arab collaborators could not but gain. It was a shrewd scenario, reflecting both daring and careful calculation.

Concurrently and on their own, almost all the oil-producing countries were moving by September to scrap the Teheran and Tripoli price agreements of 1971. OPEC summoned oil company representatives to Vienna on October 8 to discuss a new agreement, primarily to increase the producing countries' percentages of direct participation in oil revenues, but with price changes strongly hinted. Meanwhile, OPEC spokesmen sharply criticized the consumer countries for taking "windfall profits" from the steady increase in market prices of oil.[13] With a tight oil market, great pressure on price, and strong feelings among Arab oil producers, the oil situation at the end of September, for its own reasons, was visibly ready for revolutionary change.

. . .

During these crucial months, Henry Kissinger was personally in charge of American diplomacy, with little input from a distracted President. The summer before, he had interpreted Sadat's expulsion of the Soviet presence as a calming of the situation, and in the following months Vietnam negotiations took precedence over any Middle East move. He did take steps to set up a back channel to Sadat personally, and from the messages exchanged, however limited at first, got a strong impression that Sadat was a man of vision, realism, and sophistication.

Then, after the Paris Agreement in January 1973 had temporarily reduced the pressure of Indochina policy, he invited Sadat's emissary, Hafiz Ismail, to visit Washington for a public meeting with Nixon, followed by a secret two-day meeting with Kissinger at a private house in Connecticut. The two made little headway, however. Kissinger later claimed that he was sure that only after the Israeli elections, set for late October, could Israel be urged to make at least a show of progress. In any case, he offered no real hope of movement. Sadat was bound to conclude that the United States was simply not ready to help. Shortly after the meeting Kissinger learned (in some undisclosed way) that Sadat had informed the Saudis of this secret meeting, a fact that in itself should have sounded a warning note.[14]

Sadat kept trying, however, and seems to have taken the initiative for a second meeting in May, when Kissinger was in Paris to meet with his Vietnamese interlocutor, Le Duc Tho. Again the meeting was secret, in a private home, and again there was no progress. After it, Kissinger was told by his host that Hafiz Ismail, whom Kissinger had sized up as an exceptionally able and sensitive man, seemed utterly downcast by the outcome. Then, in late June, came the bizarre episode in San Clemente, when Brezhnev warned Nixon (and Kissinger) about the danger of an Arab-Israeli war. Though it seemed to the Americans to be an effort to get credit with Egypt, Brezhnev may have been genuinely trying to avert a conflict he saw as likely to be disastrous for both Egypt and Soviet interests in the Middle East. In all probability, this exchange was reported to Sadat, and the American response must once again have seemed clear evidence that the United States was not prepared to make any move to lessen the danger of war with Israel.

As we have noted, part of the failure to grasp what was afoot was the overwhelming American reliance on Israel's Mossad. Reports and evaluations not supported by Mossad tended to get little attention and respect. But the most basic reason for failure to anticipate Egypt's plans for war was the universal assumption—in Israeli, American, and Soviet minds alike—that an Egyptian attack would be a military debacle for Egypt itself.

Essentially, Sadat took advantage of a failure of imagination, as much in Israel as in Washington. In past Arab-Israeli wars, each side had fought to defeat the other, the conventional objective in military combat. In such a contest Israel might take losses, but could expect to emerge victorious through superior training, equipment, organization, and morale. What did not occur to Mrs. Meir and her generals in 1973 was that Sadat might aim not to achieve a conventional victory but rather to score enough success to erase the Egyptian (and Arab) loser complex vis-à-vis Israel, thus setting up a new psychological balance in the negotiations they expected to follow.

Finally, an important reason for surprise was the choice of the Yom Kippur holy day as the date for the attack. On that day, October 6, the people of Israel, including most of its front-line forces, would be celebrating this most sacred day in the bosom of their families. Sadat was doing almost exactly what Ho Chi Minh and his generals had done five and a half years earlier, when they selected the Vietnamese national holiday of Tet for their decisive offensive in the Vietnam War.

2. The Course of the October War

The war between Israel, on one side, and Egypt and Syria on the other, which raged from October 6 till October 28, 1973, was launched by Sadat for the objectives just described. His ally Assad in Syria sought to recover as much as possible of the Golan Heights, which Israel had taken over in the 1967 War. For Israel the aim was simply to defeat both Egypt and Syria, at bearable cost, and to hold on to at least the strategically important territory it had occupied since 1967. All three hoped that the war might lead to useful negotiations toward a more stable and peaceful regional structure. But they had very different ideas for such a structure.

In terms of military capability, Soviet aid in the years since 1967 had brought Egypt and Syria closer to the Israeli level, but still below the combat "edge" that the Israeli forces had through long and intense training and high skills and morale. Yet the two sides were nearly enough equal to make their battles intense and exceedingly expensive in consumable military supplies alone. Each side could hurt the other badly, and each therefore had a constant and critical need for rapid and unstinting support from its external helper—for Israel, the United States; for Egypt and Syria, the Soviet Union.

Not only the three direct combatants but the assisting powers therefore had to make decisions quickly and, in the case of the United States, with an eye to reactions outside the war theater, especially in the Arab world and in Western Europe. Moreover, the United States and the Soviet Union had to give special priority to where the war might leave Soviet-American relations, and at the same time to what it would do to their respective power positions in the Middle East. Both in military and in foreign policy terms, therefore, the conflict posed immensely complicated issues.

. . .

With the initial near-balance between the opposing forces, the importance of surprise, and the uneven effects of resupply, it was natural that the course of the war fluctuated markedly. In the first three days, Egypt made striking gains at moderate cost on the Suez Canal front, breaking through Israel's thinly held defense positions on the eastern side of the canal and inflicting substantial losses in men and equipment. On the Syrian (northern) front, Israeli forces were driven back for two days but then recovered; losses on both sides were moderate to heavy. The two superpowers, uncertain, stayed their hands. In these first days the general feeling among American officials, including Kissinger, was that although the Egyptians were showing far better ability than in the past to handle sophisticated equipment, including tanks and antitank missiles, surprise was the biggest reason for their gains. Israel would soon rebound and, as in 1967, sweep to victory. A big effort to send supplies to Israel by sea would therefore take effect only after the war was over, while a large-scale airlift was not really essential and would make it difficult for the United States to act as a mediator.

These views changed in the early morning of October 9, Washington time, when Israeli Ambassador Simcha Dinitz brought a distress signal direct from Mrs. Meir. Israel was desperately short of consumables, especially ammunition, and also needed fighter and transport planes. She said bluntly that Israel was losing the war for lack of supplies. On Nixon's orders, ammunition and Sidewinder missiles were at once made available for Israeli transport planes to pick up, and the United States pledged full replacement of expended ammunition and weapons stocks, so that Israel need not stint in their use. But it was a limited effort, with few aircraft to carry the supplies. On the Soviet side, by this time, a substantial airlift was under way, especially to the Syrian forces.

In the next four days the fighting stabilized, and the United States supported a UN Security Council resolution for a cease-fire in place (a change from earlier American suggestions that a cease-fire should call for an immediate return to prewar positions). The Soviet Union was favorable to the in-place proposal, and reported it was trying to persuade Sadat to accept. To minimize tensions, Britain became the sponsor of the resolution. However, on Saturday, October 13, after intensive consultations, the British concluded that the project would not be accepted by Egypt, which late that day formally rejected it.

During these days, Kissinger and his colleagues made a great effort to find a way of moving supplies and equipment to Israel with the least possible publicity, so as to minimize tension with the Soviet Union and Egypt and also to head off, if possible, oil sanctions by the Arab oil-producing countries. As it became clear that Israel's small commercial air fleet could not possibly handle even the moderate volume of supplies then ready to go, the Defense Department tried briefly to put together a scheme for large-scale chartering of commercial aircraft, but the operators and their insurers were not willing to accept the obvious risks, and the scheme was finally buried on October 12. Recriminations between Kissinger and Secretary of Defense Schlesinger abounded, and Kissinger repeatedly told Ambassador Dinitz that the Pentagon was dragging its feet. In his memoirs, he was to concede that this was an unjust charge designed to protect him from Israeli criticism.[15]

In the late evening of October 12 came a second frantic appeal from Dinitz: in three more days of heavy fighting, Israel would run out of key consumable supplies, notably ammunition; the need for other weapons and for fighter-bomber aircraft was even more urgent than before. Intensive study that night convinced Schlesinger that only a large-scale U.S. airlift could do the job—meaning full use of C-5A transports, giant aircraft just going into service on a substantial scale. Each of these could carry 60–80 tons all the way to Israel, with only one refueling. Kissinger briefly opposed the idea of using such conspicuous aircraft—showing again his concern about adverse reactions from the Arab oil nations—but when Schlesinger took his case via Alexander Haig to President Nixon on the morning of October 13, Kissinger dropped his objections. Then, with a new message from Mrs. Meir herself, Nixon shifted gears and ordered an all-out resupply effort, which rose rapidly to a level of 1,000 tons a day. This exceeded by about 25 percent the Soviet airlift to Syria, which had a shorter distance to cover and was being allowed to overfly all the intervening countries, including NATO members Greece and Turkey.[16]

The Arab threat to use the oil weapon was already affecting almost all the NATO nations, who made it clear that American planes headed for Israel could not overfly their territory or even draw supplies from American military depots in Europe. The principal resupply route thus had to be direct from the United States, with refueling or transshipment at the U.S.-operated Lajes Air Base in the Azores, on Portuguese territory. Discussions with the Portuguese began on October 12 and were concluded favorably the next day only after a strong personal message from Nixon to Prime Minister Marcelo Caetano, in which Nixon may have threatened that the United States would cease to give Portugal crucial military aid if it did not cooperate.

Sunday, October 14, was a dramatic day. A massive Egyptian offensive to break through the Mitla and Giddi passes on the Sinai Peninsula precipitated one of the largest tank battles in military history. Israeli forces prevailed totally: Egypt lost more than 264 tanks and Israel only 10.[17] A part of the Egyptian Third Army, at the southern end of the canal front, remained on the east bank of the canal, but its position was now threatened, and it had no chance to renew the attack. By this time, moreover, Israeli forces cleaning up along the east side of the canal had been able to determine the boundary line between the Second and Third Egyptian armies, which pointed to an area just north of the Great Bitter Lake as the most vulnerable part of their defense line. The Israeli high command quickly decided to prepare a counterattack at that point.

Meanwhile, the first three American C-5As got through to Israel. Kissinger had urged that they land in darkness to minimize Arab reactions, but crosswinds in the Azores forced a delay, and they arrived in daylight. Inevitably, their gigantic size and conspicuous Air Force markings galvanized onlookers. In the words of one later account: "As the droning American transport planes reached the skies over Tel Aviv, cars stopped in the streets, apartment windows opened, and people began to shout, 'God Bless America.' Golda Meir cried for the first time since the war began."[18] Israel's embattled citizens and armed forces took new heart. Military planners could now be confident and unconstrained by supply worries.

On October 16, two contingents crossed the canal and started operations designed to cripple Egypt's formidable antiaircraft missile complex—the "wall" built up since 1970, and now well manned and highly effective against Israeli air attacks—and to encircle and knock out the main units of the Egyptian Army. By October 18 it was clear that the attacking Israeli forces, especially the division commanded by General Ariel Sharon, were scoring dramatic gains. The balance now tilted heavily in favor of Israel. With the resupply efforts of both the United States and the Soviets in high gear, the Soviet Union on the 17th began a move at the United Nations to get a cease-fire in place.

At this point, there was movement on the oil front. The Gulf oil states announced a 70 percent rise in the posted price, to $5.11 a barrel. Separately, the Arab oil producers, meeting in Kuwait, ordered production and shipment cutbacks of 5 percent, effective immediately, with additional 5 percent cuts to follow monthly so long as Israel did not withdraw to its pre-1967 boundaries.

On October 19, when Nixon sent to Congress a request for $2.2 billion to finance the emergency military aid to Israel, the reaction in Egypt and among the Arab oil officials gathered in Kuwait was immediate. The next day, the Arab oil-producing countries ordered a complete embargo on shipments to the United States and the Netherlands, which were supporting Israel. These moves had little immediate effect on the war, since most of the consumer countries were already cooperating fully with the Arab producers and doing nothing to assist Israel. Nor did the Nixon Administration have any thought of changing its course, at least as long as hostilities continued. But the embargo posed serious and continuing problems and deepened the wedge between America and its European and Japanese allies.

Kissinger made his own move toward halting the fighting on October 19, suggesting to Ambassador Dobrynin that he would be willing to go to Moscow to work things out directly with Brezhnev, an offer that was quickly accepted. Kissinger took off secretly late that night (after a formal dinner at the Chinese Embassy, of all places), taking Dobrynin with him. On October 21, in Moscow, Kissinger and Brezhnev arrived in four hours at agreement on a cease-fire, to take effect on the next day in the late afternoon, Middle East time. Brezhnev was obviously under great pressure from Sadat, perhaps also from Assad, to stop the war at once and save the Egyptian Army from surrender or visible collapse. From Kissinger's standpoint, the delay in a cease-fire, caused by his going to Moscow rather than negotiating at a distance, was favorable to Israel, a useful offset to personal attacks on him at home for the delays in U.S. supply efforts for Israel.

Yet Kissinger was acutely aware that he had not truly consulted Israel in the last phase, when its forces had emerged on top and were about to close the circuit around the Egyptian Third Army. Nor had he insisted to Brezhnev that the cease-fire had to be contingent on Israel's assent. Pressed hard by the Soviets, on Sadat's behalf, Kissinger thought he should complete the arrangements for the cease-fire, even though this might stop Israel short of total victory. As he later explained: "We did not think that turning an Arab setback into a debacle represented a vital interest [of the U.S.]."[19] His plan was to tell Israel about the cease-fire at once, from Moscow, at the same time he reported it to Washington. The necessary messages were drafted and ready to be dispatched right after he reached agreement with Brezhnev, but for reasons never made clear — and to Kissinger's intense anger — the messages were delayed for several hours, so that Israel did not find out what had been done until late on Sunday evening.[20]

Separately, Kissinger had to deal with a direct instruction cabled to him by Nixon while he was en route. In his distraught state, Nixon went back to an idea he had toyed with from time to time, the very one that Brezhnev had emphasized in the bizarre late-night session at San Clemente the previous June. Nixon said in the cable (as summarized by Kissinger) that "he had realized the essential correctness of the views Brezhnev had put forth in San Clemente":

> The Israelis and Arabs will never be able to approach this subject by themselves in a rational manner. That is why Nixon and Brezhnev, looking at the problem more dispassionately, must step in, determine the proper course of action to a just settlement, and then bring the necessary pressure on our respective friends.[21]

This idea had lain behind Secretary Rogers's efforts in 1969 and 1970, but Kissinger had thrust it aside as dangerous and unrealistic, preferring instead to move step by step, without getting drawn into discussing ultimate outcomes, which would raise hackles and bar progress.

When Kissinger got Nixon's cable, he was naturally aghast, especially as its contents had already been conveyed to the Soviet Embassy in Washington. He at once phoned Haig to protest, and thus learned about the uproar that was taking place that weekend over the Saturday Night Massacre and about Nixon's distressed condition. In the circumstances, he decided to ignore the cable. The Soviet Union never followed up, and in his memoirs, Dobrynin was to argue that "this very important message, if implemented, could have changed the whole future course of the Middle East settlement."[22] That is most unlikely. Certainly this particular occasion, focused on the cease-fire Sadat desperately needed, was not a promising time for dealing with such far-reaching ideas.

When Kissinger arrived in Israel at noon on October 22, Abba Eban at once confirmed that Mrs. Meir was exceedingly upset and angry over his failure to consult the Israeli government, and that the cease-fire was to come into effect in only five hours. In hectic discussions engaging all the nation's top leadership, the Israelis pressed to put off the deadline for two or three days, so that they could complete the encirclement of the Egyptian Third Army. In response, Kissinger (according to his own recollection) said that there could be some "slippage," by which he meant only a few hours, to offset the communications delay. One Israeli source, however, later recalled his response verbatim, in much more sweeping terms: "Two or three days? That's all? Well, in Vietnam the cease-fire didn't go into effect at the exact time it was agreed on."[23]

Whatever interval was mentioned or implied, there is no doubt that Kissinger indicated that the United States would not object to a delay, and by implication would defend Israel from criticism. This extraordinary action was designed (Kissinger later claimed) to get Israel's acceptance of the cease-fire but also, one must conclude, to help his own personal standing with its leaders, which had been battered by the earlier controversies over supply shipments and then by his failure to consult them on the cease-fire.[24]

Thus fortified, the Israelis kept right on fighting after the deadline, as Kissinger flew back to Washington by way of London. It was the turn of the Egyptians and the Soviets to be angry, and recriminations flew back and forth for the next two days. Brezhnev sent a message on the hot line direct to Kissinger, while the Israeli government insisted, against all evidence, that it was the Egyptians who had first violated the cease-fire. Dobrynin later described the Soviet view of what happened, in unusually critical terms:

> The Israelis quickly realized that they could take advantage of a few hours' confusion at the beginning of the cease-fire and encircle the Egyptian Third Army. . . . Actually it was a premeditated violation of the agreement from the start. Later, Kissinger wrote about the Israeli action with evident approval. The only thing that remains unclear is whether Nixon knew about this at the time.[25]

There was indeed reason to wonder whether Nixon was in charge, as the uproar in Washington and all over America over the Saturday Night Massacre continued for several days. With a clamor to begin impeachment proceedings adding to the pressures, Nixon was exhausted and not on top of the war situation in the Middle East in the next critical days. On October 23, the Security Council passed a second cease-fire resolution, but Israeli forces went right ahead to encircle the Egyptian Third Army and cut it off from food and other basic supplies. On October 24 in the afternoon, Washington time, Sadat announced that Egypt was requesting a Security Council meeting to ask that American and Soviet forces be sent to the area to police the cease-fire. At seven that evening, Dobrynin (back from Moscow) reported to Kissinger that the Soviet Union was supporting the idea. Kissinger at once responded that the United States could not accept the proposal, which, as he saw it, would legitimize the continued presence of Soviet forces in the area. At the United Nations, Ambassador John Scali also registered the negative U.S. position. In reaching his decision, Kissinger did not consult with Nixon, who called him, almost simultaneously, to pour out his maudlin alarms about the emerging threat of impeachment proceedings. Kissinger and Haig were by this time convinced that Nixon was too distraught to participate in foreign policy decision making.

At 10:30 that evening, Dobrynin read over the phone to Kissinger a cable just received from Brezhnev, which responded to Kissinger's message by proposing formally that a joint Soviet-American force be sent to the Middle East. The message ended on a harsh and peremptory note:

> It is necessary to adhere without delay [to the proposal for a joint Soviet-American force]. I will say it straight that if you find it impossible to act

jointly with us in this matter, we should be faced with the necessity urgently to consider the question of taking appropriate steps unilaterally. We cannot allow arbitrariness on the part of Israel.[26]

Kissinger quickly summoned Defense Secretary Schlesinger, Admiral Moorer, and CIA Director Colby to the White House, for what was in effect a rump National Security Council meeting, and again consulted Haig, who repeated his earlier judgment that the President was not in shape to participate.[27]

Gathering at 10:40 that evening, the participants after intensive discussion finally concurred that it was necessary to make a move that would show American firmness and be quickly seen by the Soviet leadership, but that would not precipitate hostilities. They decided to put American military forces, worldwide, on what was called "DefCon [Defense Condition] 3," a notch above the normal "DefCon 4" status, but below "DefCon 2," readiness for imminent war. Just before midnight, Admiral Moorer issued the order to all military commands.[28] The decision makers assumed that Soviet intelligence and detection would quickly see what was going on but at the same time note that it included no threat of an early attacking move. Briefly, Kissinger supposed that the alert would not soon be detected by information media, but this was an unrealistic hope, with virtually every American military unit in the world taking visible actions.[29] By the morning of October 25, everyone knew of the alert, and there was intense worry and speculation — not least among America's NATO allies, who had been notified only after the decision was taken. Neither to the American people, its friends and allies, nor to the rest of the world, was it clear what the alert was intended to signal.

Yet the situation did ease markedly. Sadat and the Soviet leaders sent messages that they could accept a joint observer group that did not contain soldiers. In a press conference, Kissinger took a conciliatory tone toward the Soviets, while reiterating U.S. opposition to any joint military force. And the Security Council approved a new resolution (340) calling for a return to the October 22 cease-fire lines, for more UN observers, and for a special Emergency Force (which would not include the United States, the Soviet Union, or the other three permanent members of the Security Council). Finally, on October 25, the Pentagon announced that the alert would be ended at midnight.

It took two more days to iron out the details and get the respective military forces separated. The war in effect ended when the military representatives of Israel and Egypt met along the Cairo–Suez Road in the early morning of Sunday, October 28. The October War (or, as it was sometimes called, the Yom Kippur War) had lasted just over three weeks. Both sides had lost heavily. Enormous amounts of equipment had been used or destroyed, in what was really the first all-out conflict with the full array of state-of-the-art conventional military equipment (excluding only strategic bombers and offensive missiles). The home territories of the combatants had not been heavily damaged, but in every other respect the war had been a traumatic and fearsome experience. Its impact on the Middle East and on Soviet-American relations, as well as on U.S. relations with its major allies and on the oil and energy balance between producers and consumers, was clearly great. How great and in what ways remained to be seen.

From the U.S. standpoint, the first key feature of the war was that it ended without a clear victory for either side. Bluntly, although neither Nixon nor Kissinger ever said so in so many words, both had hoped this would be the outcome, and it was the core of U.S. policy throughout. Each knew well the history of the Arab-Israeli conflict and especially the repeated unsuccessful efforts to move toward peace after the Six-Day War in 1967, and each had reached the same central conclusion. This was that, when and if hostilities between the two sides should again occur, it was crucial that they be ended on terms and under conditions that allowed, so far as possible, successful negotiations afterward. In the absence of such progress, relations between Israel and the Arab states (and with the Palestinians) would remain a powder keg, capable of exploding at any time into increasingly bitter and destructive hostilities, given the armaments and technology available to each side.

This common-sense and hardheaded conclusion did not fit easily with the historical American inclination to seek for itself, and support for others, complete military victory, and only after that to set about making peace. Moreover, for Israel it implied that the United States would exert its influence and leverage to prevent a repeat of the complete Israeli victory of 1967. Israel must not lose or be left imperiled, but equally it should not win outright so as to humiliate the Arab states, specifically the largest and most important one, Egypt. Thus, the ambivalence of Nixon's and Kissinger's actions, especially about military aid early in the war, reflected their genuine ambivalence in objectives.

The second aim, particularly after the Moscow summit in May 1972, was that détente with the Soviet Union should not be destroyed, but rather, if possible, confirmed and shown to be useful. Again and again, in his public remarks, Kissinger took pains not to attack Soviet moves as contrary to the spirit or letter of détente. He wanted to emerge from the crisis still in good communication with the Soviet Union, and with as little tension as possible in Soviet-American relations.

Yet, at the same time, it was a prime third objective to reduce the role and influence of the Soviet Union in the Middle East, to break up completely its power in Egypt, and if possible to build up and assist the moderate

Arab states, so that those susceptible to Soviet influence — those who for one reason or another were "radical" — would be reduced and their radicalism attenuated.

Fourth, although Nixon and Kissinger during the run-up period to the war seriously underestimated the threat of an Arab oil weapon, by the end of the war Kissinger in particular saw the great future importance of oil, simply in economic terms. Since the Arab oil-producing countries were almost all moderates, Saudi Arabia notably so, he saw dual reasons to avoid provoking King Faisal. In the short term, moderate Arab leadership of the Arab oil producers was creating an oil pinch that could ripen into a full-fledged crisis; in the long run, however, the moderate Arab states had to be a principal bulwark of American policy in the Middle East. If an oil crisis could not be headed off, then at least effective communication with the moderate Arabs, preserving a sense of shared interests in keeping radical Arab states and Soviet influence at bay, should be kept alive.

Last, at the bottom of the list, was the preservation of America's European ties, above all in NATO. No deference was given to the views of these allies at any point, and even keeping them well informed was difficult in the fast-flowing pace of events. The result was a legacy of serious discontent within the Alliance, vastly compounded by the effect of the Arab oil sanctions and by the U.S. worldwide military alert on October 24. European public opinion erupted in protest over that action, with its apparent potential for leading to a nuclear exchange that would include targets in Western Europe — and especially that it had been taken unilaterally by the United States, without any consultation with them. By November, NATO was in deep trouble, deeper perhaps than at any other time in its history.

At the time, the important fact that almost no NATO allies were cooperating with the United States (the only exception other than Portugal was the Netherlands) was never announced officially, although it was obvious enough. The Nixon Administration avoided any public revelation or discussion, or any suggestion of blame. Privately, however, Kissinger in particular seethed, and was vitriolic in his comments. Yet he knew that bringing the Alliance back together would be one of the major tasks that had to follow the war.

. . .

In later years, Kissinger repeatedly argued that U.S. foreign policy decisions should be based on "the national interest," not on "Wilsonian" dreams of international action. These statements, often based on stereotyped and over-simplified summaries of the views of others, rarely identified or weighed the elements of "the national interest" in a given situation. In this respect, the 1973 October War was a welcome exception. Each of the considerations just listed formed part of Kissinger's conception of "the national interest" during this crisis. They were spelled out and balanced, more frankly and carefully than at any other critical point in his active career.

Moreover, Kissinger with some precision, and Nixon more vaguely, faced up frankly to the serious potential contradictions among their objectives. With considerable discrimination and success, they selected the most promising courses at each stage, but at the same time sought, as far as possible, to mollify the nations they were forced temporarily to offend or oppose. Again, this was more true in their dealings with the Arab nations and the Soviet Union than in their treatment of America's NATO allies.

Finally, it is fair to ask why Kissinger, proudly Jewish, did not wish to see Israel humiliate Egypt. The answer must go beyond the argument that President Nixon, despite all his troubles, was at least following the course of policy and would surely have rejected all-out support of Israel. The real point for Kissinger was the conviction that what he was doing was in Israel's long-term interest. As he put it on another occasion, in explaining the obduracy of Israeli negotiators, they knew that "a people of three million people amidst a hostile population of over a hundred million is historically weak whatever the state of armaments at any given point."[30] Lasting peace, and only lasting peace, in the Middle East would allow Israel to survive and prosper. Keeping this ultimate objective always before him, Kissinger found his way through the tangle of other national interests to well-judged policy decisions and actions. Essentially, in the long run, the interests of the United States and Israel coincided, so that the American "national interest" gave him a firm basis for policy.

3. Creative Diplomacy

For almost every American, the months from October 1973 to the spring of 1974 were, in Shakespeare's words, "the winter of our discontent." As the Watergate scandal built up relentlessly, oil shortages and high energy prices were a demoralizing—and for many, incomprehensible—revelation of American vulnerability, over a basic means of comfort and movement that had come to be taken for granted as a national strength. To many, the only bright spot in the gathering gloom, the only evidence that America could still act effectively, was a remarkable diplomatic offensive, conceived and executed principally by Secretary of State Kissinger.[31] This diplomatic effort applied to the tasks of peace the same assessments that had guided U.S. policy during the October War.

In an order dictated by tactical considerations, it aimed at four primary objectives: to strengthen U.S. ties to the moderate Arab countries, starting with Egypt; to oust the Soviet Union from any real role in the Arab-Israeli negotiating process, and to make the United States the key actor and mediator; to make visible headway, step by step, initially through a workable agreement for Egyptian and Israeli forces to disengage in the Sinai Peninsula, with disengagement on the Syrian front to follow; and to use the credit from these efforts to persuade the Arab oil-producing countries, above all Saudi Arabia, to lift their embargo on the United States.

Kissinger and the Nixon Administration also had two other, lesser, objectives: to ease the tensions with the principal Western European nations, and to strengthen the hand of the oil-consuming countries for the future — in effect, to blunt the oil weapon. Unfortunately, most of the European countries (some of which had long been annoyed by the strong position the United States had achieved with Saudi Arabia and Iran) were convinced that the war had been brought on by Israel's refusal to make any concessions about the territories it had occupied since 1967, and also attributed the U.S. failure to put effective pressure on Israel to an undue deference to pro-Israeli sentiment, for domestic political reasons. As Kissinger saw it, most of America's allies were "genuinely convinced that our failure to press a settlement on Israel had produced the war, that we had in effect put vital European interests at risk for reasons of American domestic politics."[32]

Right away, it was urgent to deal with the situation on the Suez Canal front, where the Egyptian Third Army was surrounded by Israeli forces on the east bank, and at the same time the Israeli forces were in difficulty on the west bank.

Fortunately, both Golda Meir and Egyptian Foreign Minister Ismail Fahmy converged on Washington in the week of October 29. Israel by then was permitting limited nonmilitary supplies to get through to the Third Army, and Kissinger laid the groundwork for a six-point agreement that would permit the cease-fire to become lasting, pending negotiations on territorial issues.

By the time Kissinger sat down with the much-used Washington Special Actions Group (WSAG) on November 2, his main strategy had taken shape. He told his colleagues:

We can reduce Soviet influence in the area and can get the oil embargo raised if we can deliver a moderate program and we are going to do it. If not, the Arabs will be driven back to the Soviets, the oil will be lost, we will have the whole world against us, and there will not be one UN vote for us. We must prove to the Arabs that they are better off dealing with us on a moderate program than dealing with the Russians on a radical program.[33]

It was a good and persuasive summary. The personal frictions that had marked some of the critical decisions during the war thenceforth disappeared. Kissinger was in the driver's seat, and the whole Administration was now solidly in agreement.

Although Kissinger had been deeply involved in running battles within the Nixon Administration over Arab-Israeli matters, he had never set foot in an Arab capital. He could see the big picture, but he had little experience of dealing directly with Arab leaders, and none of doing so on their terrain. What he did have was the benefit of extensive discussions within the State Department he had once undermined but now directed, and the good sense to pick from the cream of its officers to work directly with him. Joseph Sisco, Assistant Secretary of State for Near Eastern and South Asian Affairs, had long diplomatic experience (though he had never served in the areas for which he was responsible), and he was a quick study, with a sure grasp of the issues and the courage to speak out. Alfred Atherton (known as Roy), his deputy, was perhaps the most experienced Middle East hand in terms of firsthand exposure and crisis management, with a quiet manner and weight of judgment. Harold Saunders, from a varied career dealing with South Asia as well as the Middle East, was a member of Kissinger's NSC staff, but retained the detachment of a career officer. It was a powerful team, totally loyal and used to avoiding the limelight.

Kissinger's first stops were in Algeria and Tunisia. Houari Boumedienne in Algiers was a professed socialist, but also wary of Soviet influence, hence inwardly a moderate and friend of Sadat. He passed on to Sadat a message that Kissinger wanted to move quickly from war-ending arrangements to the more basic questions of disengagement. In Tunisia, Habib Bourguiba was a long-standing moderate, fearful of radicalism and Soviet influence. To him, Kissinger stated a familiar keynote: others might give weapons, but only the United States could influence Israel to give up territory.[34]

As these visits concluded, the European Community (EC) published on November 6 a declaration demanding Israel's return to the October 22 cease-fire line and adopting the Arab interpretation of UN Security Council Resolution 242. As we have noted, that resolution had been debated for months in 1967, before a compromise formula was offered that called on Israel to withdraw "from territories" it was occupying. Under this deliberate ambiguity, Israel was bound to argue that this meant only some or most of the territories, whereas Arabs claimed that it meant all of them. The EC position was still more evidence of the American-European rift, as well as of Europe's vulnerability to the oil weapon.

The most important stop for Kissinger came on November 6–8, in Cairo. On this crucial occasion, the personal chemistry between Sadat and Kissinger was good from the start, when Kissinger wisely drew from Sadat a long account of how he had decided to go to war and the measures he had taken to achieve surprise. When they got down to business, Sadat finally accepted Kissinger's argument that it was wiser not to haggle further over the situation of the Third Army, but rather to aim at a disengagement agreement that would get Israeli forces wholly withdrawn from the canal area. Sadat accepted the concept on the spot, and Sisco was dispatched to Israel, where he achieved an agreement on the main elements of a continuing hold-the-line cease-fire (formally agreed on November 14).[35]

From this initial success, the two principals moved to broader matters. Kissinger stated his position frankly, essentially appealing to Sadat for an act of faith: if Egypt and other Arab nations could make Israel confident of its own security, he could persuade it to make major territorial concessions. In response, Sadat showed himself ready to think in these terms. Above all, as accounts on both sides agree, a high degree of mutual respect and trust was created. The visit was a major breakthrough and an essential prelude to the sequence of visits to moderate Arab countries that followed, starting with Saudi Arabia.

With King Faisal, probably softened up by a favorable report from Sadat on Kissinger's visit, the talk was more formal. Kissinger quietly stressed the need to lift the oil embargo if the United States was to play a continuing role. There was no visible headway, but to have a polite reception in the most influential oil-producing country still represented a forward step. Kissinger must by this time have known (perhaps in part from Sadat) of King Faisal's importance in preparing and unleashing "the oil weapon." Now he courted Faisal unstintingly. The pressure at home to persuade the Arab oil producers to ease their cutbacks (and the embargo on the United States and the Netherlands) was unrelenting, but Kissinger knew that it was useless to tackle it head-on. The only way was to show that the United States could produce progress toward an Arab-Israeli peace.

From there, Kissinger went to meet with the Shah in Teheran. His account of the visit praises the Shah for not participating in reductions of oil exports or the embargo on oil for the United States, but is conspicuously silent about whether the possibility of increased oil prices was discussed. Next, Kissinger went to Pakistan for a meeting with Z. A. Bhutto (by this time in control) and from there to Beijing for the visit with Mao Zedong and Zhou Enlai, already recounted. He wound up his twelve-day, ten-capital trip with short stops in Korea and Japan, where the impact of the oil crisis was especially acute. Foreign Minister Masayoshi Ohira, a friend to America then and on other occasions, was a lonely holdout in a Cabinet that finally on November 22 voted a resolution similar to that of the European countries.[36]

The next development on the oil front came in mid-December, when the oil-producing countries in OPEC announced that the official posted price, already raised from $3.70 in September to $5.12 a barrel, would now be raised further all the way to $11.65. The increase had been proposed by the Shah of Iran, whose senior officials explained that Iran's oil reserves were far less than those of Saudi Arabia or most of the Arab countries: only much higher prices would reduce overall oil demand and lead to the rapid development of other energy sources. Oil supplies would then be drawn down more slowly and Iran's oil reserves would last longer and earn more. In his memoirs, Kissinger was to note that all the members of OPEC joined in the action—which he called "one of the pivotal events in the history of this century." But the Shah was certainly the most vocal advocate of the size of the increase.[37]

Meanwhile, Kissinger attended the annual NATO meeting and made a conciliatory speech in London. But his main diplomatic focus was on a project he had suggested to the Soviet leaders in October—namely, an international peace conference under the "auspices" of the Soviet Union and the United States. Possibly presuming that "auspices" meant continuing Soviet participation in a peace process in the Middle East, the Soviets had agreed with this suggestion. On November 17, Kissinger proposed to Dobrynin that the two superpowers ask UN Secretary-General Kurt Waldheim to do the inviting and then preside in Geneva. The conference was originally set for December 18, with Egypt, Israel, Jordan, and Syria the participants and the PLO an observer. But from the beginning, the Western European countries were not included, on the ground (never publicly stated) that they were now too clearly and publicly pro-Arab to be balanced contributors, and also, certainly, because their presence would only have complicated the plans that Kissinger and Sadat now essentially shared, and Mrs. Meir understood.

There was, however, an Israeli general election scheduled for the last week in December (postponed from the original October date because of the war), and the Israelis balked at a conference at that time. Kissinger finally got them to agree that there should be an initial formal meeting before the end of the year, though substantive discussions would be postponed until after the election. The meeting was set for December 21. Kissinger brought out of retirement the veteran American diplomat Ellsworth Bunker to lend credibility and weight to the project as a senior member of the American delegation. Among Bunker's many assignments in his long and varied service, he had earned the confidence of Muslim countries when he mediated a 1962 agreement among Indonesia, Australia, and the Netherlands for the transfer of West Irian, formerly Netherlands New Guinea, to Indonesia.

In fact, as Kissinger must already have revealed to both Mrs. Meir and Sadat, his real intent was to use the conference to eliminate the Soviet Union from the peace process. The first meeting would be limited to an exchange of speeches, after which the conference would set up working groups for successive disengagement negotiations, to be followed by substantive discussions of peace terms; in practice, Egypt and Israel would turn to the United States alone as the mediator, and the Soviet Union would be eased to the sidelines. Preparations for the conference went forward, with renewed visits by Kissinger to Cairo and Riyadh; a long first meeting with the always difficult Hafez al-Assad in Syria failed to persuade him to attend, although it at least started a relationship of respect between him and Kissinger.[38]

In all, the network of relationships he wove was the most important result of Kissinger's exploratory visits to the Middle East. Some writers have suggested that he also threw out hints that the United States would offer great economic and technological help in the future. In fact the new policy came to involve massive U.S. aid to Egypt as well as Israel, but in this crucial first stage it was the reasoned arguments Kissinger made, the personal rapport he established, and the sense of understanding and respect he conveyed that moved things forward. He was always well suited to be a mediator, a position in which a diplomat is justified in shading the views of A when he reports to B, in the interest of bringing the two closer.

After all these preparations, the actual Geneva Conference on December 21–22 came as an anticlimax; after a day of predictable speeches, the conference adjourned. Kissinger contributed a particularly eloquent speech, for which his preparatory encounters must have been a good rehearsal.

In the Israeli elections, the new Likud Party (set up and led by Ariel Sharon in the months before he put on his uniform again and became the outstanding Israeli hero of the war) came close to defeating the ruling coalition of Labor and the New Religious Party. Though Mrs. Meir still held a bare majority, she and Moshe Dayan were blamed for Israel's early reverses in the war, and were badly discredited. Dayan, however, remained Defense Minister and turned his imaginative mind to the largely military problem of defining withdrawal lines and buffer zones in the Sinai and the area of the canal. On January 3, he brought to Washington maps and proposals that struck Kissinger as promising. Kissinger passed them on with comments to Sadat, who at once invited him to confer at Aswan.

There the two had a real meeting of minds, and Sadat proposed that Kissinger go to Israel without delay and sew up the deal. He did so, and in four days of the first diplomatic "shuttle," back and forth between Cairo and Jerusalem, a disengagement agreement was completed by January 17, signed the next day by the opposing generals on the Cairo–Suez Road, and put into effect at once.

Although Dayan's crucial contribution to the agreement did not bring him back from the political wilderness in Israel, what he had proposed was a well-crafted deal: Egypt got a north-south strip along the east side of the canal, with a UN buffer zone and then an Israeli limited-arms zone adjacent. In return for retreating from the west side of the canal, the Israelis were left in control of the Giddi and Mitla passes in the Sinai. Neither side got all it wanted, but the lines were simple and readily identifiable, so that violations would be apparent at once.[39]

On his way home Kissinger sent messages to Assad in Syria and to King Hussein in Jordan to urge further negotiations with each. In Washington the deal was well received, although Kissinger's press conference was distracted by the fact that the Yeoman Radford spying incident of December 1971 came to public notice at just that time. As Kissinger rightly noted in his memoirs:

> America in the winter of 1973–1974 was not a happy place. It was ridden with suspicion, bitterness, cynicism. A taste for sensational revelations had developed, much of it unhappily too justified, some of it pursued almost for its own sake.[40]

Yet even in this atmosphere the disengagement agreement between Israel and Egypt was recognized as a major accomplishment. As Kissinger had sensed and then found, both sides were hurting as long as they remained almost fully deployed. Both needed peace. They would have been hard put to achieve it without Kissinger's diplomacy and mediation.

Still, it soon became clear that the key player in any decision to lift the oil embargo, King Faisal, was not disposed to do so until Israeli forces moved back at least from the salient of Syrian territory they had taken over in this war. Sadat, by now fully convinced of Kissinger's sincerity and ability to mediate disputes with Israel, took the lead in bringing together in Algiers, in mid-February 1974, Faisal, Assad, and the host, Boumedienne. There, Sadat put the case for dropping the embargo, arguing that "the Americans were leading the way toward a new political reality." Finally Faisal agreed, so long as there was a "constructive effort," led by the United States, to achieve an Israeli-Syrian disengagement.[41]

However, in the next few weeks Assad's position toughened, and it was only on March 18 that the Arab Oil Ministers (Syria and Libya dissenting) agreed to end the embargo on the United States, though not on the Netherlands — a gesture of pure pique, since the resourceful Dutch had long since found ways to get the oil they needed. By March 1974, the international oil companies, which still operated the distribution system on their own with minimum interference, had again shown that they could control and reroute shipments of oil so as to circumvent cutbacks and embargoes directed at particular consumers. But what remained, and was to be the main legacy of the fall and winter, was the enormous price increase, which stood firm from December on. This proved in the long run far more onerous, for the United States in particular, than the production cutbacks and embargoes, though these had created the conditions in which the price rise was possible. It was the high price level, and the power to adjust it without the consent of the consumers, that was now the core of the oil crisis and the reason it continued to have devastating effects on the oil-consuming nations.

The diplomacy to achieve an agreed and stable disengagement on the fighting front in Syria turned out, not surprisingly, to be a far more difficult and prolonged task than the disengagement in the Sinai between Egypt and Israel. Assad, a tougher bargainer than Sadat, had been impressed by what he heard about Kissinger, who in turn came to regard him as a testing and interesting adversary, but it was still an arm's-length relationship. Moreover, the territory involved lacked the clear definition provided by the Suez Canal as a boundary for the disengagement zones. It centered on the town of El Kuneitra, historically the capital of the Golan Heights area prior to the Israeli victory in 1967 and of great sentimental importance to Syria. El Kuneitra was located in a valley within easy shelling range of Israeli artillery positions in the hills to the west, which (along with civilian settlements) had been set up and made secure since 1967.

To deal with these difficulties, Kissinger had the influence on Assad of Sadat and Faisal, in favor of agreement. The opposing forces in the Golan had never had a true cease-fire, and a war of attrition had become stalemated so that neither side could hope to improve its position. There continued to be some casualties.

Despite the ending of the oil embargo, it was not possible for the parties to start negotiating at once. In Israel, a blunt report by a special commission on the responsibility for the initial surprise and setbacks in the war harshly criticized the Army Chief of Staff. Mrs. Meir and Defense Minister Dayan got off lightly, but the government as a whole was so weakened that a change was needed. Mrs. Meir retired for good on April 11, and after a lot of churning, Yitzhak Rabin became the new Prime Minister on April 30.

With the stage thus set, Kissinger arrived on May 2 in Israel, expecting that the negotiations would take only a week or two. As it turned out, he ended up making no fewer than thirteen round trips between Jerusalem and Damascus. Three times the negotiations appeared to have reached an impasse; each time Nixon urged Kissinger to persevere and Assad gave just enough ground to permit resumption. The negotiations were covered on a daily basis by a seasoned group that included about fourteen American journalists, who were kept well supplied with generally upbeat stories by an unnamed "senior official," correctly assumed to be Kissinger. With the Watergate scandal tending to dominate the American media and public discussion, Nixon was more than ever beleaguered. He must have welcomed Kissinger's drawing the limelight away from Watergate even a little, and showing that the Administration could still conduct serious business.

Finally, a succession of resourceful compromises resolved the last deadlocks, and agreement was reached on May 29 and signed on May 31. Syria got all of the town of El Kuneitra (heavily damaged in both 1967 and 1973), but the Israeli settlements remained on the slopes of Mount Hermon, subject to a prohibition on weapons capable of hitting El Kuneitra and on conducting guerrilla activity from the area. Thus ended, after almost exactly seven months, the intensive diplomacy needed to end the war and leave a reasonably stable situation on the Sinai and Syrian fronts. There had, however, been no progress on the West Bank, under Israeli occupation since 1967 and not involved in the 1973 War.

Kissinger had achieved his four primary objectives. It was an extraordinary performance, reflecting great diplomatic skill, enormous stamina, and a unique capacity for gaining the confidence and trust of leaders on both sides. Negotiations on strategic arms control and over the Vietnam War had resembled trench warfare, where positions were dug in and there was little room for maneuver. There, Kissinger had made several errors. Here, however, he was working under crisis conditions and dealing with Arab leaders for whom he quickly developed a remarkable feel, to go alongside his empathy with the leaders of Israel. It was genuinely creative diplomacy, in which attitudes were changed and maneuver played a big part. By his whirlwind travel between capitals he added a new phrase, "shuttle diplomacy," to the vocabulary of international relations and for the most part used it effectively. Rarely has a statesman managed a diplomatic process so fully and to the benefit of his country.

4. Searching for an Energy Policy

While this diplomatic response to the October 1973 War was masterly, the Nixon Administration's handling of the oil crisis was not. One scholar concluded on the basis of extensive research and interviews:

> During most of Nixon's second term, but especially in his last months in office, little had been done at the highest level in the way of energy planning. Pronouncements had been made and several important initiatives had come from the White House. . . . But these represented at best spasmodic interest by the President in energy, and the initiatives, each significant in itself, were neither coordinated or monitored from the top with any sense of urgency. At agency and department levels energy problems were dealt with in the manner of brush fires to be contained and put out. Moreover, not only was direction from the President lacking, but sometimes its absence caused fierce power struggles to develop . . . to the detriment of morale and efficiency. Partly for these reasons the period . . . is recalled . . . as one in which energy operations bordered on the chaotic.[42]

Was this a fair judgment? If it was, how much was the Nixon Administration to blame, given the novelty of the situation in American experience and the weight of a domestic public opinion largely ignorant of the wider realities of energy and oil?

When Nixon entered his second term in January 1973, few in the United States were focusing on the Middle East as the possible scene of disruptive events. In the summary of hopes and plans the President wrote out in longhand in Key Biscayne on January 11, the only word next to "Mideast" is "settlement" and the word "oil" does not appear in a list of about ten domestic concerns.[43]

Yet, as we have seen, the danger of an oil crisis was perceived with considerable accuracy by the international oil companies and the State Department. In February, Nixon appointed an Oil Policy Committee comprised of George Shultz, Kissinger, and John Ehrlichman, but this committee never took hold. Ehrlichman was forced to resign two months later over his role in Watergate, and the committee's only staff support was a six-man group recruited from the departments.

Peter Flanigan and James Akins, working together, did produce a report with proposals for "expanded coal use, development of synthetic fuels, stepped-up conservation efforts (including a stiff gasoline tax), and much increased research and development spending in order to get beyond hydrocarbons." However, Ehrlichman, still Nixon's chief domestic policy advisor at that point, blocked the plan, insisting that "conservation [was] not the Republican ethic."[44] Proposals for large-scale research projects with little promise of short-term payoffs got the same negative reaction. The inertia against basic change was very strong among Nixon's advisors and probably also in his own mind.

Nonetheless, Flanigan and Akins managed to get White House approval for a presidential message on energy, which was sent to Congress on April 18. This contained a long list of possible measures, including a decontrolling of natural gas prices. Such a market-based action appealed strongly to Shultz, but none of the recommendations in the message was pursued with Congress in any strong or systematic manner. It was a one-shot effort.[45]

On the very same day, the White House decided that the price control program dating from Camp David in 1971 should be extended in a new Phase III, and that petroleum products should continue to be covered. This reliance on price controls—a sop to public opinion in large part—cut squarely across an alternative policy of letting market forces operate to increase prices, stimulate domestic production (and imports), and encourage conservation. It was a built-in contradiction never resolved during the Nixon Administration.[46] Moreover, the April message's strong encouragement of expanded research on new energy sources ran head-on into Nixon's attempt to reduce government spending sharply, to the point of impounding funds voted by Congress.

The message did lead to the creation of the first government unit charged with action on the energy problem as a whole. In June, Governor John Love of Colorado was brought in and briefly touted as a new energy "czar" in charge of a new Federal Energy Office. Nixon was always drawn to organizational changes to meet domestic setbacks or crises, and for a time suggested a new Cabinet position for Energy and Natural Resources. There must have been protests from the existing departments and agencies and their constituents, for he never pushed this or any other item in the list of measures, and the whole effort was languishing when the October War broke out.

The politics of energy policy, both internationally and in America, intruded then and repeatedly thereafter. In the face of the optimistic national mood about the economy during early 1973, warnings of energy difficulties were scarcely heeded, and there was a significant body of opinion which argued that if the big consumer countries stuck together they could keep the producing countries from changing the price unilaterally simply by refusing to buy until the price was reduced.[47] Indeed, as late as September 1973, Nixon himself made a remarkable statement along these lines. Asked at a press conference to comment on a particularly threatening statement by Qaddafi of Libya, he responded by warning OPEC members that "oil without a market, as Mr. Mossadegh learned many, many years ago, doesn't do a country much good. We and Europe are the market."[48] This was an extraordinary misreading of the market situation, one of several occasions when Nixon was a prisoner of simplistic conclusions from events in the Eisenhower Administration. His comment shows how totally he failed to grasp the crisis potential or the economic and political changes that by then made any threat of a significant or concerted boycott by the United States and Europe an empty one. Each big consumer country had its own special position, in terms of both dependence on Middle East oil and attitudes toward the Arab countries, and almost every government considered that any attempt to bargain collectively with OPEC or to make even the mildest threat would be ineffectual and damaging to its relationship with OPEC. In a nutshell, whereas the producing countries could now afford a cutback in shipments for a long period, the consuming countries, lacking the cushion of American surplus capacity that had prevented attempts to use an oil weapon in 1956 and 1967, could not stand a severe supply cutback for more than a short period.

A second key feature of energy politics was the strength and political influence of the domestic oil industry. Over the years, members of Congress from Texas, Oklahoma, and other major oil-producing and oil-refining states had maneuvered themselves into controlling positions on Capitol Hill.

In the 1950s and 1960s, Robert Kerr of Oklahoma—himself an oil mag-nate—was reckoned by many as the Senate's most powerful single member, at least on issues where his interests and those of his state were engaged. Natural gas and coal also had powerful bases in Congress, but the inter-national oil companies had no regional base and little power in Congress, while people in the Northeast, with almost no energy production, had their own special concerns for adequate supplies, especially for heating.

The executive branch was almost equally Balkanized. Atomic energy had its own agency, coal for historic reasons was the province of the Department of the Interior, and natural gas—originally a by-product and neglected step-child of oil production—had its own regulatory agency, the Federal Power Commission, since it could only be distributed by interstate pipelines. On the other hand, coal for heating was not regulated; its price hovered between that of oil and natural gas and was heavily dependent on the proximity of the coal source to the consuming area.

These divisions would have been enough in themselves to make the framing of any true national energy policy an enormously complex under-taking. A further complication was that environmental concerns had be-come a major factor, especially after a large oil spill in early 1969 from an offshore well in the Santa Barbara Channel, a renowned beauty spot. That year also saw the passage of the National Environmental Policy Act, enacted by a bipartisan vote and public effort in which Senator Edmund Muskie was a leader. Under that act the promoters of large-scale energy projects (and similar undertakings) had first to submit Environmental Impact State-ments, which were vigilantly monitored by a number of new citizens or-ganizations, local and national, with formidable scientific and legal capacities as well as patience.

The newly created Environmental Protection Agency, headed by mod-erate Republicans, led the way in publicizing environmental problems. Al-most every major new coal project was contested, for example, and the effect on American oil development was particularly dramatic. In the late 1960s, it had been predicted that the remote North Slope of Alaska might produce as much as 2 million barrels per day by the early 1970s. Now, intense con-troversies and legal actions arose over the route of the necessary pipeline—whether to the port of Valdez on the south coast of Alaska and thence by sea, or across northwestern Canada and down by pipeline. North Slope oil was not approved for production until 1973 and did not start to reach the continental United States until 1977.

By the fall of 1973 the politics of energy was thoroughly confused and unpredictable, with no government organization to sort out the various claims, or even to reach a roughly agreed estimate of the possibilities. The oil companies were particularly closemouthed, lest disclosures affect their competitive situations or their bargaining with the oil-producing countries.

There was not even any repository of basic data from which to frame policy options. The result was widespread ignorance and potential gridlock—region against region, one resource against another, producers versus consumers, vested interests against promoters of new resources or methods of discovery or production—with many disputes especially heated because of conflicting claims and basic ignorance. The evidence is strong that Nixon himself was never abreast of the situation, let alone prepared to provide leadership.

Against this background of confusion and ignorance, the Arab embargo announced in the midst of the October War on sales of oil to the United States aroused immediate and widespread resentment among many groups in the United States. All sorts of stories were believed, including the claim (almost certainly inaccurate) that tankers bringing oil from Arab countries were being turned around just as they reached the United States, as part of the oil companies' compliance with the embargo. With no clear leadership, the natural tendency was to seek scapegoats, and the two foremost candidates were the international oil companies and the American government itself, with the Arab countries a distant third, according to one poll. In contrast, few pointed to the rapid rise in demand, especially in the United States, and almost none shared the view (common among European leaders) that Israel too deserved to be blamed for the October War.[49]

In whipping up sentiment against the oil companies, Senator Henry Jackson was once again in the forefront, this time as chairman of the important Senate Permanent Committee on Investigations, which had a standing charter to look into areas of supposed wrongdoing. With an able and aggressive committee staff, Jackson initiated a series of hearings in which officials from the international oil companies were called to testify on their ties to the producing countries and especially on their profits. It was a Grade A congressional spectacular, with klieg lights and maximum publicity, and ran for several months as additional material became available. One particular target was the "obscene" profits of the largest companies, which in fact did rise from $6.9 billion to $11.7 billion in 1973, and then to $16.4 billion in 1974. One telling disclosure was that the profits of Exxon, the most conspicuous international, for the last quarter of 1973 were 79 percent greater than in the same period the year before. Few stopped to note that the dramatic oil price increases in late 1973 were bound to mean highly profitable sales in those months from inventories accumulated at much lower prices. In fact, after 1974, the rates of return of the big oil companies fell back to "somewhat below the average rate for all American industry."[50] But at the time the oil companies took a ferocious going-over at Jackson's hands, and he became a major player on the energy front, as he already was on arms control agreements and trade with the Soviet Union.

In fact, the much reviled international oil companies were doing a tremendous job for which they got no credit with the public. Even in normal times, bringing oil to the American market was a complicated business, for the wrong kind of oil could easily get to the wrong destination. Now the companies had to sort out their oil shipments in terms of the country of origin as well. Many Americans thought the oil companies were so powerful that they could disregard the dictates of the Arab producers, but the companies knew better. The Arabs were both vigilant and, by now, well able to shut off the tap and do without the revenue for a time, or even to break off relations with any violating oil company. Both for patriotism and self-interest, the people in the international oil companies worked frantically to see that the embargo was observed, but that the United States got what it needed from non-Arab sources. In this international distribution effort, they were remarkably successful.

As we have seen, Nixon was intensely preoccupied with Watergate-related problems in the weeks after October 20, but he finally pulled himself together to deliver a major energy speech on television on November 7, a few days after the guns of the October War had finally gone silent. This long, diffuse effort was much less effective than other speeches he had given at critical times. It stressed that the United States confronted the clear prospect that for some time energy supplies were going to fall 10 percent short of normal needs, and proposed a long list of actions Americans could do for themselves (lower nighttime temperatures, car pooling) and a few modest government restraints (a return to daylight saving time through the whole year, a fifty-mile-an-hour speed limit on federal highways). His main emphasis was on the supply side, however. He proclaimed that the United States could and should produce itself out of the crisis by a great national effort, which he christened "Project Independence," on the model of the great World War II production programs such as the Manhattan Project that built the first atomic weapons. The goal should be to make the United States self-sufficient in energy resources by 1980.

As experts in and out of government well knew, such an objective was uncertain in any time frame and totally unrealistic for 1980. Whether President Nixon truly believed it could be reached was not clear. His habit was to minimize difficulties and make his speeches upbeat—as he had done with such short-term success in launching the Camp David economic program in August 1971. In this case the choice of 1980 as the target date was his personal decision.[51]

The speech contained passages contributed by two groups of advisors whose basic views diverged sharply. William E. Simon, Deputy Secretary of the Treasury, who had just been appointed to head the Federal Energy Office in November, deprecated the power of the Arab producers and believed that the oil market would shortly respond to economic factors by a sharp drop in overall demand, so that prices would then ease. On the other hand, John Sawhill, nominated by Roy Ash of OMB as Simon's deputy, thought the crisis was far more serious and likely to be lasting, and thus stressed conservation measures, even drastic ones, and the need to develop new technologies as quickly as possible. This split was never resolved, and during the winter the new Energy Office was overwhelmed by immediate problems, especially the domestic allocation of oil supplies. Simon made a constant but vain effort to ease the feelings of near-panic in many quarters and create a climate for rational decision.

The Emergency Petroleum Allocation Act that had been put together and passed by the Senate in June 1973 did not get through the House until December. The act confirmed the extension of price controls for petroleum products and required the government to make plans to allocate these, and crude oil as well, "in all regions of the country, as equitably and efficiently as possible." In effect, government now took over the role of the market for a substantial part of oil distribution.[52] The act was an understandable response to the alternative of straight political pressure. But it obviously opened the way for endless arguments from affected consuming regions, from companies at all stages of the oil market, and from their political representatives. Through the winter and spring, the Federal Energy Office and the rest of the government had their hands full scrambling from one shortage situation to another. It was another reason that a real energy policy never was even formulated, let alone set in motion.[53]

In this atmosphere, the latent debate between primary emphasis on increasing energy supplies of known character versus conservation and the development of new energy sources was never engaged. The struggle between Simon and Sawhill, and the views each represented, simmered on, the kind of struggle that only leadership from the President might have resolved. By then, however, Nixon was even more out of the action, busy with fighting off Watergate prosecutor Leon Jaworski over White House tapes. Yet the evidence is strong that, Watergate or not, taking charge of an issue of this sort was never in Richard Nixon's makeup.

With energy policy mired down, Henry Kissinger took a hand in dealing with the international aspects of the problem. The major speech he gave on December 12 in a traditionally friendly forum, the Society of Pilgrims in London, was basically a fervent reaffirmation of the importance of Atlantic ties. At the close he also addressed the energy crisis, appealing for cooperation with a proposal to set up a small group of top officials (following a Marshall Plan precedent from the 1940s) to outline a possible joint policy. The idea did not take hold, but in January 1974 Kissinger proposed a broad Energy Conference, among all the major oil-consuming nations.

This conference convened in Washington on February 11–12, 1974, with Foreign and Finance Ministers from Japan, all the members of the European Community, and Norway.[54] British Foreign Minister Sir Alec Douglas-

Home and Japan's Ohira were especially cooperative with Kissinger, and Helmut Schmidt of West Germany supported the American proposals; the dissident, Michel Jobert of France, was effectively isolated.[55] The conference declaration deliberately shied away from appearing to envisage or plan a confrontation with the Arab producers. Instead, it focused hardest on conservation measures, technical cooperation, financial safety nets, and help (largely rhetorical) for developing countries hard hit by the scarcity and high price of oil. Special emphasis was given to emergency sharing measures in the event of another crisis. Finally, it was agreed to set up an international energy agency, which was headed by an able West German, Ulf Lantzke.

The conference and Kissinger's diplomacy helped to ease the strains that had been so evident during the October War, and thus strengthen the Western Alliance. On the other hand, the conference's effect on the participants' energy policies was not great. In the United States, it was scarcely noted. The preparatory work did bring senior American officials into closer consultation about energy than had been the case up to that point, but after the conference the Administration was no nearer a coherent and agreed energy policy.

Two weeks later, on February 25, Richard Nixon made headlines by declaring at a press conference that "the crisis has passed." It appeared that he was at first referring to an easing in the very difficult shortage of home heating oil, but by the end of the press conference he had expanded his original statement. In *The New York Times*'s summary, " 'The prospects for avoiding a recession are good,' the President said, 'because we are going to be dealing with the energy crisis—what was a crisis—as a problem.' "[56]

The statement was at best premature, another example of Nixon's strong tendency to make rosy assessments for political effect. Supplies were still short, and the Arab embargo, though weakened (it soon ended on March 18), still meant serious reductions in the amount of imported oil reaching the United States. Above all, OPEC's immense December price rise, to $11.65 a barrel, remained in full effect. As George Shultz later wrote:

> It was, after all, not the OPEC oil embargo that created the key economic problem. . . . Rather, it was the restriction of production by OPEC governments that, by facilitating the imposition of sharp price increases on the consuming world, created the more serious and lasting problem.[57]

The increased price of oil from the Middle East was offset in part by being averaged against the controlled price of domestic oil in some areas, but prices at the gasoline pump remained far above their previous levels. High oil prices, in turn, meant high overall price levels for a whole range of necessities, thus continuously stimulating the inflation that had been mounting steadily for a year. At the same time, economic growth seemed virtually to cease, and the country found itself increasingly, as 1974 went on, in the grip of a totally unfamiliar situation, christened "stagflation," in which the normal tendency of reduced economic activity to lead to lower price levels was stood on its head and the unemployment and inflation rates went up together.

The oil crisis was thus far more than a temporary blip on the economic screen. Rather, it resulted in a continuing severe drag on the American economy, which in a real and substantial sense reduced the power of the United States abroad. Other consuming nations, of course, faced similar problems: Western Europe, significantly affected, took in its belt, and the nation most dependent on Middle East oil, Japan, seized the occasion to make an extraordinary adaptation, with a successful energy policy that probably did more than any other factor to make possible Japan's immensely increased economic standing in later years. The energy situation required major decisions to be taken by national leaders, and the United States suffered more than most, in large part avoidably.

5. Watergate: The Last Phase

By January 1974, the new Watergate Special Prosecutor, Leon Jaworski, was in stride, keeping the staff that his dismissed predecessor Archibald Cox had recruited and showing no inclination to let up in pursuit of the appropriate legal measures. In his State of the Union message, Nixon said flatly that he had given Jaworski all the material he needed, and that the time had come to bring the various investigations to an end: "One year of Watergate is enough." Jaworski promptly challenged him with a further request for tapes, on which the White House stalled.[58] But the scandal never lost momentum. On February 6, the House formally authorized its Judiciary Committee to proceed with consideration of articles of impeachment, and on March 1, a grand jury handed down indictments of all the senior White House and campaign staff, notably John Mitchell, H. R. Haldeman, and John Ehrlichman, for conspiracy to obstruct justice. A separate report, naming Nixon himself as an "unindicted co-conspirator," was sealed for the time being.

Meanwhile, in late February, Rodino's Judiciary Committee subpoenaed 42 tapes, and the White House decided it would transcribe these but not release the original tapes. On April 16, Jaworski asked Judge Sirica for an order covering an additional 64 tapes, and on April 30, the White House released the edited transcripts of the 42 tapes demanded by the Judiciary Committee, along with 20 of the 64 demanded by Jaworski.

It was another climactic moment. Key parts of the taped conversations had been excised with the notation "(expletive deleted)," which passed into the national store of memorable phrases — and the public now learned of the President's endless discussions with his aides of ways to put pressure on people and corrupt them. The mind-set of the White House was revealed as that of the gutter, with President Nixon himself setting the tone. By then, too, the Joint Committee on Internal Revenue Taxation, chaired by Congressman Wilbur Mills, had come up with a report that Nixon owed nearly a half million dollars in back taxes, in part for taking unjustified deductions on gifts of officially related papers and other subjects.[59] By late April, Nixon's approval rating had dropped to 26 percent.[60]

As it made public the edited transcripts of some tapes, the White House moved to quash Jaworski's motion for the release of the rest. On May 5, Jaworski offered to settle for 18 named tapes and to withhold announcing the reference to Nixon in the grand jury's March report. The White House turned down the deal. On May 9, Judge Sirica ruled in favor of Jaworski's request for all 64 tapes, which the White House appealed, this time directly to the Supreme Court (under a procedure authorized in exceptionally important constitutional cases). The same day, John Doar began to present a detailed compilation of the evidence to executive sessions of the House Judiciary Committee. It was still another climactic moment. By now, Nixon was seriously weakened and totally distracted. Impeachment had become a strong possibility, although by no means certain. At this point (as became known only later), Nixon closeted himself for days on end to play key tapes. As an experienced lawyer, he must have seen that if the Supreme Court upheld Sirica's order, he was doomed.

Then the noose closed. After eleven exhausting weeks of executive sessions, the Judiciary Committee heard Doar's final summation on July 19 and began its public meetings on July 24. By coincidence, on that same day the Supreme Court gave its decision on Judge Sirica's order for the release of the 64 tapes. Everyone had known that this would be a landmark decision on "executive privilege," a doctrine that Presidents over the years had often successfully invoked to deny Congress inside information about decisions and actions and the process behind them. A few lawyers challenged the very existence of such a privilege, which is not explicitly mentioned in the Constitution and rests on precedents from British constitutional practice. Never had its scope been defined.

Now, in a unanimous 8–0 decision,[61] with a single opinion written by Chief Justice Warren Burger, whom Nixon himself had appointed, the Court affirmed the existence of executive privilege in general, as a prerogative implicitly embraced by the Constitution, and therefore a normally valid defense against release of information on deliberations at the top levels of the executive branch. But it went on to rule emphatically that the privilege could not prevail against a subpoena solidly based on needs for a criminal investigation involving senior executive branch officials. For more than 180 years, the Court had never felt compelled to address either issue. Now the force and unanimity of its decision surprised many and were a devastating setback for Nixon.

Before the White House could turn over the tapes, the Judiciary Committee independently deliberated for three days and on Saturday evening, July 27, voted 27–11 to approve a first article of impeachment on obstruction of justice. On July 29 and 30, it adopted two more articles, the second under the broad heading of "abuse of power" (by 28–10) and the third on the more technical charge of failing to comply with congressional subpoenas (by a close 21–17). However, the committee rejected, 26–12, a proposed fourth article based mainly on Nixon's secret bombing of Cambodia in 1969–70, as well as a fifth, on money and tax charges.

On July 30, Alexander Haig and Nixon's lawyers reviewed the tapes, seeing at once that the tape for June 23, 1972, was conclusive proof of Nixon's personal involvement in obstruction of justice. It recorded Nixon himself giving the order, via Haldeman, six days after the burglary, for Richard Helms and Vernon Walters, then heading the CIA, to make a spurious claim of interference with CIA operations and thus thwart a key part of the ongoing FBI investigation of the Watergate burglary. It was the "smoking gun" many members of Congress had been claiming was needed for them to make up their minds.[62]

Nixon held out briefly, but after key Republican senators had persuaded him that the Senate would now surely vote his impeachment, he finally agreed on Wednesday, August 7, to resign. He addressed the nation to this effect on Thursday evening, and took off for California on the morning of August 9 after a farewell meeting in the East Room of the White House with his staff and others close to him.

6. Not with a Bang

By early June 1974, with Watergate visibly approaching its climax, and public attention overwhelmingly focused on the steadily growing possibility that the President would be forced out of office, Nixon — by now in bad health, with phlebitis in one leg requiring constant treatment — made a gallant effort to show that he was still effective in foreign policy and that he was still widely admired in key countries abroad. This trump card, foreign policy success, had saved his standing at least twice before: the opening to China in July 1971 stemmed a nearly overflowing tide of congressional sentiment to get out of Vietnam more rapidly; and in May 1972, the first summit meeting with the Soviet Union, held despite the U.S. mining of Haiphong Harbor, neutralized domestic opposition to the war and enabled Nixon to go ahead with the relentless bombing of North Vietnam that led to the Paris Agreement.

Now, however, with his political survival at stake, there were no opportunities for striking new diplomatic achievements. Still, he could show that NATO held firm, and he could dramatize what had been achieved in the Middle East, by making a "victory lap" series of visits to celebrate the genuine diplomatic successes there. It would all add up to show that he was, after all, still the respected leader of the free world, whose continuing performance made the attacks on him over stupid political excesses relatively unimportant.

It was a bold script, and one in which many leaders abroad were ready to play their parts. Arab countries in particular, with Anwar el-Sadat the bellwether, were genuinely admiring and grateful for all that Kissinger had accomplished; none paid much attention to Watergate or was disturbed by it. In Western Europe, also, a poll of leaders would surely have shown a majority favorable to Nixon's continuing in office, only partly comprehending the force of the case against him. Most important and dramatic, the good will of Leonid Brezhnev was conveyed to Nixon in dramatic fashion as he put his schedule into final form. As often, Ambassador Dobrynin is a vivid witness. It was, he thought,

> increasingly evident that Nixon was becoming oblivious to matters of foreign policy and that Watergate was taking an ugly turn. But the Kremlin still believed that the real source was some conspiracy by anti-Soviet and pro-Zionist groups trying to scuttle Nixon's policy of good relations with Moscow. Even Gromyko held that opinion. Our embassy tried to explain to our leaders that Nixon was being accused of violating American laws and the Constitution. But Moscow did not (or would not) understand how the president of the United States could be prosecuted for what it viewed as such a "small matter." The minds of the Soviet rulers simply could not grasp the situation, because they never even thought possible such a thing as the criminal prosecution of the highest authority. In any case, Moscow did not believe until the last moment that Nixon could be forced to resign.[63]

On May 28, the ambassador brought Nixon a personal message from Brezhnev. While the Kremlin did not really understand the Watergate events,

> [We] still can see that there are forces that are apparently very powerful and that they are up in arms against you. . . . In such cases you really need stamina and spiritual strength. Surely there are people in the United States and elsewhere who expect Richard Nixon to give way and break down. But, as we note with satisfaction, you are not going to please them

in that respect. We are stating this on the basis of our good relations and our confidence in the success of the new meeting.[64]

As Dobrynin noted, "such an extraordinary message from a Soviet leader to an American president was unprecedented in the history of our relations." It led the ambassador to call Brezhnev "Nixon's last friend." Nixon could be sure that the Moscow summit would at least be free of visible incident or controversy.

Nixon's trip to the Middle East got off to a bad start, however, with some homemade fireworks at what was planned as a transit and rest stop in Salzburg, Austria, on June 11. Kissinger decided on his own to present himself to the press there, to deal with new allegations that he had not told the full truth about his part in the wiretaps placed on his staff in 1969. Since the subject had been thoroughly aired and apparently dealt with in his confirmation hearings as Secretary of State the previous September, his decision to discuss it again was surely very bad judgment, stemming perhaps from the strain of recent months but also from his egotism, perennially thin skin, and tendency to overreact to attacks he perceived to reflect on his character. The result was an emotional response to a fair but provocatively phrased question, in which Kissinger said that if the matter were not cleared up, he would resign. This gave the press screaming headlines. For the White House, it was a gross distraction from the planned effect of Nixon's trip. For the next weeks, until the very end, the relationship between Nixon and Kissinger appears to have been cool.[65]

Once under way, the Middle East trip went very well. In Egypt, Sadat saw to it that vast crowds, estimated in the millions, turned out; old-timers in the media could recall for comparison only Eisenhower's reception in India in 1959. The enthusiasm of the populace had to have been mostly genuine, in a country where the outcome of the war followed a long period of defeat and apparent decline. As in China in February 1972, the show was the most important thing—a clear signal of the new cordiality between onetime enemies, of Egypt's restored prestige, and of a new and, from the Arab standpoint, more balanced U.S. policy in the Middle East.[66]

After that opening triumph, in quick succession, came stops in Jidda, Damascus, Jerusalem, and Amman. In Jidda, Faisal sounded his familiar anti-Zionist themes and Nixon his familiar urging that oil prices be moderated. (Saudi Arabia did indeed exert modest influence in that direction in the rest of the decade.) In Damascus, where no American President had ever visited before, it was agreed that formal diplomatic relations, broken in 1967, should be resumed—a significant step for a country with continuing radical tendencies. Assad made a strong personal impression on Nixon and vice versa, to the point of Assad kissing his guest on both cheeks as he departed.

Israel was a contrast. Troubled by the grinding compromises of the withdrawal agreement on the Golan Heights, and by the new cordiality between the United States and Arab nations, the government and people of Jerusalem extended only a cool reception to the President, though an impromptu glowing toast by Nixon to Mrs. Meir eased the atmosphere. The groundwork was laid for continued U.S. economic and military aid at high levels, and Nixon also offered Israel a nonmilitary research nuclear reactor, matching a similar offer he had made to Sadat. Finally, in Amman, King Hussein was ready to start discussing Israeli withdrawals from the West Bank, but with a brand-new Israeli government in place, the subject was not pursued, perhaps a neglected opportunity.

As Nixon flew home on June 19, the NATO Foreign Ministers were concluding their annual business meeting in Ottawa, with the signing of the long-planned and once controversial Atlantic Declaration, Kissinger's project since April 1973. Frictions over the October War had left their residue, but the energy conference had helped somewhat. In particular, the link between the key economic ministers, two of whom (Helmut Schmidt and Valéry Giscard d'Estaing) had now succeeded to the top jobs, was firmly enough in place to survive the departure in May of George Shultz, after six and a half remarkable years of service in steadily more important jobs.

The core Alliance was at last recovering from a bad patch. All had seen the damage of disunion, Kissinger himself had learned many lessons, and the way was open for a closer drawing together in the coming years.

On his return from this fairly successful trip, Nixon presided over final discussions on the SALT II negotiations. But Kissinger's extremely tight schedule had prevented him from playing his usual role in framing the issues for Nixon to decide and coming up with his own proposals. A quick Moscow trip in March and a detour to Cyprus to talk to Gromyko in April fell well short of the need. Thereafter, while Kissinger was absorbed in his Syrian "shuttle diplomacy," the skeptical, if not negative, Pentagon leaders—the Joint Chiefs of Staff, but above all Schlesinger and Clements—were putting up hard-line positions that were patently not negotiable; moreover, Schlesinger was keeping Senator Jackson informed at every turn. The President's heavy reliance on a single individual always had the danger that key subjects might be neglected at a climactic time. This now happened.

The biggest problem was setting ground rules for counting MIRVed missiles, as the Soviet deployment charged ahead, along with the U.S. Trident submarine program. Jackson's pressure for "equal aggregates" was by this time broadened so that the unit of measure included all the key offensive missile systems as a group, not one by one (which would have been wholly impracticable). Yet it was still basically less realistic than looking at the two arsenals in terms of "offsetting asymmetries"—that is, weighing a Soviet superiority in some aspects against an American superiority in others, to come at a fair comparison of effective striking power.

By early June, there appeared to be a consensus on a concept of "unequal MIRVs offsetting unequal aggregates," in Kissinger's summary phrase— more American warheads, more Soviet missiles. But Jackson had weighed in with his own public proposal, calling for reductions and equal aggregates in a manner designed to constrain the Soviet Union while leaving the United States relatively unaffected. Kissinger had no time to come to grips with this when Schlesinger responded to Jackson's (doubtless prearranged) request for his views, in a June 3 letter that in effect approved Jackson's approach! It was a flagrant end run by all the norms of loyalty and discipline within the executive branch, to which the weakened Nixon could only respond by a mild private rebuke to Schlesinger, leaving the letter un- touched on the public record. The episode testified to a sense that Nixon was no longer really involved, also perhaps to resentment over Kissinger's past use of access to Nixon for his own ends. As the Secretary of State saw it, not unreasonably, the combination of dissent within and without, sure to be revealed even if a new agreement was reached and submitted to Congress, meant that it would be feckless to attempt agreement at this time. His later assessment was surely on target: "serious prospects for SALT in the Nixon Presidency ended by early June with the Schlesinger letter."[67]

On June 14 came a second blow. Paul Nitze had been in the thick of SALT I from the outset. Yet, as we have seen, he and Gerard Smith had been left in Helsinki in May 1972 when debatable deals were made in Moscow on submarines and missile replacement, and barely got to the final signing ceremony after a lot of indignity. Nitze was too big to hold a full- time grudge about such treatment, but it certainly left him wary. Now, with the President's very political life threatened, and the courts and Congress poised for decision, Nitze thought it all too likely that the President would try to extricate himself by some dramatic and ill-judged last-minute deal on SALT II. In late May he decided that he must contribute to forestalling such a development and wrote to both Nixon and Schlesinger announcing his intent to resign at once. When he got no reply from the White House, he took the advice of a friend who was a judge and wrote a second letter making his resignation unilateral and immediate. At the same time he is- sued a public statement speaking bluntly of the

> depressing reality of the traumatic events now unfolding in our nation's capital and of the implications of those events in the international arena.
>
> Until the Office of the Presidency has been restored to its principal function of upholding the Constitution and taking care of the fair exe- cution of the laws, and thus be able to function effectively at home and

abroad, I see no real prospect for reversing certain unfortunate trends in the present evolving situation.[68]

Nitze's status as a nonpartisan elder statesman caused his statement to reverberate in Washington as in effect a call for Nixon's resignation.

On June 20, in the brief interval between overseas trips, Nixon chaired an NSC meeting to consider and decide on the position to be taken in Moscow on the SALT II issues. The meeting was a disaster. Schlesinger came in with new and patently unnegotiable proposals, and Kissinger could only fall back on exploring the Soviet positions at the summit. Fortunately for public impressions, the negotiations between Alexis Johnson and his Soviet counterparts had produced two sensible lesser agreements, one to reduce the number of ABM installations to one on each side instead of the two that had been agreed in Moscow in 1972, a second on a Threshold Test Ban, barring tests with explosive power higher than 150 kilotons. The Soviet Union — perhaps to put pressure on China — had wanted a comprehensive ban covering all tests, but with scientific studies indicating that the chances of detection were low for tests below the proposed threshold, the United States held out for that figure, and got it.[69] These were not big steps forward, but indicated that negotiations in the symbolic arms control area were still possible.

At the very end of the Moscow summit, moreover, SALT II took on new life. In preparatory discussions, Kissinger had suggested to his Soviet counterparts that they aim not at a permanent agreement or a simple short extension, but at a new agreement to run perhaps from 1975 to 1985. The two sides would be free to propose either equal aggregates or offsetting asymmetries. That way, the Soviet Union could change the numbers in the 1972 Interim Agreement without loss of face, and the United States could look again at the MIRV problem. There had been no Soviet reply until Gromyko in Moscow suddenly accepted the proposal on behalf of the Politburo. It was then agreed that there should be a midwinter mini-summit in the Soviet Union, with each side free to present new proposals on either of the alternate bases. The Soviet leaders were probably uncertain whether Nixon would still be in office; they may have wished to make a gesture that would strengthen his hand against his critics. Finally and perhaps decisively, Brezhnev may have wished to keep the atmosphere friendly, for the sake of one unfulfilled objective concerning, as usual, China.

In the schedule for the summit, the Soviet hosts had inserted a day and a half's visit to the Crimea, the all-season site for rest and relaxation of Soviet leaders. It had also been the scene of the 1945 Yalta Conference, later reviled in the United States. This time the Soviet leaders resourcefully redrew the map so that the suburb in which the meeting was held was renamed Oreanda. Thither the two teams repaired from Sunday afternoon, June 30, to Tuesday morning, July 2.

In this setting Brezhnev went after his objective, once again using an element of surprise, as he had done at San Clemente the year before, over the Middle East. He isolated Nixon for a three-hour conversation in a beautiful grotto looking out to sea, as the respective staffs watched from a distance.[70] No American record of this conversation has been published; the odds are that none exists. Its thrust, however, became clear enough as the two adjourned. Once again, the Soviet leader was aiming to loosen or remove the tie between the United States and China—picking up once more, with a battered President, the effort that went back to 1969, with additional tries in 1970 and 1971. His gambit this time was a classic nineteenth-century maneuver. He proposed a nonaggression pact with the Soviet Union, under which neither the Soviet Union nor the United States would attack the other or, by implication, cooperate with any nation that might do so. As the Molotov-Ribbentrop nonaggression accord of August 1939 had freed Hitler to attack Poland without fear that the Soviet Union would respond, so what Brezhnev now proposed would permit the Soviet Union to put any kind of pressure on China, including the threat or use of military force, with much greater confidence that the United States would stand aside. Over time, such an agreement had a good chance of eroding Sino-American confidence and cutting the heart out of the tie formed since 1971.

Brezhnev's appeal must have been aimed to arouse some of the old 1950s anti-China impulses in Nixon's political makeup; it was probably accompanied by fulsome personal sentiments. Kissinger, himself susceptible on occasion to flattery and personal appeals, was in this case detached. He saw at once that Brezhnev's proposal was simply an old wolf in sheep's clothing, and that to pursue it in any way would be at best fruitless, at worst dangerous. In Moscow for the final banquet on July 2, Kissinger was at the same table as the two leaders when Nixon turned to him and told him to pursue the idea with Gromyko. Kissinger did not demur on the spot, but he never lifted a finger, and within a few weeks told Dobrynin that discussions in this direction would not be useful. In the Soviet view, nothing had been lost by trying. How Nixon responded can only be taken as evidence of his disabled condition.[71]

On the last day of the summit, July 3, it was Kissinger who made news, through a memorable press conference that went on, after the ritual wrap-up of the meeting, into fundamental questions seldom discussed frankly in public. What he said and how he later explained it were immensely revealing—about the institutional obstacles to arms control and the sincerity of his own efforts to surmount these obstacles, and ultimately about the state of America and the world in the face of the strategic nuclear arsenals assembled and in prospect.

At the press conference, after an early response that appeared to blame the lack of SALT II progress on the military leaders in both countries (a view that he modified in his memoirs to saying it was up to political leaders to "strike the balance on which restraint may be based"), Kissinger was asked what would happen if a new SALT agreement was not reached before the 1977 deadline. He responded ("with passion," by his own account):

> If we have not reached an agreement well before 1977, then I believe you will see an explosion of technology and an explosion of numbers at the end of which we'll be lucky if we have the present stability, in which it will be impossible to describe what strategic superiority means. One of the questions which we have to ask ourselves as a country is: *What in the name of God is strategic superiority?* What is the significance of it, politically, militarily, operationally, *at these levels of numbers?* What do you do with it?[72]

The response was immediately picked up and widely quoted. In later years, particularly after conservative Republicans had savagely attacked him during the 1976 campaign, Kissinger put out a statement to the effect that in the Moscow press conference he had not intended to say, and did not believe, "that strategic superiority had lost all significance." In 1979, he again tried to define his view with greater precision. These efforts do not change this historian's conclusion that his original statement was a valid expression of underlying feelings for which he deserved and deserves credit.[73]

. . .

Nixon arrived home late on July 3, received at a remote Air Force base in northern Maine rather than, as in 1972, triumphantly in Washington. Neither his Middle East trip nor the Moscow summit had arrested the now rapid decline in his political standing. Nixon's last serious diplomatic moves had been gallant but hopeless efforts, typical of this last phase of his presidency, when he was grasping at straws, hoping in vain for a miracle. His active foreign policy career ended, in the words of T. S. Eliot, "not with a bang but a whimper."[74]

7. *Watergate in Perspective*

As it evolved, "Watergate" became an all-embracing label for a host of events and illegalities. Some were obviously for straight political advantage. In other cases, Nixon's supporters and associates claimed that there had been a national security purpose. A short discussion thus seems in order.

The original burglary of the Democratic headquarters on June 17, 1972, came about because senior officials in Nixon's aggressive campaign organ-

ization—the Committee to Re-elect the President, or CRP—decided they
must have certain information on the chairman of the Democratic National
Committee, Lawrence O'Brien, who had once been a member of President
Kennedy's Cabinet and was a well-known political figure. An earlier, undetected, burglary of Democratic headquarters in late May had failed to
produce the wanted information, so the team of five men went back on the
night of June 17 to ransack files and put recording "bugs" on phones. When
they were caught by an alert guard, documents on them pointed to CRP,
along with large sums of money readily traced to its campaign funds.

According to the evidence revealed in a series of trials, the official specifically responsible for ordering the burglaries was John Mitchell, former
Attorney General and then head of CRP. Throughout the crisis, Nixon
denied that he had ordered the project or even known of it in advance; his
denial was rejected by much of the public, but not contested by grand juries
or Congress. (Many suspected that he had simply made clear how badly he
wanted the information, in the manner of King Henry II of England suggesting the murder of Thomas à Becket.) Instead, the Judiciary Committee
focused on the ensuing attempt by Nixon and his staff to conceal and deny
any involvement in the burglary. This cover-up was the core of "Watergate."

Evidence established that, when informed of the arrests, Nixon was responsible for the decision to claim that the operation was only an unauthorized low-level caper, and that he personally put John Dean of his staff
in charge of covering up any White House participation. From the testimony of Dean and others, it also became abundantly clear that Nixon had
been part of several cover-up actions, notably the diversion of CRP funds
to support the burglars and keep them from talking about higher-ups. These
actions formed the basis for the first article of impeachment, which the
Judiciary Committee approved before the release of the "smoking gun"
tape. No national security purpose could be claimed for the burglary or
cover-up. Both were criminal actions for the political purpose of helping
Nixon win the record majority he craved.

The highlights of the second article, which concerned the abuse of government power, included an illegal wiretap, the use of the Internal Revenue
Service to harass Nixon's political opponents, and the actions of the "plumbers" unit which had been set up in the White House after the disclosure
of the Pentagon Papers. This unit had been responsible for the break-in of
the office of Daniel Ellsberg's psychiatrist in Los Angeles; the "plumbers"
hoped to obtain information that would depict Ellsberg as mentally unbalanced, with no pretense the break-in might produce national security information. As for the wiretaps, mostly dating from the 1969 news story about
the first bombings in Cambodia, the striking thing was that the committee
rejected almost all of these on the ground that they had had an arguable
national security justification. The only one it retained as a charge was the

wiretap put on Anthony Lake, who had resigned from Kissinger's staff in May 1970 and later worked in Senator Muskie's presidential campaign. The tap had been kept in place long after Lake had any access to government secrets, when he was in the opposing political camp! In this instance, the same careful distinction was evident: only if an action had no tenable national security purpose was it grounds for impeachment.

The third article, covering Nixon's failure to comply with committee subpoenas—essentially part of the cover-up—was approved largely for the sake of future precedent. The committee wished to establish that a President could not reject congressional subpoenas as a matter of right or prerogative, but must respond to them through the normal judicial process.

Finally, the committee's handling of the 1969–70 secret bombing of Cambodia showed its standards clearly. When the bombing had first been revealed in July 1973, many in Congress and the public considered it a substantial violation of the constitutional allocation of warmaking powers. In 1974 some went further, contending that it was a more basic and important offense even than obstruction of justice or misuse of government power. The Judiciary Committee's staff, presumably with the blessing of Chairman Rodino, put forward the "illegal bombing of Cambodia" as the principal item in a proposed fourth article of impeachment, which, however, was voted down by a majority of the committee, 26–12, with nine Democrats voting with the majority. The dominant view, clearly, was that this action (and others directly related to the conduct of the war), however illegal, had been taken in wartime and for the protection of American forces, and in any event embraced political factors of a different nature than the other offenses.[75]

Many of Nixon's associates later advanced the argument that at least some of his actions were a justifiable response to the atmosphere created by the controversy over the Vietnam War and the pressures of the antiwar movement. Yet, as we have just seen, the core actions comprising "Watergate"—the burglary and cover-up—were aimed squarely and solely at ensuring Nixon's reelection, and were carried out through political members of the White House staff or the CRP organization. All the participants in the cover-up, including Nixon, were imbued with a common passion: not only that he should win but that the margin of victory should be overwhelming, the largest in history.

Even Nixon's key initial decision, to conceal John Mitchell's involvement, was undoubtedly taken to prevent any dent whatever in the overwhelming victory that by late June looked within reach. Most political observers would have agreed that Nixon was so far ahead that even if Mitchell had been persuaded to confess his responsibility (while clearing Nixon), the effect would only have been a drop of, say, 5 points in Nixon's actual 21-point win in November.[76] But it was just those extra points that, in Nixon's eyes, were needed to vindicate his political career and give him, at last, the mandate he needed to govern as he pleased.

. . .

There remains the later effort of prominent Nixon partisans to use the intense political controversy that raged over Vietnam War policy as a plea in mitigation, even perhaps a justification, of his role in Watergate. In a variant of this argument, H. R. Haldeman and John Ehrlichman contended in their memoirs that without the leak of the Pentagon Papers, a Vietnam-related event, the "plumbers" and the burglary team would never have been created. Without the Vietnam War, "there would have been no Watergate."[77]

Henry Kissinger has offered a more subtle and plausible version of the thesis that Vietnam was responsible for Watergate. In his memoirs, he devoted several pages to disruptive conduct by the opponents of the Vietnam War, blaming them for bringing on the President's feeling that he had to crush these "radicals" and all they stood for, and arguing that this in turn was the biggest reason why he became obsessed with winning overwhelmingly in 1972, whatever it took.

> Most of the voluminous literature of Watergate . . . treats it as a personal aberration of Richard Nixon as if there had been no surrounding circumstances. And in truth Watergate is unthinkable apart from Nixon's driven personality. But there was also a deeper background. Historians will misunderstand Watergate who neglect the destructive impact on American politics, spirit, and unity of the war in Vietnam.[78]

Kissinger's theme has variations expressing his own often extreme reaction to criticism and opposition. As an explanation of Richard Nixon's motives, it is in the end unpersuasive. That Nixon was a driven man can be agreed by any observer or student of his career. Equally, it is evident that intense controversy over the Vietnam War changed the terms and tone of debate and polarized the country to an extraordinary degree. But only a President with Nixon's history of passionate political concern and lack of scruple could have gone to the lengths he did in the actions that came to justice in Watergate.

The judgments at the time were right. The central Watergate actions were in the realm of domestic politics, aimed at partisan success and personal power. Controversies over Vietnam War policy were at most a secondary factor. Their exclusion from the final articles of impeachment remains a valid measure of their lack of basic importance. One could say that Nixon's past caught up with him, or more simply that his pride and ambition had become, in the classic Greek word, overweening.

Chapter Nine

WHAT CAME AFTER

1. *Détente Dismantled, Détente Expanded*

Nixon had chosen Gerald Ford to be Vice President in the fall of 1973, when Spiro Agnew was forced to resign. Previous Vice Presidents succeeding to the presidency had at least been elected to the lesser office. Ford was the first with no such standing, but the choice was generally welcomed. He was experienced, he was honest, and he had worked his way up to House Minority Leader without benefit of special favors. He had been a steady, informed supporter of the Cold War policies of successive Administrations, particularly in backing military budgets and military aid to allied or vulnerable nations, but also ready to approve economic assistance and moderate international economic policies. Offsetting Ford's considerable strengths was his lack of great personal charisma. And his deserved reputation as a team player, able to work with the opposing party on occasion, had its negative side: like Robert Dole at a later period, he was often not taken seriously as a policy thinker in his own right.

In all, Ford could hardly have been a greater contrast to Richard Nixon. He was straightforward where Nixon was devious and calculating, was political only in a broad sense, arrived at foreign policy positions on the merits as he saw them, and let domestic political concerns enter only later. These qualities were bound to tell in his favor in the first phase of his presidency.

It was significant that Ford had always been a man of the House of Representatives. Numerous, diffuse, always less in the public eye than the

Senate, the House comes to the fore on matters of appropriations, trade, and the like. On the more dramatic aspects of foreign policy, it is by long tradition, and because of its size and unwieldiness, far less prominent and influential than the Senate. Many senators regard representatives, even those with high rank in the structure, as second-class participants in foreign policy matters. While the new President was respected from the start, he never generated fear of his power or concern over his ability to rouse the country in support of his positions. All wished him well; still, some saw him as a leader who could be beaten in a tough contest. Senator Henry Jackson fell into that category.

Unfortunately, Ford had to deal first with the Watergate legacy. It was now obvious that many of Nixon's Watergate-related offenses amounted to crimes. (Prosecution for obstruction of justice could hardly have failed, for example, and several other charges would have lent themselves to trial and possible conviction.) The immediate question was whether the new President should exercise his plenary power and extend a pardon to his predecessor. For Nixon to accept a pardon would amount to an admission that he had in fact committed crimes, but this was hardly in doubt after the evidence before the House committee, above all the "smoking gun" tape of June 23, 1972. Nixon had made it clear that he wanted a pardon. On August 1, Alexander Haig, on Nixon's behalf, had conveyed a proposal that Nixon would resign at once if Ford would assure him of a pardon. Consulting only his wife and closest advisors, Ford wisely turned down the proposal. In October, he took the unusual step of volunteering to testify to a congressional committee about Haig's approach and his rejection. His testimony credibly dispelled the idea of any deal or improper motive, but it emphatically did not end the dispute about whether a pardon should be given.

The strongest practical argument for a pardon was that it would avoid a long-drawn-out rehash of the charges against Nixon, possibly supplemented by others newly discovered or emphasized, such as the questions about his expenses and taxes that had been put aside in the last phase of the Judiciary Committee's voting. Leon Jaworski gave Ford his private opinion that it could take as long as two years to prepare and complete a Nixon trial. The new President finally concluded that such a prolonged airing of dirty linen would distract the country from dealing with its serious problems, without adding substantially to the already overwhelming conclusion that Nixon had been guilty of serious breaches of the Constitution and laws.

These considerations were persuasive to many Americans, particularly those close to the processes of government. Among the general public, however, substantial majorities opposed a pardon. It was clear that a new Republican President would be strongly attacked if he extended one, with the impact likely to make his task of governing more difficult for months if not years. Though Ford's reputation for personal integrity was high in Washington, this counted little with the general public. Many would still see a pardon as the result of a deal, and many more as a reward for past favors, including his own selection as Vice President.

To his great credit, Gerald Ford did not dither or hold a finger up to test the wind of public opinion. After selective private consultations, he announced on September 8 that he was giving Nixon a full pardon on all criminal charges related to his actions during his presidency. For this decision, and the prompt manner of it, most historians have honored him, but that hardly made it easier or less damaging at the time.

. . .

A second immediate concern was the economic situation. In both human and political terms, the new disease of "stagflation" was nasty. Economists and the public had thought they could console themselves that stagnant growth would at least undo inflationary trends, and vice versa, but the two together were like a high fever and a severe itch combined. With a holdover team of conservative economic advisors disinclined to take any significant government action, Ford tried to tackle the inflationary threat by exhortation. He introduced in September the slogan "Whip Inflation Now," with the acronym "WIN" for buttons and posters calling on citizens to refuse to pay higher prices and the like. The results were small, the opportunity for ridicule promptly seized.

Inevitably, the congressional elections were a nightmare for the Republican Party. The lessons of Watergate were still center stage. To the normal swing against an incumbent party were added a general tendency to emphasize domestic issues rather than foreign policy; a trend to revive liberal and activist domestic policies; and a high tide of moralism, decrying all forms of political corruption and linking these to the party of Richard Nixon. A resounding Republican defeat was a foregone conclusion, and on November 5, the Democrats gained in both chambers, locking in solid majorities with a marked liberal tinge. Ford hardly campaigned; he simply took his lumps.

A minor distraction during this period was the selection and eventual confirmation of a new Vice President. Ford's choice was former governor Nelson Rockefeller of New York, runner-up to Nixon for the presidential nominations in both 1960 and 1968, the symbol of internationalist Eastern Republicanism, and perhaps not coincidentally an early patron of Henry Kissinger. The selection broadened the White House lineup geographically but hardly in terms of viewpoint, and brought in a man better known for original ideas than for teamwork. With many in Congress happy to seize the occasion of confirmation hearings to explore his extraordinary family wealth, Rockefeller was not in place until mid-December. In a position where few have been happy or productive even when duly elected, he never found a niche.

From the start, President Ford made clear that he would continue Nixon's basic foreign policies, above all détente with the Soviet Union, and affirmed his strong support for Henry Kissinger as Secretary of State. Ambassador Dobrynin, whose reports undoubtedly had great influence on the Kremlin's response to Ford, was at first dubious, seeing him as "a typical American congressman-patriot of the cold war era." However, Kissinger brought the two together within hours of the swearing-in, and also sent a letter to Gromyko saying that Ford could be relied on to adhere to détente. With warm feelings between Ford and Kissinger evident, Dobryinin judged that "Kissinger remained the incontestable captain of American diplomacy."[1]

Only five days later, Ford again invited Dobrynin to the White House. In the meantime, Brezhnev had pressed once more for a business meeting toward the end of the year. Kissinger came up with the idea of linking a Brezhnev mini-summit to a Ford visit to Japan, a high initial priority. This led Ford, with Kissinger's agreement, to propose Vladivostok, right on the Pacific, as the meeting place. It was an extraordinary choice: there was a long history of Sino-Soviet friction along that Far Eastern border, where the Ussuri River clash of 1969 had taken place, and Vladivostok itself lay in an area China claimed as lost territory. The location was bound to be taken badly in Beijing, as a gratuitous insult. Kissinger later acknowledged that it had been a mistake.[2] That he and Ford were thus prepared to make an opening move clearly tilted to the Soviet side of the vaunted triangle was in sharp contrast to the earlier practice of favoring the Chinese by being much franker with them than with the Soviets. It suggested that by this time, with Zhou Enlai ill and out of action, they cared little about Chinese reactions.[3]

Brezhnev snapped up Ford's proposal. With this promising beginning, and consistent backing from Ford—in contrast to the passivity and frequent ambivalence of Nixon's attitude toward arms control—a new U.S. SALT II position was put together by September. This treated existing programs as beyond revision—as SALT I had shown, particularly in its last phase—and focused on equal overall totals of offensive launchers and launchers tested with MIRV. This meshed with the "equal numbers" interpretation of the Jackson Amendment and at the same time got away from comparing widely different types of weapons as if they were equal. Accepting such a broad measure of "essential equivalence" was a realistic recognition of the lack of symmetry between the two arsenals. Neither was prepared to limit or transform existing programs, and with the numbers of warheads that now loomed on each side, any attempt to measure true equality was delusive.[4] In contrast to the gridlock of the spring and early summer, and to the surprise of the U.S. negotiator, Alexis Johnson, a new position was hammered out in Washington. The key was that Kissinger got Ford's support in overcoming the reservations of the hard-liners in the Pentagon. As Johnson saw it, Nixon's departure had made a crucial difference.[5]

Thus equipped with new proposals, Kissinger made progress in Moscow in late October, paving the way for significant agreements at Vladivostok a month later. The most important of these specified equal overall ceilings on both sides — 2,400 for delivery vehicles of all sorts, and 1,320 for MIRVed delivery vehicles, defined as those types that had been tested with MIRV. By this time, however, new weapons were complicating the problem. The Soviets wanted to take account of the new air-to-surface cruise missiles (ASMs), which the Pentagon was close to producing in response to Kissinger's prodding in 1973. The Soviets in turn had a new bomber, named Backfire within the American government, which they called medium-range but which, Pentagon experts argued, could be refueled en route so that it reached parts of the continental United States. Neither weapon, the Backfire especially, could significantly affect the overall balance. The military on both sides were simply trying to keep their freedom for all future plans.

It was not possible to iron out such detailed issues at Vladivostok, and at home the framework was strongly criticized by conservatives and also by sometime supporters of strategic arms control such as Paul Nitze. In 1975, several more negotiating attempts failed, and by early 1976, with the presidential election looming and a strong hard-line tide running in the Republican Party, SALT II was dormant. Many Americans still believed that the whole SALT process was important in tamping down the arms race and getting the two sides to understand each other better. A naked arms race would also have serious negative effects on U.S. relations worldwide, and probably on the willingness of a more liberal Congress to support large defense budgets (always Kissinger's ultimate argument throughout his memoirs). But such supporters could point to little in the way of genuine verifiable restraint. What was passed on to the Carter Administration was a mediocre deal at best, finally agreed in 1979 but then not ratified when the Soviet Union moved into Afghanistan at the end of that year.

Strategic arms control negotiations thus ran into serious difficulty after Nixon's departure. The gauntlet of military orthodoxy and planning on both sides would have been hard to deal with in any circumstances. It took in the end only a shove from new Third World confrontations — first in 1975–76 (Angola) and then in 1979–80 (Afghanistan) — to ditch strategic arms control until 1985–86.

. . .

After Vladivostok, Kissinger went on to Beijing to mend fences with the Chinese leaders. His trip served only to demonstrate how distant and essentially meaningless the Sino-American relationship had become, despite Mao's apparent effort the year before to give it his blessing. This time Mao himself was said to be ill and resting. Zhou was in the hospital, his cancer so advanced that he could stand only a half-hour call by Kissinger that must have been poignant for both men but did not count in substantive terms. Zhou had become, in the ways of totalitarian regimes, a nonperson, a relic of the past. The radical Gang of Four was moving steadily to take power and exert a decisive influence on the scope and temperature of the American relationship.[6]

. . .

Offsetting the apparently successful meeting at Vladivostok, the prospects for expanded Soviet-American trade suffered a devastating blow in December, when Congress passed the long-pending Jackson-Vanik Amendment to the Trade Act. Behind this denouement lay a running battle that had raged for more than two years. As we have seen, one early confrontation had come in April 1973. When Senator Jackson refused to accept the Soviet cancellation of an exit tax on émigrés as a sufficient concession, he demanded assurance that a stated number of Soviet citizens would be allowed to emigrate annually. (He had not specified Jews, but clearly had them in mind as a major percentage.) For more than a year, the numbers issue had not been pressed, and the House approved Jackson-Vanik, first in the powerful Ways and Means Committee in September 1973, and finally, in December, by a vote of the full House. The Trade Act then moved to the Senate, to be decided in its 1974 session. By this time Kissinger had become a reluctant mediator between Jackson and the Soviet negotiators — occasionally Dobrynin, more often Gromyko himself on behalf of the Politburo.

The Jackson-Vanik Amendment had become a "make or break" issue for the continuation of any genuine détente, yet Soviet economic factors had changed. The need to improve the Soviet foreign exchange balance and expand trade ties with the West had seemed acute in 1972, but now that need had been reduced by large-scale trade and investment deals with other Western countries, West Germany in particular; moreover, as the oil crisis and the attendant downward pressure on the dollar weakened the United States economically, so they also strengthened the Soviet Union's foreign exchange balance and made it need large-scale trade with America less. (The value of Soviet oil exports and gold holdings must have increased several times.) In 1971 and 1972 the Soviets had been eager for grain deals, export credits, and (least significant) most-favored-nation status. None of these, except export credits, now had the same importance.

In 1974, the dispute was raised to maximum bitterness by an inept (or, in Jackson's case, deliberately destructive) mediation process over the future annual level of emigration. During 1973, there had been informal and apparently satisfactory Soviet indications that a level of 30,000–40,000 emigrants a year would be permitted; in the spring of 1974, moreover, Gromyko had suggested a level of 45,000, and in August, Dobrynin told Ford that the Soviet Union was prepared to give "an unwritten guarantee that it would allow 50,000 Jews to leave the Soviet Union each year." Jackson, however, now talked of a firm undertaking of at least 60,000 — in one conversation, 100,000.[7]

As the two sides bargained back and forth through Kissinger, the idea emerged of avoiding a direct Soviet assurance by an exchange of letters: in one, Kissinger would tell Jackson what Soviet policy would be; Jackson would then reply, interpreting Kissinger's statements and expressing (it was hoped) his satisfaction. In all the discussions, the Soviets were adamant that no figure could be stated publicly and that while the existence of the exchange could be revealed, its contents would never be.

On this basis, the two letters were exchanged on October 18, 1974. Contrary to what had seemed firm understandings, however, Jackson rewrote Kissinger's letter to make it a Soviet pledge, made the letters public, and for good measure gave to the press an expected figure of 60,000 emigrants a year — a figure that had been implied in the exchanges, but never accepted by the Soviet side. Such sharp practice would have caused a private citizen to suspend all relationships with him, but this hardly bothered Jackson. He believed that any form of pressure on Soviet negotiators was justified, and he could only gain with his American supporters by being tough. Kissinger told Dobrynin that when he informed Ford of the episode, the normally even-tempered President exploded that the Senator had "behaved like a swine."[8] Kissinger's inability to stand up to Jackson only made the situation worse.[9]

The Soviets responded vigorously. A few days later, at the end of Kissinger's visit to Moscow, Gromyko handed him a letter saying that Jackson's interpretations were "categorically rejected." Kissinger concealed this letter even from President Ford, perhaps hoping that if Vladivostok was a success, further negotiations might still make a trade agreement possible.[10]

By December, Senator Adlai Stevenson III, sponsor of the export control bill, had adopted as his own an amendment to the effect that any credits to the Soviet Union could not exceed $300 million without express congressional approval. It was a derisory figure: no such limitation had been placed on credits for other Communist countries, and billions of dollars had been extended in credits to Poland and Yugoslavia. Soviet leaders at once saw the limit as a slap in the face and could not understand why the Administration had not strongly opposed it.[11] Though Stevenson was a moderate liberal who favored détente, his amendment was a far more important impediment to future trade dealings than Jackson-Vanik, since prospective U.S. exports far exceeded the imports that might have come in under lower tariff levels. One is forced to conclude that neither the Nixon nor the Ford Administration ever came into clear focus on the two proposals. Far too much was left to the overextended Kissinger.

In response to both amendments, the Soviet leadership, predictably but with special vehemence, rejected the whole trade agreement early in January 1975, on the grounds that the amendment was an unacceptable invasion of their domestic sovereignty. This action, which crippled the Soviet-American détente that was Nixon's primary legacy, was in considerable part due to the failures of both Nixon and Ford to explain more forcefully to Congress and the public their trade proposals and their position on the link to emigration. It was due also to Nixon's initial coddling of Jackson and failure to see his threat to the policy. Kissinger had given it his best try, as Watergate undermined Nixon's power, but a Secretary of State's effect on public (or congressional) opinion is inherently limited save at moments of special success. Kissinger's appeal in Congress had always been principally to members of the Senate Foreign Relations Committee, not to the main body of senators or to any significant segment of the House. He simply did not have much empathy with most congressmen or, with many, even solid credibility.

·   ·   ·

With Soviet-American détente in deep trouble in 1975, the contrast with the détente between the Soviet Union and the countries of Western Europe was striking.[12] Its peak in 1972 had been the ratification by the West German Bundestag of the Eastern treaties between the Federal Republic of Germany and the Soviet Union and Poland. Briefly, as we have seen, when the close fight in Bonn over ratification played a big part in the Soviet decision to go ahead with the Moscow summit in May 1972, the two versions of détente ran in parallel. But for almost all Americans and even many Europeans, the Eastern treaties and the Berlin agreements were overshadowed by the Nixon-Brezhnev summits, deliberately glamorized by Nixon and Kissinger.

The next step, on which the Soviets and Europeans were agreed, was the long-pending Conference on Security and Cooperation in Europe (CSCE). Under Nixon, support for that project had never been more than lukewarm, but Ford was more favorable, so that American negotiators became more active. In July 1975, Ford himself was a leading participant in the founding meeting of the CSCE, held in Helsinki, Finland, to sign a Final Act worked out over the previous two years among thirty-five participating nations. These embraced all of Europe on both sides of the Iron Curtain, including the full array of nonaligned European states, with Canada and the United States included on the basis of their deep wartime and postwar involvement in the defense and rebuilding of Europe. The conference was the closest Europe was ever likely to come to a genuine peace conference to end World War II. Now, with nations marking the thirtieth anniversary of the ending of that war in Europe, there was a widespread sense that if a full-fledged peace treaty could not be reached, efforts should be made to approximate one, including setting forth principles of future behavior.

The urge to do this turned out to be very strong indeed. When the negotiators started their work in September 1973, the Soviet Union insisted on security provisions that would have the effect of ratifying and legitimizing its territorial gains, and would also not put in question its spheres of influence in Eastern Europe and the Baltic States. Several nations opposed such legitimization, and sought formulas to enable it to be eased or even removed over time. But all recognized, as Willy Brandt had done in memorable terms in 1970, that the war and postwar changes could not be undone without new bloodshed. In the United States in particular, "Yalta"—site of the last meeting between Roosevelt and Stalin in February 1945—was still a dirty word in conservative and right-wing, primarily Republican, circles. Any European territorial deal with the Soviet Union was thus highly suspect, although the fact that Richard Nixon had accepted Brandt's Eastern treaties had weakened opposition from these quarters.

The result was an effort at balance. In return for the painful acceptance of changed borders, many European negotiators, shortly joined and supported by the Americans and Canadians, tried at least to lay down principles of national behavior that might make future European wars less likely. With British diplomats and Max Kampelman for America to the fore, a series of laborious meetings, over nearly two years, produced an array of principles from which it was difficult for any nation to dissent.

In the Final Act at Helsinki, the first Basket (a British label) covered security issues, in effect confirming the postwar territorial arrangements and barring any change by force, while a second Basket concerned "Cooperation in the Field of Economics, of Science and Technology and of the Environment." The Soviet Union favored this second Basket and while, as the fight over the Trade Act had amply demonstrated, many Americans might demur at all its possible ramifications, the principles were ones the United States had supported, often pioneered. In any case they imposed no action obligations.

If the Soviet leaders had had their way, the Final Act would have stopped there. But as the preliminary meetings went on, a groundswell of feeling developed that there should also be principles favoring the greatest possible degree of interaction among European nations. From there it was only a short step to adopting common principles of behavior within individual nations. The result, built up line by line in the preliminary sessions, became a famous Basket Three, "Cooperation in Humanitarian and Other Fields." From the relatively safe terrain of contact across borders between family members, to wider freedom of travel and encouragement of tourism, its text went on to exchanges in the fields of culture and education, and finally to the sensitive areas of freedom to gather and disseminate information. All this was done with an occasional nod in the direction of traditional notions of sovereignty and national controls, but with the evident effect of moving toward a code for the internal behavior of the nations of Europe. Basket Three amounted to a Europe-wide repudiation of the forces that had produced not only the vicious totalitarianism of the first half of the twentieth century, but excesses of nationalism, custom, and convention everywhere.

This Basket Three was perhaps the most idealistic document ever subscribed to by a coherent group of nations. A few among the negotiators and among the final signers at Helsinki must have harked back in their minds to such sweeping and totally ineffectual declarations as the Kellogg-Briand Pact of 1928, purporting to outlaw war among nations, just as Stalin came to power in Russia and a short five years before Hitler galvanized Germany into manic militarism. Others, however, could point to the fact that the 1975 proposals came not from Foreign Ministries but in large part from private organizations in "civil society," with roots and international ties already developing on their own. Many Americans may have thought of the long-term influence of language in their own Declaration of Independence and in the Constitution itself, wording belied by conditions at the time but invoked to great effect to support and legitimize later civil rights movements and other efforts to create a more humane and liberal social structure.

Not until Ford went to Helsinki to sign the Final Act, and then only briefly, did the American public focus on the Helsinki Accords. Congress was only barely informed, and the Ford Administration made no effort to prepare public opinion—a job that would have been complicated by the distracting events of early 1975, notably in Indochina. From the start, moreover, Kissinger was profoundly skeptical of the whole enterprise, as he had been of Brandt's earlier initiatives, regarding it "with disdain."[13]

For some time the American government regarded American participation in this project as a concession more to its allies than to the Soviets, a way of easing the acute tensions with Western Europe over the Middle East war and the oil crisis. Only in early 1975 was Kissinger moved by the pleas of Marshal Tito of Yugoslavia and Nicolae Ceauşescu of Romania that this was a chance to get agreed-on principles that would help to tie down the Soviet Union in its dealings with Eastern Europe. Already Ford had followed Nixon's lead in making selective visits to Eastern European capitals to show that American concern for them was not dead. As Helsinki came to be seen in anti-Soviet terms, Kissinger's interest increased.[14]

Gerald Ford, by temperament and from his long experience of accom-modation within Congress, was probably all along more inclined to treat all forms of détente seriously, for their own sake and not just when they might give the Soviet Union problems. At any rate, he risked, and aroused, opposition from the Republican right wing by a forthcoming speech at Helsinki and ungrudging acceptance of the accords, noting only that their ultimate effect depended on future actions. An initial burst of criticism, chiefly from conservative quarters, lasted only a short time. More serious controversy and criticism was stirred up at the end of 1975, however, when private briefings given for American diplomats in London by Kissinger and his top staff man on European matters, Helmut Sonnenfeldt, were made public (through a leak, apparently) and were interpreted as acquiesence in Soviet domination of Eastern Europe. Attacks on Ford and Kissinger then revived and persisted through the 1976 election year, reaching a climax in a famous gaffe by Ford in a campaign TV debate with Jimmy Carter, when he got mixed up and through a slip of the tongue said that Poland was not dominated by the Soviet Union. It was a costly blunder, inconsistent with his true views.[15]

If the security provisions bothered some Americans, it was Basket Three that hit Moscow hard. Dobrynin gives a vivid description of what happened when the whole Final Act was put before the Politburo members for ap-proval, shortly before the conference:

> [T]hey were stunned. . . . Many in the Politburo (Podgorny, Suslov, Ko-sygin and Andropov) had grave doubts about assuming international ob-ligations that could open the way to foreign interference in our political life. Many Soviet ambassadors expressed doubts because they correctly anticipated difficult international disputes later on. Moscow had to take a fundamental decision with serious domestic consequences.[16]

Gromyko countered by arguing that recognition of the political map of Europe "would amount to a major political and propaganda victory for Moscow," that the second Basket would further economic cooperation, and above all that the Soviets would remain in control of their own actions ("masters in our own house"). Reluctantly, the Politburo assented. The Soviets probably dared not ditch the conference at the last moment. Their refusal to challenge aroused world opinion reflected the occasional force and reality of that sometimes derided factor in international dealings.

Yet the warnings of the Soviet ambassadors were not misplaced. In years to come, not only Soviet dissidents but activists in Poland and elsewhere invoked Basket Three of the Helsinki Accords as constant prods to their regimes. In William Hyland's words:

Helsinki . . . gave the East Europeans a legitimate means to widen contacts with Western Europe, and a framework to expand contacts at future meetings. In those terms the Helsinki conference was and remains a clear success. Indeed, it provided the soil in which the Solidarity movement in Poland could flourish; it allowed the two German states to move closer; it gave the Romanians, Hungarians and Yugoslavs more freedom of action. And it made Western Europe feel that it was participating in, indeed contributing to, the détente of the superpowers. In this sense it was psychologically important.[17]

The last sentence of this persuasive appraisal contains a note of condescension, as if Europe had been backward on this front and was only now catching up with the superpowers. This was indeed the attitude of Kissinger and his associates, perhaps of many Americans. Yet, if one went back to the origins of détente in the 1960s, Western Europeans could point to NATO's Harmel Report of 1967 as the first collective endorsement of the word, and especially to Brandt's treaties in 1970, well before the Soviet-American summits.

Initial timing apart, the historical truth was that the two forms of détente operated differently, often but not always complementing each other. Soviet-American détente faltered in 1974 and 1975, recovering only in 1979, and then marginally, through a belated SALT II Treaty. When the United States responded to the Soviet invasion of Afghanistan at the end of 1979 with trade sanctions and a boycott of the 1980 Olympics, the Europeans reacted much more mildly and kept the main détente measures in place. Which version of détente contributed most, in the end, to the breakup of the Soviet empire in 1989–91 is a broad and necessarily speculative question, but the case for the European version is strong. Hyland concluded: "If it can be said that there was one point when the Soviet empire finally began to crack, it was at Helsinki."[18]

As of 1974–75, the Helsinki Accords brought the European version of détente at least abreast of the faltering Soviet-American version. The latter was demonstrative and linked to high-level agreements; the former relied more on slow day-by-day changes and increased contacts.

2. The End in Indochina

"Our friends [in South Vietnam] have every opportunity to demonstrate their inherent strength," said Richard Nixon in his annual report to Congress on foreign policy, May 3, 1973. He regarded the continued legitimacy of Nguyen Van Thieu's government, along with freedom for the United States to resupply military equipment, as major accomplishments of the

Paris Agreement. With continued U.S. military and economic aid, it was now up to Thieu to strengthen South Vietnam and hold off the North Vietnamese.

Thieu's first concern was always to maintain his power structure, now more than ever dominated by his military colleagues in the South Vietnamese Army. Not only liberal or independent-minded civilians but almost all those with experience had been sloughed off. With the Army's long dominance and its unwieldy size by 1973, it would have been extraordinary if corruption had been kept even to the levels "normal" in Asian military forces. It had not. From senior officers right down the line, military personnel accepted and demanded rake-offs of all sorts from the civilian population and often from each other. Graft was rampant and was condoned from the very top, where Madame Thieu was a particular target of rumor and suspicion. Arnold Isaacs, the best historian of the post-1973 period, rightly stresses that "for Thieu the Army and the Americans were allies enough. Never in his years in power did he seek associates with a different perspective from his own, who might have given his regime and the nation a stronger sense of common purpose."[19]

On the American side, Ellsworth Bunker's departure in May 1973 symbolized a sharp change. American influence on every aspect of South Vietnamese life, slowly reduced after 1969, now became suddenly very much less. By mid-1973 the order of the day was American passivity, not only on Vietnamese internal politics but on military and economic policy. The new American Ambassador, handpicked by Nixon, was Graham A. Martin, a veteran Foreign Service officer who had been Ambassador to Thailand in the 1960s and then to Italy. Martin had special ties to Nixon and a more ambivalent relationship with Kissinger. He was, above all, a "take charge" ambassador, authoritarian and at times imperious to his associates, secretive and impatient of interference from Washington, but bent on getting along with Thieu.[20] And he was more than ever the key American. With all American organized units withdrawn, the senior military officer, Major General John Murray, came from the Army's supply and logistics branches. His Defense Attaché's Office, created for the occasion, had a small core of operations and intelligence personnel in uniform, but was barred by the Paris Agreement from giving advice to military units and in practice had little observation of military operations. Initially one of its main jobs was to help the South Vietnamese distribute and service the vast quantities of American equipment provided under the Enhance programs of the fall of 1972. With much of the equipment new to the South Vietnamese, the resulting problems were formidable and never resolved; most of the Enhance Plus shipments were never effectively used.[21] Instead, the principal function of Murray's team was to direct the continuing flow of American ammunition, petroleum products, and the other consumables that armies in action devour.

In April 1973, as the last American military forces pulled out, Nixon asked Congress for $1.6 billion in military aid to South Vietnam for fiscal 1974 (from July 1973 through June 1974).[22] In the past, supplies for South Vietnamese forces had in effect been melded with supplies for American forces. Congress had delayed in approving requests ticketed for the South Vietnamese, but in the end had almost always voted the full requested amounts. With no guidance from Washington, Murray now assumed that this would again be the case. Instead the House voted in July to cut the authorization to $1.3 billion, and with the Senate going still further, in October the authorized amount was set at just over $1 billion. Further cuts at the appropriations stage were common, but Murray had made no allowance for this and by the end of the calendar year, halfway through the fiscal year, had expended a total of $800 million.

As the record of these decisions shows clearly, neither chamber of Congress thought it was imposing sharp or draconian cuts. The picture they were given was that fighting continued but that the government forces were doing well and that the level of fighting (as measured by South Vietnamese combat deaths) was only a third or quarter of what it had been in 1972. Since Congress habitually suspected that requests for military aid were overstated, even a cut of this size seemed bearable. At the end of 1973, however, each American armed service, especially the Army, had to find money to replace equipment stocks that had been sharply depleted in resupplying the Israeli Army. The Pentagon itself reduced the amount actually available for Indochina during the fiscal year, and Murray suddenly had virtually no money at all for the next six months.

In February 1974, the Pentagon therefore appealed to Congress to restore the full $1.6 billion originally requested. However, the Senate Armed Services Committee, up to then a bastion of support for all Vietnam-related Pentagon requests, dug in and recommended a considerable reduction. In May a group of Democrats led by Senator Edward Kennedy moved to cut the amount further, and won the test: the Senate vote followed almost exactly the tally in June 1973 over banning military operations in Southeast Asia. The Administration made no case of privation, serious supply shortage, or growing danger, either to Congress or in its public statements. In March, for example, Kissinger wrote to Kennedy, arguing that the Paris Agreement was not working badly since South Vietnamese casualties were, he said, only about one-third those before the agreement.[23]

Meanwhile, the North Vietnamese put massive resources and manpower into improving supply routes and slowly building up their forces and equipment within South Vietnam, laying the groundwork for a major conventional offensive. The famous Ho Chi Minh Trail in Laos was expanded into a well-kept road complex that could handle large volumes of heavy truck traffic, and a new set of roads, with a pipeline alongside, was built through the western areas.

By the spring of 1974, South Vietnam was beset by serious economic problems. The fourfold global oil price rise, plus big increases in rice prices, raised inflation to the 50 percent level, imposing hardship on all classes but particularly on underpaid enlisted men in the armed forces. In contrast, the military situation still did not appear threatening. From May to July, Congress held hearings on the proposals for aid in fiscal 1975, the authorization figure having been set at $1 billion. Two congressional committees also sent staff members out to Vietnam, and their long reports were published and were available to the House and Senate that summer. Each report, like the testimony of Administration witnesses in the hearings, stated at the outset that the South Vietnamese military had lost 13,500 men in 1973, fewer than half those killed in 1972; the House report concluded that it was "unlikely that the North Vietnamese can win a military or political victory in the South in the foreseeable future, if ever," and the Senate report stated that "the official American view in Saigon [doubtless Ambassador Martin's] is that the South Vietnamese are in a very strong military position and getting stronger every day."[24]

After a prolonged floor debate in which many members referred to the two staff reports, on August 6 the House reduced the appropriation for Vietnam to $700 million. Backers of the cut again made much of the low Vietnamese casualty rate, and with defenders of the Administration's position venturing only general replies, it was a one-sided contest. Moreover, the fact that Nixon was on the verge of resignation must have cast a shadow over the debate. On August 20 and 21, with Ford now President, the Senate approved the same $700 million, barely rejecting a motion to reduce the amount still further. As in 1973, the votes that made the difference came from moderates who had once been prepared to give the Administration the benefit of the doubt.

Nixon's departure from office on August 9, coming right after the House vote, was an especially hard blow to the political establishment in Saigon. One Assembly member noted that Nixon had been "the most enthusiastic supporter" of Thieu: "Now Mr. Nixon is gone and Mr. Kissinger, who is unfriendly to Thieu, is still there."[25] Ford made an effort to rally moderates and conservatives who had been his longtime friends and allies on the Hill, but both chambers stood firm, finally passing the appropriation bill in October at $700 million.

As the winter campaign season loomed, Murray's staff made a discovery that sharply revised the picture of the previous twenty months he had been conveying to Washington and to Ambassador Martin, and they in turn to Congress. Murray's small and inexperienced staff had reverted in 1973 to an old pre-1965 practice of relying on the daily casualty reports of South Vietnamese units in the field, relayed to Saigon. Previous American officials had found that such figures were only preliminary and for many reasons badly understated; however, later revised estimates were either not available to Murray or not recognized as significant. Now, he realized, the estimated totals for South Vietnamese killed in action during 1973 and the first nine months of 1974 were nearly double what they had thought; the losses had been almost as high as in the peak years of 1968, 1969, and 1972. The revised data contradicted the picture Kissinger and others had been presenting to Congress and the American public.[26] The American government, both in the field and in Washington, had lost touch with the war.

At this point, events unfolded rapidly. In October, a high-level civilian and military conference in Hanoi quickly agreed that North Vietnam now had the upper hand. Noting "the Watergate scandal, Nixon's resignation, the economic woes following the 1973 Arab oil embargo, and the sequence of congressional votes," it concluded that the possibility of a new American intervention was now remote. "The United States could hardly jump back in, and no matter how it might intervene it would be unable to save the Saigon administration from collapse."[27] Thus Hanoi stepped up the pace and scale of its operations, battering the South Vietnamese forces in the northern area, retaking coastal areas it had lost in 1973, gaining ground in the central highlands, and conducting major attacks north of Saigon itself. By the end of the year, "the advantage was tilting irreversibly toward the Communists."[28] Yet Thieu made no effort to change tactics or strategy. Rather, he insisted that commanders stand and fight for meaningless places and areas, which only added to the snowball effect. By the end of 1974, ARVN was in poor shape.

The fighting had taken a heavy toll on experienced junior officers and noncoms, removing the combat "edge" restored in 1972, and the rate of desertion for 1974 was extraordinary—more than 200,000 from a total strength of about a million in all units.[29] Moreover, supply and equipment limitations had steadily worsened during the year, even before the reductions in the military aid program came into effect. Draconian restraints were put on many supply categories, including ammunition.[30] The cumulative result—from the pressure of Hanoi's gains; from concern for families beset by inflation and privation; from scandal and shuffle at the top of a government that had never commanded deep respect; and from equipment and supply shortages—was that, in Isaacs's summation, "South Vietnam's army was a tired, dispirited and frightened force, lacking confidence in its leaders, its future and itself."[31]

Against this background, surely accurately perceived in Hanoi but not in Washington, the North Vietnamese leaders met again in late December and early January to set final plans for the campaign year. On January 8, the meeting affirmed a two-year strategic plan that called for "large, wide-spread offensives" in 1975, which would "create conditions to carry out a general offensive and uprising in 1976." At the last moment, however, word came that the North Vietnamese forces had taken, on January 6, an important provincial capital, Phuoc Binh, against determined but ineffective resistance reinforced by Thieu only at the last minute. At once an alternative was added to the 1975–76 plan: "if the opportune moment presents itself at the beginning or the end of 1975, we will immediately liberate the South in 1975."[32]

In Washington, however, a National Intelligence Estimate completed in December foresaw real trouble only in 1976. Promptly criticized as too optimistic by officers on Murray's staff and in the Saigon embassy, this estimate nonetheless reflected the state of mind of official Washington.[33] One capable and experienced journalist, Maynard Parker, who visited South Vietnam in the fall, also believed that no military crisis loomed.[34]

At the time of the Paris Agreement, as we have noted, one of Kissinger's hopes was that the Soviet Union and China would both refrain from major resupply of North Vietnam. He even went so far as to tell the hesitant South Vietnamese that he had firm assurances to this effect. Through 1973 and much of 1974, American intelligence had believed that both nations were indeed limiting their military aid to Hanoi to levels below those of 1971 and 1972. In early 1974 Ambassador Martin said as much to visitors in Saigon, in remarks that found their way into the *Congressional Record*.[35] An excellent later historian, Stanley Karnow, has written that Hanoi sent emissaries to both Moscow and Beijing in October 1973, seeking stepped-up military aid, but was rebuffed in both capitals. Zhou Enlai even went so far as to advise the North Vietnamese to "relax for, say, five or ten years."[36] China's aid efforts were probably now focused on the Khmer Rouge in Cambodia, where it had the predominant role and meant to keep it.

However, the Soviet Union must have kept up a substantial flow to North Vietnam. In December 1974, as Hanoi enlarged its plans for a 1975 campaign, it appears to have put great pressure on the Soviets for large quantities of the expendable supplies a big offensive would need. That month, General Viktor Kulikov, chief of the Soviet armed forces, visited Hanoi. He could hardly have come empty-handed; a new and increased flow must have started no later than February. At this point, Moscow may have feared China's growing influence in Cambodia and felt under special pressure to strengthen its own ties with North Vietnam. Karnow's conclusion is persuasive: both Moscow and Beijing considered the Saigon regime doomed and "were now preoccupied with their coming rivalry for increased influence in Southeast Asia."[37]

The capture of Phuoc Binh, the first provincial capital to fall to the Communists since 1972, was a profound shock to Thieu, made worse by

Washington's tepid reaction. At a news conference on January 14, Secretary Schlesinger minimized the event, saying that he did not anticipate "a major, country-wide offensive of the type of 1972."[38] The North Vietnamese continued to respect U.S. military capabilities and were "reluctant to take those steps that they fear might conceivably lead to a reintroduction of American power." His threat was backed by sending an aircraft carrier in the direction of Vietnam and alerting the Marines on Okinawa, but Hanoi almost certainly saw it all as a bluff, and Saigon was not reassured by what the American press thought a "delphic pronouncement."[39]

In late January, Thieu appealed to President Ford for prompt military aid, but he did not invoke the "full force" pledges Nixon had made in late 1972 and early 1973. These he sought to revive in typically indirect fashion, sending an emissary to the only man still in the American government who knew firsthand about the pledge letters and whom he personally trusted— Alexander Haig, by then NATO commander in Brussels. Moved by the appeal, Haig went to Washington and saw Ford personally in February, urging him strongly to "take a stand on resuming the bombing, even if the Congress overrules you." Ford replied: "Al, I can't. The country is fed up with the war." It was a realistic judgment. The Nixon pledges were dead.[40]

. . .

In Cambodia, the intensified bombing after February 1973 had never stopped the Khmer Rouge. They simply kept coming on, despite what American officials estimated as more than 10,000 killed. In 1971 and 1972 their control of areas next to the South Vietnamese delta had been marked by only limited brutality, and in general they had relied on local leaders. One experienced reporter wrote early in 1973: "There are no real hatreds among the population," and with an end of the war in Vietnam a reconciliation in Cambodia should be easily achievable.[41] But all this changed dramatically between April and August 1973, exactly at the time of the stepped-up American bombing. Again Isaacs:

> From 1973 on, Cambodia seemed an entire country gone amok. All its psychological anchors were ripped loose in the hurricane of violence that had fallen on it. American decisions and American bombs had helped destroy peacetime Cambodian life, and it is in that sense that some connection can be said to exist between American actions and the savagery of the Khmer Rouge.[42]

From then on, the war in Cambodia saw constant grinding pressure from the Khmer Rouge and gradual yielding by Lon Nol's increasingly demoralized forces. By the end of the year the Khmer Rouge lines were about ten miles from Phnom Penh and they could conduct artillery attacks at will on its outlying areas, filled with rural refugees who had swelled the city's population to nearly 2 million. The Cambodian Army had become for the most part an undisciplined mob. Yet to keep it supplied, principally with ammunition, U.S. military aid to Cambodia in fiscal year 1974 was apparently about $200 million![43]

Meanwhile, the political and economic situation went from bad to worse. Lon Nol held on to power by sheer inertia, the economy barely functioned, and corruption was all-encompassing. Finally, in March 1974, a new American Ambassador, John Gunther Dean, who as Ambassador to Laos had helped to get a cease-fire and agreement on a new government there, proposed to Washington that a similar approach be used in Cambodia. He knew that this would probably mean, as was already evident in Laos, Communist dominance in any resulting regime, but considered this inevitable. It would be less bad, he believed, in human terms and also less damaging for the United States than the "ignominious flight" for Americans he foresaw if the military situation simply took its course.[44]

Dean's proposal was turned down in March and again in June, when he submitted a long assessment concluding that time was not on the government's side and that "steps must be taken to find . . . a compromise settlement." By this time the usually implacable Graham Martin in Saigon had similar ideas, but Dean was told in emphatic terms by the State Department that any "Laos-type compromises" were out and that his job was to strengthen the military position so that "we can negotiate from strength."[45] How Secretary Kissinger can have been persuaded, if indeed he was, that negotiating from "strength" was a serious hope must remain a mystery. It may be, as William Shawcross later suggested, that in the first six months of 1974 Nixon still controlled policy in this one country. In any event, only in October 1974, in desultory fashion, and more seriously in December in response to a French initiative, did Kissinger again open the door a crack to the return of Sihanouk. The feelers were ineffective and far too late in any case.[46]

Within Cambodia, the picture throughout the year remained one of "despair, devastation, death and defeat" (Isaacs once more). In April the Khmer Rouge sent one of their top men, Khieu Samphan, to Beijing to ask for military aid, and the Chinese agreed. In Washington, on the other hand, the aid program for Cambodia for fiscal 1975, for both military and economic purposes, was cut in the fall of 1974 from the previous year's $705 million to $377 million.[47]

On January 1, 1975, the Khmer Rouge launched a big push to take over Phnom Penh and end the war. By the end of the month they had closed the Mekong River to shipping, so that an improvised American airlift from Thailand and Saigon became the only supply channel, unloading under fire at the Phnom Penh airport. Yet, as President Ford on January 28 asked

Congress for an emergency supplemental appropriation of $222 million for aid to Cambodia, a Pentagon witness still testified that the overall outlook was "promising" if there was adequate logistic support.[48] In fact, the situation was already desperate. The Army was running out of ammunition and the city was starving. Officials argued to Congress that U.S. emergency aid might help the government to hang on at least until the rainy season in May, at which point, some claimed, the Khmer Rouge—who were indeed hard pressed themselves—might negotiate.

It was surely an imaginary scenario. Ambassador Dean was convinced that Lon Nol had to go and that the only possible deal would put the Communists in control. Yet Kissinger continued to press for the emergency aid, largely on the familiar ground that it would have "the most serious consequences" for the credibility of U.S. commitments worldwide for the United States to let down those to whom it had become committed. President Ford issued less blunt statements to the same effect, but Congress was not persuaded. Not only liberals, with new power since the fall elections, but conservatives felt the cause was hopeless. Polls showed that Americans wanted no more to do with the whole war in Indochina. Such a former staunch supporter as Democratic congressman George Mahon of Texas said bluntly that it was "just almost impossible to convince rank-and-file Americans that there is any end to this." To others on Capitol Hill, Cambodia in particular had become the "tragic shambles" of a disastrous U.S. policy. In the Senate the Republican Minority Leader, Hugh Scott of Pennsylvania, confessed that he had "not supported a dollar for this war without feeling guilty."[49]

Early in March, members of a congressional delegation visiting Phnom Penh were appalled. Paul McCloskey of California concluded that American policy represented "greater evil than we have done to any country in the world." At the same time, he argued, America had been so responsible for the horror that it should now at least give Cambodia one final chance to avoid outright defeat and work out some negotiated outcome. The compromise he proposed on his return, offering limited emergency aid with a firm cutoff date of June 30 for all aid, attracted some support. However, President Ford refused to accept it, and by early April the fall of Neak Luong (the town on the Mekong devastated by American bombs in August 1973 by mistake) had made the situation in Phnom Penh clearly hopeless.[50]

On April 10, as President Ford addressed Congress to appeal for emergency aid for Vietnam, he did not renew the request for similar aid to Cambodia, but spoke sadly of it in the past tense, blaming Congress mildly. Ambassador Dean engineered the departure of Lon Nol in late March and worked out a careful plan for the evacuation of Americans and of Cambodians who might be especially subject to vengeful treatment when the

Khmer Rouge took over. The evacuation was held up briefly by Kissinger, who made one last try to engage Sihanouk—for the record and with no serious hope, one is forced to conclude.[51]

Finally, on April 12, the evacuation was carried out without incident, using Marine helicopters from Navy ships in the Gulf of Thailand. Although several hundred places had been reserved for Cambodians, only 159 accepted the invitation. One who declined to go was Sirik Matak, the stoutest of the country's few able leaders, who had been shunted aside by Lon Nol but was still on the Khmer Rouge death list. His hand-delivered letter to Ambassador Dean on the final morning probably spoke for many in Cambodia:

> I thank you . . . for your offer to transport me towards freedom. I cannot, alas, leave in such a cowardly fashion.
>
> As for you and in particular for your great country, I never believed for a moment that you would have this sentiment of abandoning a people which has chosen liberty. You have refused us your protection and we can do nothing about it. You leave and my wish is that you and your country will find happiness under the sky. . . . I have only committed this mistake of believing in you, the Americans.

The note is poignant evidence of the trust that a great power, whatever its disclaimers, is virtually sure to arouse in a small client country. Cambodia was indeed a black page in the history of American foreign policy.

The handling of the very last phase, from December onward, however, was as good as the circumstances permitted. Ambassador Dean and the American contingent were cool, objective, and resourceful, with considerable courage and many instances of heroism. Even if U.S. aid had not been reduced, or if the January request for a supplement had been granted at once, the Cambodian regime could not have held out for more than a few weeks at the most. The Khmer Rouge had become far too strong, combining powerful nationalist feelings with Communist ruthlessness. On the American side, it was not Congress or the American people but Nixon and, acting under his orders, Haig and Kissinger who were the architects of this tragic disaster.

Five days after the Americans left, the Khmer Rouge entered Phnom Penh in triumph, received at first with relief and then with horror as they proceeded, in the most brutal fashion, to drive out virtually the whole population of the city. Very shortly, the regime of Pol Pot (a pseudonym for Saloth Sar, the leader who had taken command) showed itself perhaps the most horrible and cruel of any in the late twentieth century. In Cambodia's history, the United States was henceforth to play little part for at least a decade.

. . .

In South Vietnam, the North Vietnamese forces made their next major move on March 10. Three divisions surrounded and then attacked a much fought-over provincial capital and route junction, Ban Me Thuot, northwest of Saigon. Complete surprise was achieved and the town rapidly overrun, and at the same time other main access routes to the central highlands were cut.[52] Thieu panicked and ordered the hapless commanding general, a crony, to evacuate his forces and the civilian population to the coast. This impossible order led to a shambles on the mountain roads. A large chunk of the Army simply melted away into throngs of civilian refugees, spreading panic and a sense of defeat in all directions. The territory under government control was now cut in two.

The next phase of the offensive came in the north, where the able General Truong was whipsawed by conflicting orders from Thieu, deprived at the last minute of a good reserve division, and unable to fend off determined North Vietnamese attacks. Quang Tri and Hue were emptied in haste, and swarms of refugees descended on Danang, making its defense impossible. The result was a harrowing evacuation by boat and helicopter, with thousands of Vietnamese left behind. South Vietnamese soldiers not only failed to keep order but ousted civilians by force from places on the barges and planes. By this time American television crews were again covering the war intensely, and they conveyed a picture of misery and a collapse of discipline and authority that sank in right across America.

At the end of March, Ambassador Martin returned to South Vietnam (from a poorly timed home leave) with a high-level mission headed by General Frederick Weyand, who had been the last American commander in South Vietnam in 1972–73 and was now Army Chief of Staff. The Weyand mission concluded that the chances of restoring the military situation were bleak, but that a rump southern area might still be held. It recommended an emergency military aid program of $722 million, designed to hold this reduced area and give Saigon some leverage for a making a deal with Hanoi. It was a forlorn hope. When President Ford took the extraordinary step of giving a personal address to Congress on April 10 to present the program, he was met with almost total silence. Afterward, conservatives were among the first to say flatly that such aid was out of the question.

Meanwhile, the loss of Hue and Danang had been followed by the quick collapse of South Vietnamese resistance, including the loss of the onetime major American base at Cam Ranh Bay. Any hope of defending Saigon was now abandoned, and the question became how fast to evacuate the remaining 8,200 Americans there and as many as possible of those South Vietnamese—numbering at least 100,000, by some estimates 200,000—who had been so clearly identified with the Vietnamese government or the American effort that they were sure to be harshly treated when the North Vietnamese took over.

Washington kept pressing for an immediate all-out evacuation, but Martin held back for ten days, arguing that such action could set off a panic that would make any further evacuation difficult, even impossible. Finally, on April 19, the evacuation was speeded up. Concurrently, Martin put pressure on Thieu to abdicate, which he did on April 21, with a bitter speech blaming America for betraying South Vietnam. Briefly, old-line leaders took over, ironically the same ones who had been brought into government back in 1963 after the coup against Diem. They were still ineffectual. All could see that the end had come.

Some 6,800 Americans and 45,000 South Vietnamese were taken out by aircraft, and many more at the very end by a helicopter airlift to American ships offshore. Ambassador Martin left in this way, from the embassy roof, on April 30, followed in the last helicopter by the embassy's Marine guards. At the end, some tens of thousands of South Vietnamese with damning American ties were left to spend years in harsh "reeducation camps" or to suffer worse fates.

Those last weeks saw a great many Americans, from the ambassador down, doing heroic and selfless acts in an atmosphere of almost total confusion. Likewise, the assisting military force operating from offshore performed well under great stress. Yet as television carried dramatic pictures all over the world, the reality and image alike were of an ignominious finale to America's involvement in the Indochina War. South Vietnam had ceased to exist, its armed forces had been completely defeated, and the Americans at the end had left the people to their fate. North Vietnam was now totally victorious, with booty that included American-supplied military equipment that had originally cost more than $5 billion.[53]

Later on April 30, North Vietnamese forces entered Saigon unopposed. The city was renamed Ho Chi Minh City and a Communist regime installed. Although the new regime was nominally separate from the North until July 1976, from the start it was totally dominated by and controlled from Hanoi.

As President Ford prepared his futile appeal for emergency aid for South Vietnam on April 10, Kissinger advised him to take a confrontational line and blame Congress for the situation. But the President sought to put the war behind the nation and start healing the deep divisions that had had such devastating effect over the years. It was in that spirit that he personally inserted into a speech he delivered in New Orleans on April 23, several days before the end in Saigon, a passage that, in Karnow's words, "relegated Vietnam to the history books":

Today, Americans can regain the sense of pride that existed before Vietnam. But it cannot be achieved by refighting a war that is finished.... These events, tragic as they are, portend neither the end of the world nor of America's leadership in the world.[54]

As he reached the word "finished," his audience of students at Tulane University burst into deafening applause. The President's conclusion fitted the overwhelming national mood.

An important additional factor held back the Ford Administration from blaming Congress or the Democratic Party. In late April, Nixon's secret 1972–73 pledge letters to Thieu were disclosed by the South Vietnamese. The story behind that action was recounted years later by Thieu's confidant and aide Nguyen Tien Hung.

When General Weyand's mission was in Vietnam in March, President Thieu had once again raised the possibility of B-52 bombing. General Weyand gave him no encouragement, and Thieu then had Hung give copies of Nixon's two key letters to a civilian member of the mission, Erich von Marbod, who in turn gave them to Weyand. Immediately on his return, the general gave the copies to Ford and Kissinger in Palm Springs, California, on April 5. Kissinger at once opposed the idea of renewed bombing, in much the same terms that Ford had used with Haig in February: "If you do that, the American people will take to the streets again." Von Marbod then delivered a set of the copied letters to his civilian superior, Defense Secretary Schlesinger, who on April 8 disclosed their substance to his close friend Senator Jackson. That day the senator described the pledges, in general terms, on the Senate floor, stressing that he did not believe that Ford had been fully aware of the commitments stated. In this he may well have been right.[55]

In this convoluted way, Congress and the American public became aware, for the first time, of what Nixon had promised the President of South Vietnam, in utmost secrecy and without any congressional consultation, nearly two and a half years earlier. Sensational as the disclosure would have been at a normal time, it was now almost submerged by the crisis. The White House, surely on Kissinger's advice, adopted the line that there was nothing in the letters inconsistent with vague threats of resumed hostilities in the early months of 1973 by Kissinger and by other Administration officials. This claim was a serious distortion of the record. The prevarication sufficed, however, to keep the issue from exploding for nearly three weeks, with the White House adamantly refusing to release the text of the letters despite a strong demand for them from the Senate Foreign Relations Committee. Finally, the frustrated Hung acted on his own. On April 30 he released the letters in verbatim form at a Washington press conference, using them primarily to appeal to the conscience of

Americans in getting many more Vietnamese out and allowing them to settle in America.[56]

Whatever the disclosure's effect in that respect, the dominant American reaction was one of outrage against Nixon, expressed in a host of editorials and comments in the following days. The revelation of presidential secret pledges, at once challenged on constitutional and other grounds, did much to head off later debate about whether the executive branch or Congress was more to blame for the tragic outcome in Indochina. Thereafter, debate on "who lost South Vietnam?" was mostly subdued and tinged with the same exhaustion that pervaded public opinion from mid-1973 on.

One final reaction from Henry Kissinger deserves mention. In a speech on April 17, in which for the most part he tried to look beyond the debacle, reaffirm basic policies, and reassure other nations, he included one short paragraph on the relationship between détente and Vietnam:

> We must continue our policy of seeking to ease tensions. But we shall insist that the easing of tensions cannot occur selectively. We shall not forget who supplied the arms which North Viet Nam used to make a mockery of its signature on the Paris accords.[57]

This thrust at the Soviet Union was a sad epitaph to a clear failure of détente to do what Nixon and Kissinger had suggested in 1972 it could do — restrain the Soviet Union in contested Third World situations. As for "triangular diplomacy," by this time the Soviet Union and China were now competing intensively for future influence in Southeast Asia, doing more for their Communist clients than they might have done otherwise.

3. Judging Nixon's Indochina Policies

The final collapse of South Vietnam had many causes. First, the weaknesses of the Paris Agreement of January 1973. Second, the extraordinarily rapid North Vietnamese recovery. Third, large-scale aid from the Soviet Union and China. And fourth (and most important), Thieu's inability to remedy any of the long-standing weaknesses of his regime. South Vietnam never found itself, and a significant part of the problem was its prolonged dependence on the United States. Nixon's secret pledge to Thieu that "full force" bombing would follow a North Vietnamese military victory only reinforced Thieu's dependence on Nixon and on America, the very opposite of the increased self-reliance that was the only way South Vietnam could have rallied to preserve itself.

. . .

If the story of American involvement in Indochina were a Wagnerian opera, with musical themes to set moods and foreshadow events, a sinister theme labeled "Cambodia" would recur again and again, signaling dark events to come. Nothing got Nixon into deeper trouble, or distinguished the Nixon Administration more from its predecessors, than his handling of Cambodia. William Shawcross's much noted book *Sideshow* and some other accounts attribute policy on Cambodia largely to Henry Kissinger, but the evidence is overwhelming that the key decisions concerning Cambodia were always those of President Nixon himself. Once the United States was deeply involved, moreover, the action officer was Alexander Haig. Kissinger was hardly an innocent bystander, but he does not deserve to be singled out.

Cambodia was the site for bad decisions on no fewer than five occasions: the 1969–70 secret bombing of the border areas; the incursion of May 1970, with its devastating effect on key sectors of American opinion and negligible offsetting military gains; the decision in the fall of 1970 to provide continuing military and economic aid to Cambodia (leading Congress to ban American military advisors in both Laos and Cambodia, which in turn hamstrung the disastrous Laos offensive of early 1971); and (less noted in most accounts) the failure to understand that North Vietnam by the summer of 1972 no longer controlled the Communist side in Cambodia—that the Khmer Rouge had taken over. This led directly to the fifth grave error, the inhumane and ineffectual bombing of Cambodia in the spring of 1973, which finally persuaded Congress to ban all future American military action in Southeast Asia.

The policy behind these five decisions produced extraordinarily tragic consequences in human terms, with no remotely offsetting strategic benefits. If the United States had stayed out, the alternative outcome—most likely a North Vietnamese takeover of Cambodia, or a struggle for control between China and North Vietnam, with a puppet regime set up by either—could never have been as devastating as what happened.

For the United States to have stayed out of Cambodia would have had some military disadvantages for the defense of South Vietnam. North Vietnam would probably have taken control of the country, reopened the sea supply route, and used the border areas at will, adding somewhat to its capabilities in south-central South Vietnam and in the Delta. But such gains would not have been very important. The war would never have been decided in those parts of South Vietnam. American military officers (and some civilians) who kept stressing the importance of Cambodia were influenced more by understandable frustrations than by considered analysis.

Above all, Cambodia—Nixon's war—was a major deviation from the policy of Vietnamization and of steady U.S. withdrawal for which he had, in November 1969, sought and obtained public support. Had that declared policy been followed in straight-line fashion—as urged by William Rogers and Melvin Laird among his close advisors—there might still have been a case for a residual use or threat of U.S. airpower at some point, to permit the withdrawal to be completed in orderly fashion. A limited formal agreement with Hanoi would probably have been necessary, at least to get the American prisoners out. But such a policy would have stood no more than a modest chance of preserving South Vietnam's independence. It would have needed frank statements to Thieu and other South Vietnamese leaders that the United States would not remain in strength as the level of fighting decreased, that South Vietnam would have to handle its own defense. Telling the South Vietnamese for years, and meaning it, that they would be on their own would have been harsh medicine that might have brought on an earlier collapse. But it was also the only hope of arousing the necessary strong spirit of nationalism and self-reliance, a spirit impossible to visualize as long as the United States was so pervasive—and perhaps as long as Nguyen Van Thieu was the ruler.

In the end, unless South Vietnam had rallied in remarkable fashion, from late 1968 onward a North Vietnamese victory in South Vietnam and in Laos was the likely outcome. In Cambodia, the Khmer Rouge might have put together a guerrilla movement in opposition to the North Vietnamese, and Hanoi might have decided that outright victory there was not worth the cost, but the result would still have been Communist regimes in all of Indochina.

From the standpoint of U.S. cohesion and strength, however, a policy of clear-cut gradual withdrawal would surely have been far less damaging than what actually occurred. The pain and shame would still have been acute, but the aftermath, with all its divisions and lasting scars, would have been less severe and the country would have recovered more rapidly. Whether U.S. prestige would have been as sharply affected can be debated. Accepting defeat and limits to a great nation's power is always easy to depict as weakness, even cowardice. It is hard to imagine that the effect in this respect could have been worse than what finally happened, with the United States linked to disgraceful defeat right to the bitter end.

. . .

In the turmoil and anguish of the spring of 1975, few paused to note what was happening in the rest of Southeast Asia as Hanoi unified Vietnam, the Khmer Rouge took over Cambodia, and the Pathet Lao, under Hanoi's control, consolidated their hold on Laos. To the surprise of some observers, there was no significant effect elsewhere in the area, immediately or in the months and years that followed. Thailand, Malaysia, Singapore, Indonesia, the Philippines—all remained independent and in due course prospered.

The "domino theory" and its more sophisticated variants—the belief that a Communist takeover in Indochina would so weaken and demoralize the rest of Southeast Asia that it would fall easy prey to some combination of Chinese and North Vietnamese expansionism—simply did not take effect. A natural reaction, then and later, was that this view had always been exaggerated to the point of total error, as wrong at the previous points of American policy decision—1951, 1954, 1961, 1964–65, and 1969—as it proved to be in 1975.

The alternative conclusion is that Southeast Asia was indeed very shaky and vulnerable, especially in 1964–65, and that its enormous gains in confidence and stability after that time owed much to America's firm stand in South Vietnam. That is my personal belief, though I would at once agree that the costs of those gains were far too great. On any reading, American policy in Indochina, from the early 1950s right through to 1975, was a disaster. One may argue which Administrations were more or less to blame, but the overall judgment must be that all erred badly.[58]

Between 1969 and mid-1974, the phase of the Second Indochina War for which Richard Nixon was responsible, the prospects for lasting peace and progress in Southeast Asia continued to improve, but the part played by American actions was smaller than at earlier and more critical periods. With a measured American policy of withdrawal from South Vietnam, as Nixon himself seemed to be promising in 1969, Southeast Asia would have had a substantial chance to cope with threats to its security. The price that was paid to sustain Nixon's Indochina policy—especially in Asian lives, in destruction in Indochina, and in continued disunion and demoralization of the American people—was even more out of proportion to results achieved than in earlier periods.

4. Postscripts

On the Arab-Israeli front, the fourteen months after Nixon's resignation saw a major setback to the chances for progress over the West Bank and Gaza, but then a significant gain in the Sinai. Kissinger handled both; they were a continuum to the Nixon era. Two other events were so closely linked to Nixon's policies and to congressional and public reaction to them that they belong in an account of his presidency: a massive public and congressional outcry over the CIA and covert operations generally; and a disastrous attempt to intervene through the CIA in a civil war in Angola. Finally, any retrospective judgment on Nixon's policies must examine their effect on Iran—particularly the considerable evidence that his close embrace of the Shah, and the massive military sales to Iran he initiated in 1972, ended up playing a large part in the character of the Iranian Revolution of 1978–79.[59]

THE ARAB-ISRAELI FRONT

With the two withdrawal agreements in the winter and spring of 1973–74, along the Suez Canal and in the Golan Heights, step-by-step diplomacy proved itself. Two immediate tasks loomed: a further Israeli withdrawal from the Sinai and some agreement on the West Bank and Gaza. (Another possible task, final agreement on the Israel-Syrian border, was put on the back burner, where it remained twenty-five years later.)

As the Syrian withdrawal agreement was signed in late May 1974, many thought the way was now clear for a negotiation between Israel and Jordan over the West Bank and Gaza. Historically, many in the Israeli Labor Party establishment had at times considered this area more negotiable than the whole of the Sinai.[60] The accepted Arab interlocutor for the West Bank in June 1974, King Hussein of Jordan, had shown himself ready to deal with Israel, and there had been occasional secret exploratory talks with senior Israeli officials. By virtue of position, territorial control, temperament, and reciprocal trust, Hussein appeared the logical and preferable Arab negotiator to most nations outside the area and to all but the radical Arab groups and states within it.

In 1974, if Henry Kissinger had been able to bring off the Syrian disengagement sooner and then to open a West Bank–Gaza negotiation by the early summer, there might have been a chance for a workable agreement. The chance was lost, in part because the Syrian negotiations dragged on over small bits of territory and because the second Moscow summit loomed, but in large part also because of Nixon's health and political crisis. It was simply impossible for Kissinger to take on another negotiation with the care and attention it would have needed.

In the following months, unfortunately, the hope of moving toward agreement on the West Bank and Gaza (the Jordanian front) was knocked out by developments in the Arab world. The radical Arab nations had always been reserved or downright hostile toward King Hussein, and were acutely conscious of how negotiations during the winter and spring had worked to strengthen the hand of the moderate Arab nations and to draw them closer to the hated United States. Through the spring and summer they must have consulted feverishly on ways to hit back at the moderates. Hussein was an obvious target.

Kissinger was not idle, arranging summer visits to Washington by Israeli and moderate Arab officials. His first trip abroad after Ford became President was a quick September swing around Middle East capitals. The crucial struggle, it was clear, would come at a plenary meeting of Arab heads of state, in Rabat at the end of October, at which Kissinger hoped, and for a time expected, that the participants would give Jordan and King Hussein a formal mandate to negotiate for the West Bank. Instead, after an intense inter-Arab struggle, the mandate went to the Palestine Liberation Organization, whose radical tendencies had been demonstrated repeatedly, notably in the 1970 Jordan crisis and in its murder of Israeli athletes at the 1972 Olympic Games.

The designation of the PLO was a devastating blow to Kissinger's Middle East policy. Yasser Arafat, its head, at once took on new stature. On November 13, 1974, he made a triumphal appearance at the UN General Assembly, to wild cheers from parts of the membership, cool reserve from others including the United States, and a deeply pained and hostile reaction in the American media and public. It was another diplomatic revolution, offsetting to a considerable degree the gains for the moderates that Kissinger had helped bring about in the preceding nine months. Israel (and the United States) now faced far greater difficulty in the always formidable task of getting agreement over the West Bank and Gaza. This goal had to be postponed indefinitely.

The Sinai front was more hopeful. For months, Kissinger worked hard to bring the Egyptian and Israeli positions within range of each other, so as to make possible a further Israeli withdrawal from the peninsula. When his first effort broke down in March 1975, he and Ford considered small reductions in aid to Israel to bring pressure on its government, now headed by Yitzhak Rabin, to make concessions. The reaction both in Israel and among its supporters in America was sharp and decisive. In a few days the Jewish lobby had mobilized no fewer than seventy-six senators to sign a letter to Ford opposing any such reduction. The President and Kissinger had to lower their sights to seeking a second but still partial Israeli withdrawal (sometimes called Sinai II).

After intensive months, with both Israel and Egypt under varied pressures to reach agreement, the United States got Israel to accept withdrawal from the Sinai, by taking part in an international monitoring system and making massive commitments for future economic aid and other forms of bilateral support, matched by similar commitments to Sadat's Egypt. For the next two decades more than half of the U.S. external aid budget went to Israel and Egypt.

The reward was that the situation between Israel and most of its neighbors was now tenable (with the exception, then and later, of the Lebanon front). The Arab-Israeli front was still unsettled and threatening, but Ford and especially Kissinger deserve great credit for steps that helped keep it from a high and constant level of danger.

COVERT OPERATIONS

When Nixon resigned, majorities in Congress and the American public were outraged over revelations not only of his secret political conduct but also of his covert political actions abroad. What he had done in Chile was not yet known, but the secret bombing of Cambodia in 1969–70 had been revealed in the summer of 1973. More broadly, as we have seen, a strong feeling of having been misled and deceived lay behind the congressional revolt in June that terminated the bombing of Cambodia and any further U.S. military action in Southeast Asia. By the fall of 1974 Americans were fed up and disposed to judge the actions of their government harshly.

In September 1974, *The New York Times* published several articles by the investigative reporter Seymour Hersh that gave a detailed account of CIA operations to upset and "destabilize" Allende's regime in Chile between late 1970 and the Pinochet coup of September 1973. (A direct CIA role in the coup was not alleged, although others later added this charge on the basis of inconclusive evidence.) Hersh's stories were based on information from officials who made clear that the actions had been on Nixon's orders.

Two months later, in December, Hersh hit an even richer lode of secrets, compiled by the government itself. It was a bizarre story, embedded in the events of Watergate. In May 1973, when it had been revealed that in reaction to the disclosure of the Pentagon Papers by Daniel Ellsberg, members of the White House "plumbers" unit had raided the Los Angeles office of Ellsberg's psychiatrist, it shortly emerged that the burglars had turned to the CIA and been given equipment and technical help used in the burglary. James Schlesinger (in what turned out to be his last weeks as head of the Agency) decided that a total housecleaning was in order and issued a directive calling on all CIA employees to report any episode involving possible illegality or action outside the Agency's prescribed functions and purposes.

The result was an outpouring of some seven hundred revelations, ranging from misjudged or trivial cases up to a number of truly important ones, going back over the entire twenty-six-year history of the Agency. Schlesinger's successor, William Colby, assembled the material—CIA people labeled it "the family jewels"—and put it under tight physical security. Yet a number of Agency people came to know at least some of the contents. Many were indignant, some appalled, and at least one knew where to turn.

Published in mid-December in *The New York Times*, this Hersh story revealed that the CIA and FBI had carried on extensive operations to penetrate and disrupt organizations and individuals engaged in opposition to the Vietnam War. This activity—named Operation Chaos—was doubly repugnant to most Americans and almost all members of Congress, as an interference with freedom of expression and a clear-cut violation of the

Agency's charter barring involvement with domestic activities. Shortly thereafter, an offhand remark by President Ford himself at a small meeting with journalists indicated that the CIA had also been involved in operations to assassinate foreign leaders. Ford set up his own commission to look into this subject, chaired by Vice President Rockefeller, but its work was soon overshadowed by Congress, which established new Senate and House special committees to go into the whole range of CIA activities. These were chaired by Senator Frank Church of Idaho and Representative Otis Pike of New York, respectively.

Church, an articulate lawyer and moderate liberal, at once recruited an able staff and set to work to complete its investigations by the assigned deadline of the fall of 1975. Historically minded members of the staff put together comprehensive accounts of the CIA's record in collecting information and publishing estimates of the present and future, and a team led by a prominent New York trial lawyer took aim at assassination plots and other extreme examples of Agency covert operations. From the start, the Church Committee outpaced its House counterpart in the quality and scope of its investigations, and also in its ability to keep its findings secret until they were carefully reviewed and judged. Church shot from the hip only once, with an early remark that the CIA had acted like "a rogue elephant"—a conclusion refuted by massive evidence that almost all the Agency's misdeeds, including the assassination projects, had been in effect ordered by successive Presidents.

In American political history, reform movements such as this one have tended to peter out fairly quickly. Church managed to avoid a bad backlash, but the Pike Committee discredited itself by the extreme language of its draft reports and then by allowing a long version of its final report to leak to a liberal newspaper in late 1975. The resulting turmoil virtually destroyed its influence, and reduced that of the Church Committee. As the public and Congress were visibly turning away from the effort, the Church Committee did get out a creditable Final Report in the spring of 1976, and in late 1976 the Senate set up a watchdog committee. Stringent provisions required the CIA to make intelligence reports available on a continuing basis to the Intelligence Committee and, most important, forbade covert operations unless a prior presidential "finding" spelling out the nature and purpose of the operation had been conveyed to the Congress. In due course, the House followed suit and the requirements for disclosure of reports and for findings prior to covert operations became standard practice.

In effect, in the words of Robert Gates, a CIA official through the reform period, "the CIA moved from its exclusive relationship with the President to a position roughly equidistant between the Congress and the President— responsible and accountable to both, unwilling to act at presidential request without clearance from Congress." Among the intelligence agencies of major nations in the world, giving legislative bodies a strong and accepted role was a rare, perhaps unique, arrangement. In the Reagan Administration, a hyperactivist Director of Central Intelligence, William Casey, circumvented the arrangements and was caught at it, with the result that they became more firmly entrenched.

This was a major change in the balance of power and participation between the presidency and the executive branch on the one hand and Congress on the other, in an area inextricably linked to foreign policy. The change was by no means due solely to events in the Nixon presidency: "the family jewels" (and separate leaks) included practices that dated back to the CIA's early years under Truman and, especially, Eisenhower. Moreover, the Bay of Pigs fiasco under Kennedy was a major contributor to distrust of the Agency, and it was in the Johnson Administration that Operation Chaos was first set up on a small scale, and that the Agency's relationships to ostensibly private groups were aired and forced to be modified or ended. Yet it was the Nixon Administration that carried secrecy and covert operations to new heights (or depths), and it was the revelations of Nixon's personal misuse of the Agency that were crucial in triggering the Church Committee investigation and the ensuing watchdog legislation. To an important degree, therefore, it was Richard Nixon who brought about a constitutional change in the conduct of intelligence and covert operations.

ANGOLA

The Civil War that broke out in far-off Angola (in southwestern Africa) in 1975 did not come, strictly speaking, on Nixon's watch. Its denouement came seventeen months after he left the White House for California, yet it was Nixon's actions and the holdover effect of his approach to such Third World crises, as carried on by Kissinger, that virtually committed President Ford to vigorous intervention in Angola.

Two events set off the Angola crisis: the advent of a new regime in Portugal, resolved to let go of colonies in Africa, and the creation by the Soviet Union of a new military capability, Cuban armed forces, for use in Third World situations. The Portuguese revolution of 1974, which came just before Nixon left office, had not been predicted by the CIA, and no contingency plans appear to have been made. Through 1975 and 1976 the dominant worry in Washington was that the new governing group, which included some Communists from the start, might become outright Communist. Kissinger in particular saw a parallel to Lenin taking over from Kerensky in Russia in 1917, and became almost paranoid about the danger of a Communist regime in Portugal. Eventually, however, he gave way to the advice of a newly appointed ambassador, Frank Carlucci, a Foreign

Service officer, that this was not happening and need not happen if the United States took a correct posture and accepted the socialist regime. Meanwhile, the new regime was going ahead with its declared program of soon freeing the Portuguese colonies in Africa.

Angola became an independent state in 1975, with three factions competing for power. One, Communist-leaning but not at first downright Communist, was the MPLA, centered in the capital city of Luanda and supported by the Soviet Union; the second, the FNLA, had been formed and supported by the government of the Congo under Mobutu Sese Seko, with modest U.S. aid funneled through Mobutu; and the third, the UNITA, in the southwest next to Namibia and close to South Africa, was supported only by South Africa at first. The leaders of the three groups were, respectively, Agostinho Neto (MPLA), Holden Roberto (FNLA), and Jonas Savimbi (UNITA). Their external supporters, in early 1975, were the Soviet Union, the United States, and South Africa.[61] In early 1975, the departing Portuguese brokered an accord among the three at Alvor, but this soon broke down and during the summer an armed conflict began. The Soviet Union led in raising the stakes by initiating a very large military aid program to the MPLA. Above all, the Soviets began to bring in, by air and sea, large contingents of forces from Cuba. It was a "first" of historic proportions, which must have been based on years of training and support. Part of the preparation may have included the 1970 Soviet attempt to establish a naval installation at Cienfuegos in Cuba. This (as we have seen) produced a diplomatic record that for the first time formally committed the United States to refrain from military action against Cuba in any circumstances. When the Soviets started to dicker with Fidel Castro about training Cuban forces for use in Third World "wars of liberation" — probably just about 1970 — Castro must have insisted on an ironclad assurance that if he did this the United States would not retaliate by attacking, perhaps invading, Cuba itself. The Cienfuegos record provided such an assurance.

Thus fortified, and with increased Soviet aid and sugar purchases to stabilize the Cuban economy, Castro had gone at the project with a will. By midsummer of 1975, Cuban military forces in Angola numbered roughly 46,000 men, well trained and used to operating in tropical climates. Later estimates were that the Soviets also put up not less than $300 million in support of the MPLA. The Cuban troops were the decisive move. In response, South Africa sent its own forces to enable Savimbi's UNITA to hold on in the south. Roberto's FNLA forces, with comparatively small U.S. aid and no help from external military forces, were quickly routed by the Cuban-reinforced MPLA, and by early fall of 1975 it was clear that the Communist side would win in short order unless something drastic was done. By then, the CIA had exhausted its contingency funds and could not even come up with a token $20 million to support Roberto. Ford, and Kissinger as the man in charge, faced the need to get Congress to approve larger amounts for "covert" aid to Roberto, with some also intended for Savimbi. The amounts requested were only a fraction of what the Soviets were pouring in for the MLPA, but getting money from the post-1974 Congress was a hopeless cause. It was made even more difficult as word leaked out that South Africa, whose apartheid regime was abhorrent to the great majority of Americans, had sent forces to support UNITA, on the same anti-MPLA side the United States was backing.

Neither the House nor the Senate acted on the aid request, and in December the Senate passed an amendment proposed by Senator John Tunney of California, denying any form of U.S. aid to either of the non-Communist groups. Roberto pulled his forces out, Savimbi retreated to the southeastern bush country, and Neto took over in the capital of Luanda, with Cuban troops on every hand helping him to establish solid control. The fiasco was total and the commentary in America sulfurous, with few defending the course followed by the Ford Administration. As later events were to confirm, this was more than a Communist takeover in a distant regional situation. It signaled a turn in Soviet policy to much greater assertiveness in Third World situations; controlling elements in the Soviet leadership ceased to be held back by détente, at least in selected regional situations.

The Angola affair in 1975–76 was a disaster for American policy in both regional and global terms, a severe blow to the whole détente policy with the Soviet Union that had been a centerpiece of Nixon's policies and of Ford's intentions. Forces set in motion under Nixon had come together to disable his proclaimed policy within eighteen months of his resignation.

IRAN

Chapter 5 has recounted how Nixon's visit to Iran in June 1972, on his way back from the Moscow summit, led to American support, through the CIA, to Kurdish forces fighting in Iraq. But in early 1975, the Shah made up with Saddam Hussein of Iraq and the Kurds were left defenseless. It was a sorry story, aired as part of the exposure of covert activities in 1975–76.

In Iran itself, Nixon's policy had even graver consequences. During the years from 1972 to 1977, by Nixon's personal decision, what had been steady, low-key American support for the Shah's regime from 1953 to 1970 became a conspicuous embrace, marked by massive military sales and the sending of a large American contingent of technicians to make the new military equipment serviceable. Overnight, in historical terms, a largely traditional and rural Muslim society was in the throes of transformation into what its ruler visualized as a rich, sophisticated, and powerful state, able to deter any Soviet threat and exert increasing control and influence in its own Middle East area.

Under Nixon, the United States aided and abetted these policies of the Shah. To many Iranians, they must have seemed the result of American influence—more than was actually the case, for the Shah had his own soaring ambitions and sense of the past historical greatness of the Persian Empire. American officials and a host of private American citizens in high positions in business and industry applauded and encouraged the Shah, drowning out the few critical voices. In the eyes of almost all Iranians, America and Richard Nixon became closely identified with the Shah's regime, much more than had been the case under prior U.S. Administrations.

Three areas of practical cooperation stood out. One was the long-standing relationship between the CIA and the Shah's security service, the notorious SAVAK. As discontent grew, so did the harshness of SAVAK, with the United States inevitably linked. Another long-standing relationship linked the Iranian military establishment and U.S. advisory teams in uniform. And in 1973–74, a third U.S. presence came into being. After Nixon made the commitment in June 1972 to sell to the Shah whatever military equipment he desired, leaving the decisions entirely to him, military sales built up rapidly; the biggest items were aircraft and helicopters, sophisticated equipment requiring extensive training and maintenance supervision within Iran. For these purposes, an American contingent poured in, amounting by the late 1970s to about 25,000 mostly civilian technicians, some of them fresh from having performed similar functions in South Vietnam before it fell.[62] This technician component appears to have been especially conspicuous. In the Shah's sense of haste, for example, he allowed a large helicopter maintenance organization to set up in the ancient Persian capital of Isfahan. This group and other smaller ones, usually not under military discipline, often behaved offensively. In all, the American presence was a significant disturbing element, in contrast to earlier periods when the far fewer Americans in Iran were dedicated and carefully behaved civilians and uniformed military personnel.[63]

The American presence and perceived association with the Shah's most unpopular policies were not basic and primary causes of the Iranian Revolution of 1978–79. The policy and personality of the Shah was by far the most important cause, followed by the disruptive effect of the new oil wealth. The American role and presence did, however, contribute greatly to the anti-American character the revolution took on and to its extreme radicalism. Without these American factors, the Shah might still have been ousted and an Islamic regime installed, dealing a heavy blow to U.S. policy and influence in the area. But such doubly painful and humiliating events as the seizing of U.S. Embassy hostages in the fall of 1979—not to be released until January 1981—would have been much less likely.

In short, American involvement with Iran became in the 1970s disastrous in policy terms and deplorable in human terms. By the mid-1990s, Iran was among the most threatening of the radical regimes in the Middle East and a center of the assertive Muslim fundamentalism that loomed as a serious threat to stability in that area and beyond. The United States had played an important role in holding off a Soviet threat to Iran in the Azerbaijan crisis of 1946, and in the next three decades there had been long periods of constructive interaction and American-assisted progress. Now that record was drowned out, and the policies of the Nixon era bear a large share of the responsibility.

Chapter Ten

Summing Up

1. Nixon and His Colleagues

Richard Nixon brought to the presidency, and especially to the conduct of foreign policy, extraordinary ability and experience. The men he chose for key positions in foreign policy, including international economic policy, were with few exceptions extremely able and well qualified. He had the men he wanted, in the positions he wanted them in and reporting to him through procedures he set up. His was always the ultimate responsibility.

From his selection in November 1968 to the very end, Henry Kissinger was the foremost advisor and actor, progressively more during his years as National Security Advisor, clearly and decisively from September 1973 to Nixon's resignation in August 1974. As Nixon became totally preoccupied by Watergate, his hand could barely be seen, even in decisions for the 1974 Moscow summit.

But before this final period, Nixon was not only the court of last resort and the ultimate decider but the moving force most of the time. Opening channels to China was his idea, although its execution in 1971 owed much to Kissinger. Likewise, starting a back channel with the Soviet leadership was his doing, which again Kissinger developed to the full. Nixon's personal imprint can be seen in many key attitudes and policies: dislike and suspicion of Willy Brandt and Indira Gandhi and of Japanese leaders in general; close and uncritical friendship with the Shah of Iran and General Yahya of Pakistan; immense admiration of Charles de Gaulle; and a special relationship with Nguyen Van Thieu in South Vietnam, cemented when Thieu gave him crucial political help in the last days of the 1968 presidential campaign. Nixon's style also dominated the way the Administration handled confrontations, stressing the dramatic stroke rather than gradual steps, relying in key cases on the threat of extreme military action and on occasion its unleashing, using concealment and covert action to the utmost. Again, Kissinger was a willing executor, but the choice of measures was almost always Nixon's.

Perhaps most important, Nixon's passionate belief in an American commitment to Southeast Asia as a whole, and to South Vietnam in particular, led directly to his key decisions to extend the war to Cambodia and expand it in Laos—decisions that at critical times affected his policies toward China and the Soviet Union. Finally, Nixon's other passionate objective, his own overwhelming reelection, strongly influenced the timing and sometimes the substance of his policies. Of this we may learn more from the massive store of inner-circle tapes and materials still undisclosed.

All this is worth emphasizing, since some historians, and many in the media, were at the time and later so impressed by Kissinger's explanations of policy that they tended to describe the policy as "Kissinger's." To the contrary, I believe that Nixon set the framework from the outset, as well as the priority of objectives, with his own reelection at the very top. His temperament and past experience, however, led him to immerse himself in some problems and pay little attention to others. Negotiations bored Nixon and fascinated Kissinger, whose enthusiasm was not always matched by his skill. He was unnecessarily sloppy in the final stages of the negotiations with North Vietnam. In the SALT I arms negotiations, with a highly qualified negotiating team in place, Kissinger's use of his back channel with Dobrynin did more harm than good, and in 1972 his record was at best mixed. By contrast, in the Middle East negotiations of 1973–74, with good staff support and essentially on his own, Kissinger was both persuasive and in command, producing not only important agreements but crucial changes in Arab attitudes.

Moreover, with Nixon's blessing, Kissinger kept a tight hold on the policymaking process and was uniquely active as a presenter and explicator of foreign policy, through background talks with media representatives and others specializing in foreign policy. These contacts served his personal reputation, but also helped put the Administration in a good light and kept up communication to the country, via the media, so that the President could concentrate more, following the de Gaulle model, on rare but forceful statements and speeches.

· · ·

Among other top officials, the outsized John Connally used his brief hour upon the Treasury stage to the full, and in the spring of 1972 played a crucial part in persuading Nixon to go ahead with the mining of Haiphong at the risk of losing the Moscow summit. In their handling of the 1971 dollar crisis, Connally and Nixon relied heavily on a first-class economic team, some of whom—notably George Shultz and Paul Volcker—went on to greater responsibilities in later years.

In national security policy, three other figures stand out as heavyweights, less influential than Kissinger but each with major contributions. Melvin Laird took hold rapidly in the Pentagon, forming with an outstanding business executive, David Packard, an exceptionally strong team. His influence on Capitol Hill was greater than that of any other Administration official. He sustained defense budgets in a period of strain and strong opposition, and was effective on many other issues as well. It was Laird who put over the basic policy of periodic troop withdrawals from South Vietnam, locking in the program by making it the basic assumption for budgetary planning, so that it became the foundation stone for policy on the Vietnam War, as well as essential for maintaining popular support. On key policy decisions, starting with the incursion into Cambodia, Laird often opposed the course the President decided to follow, showing a strong sense of what the reactions in the country and in Congress would be, yet he was always totally loyal in carrying out Nixon's decisions.

Alexander Haig, at almost an opposite pole to Laird, was his unrelenting adversary in backstage conflict. In the great divide that went back to the firing of MacArthur in 1951, Haig was always "a MacArthur man" in urging strong courses of action and maximum military autonomy.[1] More than any other associate of Nixon, Haig had a mind-set and temperament akin to the President's. He must have had Nixon's backing in developing the habit of circumventing not only Laird but formal channels to the Joint Chiefs of Staff, working directly with its Joint Staff for military planning in key instances. In that way, as we have seen, he became the promoter of the "Duck Hook" planning of 1969, with the mining of Haiphong as its centerpiece—planning that was discarded then but revived in May 1972 to crucial effect.

The evidence also points to Haig as the main instigator of the secret pledges to Thieu. He gave thrust and muscle, such as these could be, to Nixon's disastrous commitment to Lon Nol in Cambodia. He promoted the badly misjudged Lam Son 719 operation into Laos in 1971 and then urged Nixon to defy a congressional ban and send in American forces when the operation got into trouble. And it was he who, in the Watergate crisis phase of October 1973, cobbled together the attempt to foreclose further requests for presidential tapes that drove Elliot Richardson to resign as Attorney General. Less definitely, circumstantial evidence suggests that his presence and views sometimes had a considerable effect on the positions taken at critical times by Henry Kissinger, who was always hyperjealous of any threat to his personal position and could see how much Haig resonated with the President.

Haig emerges from the record as a major influence on policy, especially in confrontation or crisis situations. He shared, and reinforced, Nixon's stress on the use or threat of massive airpower, his convictions about Southeast Asia and South Vietnam, and his belief that the Soviet hand lay behind most disruptive developments. Nixon surely played a role in Haig's later becoming Ronald Reagan's first Secretary of State.

A third heavyweight was Kenneth Rush, who would almost certainly have become Secretary of State in mid-1973 had it not been for Nixon's need for Kissinger's prestige to hold off the impact of the Watergate scandal. Rush had performed ably in successive years as Deputy Secretary, first of Defense and then of State, and would surely have brought to the office of Secretary a greater capacity for mastering issues and giving weight to the department's views than William Rogers was ever able to muster. Such might-have-beens to one side, Rush performed with rare distinction as Ambassador to West Germany, the most testing overseas post in the Nixon era. It was no mean feat to maintain smooth working relations with a head of government, Willy Brandt, when Nixon and Kissinger were audibly critical and in constant touch with the opposition. If the West German–American relationship had gone sour, it would have been a major blow to the core Alliance.

Then, when the Berlin negotiations became the centerpiece of Brandt's "German package" and the key to Alliance relationships, Rush (with able advice) mastered a complex set of issues and worked through an equally complex negotiating process, involving the West Germans, French, British, and Soviets as well as the White House and State Department. Rush was not one to grasp for credit, but his performance certainly ranks high in the annals of Alliance diplomacy during the Cold War.

. . .

In the decision-making process during the Nixon presidency, two features stand out: crisis management and the neglect of the professionals in the State Department. One was innovative and constructive, the other a serious defect.

The Washington Special Actions Group (WSAG), initiated in the summer of 1970, was a genuine executive committee for national security issues, especially but not only in crisis. Chaired by Kissinger and manned by officials just below the top in State and Defense, with the Chairman of the Joint Chiefs of Staff and the Director of Central Intelligence almost always present, WSAG was often simply a place where Kissinger passed on the President's desires or decisions. But the very fact that it brought together top policy people, usually the same ones, over and over, and that, when the

President was away, it followed Kissinger wherever he went, mostly to San Clemente, occasionally to Florida, had the effect of separating its members to some extent from their staffs. Accounts by participants suggest that there developed a strong group spirit and a candor rare in high-level deliberations in many Administrations.

WSAG came into its own in the Jordan crisis of 1970. Thereafter it acted repeatedly to manage crises and to make recommendations for presidential decisions. In crisis management, the evidence indicates that it was singularly effective. The participants were much more aware than the Cabinet-level members of the National Security Council itself could normally be of the inner workings and thoughts of the other participants, in particular the Joint Chiefs of Staff, who under Kennedy and Johnson had often lacked the ready and frank access to civilian policymakers that WSAG provided under Nixon.

All in all, both the individuals and the national security policy process under Nixon were of high quality, well organized to meet crises. However, the structure was far less effective in policy planning, a function Kissinger and his staff readily assumed but not always from a rounded viewpoint. In particular, the process failed to make proper use of the State Department.

In one of his last recorded utterances, Richard Nixon inveighed against a trio of bugaboos—the United Nations, human rights, and the Foreign Service of his country.[2] The private remarks of aging political figures are often not to be taken at face value, but the evidence is massive that all three antipathies were real and strong. Henry Kissinger's first volume of memoirs, and to a lesser extent his second, are loaded with disparaging remarks about the State Department as a whole and about the Foreign Service in particular—in addition to a constant strong undercurrent of digs at Secretary of State Rogers.[3]

In the Nixon Administration, until Kissinger became Secretary of State, the State Department had less influence than in any previous postwar period. William Rogers and his staff were responsible for an abortive Rogers Plan, but also, to their great credit, for the Rogers Initiative of 1970, which brought about an important cease-fire between Egypt and Israel at a time when the situation (with Nasser still in charge) looked as if it was running out of control. In the handling of Berlin, Foreign Service officers provided vital help to Kenneth Rush, while Kissinger's dealings with the Chinese rested, more than he ever admitted, on ideas and verbal formulas framed in State over the years. Rogers paired with Laird in opposition to many unwise moves in the Indochina War, but on many matters he was hampered, even crippled, by White House use of back channels and withholding of important information. The situation was evident and demoralizing to State Department people, at home and even more abroad.

This neglect was bound to affect the substance of policy, and the evidence is strong that it did so on many occasions. Contrary to the repeated claims of Kissinger in particular, neither he nor Nixon operated solely, or even habitually, on the basis of dispassionate analysis of the U.S. national interest. Both were strongly influenced by personal impressions of individuals — Nixon also by the policy views he had lived with and supported in the Eisenhower era, Kissinger also by his study of European diplomacy and political history. Every President or senior policy advisor has such background factors; more than most, Nixon and Kissinger steered by examples and stereotypes drawn from their own experience.

An outstanding example was their views of relationships in the Communist world. They were open-minded about China and trumpeted their ability to discern that Nationalist factors outweighed Communist ideology in Sino-Soviet relations. But in Chile, several Middle Eastern countries, South Asia, and Africa, any Communist interest meant to them an early Soviet grab for power, at the expense of the United States. Likewise, neither ever modified the beliefs they started with, that Communist regimes in small countries were essentially controlled by more powerful Communist regimes, and that Communist movements such as the Khmer Rouge were under the control of the regimes that supported them. The result was a series of misjudgments, running from 1969 at least through the negotiation of the Paris Agreement on Indochina.

Closely related was their neglect, or misreading, of regional and local factors. Virtually every American who worked on problems affecting India in the postwar period knew that Indian nonalignment was deeply rooted in national and cultural pride. Nixon joined with John Foster Dulles (though not apparently with Dwight Eisenhower) in regarding this posture as immoral. Kissinger, with little exposure to India, appears to have been simply put off by Mrs. Gandhi.

Among the professionals in the State Department (and in the analysis offices of the CIA, which were also on Nixon's hit list), much less monolithic views were present and usually prevalent. Not with rose-tinted glasses: it was, after all, a Foreign Service officer, George Kennan, who most trenchantly described the roots of Soviet expansionist tendencies and laid out the policy of containment that the United States essentially followed for the next forty years. But whether long-term ambition amounted to present intent, whether the Soviets and other Communist regimes were prone to take chances, and whether the Soviets, or in East Asia the Chinese, really dominated and guided red-tinted regimes — all these questions had categorical answers for Nixon and Kissinger, but often not for experienced diplomats and intelligence officers. On the record examined in this book, the latter were often right, and too seldom heeded.

Another characteristic of Kissinger in particular was to misjudge real or apparent commitments between other nations or even between the United States itself and others. The record shows many instances of this blurred vision: two were the Friendship Treaty between India and the Soviet Union and the formal obligations between the United States and Pakistan. Along the same lines, Kissinger was totally insensitive to whether American statements of intent, even at top levels, had binding weight in the absence of congressional knowledge and approval. The clearest example of this failing was Kissinger's claim that various public statements of American resolve after the Paris Agreement of 1973 (with no congressional endorsement) truly conveyed, and signaled to the American public, an intent to resort to military action if Hanoi breached the agreement.

Finally, there was a strong "heroes and villains" tendency in the thinking of both Nixon and Kissinger. Such thinking can have its place: the generation that knew Hitler and then Stalin had reason to look at the possible dark side of regimes and their relations to like-minded regimes. But the tendency to jump or cling to categorical judgments needs a responsible counterweight. Career officers in State and in the analytic offices of CIA were, with rare exceptions, somewhat detached in their appraisals and more conscious of the often ambiguous influence of historical parallels and of the underlying currents and popular moods in individual countries. Nixon and Kissinger needed their input and participation far more than their system permitted.[4]

. . .

Until Watergate made its mark, the Nixon Administration was remarkably effective in holding congressional and public support for its foreign policies. The President's statements and speeches (except for the one on going into Cambodia), Kissinger's backgrounding of influential reporters, as well as Laird's work on the defense side, maintained support especially against the steadily rising sentiment for early withdrawal from South Vietnam. Although the Cambodian incursion outraged much of Congress and the public, the Administration managed nonetheless to get congressional approval for a continuing aid program there. In perspective, the fact that, in June 1973, Congress finally cut off funds for future U.S. military activity in Southeast Asia was less remarkable than that it did not happen much earlier. Part of the explanation was that the Democratic majority in both houses of Congress obscured the fact that there were always enough conservative Democrats to give the President a working majority for carrying on the war while withdrawing. The same was true of the public at large. Vocal and dramatic as the antiwar movement was, it was always outweighed by Nixon's "silent majority"—a loose coalition of those truly persuaded that he was right and those ready to give him the benefit of the doubt.

On the face of things, one might have thought, and Nixon clearly did think, that after he won the 1972 election and then got the Paris Agreement he would have strong congressional and public support for whatever he did that seemed directed at securing the peace. Instead, his support faltered at the first test, in the spring of 1973, and then fell apart. The onset of Watergate was only part of the reason, I am convinced. The key factor was that Congress and the people were rebelling at last against inadequate participation and consultation, most of all because of their sense that the President had never really leveled with them. Again and again Nixon had sneaked loans from his store of political capital, by exaggerated claims and rhetoric and by other forms of deception. In early 1973 he ran out of capital and the effect was devastating.

. . .

So we turn now to the personality of the President himself, his great strengths and serious weaknesses. No President in American history presents greater contrasts in qualities, tendencies, and abilities than Richard Nixon. In articles and books, in TV series and long motion pictures, his character and personality continue in the 1990s to fascinate observers and, to an unusual degree, the general public. Many have attempted a coherent synthesis of his personal characteristics. Let us focus rather on Nixon's qualities, capacities, and handicaps as these bore on his conduct of foreign policy. Since almost every one of his positive qualities had its negative counterpart, the overall picture is one of paradox. He was both leader and misleader, a clearheaded planner and analyst but with a low boiling point, a canny strategist and a not always scrupulous schemer. Most fundamentally, he lacked the qualities of a statesman and builder.

That Nixon had tools of leadership cannot be questioned. He was a capable if not inspiring administrator, projecting an image of competence and control. Managing his time more tightly than almost any other President, he reserved for himself long periods of privacy for reflection. In the capacity to absorb and synthesize large amounts of information and to articulate his views both in private and in public, he stood near the top among modern Presidents.

As we have had several occasions to note, the model of Charles de Gaulle was always with him: saying little until the timing was right and then speaking with the greatest possible force. Nixon not only gave well-crafted speeches, helped by a talented team of writers but in the end his own; he also planned and timed them, often masterfully. Two examples that stand out in the narrative were his speech of November 3, 1969, which rallied the country in support of his stated Vietnam policy and gave him months of political space; and that of January 25, 1972, reporting Kissinger's secret contacts with the North Vietnamese to capture the banner of peace and give himself crucial freedom of action in that climactic year.

In these and other cases, he showed a sure sense of the state of public opinion, letting tension build but not get out of hand before he spoke. Such a sense of timing has been a powerful asset to other Presidents. Outstanding historical examples were Abraham Lincoln's finally deciding to speak out on emancipation in the fall of 1862 and Franklin D. Roosevelt's launching the Lend-Lease program in early 1941. Yet these examples illustrate another Nixon characteristic. Lincoln and Roosevelt had follow-up actions ready. With Nixon, there was rarely a new program or policy waiting to be launched. He sought only to change the national mood, buy time, and prepare a background for actions he expected to take on his own.

Equally characteristic was his emphasis on spectacular occasions. The record shows that from the opening feelers with China on, Mao Zedong and Zhou Enlai grasped that Nixon set great store by a summit visit to China in the 1972 election year, as visible and dramatic as possible. The result was one of the greatest public triumphs ever for an American President. The publicity was good for the image of America and for the Sino-American relationship, but the chief beneficiary was Richard Nixon himself, both for his reelection and for his future reputation as a statesman. Even twenty-five years later, after all that has intervened, that TV image lingers when people over forty-five think of Nixon—not canceling the impact of Watergate but counteracting it—and it was that image he invoked again and again in the unrelenting effort of his last years to win back public favor.

Another great asset for a President can be the ability to give his policy actions a colorful and systematic image, by keynote themes and by the use of labels and slogans. In his first two years, the President met this desire by the Nixon Doctrine and by the withdrawal and Vietnamization themes. After the opening to China through Kissinger's visit in July 1971, "triangular diplomacy" and "a structure of peace" were for a time effective signposts of policy, leading Americans, in Congress and the public, to feel part of a large enterprise from which would emerge not only great credit for the United States but a more peaceful and prosperous world.

Nixon was also capable of courage and tenacity, even if these qualities were sometimes displayed in the execution of unwise policies. His decisions concerning the Vietnam War in 1972—the mining of Haiphong in May and the Linebacker air bombing in the summer and again at Christmas—were taken in the face of predictable outcry, and persevered in until they made possible the Paris Agreement. In other cases, however, he showed a kind of reckless courage at first, but then retreated in the face of opposition, real or feared. One example was the failed ultimatum to the Soviets in 1969; another his pulling back in Cambodia in 1970. In later years, he often claimed that he would have acted strongly on several occasions but for the restraints imposed by public opinion. Such claims were hardly a sign of firmness or courage at the time of decision—rather the reverse. That he worshipped physical courage is evident. The quieter forms of political courage he occasionally lacked.

But, with all his talents, what mainly undid Nixon was his unshakable
bent to deceive. Robert Gates served in the Nixon Administration in a
middle-level White House position, and then under five other Presidents
in senior posts at the National Security Council and the Central Intelligence Agency. Although he was in basic agreement with Nixon's policies,
he concluded that the years from 1969 to 1974 had been "a time of secret
deals and public obfuscation (and deception), all reflecting more accurately
than they imagined the personalities of its principal architects."[5]

Deception did permeate the Nixon Administration, more than any other
not only during the Cold War but throughout American history. There was
deception within the government—in no other Administration would an
episode such as the Radford spying operation on the NSC staff have been
conceivable—as well as deception of Congress and the American people,
and, ironically more rarely, deception of nations abroad. It was a way of
thinking and acting that was deeply ingrained in Richard Nixon, reflected
in his political behavior, instinctively adopted when he confronted or anticipated obstacles, a frequent practice in the conduct of foreign policy and
especially in its explanation and presentation.

Deception often depends on secrecy; it is not, however, identical. Defenders of the Nixon Administration have argued that without secrecy at
least two of its foremost achievements—the opening to China and the Paris
Agreement on the Vietnam War—could not have been achieved. They
have a point. In both cases a visible negotiating process would have attracted
criticism and upsetting reactions that would have made the final result
difficult if not impossible to reach. But in each case there was no positive
deception. The objectives were consistent with what the Administration was
saying or not saying in public.

"Secret deals" and "public obfuscation," in Gates's words—the two are
again related, but they are not the same. Few Presidents have altogether
avoided actions that could be accused of being deceptive, or lacked a taste
for secret information. (Others besides Nixon yielded, for example, to the
blandishments of J. Edgar Hoover, offering them damaging FBI information
on their political opponents.) With Nixon, however, the taste for acting
secretly was obsessive. Covert operations run through the narrative like a
red thread: the secret bombing of Cambodia ordered in his first month in
office; the infamous Track II effort in Chile in the fall of 1970, followed by
the silent blockade to undermine Allende; the unacknowledged "tilt" in
policy during the India-Pakistan crisis of 1971; joining with the Shah of Iran
in arming and arousing the Kurds to their deaths in 1972–75.

Only a few of these were known at the time. Many surfaced only when the Church and Pike committees went to work in 1975. Thus, one must look elsewhere as well for the reasons Nixon's hold on the trust and confidence of Americans was shaken on several occasions even during his first term, and was precarious and vulnerable when the Watergate scandal broke open in March 1973.

In the end, Richard Nixon's use of covert operations was less important than his persistent record of misrepresenting his policies and pursuing strategies and actions at odds with what he told Congress and the American people. With Nixon an act of leadership became, in case after case, an exercise in misleading the American people and their Congress, for the sake of short-term freedom of action or for his own personal political purposes. In this respect his was unlike any other postwar American Administration — perhaps any Administration in American history — and in the end he paid a high price in loss of public confidence. This largest habit of deception can be seen in almost every one of the policies that were trademarks of his administration.

The Nixon Doctrine, for example, seemed to promise that the United States, in the wake of its experience in Vietnam, would now move away from the tendency to promise or commit U.S. forces to the defense of countries under Communist threat. Yet, at the time the doctrine was announced, American B-52 bombers had been systematically hitting targets in Cambodia for three months, and continued to do so for another year. In 1973 they bombed Cambodia again, this time massively, until Congress intervened. The disastrous sequence of Nixon's actions concerning Cambodia, summarized in the preceding chapter, rested in large part on deception and concealment.

On rare occasions, there may be tenable reasons for avoiding public statements of policy. In this narrative, the refusal of Presidents from Eisenhower to Nixon to acknowledge frankly what they were doing in Laos rested on such reasons (the wishes of the courageous and threatened ruler). But in most cases deception goes hand in hand with bad policy, as Americans who followed the Iran-Contra affair in the 1980s should hardly need to be reminded.

In sum, Nixon's outstanding leadership capacities were in large measure offset or made worthless by his consistent practice of deception, through secret actions and especially through actions inconsistent with his public positions.

. . .

Finally, there is one overarching paradox in Nixon, which as much as his instinct to deceive marred his performance in foreign policy. As a strategist he could be brilliant, farsighted, and resourceful; where maneuver and manipulation were needed he was skilled in their exercise. But as a statesman in the American democratic system, he fell short for simple reasons. He had no taste for the arduous processes of consultation and seeking congressional and public support, and he hated to relinquish personal control or to commit himself for the future.

In the domestic political arena, his strategic skill showed itself over and over. Yet when it came to the reelection year, 1972, Nixon never shared his high personal standing with his party. Only the use of a personal election organization (the notorious CRP) gave him the kind of control, and credit, he craved — including the freedom to raise money and engage in dirty tricks without worrying about the concurrence of others.

In key foreign policy decisions the mix was the same: skillful maneuver, no lasting structure. In his first term he knew from the outset that he would face a formidable military problem when U.S. forces were sharply reduced through withdrawals and when North Vietnam, predictably, launched an offensive designed to be decisive. He intended to blunt that offensive with U.S. airpower, yet he knew that unless he had the image of a man of peace, the country would reject such military action. The China opening, his January 1972 speech to the nation, and the Beijing and Moscow summits gave him the standing he needed, as he assembled the airpower to do the job. He had thought and planned a long way ahead, and his plan worked long enough for him to reap its political benefits. Yet he had no plan beyond the Paris Agreement, other than his secret bombing pledges and a large-scale economic aid program for North Vietnam that had never been discussed with Congress or fully disclosed to the American public.

Even more to the point was his failure to lay foundations for his key policy, to bring about a new relationship with the Soviet Union. Watergate, from March 1973 on, took Nixon progressively out of play and left the defense of his trade policy to Henry Kissinger, whose skills did not extend to dealing effectively with Congress. But deep down, Nixon was never inclined to lay down a firm basis for his policy, in Congress or in the minds of the American public. He should have presented the SALT I agreements candidly, as inescapable compromises on lesser points. And he should have told congressional leaders firmly that the trade agreement had great importance and that he would address the question of free emigration of Jews and others in his new term. Such candor might have lost him some of his overwhelming majority over George McGovern in the 1972 election, but it would have built a much firmer foundation for a détente-guided Soviet policy to continue.

Nixon was on many occasions a brilliant strategist. He lacked the candor and the steady and larger vision that make a statesman. Two examples from the Cold War period illustrate the difference — Harry Truman and Willy Brandt.

Truman, in many ways less skilled than Nixon, responded to the demands of his presidency with the Truman Doctrine (laying down the policy of aid to countries threatened by the Soviet Union and exemplifying it in Greece and Turkey); with the Marshall Plan for massive economic aid to Western Europe; with the negotiation of the NATO treaty in 1948–49; and in 1951 with the sending of substantial American forces to Europe after an impassioned "Great Debate" with Senator Robert Taft and the remaining voices of isolationism. In each of the four cases, Truman laid out his proposals candidly and fought successfully to win the approval of Congress.

As a result, his policies became the foundations of American foreign policy for the next two generations, even as he himself, weighted down by the Korean War, sank in public favor. Truman had undaunted courage, and he was a builder: recent ratings of American Presidents put him high on the list. He and his principal colleagues (George Marshall, Dean Acheson, and Robert Lovett) were statesmen.

The second example is Willy Brandt, leading his country in the same five years as Nixon. His performance — in a political system modeled largely on America's — was, and remains, a case study in effective statesmanship in a democratic country. He announced his proposed policy in advance when he was in opposition, pursued it openly and at once when he became Chancellor, conducted the major negotiations as publicly as their nature permitted, and finally submitted the resulting package for the approval of his country's legislative body, the Bundestag. The struggle there was prolonged and epic. In the end, Brandt embedded his policy in concrete, with the lasting support of all the major political parties.

Richard Nixon, as his memoirs show, developed a considerable admiration for Harry Truman, though he had opposed him relentlessly at the time. Brandt he always suspected and disliked. Each had a lesson for him that he would have done well to learn.

2. *In the Light of History*

In a moving eulogy at the memorial service for Richard Nixon on April 27, 1994, with President Clinton and the four living ex-Presidents (Gerald Ford, Jimmy Carter, Ronald Reagan, and George Bush) in attendance, Henry Kissinger concluded that Richard Nixon as President "advanced the vision of peace of his Quaker youth." In contrast to the situation of the nation when Nixon became President,

[w]hen Richard Nixon left office, an agreement to end the war in Vietnam had been concluded, and the main lines of all subsequent policy were established: permanent dialogue with China, readiness without il-

lusions to ease tensions with the Soviet Union, a peace process in the Middle East, the beginning via the European Security Conference of establishing human rights as an international issue, weakening the Soviet hold in Eastern Europe.

Few eulogies should be held to literal truth, but this passage at least gives a list of headings by which to appraise the Nixon presidency in the light of history. The first item can be commended only for brevity. The participation of American ground forces in the Second Indochina War did end in early 1973, but for all others involved, the Paris Agreement was never more than a frail cease-fire. Within a month, Richard Nixon was the first to resume serious hostilities through the disastrous bombing of Cambodia in 1973, which ended only when Congress forbade further American military action in Southeast Asia. The true "end" to the war came in 1975 in the form of defeat.

· · ·

On the wider global front, the place to start is the relationship with China. The restoration of effective Sino-American dialogue was possible mainly because China and the Soviet Union stood at the verge of war in mid-1969. In the confused sequence of events from that point to the decisive invitation of December 1970, it was the Chinese at least as much as the Americans who took the initiative. China needed the goodwill and political support of America badly, and America was ready for change — both within the government and in a now temperate public opinion that was a far cry from the hostile emotionalism rampant in the 1950s. The dramatic character of Kissinger's secret initial trip to Beijing in July 1971, and of Nixon's visit the following February, underlined the importance of the change and brought it home to the whole world. Privately, moreover, the dialogue between Zhou Enlai and Henry Kissinger over the next two years was searching and intimate.

Yet, as the relationship developed even during the Nixon era, its limits became evident. It had little effect on Soviet behavior after the immediate push to schedule a Moscow summit. After that it played a big part in luring the United States into an exaggerated and dangerous role during the India-Pakistan crisis of 1971, a prime example of "balance of power" thinking gone astray. And in 1973–74 the Chinese, with their strong tie to the Communist Khmer Rouge in Cambodia, evaded ever giving help toward any kind of compromise in that much injured country, They let Henry Kissinger down then, and the Sino-American tie steadily weakened and reached a low point in December 1974, when Ford and Kissinger decided to meet with Leonid Brezhnev at Vladivostok, on territory the Chinese regarded as theirs.

Thus, it was a three-year affair at best, likely to fade when Mao and Zhou became ill, always at the mercy of political tides within China that no outsider could influence more than marginally. Moreover, the enormous domestic political benefit Nixon got from the China opening almost certainly had its negative side. China's leaders must have felt that they were being used to get American public support for policies that included a much too friendly U.S. relationship with the Soviet Union. When a moderate Chinese regime again emerged in 1978 under Deng Xiaoping, Jimmy Carter and Zbigniew Brzezinski were able to achieve the goal of formal diplomatic recognition Nixon had planned and virtually promised for his second term, but with nowhere near the warm atmospherics of the Nixon-Kissinger era. China, the great Middle Kingdom, was too proud to be used for long. As the history of later Sino-American dealings had tended to confirm, China — whether weak or powerful — cannot readily be fitted into any other nation's "structure of peace."

While it lasted, however, Nixon's policy toward the Sino-Soviet rift may have had one crucial and little noted effect. The evidence in the summer of 1969 that the Soviet Union was seriously threatening a massive air attack on China's nuclear weapons facilities was strong at the time and has never been questioned since. The Richardson statement — that the United States "could not fail to be deeply concerned" if the quarrel should escalate "into a massive breach of international peace and security" — was a clear signal that the United States would not support the Soviet action and would probably exert pressure to bring it to an early end.[6]

In effect, the United States put its toe on the scales against Soviet pressure on China, and the Soviets drew back. We are not likely to know soon, if ever, whether war between China and the Soviet Union was indeed likely that year. But the circumstantial evidence is strong that the U.S. position played an important part in heading off a conflict that could have been appalling and unpredictable. Probably another American President would have taken the same position, but that should not prevent giving credit to the Nixon Administration for doing the right and important thing on this key front, and in timely fashion.

Moreover, Kissinger, in his first talks with Zhou Enlai, not only eased Chinese concerns that the Japanese-American Security Treaty would encourage a revival of Japanese militarism but influenced Zhou toward the Sino-Japanese reconciliation of 1972. In previous periods in the twentieth century, the United States had been perceived as siding with either Japan or China. Now, with the United States dealing with both, the great-power "structure" in Northeast Asia was undoubtedly more stable and sound than it had been for two generations. Again, another American Administration coming to office in 1969 would probably have made essentially the same effort, but Nixon, and in this case especially Kissinger, deserve credit for playing a significant part in a transforming change.

. . .

Kissinger's eulogy gave Nixon credit for establishing a lasting U.S. policy of "readiness without illusions to ease tensions with the Soviet Union." Certainly the Soviet-American relationship, alongside the health and solidity of the core Alliance, had to be among the foremost concerns of any American policy then and later. If that relationship had become more solid in the Nixon era — if there had been a genuine easing of Soviet-American tensions without sacrifice to any significant U.S. national interest — Nixon and Kissinger could indeed lay claim to a historic achievement.

As often, Ambassador Dobrynin has expressed a dispassionate judgment. Writing in the 1990s, after much opportunity for reflection, he concluded:

> But when I assess their [Nixon and Kissinger's] activity in retrospect . . . I cannot escape the conclusion that they were not really thinking in terms of bringing about a major breakthrough in Soviet-American relations, and of ending the Cold War and the arms race.
>
> Underlying their policy toward the Soviet Union was a combination of deterrence and cooperation, a mosaic of short-term and long-term considerations. Both Nixon and Kissinger sought to create a more stable and predictable strategic situation without reducing the high level of armaments, which remained the basis of a policy that was essentially based on military strength, and on the accommodation of national interests only when they found it desirable to do so. . . . Their arms control effort thus disguised this policy of strength, but only slightly. *Essentially, neither the president nor his closest aide proved able (or wanted) to break out of the orbit of the Cold War, although their attitude was more pragmatic and realistic than other Cold Warriors in the White House.*[7]

Dobrynin was right that Nixon and Kissinger envisaged a continuing arms race and also intense competition with the Soviet Union in the Third World. But he was wrong in implying that his own country was ready for a genuine "détente," without an arms race or Third World confrontations. Although we shall not know as much as we need for judgment until Soviet files for the Nixon period are opened, there is little reason to believe that these will show Soviet policy in a more pacific light than it was perceived at the time in America and elsewhere. Brezhnev in 1972, less strident than his predecessors, was still a believer in the ambiguous label of "peaceful coexistence."[8]

Looking back at the record of Nixon's first term, one cannot escape the conclusion that easing U.S.-Soviet tensions was a top-priority objective in large part because it furthered Nixon's reelection prospects and, closely second, might produce help from the Soviet leaders over the Vietnam War. In September 1972, when Nixon's reelection was in the bag and he had gotten all he could hope for in the prospective Indochina agreement, Nixon made the important and revealing Rose Garden deal with Senator Jackson, which was bound to weaken the two principal pillars of détente, expanded trade and strategic arms control. It may be argued that, but for Watergate, Nixon could later have stood up to Jackson more effectively than Ford and Kissinger were able to do. But the evidence suggests that Nixon never really wanted to take on Jackson, because a large piece of him agreed with what Jackson and his ally, James Schlesinger, were advocating.

Moreover, Nixon's 1950s reflexes over the Soviet role in political struggles in troubled countries, especially in the Third World—always fed by Alexander Haig and usually by Kissinger—never let up with the détente agreements of 1972. Nixon and Kissinger exaggerated the Soviet role and influence in some situations—India and Chile, for example. They dealt with developments in Portugal and Angola in 1973–75 much as Eisenhower might have done, but not Kennedy or Johnson. On the other hand, they did not exaggerate the importance of the Soviet Union as a disruptive force in the Middle East. There the goals of American policy, regional stability above all, depended on the sharp reduction in Soviet influence Kissinger achieved while Nixon was still President.

Nixon's "détente" with the Soviet Union foundered in the end, for lack of political support at home. For a time the tide turned to the hard-line side. Yet Nixon had carried further than any of his predecessors the pursuit of serious negotiations with the Soviet Union. His was far from being the "era of negotiations" he proclaimed in 1969, but it did help to accustom the American people, especially those with conservative leanings, to the idea that America could oppose a Communist great power on many fronts and still deal with it on others. It is an idea that applies also to dealings with China in the 1990s and into the next century.

Not least, the "political" (that is, noncareer) senior officials who played large parts in the Nixon Administration and returned to service under Reagan and Bush were, in themselves, an important part of Nixon's influence and place in history. There was, in these years, a Republican foreign policy "establishment" somewhat comparable to the more bipartisan establishment of the 1950s and 1960s. Among its members, one in particular stood out: George Shultz, Reagan's Secretary of State from 1982 to 1989.

. . .

In his eulogy, Kissinger also credited the Nixon Administration with laying a foundation for American support of the European Security Conference and the human rights provisions of the Helsinki Accords of 1975. Here the historian is bound to gulp in disbelief: in the whole range of Nixon's writings there is hardly a favorable reference to human rights either as an ideal or as a practical force in international affairs.

Moreover, as the narrative has shown, Nixon was cool to frigid over the moves that led up to the 1975 Helsinki conference, and only tolerated it in exchange for Soviet willingness to discuss reduced conventional arms levels in Europe (MBFR), which in turn helped hold at bay the Mansfield Amendment to force such a reduction in U.S. forces. In particular he disliked the principal architect of this whole European policy, Willy Brandt of West Germany, and all his works. Yet Brandt's *Ostpolitik* not only was crucially important in an immediate way for Nixon's summer of triumph in 1972, but was the first time in the Cold War that a member of the core Western Alliance other than the United States took a major initiative. In fact, the Soviet–West Germany détente — shortly expanded to the Western Europe–Soviet détente of the Helsinki Accords — was the most solid structural change in international politics in the Nixon era. In terms of enduring effect, it was more important than the U.S. opening to China, not as important for the near future as the U.S.-Soviet détente, but more solid and "structural" than either.

It was also the beginning of a greater role for Western Europe, not only in controlling its own affairs, but — as Kissinger's eulogy accurately noted — in reaching out to Eastern Europe in ways that played a big part in the eventual ending of the Cold War in 1989–90. It should not be forgotten that the precipitating event for the Soviet decision to knock down the Berlin Wall in 1989 was the spreading influence of democratic elections in formerly Communist Poland, made possible by the evolution in Eastern Europe that flowed from the Helsinki Accords. To be sure, the United States under the Ford Administration supported those accords — and in later years American diplomats were in the forefront in using the famous Third Basket to put pressure on the Soviet Union over its internal denials of human rights — but they were a European idea to begin with.

. . .

In the whole course of the Cold War, the solidity of the Western Alliance (the United States, Western Europe, and Japan) provided both security assurance and constant economic cooperation. Over those forty years "the West" made solid gains and it was this great success — highlighting the failures of the Soviet system — that was the most important single cause for Soviet defeat and collapse from 1989 on. During the Nixon era, the Alliance was strained but in the end came back together. Long disapproval of American involvement in Indochina eased as American troops withdrew, although it was temporarily rekindled by the Christmas bombing at the end of 1972. Then the Middle East war and the effect of the Arab oil weapon on European behavior brought Alliance relations near to an all-time low. Yet again the effect was temporary. Common economic interests (aided by the European ties of George Shultz as Secretary of the Treasury) righted the ship, and the Alliance came back together under Ford (and Kissinger). Troubled as the Nixon era was, it highlighted the problems and led to new structures for consultation. As the end of the century approaches, the Alliance is more diffuse and much more focused on economic issues. But it remains the centerpiece of the international system.

In all this Japan was, as often, a special case, moving from strong dependence on the United States to a more independent posture. After the strains of 1969 and the twin "shokkus" of 1971, Japan might have been ready to move to close economic ties with China, diluting its participation in the Western economic system. When the Chinese once again showed their political instability under the radical Gang of Four, however, that possibility vanished and Japan stayed glued to the West. In time, the scars of the Nixon era healed after a fashion, but the trust built up in the Occupation and then in the 1950s and 1960s never came back. The handling of Japan was a clear negative entry in Nixon's record.

. . .

Perhaps the most important claim in Kissinger's eulogy was that in the Middle East the Nixon Administration inherited a stalemated and dangerous situation on the Arab-Israeli front and left to its successors an ongoing peace process. This claim has a high measure of validity. Obviously, the record of Nixon and Kissinger (after 1972 really Kissinger alone) was not one of steady or even progress. After the pivotal Jordan crisis of 1970 and the death of Nasser, the Americans were slow to size up the now key figure of Anwar el-Sadat, and in 1972 let their Vietnam preoccupations prevent earlier close contacts with him. Perhaps Sadat's highly sophisticated preparations for the 1973 War could have been grasped, and the war headed off — but more likely not. When the war came, it produced an American balancing act that was, on the whole, well handled. The cementing of ties to Sadat's Egypt was a major breakthrough by Kissinger, and his diplomacy through the troubled winter of 1973–74 produced a diplomatic revolution, with the moderate Arab nations stronger and above all much closer to the United States, and the radicals reduced and isolated. It was a major gain for both regional stability and American interests, as well as a setback for the Soviet Union.

At the end of the decade of the 1970s, revolution in Iran changed the Middle East balance in favor of the radicals — and this book has argued that Nixon's too close embrace of the Shah played a significant part in giving that revolution a sharply anti-American twist. Yet the relations formed in the Nixon era with moderate Arab nations, Egypt in particular, held up into the 1990s. As I write in 1997, the Arab-Israel conflict has again come into sharp focus over Palestinian issues, and the ties between America and Israel, strengthened in the Nixon era, remain central to U.S. policy. Neither the Arab-Israeli conflict nor the Middle East as a whole promises lasting peace or stability.

If history gives a generally favorable judgment of the Nixon Administration's political and military policies in the Middle East (with the large exception of Iran), I believe it must conclude that U.S. policy on the oil crisis—inevitably that of Nixon himself—was a disastrous failure of both will and skill. It showed again that Nixon could not build, or truly grasp economic factors. Since his time, oil discoveries (and more efficient use of energy, sometimes taken for granted) have made the energy problem seem less critical than it did in the early 1970s. But the enduring addiction of the American public to the automobile may still turn out to be one of the major headaches of the twenty-first century, in both economic and political terms. If this should be the case, the Nixon era may be seen as a time when great opportunities to change course existed, and were not seized.

Richard Nixon's way of thinking—with all its successes and failures, good and bad judgments—was formed by his times, though it lacked a crucial dimension of humanity and genuine cooperation with the international community as a whole. He was the archetype, perhaps even the caricature, of the Cold Warrior. Presiding over a time when the United States should have been moving out of the mold of the Cold War and into the era when local and regional crises were more important than superpower rivalry, and economic factors more influential than geopolitics at any level, he never made the leaps that history called for, on either front.

· · ·

Finally, the Nixon presidency contained fundamental lessons for the conduct of foreign policy in the American democratic system. Nixon and Kissinger were in many respects a strong foreign policy team. Their judgment was erratic and often subjective, and their vision too narrow. But they knew how to wield the levers of power and were capable of eloquent and effective presentations to the American public (and to audiences abroad). Yet they deceived that public, and especially Congress, far too often. Major defeats in Congress undermined and seriously weakened their détente policy with the Soviet Union, and finally forbade the military threats they planned in Indochina. These were not simply failures of tactics, but failures of trust brought on by years of neglect and deception. If there is any single lesson from the Nixon era that stands out above all others, it is that a pattern of deception, of Congress and of the American people, is in the end doomed to failure.

Chronology of Events

1968

January 31	North Vietnamese and Vietcong Tet offensive begins.
March 25	Wise Men advise President Lyndon Johnson against force increase or escalation in Vietnam; majority urge effort to negotiate.
March 31	Johnson orders partial bombing halt, limits additional troops, and announces that he will not run for reelection.
May 10	Talks on terms for complete bombing halt begin in Paris.
July 12	Nixon meets in New York with Anna Chennault and South Vietnamese Ambassador Bui Diem, and designates Chennault as his channel to President Nguyen Van Thieu of South Vietnam.
July 25–26	Johnson briefs Nixon and Democratic candidate Hubert Humphrey on status of Paris talks and U.S. position. Does so again on August 8, 10.
August 8	Nixon nominated at Republican convention in Miami.
August 29	Humphrey nominated by Democrats in Chicago.

Early October	Intensive negotiations with North Vietnamese in Paris over terms for complete bombing halt.
October 31	Johnson announces full bombing halt, with substantive peace talks to start in Paris.
November 2	Thieu announces South Vietnam will not attend peace talks.
November 5	Nixon elected President with 43.5 percent of popular vote.
Mid-November	South Vietnam agrees to join Paris peace talks, which finally commence in January 1969.
December 2	Nixon appoints Henry Kissinger National Security Advisor. Cabinet appointments announced.

1969

February 17	Nixon meets with Soviet Ambassador Anatoly Dobrynin and sets up private "channel" between him and Kissinger.
March	In tour of major European capitals, Nixon has special talks with French President Charles de Gaulle, who urges getting out of Vietnam and seeking relationship with China. Nixon sends message via French that he is interested.
March 2	Chinese and Soviet armed forces clash over an island in the Ussuri River, their border.
March 14	Nixon announces new antiballistic missile program (Safeguard).
March 15	Nixon approves program of "Vietnamization" and Defense Secretary Laird's plan to start withdrawing U.S. forces from Vietnam.
March 18	Nixon starts secret bombing of targets in Cambodia, partly to reinforce air threat against North Vietnam itself.
May 14	Nixon TV speech proposes that ultimate U.S. and North Vietnamese troop withdrawals be simultaneous.
June 8	Thieu, with Nixon at Midway, announces first withdrawal of 25,000 American troops.
July–August	Intense struggle in Congress ends with tie vote rejecting amendment to delete funds for new Safeguard program. Program goes ahead.

July 15	Nixon sends secret ultimatum to Ho Chi Minh threatening drastic measures if progress toward peace not achieved by November 1.
July 25	On Guam starting world trip, Nixon announces U.S. policy that threatened nations supply own manpower. Policy labeled Nixon Doctrine.
August	Kissinger meets secretly in Paris with Xuan Thuy, conveys ultimatum in blunt terms.
August–October	Nixon conveys to Soviets and to Romanian and Pakistani heads of government his ultimatum with November 1 deadline. Date passes without action.
September 3	Ho Chi Minh dies. No change in North Vietnamese policy or actions.
September 16	Nixon announces withdrawal of 35,000 more men as war pace slackens.
September 29	Willy Brandt and Social Democratic Party win West German elections, in coalition with Free Democratic Party. Brandt installed as Chancellor and Walter Scheel as Foreign Minister.
October 15	Big antiwar demonstration in Washington.
October 20	Soviet Union accepts U.S. proposal for Strategic Arms Limitation Talks (SALT I).
November 3	Nixon states Vietnam war policy on national TV, stressing Vietnamization, troop withdrawals, and negotiation. Appeals to "silent majority" of public. House overwhelmingly votes approval resolution, and majority of senators make supporting statements.
November 15	Another antiwar demonstration in Washington.
November 17–December 22	First round of SALT in Helsinki.
December	U.S. Ambassador in Warsaw makes contact with Chinese Ambassador to renew talks suspended in January 1969. Two sessions in January and February 1970 reach verge of agreement for U.S. emissary to go to Beijing.
December	After negotiations with Soviet representatives, State Department launches Rogers Plan outlining possible solution to Arab-Israeli conflict. Plan rejected by both sides.
December 15	Nixon announces third withdrawal of 50,000 troops.

1970

January	Brandt emissary, Egon Bahr, goes to Moscow for exploratory talks on a peace treaty with the Soviet Union.
January 7	Israel begins deep penetration bombing of Egypt; Nasser requests additional military help from Soviet Union.
February 20	Kissinger begins secret peace talks with Le Duc Tho, a senior North Vietnamese official.
March 18	Coup in Cambodia ousts Prince Norodom Sihanouk. Replaced by General Lon Nol and Prince Sirik Matak.
April 16–August 14	Second round of SALT in Vienna.
April 20	Nixon announces fourth withdrawal of 150,000 troops over the next year.
April 30	Nixon announces that American and South Vietnamese forces have attacked Communist sanctuaries in Cambodia. Sharp protests at home, especially in colleges. Members of Ohio National Guard kill four demonstrating students at Kent State University. China shortly cancels next session in Warsaw talks.
May–June	U.S. forces operate in border areas of Cambodia, capturing supplies but not finding predicted Communist headquarters.
June 30	Senate passes Cooper-Church Amendment, prohibiting U.S. combat activity in Cambodia. Nixon announces completion of withdrawal and states on TV that basis for continued U.S. force activity in Indochina is protection of U.S. forces in South Vietnam.
August	New Rogers Initiative leads to August 7 cease-fire on Egypt-Israel front, but situation remains tense.
August–October	United States detects evidence of Soviet Union planning to turn a small base at Cienfuegos in Cuba into a large submarine-supporting installation. United States protests vigorously and Soviet activity ceases. Soviets inquire whether apparent 1962 U.S. pledge not to attack Cuba remains in force. Diplomatic exchanges confirm pledge.
August 12	West German–Soviet Treaty signed, recognizing post-1945 German borders.
September	Palestinians in Jordan launch effort to throw out King Hussein. Extremists hijack four Western aircraft in Jordan. Syrian forces

briefly cross the border to assist Palestinians. King's forces regain control, as Syrians pull back from border, with U.S. and Israeli forces nearby.

September 4   In Chile, Salvador Allende Gossens wins plurality in presidential elections. Nixon initiates intense internal discussion of U.S. response.

September 28   Gamal Abdel Nasser dies; Anwar el-Sadat shortly becomes President of Egypt.

October   Nixon orders CIA Director Helms to mount all-out covert operation (Track II) to prevent Allende from taking office in Chile. Moderate Chilean general killed by officers in touch with CIA. Covert operation suspended.

October 7   Nixon announces "standstill cease-fire" plan for Vietnam, tacitly abandoning previous insistence that ultimate total withdrawal of U.S. forces be matched by parallel North Vietnamese withdrawal.

November 2   Third round of SALT resumes in Helsinki.

November 3   Congressional elections a setback for Nixon.

December   American troops in Vietnam down to 280,000.

December 8   Zhou Enlai sends handwritten note to Nixon, via Pakistan Ambassador, inviting a high-level American envoy to come to Beijing.

1971

February 8–
March 25   South Vietnamese troops attack military supply installations at head of Ho Chi Minh Trail in Laos (Operation Lam Son 719). Forced to withdraw in disarray.

March   Pakistan President Yahya Khan quells riots in East Pakistan, sending millions of refugees into neighboring India.

May 19   Mansfield Amendment to cut U.S. forces in Europe rejected by Senate after Brezhnev speech that Soviets will definitely engage in European conventional force reduction talks (MBFR).

May 20   Soviet-U.S. agreement to work to limit both ABM and offensive nuclear weapons announced, the result of back-channel negotiating by Kissinger.

June 13   *The New York Times* begins publishing the Pentagon Papers. Nixon seeks to prevent publication but is turned down by Supreme

Court. Initiates covert operation by White House "plumbers" to discredit Daniel Ellsberg, who gave papers to the *Times*.

July 8   SALT resumes in Helsinki through September.

July 15   On Kissinger's return from secret visit to China, Nixon announces Chinese invitation for him to visit China early in 1972. Reports make clear that Pakistan played major intermediary and supporting role.

August   India and Soviet Union sign Friendship Treaty in apparent reaction to new U.S.-Pakistan-China ties.

August 15   Nixon suspends convertibility of the dollar into gold, ending U.S. leadership in the Bretton Woods system. Negotiations over new exchange-rate structure continue through the fall.

September 3 Quadripartite Agreement on Berlin signed.

October 3   Thieu reelected as President in South Vietnam.

Mid-October Second Kissinger visit to Beijing works out arrangements for 1972 Nixon visit and draft communiqué for that occasion.

October 25   United Nations votes to recognize the People's Republic as the official "China" in both Security Council and General Assembly.

November 4–5 Indira Gandhi visits Washington to discuss the Indo-Pakistan crisis. Meeting goes badly.

November 15 SALT reconvenes in Vienna through January.

December   American troops in Vietnam down to 140,000.

December 3   Fighting breaks out along western India-Pakistan border, as Pakistan sends large forces to pacify turbulent East Pakistan.

December 8   United States suspends economic aid to India and criticizes India as aggressor at United Nations.

December 10 Nixon orders powerful naval task force into Strait of Malacca en route to Indian Ocean and possibly Bay of Bengal.

December 15 India agrees to cease-fire offer from East Pakistan.

December 16 Exchange-rate agreement reached at Smithsonian Institution in Washington. Dollar devalued by about 10 percent.

December 17	Pakistani forces surrender in the East, ending the Indo-Pakistan war. Bangladesh promptly created, breaking away from Pakistan.

1972

January 25	In major televised speech, Nixon reveals Kissinger's secret negotiations with North Vietnam since 1969. Says that the United States is prepared for a cease-fire and for withdrawal of U.S. forces in return for release of U.S. POWs, but continues to insist that North Vietnam accept Thieu regime.
February 21–27	Nixon visits China. Enormous publicity and a communiqué in which each side states its views on disputed issues.
March 30	North Vietnam launches Easter offensive into South Vietnam northern province of Quang Tri, with parallel attacks in highlands.
April 13	Senate passes Javits bill limiting President's war powers.
April 15	Nixon authorizes bombing of Hanoi and Haiphong.
April 27	Brandt survives "no confidence" motion in Bundestag.
May 1	Quang Tri falls to North Vietnamese.
May 8	Nixon orders mining of Haiphong Harbor.
May 10	Bundestag votes to approve Soviet and Polish treaties recognizing postwar borders.
May 22–29	Moscow summit. SALT I Treaty and Interim Agreement signed May 26.
May 29–30	Nixon visits Teheran on way home. Agrees that Shah may purchase U.S. weapons as he chooses. Also agrees for CIA to assist Iran in supporting Kurdish autonomy movement (confirmed in June).
June	With triumphs in Moscow and Beijing, Nixon at peak of prestige and political strength.
June 17	Five men arrested for break-in at Democratic National Committee offices in Watergate complex in Washington. White House and Nixon reelection organization (CRP) deny any connection and call it unauthorized "third-rate burglary."
July	American companies complete first large sales of grain to Soviet Union. Others follow during summer, without announcement.

July 18   Sadat evicts Soviet military presence from Egypt.

July 19   Kissinger resumes secret meetings with Le Duc Tho in Paris.

August   Another 10,000 American soldiers return from Vietnam, leaving about 39,000.

August   Kissinger meets in Saigon with Thieu, who rejects U.S. position on key points despite earlier apparent acceptance. Haig also visits without success.

August 14   Kissinger and Le Duc Tho meet secretly again in Paris.

September 14   Jackson Amendment to SALT I agreements approved by Senate, requiring "essential equivalence" in future agreements on offensive weapons.

September 16   South Vietnamese troops recapture Quang Tri.

September 26–27 Le Duc Tho resumes Paris talks with Kissinger.

September 30   Nixon signs SALT I agreements. In Rose Garden talk with Jackson, Nixon agrees to give him effective veto over future arms control appointments; also indicates no objection to Jackson's attaching emigration conditions to Senate action on Soviet trade agreement.

October 4   Jackson Amendment linking American-Soviet trade to relaxed Soviet emigration introduced in Senate.

October 8–12   Kissinger and Le Duc Tho reach draft agreement, after four intense final days of negotiation. Kissinger returns to Washington to prepare for visit to Saigon to get Thieu's concurrence. Text available only in English and no copy or translation sent ahead to Saigon.

October 19–23   Kissinger visits Saigon, but Thieu digs in against draft agreement. On October 23, pursuant to earlier Kissinger promise to North Vietnamese, bombing of North Vietnam ceases. United States proceeds with massive Enhance Plus program of arms deliveries to South Vietnam, supplementing earlier Enhance program to replace equipment and supplies expended in beating back North Vietnamese offensive.

October 26   Despite Thieu's attitude, Kissinger announces at a Washington press conference that "peace is at hand."

November 7   Nixon reelected in landslide.

November 20–25   Kissinger resumes talks with Le Duc Tho, presenting without success a long list of amendments urged by Thieu.

December 4–13	More peace talks in Paris, ending with an impasse.
December 14	Kissinger threatens Hanoi with "grave consequences" if negotiations not resumed in seventy-two hours.
December 18	Nixon orders Christmas bombings of Hanoi and Haiphong, which continue through December 29.

1973

January 8	Peace talks resume in Paris.
January 23	Kissinger and Le Duc Tho sign initial agreement.
January 27	United States and North Vietnam, with South Vietnam and Vietcong (NLF), sign Paris Agreement for cease-fires and provisions to preserve the peace. Cease-fires come into effect in South Vietnam, North Vietnam, and Laos.
February	Nixon resumes bombing of Cambodia, without announcement, on basis that North Vietnamese have not made proper effort for cease-fire there. In next four months, United States drops over 80,000 tons of bombs over Cambodia.
February 15–19	Kissinger meets with Zhou Enlai in Beijing, at end of visit to several Southeast Asian capitals.
March 28–29	Last American POWs released in Hanoi.
March 29	Last American troops leave Vietnam.
March 30	Press reports that James McCord, one of Watergate burglars, has admitted to Federal Judge John Sirica that senior White House officials were involved in the break-in. Other revelations rapidly follow.
April 2–3	Thieu visits Nixon at San Clemente.
April 5	Senate votes to ban economic aid funds for North Vietnam unless specifically approved by Congress.
April 17	Nixon makes first public statement about Watergate.
April 18	White House sends energy message to Congress.
April 23	Kissinger major speech declares 1973 to be the "Year of Europe." Proposes new Atlantic Charter.

April 30	Nixon aides H. R. Haldeman, John Ehrlichman, and John Dean and Attorney General Richard Kleindienst resign following their implication in Watergate break-ins and cover-up.
May 10	House votes to cut off funds for military activities in Cambodia after June 30.
May 17	Ervin Committee begins televised Watergate hearings about break-ins and cover-up.
May 31	Senate votes to cut off funds for operations in Cambodia and Laos after June 30.
June 17–25	Leonid Brezhnev meets with Nixon in Washington and San Clemente for second summit. Makes intense private appeal for new peace effort in Middle East.
June 25	Former White House counsel John Dean testifies to Ervin Committee that he discussed Watergate cover-up with Nixon.
June 26	Nixon vetoes appropriation bill containing ban on future military operation in Indochina. Senator Mansfield says he will block all appropriation bills if Nixon does not yield.
June 29	Nixon accepts ban on military activities in Southeast Asia after August 15.
July	Discussions on European security (CSCE) begin in Helsinki.
July 16	1969–70 secret bombing in Cambodia revealed to Congress in confirmation hearings for new Air Force Chief of Staff.
July 18	House passes a war powers bill.
July 20	Senate passes a war powers bill.
August	Sadat meets secretly with King Faisal in Riyadh; gets Saudi support for war against Israel and agreement to use oil weapon for pressure on United States and other nations.
August 15	U.S. halts bombing in Cambodia, in accordance with Congress's prohibition.
August 22	Nixon announces appointment of Kissinger as Secretary of State, succeeding William Rogers. Senate Foreign Relations Committee holds hearings and confirms appointment, which takes effect September 22.

September 11	President Allende of Chile assassinated in coup. General Augusto Pinochet assumes power.
October 6	Sadat attacks Israel, launching October War (October 6–28).
October 10	Vice President Spiro Agnew resigns after revelations of bribery. Replaced by Gerald Ford, who is confirmed in December.
October 12	Court of Appeals upholds Judge Sirica's decision that selected White House tapes must be released to Special Prosecutor Archibald Cox. Attorney General Richardson attempts to work out compromise with Alexander Haig, on behalf of Nixon, but effort breaks down over Haig demand that Cox ask for no further tapes.
October 14	American supplies and weapons arrive in Israel.
October 16	Gulf oil states announce 70 percent increase in oil prices.
October 20	Arab oil-producing countries order embargo on oil shipments to United States and other nations supporting Israel.
October 20	"Saturday Night Massacre." Richardson and his deputy, William Ruckelshaus, refuse to carry out Nixon's order to fire Cox, and resign along with Cox, whose offices are sealed by the FBI on Nixon's orders. Storm of protest all over the country, with great pressure on Nixon to appoint at once a successor Special Prosecutor. Early the next week he selects (on Bar advice) Leon Jaworski, a top Houston trial lawyer.
October 21	Kissinger meets with Brezhnev in Moscow; the two agree to a cease-fire, but Israel, not consulted or informed at once, disregards the cease-fire for nearly two days and encircles the Egyptian Third Army near the Suez Canal.
October 24–25	With Nixon out of action over Watergate, Kissinger rejects Soviet proposal for joint Soviet-American force to impose and police cease-fire. In harsh message, Brezhnev threatens to go ahead anyway. Kissinger convenes rump NSC meeting without Nixon, and group agrees to alert U.S. forces worldwide. Alert ordered about midnight, and evident by morning of the 25th.
October 25	Soviets modify proposal to exclude both U.S. and Soviet forces from monitoring cease-fire. Alert ended. Parties proceed to preliminary cease-fire on October 28.
November 6–8	Kissinger meets with Sadat in Cairo.
November 7	Congress overrides Nixon's veto of the War Powers Act.

November 7	Nixon delivers televised energy speech stressing development of American resources as key to problem. Sets goal of "energy independence" by 1980.
November 10–14	Kissinger visits Beijing, at end of ten-nation trip devoted primarily to explaining U.S. Middle East and oil policy. Visit climaxed by long talk with Mao Zedong.
December	Oil-producing countries (OPEC), led by Iran, impose drastic price rise from $5.12 to $11.65 a barrel, a nearly fourfold increase since September.
December 21–22	Geneva Conference on the Middle East meets for a day to hear speeches, then adjourns, leaving principal parties, Egypt and Israel, to ask for help from other nations. Kissinger had already arranged that both would turn only to United States.

1974

January 17	Disengagement agreement completed between Egypt and Israel, after dramatic Kissinger shuttle in last days.
February 6	House formally authorizes its Judiciary Committee to proceed with consideration of possible articles of impeachment against Nixon.
February 11–13	Washington Energy Conference sets up International Energy Agency but avoids commitments or adversary posture toward oil-producing countries.
February 25	Nixon declares the energy crisis over.
March 1	Grand jury indicts John Mitchell, Haldeman, and Ehrlichman for obstruction of justice. Names Nixon as "unindicted co-conspirator"; this withheld from public knowledge but revealed to Jaworski.
March 18	Oil embargo lifted.
April 30	Yitzhak Rabin succeeds Golda Meir as Prime Minister of Israel.
April 30	In lieu of supplying requested tapes to Judiciary Committee and Jaworski, White House releases edited transcripts. Effort backfires when tapes prove to include rough language by Nixon.
May 9	House Judiciary Committee starts to hear from counsel John Doar a full summary of evidence concerning Nixon, preparatory to considering articles of impeachment. On same day, Judge Sirica ap-

proves Jaworski request for 64 tapes bearing on cover-up; White House appeals ruling direct to Supreme Court.

May 29 — Disengagement agreement between Syria and Israel reached after several weeks of shuttle diplomacy by Kissinger.

June 10–19 — Nixon visits Middle East, with tremendous reception in Cairo.

June 27–July 3 — Third Nixon-Brezhnev summit. No major new agreements. Meeting highlighted by strenuous Brezhnev effort to enlist Nixon against China through a Soviet-American nonaggression agreement. Effort sidetracked by Kissinger. At close of meeting, he makes impassioned statement to press, questioning value of "strategic superiority" in nuclear weapons.

July 24 — Supreme Court upholds Judge Sirica's May 9 order for release of tapes, 8–0, with opinion by Chief Justice Burger affirming doctrine of "executive privilege" but concluding it cannot prevail against subpoena seeking evidence relating to criminal conduct by President or other senior officials.

July 26–27 — House Judiciary Committee approves three articles of impeachment, those concerning obstruction of justice, abuse of power, and noncompliance with a congressional subpoena. Rejects proposed fourth article based on Nixon's secret bombing of Cambodia in 1969–70.

August 7–9 — With multiple advice that Senate would vote impeachment, Nixon yields and resigns, effective noon on August 9. Gerald Ford sworn in.

September–October — Ford tries in vain to restore military aid level for South Vietnam.

November 23–24 — Ford meets with Brezhnev in Vladivostok. Reaches tentative agreement on overall numbers of strategic nuclear weapons.

December — Congress passes Trade Reform Act with Jackson-Vanik Amendment linking Soviet trade status to much more liberal emigration policy. Politburo indignantly rejects trade agreement.

1975

January 6 — North Vietnamese forces capture provincial capital Phuoc Binh.

January 28 — Ford asks Congress for emergency aid for Cambodia. No response.

February — Haig urges Ford to resume bombing of North Vietnam; Ford declines.

March 25	North Vietnamese capture Hue.
March 30	North Vietnamese capture Danang.
April 8	Nixon's secret pledges of support to Thieu revealed to Congress.
April 10	Ford asks Congress for aid to South Vietnam. Stony reception.
April 12	Evacuation of Americans from Cambodia.
April 17	Khmer Rouge captures Phnom Penh.
April 21	Thieu abdicates.
April 29–30	American evacuation of Saigon.
April 30	Communists capture Saigon.
July 30–August 1	Helsinki conference on European cooperation and security.

Notes

Chapter 1. An Hour and a Man

1. For the Herter Committee experience, see Nixon, *RN*, 48–52; Ambrose, *Nixon: The Education*, 154–57; Parmet, *Richard Nixon*, 299–303. As an indication of how Nixon was then regarded, at a small Washington dinner in the spring of 1948 another promising young congressman, John F. Kennedy of Massachusetts, held forth to my wife on the realism and keen mind of Nixon as a particular example of what Congress needed.

2. Ambrose, *Nixon: The Education*, 154–57.

3. What Acheson said had been put publicly in almost exactly the same terms a year earlier by General MacArthur, then the U.S. proconsul in Japan and senior military officer in Asia. See Parmet, *Richard Nixon*, 308.

4. *Congressional Record,* 82nd Cong., 1st sess., April 11, 1951, 3655.

5. Ambrose, *Nixon: The Education*, 239–40.

6. In Nixon's memoirs, there is only one reference to MacArthur, in another connection. Nixon, *RN*, 238.

7. From 1953 to 1956 I regularly attended twice-weekly NSC Planning Board sessions. At one of these sessions, discussions within the NSC itself that morning were reported orally, with what seemed considerable fullness and candor. The interventions of the Vice President were frequently reported at these sessions.

As Nixon himself recounts (*RN*, 139–40), he was also involved when I came under attack from Senator Joseph McCarthy in July 1953 for having contributed money to the lawyers conducting the legal defense of Alger Hiss. Nixon says he defended me because he had seen me at meetings of the National Security Council; I do not recall ever attending such a meeting in that period, and suppose that General Walter Bedell Smith and Allen Dulles, successive Directors of Central Intelligence, vouched for me on the basis of the extensive CIA inquiry that had been conducted prior to my joining the Agency. I had contributed to the fund not because I knew Alger Hiss well, nor because I had reached any conclusion as to his guilt or innocence, but simply because he obviously needed a good lawyer and did not have the funds to pay for one. I also felt it was of major public importance to ascertain whether he or his accuser, Whittaker Chambers, was telling the truth.

8. Eisenhower, *Mandate for Change*, 181.

9. It is debatable whether the 1953 coup was indeed a long-term success. But it was so perceived at the time.

10. Nixon, *RN*, 125.

11. Berger served with special distinction as Ambassador to South Korea in the early 1960s. In 1968 he was moved to the equally senior post of Deputy Ambassador in South Vietnam, where he remained for four years.

12. *The Gallup Poll, 1935–1971*, 1235.

13. I base these views on two trips to South Vietnam, in 1956 and especially in 1958, as well as on the cable traffic and talks with my colleagues in the CIA and in the intelligence community.

14. Ambrose, *Nixon: The Education*, 346.

15. Ambrose, *Nixon: The Education*, 590.

16. Nixon thought that Allen Dulles must have secretly briefed Kennedy, but Dulles finally reassured him that he had not done so. Grose, *Gentleman Spy*, 508–9; Reeves, *President Kennedy*, 69–70.

17. See Rusk, *As I Saw It*, 428; Clifford, *Counsel to the President*, 343–44. General Andrew Goodpaster, one participant in the meeting, understood Eisenhower's remarks differently. I have not tried to sort out the controversy, which did not concern Nixon, but suspect there will never be a clear answer.

18. The memoir quote is in Nixon, *RN*, 256.

19. Ambrose, *Nixon: The Triumph*, 30–31.

20. Ambrose, *Nixon: The Triumph*, 48.

21. Ambrose, *Nixon: The Triumph*, 43–50.

22. Ambrose, *Nixon: The Triumph*, 76. In the same television appearance, however, he dismissed fears of "a fourth-rate military power." By 1967 he seems to have changed that view, probably in light of the Chinese development of a nuclear capability.

23. Ambrose, *Nixon: The Triumph*, 68–69, 77.

24. Ambrose, *Nixon: The Triumph*, 91.

25. Nixon, *RN*, 274–75.

26. Nixon, "Asia After Viet Nam," *Foreign Affairs*, October 1967: 111–25.

27. Nixon, "Asia After Viet Nam," 117. The conventional view at the time was that China had been the aggressor in that brief and indecisive conflict. Later evidence compiled by Kenneth Maxwell, however, indicated that there had been substantial provocation on the Indian side. Maxwell, *India's China War*, passim.

28. Nixon, "Asia After Viet Nam," 119.

29. Nixon, "Asia After Viet Nam," 121.

30. Nixon, "Asia After Viet Nam," 123. Emphasis added.

31. For example, in a major speech I made in August 1967: "We [the Johnson Administration] knew, as we have always known, that the action against South Viet-Nam reflected deeply held ambitions by Hanoi . . . and that Hanoi needed and wanted only Chinese aid to this end and wished to be its own master. And we knew, as again we always have, that North Viet-Nam would resist any Communist Chinese trespassing

on areas it controlled." "The Path to Viet-Nam," in Falk, ed., *The Vietnam War and International Law*, vol. 2, 22.

32. For some time, influential segments of American opinion had felt the need to reach out to China at the appropriate time. In the early 1960s the Council on Foreign Relations produced a series of books designed to focus the discussion on future possibilities. The final book in this series, A. Doak Barnett's *Communist China and Asia: Challenge to American Policy*, was much more in favor of early reconciliation than Nixon's article in *Foreign Affairs*.

33. Nixon, *RN*, 289. Ambrose, *Nixon: The Triumph*, 104, 129, seems to me misleading in suggesting that in 1967 LBJ was doing just what Nixon would have done. Almost certainly Nixon would have hit harder.

34. Ambrose, *Nixon: The Triumph*, 129.

35. White, *Making of the President 1968*, 148.

36. *The Gallup Poll*, 2109: 49 percent of Americans felt getting into the war had been a mistake; 41 percent did not; and the rest were undecided. For the change of heart of the bipartisan group, see Isaacson and Thomas, *The Wise Men*, 697–703. In another striking change of position, Senator Henry Jackson of Washington joined with Senator Richard Russell in resisting major force increases. Both believed that the U.S. role in the war simply had to be wound down. Fosdick, *Staying the Course*, 76.

37. Ambrose, *Nixon: The Triumph*, 142.

38. Nixon, *RN*, 305.

39. This was reported and discussed in a meeting held by President Johnson with his close advisors on May 8, 1968. The record is in the notes of the meeting by Tom Johnson of the President's staff—hereafter called "Tom Johnson Notes"—1, 3. These notes are valuable and in good order in the LBJ Library.

40. This formula grew out of an effort initiated and conducted by Henry Kissinger, who met two Frenchmen with possible ties to Ho Chi Minh at an international conference and found them responsive and apparently well connected in Hanoi. The government gave Kissinger authority to proceed with the new formula, which abandoned insistence on an advance understanding. Unfortunately, what seemed for a time a highly promising effort got nowhere by late September, after a last phase in which I was the official contact with Kissinger. Johnson then decided to state the new position himself, which he did at San Antonio.

41. The key point of Thieu's prior concurrence is firmly stated in the memoir of the South Vietnamese Ambassador in Washington, Bui Diem, *In the Jaws of History*, 239, but is omitted in the Thieu-serving account in Hung and Schecter, *Palace File*.

42. Solberg, *Hubert Humphrey*, 347–48. The reported tone of this unpleasant exchange did no credit to Johnson. Yet he had a point. In Paris he was trying to deal as firmly as possible with a tough negotiating adversary; to have his Vice President, the man whose presidential campaign he was supporting, take a softer line in public than did Johnson in private presented inescapable problems.

43. Nixon, *RN*, 307–8. Nixon did refer to Johnson's San Antonio speech, so he must have been familiar with the "not take advantage" formula. Tom Johnson Notes, July 26, 1968, 10.

44. The full text of Nixon's statement is in *New York Times*, August 2, 1968, 16.

45. *New York Times*, August 4, 1968, 52–53.

46. *New York Times*, August 5, 1968, story on 1, 24; text of Vietnam plank on 26.

47. Nixon's references, or lack of them, to China during the 1968 campaign are a

teasing subject. Theodore White's 1969 account of the campaign told of a private talk with Nixon in March 1968, in which Nixon said that "the very first thing he'd do [if elected President] would be to try to get in touch with Red China. There had to be an understanding with Red China. In ten or fifteen years it would be impossible to run the world if Red China weren't part of it." White, *Making of the President 1968*, 148. On the same lines, Edward Cox, Nixon's son-in-law, recalled in 1996 that Nixon told him in October 1968 (and Harrison Salisbury of *The New York Times* separately) that "the ultimate solution lay in Peking and Moscow, which he would visit in that order." Nixon felt, however, that going public would spoil the idea. *New York Times*, March 18, 1996, A14.

48. Ambrose, *Nixon: The Triumph*, 149, 154, 167–68, is sharply critical of Nixon for failing to frame clear issues for the campaign by saying exactly what he proposed to do about Vietnam and thus enabling the American people to vote unmistakably for a Vietnam policy. Such frustration was, however, seldom voiced during the campaign by serious political observers. There were far too many variables and contingencies — not only the Paris talks but whether there would be renewed North Vietnamese offensives and how the South Vietnamese shaped up during the year.

49. Tom Johnson's notes of the August 10 meeting at the LBJ Ranch refer specifically to "your side–our side" on p. 5, and on p. 3 the notes start to summarize Vance's presentation, apparently on military restraint, but then break off. Vance's recollection (interview with the author, April 1, 1991, with the notes before him) may be the best evidence available. What is clear, in this and many other references to the representation problem, is that the Americans involved never thought the exact status of the NLF at the table presented a serious problem — and that Nixon himself never raised questions about it.

50. Solberg, *Hubert Humphrey*, 349–50. At this meeting LBJ did not tell Humphrey what was afoot on the Soviet front. He seems to have been much more candid with Nixon on this. He did say that he hoped Hanoi might make some move soon, perhaps having Soviet influence in mind, but on August 18 told Humphrey this hope had vanished.

51. Plank and its origin in *New York Times*, August 21, 1968, 1, 33; August 24, 1968, 2, 19. The language about a new political structure in South Vietnam avoided the term "coalition government," but this was its sense.

52. Ambrose, *Nixon: The Triumph*, 177, 183.

53. Nixon, *RN*, 327–30.

54. Bunker's reports from August 22 to October 19, 1968, describe the failure of the "third offensive" and the improved military situation as he and the American mission saw it. Pike, ed., *The Bunker Papers*, 540, 547, 556, 563, 571, 589, 602 (review of the third quarter).

55. According to Dobrynin, "no such policy was ever proclaimed or even mentioned at Politburo meetings, but the determination never to let a socialist country slip back into the orbit of the West was in essence a true reflection of the sentiments of those who ran the Soviet Union." Dobrynin, *In Confidence*, 183.

56. Rostow-Smith Chronology, 1. This compilation was prepared in November, by Walt Rostow and Bromley Smith of the NSC staff, for Johnson's use in reviewing the record with Nixon when they met after the election. Another chronology was done at the same time by General Robert Ginsburgh of the NSC staff.

57. White, *Making of the President 1968*, 355; Ball, *The Past Has Another Pattern*, 445–47.

58. This visit is noted in several accounts. The fullest, with a slightly garbled text of the exact message, is in the Ginsburgh Chronology, 4–5, LBJ Library.

59. Christian, *The President Steps Down*, 52.

60. Tom Johnson Notes, October 14, 1968, 11–12.

61. Christian, *The President Steps Down*, 51.

62. Tom Johnson Notes, October 14, 1968, 23–25.

63. Christian, *The President Steps Down*, 55, 57.

64. Christian, *The President Steps Down*, 60.

65. Nixon, *RN*, 325. By Christian's account, *The President Steps Down*, 61, from listening in on the conversation with other key advisors on a loudspeaker arrangement, Nixon said: "I'll make no statement that will undercut the negotiations and we'll just stay right on that, and hope that this thing works out." The sense of both versions seems the same.

66. White, *Making of the President 1968*, 356–76, is excellent on trends in the campaign in October.

67. Christian, *The President Steps Down*, 104. Clifford, *Counsel to the President*, 593, has slightly different wording but the same sense. Both men were present during the call. Nixon recalled in his memoirs that Johnson made clear that South Vietnam had not yet agreed to participate in the talks and was not joining in the announcement that evening. Nixon, *RN*, 322.

68. White, *Making of the President 1968*, 381. Wicker, *One of Us*, 378–79, describes the reaction of Nixon campaign officials as "horrified."

69. Witcover, *Resurrection of Richard Nixon*, 431–42.

70. Powers, *Man Who Kept the Secrets*, 197–200.

71. Chennault and Bui Diem have given compatible accounts of what took place at the meeting, differing only on the date. Chennault says there was "snow in the air" and Bui Diem names July 12 firmly. Catherine Forslund's recent dissertation on Chennault, "Woman of Two Worlds," using her subject's datebook, concludes that there was a first meeting, also in New York, on February 16. (Forslund is also my source for the earlier relations between Chennault and Thieu.) Even if this was only a brief introduction of the parties, it is striking evidence of Nixon's meticulous advance planning.

72. Safire, *Before the Fall*, 88–91, recites communications from Chennault to Nixon in late June suggesting a meeting with Bui Diem, then gives the text of a July 3 memo from Richard Allen to Nixon urging such a meeting on an "absolute top secret" basis, with Nixon's personal annotation that it was hard to see how a meeting could meet that condition, in view of his Secret Service escort. So, Safire says, Allen dropped the idea. One can only conclude that both he and Allen were deliberately kept in the dark by Nixon, who found some other channel to set up the meeting. Safire was simply uninformed on the whole episode.

73. I have no reason to believe that she was ever directly on the Agency's payroll. As a CIA estimator in the 1950s, I had no contact with her; in the 1960s I saw her occasionally at large social functions and on one semi-official occasion, the small New York funeral of a respected Chinese (Nationalist) Ambassador to the United States and the United Nations. After that funeral I flew back to Washington with her and with her constant escort, Thomas Corcoran, whom I also knew socially. Our relations were easy and friendly, never close.

74. Chennault, *Education of Anna*, 173–74.

75. Chennault, *Education of Anna*, 176; Bui Diem, *In the Jaws of History*, 237.

76. Chennault, *Education of Anna*, 184.

77. This was the effort code-named PENNSYLVANIA. I followed it closely and was at one period the contact with Kissinger.

78. Nixon, *RN*, 323.

79. Nixon, *RN*, 323.

80. Hersh's principal source was apparently Richard Allen, a member of the Nixon entourage in New York but not in the inner circle privy to the Chennault meeting. By the early 1980s, when he talked to Hersh—indeed within the first months of the Nixon Administration—Allen had reason to be envious and resentful of Kissinger for having replaced him and eased him out of the Nixon structure. This animus may well have contributed to his statements.

Allen may be the original source of another Hersh item, that Kissinger talked on the phone to someone in the Paris delegation on the morning of October 31 and learned that the delegation was "breaking out the champagne" to celebrate an agreement to stop the bombing. This is plausible, but hardly crucial inside information. If it reached Nixon, it would have been at almost the same time he got Johnson's phone call stating his plans for an announcement that evening.

81. My conclusion that Kissinger did not convey inside information to the Nixon camp does not rule out the possibility that he said or hinted that his advice was based on his contacts with the Paris delegation. This sort of self-promotion, while unattractive, is at worst a minor and not uncommon practice, quite different from getting and reporting real secrets.

82. Powers, *Man Who Kept the Secrets*, 197–98. Chennault may also have acted through Thieu's brother, Nguyen Van Kieu, in Taiwan, who came down to Saigon shortly after October 15 and pulled out all the stops with various leaders about the dangers of going along with the halt and new negotiations. See my 1969 Oral History for the LBJ Library, Tape 5, p. 5, done when my memory was fresh.

83. Chennault, *Education of Anna*, 186, confirmed in an interview in 1996, in which she belittled the role of Bui Diem in the link. How she communicated with Thieu is not clear: it could have been by phone or perhaps via Ambassador Kieu or Chennault's sister in Saigon. I know no evidence she was physically in Saigon in these two weeks.

84. Chennault, *Education of Anna*, 186.

85. Chennault, *Education of Anna*, 190–91. In her account, Chennault noted that in placing the call to Mitchell she asked her escort, Thomas Corcoran, an experienced lawyer, to listen in on the call to be sure she had corroboration of what was said. His notes must have been the basis for her unusually full account of the talk.

86. Bui Diem, *In the Jaws of History*, 239–45. In this summary he also recounted a meeting with me on October 30 in my office, at which I expressed indignation over his contacts with "the Nixon camp" and he defended himself by claiming that these were normal. My appointment book confirms a meeting that morning, but I have no recollection of the conversation.

87. The notes of Johnson's meetings suggest that the report containing or describing "the cables" was received about 6 a.m. on the 29th in Washington, after the long early morning meeting with General Abrams.

88. Notes of Benjamin H. Read, then Executive Secretary of the Department of State, conveyed to me in 1992. Other sources corroborate this summary: see Powers, *Man Who Kept the Secrets*, 197–200, for the best account of what the FBI and the National Security Agency did and why.

89. Just which lines the FBI tapped (the South Vietnamese embassy's and/or Chennault's) was the subject of some confusion to the Senate Select Committee on Intelligence Activities (the Church Commitee) in 1975. Senior FBI officer Cartha DeLoach testified at the hearings (vol. 6, 164–95) that both lines were tapped but later (Church Comittee Final Report, Book II, 228n) said that Chennault's line was not, the view accepted by Powers, *Man Who Kept the Secrets*, 198–99. In a 1988 interview with me, however, DeLoach confirmed that the FBI had tapped both lines on national security grounds (at the request of the Attorney General).

From this evidence it seems clear that the FBI was finally persuaded that her activities could well fall within the Trading with the Enemy Act and the Neutrality Act. Certainly, evidence of interference by a private citizen with an ongoing negotiation by the American government justified intelligence activity to find out what was going on, which had a clear and direct connection to national security.

In later years William Safire attempted to argue that the taps were an interference with Chennault's free speech rights, and H. R. Haldeman drew a parallel between the taps authorized by Johnson and the Watergate break-in, claiming that the former were as "political" as the latter. Both arguments ring hollow: the latter was spurned by the Watergate committees without serious argument. Safire, *Before the Fall*, 90; Haldeman, *The Ends of Power*, 79–81. See also an exchange between Safire and me, *New York Times*, May 23, 1991 (Op-Ed page), and June 13, 1991, A28.

90. Powers, *Man Who Kept the Secrets*, 199.

91. Clifford, *Counsel to the President*, 383–84; Rusk, *As I Saw It*, 488–90.

92. Solberg, *Hubert Humphrey*, 194–98, supplemented by James H. Rowe's Oral History at the LBJ Library, Tape IV, 20–21. Solberg also gives an accurate account of a meeting between Humphrey and me on Sunday morning, November 3, at which I summarized the intelligence information (using what I had been told, since I never saw the actual messages). I advised against going public.

Max Kampelman, a long-standing close friend of Humphrey, has suggested an additional reason for Humphrey to hold his fire. In a 1996 interview, he reported that on that Saturday night he passed on to Humphrey a message from the pollster Lou Harris that Humphrey had made striking gains, passing Nixon, and was sure to win if the trend stayed as it was. According to Kampelman, Johnson and Humphrey each thought the other should make the decision about whether to go public. For what it is worth, I believe Johnson had to make the call: only he, as President, could take responsibility for the disclosure of intelligence reports, which he would need in order to be convincing.

Kampelman also believes (and I agree) that Nixon's denial and crocodile tears probably were what turned the election around. At the time, and when I did an Oral History interview for the LBJ Library in 1969, I believed that Nixon had not been personally involved, partly (as I recall arguing to Humphrey's staff) because he knew that Johnson was likely to pick up what was going on. Obviously, I was wrong. See William P. Bundy, Oral History, Tape 5, 1–5, LBJ Library.

93. White, *Making of the President 1968*, 381; Witcover, *Resurrection of Richard Nixon*, 441.

94. White, *Making of the President 1968*, 381; Witcover, *Resurrection of Richard Nixon*, 441.

95. Nixon, *RN*, 327.

96. Chennault, *Education of Anna*, 193–98.

97. *Washington Post*, February 18, 1981, M2. Emphasis added.

98. George Carver, special assistant for Vietnam matters to CIA Director Richard Helms and thus privy to the intercepted cables, later claimed to have argued that "Saigon did not need a deal with Nixon in order to resist the agreement Johnson was pushing. Thieu thought he was being sold down the river, and if Carver had been in Thieu's position, he would have felt the same way." Powers, *Man Who Kept the Secrets*, 198. However, in light of the extremely tight compartmentalization of information throughout October, Carver may well not have known about Thieu's concurrence of October 14 with Bunker and Abrams.

99. Cable reprinted in Pike, ed., *The Bunker Papers*, vol. 3, 643–44.

100. Bunker would not, in the normal course, have been informed of the intercepts or FBI material, nor did he or anyone in the Administration then know of Nixon's key role.

101. Hung and Schecter, *Palace File*, 21, confirmed by later interviews between the authors and Thieu.

102. Hung and Schecter, *Palace File*, 21, based on long conversations with Thieu. The authors noted that Thieu's pride and reserve kept him from ever referring to the debt in his dealings with Nixon.

103. Bui Diem, *In the Jaws of History*, 245–46.

104. Tom Johnson Notes, November 7, 1968, 3. These mention both Dirksen and the possibility of using Bui Diem as the messenger to Thieu.

105. After the Inauguration, Nixon had Haldeman dig out all the records of intelligence information on the subject. He did so and reported that the material did not directly implicate Nixon. Parmet, *Richard Nixon*, 522–23, based on a 1985 interview with Haldeman. In the same interview, Haldeman said he thought Nixon had been indiscreet to meet with Chennault and Bui Diem.

106. Tom Johnson Notes, November 11, 1968.

107. Nixon's account of the meeting is in *RN*, 337.

108. Quoted in Johnson, *Vantage Point*, 556.

109. Hung and Schecter, *Palace File*, 29.

110. Such a dispute, ridiculous as it may seem, was not without earlier and later parallels. I recall a similar dispute over the status of East and West Germany at a Geneva conference about Berlin in 1959, which resulted in an equally absurd table configuration.

111. The table was circular, with a boundary at its equator (to reflect the "two sides" idea), no name plates (to avoid the implication of recognizing the legitimacy of the NLF or the Saigon government), and two small outside tables at the boundary, separated from the main table by a distance of two feet (arrived at by measuring the lateral profile of a Soviet diplomat!). Over such details did the harassed negotiators struggle for weeks, with the South Vietnamese most to blame for the delay.

112. Kissinger, "The Viet Nam Negotiations," *Foreign Affairs*, January 1969: 211–34. Legend at the magazine had it that Kissinger tried at the last minute to withdraw the article lest it embarrass him with Nixon. However, the editor, Hamilton Fish Armstrong, refused to consider this, arguing that it was extraordinarily timely and important and that readers would understand its unofficial status.

113. Kissinger, "The Viet Nam Negotiations," 223–25.

114. Quoted in Johnson, *Vantage Point*, 552–53.

115. Eisenhower and Kennedy never met until just before the Inauguration, when they discussed mainly the brewing crisis in Laos.

116. Nixon, *RN*, 338; Prochnau and Larsen, *Certain Democrat*, 241–43.

117. Nixon, *RN*, 339, for Nixon's view of the Cabinet being to the left of his position.

118. In April 1964 I visited South Vietnam shortly after Nixon had been there, and was told by Lodge's deputy (a career Foreign Service officer) that when Nixon visited the Delta area, he asked for a second helicopter to carry the press. The military command routinely approved the request, but Lodge intervened to block it! The deputy quoted Lodge as saying, in earthy terms, "The **** wanted the publicity and I didn't want him to have it!"

119. Kissinger, *White House Years*, 42.

120. Kissinger, *White House Years*, 11–12.

121. Kissinger, *White House Years*, 11. Even a serving Vice President often has an uneasy relationship with senior officials, since he is rarely in the chain of command. On his foreign travels during the 1960s, Nixon was in the anomalous position of being an ex–Vice President and possible future presidential candidate with many high-level friends in the countries he visited, who was often drawing on these same contacts to pursue his law clients' private business. That this made him awkward to handle does not seem to have occurred to him; certainly, in his years in power, he would have been highly critical of ambassadors going to special lengths in their treatment of former or prospective Democratic officeholders.

122. Kissinger, *White House Years*, 50.

Chapter 2. The First Fifteen Months

1. Dobrynin, *In Confidence*, 198, describes this meeting, adding that Nixon actually proposed holding a summit, after thorough preparation.

2. Thompson, ed., *The Nixon Presidency*, passim (especially Haldeman and Rush).

3. Johnson, *Right Hand of Power*, 520.

4. For the Nixon meeting with the delegation, the apparent understanding, and the failure to follow up, I have relied on the recollection of Marshall Green, who was with the delegation before he became Assistant Secretary of State for East Asia and the Pacific (a post I held until early May).

5. Clarke, *Advice and Support*, 335–36.

6. Clarke, *Advice and Support*, 344.

7. Hung and Schecter, *Palace File*, 31–35, is a full account of this meeting as Thieu reported it to his colleagues. On withdrawal, the phrasing was: "By the time most of the Americans withdraw, so will the North Vietnamese." Thieu also said that Nixon had "firmly agreed" that withdrawal must be mutual. There is a possibility that Thieu deliberately misstated what Nixon had said, to keep up the spirits and morale of his colleagues.

8. Emphasis added. The warm and close relationship between Kissinger and both Sven Kraemer and his father, Fritz, is fully and dramatically described in Isaacson, especially 43–47. Kissinger must have taken Sven Kraemer's 1969 report seriously, but appears to have left the question of pressing Thieu entirely to Nixon.

9. Clarke, *Advice and Support*, 355. In South Korea, two combat divisions and substantial air forces remained, and significant forces stayed on the front lines into the 1990s.

10. Clark M. Clifford, "A Viet Nam Appraisal," *Foreign Affairs,* July 1969: 601–22. Clarke, *Advice and Support,* 524, has the full table of the eventual timing and scale of "troop redeployments."

11. The Acheson-Nixon reconciliation is covered at length in Brinkley, *Dean Acheson,* 262–71. See also Douglas D'Auria, "Present at the Rejuvenation: The Association of Dean Acheson and Richard Nixon," *Presidential Studies Quarterly,* Spring 1988: 393–411.

12. The tactics behind this announcement suggest the degree to which Laird was pressing Vietnamization. Laird had Nixon's written approval but feared that he might develop second thoughts (as he had apparently done on other occasions). He thus submitted the plan for Resor's announcement when Nixon was in San Clemente, saying that he would "go ahead unless countermanded." Author's interview with Robert Pursley (Laird's principal aide), March 24, 1992.

13. Interviews with Marshall Green, 1992. Kissinger, *White House Years,* 222–23. The meeting with the press came at the end of an exhausting day, which included a stop at Johnston Island to observe the splashdown of the Apollo 11 American astronauts returning from the first human landing on the moon.

14. This summary is based on Kissinger, *White House Years,* 224–25. Nixon's memoir records him as saying flatly that if a nuclear power attacked a friend of the United States, "we would respond with nuclear weapons." Nixon, *RN,* 395. The meaning of the phrase "the region as a whole" was obscure, perhaps deliberately so in later renditions.

15. I have relied heavily on the excellent short summary in Isaacs, *Without Honor,* 192–208, which for the crucial periods of decision in 1969 and 1970 draws on research in primary sources such as JCS memoranda and intelligence reports.

16. Lehman, *Executive, Congress, and Foreign Policy,* 42.

17. Most estimates at the time were that North Vietnamese forces in Cambodia totaled 25,000 to 40,000 men. In his memoirs, Kissinger omitted this figure, citing instead a figure of 300,000 for 1969–70, the number given much later by Khmer Rouge sources to American reporters. *White House Years,* 240, 1485. This figure can only have come from boasting or perhaps from the bitter hostility then prevailing between the Khmer Rouge and North Vietnam; it bears no relation to the forces encountered or observed at any time by responsible sources.

18. Kissinger, *White House Years,* 241.

19. This system came to light, along with all else, only in 1973. It may be that one reason for it related to an understanding with the Thai government that strikes from U.S. bases there had to be cleared formally and were presumed not to include Cambodian targets. Hannah, *Key to Failure,* 265–66.

20. Johnson, *Right Hand of Power,* 493–96.

21. Thompson, ed., *The Nixon Presidency,* 82–83.

22. Kissinger, *White House Years,* 253.

23. The best discussion by far that I have seen of the Soviet-Vietnamese relationship is Pike, *Vietnam and the Soviet Union: Anatomy of an Alliance* (1987). Pike dates the onset of intimate relations between Hanoi and Moscow to 1964–65 and estimates that by 1968 the Soviets were supplying 65 percent of Hanoi's needs: 74, 122.

24. Tom Johnson Notes of Meeting, July 26, 1968, second page (handwritten, not transcribed), LBJ Library.

25. Hannah, *Key to Failure,* 268–69.

26. Nixon, *RN,* 393.

27. Dobrynin's report was published by the Cold War International History Project of the Woodrow Wilson International Center for Scholars, at the Smithsonian Institution in Washington. Fall 1993, Bulletin No. 3, 63–67.

Dobrynin never took notes during his talks with Kissinger, boasting (in his memoirs) that he had an exceptional oral memory and could re-create a conversation afterward in full detail without the aid of notes. His report of the July 12 talk bears out this claim: it is precise on Kissinger's points, in sequence and in detail, with his own short summaries of Soviet positions and commentary. The report also contains Dobrynin's categorical conclusion that Kissinger was indeed the main advisor and spokesman under Nixon and for good measure the assessment of Kissinger as "a smart and erudite person . . . but at the same time extremely vain . . . and not averse to boasting about his influence."

28. Ibid., 66.

29. This apparently verbatim text is from Nixon, *RN*, 396. This appears to have been the first revelation of the whole plan and its execution. Kissinger's account of the meeting, in *White House Years*, 278–82, dwells more on the negotiation discussions.

30. Ambrose, *Nixon: The Triumph*, 301.

31. Ambrose, *Nixon: The Triumph*, 306–7.

32. Nixon, *RN*, 399–400. The meeting is also described in Kissinger, *White House Years*, 304.

33. Nixon, *RN*, 405–7.

34. Nixon, *RN*, 402, 404.

35. Brinkley, *Dean Acheson*, 279, paraphrasing a letter from Acheson to Kissinger on October 20. After the speech, Kissinger phoned Acheson to say that its last two paragraphs (which contained the appeal to the "silent majority") had been based on Acheson's letter. Ibid., 280.

36. Polls asking this question had shown a steady rise from an initial 24 percent pro-mistake in August 1965 to an almost even balance in late 1967, a consistent strong plurality by March 1968, and substantial majorities throughout 1969. In October that year, 58 percent believed that sending U.S. troops had been a mistake while only 32 percent believed it had not been. These poll results, available individually in *The Gallup Polls: Public Opinion 1935–1971*, vol. 3, 1959–71, are summarized in Hazel Erskine, "The Polls: Is War a Mistake?" *The Public Opinion Quarterly*, Spring 1970: 134. This article makes interesting comparisons with how the same question was answered in other wars, notably World War II and the Korean War.

37. Thompson had given President Kennedy an even more upbeat appraisal in the spring of 1963, just when, in hindsight, the situation was starting to worsen seriously. Many in government during the Johnson years, myself included, came to regard his judgment as greatly overrated. Nixon, however, continued until the end to set great store by Thompson's periodic visits and reports.

38. It has sometimes been argued that "counterforce" targeting could have avoided major civilian damage and casualties and was thus far more humane than what came to be called "mutual assured destruction." In the many studies I examined in my years at the Pentagon, 1961–64, it seemed clear that even the most strictly defined "military only" targeting would inflict enormous civilian damage, so close were the Soviet Union's military installations to cities and towns. In other words, the difference from this standpoint was always one of degree and usually slight.

39. The quoted language is from Kissinger, *White House Years*, 208, based on

minutes of the meeting from past files. All sources agree on the tenor and vehemence of Kosygin's negative response.

40. Talbott, *Master of the Game*, 118, noting the strong dissent of Paul Nitze himself from this view, both during the Johnson Administration and afterward.

41. Wicker, *One of Us*, 452. This and the preceding pages in Wicker are an excellent summary of the key developments in the Johnson Administration. See also Nitze, *From Hiroshima to Glasnost*, 292, and Talbott, *Master of the Game*, 102.

42. Kissinger, *White House Years*, 538.

43. Talbott, *Master of the Game*, 112–14; Brinkley, *Dean Acheson*, 271–75.

44. Nixon, *RN*, 415–18.

45. Kai Bird, *The Chairman*, 615–17.

46. In his memoirs, Kissinger caricatures the opposition as wanting simply to "abandon" MIRV—which was neither their intent nor the likely result. Kissinger, *White House Years*, 210–12.

Kissinger never indicates what advice he may have given the President at this stage. Members of his staff recall vividly the arguments that raged among them, and dramatic evidence of their differences emerged from the transcripts of the telephone taps placed on some members over the leaks concerning the secret bombing of Cambodia. See Isaacson, *Kissinger*, 318; and Hersh, *Price of Power*, 153. One staff member has speculated to me that Nixon simply could not visualize entering a negotiation offering to discuss a major new U.S. asset—although of course he was doing just that in the case of ABM!

47. Kissinger had written a much noted book, *Nuclear Weapons and Foreign Policy*, published in 1957, and had returned to the subject several times during the 1960s.

48. Nitze's strong defense posture and his key role in the ABM fight impressed the President, who met with Nitze privately and urged him to communicate directly with Nixon outside regular channels. Nitze quickly and courageously said that he could not bypass Smith and other colleagues in that fashion. Nixon reiterated the proposal and facilities were created, but Nitze never made use of them. It was a revealing example of Nixon's habitual distrust and manipulation, and of the profoundly different ethos that Nitze exemplified.

49. During the negotiating rounds, all exchanges with the Soviets were fully coordinated and reported, along with the team's assessments and recommendations. In the recess periods, the team members reported to their original agencies and worked with them in the decision-making process for the next round.

50. It was then thought that Soviet missile silos could take MIRVs without significant modification. The prospective U.S. MIRV systems were to be installed on Minuteman III and on the Poseidon naval missile, without differences discernible from the air. As it turned out, however, Soviet missile silos did require recognizable change when MIRVs were installed.

51. Hersh, *Price of Power*, 157; and Kissinger, *White House Years*, 148. Smith, *Doubletalk*, 108–9, lists the members of the Verification Panel: the Deputy Secretary of Defense (David Packard), the JCS Chairman (Admiral Thomas Moorer), the Under Secretary of State (Elliot Richardson, then John Irwin); and the Directors of ACDA and CIA (Smith and Richard Helms). In addition, Attorney General John Mitchell was formally named to the Panel, although he rarely attended meetings.

52. To his closest staff members, Nixon was inclined to belittle Kissinger's love of negotiations, including his focus on personalities and little indicators of position. Kissinger, *White House Years*, 142.

53. The authoritative annual assessment by the International Institute of Strategic Studies (London), *The Military Balance 1970–1971*, 88–89, estimated America's naval strike aircraft at 900 and land-based strike aircraft at 1,200.

54. My emphasis on Nitze in this account stems from a long conversation I had with him on his return from Helsinki in December 1969. In 1992 he corroborated this summary, although, of course, I am responsible for all inferences drawn from it.

55. Figures from Kissinger, *White House Years*, 537. He notes that the actual Soviet total at the end of 1970 was 1,440.

56. Hersh, *Price of Power*, 164–66.

57. Kissinger, *White House Years*, 534–35, 548.

58. As recounted by Raymond Garthoff, a member of the delegation, in his *Détente and Confrontation*, rev. ed. 1994, 159n; see also Isaacson, *Kissinger*, 320. Later the Soviet negotiator told Garthoff that he at least had been hoping strongly that the United States would offer a negotiable position on MIRV.

59. Such reciprocal bans would have minimized the verification problem. Production of major items, as the Soviets realized, was essentially an open matter in the United States, revealed in congressional documents or in technical journals almost without exception. Conversely, the flight-testing phase was by far the most promising for ready detection of Soviet activity: the CIA took the position all along that the Soviets would never deploy or rely on a missile system that had not been tested in a realistic mode.

60. Smith, *Doubletalk*, 174–75.

61. In his Oral History for the Office of the Secretary of Defense, Kenneth Rush described the effort he made in 1972, as Deputy Secretary of Defense, to get MIRV back into the negotiations. The effort was in vain.

62. Cited in Talbott, *Master of the Game*, 124. The statement was made on December 3, 1974, in the wake of President Ford's attempt at Vladivostok to frame a workable basis for further agreement on offensive weapons control.

63. Smith, *Doubletalk*, 471–72.

64. Hyland, *Mortal Rivals*, 43.

65. Advocates of controlling MIRV did argue, correctly, that even less than fool-proof initial verification was still a lot more than would exist once MIRVs were deployed on the Soviet side. In the end, the follow-on SALT II negotiations, during and after Nixon's tenure, had to face up to the problem of MIRV numbers. They could meet it only by agreeing, without any means of verification whatever, that a given type of MIRVable missile should be assumed to be carrying the maximum number of MIRVs its size permitted.

66. Smith, *Doubletalk*, 472.

67. This proposed initial negotiating position was worked out in great haste. All evidence suggests that Johnson — enmeshed in the Paris negotiations and much else — simply wanted agreement, a lowest common denominator with which no key player was unhappy. In the face of the JCS opposition to any restraint on MIRV, he would have had first to be persuaded that a bilateral ban on MIRV made sense and then to inject himself into the issue in a way that was rarely his practice. Moreover, Nitze himself was never persuaded that a MIRV ban was verifiable. When Morton Halperin of ISA proposed putting off the August MIRV test, Nitze forwarded the proposal to Secretary Clifford, adding his own view that it should not be accepted. The idea died. Talbott, *Master of the Game*, 102.

68. Quoted in Wicker, *One of Us*, 457.

69. Matthew 23: 24.

70. Smith, *Doubletalk*, 154.

71. Kissinger, *White House Years*, 170.

72. Kissinger, *White House Years*, 170–71.

73. Kissinger, *White House Years*, 170–71.

74. I am indebted to Nicholas Katzenbach, Under Secretary of State from 1966 to early 1969, for recalling this episode to me.

75. Marshall Green, "Memorandum for the Record," June 10, 1969, now in Green's possession.

76. Kissinger, *White House Years*, 189–90.

77. Whether the idea of using these visits for this purpose came from Nixon or Kissinger is impossible to establish from the present record. On the trip between Jakarta and Bangkok, Kissinger instructed John Holdridge, then the China expert on the NSC staff, to draft a message to be left with a head or heads of state during the balance of the trip, asking the recipient to tell the Chinese of the new U.S. interest. The instruction must have come from the President, but whether on Kissinger's suggestion is not clear. Holdridge interview, 1996.

78. Kissinger, *White House Years*, 180–81.

79. Kissinger, *White House Years*, 184. Emphasis added.

80. Interviews and correspondence with Marshall Green, 1993–94.

81. Kissinger, *White House Years*, 687. Donald Anderson, a Foreign Service officer involved in drafting the instructions for the January 20 meeting, recorded, in a private memoir done in 1997, that the original drafts had included only a suggestion for sending Red Cross representatives to China, but that this was changed to proposing a "high-level representative of the President" on orders from "on high." The abruptness and lateness of the change suggest that Kissinger had just seen the Pakistani report and knew the Chinese would probably be receptive. In his account, Kissinger conceded that State "did not know what was passing in secret channels." He can be excused for not revealing the sensitive Pakistani channel, but not for later blaming State for stodginess and lack of imagination.

82. Kissinger, *White House Years*, 787.

83. Nixon, *RN*, 545, attributes this response to the publication two days earlier of his first Foreign Policy Report to Congress, which spoke very generally about better relations with China. But this was far less specific than what had been said already in Warsaw.

84. Kissinger, *White House Years*, 687–93.

85. Nixon, *RN*, 497; Kissinger, *White House Years*, 193–94.

86. Hersh, *Price of Power*, 416. One Hersh source for Kissinger's remarks was a junior staff member, Roger Morris, somewhat given to sensationalism and a sharp critic of Kissinger after the spring of 1970. Robert Osgood was a respected senior expert on defense and NATO policy at the Brookings Institution.

87. Brandt, *My Life in Politics*, 167.

88. Brandt, *My Life in Politics*, 174–75.

89. Hanrieder, *Germany, America, Europe*, 201.

90. Brandt, *My Life in Politics*, 170–71, says that Nixon's apology the following spring when the two met at Camp David was accepted by him in good spirit.

91. Bark and Gress, *History of West Germany*, 152.

92. Bark and Gress, *History of West Germany*, 164.

93. Bark and Gress, *History of West Germany*, 165–66.

94. Bark and Gress, *History of West Germany*, 169–70.

95. Schmidt, *Men and Powers*, 146–47 on the November meeting, 148–49 on his relationship to Laird. In 1969–70 Schmidt was active in the formation of a "Eurogroup" and in organizing increases in the European contributions to NATO's infrastructure, a sore point with Congress over the years. He also wrote an important article in *Foreign Affairs* in October 1970, "Germany in the Era of Negotiations," arguing bluntly against any reduction in the level of U.S. forces committed to NATO in Europe. Carr, *Helmut Schmidt*, 65–66.

96. Nixon, *Leaders*, 64, 66.

97. Kissinger, *White House Years*, 410–11.

98. Kissinger, *White House Years*, 530–31.

99. I was a member of the American delegation at a fruitless 1959 Geneva conference on Berlin involving the four occupying powers and, in carefully subordinated roles, the two German entities. Weeks of sterile argument in the conference chamber were far less enlightening than a three-day break visit to Berlin. Having last seen the city in ruins in July 1945, I was left in awe of the constant hardships and sense of isolation of the West Berliners, and of their staying power, and deeply impressed at how sensitive their morale had to be to any perceived change in their status or in the West's resolve. In these impressions, I was of course simply tuning in, with greater emotional understanding, to what a generation of American officials had known all along.

100. In 1967, no embargo was attempted, and if it had been the United States could have increased its own oil production to cushion the impact. However, it could not have made up the difference completely, as it could have done in the 1956 Suez war, when Britain and France colluded with Israel to attack Egypt and take over the Sinai but were forced by U.S. pressures and UN condemnation to desist and withdraw. See Quandt, *Decade of Decisions*, 71.

101. Safran, *Israel*, 415.

102. O'Brien, *The Siege*, 489–90.

103. Less visibly, the Khartoum meeting was the occasion for a pledge of large-scale aid to battered Egypt by Saudi Arabia and other oil-producing countries generally regarded as moderates in the Arab spectrum. The continued need for these subsidies had some restraining effect on Nasser's behavior.

104. Quandt, *Decade of Decisions*, 77.

105. Quandt, *Decade of Decisions*, 77.

106. Nixon, *RN*, 283.

107. O'Brien, *The Siege*, 494–95, 538, citing Rabin's memoirs, argues that Rabin as ambassador had more influence than any member of the Cabinet save Moshe Dayan on Israel's foreign and defense policies generally and that he "assumed control of Israel's relations with the United States" — that Foreign Minister Abba Eban "had the responsibility, but Rabin had the power."

108. O'Brien, *The Siege*, 495, spells this out, relying in part on the recollection of Foreign Minister Eban, who opposed escalation and considered Rabin to have been in the end decisive with Mrs. Meir. In his 1977 autobiography, Eban stressed that what Rabin conveyed about the attitude of Kissinger, in particular, in favor of escalation, must have "accorded with her own impression, when she met Kissinger herself." Eban, *Autobiography*, 465.

109. Eban, *Autobiography*, 464.

110. In his 1997 memoir, Leonard Garment of the White House Staff recounts

that he was specifically instructed by Nixon to tell Mrs. Meir, as she set out on a speechmaking trip after her visit to Washington, that she should feel no compunction about attacking the Rogers Plan in emphatic terms. Garment, *Crazy Rhythm*, 192.

111. Eban, *Autobiography*, 465. Kissinger's *White House Years* does not mention his attitude, but Rabin and Eban were surely solid witnesses.

112. Kissinger, *White House Years*, 560–62.

113. Kissinger, *White House Years*, 567–68. The question of controlling guerrilla forces was to assume great importance during the summer, as recounted in Chapter 3. To anticipate, it was never clear that the Soviets had authority to speak for any Arab state, or that Arab states themselves, even though they were hosts to the guerrillas, had real control over fedayeen and PLO groups.

114. Kissinger, *White House Years*, 568.

115. Herzog, *The Arab-Israeli Wars*, 216. The author, President of Israel at the time his book on Israel's wars was published, had previously been a major general in the Israeli Army and Ambassador to the United Nations. As Quandt notes, Israeli sources have often argued that the Soviets had decided to raise the ante before the deep penetration raids, and one American scholar has marshaled evidence to this effect. Uri Ra'anan, "The USSR and the Middle East: Some Reflections on the Soviet Decision-making Process," *Orbis*, Fall 1973, cited in Quandt, *Decade of Decisions*, 95. By December the Israelis had so battered the Egyptian air defenses that the possibility of deep raids must have come up between the Soviets and the Egyptians; but the depth and extent of the raids surely precipitated a decision by late January.

116. Kissinger, *White House Years*, 568. There was also a requirement that the fighting stop simultaneously on both sides, which seemed inevitable and raised no problems.

117. Kissinger, *White House Years*, 570.

118. Kissinger, *White House Years*, 572.

119. This brief summary is based on standard sources, supplemented by a few personal memories. As a young lawyer in the Washington firm of Covington and Burling, which then represented Iran before the UN, I heard many firsthand accounts of the 1946 UN crisis. I also had the task in 1947 of drafting for Iranian Ambassador Hussein Ala (a man of great courage and influence with the Shah) a note rejecting a Soviet protest under the 1921 agreements at the sending of a U.S. team to train an Iranian gendarmerie for countryside security. The commander of that team was the father of General H. Norman Schwarzkopf. In this private capacity I met the Shah when he visited Washington in 1949. In subsequent work as a CIA staff assistant at the Eisenhower NSC, I was involved in policy papers on Iran after the 1953 coup (of which I had been unaware at the time). I was also familiar with the discussions and papers that defined the U.S. relationship to the Baghdad Pact.

120. There are several books on this covert operation, notably that of the man in charge on the ground, Kermit Roosevelt, *Countercoup*. It is summarized in Ambrose, *Eisenhower*, vol. 2, 109–12, 129–30.

121. Nixon, *RN*, 133.

122. Author's interview, December 1996, with Cyrus Ghani, an extremely knowledgeable Iranian who was exiled in the 1978–79 revolution. In 1967, he had close contact through Robert Ellsworth, a top Nixon aide, with Nixon's party.

123. The U.S. Ambassador at the time, the veteran career officer Julius Holmes, combined in rare degree tact, firmness, and clarity of view and expression; he was not

only formally instructed but immersed in the thinking that led President Kennedy to change U.S. policy significantly.

I participated in that policy review and followed Iranian developments closely for a time, from a post in the Pentagon that included a responsibility for military assistance programs worldwide. In 1962, I was charged with drawing up exact annual schedules for an unprecedented five-year commitment to Iran, a military aid package long on maintainable items and short on glamorous ones. Hence I participated in a very small private meeting at which Secretary McNamara conveyed this commitment to the Shah: "This is it" was the tone. Looking back, I can see that what seemed a wholly statesmanlike action must also have been acutely galling to the Shah, already enamored of military hardware and fancying himself a considerable expert on strategy as well as advanced equipment. Quite likely, the episode contributed to his obsessive desire to run his own military show a decade later.

124. *New York Times*, October 24, 1969, 5.

125. The concept of regional pillars is never mentioned in any of Nixon's four Foreign Policy Reports, 1970–73. Nor do any of these reports address the question of security in the area of the Gulf. (This body of water was habitually referred to as "the Persian Gulf" until at least the late 1960s, when Arab countries started to object and insist that it be called "the Arabian Gulf." At one CENTO meeting I attended, the representative of Iran made a big issue of this, threatening to withdraw if the latter label were used!)

126. In 1970 the population of Iran was 29,256,000, Iraq's population was 9,400,000, and Kuwait's, 738,000. From *Statistical Abstract of the United States*, 1972.

127. Rubin, *Paved with Good Intentions*, 128. This also notes that when substantial Saudi Arabian purchases got under way, 80 percent went to construction and support services and only 20 percent to equipment. Moderate as Iranian capacities to operate and service sophisticated equipment were, then and later, they were far greater than those of the Saudis.

128. Rubin, *Paved with Good Intentions*, 124.

129. The issue concerned smaller islands in the Ryukyu group, as well as the Bonin group of islands. For convenience, "Okinawa" is used for the whole.

130. See U. Alexis Johnson, *Right Hand of Power*, 479–80.

131. The phrase "constant irritant" is from Nixon, *RN*, 343, the only reference in Nixon's memoirs to the subject. He gives no account of the 1969 summit and never refers again to Okinawa except for the June leak (*RN*, 389). Kissinger, on the other hand, gives a careful and useful analysis of the history and the situation as it stood in early 1969. Kissinger, *White House Years*, 325–26; see also Johnson, *Right Hand of Power*, 447ff.

132. Some U.S. forces stationed in Japan were trained to use nuclear weapons if needed, and the plan was always that if necessary such weapons would be brought in at the last moment, assuming that Japanese consent would then be forthcoming.

133. U.S. imports of man-made fibers increased more than tenfold between 1964 and 1971, with Japan accounting for 28 percent of these in 1968. The total imports were still only 3.6 percent of total U.S. consumption, and the Japanese share thus roughly 1 percent of U.S. consumption.

134. Destler et al., *Textile Wrangle*, 68.

135. Kissinger, *White House Years*, 330.

136. Destler et al., *Textile Wrangle*, 8.

137. In *White House Years*, 332, Kissinger emphasizes the President's insistence

on a firm textile agreement and claims that he himself was reluctant "about linking an issue of fundamental strategic importance with a transient domestic political problem." On the other hand, Destler concluded after extensive interviews that the idea was Kissinger's, related to his strong desire at this time to establish himself as a firm negotiator who could get results where others could not, particularly on a matter regarded as a test of "toughness." Destler et al., *Textile Wrangle*, 125–26.

138. Kissinger, *White House Years*, 332–33. The source of the formula is also not wholly clear. Kissinger attributes it to Stans personally. Destler, unable to gain access to the document itself, concludes that Kissinger used the NSC staff to get from the Commerce Department, without stating the purpose, the materials for the text. Destler et al., *Textile Wrangle*, 126–27. Along the way, representatives of American industry seem to have sensed, or been told, that the matter had been raised between Nixon and Sato personally and that some sort of commitment had been extracted.

139. Operations in support of the Indochina War were not mentioned or envisaged. By early 1969 popular protests had led the United States to discontinue the use of Okinawa air bases for B-52 operations in Indochina.

140. Nixon, *U.S. Foreign Policy for the 1970's: A Report to the Congress*, February 1970, 48.

141. Hersh, *Price of Power*, 381.

142. Quoted in Hersh, *Price of Power*, 381. Sneider was an exceptionally accurate and professional officer, with long experience dealing with Japan. He had had a difficult relationship with Kissinger during a brief stint on the NSC staff in early 1969, and was one of those subjected, without his own knowledge at the time, to wiretaps over leaks. Sneider's action in quieting Japanese speculation can, of course, be judged as unwise or even insubordinate. Yet I am absolutely sure that he was right to believe that if word had got around in the Japanese establishment, the result would have been extreme confusion at best and highly destructive controversy at worst.

143. Kissinger, *White House Years*, 340; Destler et al., *Textile Wrangle*, 134–35. Destler's conclusion that to all intents and purposes Sato closed a deal is qualified only by the surmise that, given intense time pressure alone, he may not have understood the significance of the terms in any detail.

144. Johnson, *Right Hand of Power*, 550–51. I knew Shimoda well in the Johnson presidency and admired and trusted him. After leaving his Washington post in the fall of 1970, he went on to become Chief Judge of the Japanese Supreme Court.

145. Destler et al., *Textile Wrangle*, 146–48.

146. Kissinger, *White House Years*, 340.

Chapter 3. 1970: A Troubled Year

1. Kissinger, *White House Years*, 451–57, gives a good short summary of the early 1970 developments in Laos. An excellent close-up account is Jane Hamilton-Merritt, *Tragic Mountains*, 231–47.

2. Kissinger, *White House Years*, 451–52.

3. Hamilton-Merritt, *Tragic Mountains*, 236. This book provides a dramatic and moving account of the fighting in these early days, 232–37.

4. Hamilton-Merritt, *Tragic Mountains*, 238.

5. For a sophisticated Western observer's account of how it felt to be a civilian

in an area under B-52 attack, see Isaacs, *Without Honor*, 229–30, describing the view from Phnom Penh in 1973.

6. Kissinger, *White House Years*, 454–55, recounts this episode, noting that Kissinger apologized to Laird, whose staff had twice lined out the draft statement that no Americans had been killed in Laos. Obviously, Americans in the field were particularly upset.

7. Hamilton-Merritt, *Tragic Mountains*, 246.

8. John Clark Pratt was an American Air Force reserve officer flying Raven patrols from Thailand in this period. His *The Laotian Fragments* (1974), a novel, paints a vivid, authoritative account of the fighting in early 1970, the Americans involved, the role of airpower, and what a close-run engagement it was.

9. A balanced account of the intensely controversial events surrounding the Cambodian incursion is a daunting task. On the one hand, the Nixon and Kissinger memoirs (*RN*, 445–67, and *White House Years*, 457–517) continue to defend and blame, although Kissinger is a good source on the sequence of events. On the other side, William Shawcross's *Sideshow*, a sensation when published in early 1979, is a devastating critique — to which much of Kissinger's treatment, published later the same year, is a rebuttal. Isaacson on Kissinger is both an excellent short account of the events of 1970 and a discerning commentary. A conspicuous gap is the absence of serious discussion of Laos in any of Alexander Haig's substantial writings. My limited additional research into contemporary intelligence assessments, with the help of old CIA colleagues, has supported many of Shawcross's key points.

The 1980s saw a flowering of serious writing on Cambodia, notably excellent books by Elizabeth Becker, *When the War Was Over*, and Nayan Chanda, *Brother Enemy*. Becker in particular is of great value in understanding the Khmer Rouge, who, however, were of little immediate consequence in 1969–70.

10. Lehman, *Executive, Congress, and Foreign Policy*, 44, cites several evidences of Sihanouk's tolerant attitude. None of this, however, amounted to encouragement of the bombing on the scale reached by late 1969.

11. Shawcross, *Sideshow*, 64. See also Becker, *When the War Was Over*, 117, which argues that the Sihanoukville supply line was arranged directly with the North Vietnamese, and does not mention China. However, CIA analysis of materials captured in the 1970 incursion makes clear that from the very first shipment in December 1966 all ten ships that delivered cargo to the port, up to April 1969, were Chinese. See CIA Intelligence Memorandum, December 1970, "Communist Deliveries to Cambodia for the VC/NVA forces in South Vietnam, December 1966–April 1969," 2–3.

12. Kissinger, *White House Years*, 463. Kissinger cites contemporary memoranda and intelligence judgments to support this claim.

13. The most searching examinations of this question are in Shawcross, *Sideshow*, 114–22, and Hersh, *Price of Power*, 175–83. Drawing on interviews with Americans in intelligence and covert operations, both offer plausible evidence that the idea of removing Sihanouk had been considered in 1969 by U.S. intelligence circles in Saigon, and stress the continuing ties to Son Ngoc Thanh and the Khmer Serei. However, Hersh's evidence that these ties took an active turn against Sihanouk in 1969–70 or were in any way linked to Lon Nol is sketchy at best. In the end (176) he finds "no conclusive evidence that the United States was directly responsible for Sihanouk's overthrow," and falls back to the claim that the ties he describes meant that Lon Nol took power "knowing" that the United States would at once recognize and support his government.

Shawcross reached a similar conclusion, citing particularly the later statement of a member of Lon Nol's Cabinet: "We all just knew that the United States would help us." To the same effect William Colby, a CIA senior official at the time and long familiar with the ties to the Khmer groups, judged that simply from the overall situation in the area, Lon Nol would have drawn the "obvious conclusion" that the United States would support a regime he headed. Shawcross, *Sideshow*, 122.

14. Kissinger does not discuss this French initiative, except to mention Laird's support for the general idea. Kissinger, *White House Years*, 478. Green's position is described in Shawcross, *Sideshow*, 129.

15. Becker, *When the War Was Over*, 132, says that the Chinese conditions were (1) permission for the Chinese to continue supplying the Vietnamese through Khmer territory; (2) permitting the North Vietnamese to maintain their bases in Khmer territory; and (3) government statements supporting the Vietnamese Communists.

16. Shawcross, *Sideshow*, 129, quotes Green to this general effect but not so specifically, based on interviews in May 1970.

17. Sorley, *Thunderbolt*, 283–84.

18. The Vietnam scholar Douglas Pike has recalled vividly that he and other Americans stationed in Saigon were surprised and taken aback by the furor in America after the incursion. Author interview, 1994.

19. Palmer, *The 25-Year War*, 100, notes that while the JCS had long favored some action against the Cambodian sanctuaries, in the spring of 1970 they played "a minimal role." He was Vice Chief of Staff of the Army at the time. Palmer also thought that few leaders anticipated the sharp reaction at home. Since other testimony is clear that Laird, Rogers, and Nixon himself all saw the reaction as likely to be stormy, Palmer's view simply shows that the military, who rightly do not try to judge public opinion, were simply left in the dark about the likelihood of a reaction that would limit future operations.

20. I cannot refrain from a speculation based on personal experience. Admiral McCain's headquarters building and its big briefing room went back for decades: in World War II it had been the nerve center for Admiral Chester Nimitz's brilliant naval operations, which turned the tide against Japan at the Battle of Midway in June 1942 and led on to victory in 1945. It was hallowed ground, especially for former naval officers.

In December 1961, I had my first exposure to that briefing room on a business visit with Secretary McNamara. Although my wartime service had been with the Army in Europe, the setting made a powerful impression on me. On that occasion too, as with Nixon in 1970, "large red arrows" were used to depict the military threat to Saigon, making it seem like, say, Okinawa in World War II. In 1961 the unreality of such comparisons and assumptions sank in rapidly, and the effect of the setting wore off. Yet I can readily imagine the effect his 1970 visit may have had on Nixon, recalling his wartime service with the Navy in the Pacific and thinking about the American role there since 1941 and in the postwar years. It may well have contributed to an inner feeling he clearly had, that America could not let go in the Pacific, or fail the small nations that depended on U.S. help.

21. Kissinger deals at length with the background and substance of this troop withdrawal announcement, stressing his own urging of a high figure but spread over a long period. With Cambodia clearly in mind, the first new withdrawals were not promised till October. Kissinger, *White House Years*, 475–83.

22. Kissinger, *White House Years*, 499 (Helms). Kissinger's account gives consid-

erable weight to statements by Le Duc Tho during their two secret meetings in Paris, on March 16 and April 4, to the effect that neutralization of Cambodia was impossible and that the Khmer people would fight to victory, under the Sihanouk-led United Front. Ibid., 468–69. While these statements show that Hanoi definitely was dead set against compromise or recognition of Lon Nol, they were hardly evidence of an early attempt to defeat Lon Nol by a quick attack on the capital, which was the crux of the argument for immediate U.S. intervention.

23. Kissinger, *White House Years*, 496. The careful account of dealings with Congress written by Kissinger's staff man for congressional relations, John Lehman, includes a claim that there were informal advance consultations with members of Congress, including phone calls by the President. Lehman's source for these claims is a contemporary interview with Bryce Harlow, Nixon's most trusted senior liaison to Congress. Harlow was in a good position to know, but also capable of trying to put the best face on the President's actions. Lehman, *Executive, Congress, and Foreign Policy*, 45. Lehman, sympathetic to Nixon, notes the fear of any leak, and describes the President's relationship to the Senate Foreign Relations Committee as one of "very deep and bitter hostility." Ibid., 46.

24. Kissinger, *White House Years*, 1485; also Isaacson, *Kissinger*, 267. A memo from Nixon to Kissinger, written in the early morning of April 22, shows Nixon's highly emotional state. *White House Years*, 1484. During that week, Kissinger coped with sharp protests against the incursion from several members of his staff, four of whom resigned over the issue. *White House Years*, 497. Whatever his own views, Kissinger must have sensed clearly where the President would come out—recalling both the threats of 1969 and Nixon's reaction to the earlier EC-121 shootdown—and must have known that to be in dissent would sharply reduce if not eliminate his influence on other matters.

25. Palmer's reaction, *The 25-Year War*, 96–97. For the speech, see *Public Papers of the President, 1970*, 137–39.

26. Safire, *Before the Fall*, 187–88. Lehman recounts that in a background briefing to the press just before Nixon's speech, Kissinger gave a much more low-key picture of the operation, stressing that it would go no further than twenty-one miles into Cambodia and would end within weeks, although forces might later be reintroduced. Lehman, *Executive, Congress, and Foreign Policy*, 46. This suggests that Kissinger saw how violent the reaction might be, and was protecting his own press image.

27. Kissinger reports the President as inclined from the first to positive action. Kissinger, *White House Years*, 465. Alexis Johnson had considerable difficulty with Kissinger and watched closely what his influence was. His conclusion was that the decision to go into Cambodia was "unequivocally the President's." Johnson, *Right Hand of Power*, 529. I disagree on this important point with Shawcross, who throughout his brilliant and immensely revealing *Sideshow* treats the Cambodian incursion as effectively decided by Kissinger. As I have noted repeatedly, this was rarely true of any Nixon decision at least in the first three years; it was emphatically not true of this one, or of the later ones to which this led.

28. Powers, *Man Who Kept the Secrets*, 219, on what COSVN really was. The acronym stands for "Commanding Officer, South Vietnam"—a title used by Americans. Shawcross, *Sideshow*, 150, describes how U.S. forces did heavy damage to the town of Snuol, treating it still as a hub of North Vietnamese activity even though no North Vietnamese forces were there by the time of the U.S. entry.

29. *The Gallup Poll: Public Opinion, 1935–1971*, 2244, 2251, 2257.

30. Personal interviews at the time. Alsop was a valued friend.

31. Aitken, *Nixon*, 460.

32. Quoted in Aitken, *Nixon*, 410.

33. Thompson and Frizzell, eds., *The Lessons of Vietnam*, 103. White, *Breach of Faith*, 129, and Parker, "Vietnam: The War That Won't End," *Foreign Affairs*, January 1975: 356–57.

34. The Kissinger response is cited in Thompson and Frizzell, *The Lessons of Vietnam*, 103; the rest from Hersh, *Price of Power*, 200, and Shawcross, *Sideshow*, 173.

35. Draft of SNIE 14.3-1-70, June 16, 1970, 1, 5, 6–7 (supply losses), 8–9 (weapons and ammunition), 10–11 (claimed manpower losses), 14 (westward Communist gains), 19 (fear of further U.S. escalation), 24 (summary). This declassified draft is available in CIA files. It was apparently never coordinated with other intelligence agencies or formally published.

36. The retrospective CIA analysis, from the invoices, is contained in an Intelligence Memorandum by the Directorate of Intelligence, dated December 1970, "Communist Deliveries to Cambodia for the VC/NVA Forces in South Vietnam, December 1966–April 1969." The intelligence controversy, including also the withholding of a skeptical draft CIA estimate just before the President's decision in late April, is well summarized in Powers, *Man Who Kept the Secrets*, 216–19.

In his memoirs, Kissinger carried the argument one step further, stating that a pre-incursion estimate by the command in Saigon (as distinct from the Defense Intelligence Agency in Washington) had been a flow of about 10,000 tons a year through Sihanoukville in 1967–68, a level presumably maintained thereafter, and that documents captured in the invasion showed totals that "far exceeded" this. Kissinger, *White House Years*, 241–42. The invoices offer no support for the 10,000-ton figure, let alone one "far" higher. Kissinger cites no source for his statement.

37. Douglas Pike, "Road to Victory: The Ho Chi Minh Trail," *War in Peace*, Orbis Publishing Co., London, 1984, vol. 5, no. 60, 1196.

38. Pike, "Road to Victory," 1196.

39. Shawcross, *Sideshow*, 137, 165.

40. Isaacson, *Kissinger*, 270.

41. *The Gallup Poll: Public Opinion, 1935–1971*, vol. 3, 2240, 2266, 2285. The June poll used July 1971 as the cutoff date; all others used the end of 1971.

42. Acheson had some personal knowledge of the geography of Cambodia, which he had visited in 1962 when he represented Cambodia in an important World Court case concerning a temple area disputed with Thailand (and won the case). That he had also come to like and admire Sihanouk may have had a bearing on his views. As we shall see, he did not withdraw from any further association with the White House, but confined his advice and help thereafter to NATO matters. Brinkley, *Dean Acheson*, 284.

43. Only in the mid-1980s did papers come to light showing that in July 1965, just before Johnson's decision to raise the U.S. force level greatly, Cooper had joined with Senator Mike Mansfield and other moderate senators in urging President Johnson to move in the opposite direction, on the ground that the war would be too hard to bring to a successful conclusion. Thereafter, Cooper joined with other skeptics, such as Senator Richard Russell, in supporting the war, largely (no doubt) in the belief that visible divisions would make it impossible to succeed. It was clearly the Cambodian incursion that changed his position to that of an outright opponent.

44. There was a brief effort at compromise in early July, turned down by Nixon. Thomas Morgan, chairman of the House Foreign Affairs Committee and a clear-cut

opponent of the amendment, thought some compromise would eventually be needed. Lehman, *Executive, Congress, and Foreign Policy*, 69.

45. Lehman, *Executive, Congress, and Foreign Policy*, 72–73.

46. For a careful insider account of the Nixon Administration's reaction and beliefs, see Lehman, *Executive, Congress, and Foreign Policy*, 61–69.

47. *Public Papers of the President, 1970*, 547. Lehman, *Executive, Congress, and Foreign Policy*, 69, records the "acute distress" of himself and other staff members watching the exchange on TV. He also notes that Nixon's rationale opened the way to the argument that if the protection of U.S. servicemen was now the paramount criterion, this could be achieved by their simple withdrawal!

48. *Public Papers, 1970*, 550.

49. Shaplen, *A Turning Wheel*, 6.

50. Kissinger, *White House Years*, 696–97.

51. Unknown to the State Department, Ambassador Hilaly of Pakistan had given Kissinger in late January 1970 a report emphasizing Zhou's Soviet and Japanese concerns. It was an important and encouraging insight, as well as another stage in the development of the Pakistani channel for direct and indirect messages. Kissinger, *White House Years*, 687.

The East Asian Bureau of the State Department, however (contrary to Kissinger's repeated derogatory comments and despite not being informed of this and other reports from the Pakistani channel), recognized and discussed the possibility of Chinese concerns over a revival of Japanese militarism along with the possible appeal of trade concessions. The American chiefs of mission in East Asia met in Tokyo in July 1970, and sent a summary of their talks to the White House. Marshall Green, unpublished manuscript, *Evolution of U.S. China Policy, 1956–1973: Memoirs of an Insider* (cited hereafter as "Green manuscript"), 30. In fact, the East Asian Bureau tracked the subject constantly, wholly favored a new course, and was often more imaginative than the China hands on Kissinger's staff or Kissinger himself. Uninformed of Nixon's thinking or Kissinger's maneuvers, Green was consistently wise on issues of substance, erring only in not being able to imagine the degree to which the President and his advisor wished to involve themselves personally. This was one case among many where extreme White House secrecy and ambitions for credit and political timing prevented full use of the State Department's expertise and experience. See Michel Oksenberg's excellent survey, "A Decade of Sino-American Relations," *Foreign Affairs*, Fall 1982: 177.

52. Garver, *China's Decision for Rapprochement*, 79ff, a stimulating analysis of this period, argues that after the intense Sino-Soviet confrontation of 1969 had been eased by the beginning of negotiations, Chinese policy was really pro-Soviet from early 1970 to early 1971, with the moderates essentially adopting Lin's position. It seems likely that any such position on Zhou's part was purely temporary and tactical.

53. Roderick MacFarquhar, "The Succession to Mao and the End of Maoism," in *The Cambridge History of China*, vol. 15, 312ff, gives a vivid account of the Lushan meeting.

54. Kissinger, *White House Years*, 702–3; Hersh, *Price of Power*, 366–67. The sequence of events is particularly well related in Pollack, "The Opening to America," in *The Cambridge History of China*, vol. 15, 417–19. The academic was Professor Allen Whiting, at the University of Michigan, who had served in the State Department in the mid-1960s and was known especially for his landmark book on missed signals when the Chinese moved to enter the Korean War.

55. Kissinger, *White House Years*, 699. Dewey, former governor of New York, had

been the Republican presidential candidate in 1944 and 1948. Murphy was a senior retired diplomat always close to Republican Presidents and hard-line toward the Soviet Union. Both were well along in years (sixty-eight and seventy-six, respectively); one may suspect Kissinger of stacking the deck in favor of his own candidacy.

56. Hersh, *Price of Power*, 365–66, with Snow as his source. Nixon's own account of this period is sketchy, asserting that as of early 1971 "our tentative approaches to Communist China appeared to have fallen on deaf ears." Nixon, *RN*, 497. This is impossible to reconcile with the December 8 message from Zhou, and suggests that Nixon simply did not have the record before him in writing his memoirs.

57. Kissinger, *White House Years*, 701. As usual for all high-level exchanges with China, Kissinger's version is the only one available to scholars as of mid-1997, but in this case there was probably little to be read into the rest of the message. It is noteworthy that Zhou's letter was a response to Nixon's message via Yahya, sorting this out from other messages sent by the United States as being, for the first time, "from a Head [Nixon], through a Head [Yahya], to a Head [Mao]." As to the contents, it was long-standing Chinese tradition that China must never appear as a suppliant to any other nation. It was also to Nixon's advantage to portray himself as having taken the initiative.

58. Kissinger, *White House Years*, 686. Kissinger fails to note that Richardson's statement of September 1969 had already made clear that the United States would not collaborate with the Soviet Union against China.

59. Snow, *The Long Revolution*, 11–12, quoted in Pollack, "Opening to America," 419, in *The Cambridge History of China*, vol. 15.

60. Snow, *The Long Revolution*, 182–83, quoted in Hersh, *Price of Power*, 366.

61. My emphasis on the Soviet economic situation and its relation to foreign policy owes much to Robin Edmonds, a British Sovietologist with long experience in the Foreign Office. In *Soviet Foreign Policy*, 1983, 79ff, Edmonds draws on the work of the distinguished analyst of the Soviet economy Alec Nove to highlight six problems: the technological gap; the managerial gap; low qualitative indicators of progress, rather than the familiar quantitative ones; the decline in reserves of labor; unmet consumer aspirations; and the overcommitment of resources to the defense sector.

62. As Edmonds notes, official and semi-official papers presented to the Joint Economic Committee of the U.S. Congress in the fall of 1970 estimated that by then Soviet armed forces were getting 40 percent more equipment than their U.S. counterparts and that the true Soviet military budget, always concealed by various devices and headings, might be as much as five times greater by 1968 than it had been in 1958 (when Khrushchev was downsizing the military substantially). Edmonds, *Soviet Foreign Policy*, 40–41.

63. Gelman, *The Brezhnev Politburo and the Decline of Détente*, 126ff, has a good short summary of these developments.

64. Kissinger, *White House Years*, 552.

65. Dobrynin cable of July 12, 1969, Document 5 in Issue 3, Fall 1993, *Bulletin of the Cold War International History Project*, Woodrow Wilson International Center for Scholars, Washington.

66. Kissinger, *White House Years*, 552, for both the quotation and Kissinger's arguments.

67. Isaacson, *Kissinger*, 306.

68. Kissinger, *White House Years*, 557.

69. The authoritative International Institute for Strategic Studies, in London, in its *Military Balance, 1970–71*, 186, gave the following totals for Soviet missiles capable of reaching the United States.

Midyear	ICBMs	SLBMs
1967	460	130
1968	800	130
1969	1,050	160
1970	1,300	280
[1971	1,510	440]

In simplified terms, the Soviets were improving their land-based missile posture rapidly, at the rate of about 250 new installed missiles each year, with an almost equally dramatic increase in their submarine-based missile strength under way by 1970. Kissinger has slightly different figures, notably 1,440 as the mid-1970 figure for ICBMs. *White House Years*, 537.

70. According to the 1974 calculations of the respected Swedish organization SIPRI, the warhead numbers evolved as follows:

Numbers of independently targetable warheads on strategic missiles

Year end	U.S.A.	U.S.S.R.
1967	1,710	722
1968	1,710	934
1969	1,710	1,326
1970	1,874	1,722
1971	3,082	1,763
1972	4,146	1,971
1973	5,210	2,111

71. Nitze, *From Hiroshima to Glasnost*, 309.

72. There was also a running argument among American officials whether Soviet heavy missiles could be constrained by limits on their "throw weight"—that is, the warhead loads they could carry to targets in America. This was a particular concern of Paul Nitze, then and later, but no practicable way of monitoring such a restriction was ever devised or at least seriously considered.

73. As Kissinger later frankly admitted, the Soviet idea of a single installation protecting the capital cities on each side was simply not possible for the United States to carry out, with Congress well aware of the outcry if ABMs were sited in the Washington area. U.S. planning had shifted entirely to protecting wider areas, with emphasis on strategic missile sites, and the "one installation" position briefly taken at Vienna was totally out of sync with ABM plans even then being presented to Congress. Kissinger, *White House Years*, 542.

74. Ash, *In Europe's Name*, 30, notes the influence of the expellees, stronger in the CDU/CSU than in the SPD/FDP coalition. Brandt, *My Life in Politics*, 180, includes a good sample of his eloquence in appealing to this wider interest in lasting peace.

75. Bark and Gress, *History of West Germany*, 184 (reaffirmation of allied status). Ash, *In Europe's Name*, 161–71, is a succinct summary. In the wording changes, the Soviets had wished to describe the various frontiers as "unalterable," but finally agreed to accept "inviolable"—which the Germans could argue to their public did not exclude forever any change, while guaranteeing observance in the meantime.

76. Quoted in Brandt, *My Life in Politics*, 200. The reference could have been taken to mean not only Germans but the Soviets, for having failed to help the resisters in the ghetto.

77. "Acheson Urges Brandt's 'Race to Moscow' Be Cooled Off," *Washington Post*, December 11, 1970, quoted in Brinkley, *Dean Acheson*, 293. When the West German Ambassador in Washington telephoned Acheson to defend his government's policy and insist that the unity of Western Europe and NATO remained Bonn's top priority, Acheson stood his ground in ringing terms. Ibid.

78. *Time*, January 4, 1971, 6ff.

79. Heikal, *Road to Ramadan*, 92–93. The capable Israeli scholar Galia Golan offers a different picture, drawing on other Egyptian sources to argue that Nasser did not have his mind made up before going to Moscow, but instead came around to accepting the cease-fire only because he was driven to despair by Brezhnev's refusal to supply additional military items useful for an offensive crossing of the canal. Golan, *Soviet Policies in the Middle East*, 75–76. The two versions have in common that the Soviets did not oppose the cease-fire or urge Nasser to take stronger action.

80. As of midsummer it was not clear how that debate was going; the public evidence of its existence, as we have noted, was the announcement that the Twenty-fourth Party Congress was being postponed till the spring of 1971. This revelation came on July 13, right in the middle of the Nasser visit. Conceivably the Soviet leaders were simply distracted and unready for another big decision abroad; conceivably some at least argued that a really serious confrontation with the United States in the Middle East could operate to limit if not bar the increased economic links to the West that must have figured in the internal policy debate.

Galia Golan's account claims that Soviet officials in early July also put forward privately to American representatives a proposal containing significant concessions on Israel's borders and accepting that Israeli withdrawal need not take place till after a settlement was reached. Both points were contrary to the positions Egypt had been taking. Golan, *Soviet Policies in the Middle East*, 75. No such proposal is mentioned in American memoirs or accounts.

81. Quandt, *Decade of Decisions*, 102.

82. Kissinger, *White House Years*, 585–86.

83. O'Brien, *The Siege*, 469, using 1975 figures compiled by a scholar of the sociology of the Palestinians.

84. On occasion, false messages were also sent for psychological effect, suggesting greater U.S. capabilities and more immediate intentions than were actually the case.

85. Kissinger, *White House Years*, 610, 614.

86. Kissinger says that Syria's move into Jordan did not start until September 20. Kissinger, *White House Years*, 617. Both Quandt, *Decade of Decisions*, and Safran, *Israel*, date it on September 19; convincing evidence supports that date. The explanation may be that the incursion started on the 19th but only became formidable when substantial reinforcements were sent on the 20th.

87. Quandt's account appears to compress September 19 and 20 into a single day of Washington decision making. After recounting WSAG meetings on the 19th, he

says it was on the same evening that Hussein made his frantic appeal for help and Kissinger turned to Rabin. Other accounts make clear that these events came on the evening of Sunday the 20th.

88. Safran, *Israel*, 454.

89. Haig, *Inner Circles*, 251.

90. Strength estimates from *New York Times*, September 17, 1970, 19, presumably from U.S. official sources.

91. Golan, *Soviet Policies in the Middle East*, 144, analyzes the Soviet position in the Syrian intervention at length. She accepts that through their advisors, and directly from Syrian President Nureddin al-Attassi, the Soviets knew in advance that the Syrians were going to invade Jordan. Yet she takes seriously the various subsequent Soviet urgings for restraint, and concludes that, as the threat of Israeli counterintervention loomed, the Soviets did urge the Syrians to retreat.

92. Nixon, *RN*, 482.

93. While critical of the 1962 windup negotiations, Michael Beschloss notes that both countries treated the Kennedy-Khrushchev agreement with "almost the same reverence" as if it were a treaty. Beschloss, *Crisis Years*, 562n. Reeves, *President Kennedy*, 412–25.

94. Kissinger, *White House Years*, 634.

95. Kissinger, *White House Years*, 637.

96. Beschloss, *Crisis Years*, 554, 558. Kissinger, *White House Years*, 633.

97. Isaacson, *Kissinger*, 292–93.

98. Isaacson, *Kissinger*, 298.

99. Isaacson, *Kissinger*, 302.

100. Nixon, *RN*, 486; also Isaacson, *Kissinger*, 304.

101. Isaacson, *Kissinger*, 307; Kissinger, *White House Years*, 648, on Mansfield and Reston.

102. Kissinger, *White House Years*, 647; Isaacson, *Kissinger*, 308.

103. Haig, *Inner Circles*, 254–55. ("Either you . . . dismantle the base . . . or we will do it for you.") I find his account credible, though neither Nixon nor Kissinger mentions such action. According to Haig, the rarely flappable Dobrynin got quite irate and said this kind of threat was intolerable. He may well have surmised that Haig was exceeding his instructions, or at least interpreting them as a military man rather than as a diplomat might do.

104. Kissinger, *White House Years*, 649–50.

105. Zumwalt, *On Watch*, 311; Isaacson, *Kissinger*, 310.

106. This "parity" objective is stressed by Garthoff, *Détente and Confrontation* (1985 ed.), 16.

107. Beschloss, *Crisis Years*, 560–61.

108. Hersh, *Price of Power*, 251.

109. Nixon's memoirs devote only two pages to policy toward Chile during his tenure. Kissinger makes a strenuous case for what was done in 1970, but has significant evasions and omissions. *White House Years*, 653–83. In a later chapter on U.S. policy toward Chile after Allende took office, he reverts briefly to events of 1970. *Years of Upheaval*, 374–413. Exhaustive congressional hearings in 1975 went deeply into the events of 1970, and later writers have covered the ground well and in close overall agreement. These include a strong chapter in Hersh, who as a reporter had first revealed the extent of CIA activities in the fall of 1974; an excellent chapter (220–39) in Powers, *Man Who Kept the Secrets* (1979), centered on Richard Helms and the role

of the CIA; and an incisive summary in Nathaniel Davis, *The Last Two Years of Salvador Allende* (1985), by the American Ambassador to Chile in 1971–73. Of special overall value are Sigmund, *The Overthrow of Allende* and *The United States and Democracy in Chile*, covering the background and later events as well as the 1970–73 period, and giving due weight to underlying political and social trends.

The findings from the congressional hearings are summarized in the report of a Senate Select Committee (the Church Committee), *Covert Action in Chile, 1963–73*: since the main outlines seem clear, I have not tried to go through this report in detail.

110. Powers, *Man Who Kept the Secrets*, 223, has a good summary of the 1964 effort. Kissinger, *White House Years*, sets its cost at $3 million, the same figure reached by the Church Committee in 1975. Hersh's far larger estimate of $20 million between 1961 and 1964 includes an unstated percentage of economic aid through the Agency for International Development (AID).

111. Hecksher is described well in Powers, *Man Who Kept the Secrets*, 225.

112. Hersh, *Price of Power*, 263.

113. Powers, *Man Who Kept the Secrets*, 228.

114. Sigmund emphasizes that the Frei "revolution" had stalled at that historically dangerous point where expectations had been roused but cannot yet be satisfied by gradual, moderate measures. Sigmund, *Overthrow of Allende*, 57–76.

115. Nixon's report from the Italian businessman was recounted by him in a 1977 television interview. Powers, *Man Who Kept the Secrets*, 234. Nathaniel Davis, a Foreign Service officer who succeeded Korry as ambassador in 1971, disparaged it scathingly: "four thousand miles of heterogeneous societies and regimes would lie between those two slabs of Marxist pumpernickel." Davis, *Last Two Years*, 6. Charles Meyer, then Assistant Secretary of State for Latin America, a businessman with wide experience and contacts in the area, recalls that after the election the tenor of the comments he got from senior Latin American businessmen and officials reflected concern and a need to watch the situation closely, but nothing approaching alarm or a need to take drastic action. Meyer interview, 1994.

116. Hersh, *Price of Power*, 287; Kissinger, *White House Years*, 676. Writing in 1982, Kissinger claimed that "these efforts were called off before they could produce any result." *Years of Upheaval*, 377. It would be more precise to say that the American part was called off and the Chilean action was bungled.

117. Hersh, *Price of Power*, 286.

118. Powers, *Man Who Kept the Secrets*, 220.

119. Powers, *Man Who Kept the Secrets*, 237. That Nixon and Kissinger ignored the momentum a covert operation may acquire, and how hard it may be to control or limit, is particularly striking in view of the deep interest Nixon took in the question of U.S. complicity in the assassination of Ngo Dinh Diem in Vietnam in November 1963. Not in sympathy, in any event, with the removal of Diem, Nixon went to great lengths to try to find evidence that Kennedy had been directly involved or had encouraged the killings of Diem and his brother Ngo Dinh Nhu. *Haldeman Diaries*, 606. These efforts to get at the files grew to the point of obsession in 1971, especially after the publication of the Pentagon Papers. Did Nixon see a resemblance to what he had set under way in Chile?

120. Hersh, *Price of Power*, 297–303, is an excellent short summary of this election period in relation to Vietnam, including postwar interviews with North Vietnamese leaders about their attitude at the time. Kissinger, *White House Years*, 968–86, is

revealing and discursive, and includes the private recommendations of key hawkish senators.

121. Kissinger, *White House Years*, 972–74, and Hersh, *Price of Power*, 300–3, cover the factors and the debate, in sharply different fashion. See also Lankford, *The Last Aristocrat* (biography of Bruce), 361. Habib was a Foreign Service officer who had served in Vietnam in 1965–67, then been in the East Asian Bureau and deeply involved in the 1968 policy review that led to Johnson's decision to move toward peace talks. He was with Harriman and Vance through 1968, then with Lodge and Bruce, and was always the model of a nonpartisan officer. He went on to be Ambassador in Korea and Under Secretary for Political Affairs, the highest post to which a career Foreign Service officer could normally aspire. I considered him a great man, sophisticated and with excellent judgment, blunt and courageous in stating his views.

122. Safire, *Before the Fall*, 383–87.

123. Hersh, *Price of Power*, 302.

124. Hersh, *Price of Power*, 302n. In later summaries, the Administration consistently disregarded the October 7 speech as an important change of position. Only in 1973, in an obscure passage in the annual Foreign Policy Report, was it admitted candidly that not since October 7, 1970, had the Administration insisted on North Vietnamese withdrawal from the South as part of a settlement. Nixon, *U.S. Foreign Policy for the 1970's*, 1973, 59.

125. Stein, *Presidential Economics*, 133–38.

126. Safire, *Before the Fall*, 571; Garment, *Crazy Rhythm*, 161ff.

127. Nixon, *RN*, 492.

128. An excellent recent biography is James Reston, Jr., *The Lone Star* (1989), which deals with how he came into the Nixon Cabinet at 372–88. Connally's own memoir, *In History's Shadow: An American Odyssey* (1993), is scattershot and disappointing.

129. The report, *Goals for Americans*, was published by a citizens Commission on National Goals initiated by President Eisenhower and privately funded and managed. As its staff director, on leave from my government post, I canvassed a considerable spectrum of supposedly expert opinion about whether the report should have as one of its dozen priority subjects the question of adequate raw materials and natural resources, oil first and foremost. The opinion was virtually unanimous that this question did not qualify as a priority.

130. For the economic section of this and later chapters, I have relied heavily on Stein, *Presidential Economics*, 133–207; Volcker and Gyohten, *Changing Fortunes*, 59–90; and Shultz and Dam, *Economic Policy Beyond the Headlines*, 67–68 and passim. I am also much indebted to Professor Peter Kenen of Princeton for initiating me into the mysteries of international economic policy.

131. Volcker and Gyohten, *Changing Fortunes*, 45.

132. Martin and I were colleagues on the Yale governing board through the late 1960s and early 1970s. In drives back and forth to New Haven, he consistently took a deeply alarmist view of the dangers of inflation. In November 1965, when President Johnson had just committed major ground forces in Vietnam, Martin invited me to talk informally to members of the Federal Reserve organization about the prospects for the war. Naively, I did not check with my superiors or with senior economic officials. My best recollection is that I said it would be a difficult and fairly long undertaking and could not start to turn better for at least eighteen months. Shortly

after, the Reserve Board raised interest rates to check inflation, to the displeasure of President Johnson.

133. Volcker and Gyohten, *Changing Fortunes*, 45, 71.

134. Volcker and Gyohten, *Changing Fortunes*, 61.

135. For this section I have relied heavily on the sophisticated and authoritative work of Daniel Yergin, especially *The Prize: The Epic Quest for Oil, Money, and Power*, 500–90, supplemented by Dankwart Rustow and John F. Mugno, *OPEC*.

136. Quoted in Yergin, *The Prize*, 525.

137. Yergin, *The Prize*, 577–80, is a vivid description of the first stage of the "Libyan squeeze."

138. Yergin, *The Prize*, 580.

139. Yergin, *The Prize*, 581.

140. Years later, the CBS-TV show *60 Minutes*, always given to exposing supposed error and betrayal in or out of government, investigated the charge that Nixon and Kissinger, the latter especially, let the Shah have his way on raising oil prices so that he would have the money to pay for his arms purchases from the United States. The charge was not tied specifically to the events of early 1971, but these could have been seen as the starting point for such a policy. I believe (and told the producers of the program at the time) that the charge is false. The Shah held the cards and the United States was in a very weak bargaining position.

141. Levy, *Oil, Strategy and Politics*, 181. This essay was originally published as "Oil Power," in *Foreign Affairs*, July 1971: 652–68.

142. Levy, *Oil, Strategy and Politics*, 182. In fact, within three years the quota system was discarded and over 30 percent of U.S. oil needs was being met by OPEC sources!

143. There is no coherent or comprehensive account of what happened in Cambodia in 1970–71, or for that matter during the climactic months from February to July 1973. Among Western writers on Cambodia, William Shawcross's *Sideshow* remains the best overall account of events in Cambodia and how the Nixon Administration sought to deal with them. But it does not get deeply into what may have been happening within that unhappy country. On the American side, Nixon's memoirs and other writings are totally silent on this whole period, as are Kissinger's save for occasional glancing references. More striking is the absence of any serious discussion by Alexander Haig (*Inner Circles*), since Haig was much closer to the situation than most others. Lewis Sorley's excellent biography of General Abrams, *Thunderbolt*, is helpful but sparing about Cambodia. A helpful source for feel and substance is the short oral history of Emory Swank, U.S. Ambassador from September 1970 to September 1973. Elizabeth Becker's *When the War Was Over* and Ben Kiernan's *How Pol Pot Came to Power* are each sensitive and the fruit of extensive research, but stronger on the periods preceding and following 1970–73.

144. Quoted in Shawcross, *Sideshow*, 175.

145. Becker describes Lon Nol as having very poor military skills, while being strongly antiforeign, a religious reactionary, a firm devotee of the occult, and a practicing mystic. Becker, *When the War Was Over*, 135.

146. Becker, *When the War Was Over*, 140. With American advisors withdrawn, Ambassador Bunker and others in Saigon appear to have had little clear or accurate information on what ARVN was doing in Cambodia.

147. There are very few accounts of the important confrontations between the

executive and Congress that were not in the full glare of public attention. In the present case, however, we have the careful and balanced account of a key participant, John F. Lehman, later Secretary of the Navy under President Reagan, in 1970–71 a young member of the NSC staff charged with responsibility for congressional liaison. His *The Executive, Congress, and Foreign Policy*, written when his memory was still fresh and other participants were fully available, is a first-class analysis, with two particularly useful chapters on the initial clash over the Cooper-Church Amendment and on the confrontation of December and January over that amendment and military aid for Cambodia. Lehman shows President Nixon not only giving the basic orders but intervening at critical points. He also refers frequently to important actions and statements by "a senior official" who is obviously Kissinger.

148. Lehman, *Executive, Congress, and Foreign Policy*, 208, called this confrontation "the most intensive period of consultation and debate between the branches on foreign policy since the Marshall Plan." This overlooks the great debates over sending forces to Europe in 1950–51 and over MacArthur's dismissal in the spring of 1951. But it is true that in the Eisenhower, Kennedy, and Johnson eras there were no similar debates or confrontations over foreign policy.

149. Kissinger, *White House Years*, 991; Fulghum and Maitland, *South Vietnam on Trial*, 66.

150. Clarke, *Advice and Support*, table on 524.

151. Kissinger, *White House Years*, 1002. Fulghum and Maitland, *South Vietnam on Trial*, 70–75, stress the lack of coordination in the field persuasively, based on the retrospective judgment of American senior officers.

152. Palmer, *The 25-Year War*, 109 (evaluation of Lam). It was later learned that Thieu had all along expected to terminate the operation if South Vietnamese casualties reached a certain level.

153. Fulghum and Maitland, *South Vietnam on Trial*, 71–72.

154. Sorley, *Thunderbolt*, 310.

155. Sorley, *Thunderbolt*, 312.

156. Fulghum and Maitland, *South Vietnam on Trial*, 60–61. Other sources agree on the manner of Tri's death, but do not confirm that he was on his way to take command of the Lam Son 719 offensive.

157. Palmer, *The 25-Year War*, 108–15, makes clear that for this operation (and probably others), Nixon and Kissinger took Haig's judgment in preference to the advice of the field command and the JCS. Palmer's account and that of Lewis Sorley, *Thunderbolt* (a biography of General Abrams), 305–16, are painful reading even at a distance of many years.

158. Haig, *Inner Circles*, 272–76.

Chapter 4. 1971: Progress and Preparation

1. Text in Kissinger, *White House Years*, 760.

2. Kissinger, *White House Years*, 702. The last sentence was essentially the same as one drafted in the State Department and used in the Warsaw exchanges in early 1970.

3. Kissinger, *White House Years*, 703.

4. Hersh, *Price of Power*, 368–69.

5. Kissinger, *White House Years*, 706–7.

6. Kissinger, *White House Years*, 710. Fulghum and Maitland, *South Vietnam on Trial*, 23, has a table with the dates of withdrawal of principal combat units and the remaining strength figures for each occasion.

7. Kissinger, *White House Years*, 724.

8. Kissinger, *White House Years*, 725.

9. At the time of the release, Ellsberg was a Visiting Fellow at the Center for International Affairs at the Massachusetts Institute of Technology, where I was also in residence, working on an account of decision making for the Vietnam War in 1961–66. In 1970, when my generous hosts at the Center told me that they wished to have another Vietnam project under way from the standpoint of a dissenter and critic, I suggested Ellsberg. I had worked with him at Defense in the summer of 1964, had read his recent writings and speeches, and thought him extremely bright and capable. He kept largely to himself during his academic year at the Center, and I had no inkling of what was stirring in his mind.

10. Kissinger, *White House Years*, 730.

11. Kissinger, *White House Years*, 743–46, contains his warm and obviously sincere tribute to Zhou.

12. Holdridge, *Crossing the Divide*, 57–58.

13. Kissinger, *White House Years*, 750.

14. Kissinger, *White House Years*, 689.

15. Kissinger, *White House Years*, 757. Kissinger has also said that before he left on his July 1971 trip Nixon urged him to stress that he, Nixon, could "turn hard on Vietnam" and to keep in play a "possible move toward the Soviets." *White House Years*, 735. Kissinger does not say that he carried out such an instruction. I am inclined to doubt that he did so, certainly not with the force its wording suggests. To do so would have been out of key with his early conclusion that the worst way to approach Zhou was to appear to threaten him in any way. We shall come to other instances where Kissinger disregarded instructions from Nixon.

16. It was part of the important report from the Pakistani Ambassador of a talk with Zhou in February 1970, and after a July 1970 meeting of American chiefs of mission in East Asia, those present concluded, in a report passed on to the President, that "Peking is worried that the U.S. will be pulling back militarily from the Western Pacific, and is much concerned over future Japanese capabilities and interests." Marshall Green, unpublished manuscript, *Evolution of U.S.-China Policy, 1956–1973: Memoirs of an Insider*, 38.

17. Hersh, *Price of Power*, 382. Kissinger would not, of course, have known of this conversation at the time.

18. Kissinger, *White House Years*, 749.

19. Kissinger, *White House Years*, 334.

20. Under questioning by the Watergate prosecutors in 1975, Nixon painted a similar but cruder picture of what he himself later told the Chinese on this subject: "We told [the Chinese] that if you try to keep us from protecting the Japanese we would let them go nuclear. And the Chinese said, 'We don't want that.'" Hersh, *Price of Power*, 380–81.

21. Kissinger, *White House Years*, 747; Hersh, *Price of Power*, 376. Hersh adds that Kissinger brought a still fuller book of such information on his second trip in October. One may surmise that the first collection was broad and summary in nature, and that the second went further, perhaps to the point of providing the "raw" material itself, certainly the photographs. Either way, such sharing was an extraordinary act for

material not customarily shared except with the most intimate allies of the United States.

22. Kissinger, *White House Years*, 764.

23. Kissinger, *White House Years*, 765. Emphasis added.

24. Johnson, *Right Hand of Power*, 553–55.

25. *The Gallup Poll, 1959–71*, 2309, 2323.

26. Kissinger, *White House Years*, 768, noting that the exchanges also included the South Asia crisis.

27. The power struggle and Lin's disaster are vividly recounted in MacFarquhar, *The Cambridge History of China*, vol. 15, 323–36.

28. This episode appears consistent with Alexander Haig's experience when he visited Beijing in January 1972 to help prepare for Nixon's visit. Zhou urged that the United States stand fast in Vietnam. Author interview with John Holdridge, 1996.

29. Kissinger, *Diplomacy*, 729.

30. Kissinger, *Diplomacy*, 729.

31. For years members of the East Asian Bureau had regularly discussed the question of opening relations with Beijing as a question of "when" rather than "if." And care was always taken to send Chinese-language officers to posts where they could stay in touch with affairs in China and keep their language skills fresh, as far as possible.

32. Kissinger, *White House Years*, 821. This comes at the close of one of the most important (and often cryptic) passages in Kissinger's memoirs, discussing the situation in early 1971, 802–23.

33. Sutterlin and Klein, *Berlin*, 95–96; interviews with Hillenbrand, 1994–95.

34. Quoted in Hersh, *Price of Power*, 420n. For the views of Hillenbrand and Sutterlin, see Hersh, *Price of Power*, 419, and Sutterlin and Klein, *Berlin*, 421–22. Both have confirmed in interviews in the early 1990s that they remain of the same view. Jonathan Dean, who worked closely with Rush, concurs (1997 interview).

35. Smith, *Doubletalk*, 226. On the 1971 SALT negotiations, the differences between the accounts of Henry Kissinger and what his staff told John Newhouse, on the one hand, and those of Gerard Smith, Paul Nitze, and others in the delegation, on the other, were sharper than for any other period save May 1972.

36. Smith, *Doubletalk*, 196–98. In the same passage, Smith notes that all through 1970 "the Soviets seemed to be marking time," a shrewd judgment.

37. Nixon, *U.S. Foreign Policy for the 1970's, 1971*, 193. Kissinger, *White House Years*, 811–14, on the critics.

38. Kissinger, *White House Years*, 814–15.

39. Kissinger, *White House Years*, 820.

40. Hersh, *Price of Power*, 342, is totally convincing on this point. No doubt the same sort of cleansing was done for the documents leaked later to John Newhouse. His book on the SALT negotiations, *Cold Dawn*, is thus deprived of the authority the work of that capable and honorable scholar should have had.

41. Smith, *Doubletalk*, 223–35, especially 234–35.

42. Interview with Peterson, 1994.

43. Hersh, *Price of Power*, 343.

44. Hersh, *Price of Power*, 346.

45. This summary is based on the useful, and rare, discussion in Peter M. E. Volten, *Brezhnev's Peace Program*, 58–62.

46. This first group included, in addition to Acheson, former High Commissioner to West Germany John J. McCloy, George Ball, and Cyrus Vance, and Generals

Lucius Clay, Alfred Gruenther, Lauris Norstad, and Lyman Lemnitzer. Kissinger, *White House Years*, 944. The whole episode is covered at length in Bird, *The Chairman*, 622–24; and Brinkley, *Dean Acheson*, 297–300.

47. *Congressional Record*, 92nd Cong., 1st sess., 14, 672–15, 960, contain the whole final debate. The key early exchanges are at 15, 113–135.

48. Ibid. For Nelson's remarks, see 15, 363–68 and 15, 943–45. No doubt for reasons of personal loyalty, he nonetheless voted with Mansfield in what was by then a lost cause.

49. Kissinger, *White House Years*, 946–47.

50. Smith, *Doubletalk*, 252–53; see also Haldeman, *Diaries*, 329.

51. The exotics are discussed in Smith, *Doubletalk*, 343.

52. Smith, *Doubletalk*, 277.

53. Smith, *Doubletalk*, 485–86.

54. Smith, *Doubletalk*, 343.

55. The main sources for this section are Volcker and Gyohten, *Changing Fortunes*; Stein, *Presidential Economics*; and Shultz and Dam, *Economic Policy Beyond the Headlines*. There are vivid accounts of the decisive Camp David meeting in Safire, *Before the Fall*, and Haldeman, *Diaries*. What happened and why are probably more clear and undisputed than for any other major event in the Nixon Administration.

56. Shultz, *Economic Policy*, 114.

57. Stein, *Presidential Economics*, 166–67.

58. Volcker and Gyohten, *Changing Fortunes*, 71–76, is an excellent short account of these developments. Both Stein and Shultz discuss the question of incomes policy at length, making clear that each was opposed in principle to such action, and that this had been the consistent position of the Council of Economic Advisors, of which Stein was a member. Shultz and Dam, *Economic Policy*, 80; Stein, *Presidential Economics*, 143–44, 168.

59. Volcker and Gyohten, *Changing Fortunes*, 76–80; Stein, *Presidential Economics*, 165–67.

60. Stein, *Presidential Economics*, 135, is vivid on this well-recognized point, recounting a talk with Nixon in December 1968 in which the newly elected President blamed his 1960 defeat on "economic officials" and "financial types" who put curbing inflation ahead of curbing unemployment. He also recounts that the orthodox anti-inflationary program adopted in 1969 on the recommendation of the CEA was designed to ease the situation before the 1970 congressional elections but worked more slowly than its advocates had predicted. This weakened the force of the CEA's objections in 1971 to a freeze.

61. Haldeman, *Diaries*, 327.

62. Haldeman, *Diaries*, 335–36.

63. Haldeman, *Diaries*, 127, on Nixon's regard for Shultz.

64. Stein, *Presidential Economics*, 180. Shultz and Dam, *Economic Policy*, 117, reach similar conclusions.

65. Shultz and Dam, *Economic Policy*, 118.

66. Shultz and Dam, *Economic Policy*, 110; Volcker and Gyohten, *Changing Fortunes*, 92.

67. Volcker and Gyohten, *Changing Fortunes*, 81–84.

68. Volcker and Gyohten, *Changing Fortunes*, 79, 96.

69. Volcker and Gyohten, *Changing Fortunes*, 86–87.

70. Volcker and Gyohten, *Changing Fortunes*, 80; Shultz and Dam, *Economic Policy*, 115–16.

71. Stein, *Presidential Economics*, 178.

72. Van Hollen, "The Tilt Policy Revisited: Nixon-Kissinger Geopolitics and South Asia," *Asian Survey*, 20 (April 1980): 339–61, 341; Kissinger, *White House Years*, 851–52.

73. Van Hollen, "The Tilt Policy," 342; Hersh, *Price of Power*, 445. The cable was sent in the authorized "dissent channel," initiated during the Vietnam War to permit Foreign Service officers at any level to register dissent from policy. Nonetheless, on Nixon's orders, Consul General Archer Blood was transferred, with only the consolation of an award from the American Foreign Service Association for courage and "creative dissent." Kissinger's memoir is semi-apologetic about this episode, sharply criticizing the officers for giving their cable a low security classification (as if it would not have leaked anyway!) but conceding there was "some merit to the charge of moral insensitivity." Kissinger, *White House Years*, 854.

74. Van Hollen, "The Tilt Policy," 344. A principal critic, Senator Edward Kennedy, chairman of the Senate Judiciary Committee's subcommittee on refugees, claimed that the overlooked shipments had a value of $50 million. While the size of the total deal was on this order, a later study by the General Accounting Office concluded that the value of these particular shipments was only $3.8 million. *New York Times*, February 5, 1972. The question of value was, of course, secondary to the basic fact that any shipments at all had continued.

75. Kissinger, *White House Years*, 863.

76. Quoted in Van Hollen, "The Tilt Policy," 347.

77. Van Hollen, "The Tilt Policy," 346.

78. Kissinger, *White House Years*, 767, has Kissinger's judgment and key parts of a memorandum from Hal Sonnenfeldt and William Hyland. A far more balanced judgment, with additional history on the Indo-Soviet relationship, is in Kux, *Estranged Democracies*, 286, 292, 295. The treaty provided only for consultations in the event of crisis and pledged that neither country would support a third party against the other.

79. Jackson, *South Asian Crisis*, 48–49, notes a number of Soviet actions in the spring to enlarge Soviet economic activity in cooperation with Pakistan.

80. Jackson, *South Asian Crisis*, 41ff.

81. Kissinger, *White House Years*, 864.

82. At an NSC meeting on July 16 and again at a senior meeting on August 11, Nixon did state his resolve to cut off aid to India if it went to war, and roundly denounced Soviet policy. Kissinger, *White House Years*, 863, 869. However, the "five minutes" to make the President's views clear never took place except with his personal staff, nor did Kissinger himself, in conveying the President's wishes, apparently go beyond strident urging of a "tilt" and one early mention of the importance of Pakistan as a channel to China.

83. Jackson, *South Asian Crisis*, 76–77.

84. Kissinger, *White House Years*, 866. Jha was a remarkable figure, an economist and administrator who had played a big part in India's progress in the 1960s. Senior American officials regarded him as a pillar both of his country and of a good relationship with the United States.

85. Kissinger, *White House Years*, 874. Presumably the source was the same Indian official whose reports became crucial in December.

86. Jackson, *South Asian Crisis*, 90–92.

87. Kissinger, *White House Years*, 878ff.

88. Kissinger, *White House Years*, 880–81. Van Hollen, "The Tilt Policy," 348–49, is especially convincing in rebutting Kissinger's claim. A comparison with South Africa in the mid-1980s is to the point: until President De Klerk reversed the policy of his predecessors and agreed to talk directly to Nelson Mandela, the situation was totally stalemated. Similar examples are legion in the history of independence movements, including those of India and Pakistan themselves.

89. Jackson, *South Asian Crisis*, 95–96; Kux, *Estranged Democracies*, 303. Kux was a Foreign Service officer with long service in both India and Pakistan; his survey of Indo-American relations in the Nixon era has balance and perspective.

90. This 1959 agreement was one of the high points of the U.S. embrace of Pakistan during the Eisenhower Administration. That it remained without treaty status and constitutionally not binding showed caution about supporting Pakistan in all contingencies. The accepted view was that the United States, through the SEATO Treaty, of which Pakistan was a signatory, had indeed committed itself to come to Pakistan's aid against any aggression *from the Soviet Union*, but that there was no such obligation, express or implied, in case of conflict with India.

91. Kissinger, *White House Years*, 896. Jackson, *South Asian Crisis*, 106ff, has a careful discussion of the factors behind Yahya's action, as well as a detailed comparison showing how vastly superior India's military forces were by 1971.

92. Kissinger's memoir was to claim that "we enjoyed more support in the world community than on any other [issue] in a decade." *White House Years*, 899. On the substance of the dispute, the resolution was neutral. Key countries made clear that they simply favored a cessation of hostilities. Jackson, *South Asian Crisis*, 127–28.

93. Two criticisms that morning may have aroused Kissinger especially, a strong editorial in *The Washington Post* and a critical column by the usually friendly Joseph Kraft. Jackson, *South Asia Crisis*, 207–9, contains excerpts from Kissinger's briefing. The full text is in the *Congressional Record* for December 9.

94. Kissinger, *White House Years*, 901. Emphasis in original.

95. Jackson, *South Asian Crisis*, 225–26. Throughout the crisis, Sisco consistently urged a cool and correct posture, discounting Kissinger's alarmist views and great-power factors. Marvin Kalb and Bernard Kalb, *Kissinger*, 259–60. There was an important complication that bedeviled efforts to get assurances regarding Kashmir. This was that neither Pakistan nor India recognized the other as sovereign in the areas of Kashmir it controlled under cease-fire lines dating back to the original conflict over Kashmir in 1948. Thus India declined to say whether assurances that it did not threaten "West Pakistan" applied to Kashmir, while Pakistan was equally reluctant to give assurances that it would not take Indian-controlled areas. When Ambassador Jha, through the State Department, asked for such assurances, there was no response. Van Hollen, "The Tilt Policy," 352, and 1994 interview with author.

96. Kissinger, *White House Years*, 904. As a former intelligence officer, I share the view held by many that "raw" intelligence reports such as this one should be handled with special care and efforts at evaluation. Anything "hot"—and in tune with the inclinations of the policymaker—may be given disproportionate weight. Everyone familiar with intelligence reporting from agents has known overzealous sources eager to prove their value by simplifying and dramatizing their reports.

97. Kissinger, *White House Years*, 903.

98. This was an even more startling claim than that based on the 1959 Executive Agreement, which was at least a formal document. The 1962 message, conveyed orally

by the American Ambassador on instructions, came at the time of the Sino-Indian border war and the initiation of a modest U.S. military aid program to India, with which I was involved. Apparently, some in the State Department feared that Pakistan would react negatively to the program. Hence the message of reassurance, to the effect that the United States would support Pakistan against India *if India used U.S.-supplied equipment against it.* In later years, when the brief period of American military aid to India ended, this assurance was no longer relevant. At no time could such a message be regarded as a categorical "pledge," and certainly not when the circumstances that gave rise to it had ceased to exist.

99. Kissinger, *White House Years,* 906–7. In an interview in October 1994, Kissinger confirmed to me that this talk was very important in his perceptions and later actions.

100. Jackson, *South Asian Crisis,* 141, records this change of decision, with the additional note that the authorities in East Pakistan were told that the help from "friends" referred to "Chinese support and an American naval-air intervention"!

101. Kissinger, *White House Years,* 910.

102. The "daylight" order, omitted by Kissinger, is in Admiral Zumwalt's vivid account, *On Watch: A Memoir,* 367–68, along with the important change in the course. Kissinger's memoir sticks to the Bay of Bengal as the sailing area, but Zumwalt was the responsible officer, more familiar with the geography, and surely the more reliable witness.

103. *New York Times,* December 15, 1971. The Kalbs, one or both of whom were aboard the President's plane, have a colorful account of this episode; see Kalb and Kalb, *Kissinger,* 261–62.

104. Zumwalt, *On Watch,* 368.

105. Quoted in Jackson, *South Asian Crisis,* 140. The issue of *Time,* forward-dated "December 26" in customary newsmagazine fashion, actually came to newsstands about December 19. Nixon's interview must have been conducted almost as soon as the war ended on December 16.

106. Kalb and Kalb, *Kissinger,* 262.

107. Nixon's account, *RN,* 531–32, says that Radford was not established beyond doubt as Anderson's source, but relates how he was transferred forthwith to Oregon. At the time, Radford stuck to his denial in the face of a failed polygraph test, but later admitted his responsibility to Seymour Hersh. Colodny and Gettlin, *Silent Coup,* 393.

108. Colodny and Gettlin report interviews with John Ehrlichman, in which he quoted Nixon as saying at the time, in substance, that if he kept Moorer on, he would be "even more pliant than he had been in the past, and that would be good for Nixon." *Silent Coup,* 49. Although I treat this source with reserve on many matters, it is persuasive here. Zumwalt, *On Watch,* 374, defends Moorer's claim that he did not know the materials were special and already knew their substance, and also defends Admiral Welander, the liaison officer, on the ground that Moorer was entitled to the information, and that Haig was keeping General Westmoreland, Army Chief of Staff, informed of similar matters withheld by Kissinger. In the end Zumwalt was harshly critical of Nixon, for failing to get the facts, and for the general atmosphere of conspiracy he created in the White House and between it and the armed services.

109. Zumwalt, *On Watch,* 376.

110. Writing in 1983, Seymour Hersh concluded from intensive inquiry that the Indian source of the CIA report was Morarji Desai, a very senior Indian figure, close colleague of Nehru, and contestant for the prime ministership after his

death. Desai was a perennial critic of Mrs. Gandhi and was eased out of the Cabinet in 1969. Hersh, *Price of Power*, 450, 453. In a 1994 interview with me, Hersh gave as his best recollection that the source was someone familiar with the records of Cabinet discussions, but not in a position to interpret their ultimate thrust. At the time Desai was an ordinary member of parliament, not in the Cabinet. Even if he had access to such records, his interpretation of them would have been secondhand at best.

111. David K. Hall, "Laotian War of 1962 and the Indo-Pakistani War of 1971," in Blechman and Kaplan, eds., *Force Without War*, citing an apparently well-informed Indian source, Pran Chopra, *India's Second Liberation* (MIT Press, 1974), 212–13.

112. On Nixon's displeasure and Kissinger's chagrin, Haldeman's diary is clinching evidence. "[Kissinger] knows he made the mistake in India-Pakistan and doesn't know how to cope with it." Haldeman, *Diaries*, 392. Other references make clear that "the mistake" was the remarks to the media on the plane returning from the Azores, threatening to abandon the Moscow summit. At no point did Nixon or his aides challenge the naval move or Kissinger's other policy actions.

113. Zumwalt himself had a strong background in Soviet studies and had been a protégé of Paul Nitze in the Pentagon's Office of International Security Affairs in the early 1960s. I knew Zumwalt and respected him highly.

114. Zumwalt, *On Watch*, 362.

115. Hall "Laotian War of 1962 and the Indo-Pakistani War of 1971," 195, in Blechman and Kaplan, *Force without War*.

116. Kalb and Kalb, *Kissinger*, 257. To the same effect, see Kux, *Estranged Democracies*, 307. Kux goes on (307–19) to describe the modest easing of Indo-American relations during the ambassadorship of Daniel Patrick Moynihan, from early 1973 to early 1975, while still concluding that the damage from the American handling of the 1971 crisis and war was severe.

117. Kissinger, *White House Years*, 913. Kissinger may well have primed Bhutto to raise the question with Zhou.

118. Kissinger, *Diplomacy*, 728. Emphasis added.

119. Nixon, *RN*, 527. Emphasis added. Kissinger's remark was obviously made to Nixon privately.

120. Kissinger, *Diplomacy*, 199. Kissinger goes on to extol Bismarck's diplomacy precisely because it avoided exclusive commitments and left the way open for flexible responses.

121. These casualty figures are from Braestrup, ed., *Vietnam as History* (1984). I have rounded the South Vietnamese figures to emphasize their approximate nature.

122. Colby, *Lost Victory*, 310.

123. Palmer, *The 25-Year War*, 118.

124. Reporting Cable, December 21, 1970, Pike, ed., *The Bunker Papers*, 802.

125. Pike, ed., *The Bunker Papers*, 802.

126. Palmer, *The 25-Year War*, 94.

127. Text in Kissinger, *White House Years*, 1012.

128. Kissinger, *White House Years*, 1018, with full text at 1488–89.

129. *The Gallup Poll: Public Opinion, 1972–1977*, 13, poll taken February 4–7. The text of the speech is in *Public Papers, 1972*, 1/25/72.

Chapter 5. The Triumphs of 1972

1. Haig, *Inner Circles*, 260.
2. Nixon, *U.S. Foreign Policy for the 1970's*, 1972.
3. Kissinger, *White House Years*, 1061ff, is much more revealing than Nixon, *RN*, 562–64, on this conversation.
4. Kissinger, *White House Years*, 1066.
5. Kissinger, *White House Years*, 1086.
6. Fulghum and Maitland, *South Vietnam on Trial*, 128–42, is a vivid account of the early days of the offensive, with pictures also of the new North Vietnamese weapons.
7. Fulghum and Maitland, *South Vietnam on Trial*, 127, sums up the part played by these highly secret intelligence operations in the field, guided and feeding back to the National Security Agency in Fort Meade, Maryland. It appears that these often detected enemy moves at an early stage and were also able to identify and pinpoint enemy headquarters, permitting air attacks and constant harassment. See also Colby, *Lost Victory*, 320–21.
8. Nixon, *RN*, 590.
9. Text in Stebbins and Adam, eds., *American Foreign Relations 1972*, 152–56. Also in *Public Papers of the President, 1972*, 550–54.
10. Kissinger, in *White House Years*, 1493 (endnote 3), admitted as much.
11. This account of the origin of the SLBM position is based primarily on John Newhouse, *War and Peace in the Nuclear Age*, 230–31. The author relied on an interview with Kissinger in June 1973.
12. Nixon, *RN*, 592.
13. The meetings are fully described in Smith, *Doubletalk*, 370–78, in a chapter entitled "Bullshit," the expression Nixon used to him at the NSC meeting.
14. Kissinger, *White House Years*, 966.
15. Turner, *The Two Germanies*, 154.
16. *New York Times*, April 18, 1972, 3.
17. Kissinger, *White House Years*, 1150.
18. For the highlights of the ratification struggle, I have relied on Bark and Gress, *A History of West Germany*. For a full understanding of the byplay in 1972, I have turned also to Baring, *Machtwechsel*, a balanced account.
19. Bundestag votes were taken by electrical signal, with no tally by individuals. For years, politicians and experts tried to establish where Barzel had gained and lost votes. Baring's best guess is that he lost two or three CDU or CSU members, enough to barely offset well-identified FDP defections. Baring, *Machtwechsel*, 420.
20. Baring, *Machtwechsel*, 421–25. In later years, reliable evidence appeared to establish that the East German intelligence service, the notorious STASI, had bribed one Bundestag member and blackmailed another, to change their votes from Barzel to the government side. This was the conclusion of the prominent West German weekly magazine *Der Spiegel*, July 22, 1991, 57–58. I am indebted to Ben Fischer of the CIA historical office, the Center for the Study of Intelligence, for bringing this source to my attention.
21. Sorley, *Thunderbolt*, 322.
22. Haldeman, *Diaries*, 450.
23. Fulghum and Maitland, *South Vietnam on Trial*, 174.
24. Kissinger, *White House Years*, 1175; also Haldeman, *Diaries*, 450–51.

25. Nixon's memoir, *RN*, is brief on the next decisions. His *No More Vietnams*, written several years later, is more revealing, 140–51. Kissinger's *White House Years*, 1174–86, is as usual full; in it he takes credit for proposing the mining of Haiphong. It seems likely that Alexander Haig also had a significant input.

26. Kissinger, *White House Years*, 1184–85. In his memoirs, Alexis Johnson of the State Department tells an unattractive story, but one that seems in character for Kissinger. He reports that in a conversation just before the climactic NSC meeting of May 8, Kissinger expressed to him a hope that Secretary Rogers would oppose the mining, saying that he himself opposed it, but had exhausted his arguments without persuading Nixon. Johnson doubted that he was being truthful, and on the basis of past experience thought Kissinger entirely capable of setting up Rogers for a rejection and rebuke by Nixon that would further damage his standing and influence. He warned Rogers, who at the meeting was "ambiguous." Johnson, *Right Hand of Power*, 535.

27. Kissinger, *White House Years*, 1184–85.

28. Haig, *Inner Circles*, 287.

29. Text in Stebbins and Adam, eds., *American Foreign Relations 1972*, 257–61. Also in *Public Papers of the President, 1972*, 583–87. The principal authors of the speech draft were Kissinger, Winston Lord of his staff, and John Andrews. All worked hard to remove from the original draft the apocalyptic tone of the Cambodian address two years earlier. Kissinger, *White House Years*, 1189.

30. Dobrynin, *In Confidence*, 246. Nixon's language did have a direct and emotional flavor: "Let us not slide back toward the dark shadows of a previous age. We do not ask you to sacrifice your principles, or your friends, but neither should you permit Hanoi's intransigence to blot out the prospects we together have so patiently prepared." Stebbins and Adam, eds., *American Foreign Relations 1972*, 261.

31. Kissinger, *White House Years*, 1191, quotes the initial comments of *The New York Times*, *The Washington Post*, and other papers. Most were alarmed, primarily by the Soviet reaction they anticipated.

32. Dobrynin, *In Confidence*, 247. Kissinger's account does not mention such an exchange, or suggest that the bombing of Haiphong Harbor was suspended, the only sure way to avoid a recurrence.

33. Kissinger, *White House Years*, 1194. Nixon, *RN*, 607, has essentially the same version, obviously provided by Kissinger to Nixon, probably right away. Dobrynin, *In Confidence*, 247–49, gives a conflicting account of this meeting on the 11th, saying that Kissinger did not treat his message as a clear-cut reply that the summit was still on. I have not tried to reconcile the two accounts, since their differences bear only on timing.

34. *New York Times*, May 10, 1972, 2.

35. All quotations from Kissinger, *White House Years*, 1201. Kissinger's listing also included Soviet concern over the possibilities of confrontation, especially in the Middle East, but this was a minor part of his analysis.

36. For Dobrynin's account, see *In Confidence*, 246–49.

37. Isaacson, *Kissinger*, 422–23, quoting the author's interview with Arbatov in 1989.

38. Dobrynin, *In Confidence*, 249.

39. See Kissinger, *White House Years*, 1202–57. For a contrasting view of the SALT negotiations at the summit, the best source is Smith, *Doubletalk*, 407–45, written shortly after the events but not published until 1980, after the publication of *White House Years*. Smith delayed publication because he undertook other government re-

sponsibilities and was concerned that early publication might diminish his effectiveness in the new post. It was another selfless decision, among many by him.

40. Kissinger, *White House Years*, 1229. Smith, *Doubletalk*, 417, quotes a biting contemporary comment on the procedural arrangements by his colleague Paul Nitze.

41. Full texts are in Stebbins and Adam, eds., *American Foreign Relations 1972*, 61–78, along with Nixon's speech.

42. In fact, the U.S. side would never build a Washington complex because of the popular objections, yet the agreement did mean that neither side would have a strategically significant missile defense system. Isaacson, *Kissinger*, 429. The summit did resolve the remaining issue of distance between major ABM radar installations, accepting the U.S. position that this should be 1,300 miles, against the Soviet preference for 1,500 miles.

43. Willrich and Rhinelander, *SALT*, 145. A "launcher" and a "missile" were essentially equivalent in numbers for many missile types but not for all. Thus agreements were framed in terms of numbers of launchers.

44. The conversion possibility was negligible for sea-based missiles. Any alteration in their physical characteristics would have needed wholesale redesign and rebuilding of the submarines themselves.

45. Kissinger, *White House Years*, 1239. In one other case, however, the U.S. side used the unilateral statement approach, but with a much more forceful statement of the consequences of breach. This was the important issue of future mobile missiles. In a unilateral statement, labeled "B," the United States agreed to defer to future negotiations the question of a ban on deployment of mobile land-based ICBM launchers, but added that during the life of the Interim Agreement it would consider deployment of such launchers "inconsistent with the objectives of the agreement" — implying that the United States might then scrap the whole Interim Agreement. Text in Willrich and Rhinelander, *SALT*, 306.

46. Mathematically, the total top and bottom circular surface area of the missile in its upright position would be, as schoolboys know, the constant known as pi, times the radius (half the diameter) squared. A radius increase of 15 percent could thus produce a 32.25 percent increase in surface area (1.15 squared equals 1.3225). This would also have to be multiplied by the depth measurement. It was judged at the time that depth could be increased up to a near doubling, so that overall volume could go up by over 50 percent!

47. The two points were separately stated in the "Agreed Interpretations" section that followed the basic text of the Interim Agreement. Willrich and Rhinelander, *SALT*, 303–4. U.S. negotiators later said that by "dimensions" they had meant *either* diameter or depth, but not both, but this view was certainly not established in the text or any interpretation. Smith, *Doubletalk*, 432, and Willrich and Rhinelander are sources for the view that no tighter control was attainable.

Hersh, *Price of Power*, 547, reports that U.S. electronic intelligence at the time could intercept car phone exchanges with Soviet official vehicles. On the final day of the summit, these picked up a conversation between Brezhnev and a high-ranking defense official, in which the official assured Brezhnev that the next planned Soviet missile could be fitted within the greater silo dimensions under the agreement.

48. A useful summary of the strategic missile balance under the Interim Agreement is in International Institute for Strategic Studies, *The Military Balance, 1972–1973*, 83–86.

49. International Institute for Strategic Studies, *The Military Balance, 1972–1973*, 83–86. Intercontinental bomber figures are from Johnson, *Right Hand of Power*, 581.

50. Both purposes were strongly supported by experts who had studied the problem of strategic stability, and had been much written up in the literature since the late 1950s.

51. Hersh, *Price of Power*, 553, states convincingly that this concession was not disclosed to Congress during the ratification process or publicly revealed until 1974!

52. Kissinger, *White House Years*, 1232, describes the *Times* story, and Smith, *Doubletalk*, 420–21, describes his views and actions. Smith says that he found out only later that the Soviets were insisting by this time that SLBMs be part of the overall agreement. Kissinger's account makes no mention of such a Soviet position, which could have been an important part of Nixon's "massage table" decision to persist on including SLBM launchers.

53. Kissinger, *White House Years*, 1233. After the meeting with the President, Kissinger sent "a sharp cable" to Haig telling him to rally support in Washington, not simply transmit concerns.

54. In the case of the 1963 Partial Test Ban Treaty, the Joint Chiefs had taken a similar position and been given assurances of detection measures. This time they were more vehement, and the enlarged programs they sought much greater.

55. The visit is well described by Kissinger, *White House Years*, 1260–65. He returns to the argument in *Years of Upheaval*, 667–77. Other useful sources are Rubin, *Paved with Good Intentions*, and Bill, *The Eagle and the Lion*.

56. Kissinger, *White House Years*, 1263; Rubin, *Paved with Good Intentions*, 125–27.

57. Rubin, *Paved with Good Intentions*, 126, and Kissinger, *White House Years*, 1263, for the regional situation as Kissinger saw it.

58. Sorley, *Arms Transfers Under Nixon*, tables at 194. Sorley defends the sales as wise and necessary (114–25), as did Kissinger in both volumes of his memoirs, *White House Years*, 1263–65, and *Years of Upheaval*, 668–70. Rubin, *Paved with Good Intentions*, 142, and Bill, *The Eagle and the Lion*, 209–11, are critical, especially of the long-term political impact within Iran of the massive weapons program.

59. Kissinger, *White House Years*, 1265; *Years of Upheaval*, 668–70. In his first volume, Kissinger said that he would discuss the policy of aid to the Kurds, and then its withdrawal, in greater detail in his second volume. He did not do so, suggesting the weakness of his case.

60. *The Gallup Poll, 1972*, 36–37.

61. *The Gallup Poll, 1972*, 45.

62. *The Gallup Poll, 1972*, 50, 55.

63. These figures are from Nixon, *RN*, 670–71. For a balanced view of Nixon's domestic record, see Hoff, *Nixon Reconsidered*. On the environment, an excellent summary is by its chief figure, Russell E. Train, in Hoff and Ink, eds., *The Nixon Presidency*, 185–96. Train lists considerable achievements, but also concludes that Nixon "had little personal interest in or enthusiasm for the environmental program his Administration pursued so vigorously and effectively." Ibid., 196.

64. Sheehan, *A Bright Shining Lie*, 3–28.

65. Kissinger, *Years of Upheaval*, 341.

66. Author's interview with Philip Habib, 1973.

67. Kissinger, *White House Years*, 1284.

68. Kissinger, *White House Years*, 1294–95. Some sources give higher figures for

the Soviet military presence in Egypt. Mohammed Hassanein Heikal, a prominent newspaper editor always close to the leadership, gave a figure of 21,000 in his important account of the period. Heikal, *Road to Ramadan*, 175.

69. Another factor may have been that relations with Egypt were apparently handled not by the Soviet Foreign Office but by a succession of Politburo members working through the Central Committee. Visiting Egypt in April 1972, I was told on several occasions of the low opinion Egyptians had of the crude behavior of Soviet troops.

70. Kissinger, *White House Years*, 1298.

71. Trager, *Great Grain Robbery*, is a vivid account of the events and personalities of the 1972 grain sales, with supporting material on the grain market and Soviet agriculture generally.

72. Trager, *Great Grain Robbery*, 16.

73. Trager, *Great Grain Robbery*, 10. At this time, when Peter Peterson was brought in to head the International Economic Policy Council, he was not given any policy responsibility on agriculture matters.

74. Trager, *Great Grain Robbery*, 10–11.

75. Kissinger, *White House Years*, 1269.

76. Trager, *Great Grain Robbery*, 36.

77. Trager, *Great Grain Robbery*, 20–30, records many individual purchases from the grain companies, but does not give overall figures. No doubt the Department of Agriculture did not have such figures. They and the rest of the government were flying half blind.

78. In 1972 the subsidy level for exported wheat was about 14 cents a bushel. Trager, *Great Grain Robbery*, 20–30, gives a vivid account of the role of Carroll Brunthaver, the new official in charge of subsidies.

79. Trager, *Great Grain Robbery*, 18–19.

80. Kissinger, *White House Years*, 1270.

81. Kissinger, *White House Years*, contains only a handful of references to Jackson, all favorable, before the fall of 1972.

82. The Rand Corporation, based in Santa Monica, California, was a large research organization set up in the 1950s and originally relying primarily on funds from the Pentagon for specific projects. In the 1960s and 1970s it steadily broadened its funding base and range of interests, while keeping a strong defense component in its work.

83. Stern, *Water's Edge*, 19 ("a bad one").

84. *Congressional Record*, 92nd Cong., 2d sess., 1972, 118, pt. 23: 29725–26 (Cooper argument) and 30649 (approval of amendment).

85. *Congressional Record*, 92nd Cong., 2d sess., September 14, 1972, 118, pt. 23: 29725.

86. This section is based largely on Stern, *Water's Edge*, a masterly case study of the controversy over trade and emigration in the early 1970s. Stern was at the time an assistant to a liberal senator, Gaylord Nelson of Wisconsin, with good access to practically all the key actors in the Senate.

87. Stern, *Water's Edge*, 4–7.

88. Stern, *Water's Edge*, 14–15. Jewish leaders who saw Nixon before the summit got the impression he would bring the subject up, but he did not do so.

89. Stern, *Water's Edge*, 16, 19.

90. "Jackson . . . opposed the basic direction of Soviet-American trade negotiations." Stern, *Water's Edge*, xiv. I have called the tax an "exit tax." At various times it

was referred to as an "emigration tax" or, since those affected were mostly educated, an "education tax."

91. Dobrynin, *In Confidence*, 268.

92. Stern, *Water's Edge*, 7–10.

Chapter 6. "Peace" Comes to Indochina

1. Morrocco, *Rain of Fire*, 136–37.

2. In hearings before the House Committee on Appropriations, Thomas Moorer, Chairman of the Joint Chiefs of Staff, testified that air bombing had reduced overland imports from 160,000 tons a month to 30,000, and the mining had reduced seaborne imports from 250,000 tons a month to near zero. See House Committee on Appropriations, *Briefings on Bombings of North Vietnam: Hearings Before Subcommittees of the Committee on Appropriations*, 93rd Cong., 1st sess., January 9–13, 1973, 2, 27.

3. Porter, *A Peace Denied*, 121, quoting the able correspondent Joseph Kraft's report of North Vietnamese views expressed to him in a visit to Hanoi in that month.

4. See Porter, *A Peace Denied*, 114. The January 1973 testimony of Admiral Moorer was to the same effect, stressing especially the drop in civilian but not in military flows.

5. Porter, *A Peace Denied*, 115–16.

6. Kissinger, *White House Years*, 1322–23.

7. Then and later, Kissinger purported to set great store by provisions that barred later infiltration of new forces. The chances that these would be observed, or that an international commission could report and act on any violations, were about zero, as experience in Laos after the 1962 Geneva Accords had conclusively demonstrated.

8. Porter, *A Peace Denied*, 121.

9. Kissinger, *White House Years*, 1347.

10. Becker, *When the War Was Over*, 109; Chanda, *Brother Enemy*, 59–60; Shawcross, *Sideshow*, 238, 250–51.

11. Nixon, *U.S. Foreign Policy for the 1970's*, 1972, 116, 119. In one of these passages, there was specific reference to the need for congressional approval.

12. Nixon, *RN*, 692.

13. Hung and Schecter, *Palace File*, 33.

14. Goodman, *Lost Peace*, 130–31, says that Kissinger rejected urgings by his staff to be tougher on these issues in his last sessions with Le Duc Tho.

15. It is not clear whether Nixon authorized what Kissinger said on this occasion. The President and his staff were focused overwhelmingly on the election and on a spate of stories about dirty tricks that were appearing in *The Washington Post*. See Haldeman, *Diaries*, passim.

16. *Washington Post*, Op-Ed pages, October 29 and 30, 1972.

17. Ehrlichman, *Witness to Power*, 179.

18. A few of these were revealed in April 1975 at the time of the fall of Saigon. The apparently complete file was not published until 1986 in Hung and Schecter, *Palace File*, 365–98, and includes a number of letters to Nixon's successor, Gerald Ford, right down to the fall of Saigon in April 1975. The body of that book contains long discussions of Thieu's reaction to particular letters.

19. Admiral Moorer's January 1973 testimony before the House Appropriations Committee, *Briefings on Bombings of North Vietnam*, 93rd Cong., 1st sess., 1973, 32,

giving the above figures, also estimated a figure of 2 million tons for the *annual* flow of Soviet and Chinese supplies into Haiphong before it was mined. The comparison is obvious.

20. Le Gro, *Vietnam*, 17.

21. Secretary Laird, on November 7, explicitly admitted this aim. Porter, *A Peace Denied*, 144. Actually, when the original schedule for completing an agreement was abandoned, by October 26, U.S. deliveries were extended through November.

22. House Appropriations Committee, *Briefings on Bombings of North Vietnam*, Moorer testimony, 4.

23. Hung and Schecter, *Palace File*, 121–25, describe the Thieu-Haig talks and Thieu's reaction to the letter that arrived shortly after Haig had returned to Washington. The authors also report (354) that in a 1985 interview Melvin Laird said he had been told by Kissinger, apparently in 1975 after the letters had been released, that the pledges were "a deal between Haig and the President."

24. Hung and Schecter, *Palace File*, 388, has a photostatic copy of the letter, with Thieu's vehement marking of the passages quoted.

25. For a vivid, full account of Linebacker II, see Morrocco, *Rain of Fire*, 146–69; A more analytic account is Clodfelter, *Limits of Air Power*, 183–202.

26. Turley, *The Second Indochina War*, 147, quotes Hanoi's original official estimate (frequently cited by other writers) of 1,318 killed, but notes that this was later raised to 2,196.

27. The poll of senators was by the *Congressional Quarterly*. Hersh, *Price of Power*, 627. For a sample of domestic and foreign reactions, see Clodfelter, *Limits of Air Power*, 191.

28. Hung and Schecter, *Palace File*, 144–45, 392.

29. Kissinger, *White House Years*, 1465, also 1372, 1383, 1414, and especially 1495–96.

30. To the same effect, Sir Robert Thompson in 1975 judged that after the eleven days of bombing, North Vietnam was at the mercy of the United States and would have accepted any terms. Thompson and Frizzell, *Lessons of Vietnam*, 105.

31. It was symptomatic that on January 2 the House Democratic Caucus had voted 154–75 to cut off all funds as soon as American troops and the POWs were out, and on January 4 the Senate Democratic Caucus followed suit by a 36–12 vote. Hersh, *Price of Power*, 631. Nixon noted both votes and found them confirmed by the chill tone of meetings with the Democratic leadership right after that. He knew the handwriting was on the wall. Nixon, *RN*, 742–43.

32. In his opening talk with Thieu on October 18, Kissinger had said, "The United States believed that secret understandings" with the two major Communist countries "would drastically reduce the supply of war material to North Vietnam." Hung and Schecter, *Palace File*, 87. The January assurances were given to Foreign Minister Tran Van Lam: in an account apparently from Lam, the veteran Australian correspondent Denis Warner says that Kissinger told Lam he had "firm assurances" from both Beijing and Moscow that "the flow of offensive weapons would stop." Warner, *Not with Guns Alone*, 5. The degree to which Kissinger's claim sank in is suggested by its being mentioned on background in April 1973, by Vietnamese sources, when Thieu visited Nixon in San Clemente. *New York Times*, April 7, 1973.

33. Nixon, *No More Vietnams*, 169. Kissinger, *White House Years*, 1470.

34. Alsop column, *Washington Post*, October 30, 1972, A21.

35. Kissinger, *Years of Upheaval*, 37–41.

36. Isaacs, *Without Honor*, 60, rightly stresses this point.

37. Isaacs, *Without Honor*, 62–63.

38. See Isaacs, *Without Honor*, 68ff, for an excellent summary.

39. Isaacs, *Without Honor*, 94, notes that General Frederick Weyand, the last U.S. commander in Vietnam, pushed for the delineation of areas of control from November on, foreseeing rightly that the cease-fire could hardly hold without them. Apparently, the negotiating team did not feel it could take on anything else, perhaps in part because it surmised that delimiting, and thus legitimizing, areas of Communist control in the South would be extremely objectionable to Thieu.

40. Kissinger, *Years of Upheaval*, 10. It is striking both that the claim is undocumented and that nothing resembling it appears in any of the extensive quotations from records of conversation and cables in Kissinger's first volume.

41. Chanda, *Brother Enemy*, 68.

42. Isaacs, *Without Honor*, 211–12, is an excellent summary on the legal position. Kissinger, *Years of Upheaval*, 10, describing the final exchanges with Le Duc Tho on this subject, says it was Nixon who finally decided not to press further for the kind of assurance Tho was plainly not ready to give.

43. See Herz, *Vietnam War in Retrospect*, 65; Ambassador Herz was an experienced Foreign Service officer who had served in Saigon and was in the State Department at the time of the negotiations, although not directly involved.

44. *The Gallup Poll: Public Opinion, 1972–1977*, 93–94.

45. Ehrlichman, *Witness to Power*, 288.

46. Kalb and Kalb, *Kissinger*, 422. This report seems the most reliable picture of how Kissinger saw the Paris Agreement and the situation at the time.

47. Nixon, *RN*, 689, 730.

48. Nixon, *RN*, 742. Emphasis added.

49. Nixon, *RN*, 860, gives the figure of 591, but so worded that he may have been including some allegedly held back or recently dead.

50. *The Gallup Poll, 1972–1977*, 93–94.

51. Kissinger, *Years of Upheaval*, 13–71.

52. Seventh Air Force headquarters had been moved from Saigon after the cease-fire in Vietnam went formally into effect in January. In addition to 419 strike aircraft and 56 B-52 bombers in Thailand itself as of April 1, 1973, the Air Force could bring to bear additional B-52s from Guam. *Thailand, Laos, Cambodia, and Vietnam: April 1973*, a staff report to a subcommittee of the Senate Foreign Relations Committee, June 11, 1973, 4.

53. Isaacs, *Without Honor*, 217–20, is especially vivid on the situation in Cambodia at this time and the effect of the bombing.

54. Examples were that 175 military trucks had crossed the demilitarized zone in a single day and that 223 tanks had been detected moving through Laos and Cambodia into South Vietnam. Kissinger, *Years of Upheaval*, 32.

55. Kissinger, *Years of Upheaval*, 317.

56. Kissinger, *Years of Upheaval*, 317–18.

57. When Nixon's secret pledges to Thieu became public in 1975 (in circumstances to be recounted in Chapter 9, part 2), Kissinger was to contend that these Nixon warnings in March 1973, along with other statements in this period, amounted to a public statement of the secret pledges Nixon had made to Thieu, making clear to the American public the policy behind those pledges. Kissinger, *White House Years*,

1373, 1495. He was at once challenged in an article by McGeorge Bundy, "Vietnam, Watergate and Presidential Powers," *Foreign Affairs*, Winter 1979–80, 397–407, and returned to the issue, with others, in *Years of Upheaval*, 305. The quality of Kissinger's argument can be judged by the fact that he characterizes the Nixon-Thieu letters as saying only that "we [the United States or Nixon and Kissinger?] were prepared to defend the Paris Agreement by military action if necessary." This is a ludicrous understatement of the language used in the two pledge letters.

58. John Osborne, "Nixon Watch," *New Republic*, March 31, 1973: 13. Osborne was an astute observer not basically hostile to Nixon and a good friend to one member of his staff, Leonard Garment. Garment, *Crazy Rhythm*, 287.

59. Quoted in Kissinger, *Years of Upheaval*, 305–6.

60. Kissinger, *Years of Upheaval*, 323.

61. Block, *Herblock Special Report*, 132.

62. Graham's chapter on Watergate in her memoir, *Personal History*, 485–508, is a spine-tingling account of the paper's actions and her own experiences. The handling raised the *Post*'s reputation deservedly to the highest levels, symbolized by a Pulitzer Prize for Public Service. Incidentally, it is a sign of the delay in the country's reactions that, as she recounts, the Pulitzer Prize jury in the early spring of 1973 did not have in mind any recognition of the *Post* on this account. Only when McCord and others after him greatly amplified the thrust of the *Post* stories did the Pulitzer committee scramble to give the paper their top award. Graham, *Personal History*, 487–88.

63. As a student at the Law School in 1946, I took Cox's course in Labor Law, based extensively on the opinions of the recently created National Labor Relations Board. During his several years as a member of the board, his opinions frequently diverged from what was then a liberal majority. His reputation (and my experience) was that he was a relentless teacher and exemplar of objective probing and analysis.

64. House Armed Services Committee, *Bombing in Cambodia: Hearings*, 93rd Cong., 1st sess., July–August 1973. The Appendix (496–512) contains excerpts of testimony by General George C. Brown at an executive session on July 13, 1973, in relation to his nomination as Air Force Chief of Staff.

A few members of the Senate had actually learned the essential facts about this in late 1972, from a disillusioned Air Force officer, Hal Knight. The reluctance of these senators to make an immediate issue of the bombing and its secrecy is evidence of how strong Nixon's position and image were until March.

65. *The Gallup Poll, 1972–1977*, 156–58. Similarly, a *Time* magazine poll in August had 60 percent favoring Nixon continuing in office, 20 percent for resignation, only 10 percent for impeachment. White, *Breach of Faith*, 297.

66. *The Gallup Poll, 1972–1977*, 95, 114, 115, 118.

67. Hung and Schecter, *Palace File*, 163.

68. Gallup polls had shown a significant switch in public opinion on the question of future military aid, from 51–39 in favor in September 1972 to 52–37 against in late November, and 50–38 against in a special January 25 poll. *The Gallup Poll, 1972–1977*, 55–56, 74, 94. This suggests that the massive Enhance programs may have struck many Americans as fulfilling future needs and obligations, a reaction Nixon does not seem to have anticipated.

69. Kissinger, *Years of Upheaval*, 311.

70. *New York Times*, April 8, 1973, E15.

71. Kissinger, *Years of Upheaval*, 324. Kissinger went on to conclude (327) that the chance for action in the first months of 1973 was lost by "Watergate's enfeeblements."

72. Nixon, *No More Vietnams*, 178.

73. *New York Times*, April 24, 1973, A5 (Kissinger's remarks); *Washington Post*, April 26, 1973, A1 (Marder).

74. Isaacs, *Without Honor*, 225

75. Isaacs, *Without Honor*, 225. Another example of contemporary reporting was a long feature story on Cambodia by the veteran H. G. S. Greenway, *Washington Post*, April 8, 1973, A1.

76. *Washington Post*, March 30, A14; April 3, A18.

77. Senate Foreign Relations Committee, *U.S. Air Operations in Cambodia: April 1973*, 93rd Cong., 1st sess., April 27, 1973, 1, 8.

78. House Appropriations Committee, *Department of Defense Appropriations for 1974: Hearings Before a Subcommittee of the House Appropriations Committee*, 93rd Cong., 1st sess., January 9–13, 1973, 153–54.

79. Senate Foreign Relations Committee, *Department of State Appropriations Authorization, Fiscal Year 1974: Hearings Before the Senate Foreign Relations Committee*, 93rd Cong., 1st sess., 1973, 449–517. The key pages of argument are 452, 485–86, 489–93, and 511. Rogers's original legal memorandum is also in Kissinger, *Years of Upheaval*, 1240–43.

80. Senate Foreign Relations Committee, *Department of State Appropriations Authorization, Fiscal Year 1974*, 485–86.

81. Senate Foreign Relations Committee, *Department of State Appropriations Authorization, Fiscal Year 1974*, 511.

82. Before reaching this point, Rogers had conceded that the theory of a residual authority was a "very close" question. Senate Foreign Relations Committee, *Department of State Appropriations Authorization, Fiscal Year 1974*, 490.

83. Senate Foreign Relations Committee, *U.S. Air Operations in Cambodia: April 1973*. Lowenstein and Moose later published a fuller report of their trip: *Thailand, Laos, Cambodia, and Vietnam: April 1973*, June 11, 1973.

84. Senate Appropriations Committee, *Second Supplemental Appropriations for Fiscal Year 1973, Department of Defense: Hearings Before a Subcommittee of the Senate Appropriations Committee*, 93rd Cong., 1st sess., 1973, 1995.

85. Senate Appropriations Committee, *Second Supplemental Appropriations*, 1996–97, quoted in Isaacs, *Without Honor*, 135–36.

86. An earlier amendment to bar the transfer of funds to support bombing activities during the current fiscal year (that is, up to June 30) was also passed, 219–188, in what members saw as the true breakpoint for their chamber. The Long Amendment, a more categorical action for the new fiscal year, attracted greater support. See *Congressional Record*, 93rd Cong., 1st sess., 1973, 15318–23 (Leggett speech, 15296–98).

87. Among the Democrats who switched were Richard Bolling of Missouri (chairman of the Rules Committee), Thomas Foley of Washington (former assistant to Senator Henry Jackson), Henry Gonzalez and Jake Pickle of Texas (both strong followers of Lyndon Johnson, who had supported Nixon over Vietnam right up to his death in late January 1973), Otis Pike of New York, Melvin Price of Illinois, and Clement Zablocki of Wisconsin (long the chairman of the Asia subcommittee of the House Foreign Affairs Committee). Among the Republicans who felt differently in 1973 was John B. Anderson of Illinois.

The record of the House in the Vietnam War is a fascinating and neglected study. By far the most illuminating, concise, and colorful analysis I have found is the chapter "The House at War," in Rapoport, *Inside the House*, 201–44.

88. Kissinger, *Years of Upheaval*, 351.

89. The fact that the House vote in late June was almost identical to that in early May is another indication that Watergate had little impact.

90. Two substantially different accounts are in Kissinger, *Years of Upheaval*, 355–59, and Hung and Schecter, *Palace File*, 203–4. The language of the ban actually covered only North and South Vietnam, Cambodia, and Laos, so that Ford's pledge went a notch further, in exchanges that were clearly hectic and confused. The Hung-Schecter account, based on an interview with Melvin Laird, then Nixon's point man with Congress, is the more convincing.

91. Hung and Schecter, *Palace File*, footnote 22 on 508, quoting a 1985 interview with Laird. Another and fuller account, based on a long interview with Ford right after the crucial day, is in Rapoport, *Inside the House*, 239–43.

92. Nixon, *No More Vietnams*, 181–83.

93. Compare Vogt's long letter, Tab C of the Appendix in Kissinger, *Years of Upheaval*, 1227–30, with Isaacs, *Without Honor*, 229, and Shawcross, *Sideshow*, 294.

94. *Washington Post*, September 5, 1973, F7, quoted in Shawcross, *Sideshow*, 310–11; see also 269. In his three years as ambassador, Swank had become more and more pessimistic about the war, and more and more frank in saying so in closely held cables, while keeping his thoughts to himself in the field and carrying out policy faithfully and diligently. To Kissinger and his staff he had come to seem defeatist, especially about the 1973 bombing. On returning to Washington he was put in a blind alley assignment, and retired from the Foreign Service in 1975.

95. Hung and Schecter, *Palace File*, 204, quoting from the authors' interview with Haig in 1985.

96. Kissinger, *Years of Upheaval*, 351–52; see also Isaacs, *Without Honor*, 234–35.

97. Having failed to mention the Cambodian negotiating effort in his 1978 memoirs, *RN*, Nixon gives it considerable emphasis in *No More Vietnams*. At 177 he asserts that as of mid-June "both Cambodian parties turned out to be responsive to our plan." Kissinger's more detailed account makes no such claim even as to Sihanouk. Kissinger, *Years of Upheaval*, 353.

98. Kissinger, *Years of Upheaval*, 365.

99. Isaacs, *Without Honor*, 216, 233–34.

100. This trip, not mentioned by Isaacs and perhaps not even known to Kissinger at the time, is recounted authoritatively in Chanda, *Brother Enemy*, 70–71. This remarkable book is by far the most thorough study of the relations between North Vietnam (Vietnam after 1975) and Cambodia, with many illuminating flashbacks to the events before 1975, drawn from an extraordinary range of personal interviews and acute observation. This particular description of the April trip came in part from personal interviews with Sihanouk himself, in part from Khmer Rouge sources.

101. Isaacs, *Without Honor*, 237.

102. As we have seen, these hearings were held by a subcommittee of the Senate Foreign Relations Committee, chaired by Senator Stuart Symington of Missouri. For a good short account of this and other events in Congress at this period, see Alton Frye and Jack Sullivan, "Congress and Vietnam: The Fruits of Anguish," in Lake, ed., *Vietnam Legacy*, 202–7.

103. John W. Finney, then covering Congress for *The New York Times*, gave a

good short account of the bill's origins in *New York Times,* April 16, 1972, E1. Much of my account of the act's history comes from Finney's thoughtful reporting.

104. An early example of invoking that power, albeit in vain, was the 1846 vote of a young congressman named Abraham Lincoln against funds for President Polk's Mexican War.

105. Quoted in *New York Times,* October 7, 1971, A3.

106. See Schlesinger in *New York Times,* January 5, 1972, 37, and at greater length in "Not This War-Powers Bill," *New Republic,* February 5, 1972: 13–14, 106.

107. *New York Times,* April 14, 1972, 1.

108. *New York Times,* November 18, 1973, 8.

Chapter 7. Under Pressure

1. Kissinger, *Years of Upheaval,* 44–71.

2. Quotations from Kissinger, *Years of Upheaval,* 55.

3. Kissinger, *Years of Upheaval,* 47.

4. Kissinger, *Years of Upheaval,* 53.

5. Kissinger, *Years of Upheaval,* 295.

6. Bruce had been Ambassador to France, the Federal Republic of Germany, and Britain, as well as Under Secretary of State in the final year of the Truman Administration.

7. Kissinger, *Years of Upheaval,* 678.

8. Holdridge, *Crossing the Divide,* 143–63. The author was Bruce's deputy.

9. On the date of onset of Zhou's cancer, Wilson, *Zhou En-lai,* 282.

10. Kissinger, *Years of Upheaval,* 687–88.

11. Kissinger, *Years of Upheaval,* 695.

12. Kissinger, *Years of Upheaval,* 696.

13. See Ikle's article "Can Nuclear Deterrence Last Out the Century?" *Foreign Affairs,* January 1973: 267–85.

14. Kissinger, *Years of Upheaval,* 263–65. Johnson, *Right Hand of Power,* 591–92, records that it was just at this time that there was published an account of SALT I that was heavily favorable to Kissinger, denigrating the role of the negotiating team, and obviously based on massive leaks from Kissinger's office. This was John Newhouse, *Cold Dawn.* When Alexis Johnson remonstrated to Kissinger by cable over the Newhouse book, he got only an anodyne reply denying leaks. Johnson's comment: "I did not believe him, and I think Henry and I understood each other on this. It was this sort of reflexive deceptiveness that made the whole administration seem unworthy to the public, and very difficult to work for."

15. Kissinger, *Years of Upheaval,* 271–73; see also Johnson, *Right Hand of Power,* 587–88.

16. Kissinger, *Years of Upheaval,* 1011.

17. Kissinger, *Years of Upheaval,* 253. Full text at 1234.

18. Kissinger, *Years of Upheaval,* 253–54.

19. Kissinger, *Years of Upheaval,* 254.

20. Kissinger, *Years of Upheaval,* 274–76. Kissinger's full account of the negotiating history of this project is the basis of what follows, except as noted.

21. Brimelow's role, a tight secret at the time, could hardly have been admitted to other European governments. They would have seen it as a particularly objection-

able example of the detested Anglo-American "special relationship"—on an issue where other European nations had as much at stake as Britain.

22. European reactions and resentment are fully discussed in Garthoff, *Détente and Confrontation* (1st ed., 1985), 338–40.

23. Nixon, *RN*, 880–81; Kissinger, *Years of Upheaval*, 286. The Soviets did go on to make much of the document in various settings, and to their own public, while interpreting it to their military as not affecting the need for strong defense. Garthoff, *Détente and Confrontation* (1st ed., 1985), 344–53.

24. Garthoff, *Détente and Confrontation* (1st ed., 1985), 333.

25. Nixon, *RN*, 882.

26. Kissinger, *Years of Upheaval*, 295. Nixon's memoir makes no mention of Kissinger's comment or of anything to that effect said by himself.

27. As an editor, I attended a conference of senior Europeans and Americans in the spring of 1973. Oil officials joined with European political officials and businessmen to express their concern about U.S. energy policy in the strongest terms politeness would permit.

28. Palmer, *The 25-Year War*, 94.

29. Kissinger, *Years of Upheaval*, 130.

30. The original Atlantic Charter was worked out by Roosevelt and Churchill in Argentia Bay, Newfoundland, in August 1941, and formed the public basis of their common policy during World War II. Kissinger used this title at first, but Europeans deleted it from an early summary of a meeting, perhaps because it connoted the Anglo-American special relationship formed during World War II. The final title was "Atlantic Declaration."

31. Kissinger, *Years of Upheaval*, 729.

32. Stebbins and Adam, eds., *American Foreign Relations 1973*, 181–89.

33. Shultz, *Turmoil and Triumph*, 147.

34. Shultz, *Turmoil and Triumph*, 148.

35. Nixon, *RN*, 674.

36. My informant was Thomas G. Corcoran, of New Deal fame, who had stayed on in Washington as a lawyer and, like Connally, moved to the right in the Nixon era. As we have seen, Corcoran in 1968 was a bit player in the Chennault affair.

37. *The Gallup Poll, 1972–77*, I, 113.

38. Drew, *Washington Journal*, 21. The same source quotes Connally, in September, taking a very tough position on the President's right to protect the tapes, to the point of saying that there were times when a President would be right not to obey even a Supreme Court decision.

39. Haldeman, *Ends of Power*, 205. The possible reactions to such destruction are discussed in Ambrose, *Nixon: Ruin and Recovery*, 196.

40. Ambrose, *Nixon: Ruin and Recovery*, 500, 526. In August 1974 Connally was indicted on a charge of accepting a bribe of $10,000 from a lobbyist for the milk industry. He was tried and acquitted. In 1980 he sought the Republican presidential nomination, but proved more successful at raising money in corporate boardrooms than at attracting votes in primaries. In private life he amassed a considerable fortune, but when he tried to add to it in the go-go Texas economy of the 1980s, its collapse left him spectacularly bankrupt in 1987. It was a roller-coaster career and in the end as dramatic a fall from a high political altitude as any in American history.

41. Kissinger, *Years of Upheaval*, 425–27. This was an extraordinarily conciliatory posture toward Kissinger personally, by a chairman always sensitive to prerogative.

42. Kissinger's defense of his conduct, with quotations from the report of Attorney General Richardson to the committee on this occasion, is in *Years of Upheaval*, 427–29. At the time of the first wiretaps—May 1969—Kissinger was new to the Nixon entourage and had to worry about maintaining his position on substantive matters. He could hardly have opposed his judgment to that of J. Edgar Hoover on the legitimacy and past use of wiretaps. Nevertheless, in view of his passionate concern about leaks, one must doubt that his role was as passive as his memoirs claim. Evidence later unearthed by Seymour Hersh is persuasive that once wiretap authorizations became common practice, Kissinger participated in initiating them in several other cases where national security was at most marginally involved, especially against journalists critical of the Administration. Hersh, *Price of Power*, 81–95.

43. As the White House saw it, Helms's deputy, Vernon Walters, surely in consultation with Helms, "finked out" and refused to give such a message to the FBI. Haldeman, *Diaries*, 481. Other references to Helms by Haldeman make clear that the White House wanted to get rid of him in Washington by at least the fall of 1972. The June episode was recorded in the famous "smoking gun" tape that was decisive in the closing phase of Watergate. See below, Chapter 8, section 5, for further discussion.

44. Senate Foreign Relations Committee, *Nomination of Richard Helms to Be Ambassador to Iran, and CIA International and Domestic Activities: Hearings*, 93rd Cong., 1st sess., February 5, 7, 1973, 44–55.

45. Helms also judged that to refuse to answer on the grounds of security would be taken as a tip-off that there had been CIA involvement. As he knew, the ambiguous effect of any such response was one reason the convention of the Russell era insisted that senators and members of Congress should not even ask questions concerning covert operations. But Russell had died in 1971, and in 1973 no senator had taken his place as the Senate's accepted arbiter in this area.

46. In 1977 the Carter Administration decided to prosecute Helms for perjury, and after protracted negotiations he pleaded "no contest" to charges of having failed to testify "fully and completely" to Congress, and was given a small fine and a suspended prison sentence. Almost everyone in Washington concerned with foreign policy and intelligence activities, notably his former CIA colleagues, felt that he had acted properly and understandably in the circumstances and had been given a raw deal. I share this view and have expressed it frequently. The real culprit was Senator Symington for not saving the matter for executive session or private discussion. The best account of the whole matter is in Powers, *Man Who Kept the Secrets*, 10–11, 299–305.

47. Kissinger, *Years of Upheaval*, 377, denies U.S. involvement in any coup plotting after November 1970.

48. Kissinger, *Years of Upheaval*, 408–13, gives a fair picture of what was happening and the Administration's rationale for proceeding as it did at this early stage.

49. Interview, October 10, 1973, with a Madrid paper. Quoted in Kissinger, *Years of Upheaval*, 406, 1245.

50. Paul E. Sigmund, "The 'Invisible Blockade' and the Overthrow of Allende," *Foreign Affairs*, January 1974: 322–40. Sigmund's later book *The United States and Democracy in Chile* covers the matter more systematically in the light of later evidence. This full treatment (56–84) deals with American economic policy, nationalization controversies, disclosures in the congressional investigation of early 1973, CIA activities after 1970, and other materials that have contributed to a widespread belief

that the United States was involved directly in the coup. Sigmund argues that there is no evidence of this, but concedes that through various pressures the United States did play a role, and that this made a major contribution to public and congressional efforts to avoid such action in the future. On any reading, U.S. policy toward Allende, both before and during his rule, was deplorable.

51. As far back as early March, well before Watergate, Nixon had expressed to Kissinger an extremely gloomy prognosis that, except for Jackson and Tower, the Senate "won't back us on these issues." Kissinger, *Years of Upheaval*, 262.

52. Full texts of these speeches are in Stebbins and Adam, eds., *American Foreign Relations 1973*, 359, 433.

Chapter 8. The Middle East War and the Oil Crisis

1. Kissinger, *Years of Upheaval*, 206. In their later dealings, Sadat and Kissinger were exceptionally candid with each other, as Kissinger repeatedly notes in his writings.

2. Holden and Johns, *House of Saud*, 120, 128.

3. Until the 1970s, British and American commentators referred to the Gulf as the Persian Gulf, but Arab nations then insisted that it be called the Arabian Gulf. With Persia and Arabia dominating roughly equal portions of the coastline, the body of water has come to be called simply "the Gulf."

4. Holden and Johns, *House of Saud*, 265 ("a man . . ."), 289; also 229 (CIA ties), and passim. At a later point (495), this refers to Adham as having been "chiefly responsible for the entente formed with Egypt in 1970–71."

5. It is notable that Kissinger's voluminous memoirs never mention Adham. This may well suggest how important he was, not the reverse. Kissinger delighted in working with covert agencies; rarely did he mention names. In the case of Saudi Arabia, to have admitted this kind of close collaboration with a fervently anti-Zionist government might have been disturbing to important sectors of American opinion, as well as to Israel.

6. See Yergin, *The Prize*, 594; James E. Akins, "The Oil Crisis: This Time the Wolf Is Here," *Foreign Affairs*, April 1973: 467.

7. A prominent spokesman for this view was M. A. Adelman of MIT, "Is the Oil Shortage Real? Oil Companies as OPEC Tax Collectors," *Foreign Policy*, Winter 1972–73: 69–108.

8. The debate of that period is vividly summarized in Yergin, *The Prize*, 589–91.

9. Yergin, *The Prize*, 599, notes that "one visitor," perhaps Yergin himself, visited Tokyo in the summer of 1973 and found that "almost every Japanese policymaker concerned with energy" had read the Akins article.

10. Much more could be said about the scarcely concealed fault line between the American international oil companies and strong American supporters of Israel. Barely beneath the surface were the contrasting beliefs on each side that the other was not as patriotic as it should be: putting either their company or Israel ahead of their concern for American national interests.

11. In the spring and summer of 1973, debate did rage vigorously, some going so far as to argue that expressions such as the Akins article were to be blamed for putting ideas into the heads of the oil producers. Given the sophistication of Yamani and his colleagues, the argument was ridiculous and not without a note of condescension. For a telling refutation, see the article by Jahangir Amuzegar, a top Ira-

nian official, "The Oil Story: Facts, Fiction and Fair Play," *Foreign Affairs*, July 1973: 681, 684.

12. Quoted in Yergin, *The Prize*, 597.

13. Yergin, *The Prize*, 599.

14. Kissinger's principal reaction, instead, was to revile the American diplomat in Cairo who had learned of the disclosure from a Saudi counterpart and passed it on by regular cable to the State Department. *White House Years*, 224–26. Kissinger's reaction ignored the risks inherent in his kind of diplomacy, and above all skipped over the key fact that the Egyptians had shared the substance of the exchange with the Saudis, who up to that point had not been involved in diplomacy with Israel. The Saudi knowledge also supports the hypothesis that Kamal Adham was involved in setting up the meeting.

15. This controversy, discussed in Isaacson, *Kissinger*, 513–17, continued to rage after the war. Most accounts have concluded that the Pentagon was not deliberately holding up the shipments, although it may not have been going all out. The charter scheme was probably impractical from the start; the real error was failure to face this fact sooner.

16. Garment, *Crazy Rhythm*, 196–99, is a vivid account of this debate, which gives primary credit to Nixon for resolving disagreements between the Pentagon and Kissinger. This is the only time Nixon appears to have made an important decision about the war.

17. Herzog, *The Arab-Israeli Wars*, 260.

18. Isaacson, *Kissinger*, 522. This goes on to note that more supplies and equipment arrived on this first day of the big airlift than the Soviets had delivered to Egypt, Syria, and Iraq in the preceding four days! Included in the deliveries were forty Phantom fighter-bomber aircraft; earlier there had been a hang-up over finding four.

19. Isaacson, *Kissinger*, 526–27.

20. Whether the cause was atmospheric factors or Soviet deliberate interference for some murky reason is discussed in Kissinger, *Years of Upheaval*, 557, with the evidence inclining to the former explanation.

21. Kissinger, *Years of Upheaval*, 550–51. Dobrynin, *In Confidence*, 292, also quotes the text directly. As Kissinger notes, it was delivered to the Soviet Embassy in Washington simultaneously with Nixon's cable to Kissinger.

22. Dobrynin, *In Confidence*, 292–93.

23. Isaacson, *Kissinger*, 528; Kissinger's recollection is in *Years of Upheaval*, 569. In the Vietnam situation, as Kissinger surely knew, the far-flung character of the fighting was entirely different from the confined and carefully observed situation on the Egyptian Third Army front in 1973.

24. Kissinger's rather lame defense is in *Years of Upheaval*, 569.

25. Kissinger, *Years of Upheaval*, 570–71; Dobrynin, *In Confidence*, 293.

26. Kissinger, *Years of Upheaval*, 583. Describing what he later learned about this message, Dobrynin says in his memoir that there had been a hectic meeting of the Politburo to review the text, but that a sentence was added later, possibly because of an urgent appeal from Sadat. This must have been the "I will say it straight" sentence, which is stiffer than the rest. Dobrynin, *In Confidence*, 295. Of course, the ambassador may have been trying to present his government in a more accommodating light than was the case.

27. The others present were General Brent Scowcroft and Commander Jonathan Howe of Kissinger's NSC staff. The status of the meeting raises serious questions. It

has long been accepted that a presidential decision cannot be challenged on the basis of who was consulted, or what the tenor of their advice was. However, this may not cover the case of a meeting of advisors acting in the President's name, especially in his capacity as Commander in Chief, without his personal participation in any form. A standard example of this was the case of Woodrow Wilson after his 1919 stroke, when many believed that decisions in his name were actually being taken by Mrs. Wilson alone. These were never challenged, but the subsequent Twenty-fifth Amendment provided elaborate procedures for dealing with a situation where a President is "unable to discharge the powers and duties of his office." I have not dug into the obvious question whether a President's temporary inability to function, absent serious medical symptoms, is covered by the amendment. One can only conclude that it was fortunate that the decision the NSC group took that night did not arouse controversy, then or later.

28. Kissinger, *Years of Upheaval*, 586–91.

29. Kissinger, *Years of Upheaval*, 591, citing his *White House Years*, 614–30.

30. Kissinger, *Years of Upheaval*, 789.

31. For this section I have relied on Kissinger, *Years of Upheaval*, in large part. I have also consulted two well-informed studies from different vantage points: Edward R. F. Sheehan, *The Arabs, Israelis, and Kissinger*, and Matti Golan, *The Secret Conversations of Henry Kissinger*. As their introductions make clear, Sheehan benefited from special cooperation with Kissinger's staff—a practice that I have deplored in other instances, but which seems to have had few drawbacks in this case—and Golan, then a correspondent for the Israeli paper *Haaretz*, from extensive access to Israeli sources. In both cases, the material was sharply criticized for revealing secrets. Some of Kissinger's colleagues were actually reprimanded in response to these criticisms (perhaps a charade, since their careers did not suffer), while Golan was forced to rewrite his text, which he seems to have done only in a limited way. Both thus contain material that brings alive the negotiations, and makes clear the strength of the emotions with which Kissinger had to cope.

32. Kissinger, *Years of Upheaval*, 707.

33. Kissinger, *Years of Upheaval*, 616.

34. Kissinger, *Years of Upheaval*, 630–32.

35. The six-point agreement is in *Years of Upheaval*, 641.

36. I met Ohira on several occasions in the late 1960s and found him, as Kissinger did, taciturn but solid and conveying goodwill. In later years, when former senator Mike Mansfield, equally taciturn and inwardly warm, became U.S. Ambassador in Tokyo, the two were proverbial for the brevity and subtle substance of their exchanges. Both were remarkable men.

37. Kissinger, *Years of Upheaval*, 885.

38. Kissinger, *Years of Upheaval*, 777–86, especially 781.

39. See Kissinger, *Years of Upheaval*, 801, 813, 839.

40. Kissinger, *Years of Upheaval*, 853.

41. See Yergin, *The Prize*, 631–32.

42. Neil de Marchi, "Energy Policy Under Nixon," in Goodwin, ed., *Energy Policy in Perspective*, 395. So far as I can determine, no senior participant ever wrote at length about energy policy in 1973–74. This account owes much to a paper done for me in 1991 by a research assistant, Mark Sandy, then a graduate student at the Woodrow Wilson School at Princeton.

43. Nixon, *RN*, 765.

44. See Yergin, *The Prize*, 591, for the summary of the report. Ehrlichman's re-action was related by James Akins in an interview in 1991 with my assistant, Mark Sandy.

45. Shultz and Dam, *Economic Policy*, 185.

46. De Marchi, "Energy Policy," 427.

47. Adelman, "Is the Oil Shortage Real?"

48. Quoted in Rustow and Mugno, *OPEC*, 155.

49. *The Gallup Poll, 1972–1977*, I, 226.

50. Yergin, *The Prize*, 659.

51. In a 1995 interview, John Sawhill recalled vividly that when drafts of the speech were circulated for comment within the White House circle, he changed "1980" to "2000" at least twice. Finally he was told to lay off: the target date came straight from the President personally.

52. Quoted in Vietor, *Energy Policy*, 244.

53. De Marchi, "Energy Policy Under Nixon," 395.

54. After the war, Japan had been under great pressure to endorse the Arab position, and finally did so on November 22. Given its especially great dependence on Arab oil — 76 percent, versus 59 percent for the countries in the European Community and only 17 percent for the United States — the action was at least understandable. Figures from Rustow and Mugno, *OPEC*, 42.

55. Kissinger, *Years of Upheaval*, 905–25.

56. *New York Times*, February 26, 1974, 1.

57. Shultz and Dam, *Economic Policy*, 184.

58. Jaworski, *Right and the Power*, 89.

59. White, *Breach of Faith*, 294.

60. According to a periodic public opinion survey conducted by *Time* magazine, in April 1974, 38 percent of the public favored resignation, and an additional 17 percent called for impeachment. White, *Breach of Faith*, 297–98.

61. Justice William Rehnquist recused himself because he had participated in rel-evant Justice Department work before joining the Court.

62. The best account of this episode is in Thomas Powers, *Man Who Kept the Secrets*, 259–67. In the end Nixon's order produced only a short delay in the FBI inquiries into the money's history; these were resumed when Helms and Walters, by then sure there was in fact no CIA concern, declined to put their original oral request into writing.

63. Dobrynin, *In Confidence*, 310.

64. Dobrynin, *In Confidence*, 310–11.

65. Kissinger recorded in 1982 that Nixon was so upset at the time that if Watergate had not overwhelmed him, Kissinger doubted "whether I could have maintained my position in his Administration." *Years of Upheaval*, 1122. The Senate Foreign Relations Committee, led by the always fair-minded Hubert Humphrey, helped Kissinger to dig out. It started another set of hearings on July 10, and on August 6 issued a report saying that new information did not change the conclusions they had reached the previous September, that Kissinger's role in the wiretapping should not be a bar to his service as Secretary of State.

66. Nixon, *RN*, 1010–18.

67. Kissinger, *Years of Upheaval*, 1028, and in greater detail, 1153–57.

68. Nitze, *From Hiroshima to Glasnost*, 340; also Kissinger, *Years of Upheaval*,

1151–52. The judge was Gerhard Gesell, widely considered an outstanding trial judge on the federal bench and a man of exceptional experience and wisdom.

69. Kissinger, *Years of Upheaval*, 1167–69.

70. Hyland, *Mortal Rivals*, 62–63.

71. Kissinger, *Years of Upheaval*, 1174.

72. Kissinger, *Years of Upheaval*, 1175. Emphasis added.

73. See McGeorge Bundy, *Danger and Survival*, passim. This book argues that although the nuclear *danger* had great significance in the conduct of foreign policy crises, the *balance* between major nuclear weapons countries (above all the United States and the Soviet Union) had much less significance.

74. T. S. Eliot, "The Hollow Men."

75. Shawcross, *Sideshow*, 330–33, is a vivid account of the history of this article and the final debate and vote on it.

76. White, *Making of the President 1972*, 298.

77. Haldeman, *Ends of Power*, 79, 110–13.

78. Kissinger, *Years of Upheaval*, 81.

Chapter 9. What Came After

1. Dobrynin, *In Confidence*, 319–23. As early as January 1974, Ford confided to Dobrynin that if and when he should become President, he would keep Kissinger as Secretary. It was a significant early gesture of continuity, as well as confidence in the discretion of the ambassador—also striking evidence of how early Ford grasped where matters were headed.

2. Hyland, *Mortal Rivals*, 77.

3. Since Kissinger's memoirs stop with Nixon's resignation, we do not have his explanation. One cannot rule out his having taken personal offense at some Chinese act or omission; more likely, he wanted a visible early move that would emphasize the policy of détente with the Soviets.

4. A final factor from the U.S. standpoint was that the ongoing MIRV program, which had given the United States three times as many deliverable warheads as the Soviets in 1972, had expanded the ratio to 4–1 by 1974. Shortly, of course, the Soviets would catch up and eventually move ahead, as the U.S. negotiators recognized. Johnson, *Right Hand of Power*, 602.

5. Johnson, *Right Hand of Power*, 604. Isaacson, *Kissinger*, 621–28, gives a devastating account of the disagreements and devious tactics that attended the early months of the Ford Administration, especially over arms control. He is almost equally critical of Kissinger and Schlesinger.

6. One experienced American participant described the atmosphere of this 1974 visit as "frigid." After a perfunctory session with Deng Xiaoping, the Chinese shipped the party out into the countryside for a picnic, with no further substantive talks. Author interview with John Holdridge, 1995. Holdridge had been on Kissinger's staff for previous visits going back to the very first one, and was by then in charge of the U.S. mission in Beijing, between the tenures of David Bruce and George Bush. In his opinion, the new influence of the Gang of Four was decisive, not any error on the U.S. side: the "window of opportunity" had closed.

7. Dobrynin, *In Confidence*, 334ff.

8. Dobrynin, *In Confidence*, 335.

9. Isaacson, *Kissinger*, 615–21, is a full account of this episode, unsparingly critical of Kissinger, less so of Jackson.

10. This is my own supposition. Kissinger's *Years of Upheaval* ends with the resignation of Nixon.

11. Ford's State of the Union speech in January, to make the point of how much business America was losing because of the Jackson-Vanik and Stevenson amendments, gave the figure of $8 billion for trade and financing commitments already made by Western European nations. Ford, *A Time to Heal*, 138–39; Dobrynin, *In Confidence*, 336 (Soviet view on the failure to fight the Stevenson Amendment).

12. This section is based on Dobrynin, *In Confidence*, 345–47; Hyland, *Mortal Rivals*, 114–29 (an unusually candid view from a top Kissinger aide); Garthoff, *Détente and Confrontation* (rev. ed., 1994), 527–33; Ford, *A Time to Heal*, 298–306; and Stebbins and Adam, eds., *American Foreign Relations 1975*, 283–360, for the full texts of the documents. The first two in particular fill out and amplify earlier sources as to the Soviet and American viewpoints.

13. Hyland, *Mortal Rivals*, 114.

14. Hyland, *Mortal Rivals*, 115.

15. The substance of the Kissinger and Sonnenfeldt briefings, in mid-December, was cabled to Washington and promptly leaked in partial versions. "Nonverbatim summaries" were finally published in *New York Times*, April 7, 1976. They are also available in Stebbins and Adam, eds., *American Foreign Relations 1975*, 561–69. Sonnenfeldt's briefing suggested a readiness to accept a special Soviet national interest in the area, along with a wish that the Eastern Europeans would accommodate to it peacefully. My surmise is that both men had a long-term concern lest Germany once again exert pressure on Eastern Europe, the historical *Drang nach Osten*.

16. Dobrynin, *In Confidence*, 346.

17. Hyland, *Mortal Rivals*, 127–28. The British scholar Timothy Garton Ash has given an extremely thoughtful appraisal of the links between *Ostpolitik* and the end of the Cold War. Ash, *In Europe's Name*, 362–71.

18. Hyland, *Mortal Rivals*, 128.

19. Isaacs, *Without Honor*, 105. William Colby, *Lost Victory*, 346–47, is critical both of the congressional cuts in aid and of Thieu's rejection of new blood and nascent democratic practices at the village level.

20. I base this assessment on several years of dealing with Martin (1964 to 1969) when he was Ambassador to Thailand. I found him patriotic and capable, but rarely candid.

21. After the war, Murray contended that the equipment sent in the Enhance Plus shipments was "inferior" and not wanted by ARVN. Braestrup, ed., *Vietnam as History*, 109.

22. The best short account of the running struggle over aid appropriations is in Isaacs, *Without Honor*, 313–21, with extensive citations to congressional materials.

23. Quoted in Isaacs, *Without Honor*, 311.

24. The House report, to its Foreign Affairs Committee (later, for a time, renamed the International Relations Committee), was *U.S. Aid to Indochina*, Report of a Staff Survey Team, July 25, 1974. The Senate report, to the Foreign Relations Committee, was *Vietnam: May 1974: A Report to the Committee*, August 5, 1974.

25. Isaacs, *Without Honor*, 321.

26. The full story, with the relevant figures, is in Isaacs, *Without Honor*, 310–13.

27. Resolution quoted in Isaacs, *Without Honor,* 339.

28. Isaacs, *Without Honor,* 327. Lipsman and Weiss, *False Peace,* 160–66, has maps and details on the 1974 military operations.

29. Significant desertion rates had often been experienced before, but these were the worst ever. Lipsman and Weiss, *False Peace,* 146–53, has excellent material on the progressive deterioration of ARVN between early 1973 and late 1974. It assesses carefully the role of reduced supplies as compared with other factors, concluding that leadership problems and the economic pinch were as significant.

30. Le Gro, *Vietnam,* 87.

31. Isaacs, *Without Honor,* 329.

32. Dung, *Our Great Spring Victory,* 21–25.

33. These estimates had input from all the intelligence agencies, but were issued on the ultimate authority of the Director of Central Intelligence, then William Colby, a veteran of many years of service in South Vietnam. Colby's own memoir of the war has poignant pages on this last phase, basically in accord with this account. Colby, *Lost Victory,* 347–55.

34. Maynard Parker, "Vietnam: The War That Won't End," *Foreign Affairs,* January 1975: 352–74. This article went to press before the battles of December and January.

35. Isaacs, *Without Honor,* 334.

36. Karnow, *Vietnam,* 660.

37. Karnow, *Vietnam,* 664.

38. Hung and Schecter, *Palace File,* 149–50.

39. Dung, *Our Great Spring Victory,* 22–23; Hung and Schecter, *Palace File,* 250.

40. Hung and Schecter, *Palace File,* 251, quoting a 1986 interview with Haig.

41. Henry Kamm in *New York Times,* February 6, 1973, quoted in Isaacs, *Without Honor,* 233.

42. Isaacs, *Without Honor,* 232.

43. Senate Foreign Relations Committee, *Vietnam: May 1974,* August 5, 1974.

44. Shawcross, *Sideshow,* 325.

45. Isaacs, *Without Honor,* 259, and Snepp, *Decent Interval,* 97 (Martin's views).

46. Isaacs, *Without Honor,* 260; Shawcross, *Sideshow,* 337–43.

47. Isaacs, *Without Honor,* 255.

48. Isaacs, *Without Honor,* 243.

49. Quotations from Isaacs, *Without Honor,* 270–71.

50. Isaacs, *Without Honor,* 270–73.

51. Shawcross, *Sideshow,* 361.

52. Snepp, *Decent Interval,* 197, 207, is an excellent account of the March campaign.

53. Pentagon estimates cited in Snepp, *Decent Interval,* 567. Specific items included 550 tanks, 73 F-5 jet fighters, 1,300 artillery pieces, and 1,600,000 rifles.

54. Quoted in Karnow, *Vietnam,* 667.

55. In Ford's later recollection, when he signed his first letter to Thieu after taking office in August 1974 he was told in general terms of the Nixon letters but did not actually read them. Hung and Schecter, *Palace File,* 310, based on an interview with Ford in 1986.

56. Hung and Schecter, *Palace File,* 346–47, describes vividly this press conference and its effect on the refugee issue.

57. Stebbins and Adam, eds., *American Foreign Relations 1975,* 117.

58. In 1967, I wrote a short history of American policy in Indochina up to that point, published as "The Path to Viet-Nam" in Falk, ed., *The Vietnam War and International Law.*

59. Conversely, the Cyprus crisis of 1974–76, which had simmered for more than a decade, boiled over again in the last month of Nixon's presidency. But no decision in Nixon's time played a special or unique role in it. It was not truly part of the Nixon era.

60. I well recall a long personal interview in the spring of 1972 with Golda Meir, in Jerusalem, in which she held forth eloquently to the effect that Israel must retain key parts of the Sinai, but that it could not indefinitely hold on to the whole of the West Bank and Gaza. Her argument ran as follows: (1) large numbers of Arabs could not be admitted to full citizenship in Israel without distorting the voting balance to an unacceptable degree; (2) consistent with the ideals on which the state of Israel had been founded, Arabs in Israel could neither be treated as second-class citizens nor expelled by pressure or force; (3) therefore, Israel must accept that Arabs, in some organized form, should control the areas in which they predominated, outside the internationally recognized borders of Israel. (An Arab state, though already discussed, did not come up in our talk. Nor did we discuss expanded Jewish settlements, an idea not then widespread.)

61. For the background and status in early 1975, see Kenneth Adelman, "Report from Angola," *Foreign Affairs*, April 1975: 558–74.

62. Rubin, *Paved with Good Intentions*, 135–37, gives a figure of 24,000 for 1976. Bill, *The Eagle and the Lion*, 209, notes that as early as 1975 no fewer than thirty-nine American defense contractors were active in Iran and estimates the total American presence at 50,000 by the end of 1977.

63. Bill, *The Eagle and the Lion*, 209ff.

Chapter 10. Summing Up

1. Chapter 1 has described the 1951 controversy. Haig believed that Truman had been entitled to dismiss the general, but that MacArthur had been "right on the military and strategic issues." Haig, *Inner Circles*, 66.

2. Crowley, *Nixon Off the Record*, 137.

3. It was ironic that Kissinger later dedicated his major history work, *Diplomacy*, to "the men and women of the Foreign Service . . . whose professionalism and dedication sustain American diplomacy."

4. The small and specially selected contingent of State and CIA officers on the NSC staff was not a substitute for constant input from the agencies themselves. After several staff members resigned over the Cambodian incursion, those who remained were by no means yes-men, but they were more and more separated from their original associations.

5. Gates, *From the Shadows*, 49. His judgments of other presidencies are not uncritical. That of the Nixon era, and of Nixon and Kissinger personally, is unique in its sharpness.

6. Kissinger himself called this a "revolutionary step" in the first volume of his 1978 memoirs (*White House Years*, 184). By 1994 he saw the statement as "the most daring step of [Nixon's] presidency," contending that it as much as committed the United States to positive action, presumably military, if the Soviets had carried out

their threats to the Chinese nuclear facilities. Kissinger, *Diplomacy*, 723–24. This latter-day interpretation of the statement's meaning is nonsense, in terms both of its language and how it was then interpreted. Nor did such a discreetly worded statement require courage. He was right about its importance, but wrong about the degree of commitment it stated.

7. Dobrynin, *In Confidence*, 195. Emphasis added.

8. It is relevant to note that the release in recent years of extensive Russian materials on Soviet policy in the early Cold War years has tended more to confirm the dark views of American policymakers at that time than to support the arguments of revisionist historians. For an objective and persuasive account incorporating the released materials, see Gaddis, *We Now Know: Rethinking Cold War History*.

Bibliography

Books

Abramson, Rudy. *Spanning the Century: The Life of W. Averell Harriman, 1891–1986*. New York: William Morrow, 1992.

Aitken, Jonathan. *Nixon: A Life*. London: Weidenfeld and Nicolson, 1993.

Ambrose, Stephen E. *Eisenhower*, vol. 2: *The President*. New York: Touchstone, 1984.

——. *Nixon: The Education of a Politician, 1913–1962*. New York: Simon & Schuster, 1987.

——. *Nixon: Ruin and Recovery, 1973–1990*. New York: Simon & Schuster, 1991.

——. *Nixon: The Triumph of a Politician, 1962–1972*. New York: Simon & Schuster, 1989.

Andrade, Dale. *Trial by Fire: The 1972 Easter Offensive, America's Last Vietnam Battle*. New York: Hippocrene Books, 1995.

Andrew, Christopher. *For the President's Eyes Only: Secret Intelligence and the American Presidency from Washington to Bush*. New York: HarperCollins, 1995.

Ash, Timothy Garton. *In Europe's Name: Germany and the Divided Continent*. New York: Random House, 1993.

Ball, George. *The Past Has Another Pattern*. New York: W. W. Norton, 1982.

Baring, Arnulf. *Machtwechsel*. Stuttgart: Deutsche Verlag, 1982.

Bark, Dennis L., and David R. Gress. *A History of West Germany: Democracy and Its Discontents, 1963–1988*. Oxford: Blackwell, 1989.

Barnett, A. Doak. *Communist China and Asia: Challenge to American Policy*. New York: Council on Foreign Relations, 1961.

Becker, Elizabeth. *When the War Was Over: The Voices of Cambodia's Revolution and Its People*. New York: Simon & Schuster, 1986.

Berger, Carl, ed. *The United States Air Force in Southeast Asia, 1961–1973.* Washington: Office of Air Force History, 1977.

Berman, William S. *William Fulbright and the Vietnam War: The Dissent of a Political Realist.* Kent, OH, and London: Kent State University Press, 1988.

Beschloss, Michael. *The Crisis Years, Kennedy and Khrushchev, 1960–63.* New York: Edward Burlingame Books, 1991.

Bialer, Seweryn, ed. *The Domestic Context of Soviet Foreign Policy.* Boulder, CO: Westview Press, 1981.

Bill, James A. *The Eagle and the Lion: The Tragedy of American-Iranian Relations.* New Haven: Yale University Press, 1988.

Bird, Kai. *The Chairman: John J. McCloy and the Making of the American Establishment.* New York: Simon & Schuster, 1992.

Blechman, Barry M., and Stephen S. Kaplan, eds., *Force Without War: U.S. Armed Forces as a Political Instrument.* Washington: Brookings Institution, 1978.

Block, Herbert L. *Herblock Special Report.* New York: W. W. Norton, 1974.

Blum, John Morton. *Years of Discord: American Politics and Society, 1961–1974.* New York: W. W. Norton, 1991.

Braestrup, Peter, ed. *Vietnam as History: Ten Years after the Paris Peace Accords.* Washington: The Wilson Center/University Press of America, 1984.

Brandt, Willy. *My Life in Politics.* New York: Viking, 1992 (originally published in Germany in 1989).

Brauer, Carl M. *Presidential Transitions: Eisenhower Through Reagan.* New York: Oxford University Press, 1986.

Brinkley, Douglas. *Dean Acheson: The Cold War Years, 1953–71.* New Haven: Yale University Press, 1992.

Bundy, McGeorge. *Danger and Survival: Choices About the Bomb in the First Fifty Years.* New York: Random House, 1988.

Butler, David. *The Fall of Saigon: Scenes from the Sudden End of a Long War.* New York: Simon & Schuster, 1985.

The Cambridge History of China. Edited by John Fairbank and Roderick MacFarquhar. Vol. 15. London and New York: Cambridge University Press, 1991.

Carr, Jonathan. *Helmut Schmidt: Helmsman of Germany.* London: Weidenfeld and Nicolson, 1985.

Carter, Jimmy. *Keeping Faith: Memoirs of a President.* New York: Bantam Books, 1982.

Chanda, Nayan. *Brother Enemy: The War after the War.* New York: Harcourt Brace Jovanovich, 1986.

Charlton, Michael, and Anthony Moncrieff. *Many Reasons Why: The American Involvement in Vietnam.* London: Scolar Press, 1978.

Chennault, Anna. *The Education of Anna.* New York: Times Books, 1980.

Chester, Lewis, Godfrey Hodgson, and Bruce Page. *An American Melodrama: The Presidential Campaign of 1968.* New York: Viking, 1969.

Christian, George. *The President Steps Down.* New York: Macmillan, 1970.

Clarke, Jeffrey J. *Advice and Support: The Final Years, 1965–1973.* The United States Army in Vietnam Series. Washington: U.S. Army Center of Military History, 1988.

Clifford, Clark, with Richard Holbrooke. *Counsel to the President.* New York: Random House, 1991.

Clodfelter, Mark. *The Limits of Air Power: The American Bombing of North Vietnam.* New York: The Free Press, 1989.

Cohen, Warren I. *America in the Age of Soviet Power.* Vol. 4 of *Cambridge History of American Foreign Relations.* Cambridge, Eng.: Cambridge University Press, 1993.

———. *Dean Rusk.* Vol. 19 of *American Secretaries of State and Their Diplomacy.* Totowa, NJ: Cooper Square Publishers, 1980.

Colby, William, with James McCargar. *Lost Victory: A Firsthand Account of America's Sixteen-Year Involvement in Vietnam.* Chicago: Contemporary Books, 1989.

Colodny, Lon, and Robert Gettlin. *Silent Coup: The Removal of a President.* New York: St. Martin's Press, 1991.

Connally, John, with Mickey Herskowitz. *In History's Shadow: An American Odyssey.* New York: Hyperion, 1993.

Cook, Don. *Charles de Gaulle: A Biography.* New York: Putnam, 1983.

Craig, Gordon, and Francis Loewenheim, eds. *The Diplomats, 1939–1979.* Princeton: Princeton University Press, 1994.

Crowley, Monica. *Nixon Off the Record.* New York: Random House, 1996.

Davis, Nathaniel. *The Last Two Years of Salvador Allende.* Ithaca: Cornell University Press, 1985.

Destler, I. M. *Presidents, Bureaucrats, and Foreign Policy: The Politics of Organizational Reform.* Princeton: Princeton University Press, 1974.

———, with Haruhito Fukui and Hideo Sato. *The Textile Wrangle: Conflict in Japanese-American Relations, 1969–1971.* Ithaca: Cornell University Press, 1979.

Diem, Bui, with David Chanoff. *In the Jaws of History.* Boston: Houghton Mifflin, 1987.

Dobrynin, Anatoly. *In Confidence: Moscow's Ambassador to America's Six Cold War Presidents.* New York: Random House, 1995.

Dommen, Arthur J. *Laos: Keystone of Indochina.* Boulder, CO: Westview Press, 1985.

Dougan, Clark, and Samuel Lipsman. *The Vietnam Experience: A Nation Divided.* The Vietnam Experience Series. Boston: Boston Publishing Co., 1984.

Doyle, Edward, and Terrence Maitland. *The Vietnam Experience: The Aftermath, 1975–1985.* The Vietnam Experience Series. Boston: Boston Publishing Co., 1985.

Drew, Elizabeth. *Washington Journal: The Events of 1973–1974.* New York: Macmillan, 1984.

Duiker, William J. *The Communist Road to Power in Vietnam.* Boulder, CO: Westview Press, 1981.

Dung, Van Tien. *Our Great Spring Victory.* New York and London: Monthly Review Press, 1977.

Eban, Abba. *An Autobiography.* New York: Random House, 1977.

Edmonds, Robin. *Soviet Foreign Policy, 1962–1973: The Paradox of Power.* London: Oxford University Press, 1975, 1977.

———. *Soviet Foreign Policy: The Brezhnev Years.* New York: Oxford University Press, 1983.

Ehrlichman, John. *The Company: A Novel.* New York: Simon & Schuster, 1976.

———. *Witness to Power: The Nixon Years.* New York: Pocket Books, 1982.

Eisenhower, Dwight D. *Mandate for Change, 1953–56.* New York: Doubleday, 1963.

Falk, Richard, ed. *The Vietnam War and International Law.* Sponsored by the American Society for International Law. 2 vols. Princeton: Princeton University Press, 1969.

Fischer, David Hackett. *Historians' Fallacies: Toward a Logic of Historical Thought.* New York: Harper & Row, 1970.

Fischer, Michael M.J. *Iran: From Religious Dispute to Revolution.* Cambridge: Harvard University Press, 1980.

Fisher, Louis. *Constitutional Conflicts Between Congress and the President.* Princeton: Princeton University Press, 1985.

———. *Presidential Spending Power.* Princeton: Princeton University Press, 1975.

Ford, Gerald. *A Time to Heal.* New York: Harper & Row, 1979.

Fosdick, Dorothy, ed. *Staying the Course: Henry M. Jackson and National Security.* Seattle: University of Washington Press, 1987.

Franck, Thomas M., and Edward Weisband. *Foreign Policy by Congress.* New York: Oxford University Press, 1979.

Friedman, Leon, and William F. Levantrosser, eds. *Richard M. Nixon: Politician, President, Administrator.* New York: Greenwood Press, 1991.

Fulghum, David, and Terrence Maitland. *The Vietnam Experience: South Vietnam on Trial.* The Vietnam Experience Series. Boston: Boston Publishing Co., 1984.

Gaddis, John Lewis. *Strategies of Containment: A Critical Appraisal of Postwar American National Security Policy.* Oxford: Oxford University Press, 1982.

———. *We Now Know: Rethinking Cold War History.* Oxford: Clarendon, 1997.

The Gallup Poll: Public Opinion, 1935–1971. Wilmington, DE: Scholarly Resources, 1978.

The Gallup Poll: Public Opinion, 1972–1977. 3 vols. Wilmington, DE: Scholarly Resources, 1978.

Garment, Leonard. *Crazy Rhythm: My Journey from Brooklyn, Jazz, and Wall Street to Nixon's White House and Beyond.* New York: Times Books, 1997.

Garten, Jeffrey E. *A Cold Peace: America, Japan, Germany, and the Struggle for Supremacy.* New York: Times Books, 1992.

Garthoff, Raymond L. *Détente and Confrontation: American-Soviet Relations from Nixon to Reagan.* Washington: Brookings Institution, 1985; rev. ed., 1994.

———. *Perspectives on the Strategic Balance.* Washington: Brookings Institution, 1983.

Garver, James W. *China's Decision for Rapprochement with the United States, 1968–1971.* Boulder, CO: Westview Press, 1982.

Gates, Robert. *From the Shadows: The Ultimate Insider's Story of Four Presidents and How They Won the Cold War.* New York: Simon & Schuster, 1996.

Gelman, Harry. *The Brezhnev Politburo and the Decline of Détente.* Ithaca: Cornell University Press, 1984.

Gilpin, Robert. *The Political Economy of International Relations.* Princeton: Princeton University Press, 1987.

Golan, Galia. *Soviet Policies in the Middle East from World War II to Gorbachev.* Cambridge, Eng., and New York: Cambridge University Press, 1990.

Golan, Matti. *The Secret Conversations of Henry Kissinger.* New York: Quadrangle, 1976.

Goodman, Allan E. *The Lost Peace: America's Search for a Negotiated Settlement of the Vietnam War.* Stanford: Hoover Institution Press, 1978.

Goodwin, Craufurd D., ed. *Energy Policy in Perspective: Today's Problems, Yesterday's Solutions.* Washington: Brookings Institution, 1981.

Gowa, Joanne. *Closing the Gold Window: Domestic Politics and the End of Bretton Woods.* Ithaca: Cornell University Press, 1983.

Green, Marshall. *Pacific Encounters.* Washington: Dacor Bacon House, 1997.

——, John H. Holdridge, and William N. Stokes. *War and Peace with China: First-Hand Experiences in the Foreign Service of the United States.* Bethesda, MD: Dacor Press, 1994.

Greenberger, Martin. *Caught Unawares: The Energy Decade in Retrospect.* Cambridge: Ballinger, 1983.

Greene, John Robert. *The Limits of Power: The Nixon and Ford Administrations.* Bloomington: Indiana University Press, 1992.

Greenstein, Fred I. *The Hidden-Hand Presidency: Eisenhower as Leader.* New York: Basic Books, 1982.

Greenwood, Ted. *Making the MIRV: A Study of Defense Decision Making.* Cambridge: Ballinger, 1975.

Grose, Peter. *Gentleman Spy: The Life of Allen Dulles.* New York: Houghton Mifflin, 1994.

Haig, Alexander M., Jr. *Caveat: Realism, Reagan, and Foreign Policy.* New York: Macmillan, 1984.

——, with Charles McCarry. *Inner Circles: How America Changed the World, A Memoir.* New York: Warner Books, 1992.

Halberstam, David. *The Best and the Brightest.* New York: Fawcett Crest, 1972.

——. *The Making of a Quagmire.* New York: Random House, 1964, 1965.

Haldeman, H. R. *The Haldeman Diaries: Inside the Nixon White House.* New York: Putnam, 1994.

——, with Joseph DiMona. *The Ends of Power.* New York: Times Books, 1978.

Haley, P. Edward. *Congress and the Fall of South Vietnam and Cambodia.* Rutherford, NJ: Fairleigh Dickinson University Press, 1982.

Halpern, Paul J., ed. *Why Watergate?* Pacific Palisades: Palisades Publishers, 1975.

Hamilton-Merritt, Jane. *Tragic Mountains: The Hmong, the Americans, and the Secret Wars for Laos, 1942–1992.* Bloomington: Indiana University Press, 1992.

Hannah, Norman B. *The Key to Failure: Laos and the Vietnam War.* Lanham, MD: Madison Books, 1987.

Hanrieder, Wolfram F. *Germany, America, Europe: Forty Years of German Foreign Policy.* New Haven: Yale University Press, 1989.

Haslam, Jonathan. *The Soviet Union and the Politics of Nuclear Weapons in Europe, 1969–87.* Ithaca: Cornell University Press, 1990.

Heikal, Mohammed H. *The Road to Ramadan.* New York: Quadrangle/Times Books, 1975.

——. *The Sphinx and the Commissar: The Rise and Fall of Soviet Influence in the Middle East.* New York: Harper & Row, 1978.

Herring, George C. *America's Longest War: The United States and Vietnam, 1950–1975.* New York: Alfred A. Knopf, 1979: 2nd ed., 1986.

Hersh, Seymour M. *The Price of Power: Kissinger in the Nixon White House.* New York: Summit Books, 1983.

Herz, Martin F. *The Vietnam War in Retrospect.* Washington: Georgetown School of Foreign Service, 1984.

——. *The War of Atonement.* London: Weidenfeld and Nicolson, 1975.

Herzog, Chaim. *The Arab-Israeli Wars: War and Peace in the Middle East from the War of Independence Through Lebanon.* New York: Vintage Books, 1982, 1984.

Hirst, David, and Irene Beeson. *Sadat*. London: Faber and Faber, 1981.

Hodgson, Godfrey. *America in Our Time*. Garden City, NY: Doubleday, 1976.

Hoff, Joan. *Nixon Reconsidered*. New York: Basic Books, 1994.

—— and Dwight Ink, eds. *The Nixon Presidency*. Special issue of *Presidential Studies Quarterly*. New York: Center for the Study of the Presidency, 1996.

Holden, David, and Richard Johns. *The House of Saud*. London: Pan Books, 1981.

Holdridge, John H. *Crossing the Divide: An Insider's Account of the Normalization of U.S.-China Relations*. Lanham, MD: Rowman & Littlefield, 1997.

Howard, Michael. *The Causes of Wars*. London: Unwin Paperbacks, 1983, 1984.

Hughes, John. *Indonesian Upheaval*. New York: David McKay, 1967.

Hung, Nguyen Tien, and Jerrold L. Schecter. *The Palace File*. New York: Harper & Row, 1986.

Hyland, William G. *Mortal Rivals: Superpower Relations from Nixon to Reagan*. New York: Random House, 1987.

International Institute for Strategic Studies. *The Military Balance*. London: The Institute, 1970–   .

Isaacs, Arnold R. *Without Honor: Defeat in Vietnam and Cambodia*. Baltimore: Johns Hopkins University Press, 1983.

Isaacson, Walter. *Kissinger: A Biography*. New York: Simon & Schuster, 1992.

—— and Evan Thomas. *The Wise Men: Six Friends and the World They Made*. New York: Simon & Schuster, 1986.

Jackson, Robert Victor. *South Asian Crisis: India, Pakistan and Bangla Desh, a Political and Historical Analysis of the 1971 War*. New York: Praeger, 1975; published for the International Institute for Strategic Studies.

Jaworski, Leon. *The Right and the Power: The Prosecution of Watergate*. New York: Reader's Digest Press, 1976.

Johnson, Lyndon Baines. *The Vantage Point: Perspectives of the Presidency, 1963–69*. New York: Holt, Rinehart and Winston, 1971.

Johnson, U. Alexis, with Jef Olivarius McAllister. *The Right Hand of Power: The Memoirs of an American Diplomat*. Englewood Cliffs, NJ: Prentice-Hall, 1984.

Kaiser, Robert G. *Russia, the People and the Power*. New York: Pocket Books, 1976.

Kalb, Marvin, and Bernard Kalb. *Kissinger*. Boston: Little, Brown, 1974.

Kaplan, Morton A., et al., eds. *Vietnam Settlement: Why 1973, Not 1969?* Washington: American Enterprise Institute, 1973.

Kaplan, Stephen S., ed. *Diplomacy of Power: Soviet Armed Forces as a Political Instrument*. Washington: Brookings Institution, 1981.

Karnow, Stanley. *Vietnam: A History*. New York: Viking, 1983.

Kiernan, Ben. *How Pol Pot Came to Power: A History of Communism in Kampuchea, 1930–1975*. London: Verso (New Left Books), 1985.

Kissinger, Henry A. *Diplomacy*. New York: Simon & Schuster, 1994.

——. *White House Years*. Boston: Little, Brown, 1979.

——. *Years of Upheaval*. Boston: Little, Brown, 1982.

Kitfield, James. *Prodigal Soldiers*. New York: Simon & Schuster, 1995.

Kohler, Foy D. *Understanding the Russians: A Citizen's Primer*. New York, Harper & Row, 1970.

Kunz, Diane B. *Butter and Guns: America's Cold War Economic Diplomacy*. New York: The Free Press, 1997.

Kux, Dennis. *India and the United States: Estranged Democracies, 1941–1991*. Washington: National Defense University Press, 1993.

Ky, Nguyen Cao. *Twenty Years and Twenty Days*. New York: Stein & Day, 1976.

Lake, Anthony, ed. *The Vietnam Legacy: The War, American Society and the Future of American Foreign Policy*. New York: New York University Press (for the Council on Foreign Relations), 1976.

Lankford, Nelson D. *The Last American Aristocrat: The Biography of Ambassador David K.E. Bruce*. New York: Little, Brown, 1996.

Laqueur, Walter. *Confrontation: The Middle East War and World Politics*. London: Wildwood House, 1974.

Larrabee, Eric. *Commander in Chief: Franklin Roosevelt, His Lieutenants and Their War*. New York: Harper & Row, 1987.

Le Gro, William E. *Vietnam from Ceasefire to Capitulation*. Indochina Monograph Series. Washington: U.S. Army Center of Military History, 1981.

Lehman, John. *The Executive, Congress, and Foreign Policy: Studies of the Nixon Administration*. New York: Praeger, 1974.

Levy, Walter J. *Oil, Strategy and Politics, 1941–1981*. Edited by Melvin A. Conant. Boulder, CO: Westview Press, 1982.

Lewy, Guenter. *America in Vietnam*. New York: Oxford University Press, 1978.

Lipsman, Samuel, and Stephen Weiss. *The Vietnam Experience: The False Peace, 1972–1974*. The Vietnam Experience Series. Boston: Boston Publishing Co., 1985.

Longford, Lord. *Nixon*. London: Weidenfeld and Nicolson, 1980.

Luttwak, Edward. *The Strategic Balance, 1972*. The Center for Strategic and International Studies, Georgetown University. New York: The Library Press, 1972.

May, Ernest, and Janet Fraser, eds. *Campaign '72: The Managers Speak*. Cambridge: Harvard University Press, 1973.

McLellan, David S., and David C. Acheson, eds. *Among Friends: Personal Letters of Dean Acheson*. New York: Dodd, Mead, 1980.

Meir, Golda. *My Life*. New York: Putnam, 1975.

Merry, Robert W. *Taking on the World: Joseph and Stewart Alsop — Guardians of the American Century*. New York: Viking, 1996.

Moore, Jonathan, and Janet Fraser, eds. *Campaign for President: The Managers Look at '76*. Cambridge: Ballinger, 1977.

Morrocco, John. *The Vietnam Experience: Rain of Fire: Air War, 1969–1973*. The Vietnam Experience Series. Boston: Boston Publishing Co., 1985.

Mortimer, Edward. *Roosevelt's Children: Tomorrow's World Leaders and Their World*. London: Hamish Hamilton, 1987.

Newhouse, John. *Cold Dawn: The Story of SALT*. New York: Holt, Rinehart and Winston, 1973.

———. *War and Peace in the Nuclear Age*. New York: Alfred A. Knopf, 1989.

Nitze, Paul H. *From Hiroshima to Glasnost: At the Center of Decision*. New York: Grove Weidenfeld, 1989.

Nixon, Richard M. *In the Arena*. New York: Simon & Schuster, 1990.

———. *Leaders*. New York: Warner Books, 1982.

———. *1999: Victory Without War*. New York: Simon & Schuster, 1988.

———. *No More Vietnams*. New York: Arbor House, 1985.

———. *RN: The Memoirs of Richard Nixon*. New York: Touchstone, 1978, 1990.

———. *U.S. Foreign Policy for the 1970's: Building for Peace*. Report to the Congress, vol. 2. Washington: Government Printing Office, 1972.

——. *U.S. Foreign Policy for the 1970's: The Emerging Structure of Peace*. Report to the Congress, vol. 3. Washington: Government Printing Office, 1972.

——. *U.S. Foreign Policy for the 1970's: A New Strategy for Peace*. Report to the Congress, vol. 1. Washington: Government Printing Office, 1971.

——. *U.S. Foreign Policy for the 1970's: Shaping a Durable Peace*. Report to the Congress, vol. 4. Washington: Government Printing Office, 1973.

Nye, Joseph S., Jr., ed. *The Making of America's Soviet Policy*. Council on Foreign Relations. New Haven: Yale University Press, 1984.

O'Brien, Conor Cruise. *The Siege: The Saga of Israel and Zionism*. New York: Simon & Schuster, 1986.

Ognibene, Peter J. *Scoop: The Life and Politics of Henry M. Jackson*. New York: Stein & Day, 1975.

Osborn, George K., et al., eds. *Democracy, Strategy and Vietnam: Implications for American Policymaking*. Lexington, MA: Lexington Books/ D. C. Heath, 1987.

Palmer, Bruce, Jr. *The 25-Year War: America's Military Role in Vietnam*. New York: Touchstone, 1985. Originally published by the University Press of Kentucky, 1984.

Parmet, Herbert S. *Richard Nixon and His America*. Boston: Little, Brown, 1990.

Parsons, Anthony. *The Pride and the Fall: Iran 1974–1979*. London: Jonathan Cape, 1984.

Pierre, Andrew J. *Nuclear Weapons in Europe*. New York: Council on Foreign Relations, 1984.

Pike, Douglas. *Vietnam and the Soviet Union: Anatomy of an Alliance*. Boulder, CO: Westview Press, 1987.

——, ed. *The Bunker Papers: Reports to the President from Vietnam, 1967–73*. 3 vols. Berkeley: Indochina Research Monograph Series #5, The Asia Foundation and the Institute of East Asian Studies of the University of California, 1990.

——, ed. *Vietnam and China: A Reader*. Berkeley: University of California, Institute of East Asian Studies, Indochina Studies Project, 1987.

Podhoretz, Norman. *Why We Were in Vietnam*. New York: Simon & Schuster, 1982.

Polk, William R. *The Arab World*. Cambridge: Harvard University Press, 1980.

Porter, Gareth. *A Peace Denied: The United States, Vietnam, and the Paris Agreement*. Bloomington: Indiana University Press, 1975.

Powers, Thomas. *The Man Who Kept the Secrets: Richard Helms and the CIA*. New York: Alfred A. Knopf, 1979.

Prados, John. *Keepers of the Keys: A History of the National Security Council from Truman to Bush*. New York: William Morrow, 1991.

——. *The Soviet Estimate: U.S. Intelligence Analysis and Soviet Strategic Forces*. Princeton: Princeton University Press, 1982, 1986.

Pratt, John Clark. *Vietnam Voices: Perspectives on the War Years, 1941–1982*. New York: Penguin Books, 1984.

Prochnau, William W., and Richard W. Larsen. *A Certain Democrat: Senator Henry M. Jackson: A Political Biography*. Englewood Cliffs, NJ: Prentice-Hall, 1972.

Quandt, William B. *Decade of Decisions: American Policy Toward the Arab-Israeli Conflict, 1967–76*. Berkeley: University of California Press, 1977.

Rapoport, Daniel. *Inside the House*. Chicago: Follett Publishing Co., 1975.

Reeves, Richard. *President Kennedy: Profile of Power*. New York: Simon & Schuster, 1993.

Reich, Bernard. *Quest for Peace: United States–Israel Relations and the Arab-Israeli Conflict.* New Brunswick, NJ: Transaction Books, 1977.

Reston, James, Jr. *The Lone Star: The Life of John Connally.* New York: Harper & Row, 1989.

Rowen, Hobart. *Self-Inflicted Wounds: From LBJ's Guns and Butter to Reagan's Voodoo Economics.* New York: Times Books, 1994.

Rubenstein, Alvin Z. *Red Star on the Nile: The Soviet-Egyptian Influence Relationship Since the June War.* Princeton University Press, 1977.

———, ed. *Soviet and Chinese Influence in the Third World.* New York: Praeger, 1975.

Rubin, Barry. *The Great Powers in the Middle East 1941–1947: The Road to the Cold War.* London: Frank Cass and Company, 1980.

———. *Paved with Good Intentions: The American Experience and Iran.* New York: Oxford University Press, 1980.

Rusk, Dean, with Richard Rusk and Daniel S. Papp. *As I Saw It.* New York: W. W. Norton, 1990.

Rustow, Dankwart, and John F. Mugno. *OPEC: Success and Prospects.* New York: New York University Press (for the Council on Foreign Relations), 1976.

Sadat, Anwar. *In Search of Identity: An Autobiography.* New York, Harper & Row, 1979.

Safire, William. *Before the Fall.* Garden City, NY: Doubleday, 1975.

———. *Lend Me Your Ears: Great Speeches in History.* New York: W. W. Norton, 1992.

———. *Safire's Washington.* New York: Quadrangle/The New York Times Book Co., 1980.

Safran, Nadav. *Israel: The Embattled Ally.* Cambridge: Harvard University Press, 1981.

———. *Saudi Arabia: The Ceaseless Quest for Security.* Ithaca: Cornell University Press, 1991.

Schiff, Zeev. *October Earthquake: Yom Kippur 1973.* Tel Aviv: University Publishing Projects, 1974.

Schmidt, Helmut. *Men and Powers: A Political Retrospective.* New York: Random House, 1989.

Schulman, Robert. *John Sherman Cooper: The Global Kentuckian.* Lexington: University Press of Kentucky, 1976.

Schulzinger, Robert D. *Henry Kissinger: Doctor of Diplomacy.* New York: Columbia University Press, 1989.

Schurmann, Franz. *The Foreign Politics of Richard Nixon.* Berkeley: Institute of International Studies, University of California, 1987.

Seaborg, Glenn T. *Stemming the Tide: Arms Control in the Johnson Years.* Lexington, MA: Lexington Books, 1987.

Shaplen, Robert. *Bitter Victory.* New York: Harper & Row, 1986.

———. *A Turning Wheel: Three Decades of Asian Revolution as Witnessed by a Correspondent for* The New Yorker. New York: Random House, 1979.

Shawcross, William. *Sideshow: Kissinger, Nixon and the Destruction of Cambodia.* New York: Simon & Schuster (Touchstone), 1979, 1981, 1986, 1987.

Sheehan, Edward R.F. *The Arabs, Israelis, and Kissinger: A Secret History of American Diplomacy in the Middle East.* New York: Reader's Digest Press, 1976.

Sheehan, Neil. *A Bright Shining Lie: John Paul Vann and America in Vietnam.* New York: Vintage Books, 1988, 1989.

Shevchenko, Arkady N. *Breaking With Moscow*. New York: Alfred A. Knopf, 1985.

Showalter, Dennis E., and John G. Albert, eds. *An American Dilemma: Vietnam, 1964–1973*. Chicago: Imprint Publications, 1993.

Shultz, George P. *Turmoil and Triumph: My Years as Secretary of State*. New York: Scribner, 1993.

—— and Kenneth W. Dam. *Economic Policy Beyond the Headlines*. Stanford: Stanford Alumni Association, 1977.

Sick, Gary. *All Fall Down: America's Tragic Encounter with Iran*. New York: Random House, 1985.

Sigmund, Paul E. *The Overthrow of Allende and the Politics of Chile, 1964–1976*. Pittsburgh: University of Pittsburgh Press, 1977.

——. *The United States and Democracy in Chile*. Baltimore: Johns Hopkins University Press, 1993.

Smith, Gerard. *Doubletalk: The Story of the First Strategic Arms Limitation Talks*. Garden City, NY: Doubleday, 1980.

Snepp, Frank. *Decent Interval*. New York: Vintage Books, 1977, 1978.

Solberg, Carl. *Hubert Humphrey: A Biography*. New York: W. W. Norton, 1984.

Sorley, Lewis. *Arms Transfers Under Nixon: A Policy Analysis*. Lexington: University Press of Kentucky, 1983.

——. *Thunderbolt: From the Battle of the Bulge to Vietnam and Beyond: General Creighton Abrams and the Army of His Times*. New York: Simon & Schuster, 1992.

Spector, Ronald H. *After Tet: The Bloodiest Year in Vietnam*. New York: The Free Press, 1993.

Spiegel, Steven L. *The Other Arab-Israeli Conflict: Making America's Middle East Policy from Truman to Reagan*. Chicago: University of Chicago Press, 1985.

Stebbins, Richard P., and Elaine P. Adam, eds. *American Foreign Relations 1972: A Documentary Record*. Documents on American Foreign Relations Series, Council on Foreign Relations. New York: New York University Press, 1976.

——. *American Foreign Relations 1973: A Documentary Record*. Documents on American Foreign Relations Series, Council on Foreign Relations. New York: New York University Press, 1976.

——. *American Foreign Relations 1974: A Documentary Record*. Documents on American Foreign Relations Series, Council on Foreign Relations. New York: New York University Press, 1977.

——. *American Foreign Relations 1975: A Documentary Record*. Documents on American Foreign Relations Series, Council on Foreign Relations. New York: New York University Press, 1977.

Stein, Herbert. *Presidential Economics: The Making of Economic Policy from Roosevelt to Reagan and Beyond*. New York: Simon & Schuster (Touchstone), 1984–85.

Stern, Paula. *Water's Edge: Domestic Politics and the Making of American Foreign Policy*. Westport, CT: Greenwood Press, 1979.

Summers, Harry G., Jr. *On Strategy: A Critical Analysis of the Vietnam War*. Novato, CA: Presidio Press, 1982.

Sutter, Robert. *Chinese Foreign Policy and the Cultural Revolution, 1966–77*. Boulder, CO: Westview Press, 1978.

Sutterlin, James S., and David Klein. *Berlin: From Symbol of Confrontation to Keystone of Stability*. New York: Praeger, 1989.

Szulc, Tad. *The Illusion of Peace*. New York: Viking, 1978.

Talbott, Strobe. *Endgame: The Inside Story of SALT II*. New York: Harper & Row, 1979.

———. *Master of the Game: Paul Nitze and the Nuclear Peace*. New York: Alfred A. Knopf, 1988.

Terrill, Ross. *800,000,000: The Real China*. Boston: Little, Brown, 1972.

Thompson, Kenneth W., ed. *The Nixon Presidency: Twenty-two Intimate Perspectives of Richard M. Nixon*. Lanham, MD: University Press of America, 1987.

Thompson, W. Scott, and Donaldson D. Frizzell. *The Lessons of Vietnam*. New York: Crane, Russak, 1977.

Thornton, Richard C. *The Nixon-Kissinger Years: The Reshaping of American Foreign Policy*. New York: Paragon House, 1989.

Trager, James. *The Great Grain Robbery*. New York: Ballantine Books, 1975.

Turley, William S. *The Second Indochina War: A Short Political and Military History, 1954–1974*. Boulder, CO: Westview Press, 1986.

Turner, Henry Ashby, Jr. *The Two Germanies Since 1945*. New Haven: Yale University Press, 1987.

Udovitch, A. L., ed. *The Middle East: Oil, Conflict & Hope*. Critical Choices for Americans. Vol. 10. Lexington, MA: Lexington Books, 1976.

Ulam, Adam B. *Dangerous Relations: The Soviet Union in World Politics, 1970–1982*. New York: Oxford University Press, 1983.

Vance, Cyrus. *Hard Choices: Critical Years in America's Foreign Policy*. New York: Simon & Schuster, 1983.

Vietor, Richard H.K. *Energy Policy in America Since 1945*. Cambridge, Eng.: Cambridge University Press, 1984.

Volcker, Paul, and Toyoo Gyohten. *Changing Fortunes: The World's Money and the Threat to American Leadership*. New York: Times Books, 1992.

Volten, Peter M.E. *Brezhnev's Peace Program: A Study of Soviet Political Process and Power*. Boulder, CO: Westview Press, 1982.

Warner, Denis. *Not with Guns Alone*. London: Hutchinson, 1977.

White, Theodore H. *Breach of Faith: The Fall of Richard Nixon*. New York: Atheneum, Reader's Digest Press, 1975.

———. *The Making of the President 1968*. New York: Atheneum, 1969.

———. *The Making of the President 1972*. New York: Atheneum, 1973.

Wicker, Tom. *One of Us: Richard Nixon and the American Dream*. New York: Random House, 1991.

Willrich, Mason, and John B. Rhinelander, eds. *SALT: The Moscow Agreements and Beyond*. New York: The Free Press, 1974.

Wilson, Dick. *Zhou En-lai*. New York: Viking, 1984.

Witcover, Jules. *Marathon: The Pursuit of the Presidency, 1972–1976*. New York: Viking, 1977.

———. *The Resurrection of Richard Nixon*. New York: Putnam, 1970.

———. *The Year the Dream Died: Revisiting 1968 in America*. New York: Warner Books, 1997.

Wolfe, Thomas A. *The SALT Experience*. Cambridge: Ballinger, 1979.

Woodward, Bob, and Carl Bernstein. *All the President's Men*. New York: Simon & Schuster, 1974.

Yahya, Ali M. *Egypt and the Soviet Union, 1955–1972*. Washington: Harbinger Distributors, 1989.

Yergin, Daniel. *The Prize: The Epic Quest for Oil, Money, and Power.* New York: Simon & Schuster, 1991.
—— and Martin Hillenbrand, eds. *Global Insecurity: A Strategy for Energy and Economic Renewal.* Boston: Houghton Mifflin, 1982.
Zumwalt, Elmo R., Jr. *On Watch: A Memoir.* New York: Quadrangle, 1976.

Articles

Adelman, Kenneth. "Report from Angola," *Foreign Affairs,* April 1975: 558–74.
Adelman, M. A. "Is the Oil Shortage Real? Oil Companies as OPEC Tax Collectors," *Foreign Policy,* Winter 1972–73: 69–108.
Akins, James E. "The Oil Crisis: This Time the Wolf Is Here," *Foreign Affairs,* April 1973: 462–90.
Amuzegar, Jahangir. "The Oil Story: Facts, Fiction and Fair Play," *Foreign Affairs,* July 1973: 676–89.
Bundy, McGeorge. "Vietnam, Watergate and Presidential Powers," *Foreign Affairs,* Winter 1979–80: 397–407.
Clifford, Clark M. "A Viet Nam Appraisal," *Foreign Affairs,* July 1969: 601–22.
D'Auria, Douglas. "Present at the Rejuvenation: The Association of Dean Acheson and Richard Nixon," *Presidential Studies Quarterly,* Spring 1988: 393–411.
Ginsburgh, Robert. "North Vietnam Airpower," in *Vital Speeches,* September 9, 1972: 732–35.
Hall, David K. "The Laotian War of 1962 and the Indo-Pakistani War of 1971," in Blechman and Kaplan, eds., *Force Without War.*
Halperin, Morton. "The Decision to Deploy the ABM: Bureaucratic and Domestic Politics in the Johnson Administration," *World Politics,* October 1972: 62–95.
Iklé, Fred Charles. "Can Nuclear Deterrence Last Out the Century?" *Foreign Affairs,* January 1973: 267–85.
Kissinger, Henry A. "The Viet Nam Negotiations," *Foreign Affairs,* January 1969: 211–34.
Nixon, Richard M. "Asia After Viet Nam," *Foreign Affairs,* October 1967: 111–25.
Oksenberg, Michel. "A Decade of Sino-American Relations," *Foreign Affairs,* Fall 1982: 175–95.
Parker, Maynard. "Vietnam: The War That Won't End," *Foreign Affairs,* January 1975: 356–57.
Schmidt, Helmut. "Germany in the Era of Negotiations," *Foreign Affairs,* October 1970: 40–50.
Sigmund, Paul E. "The 'Invisible Blockade' and the Overthrow of Allende," *Foreign Affairs,* January 1974: 322–40.
Szulc, Tad. "Behind the Cease-Fire Agreement," *Foreign Policy,* Summer 1974: 21–69.
Van Hollen, Christopher. "The Tilt Policy Revisited: Nixon-Kissinger Geopolitics and South Asia," *Asian Survey,* 20 (April 1980): 339–61.
Wheeler, John. "Coming to Grips with Vietnam," *Foreign Affairs,* Spring 1985: 747–58.
Z. "The Year of Europe?" *Foreign Affairs,* January 1974: 237–48.

Government Materials

House Appropriations Committee. *Department of Defense Appropriations: Briefings on Bombings of North Vietnam: Hearings Before Subcommittees of the Appropriations Committee.* 93rd Cong., 1st sess., January 9–13, 1973.

House Armed Services Committee. *Bombing in Cambodia: Hearings Before the House Armed Services Committee.* 93rd Cong., 1st sess., July–August 1973.

House Select Committee on Missing Persons in Southeast Asia. *Americans Missing in Southeast Asia, Part 5: Hearings Before the House Select Committee on Missing Persons in Southeast Asia.* 94th Cong., 2nd sess., 1976.

Public Papers of the Presidents of the United States, 1968–75.

Senate Appropriations Committee. *Emergency Military Assistance and Economic and Humanitarian Aid to South Vietnam, FY 1975: Hearings Before the Senate Appropriations Committee.* 94th Cong., 1st sess., April 15, 1975.

———. *Second Supplemental Appropriations for Fiscal Year 1973, Department of Defense: Hearings Before the Senate Appropriations Committee.* 93rd Cong., 1st sess., May 7, 1973.

Senate Foreign Relations Committee. *Department of State Appropriations Authorization, Fiscal Year 1974: Hearings Before the Senate Foreign Relations Committee.* 93rd Cong., 1st sess., 1973.

———. *Nomination of Richard Helms to Be Ambassador to Iran, and CIA International and Domestic Activities. Hearings Before the Senate Foreign Relations Committee.* 93rd Cong., 1st sess., February 5, 7, 1973.

———. *Thailand, Laos, Cambodia, and Vietnam: April 1973: A Report to the Subcommittee on U.S. Security Agreements and Commitments Abroad.* 93rd Cong., 1st sess., June 11, 1973.

———. *U.S. Air Operations in Cambodia: April 1973: A Report to the Subcommittee on U.S. Security Agreements and Commitments Abroad.* 93rd Cong., 1st sess., April 27, 1973.

———. *Vietnam 1974: A Report to the Committee by Richard Moose and Charles Meissner on Mission to Vietnam.* 93rd Cong., 2nd sess., August 5, 1974.

Senate Judiciary Committee. *Aftermath of War: Humanitarian Problems of Southeast Asia: A Staff Report of the Subcommittee on Refugees and Escapees.* 94th Cong., 2nd sess., May 17, 1976.

Senate Select Committee on Governmental Operations. *Intelligence Activities: Senate Resolution 21. Vol. 6: FBI. Hearings Before the Senate Select Committee on Governmental Operations.* 94th Cong., 1st sess., 1975.

———. *Intelligence Activities and the Rights of Americans: A Final Report.* Book 2. 94th Cong., 2nd sess., April 26, 1976.

Oral Histories

Atherton, Alfred L. Oral History Interview. Association for Diplomatic Studies and Training (ADST), Arlington, VA, 1990.

Bundy, William P. LBJ Library, 1969.

Rowe, James H., Jr. LBJ Library, 1982.

Saunders, Harold H. ADST, November 24, 1993.

Sisco, Joseph J. ADST, March 14, 1990.

Other Materials

Forslund, Catherine Mary. "Woman of Two Worlds: Anna Chennault and Informal Diplomacy in U.S.-Asian Relations, 1950–1990." Ph.D. dissertation, spring 1997, Washington University at St. Louis.

Ginsburgh, Robert. Chronology, October 1968. LBJ Library.

Green, Marshall. *Evolution of U.S.-China Policy, 1956–1973: Memoirs of an Insider.* Unpublished manuscript.

Johnson, W. Thomas. "Notes of High-Level Meetings with the President Relating to Vietnam and Other Key Foreign Policy Issues. April–December 1968" (cited as Tom Johnson Notes). LBJ Library.

Rostow, Walt, and Bromley Smith, Chronology, October 1968. LBJ Library.

Index

A

Abdullah, King of Jordan, 183

Abrams, Gen. Creighton, 30, 33, 54, 62–66, 72, 74, 82, 151–53, 225, 227–29, 294, 298–99, 307, 309, 314, 315, 360, 550*n87*, 552*n98*, 574*n143*

Abshire, David, 223

Acheson, Dean, 5–8, 66, 82, 88, 160, 169, 178, 256, 522, 545*n3*, 555*n35*, 566*n42*, 570*n77*

Adenauer, Konrad, 111, 112, 118–21

Adham, Kamal, 430, 431, 598*n14*

Afghanistan, 403, 477; Soviet invasion of, 484

AFL-CIO, 254, 350, 407

Agnew, Spiro, 25, 42, 88, 157, 208, 221, 226, 384, 425–26, 473

Agriculture, U.S. Department of, 340

Aichi, Kiichi, 138

Air Force, U.S., 85, 90, 137, 299, 372, 406; in Laos, 145

air-to-surface cruise missiles (ASMs), 477

Akins, James E., 431, 453, 597*n11*

Ala, Hussein, 560*n119*

Alaskan pipeline, 215–16, 455

Albert, Carl, 388, 427

Aldrich, George, 386, 388

Alessandri, Jorge, 198–201, 422

Algeria, 55, 446, 450

Allen, Richard, 549*n72*, 550*n80*

Allende Gossens, Salvador, 179, 198–203, 421–23, 503, 519, 571*n109*

Alliance for Progress, 198–200, 204

Allison, Gen. Royal, 90

Allott, Gordon, 257

All the President's Men (Woodward and Bernstein), 379

Alsop, Joseph, 358

Alsop, Stewart, 157

Ambrose, Stephen, 7, 12

American Assembly, xiv